You'll Never Eat Lunch in This Town Again

Julia Phillips was born in New York. After working in magazine publishing she became a film producer, and was the first woman producer to win an Oscar for Best Picture (*The Sting*). She also produced *Taxi Driver* and *Close Encounters of the Third Kind*. She lives in Beverly Hills, where she is writing her first novel.

House Lights Dim

Before Titles

The Sting *had been nominated, two months before, in ten categories, including Cinematography, Editing, Actor, Screenplay, Director, and Best Picture.* The Exorcist, *which had garnered an equal number of nominations, had been released the same day, two days before Christmas. It had received an enormous amount of initial publicity; even* The New York Times *carried pictures of people lined up in the cold to get in.*

Warners had been far too cautious in its release of The Exorcist. *It had opened in only twenty-four theaters. At* 90/10 *deals, Leo Greenfield kept reminding us. But then, he was the guy who told us, based on the first week's figures, that our picture would gross maybe fifteen mil. We had opened in 220 theaters, with* 70/30 *deals, and kept widening the release. Warners waited a good six weeks until they went wide. But* The Exorcist *was only a three-week picture; the audience lost interest before it was available.*

The Sting, *on the other hand, had staying power. It had hung in, week after week, and it had opened in ten times the number of theaters. Not only was* The Sting *racking up some very impressive figures, but people had started to notice that it was an excellent movie. It certainly didn't send you out in the street unsure whether to hit a church or a bar, as* The Exorcist *did. And Warners had a crack at* The Sting *and turned us down.*

We'd made damn sure John Calley and Dick Shepard came to the one screening Universal permitted us before the release of the picture. As they were walking out, I collared Calley, because I knew how much it annoyed him, and asked him how he liked the picture.

'I'm going home to slash my wrists,' he said. Good. Supercilious motherfucker.

It would be them or us tonight at the Awards.

Michael and Tony had spent weeks aggravating over whether The Sting *would win for Best Picture or not. They had practiced speeches, how they would stand up, their walks to the stage. I hadn't dared to contemp!ate the possibility of winning. I was not a big believer in the power of positive thinking, although I had gone to college with Norman Vincent Peale's daughter. Didn't wanna put a mojo on it; didn't wanna tempt the evil eye.*

I translated all my anxiety into finding a dress. Joel Schumacher was my fashion consultant. We agreed I was a New York girl, most comfortable in black, and since so many Californians dressed in colors, that I would probably stand out. Where I got the chutzpah *to think I might stand out at such a gathering I don't know. We traipsed from store to store and I would try something on and I would say, 'Now I win . . .' and then see if the dress was comfortable to walk in, and he would pull at a strap and say, 'Now, when you win . . .' We finally settled on a black spaghetti-strap number by Halston at Giorgio's, a long strand of pearls, and a double feather boa made up of guinea hen and black ostrich feathers.*

I was still, six months after Kate's birth, a little wide in the hip. Joel was adamant that I should wear beautiful black sandal-heels but I couldn't find any tall enough. I needed height. I ended up buying a pair of giant platform shoes from Fred Slatten. Black satin with rhinestones They stayed hidden under the dress and they definitely gave me height. They also filled me with the quiescent fear that I might actually fall off them on global TV. A toss-up, looks or safety. The hips won out.

Trancas, California
April 2, 1974

I wake with a shudder at six thirty. The sun creates hot bounce on the sky/sea horizon. It is quite a sight, but I take this view for granted. Without pausing a moment in sincere appreciation, I automatically pop a diet pill. Bad move. Within

iv

twenty minutes, I'm dancing around the sandy living room, neatening up. I run along the beach, take a perfunctory dip in the freezing-cold Pacific, race indoors for a brief hot shower.

When I hit the bedroom, Michael is standing on his head, yoga-style, in the corner of the room. 'I gotta pick up my tuxedo,' Michael says, still upside down. The veins in his temples explode and contract on each syllable. Upstairs, I hear Kate's first baby-musings for the day. Sonia heats formula in the kitchen. I can smell it. I don't know how Kate can stand that shit.

'Good, that'll give me time to be nervous all by myself. Maybe Sonia could take Kate out for awhile.' As in: I. NEED. MY. SPACE. . . .

Within the hour, they're toast. I lay out some coke on a small mirror. Secret stash. Mine. Michael doesn't even know I have it . . . that's how it's gotten. I chop it lightly with a razor. It falls apart like butter. This is good coke. Smooth. I do a hit, then another. I roll a joint and smoke it out on the deck. Less than a hundred yards from me, the ocean beats down in heavy waves against the sand. I pace, my heart beating in triple time to the waves.

I watch the postal van ease its way toward our mailbox, vault over the deck, and scramble down the hill to meet it. The mailman has a stack, bills mostly, junk mail addressed to Occupant. Sandwiched between the telephone bill and the latest issue of *Time* is a small blue envelope. The handwriting addressing Michael and Julia Phillips is familiar. I tear open the envelope as I return to the house, yelling 'Thanks' over my shoulder to the mailman's wishes for our good luck that night. The letter is short and pithy, my favorites:

Dear Michael & Julia:
In a few days, you will be getting cards and letters and telegrams from everyone, so I wanted to get in what I had to say now. The important thing to remember is that you are nice sweet people. You are about to have a lot of temptation thrown your way, so try not to forget that.
Love, John

Maybe too pithy. The letter upsets me; just now, Michael and I are nice sweet people to everybody but each other. Marriage . . . Here today, gone today. I pop half a Valium and look at my shaking hands. Shut up, I tell them.

When they do, I set about the arduous process of blow-drying my hair, then spicing it up with a curling iron. I swallow another three Valium halves and recurl my hair as a chaser each time until it is time to get dressed. After I'm dressed, I have a little coke as a chaser for all that Val out of my secret stash. I don't offer Michael any. It would provoke a fight. I'm not into fighting with Michael tonight.

Universal has been kind enough to provide a limousine for us and Tony and Antoinette Bill, and David Ward and his wife, Chris. When I first met Antoinette Bill, everybody called her Mrs Tony. Her given name was Antoinette, but she had gone under the name Toni all her life. Tony, who was in actual fact née Gerard Anthony Bill, was also called Tony. Somehow, Tony stayed and Toni became Mrs. Tony. I, of course, was outraged.

'You sound like his chattel,' I told her at lunch at Ma Maison one day. I had just had my lip and legs painfully waxed by Charlotte at Elizabeth Arden's, which was making me bristle. The fact that Patrick had the restaurant wrapped in polyethylene, something my father participated in inventing, and that it was a hot day with too little air conditioning, might also have added to my dyspeptic world-view. 'Isn't there something else I can call you?'

She smiled. 'Well, my real name is Antoinette, but I always thought it was pretentious.'

'Maybe when you were ten, but you're a grown-up married lady now with two kids and a husband named Gerard who likes to be called Tony, not that I blame him. I'm gonna call you Antoinette from now on. Okay?' I still asked permission in certain matters . . .

She grinned and flushed. 'Why not? What the hell!' She laughed and toasted me with a glass of dry white wine.

I started calling her Antoinette; pretty soon some other people started calling her Antoinette; after awhile everyone but Tony called her Antoinette. One day she went out and had her checks, credit cards, license, passport – everything identifying her – changed to Antoinette Bill. I felt as good that day as I did the day Michael's mother, Sherry, started getting paid for finding the dresses that Michael's father, Larry, knocked off in his lower-priced dress line. I was a fucking one-woman consciousness-raising session . . .

Michael and I have to be the first to leave because we're in Trancas, which is as far away from the Dorothy Chandler Pavilion as you can be, and still live in the county of L.A. David and Chris live in Topanga Canyon, so we pick them up on the way into town. There is something very silly about being all duded up at three o'clock in the afternoon, sitting in the back of a stretch limo, but the door will be closed, the Academy has reminded us in numerous missives preceding the event, at six thirty promptly.

We have already split up Bill/Phillips Productions and there's bad blood between Tony and us. This isn't to become known until we are. Tony decides to drive himself and meet us there. He doesn't want to be Hollywood and arrive in a limo. If you really feel that way, I think, why go at all? Because we're going to win. This concept makes me as nervous as the thought of losing.

A limo provided by the studio for the producers and the writer is a truly grandiose gesture, given all previous behavior by Universal. Basically we have been treated as a nasty inconvenience to be just barely tolerated. By Zanuck and Brown. By George Roy Hill. Mostly by those who live in the Black Tower, sometimes referred to locally as the Black Mariah, the reflector-sunglass mausoleum that houses all the Universal Executives, both living and dead. To them, our youth, so chic at some of the other studios, is an impudence.

The day the nominations came out, and both those who had made *American Graffiti* and *The Sting*, a ubiquitously young group, had snagged an incredible number of honors for Universal, we received telegrams from the top two execs at Universal: Lew Wasserman and Sid Sheinberg.

SINCEREST CONGRATULATIONS AND BEST WISHES FROM ALL OF US AT UNIVERSAL FOR TEN ACADEMY AWARD NOMINATIONS, INCLUDING BEST PICTURE, FOR THE STING. LEW R. WASSERMAN

Not warm, but essentially correct

CONGRATULATIONS FOR THE ACADEMY AWARD NOMINATION FOR AMERICAN GRAFFITI. THE FILM IN OUR JUDGEMENT IS AN AMERICAN CLASSIC AND DESERVING OF ALL OF ITS ACCOLADES. LET'S HOPE THERE ARE OTHER VENTURES THAT WE CAN SHARE WITH YOU IN THE FUTURE. SID SHEINBERG

Not warm, and incorrect in all its essentials.

I have this image of Sid's secretary: Well, all young people look alike, don't they? I've always wondered if the message Western Unioned to George Lucas congratulated him on the receipt of so many nominations for *The Sting*. I wonder if he kept his, too . . .

And now, here we are: Chris and David and Michael and Julia, flying along the Pacific Coast Highway, compliments of Universal Airlines, to the Dorothy Chandler Pavilion. I have nibbled another half a Valium at the Wards'. I've decided it's okay to carry Valium to the Academy Awards. Most of the people in the Academy are from the Valium-and-Alcohol Generation. I'm becoming a tad too relaxed behind it, though. Sleepy might be a better word.

Need a little hit, I think, as my head lolls around on my neck. Need a big hit, I amend. You have a big hit. *The Sting* . . . Not that kind of a hit . . . maybe coffee. If nothing else was around. I'm pissed at myself for leaving my secret stash behind. I focus on getting downtown, like that's going to make the drive quicker.

By the time we reach the exit to the Music Center, limousines are backed up onto the ramp. Behind us they stack up quickly. Limos to the left of me, limos to the right. A limo! A limo! My kingdom for a limo! It is a boiling-hot day and all the air conditioners are blasting. The hot and the cold mingles with the poisonous air; the exhaust makes a greenish brown cloud that hangs over us. I feel I am in line for the funeral of the most popular guy in Hollywood. Who could that be, I wonder . . .

The limousines, the cloud, the heat, make me think: We are all going to die. A thought I have two, maybe three hundred times a day anyway. I concentrate on Life and it makes me realize I have to pee semi-badly. At the rate we're moving, I won't get to check my makeup. I know the only part of my face that is glowing with health right now is my shiny forehead.

It's ridiculous to worry about how I look. There's a long red carpet; it is the only route to the door. The door that closes promptly at six thirty! There are barricades and cops and fans and photographers. Everywhere. We do not rate a flicker. There is nothing quite like being the only unknown in a bevy of luminaries. Unless it is to be the only name at a gathering of nobodies. If I had to vote for the lesser of two evils, as I do for my president, I'd go with anonymity. But I didn't know that then.

We walk along that red carpet, graced by Sally Kellerman in front of us and Paul and Linda McCartney behind us. Nobody reaches out to us. No Army Archerd interview. No hail-fellow-well-met interchange with milling celebs. An all-time Humbler. A year or two before, I'd have been amazed to be here. Now that I am, I can see that the only way to attend one of these events is as a star. We traverse the gauntlet in that casual way that says: I don't care to be noticed. I feel like a walk-on in a high-school play.

Of course, Tony and Antoinette are here already. We see Tony chatting up Steve Shagan, who's in competition with David Ward for Best Screenplay, and drinking, from the look around his mouth, his third glass of wine. He looks pretty cool in his tux. He looks like he belongs. Shagan insincerely wishes us luck. That's okay, I forgive him. He's insisted we hire

Norman Garey, who acts as our lawyer and is truly our friend. I shift back and forth, no small feat on platforms four inches from the ground in the toe and probably six in the heel. It gives me the illusion that I am taking steps, presumably away, from a situation that makes me uncomfortable.

People are chatting, waving, drinking. Mostly they are checking their watches. I have felt the same palpable heat of anticipation on only two other occasions: The Band of Gypsies concert, New Year's Eve, 1968. Probably the last live Jimi Hendrix performance. The Rolling Stones at Madison Square Garden in 1972. The tour that ended at Altamont . . .

People make their way to their seats. Apparently NBC or the Academy, whoever is running the show, expects *The Sting* and the *The Exorcist* to run neck and neck because nominated personnel for each film fill up the first three rows on opposite sides of the aisle. Gives me pause about Price-Waterhouse.

The very first production number features Liza. She's fabulous. Getting to be a real show stopper. Like Mama, which is what she always calls her famous mother. She's been Tony's friend for a long time, and Michael and I have met her a few times: once or twice, in fact, as a guest at our house at the beach. We introduced her to Redford out there. When she finishes, she winks at us. The ordeal we're about to endure for the longest hours of all my hours seems a bit more personal, more friendly.

To be perfectly fair, though, I had been partaking from a panoply of mood enhancers, stimulants, and depressants all day. Every once in a while, I would strike upon the perfect chemical combination: for Oscar night it's been a diet pill, a small amount of coke, two joints, six halves of Valium, which makes three, and a glass-and-a-half of wine. So far. I have a warm and comfortable feeling of well-being.

This is greatly enhanced by *The Sting* picking up some awards. Best Editing. Best Music. Bill Reynolds and Marvin Hamlisch make nice acceptance speeches. They even thank us. Best Screenplay! David Ward, our pal, has won! My heart begins to samba in my chestal cavity. I hope it doesn't embarrass me by exploding. At least not before we win. *If* we win. I can barely hear David's acceptance speech over my internal din. Boomalacka Boomalacka . . .

One of the TV crew rushing around in front of me slips on some cable and steps on my foot. Hard. Just keeps going, too. Doesn't even apologize. He's with the team telecasting the event to one hundred million people or so, and he has more important things on his mind . . . he's only behaving the way everybody in The Business does: all is sacrificed on the altar of the show. Hey, whatever's good for the project . . .

If you're fucking over your partner for the good of the project, that's different from just plain fucking him over. In fact, if you're fucking him over just for the hell of it, but you can make it seem like it's for the good of the project, you're applauded for being 'professional.' This poor son of a bitch is hurting my toes because they're in his way. He has to step on my feet for the good of the show. He does it to me several times during the course of the festivities; I'm finally forced to grab him by his bow tie and browbeat an apology and a promise from him that he won't do that anymore.

My mind is starting to wander and my mouth is getting dry and I have to take another nerve-pee. I know it's okay to get up and walk out because people have been doing it steadily throughout the night. The reason that we never see this on TV is that the second anybody vacates a seat, one of the staff working on the show, all of whom are dressed in formal attire, sits in the empty seat.

I clunk my way to the ladies' room in the Fred Slatten platforms. I promise, Joel, I'll never go against you again. In the fashion department. The bar in the lounge holds Jack Lemmon up. Aloft. As it were. He waves as I pass. He doesn't know me at all. But he waves. Nice guy . . .

I pee, fix hair, remove shine from forehead, reapply lipstick. Have a hit of coke which I scrape from the inside of my purse. A little leftover from the last big occasion. Probably New Year's Eve. Swallow half a Valium dry. Check in the mirror. Perfect. I stop at the bar for a glass of water. On the loudspeaker I can hear the nominees for Best Actress being announced.

'We'd better go back in,' Jack says merrily. 'Our time's coming up.' He takes my arm ceremoniously and walks me to the door. When we step through, we are engulfed in darkness.

'Someone's sitting in our seats,' I whisper.

'No problem,' he says vaguely and drops my arm. He ambles to his seat and sits on the NBC stand-in's lap. It gives me a giggle and the giggle gives me a rush. I edge my way back to my seat in the darkness. It is empty.

I study my program. It's just Best Actor, Best Director, and Best Picture. Redford's nominated for *The Sting*, but he doesn't win. Jack Lemmon does, for *Save the Tiger*. Shagan's picture. Based on our relationship at the bar, I feel personally involved, a tad miffed when he doesn't thank me. Redford doesn't attend and he's assigned Eileen Brennan, a featured player in the picture, to accept on his behalf; I think he should have assigned me, so deep down I'm glad he hasn't won. Even if he is in my movie. I am at the onset of what I think of as my Hollywood Period.

Everything about John Huston, presenter of the award for Best Director, is long: the tails of his jacket, his face, his vowels, his speech. He's drunk and hurls invective in a series of unfinished sentences at the audience for a good five minutes. This can be a v-e-e-r-y long time if you're just a category away from knowing if you've won an Oscar or not. Outside of president, or mondomondo rock 'n' roll star, it doesn't get much better for shallow capitalist American youth.

'And they tell the winners, Don't take too much time,' Michael whispers. We laugh and squeeze clammy hands. Finally, Houston reads the nominees for the Best Director. And the winner is . . . George Roy Hill.

As George walks up the stairs to the stage, he winks at us. I look across the aisle and catch a brief glimpse of Billy Friedkin, nominated as Best Director for *The Exorcist*. His face seems a twisted portrait. Tentative title: Hatred and Loss. Not his fault. It's a guy thing.

During the course of the evening, the atmosphere of the Dorothy Chandler Pavilion has deteriorated to something fetid, not unlike the air in Tijuana. If you consider that a good portion of the audience is filled with nominees, you can imagine that the losing vibes become more and more profound as the ceremonies wear on. With each passing category, there are more and more – let us call them 'nonwinners' – in the crowd. It's a wonder they can applaud at all, I think.

RE: the quintessential Hollywood gathering: incredible glamour – jewels, furs, limos – accompanied by the stench of loss.

David Niven comes out to introduce Elizabeth Taylor, who is presenting the award for Best Picture. Just as she is about to enter from stage right, a streaker cuts in front of her, runs naked across the stage. People shriek and cheer and howl when David Niven says something to the effect that there's a man making much ado about very little. When, somewhat shakily, Liz finally makes her entrance, she receives a standing ovation. As Michael and Tony stand, they button up their tuxedo jackets.

'Just remember *Cabaret*,' I hiss into Michael's ear as we applaud. It won in all categories last year, but *The Godfather* won for Best Picture. Al Ruddy kept saying over and over, 'You really had us worried there,' and thanked Peter Bart and Bob Evans. Never mentioned Francis, the fool. Not the greatest public speaker. Not the greatest producer either.

Elizabeth Taylor is wearing a pastel sleeveless number. She has lost a considerable amount of weight. She is ample but still beautiful. She reads the nominees in her hushed, quasi-English voice. 'And the winner is – oh, I'm so happy – *The Sting*.'

I turn instinctively toward Michael and Tony, but they're already out of their seats and on their way to the stage. I toss my purse to Antoinette, per a prearrangement.

'See ya later,' I say, and start to rise. Something is keeping me from getting out of my chair and it is strangling me at the same time. The pearls! They're caught on the arm of the chair. Michael has turned back. I'm ready to propel myself out of the chair and fuck the pearls, but he untangles me instantly. I'm pissed he's had to rescue me. I take a breath and reach out for him. The three of us walk up to the stage holding hands.

Liz steps to one side and puts the single award into my

outstretched hands. I don't let go of it until it's wrested from me by an Academy official who says it has to be engraved. Her eyes really are violet. Tony steps up to the microphone and says something lame about being in the business for twelve years and having made all these friends and all this time in the business . . . He seems sullen, and his speech has no beginning and no end. His stepping away from the mike is the only signal that he is done, and the audience applauds pallidly.

Now it's my turn. I ease my way to the mike. I feel like I'm in a circus, walking on stilts. The lights seem very hot. I'm sweating. I can't see beyond the first three rows. Jack Lemmon and Walter Matthau are sitting next to each other in the first row. I address them. I fix a see-how-I'm-smiling grimace onto the lower half of my face.

'You can't imagine what a trip it is,' I say, 'for a nice Jewish girl from Great Neck to win an Academy Award and meet Elizabeth Taylor all in the same night.'

Jack and Walter are laughing; so is the rest of the audience. I am enfolded into Liz's very famous cleavage. WHAT! A! RUSH! For somewhere between five and thirty seconds.

Michael does a nice wrap-up boogie about David Ward making it possible and George Roy Hill making it happen. Then he thanks me and Tony for bringing him into this business. We walk quickly into the wings, where Liza and George stand waiting.

'It still sags in the middle,' Michael says to George. Liza kisses us. Liz teeters on very high heels right behind us; those amazing eyes vague somewhere in the middle distance.

'Has anyone seen my glass?' she whispers. No one has. She finds another. Beyond the darkness backstage is the Press Room, which emanates shafts of hot bright light. The group propels itself toward the light, moths toward the flame. Old Liz and old Liza know the bunch to stick with tonight. Most of the pictures in the papers the next day feature Liz and Liza, even though they aren't nominated for anything. Just now, Liza seems buzzed, Liz drunk, and I am getting sad.

Wait a second. Is this all there is? I wanna do it over. I feel cheated. Am I wrong to feel cheated? I feel like crying. I wanna go home. Take off my uncomfortable shoes. I wish the pearls had strangled me. I take a morose sip of Liz's drink and it makes my lips curl. E-e-e-u-u-uw . . . bourbon. The smell makes me pukey. The flashbulbs flash and the dumb questions commingle in the smoky air . . .

The portion of the evening that we spend at dinner at the Beverly Hilton passes in a blur. Lots of pats on the backs and people who ignored us a week before making sure to say howdy and congratulations. Hey, life's a trip . . . and then you get there.

Several days before, Frank Konigsberg, a heavy-duty agent in television at ICM, decides he's throwing us a Win Lose or Draw party. Frank has a house high on Miller Drive, where if you turn three hundred degrees your eyes are filled with both the Valley and La Cienega views. The city at night stretches around you, a land of light; from this high up it looks as if something is really going on down there. I wonder if attendance would be so high if we had lost.

We get out of the limo and walk toward the house and all Young Hollywood rushes us: Howard Rosenman ('You've given a lot of people hope'), Ron Bernstein ('Jewish girl from Great Neck – you'll go down in the annals of Oscardom'), Don Simpson ('I've got some good blow for you upstairs'), John Ptak ('J.P.'), Andrea Eastman ('Big J!'), Paul Schrader (Unintelligible, spoken into armpit), Steven Spielberg, Peter Boyle, Michelle Phillips, Larry Gordon. Kisses, kisses, kisses. Behind them, hundreds of yet-to-bes fill the house.

Michelle is first out the door. Michelle is always first; it is her special gift. She dances around us jubilantly.

Once inside, Michael, Tony, and I quickly separate. Hey, it's the seventies. There's the party downstairs. Hi, howya doin', getcha' drink? Laughter. Bass line. Then there's the party upstairs. Guys. Drugs. Silence.

I'm upstairs in a jiff.

In all the fuss, I've heard Don's voice the most clearly. Need a hit. Simpson, Schrader, and Schrader's agent sit on the edge of the bed, passing around a gram bottle. In the half-light of the room, I can see coke lines forming around their mouths and under their cheeks. Why does that hardening always improve a man's looks? I wonder. And hurt mine.

They pass the bottle to me; I do two unsatisfying snorts per nostril. The coke is mediocre. Cut burns its way up my nose. I make a face. Generally, I don't like taking other people's drugs. For many reasons, not the least of which is you never know what you're getting. More important: with drugs, it's always better in the power equation if you give rather than receive. Particularly if you're a woman. Particularly with coke.

'I'm going downstairs,' I blurt, and I'm out the door.

Antsy, I keep moving through and around people. I feel the incessant pounding of a heavy rock bass line coming from somewhere far away. Probably the next room. It syncopates with the throb of excitement around me. Now I'm being hugged and congratulated by Joan Didion and John Gregory Dunne. Joan wraps herself around me gracefully. In her profound childish whisper, sadly, 'I'm so happy for you.'

'Darling,' John bellows.

They are drinking. I remember the first time I had dinner at their house. I'd let John Dunne mix my drinks. By the time the main course was served I was on my knees in the bathroom throwing up into the toilet. Jews shouldn't drink, I thought. Jews were not meant to drink. Drugs, money, sex, and dancing they could be good at, but rarely drinking. You had to learn that from childhood.

Since I was in their bathroom anyway, I checked their medicine cabinet. I always like to do that in a new house. Outside of my mother's, it was the most thrilling medicine cabinet I had ever seen. Ritalin, Librium, Miltown, Fioranol, Percodan . . . every upper, downer, and in-betweener of interest in the *PDR*, circa 1973.

'I got your letter this morning,' I say to him as he hugs me warmly. He blushes. 'I've got it in my purse,' I lie. I move off toward the bass line.

'You don't really?' He's very pleased. He shouts after me but I'm out of verbal range. I turn, I nod, and I keep going . . .

*

Michael and Tony and I converge in the front hall of the house. What time is it? I want to know. Three thirty, Michael says. He is the only one wearing a watch.

'Let's hit it!' we say simultaneously. We've been split for months and haven't hung out much; tonight hasn't been a terrifically connecting experience, but here it is. Another case of three-way mindlink. It has kept us going for longer than we should stay. And here in this stranger's front hall, at a party that this stranger is throwing for our victory, we experience that mindlink again.

'I'll just get my purse,' I say, escaping the moment by running up the stairs. Just one little hit for the road. Something to take away this sad little feeling. The boys haven't moved from the edge of the bed.

'Anything left?'

'Sure,' Don says coldly, and hands me a glassine package that must have held an eighth at the beginning of the evening. The gram bottle has been retired, out of stash, probably hours ago. I stick the fingernail of the pinky on my right hand into the bag carefully.

It feels grainy. Like sand. I am just a speck of sand under the fingernail of a larger being . . . This is not my favorite way to do coke. Maybe I just don't like sticking my finger up my nose in front of people. I do a hasty two and two. Kiss them in the general vicinity of their cheeks. Grab my purse. Leave.

Michael, Tony, and Antoinette are in the limo already. 'Where did David and Chris go?' I realize suddenly I haven't seen them for hours.

'Chris got pissed off because David was getting too much attention,' Michael says. 'They left hours ago. Harry took them home.'

Somewhere during the course of the evening, we've gotten on a first-name basis with the limo driver, probably after we won. Why should the limo driver be different from anyone else in Hollywood? When we drop the Bills off, we hug and kiss and feel warm toward each other. Michael and I huddle together in the backseat and Harry zooms up the Pacific Coast Highway. It is nearly five ay-em. Dawn is coming on. We're hitting the beaches of Puerto Vallarta today. This afternoon.

'Should we bother to sleep?' I ask.

'Nah. Let's pack and split.'

'I'm not gonna take anything with me.' Michael knows I mean no drugs.

'Good idea,' he says. We'd had some end-of-a-long-night-doing-coke fights. Nothing heavy, just enough to be scary. Ugly epithets exchanged. Perhaps a crystal piece or two thrown against a wall. A long day, here and there, of silent tears.

'Good idea,' I repeat, trying it out. It doesn't sound too threatening. 'Definitely using this time to clean up,' I say. We'll be staying a week, per a plan we made together in happier times, not so long ago. I'll pass through my thirtieth birthday in five days, on foreign soil. I just hope I won't be deathly ill by then. I always get sick in Mexico.

I sit up. The sun creeps over the edge of the waves. It splashes the sea with an astonishing kaleidoscope of phosphorescent hues; an acid vision on the natch. Flashback to the first time I tried acid: I sat next to a pool for hours, completely enveloped in the changes on the surface of the water.

When we get home, we watch the sun come up, then fall asleep in our clothes. I awake with a start to the harsh persistent ringing of a phone. From its peremptory tone, I assume it is my mother. I pick up the phone anyway. Surprise!

'Well, well, how do you do,' my mother-in-law, Sherry Phillips, chirps. Instinctively I turn to hand the phone to Michael, but I am alone in the bed. 'Just a second,' I say, covering the mouthpiece. 'Michael,' I holler, 'your parents.'

From somewhere down the hall in the living room, I hear him cooing to Kate. He picks up the other extension. Michael's parents tell us how proud they are and how excited they are and how cute we looked. Very supportive, everything one could ask for in parents. But I don't respect them, so their support doesn't count.

I take off my clothes and hang them up. I cream my face and wipe off last night's makeup. I scrutinize my face in the mirror. I look a hundred years old.

I swallow a diet pill and head out to the garage. I retrieve our one decent suitcase from a pile of stuff that we've shipped from New York City but never unpacked. Peter Boyle, who is renting Margot Kidder's and Jennifer Salt's house down the block, is walking slowly, deliberately, up our driveway. He looks like someone with a lot on his mind. When he sees me, he shoots me a reluctant smile. Wordlessly he takes the suitcase from me.

'Soooooo, whaddya think?' I ask as he lugs the suitcase down the hall to our bedroom. Sonya is making the bed. She smiles at me, something she does rarely. I guess she's proud. 'I need some coffee,' I say and point Peter toward the living room. Let's join Michael and Kate and leave Sonya to her chores.

Peter hugs Michael. Kate gurgles up at him.

'So, whaddya think?' Michael asks.

'I think that you should prepare yourself for a real education,' Peter says seriously. 'You're about to lose a lot of friends.'

'Why?'

'Because people really like you best when you're struggling . . . when you're on the way up.'

Michael and I are shocked into silence.

'The only thing they like better is if you're on the way down. That's the only way you have to go now.'

'Hey, c'mon,' Michael protests. 'We're nowhere near where we plan to be.'

'I'm just telling you the awful truth.' Peter shrugs. 'But, hey, what the hell do I know . . .?'

The phone rings sharply. This time, no question, it's my mother. Both my parents are on the phone. They start out very excited. They liked the speeches. They want to know everything about the evening.

'I presume you wore the chicken feathers because you thought they were glamorous,' my mother says sourly.

'What are you going to do for an encore?' my father asks.

Is this to be a stereophonic assault?

'Some women were talking about your speech in the elevator this morning,' my mother adds, just for encouragement, 'and decided you must be the daughter of someone in the business . . .' Hey, where's my congrats? Oh, I guess they forgot. And what about the L-word? It isn't mentioned, although the call is a long one. Not once . . .

For the next ten days, Michael and I try to reconcile in Puerto Vallarta. I sit in the sun too long and get a rash all over my body, necessitating a house call from a local doctor, who administers a shot of cortisone amidst a torrent of Spanish. I return with an arcane flu, which swells just about every major lymph node in my system, and spend the next six weeks in solemn retreat in my bed.

When it passes, I go back to work with a vengeance, ignoring Kate, ignoring Michael. Ignoring, most of all, myself. I do things that are harmful to my health. I drive too fast. I alter my consciousness with whatever is around, usually pot and coke, constantly. I openly tempt losers and bad guys and comedy writers.

Over the next couple of months, my relationship with Michael deteriorates beyond redemption and we separate.

July 29, 1974.

It is just two days before our eighth wedding anniversary.

Everything that rises must break up . . .

Title Up:

You'll Never Eat Lunch in This Town Again

JULIA PHILLIPS

Mandarin

A Mandarin Paperback
YOU'LL NEVER EAT LUNCH
IN THIS TOWN AGAIN

First published in Great Britain 1991
by William Heinemann Ltd
This edition published 1992
by Mandarin Paperbacks
Michelin House, 81 Fulham Road, London SW3 6RB

Mandarin is an imprint of the Octopus Publishing Group,
a division of Reed International Books Limited

Copyright © 1991 Ruthless Productions, Inc.

A CIP catalogue record for this title
is available from the British Library
ISBN 0 7493 1172 X

Printed and bound in Great Britain
by Cox & Wyman Ltd, Reading, Berks

What is truth, said jesting Pilate, and did
not stay for an answer.
Francis Bacon, circa 1600

The truth changes from moment to moment.
Joel Schumacher, circa 1974

*Some names have been changed to protect
the privacy of, and me from, guilty people,
places, and things . . . the truth remains
substantially intact.*

Benedict Canyon, California
1989

She watched herself watching her nails dry and the news washed over her, a litany of chaos, lies, and despair. *Am I the only one who notices the swastikas outnumber peace symbols on the Wall tumbling down on my TV?* Yeah, guys, fight for the right to buy jeans, she overheard herself add. Long before attending therapy-school and learning the observing ego, she often out-of-bodied Life and viewed it instead. From a safe distance. Whatever the fuck that was.

Call it a film in progress. As it were. More precisely: a series of scenes, shots, takes, lines, that just needed an editorial vision to become a movie. An epic, preferably, with her as the Omniscient Voiceover. Kinda gimmicky, but then what movie was without its gimmicks? What life, for that matter?

She sprayed more quick-dry solution, the kind that really worked, even if it did mutate the skin on her fingers to reptilian scales, and held her nails up to the light. Perfect. If she could just resist the temptation to change a light bulb, feed the cats, or pick a pimple for another fifteen minutes, they'd be ding-less. Until she used her hands. Well, nothing's perfect, she amended casually, and focused on the center of the universe that was her nail. *Cogito, ergo sum.* First person, present. Third person. Past? Yeah, past. As in: incognito, ergo somebody else . . .

Since they were now telling her that eighty percent of the earth's frog population had died in the last five years, she wouldn't bother with the future anymore. She suspected she had shot her wad on the future some time ago. She'd pretty much passed on the future for awhile now. Oh, she'd work on it from time to time, to keep her chops up, but it always came up BLACK . . .

She closed her eyes for a nanosecond, then:

FADE UP with a POP DISSOLVE:
Bright shiny RED scorches through.
PULL BACK to reveal a well-manicured NAIL. Another nail flicks under, then pries, then springs a speck of sand. When it falls to the floor it REVERBERATES with a disproportionately macro sound for something so very micro. PULL BACK some more.
WIDER: A WOMAN and A MAN, laughing, creating late summer afternoon drinks in her kitchen.
WIDER: They are in bathing suits, both in good shape. On closer inspection, she is old enough to be his mother. She is not his mother. She hands him her concoction: vodka, tomato juice, splash of Rose's Lime, fresh lime, ice, straw.
HE: And what do we call this?
SHE: (looking up at him; smiling) Sunset at dawn . . .
FOLLOW her eyes . . .

He swung himself up onto her kitchen counter and said, 'I think I was an abused child.'

'What a surprise,' she said.

'Not by my mom or anything – maybe by a baby-sitter or something . . .' He grinned, his bonded teeth glittering phosphorescently in the light, looked down at his differently colored socks flopping over his combat boots and shot her a direct hit with his pale blue eyes. Hours later in the car, smoking a joint on the way to a club, he would turn to her suddenly and flash his fluorescent smile: 'I think you were the baby-sitter.'

They had engaged in this sort of repartee for a couple of years and she sparred with him over and over for three reasons: one, he was beautiful; two, he was smart; three, she was bored. Experiencing the sort of ennui Mastroianni did in *La Dolce Vita*. She was going to be forty-four in a month.

'The same age as the year I was born in,' she would muse, thinking, I was supposed to be dead and over by now.

She was born April 7, 1944. In between. Not a War Baby: fortyonefortytwofortythree; not a Boomer: fortysixfortysevenfortyeight. Dwight Eisenhower was *Time*'s Man of the Year; he was in between, too.

Her friends' eyes would glaze with lack of connection to the concept. That was probably because all her friends were so much younger than she was. First in her life friends had been contemporaries, then older, then younger. But she had never had a friend like him and she had always been surrounded by smart, handsome men.

He was a great big beautiful boy. He was twenty-five, but he seemed to her, especially from behind, like nineteen, just out of high school. Head on he was devastating: blond hair kept perpetually white by California sun and tanning salons, a girl's pretty, delicate blue eyes, contrasting with the heavy jaw and the high cheekbones of a brutal man. Altogether a pop-sexual icon for her tastes at least, and she had seen enough stares from others to know they shared her view. Star quality. No doubt about it.

Then there was a pretty good brain and a very fast mouth. Then there was her identity crisis. She had had a big career as a movie producer before women did such things, back in the seventies: meteoric rise, then something bad happened; cataclysmic fall, then something worse happened. She sank into drugs. She had always done them but with all the money she made she got to drown in them. No other period in her life had been so exquisite.

She had cleaned up and returned, but she just couldn't get it together to make a serious comeback. She ran around, she made deals, she sat at good tables in high-profile restaurants, she even made a movie, but she knew she wasn't in a cruising gear at all. She wasn't drowning, like she'd been during the last days of freebase and the first weeks of withdrawal, but she wasn't swimming either. Her life was like running on a treadmill or riding on a stationary bike; it was aerobic, it was healthy, but she wasn't going anywhere.

She had been in this state for so long it didn't bother her.

7

The free-floating anxiety, depression, and rage felt comfortable, or at least familiar, like an old bathrobe. It blanketed her and kept the world at bay. She didn't do serious drugs anymore but she didn't feel much either, and when she did she usually got the flu. Then she knew she was real because she felt so sick. Sometimes the flu would make her feel like drugs. 'Why did I think this was fun?' she wondered and then she realized the flu was more like the crash than the high. Not the fun part. But the gestalt of the trip anyway.

She had finally reached the age where she was more afraid of getting old than dying. Drugs had made her die from time to time and over and over. Wrinkles and enfeebled walking were scarier than expiration.

She remembered the second time she met him. The first time had been at Helena's on a Friday night. She was involved in optioning the Vampire books by Anne Rice ('*Star Wars* for the nineties,' she would tell the yup studio executives, quoting Jeff Berg, who had a gift for that kind of phrasemaking, and they would smile understandingly and pass) and he was in a vampire movie that Joel Schumacher had just put together at Warner Bros. Joel was a better dress designer than director, but that was show biz.

Her older, younger friend Stuart introduced them and he tried to chat with her but she was so pissed that someone besides her was doing a vampire movie that she didn't focus or listen. Besides, she was on the move and for some reason he didn't get to her at all that first time. She remembered more what she was wearing (an old Thea Porter black-and-gold jacket with a flared peplum) than what he was (a funny hat). Remembrance of *Vogue*s past. That was summer. She didn't meet him again for almost a year. She'd just finished locking reels on her little New York movie and she and Stuart were having a Friday celebration at Mortons.

'Yo, Jules, it's Stuart . . . are you there . . . pick up the goddamn phone . . .' He whistled and like a dog she came running.

8

'I'm here, I'm here . . .' She pressed STOP on the answering machine and it squealed off.

'Wanna go to an uptight screening?' Stuart was in his nervous I'm-a-baby-personal-manager-working-for-a-fag-who-has-pedicures-during-staff-meetings mode. Very Friday Night. She laughed.

'I didn't think so,' he said. 'Listen, I gotta take this kid I'm trying to sign. Could I bring him to dinner?'

'Ahhhhhh . . .' She had jet lag and she wasn't into meeting another new person.

'He's dying to meet you . . . you met him once before with me at Helena's . . . he's one of the Lost Boys . . . *Pleeeeze*.'

'Is this going to help you out?'

'A lot.'

'Okay, but I'm not drinking again and I'm dieting.' She had been 114 that morning and was freaked about her weight. It took all her self-control not to fast.

After she had given up drugs her body had gone into a six-month revolt and she had gained fifty pounds. One day she looked hard in the mirror. With the gray streak in her bangs and the chunky body, she looked like her mother. 'No!' she blurted to the mirror image. Through her drug doctor she found the obesity doctor. She was starting to drag a legion of great and famouses, as she called all the doctors lured by her case, behind her.

The obesity doctor, Leslie Dornfeld, was an angry, brilliant ex-Green Beret who had shed ninety pounds himself. He was one of a team of five doctors at UCLA who'd invented a space food called Optifast that was making them all a fortune. At first he was reluctant to put her on the fast because he was afraid she would feel so deprived she would drift back into drugs.

'I'll drift back into drugs if I continue to weigh a hundred fifty pounds.' He laughed. 'Listen,' she pitched, 'I'll be your model patient. Big losses are as moving as the big wins. I know, I used to be a compulsive gambler.'

'Okay, okay.' He held up his hands in what she called the heaven salesman gesture. Heaven salesmen were the guys who looked at the ceiling and said things like, 'She wants a size

9

seven – wouldn't I give her a size seven if I had a size seven?'
A dying breed lost to the Americanization of the Jews.

She fretted about what to wear and tore outfit after outfit
apart for two hours before dinner, a thorough workout. She
settled on a neutral blue Zoran casual suit, which she finished
off with a paradoxically flamboyant rhinestone cowboy belt
from a ten-year-old shopping spree at Nudie's. And a six-foot-
long white puckered silk scarf. If she could look in the mirror
and laugh, she could go out . . .

'Fly low and avoid the radar,' the lady d.j. purred – the one
she called Husky* – her voice not so husky anymore. Caution
to small planes landing on uncharted airstrips. The drive to
Mortons was anywhere from ten to twelve minutes from her
house, depending on time of day. If it was early enough, she
caught just the end of the Import Show. Some things were
never going to change, even though, God knows, she and
Husky did. But tell me, Husky, does the music sound the
same? Hey, just kidding . . .

'Free! huhuhuhuhuhu – Rock!' Grand Master Flash
intoned. She turned it up. So now the blow was headed for
the lowah clahsses. Inevitable . . . Finslander,* the smuggler,
nicknamed Fins because he liked to travel on water, told her:
never send a mode of transport without cargo. So when they
flew the guns to South America, what came back?

'Free! huhuhuhuhuhuhuh – Base!' Duh.

She stopped for the light at Santa Monica and Canon and
watched a slumpshouldered, malnourished black man push
the shopping cart that was the sum total of his life across the
intersection. He sported dreadlocks, but he had shaved trian-
gles over his ears and in the center of his forehead. He looked
like a homeless Klingon . . .

'Don't do it, do it, do it, do it . . .' He glanced in her
direction, Afro Travis Bickle. Boy, she thought, as she started
to turn left onto Santa Monica, away from him, comes the
revolution . . . What am I gonna do when they invade

* Names marked with asterisks are fictitious.

10

Benedict Canyon armed with Uzis? Hold up a sign that says: DON'T SHOOT, I WAS EMPATHETIC . . .?

She was only seventeen minutes late. She stepped around her scarf out of the car and handed the ancient Mexican dude five bucks. Just have it in front when I come out. With the engine running. Whenever possible. She imagined there were valets all over town who thought of her as 'T'ank you, missy, fi' dolla, hab a ni' deener . . .' I have always depended on the strangers whose kindness I purchase . . . and as she turned her back on him to head for the restaurant she thought, again, Don't shoot, I was empathetic . . .

She walked in and smiled broadly at Rick, who didn't need to show her to her table, it was close, with her back to the wall and a full view of the restaurant. What a great venue, she thought, referring to the restaurant, not the clientele . . . all pinkwhite, tables far enough away from each other so you were never crowded, ceilings high enough so you could breathe. More important, it was the only place in town where you could maintain a diet.

The boys were already there and drinking. Stuart was nursing a martini, her favorite; Brooke was drinking a Cuba Libre, a rum and Coke.

'I used to throw up on those when I was fifteen,' she said, gesturing with her head. Quick flashback: Harlem in the sixties, smiling black bartender, Johnny Harris ordering two 151 rum & Cokes. Come to think of it, Brooke looked like a neon version of Johnny Harris. Lots of bone structure, slitlike pale blue eyes that had the fire of intelligence, and big fat lips.

Johnny Harris had been her fucked-up boyfriend in college. She had known him three high schools ago and he'd found her in their freshman year when he was at Amherst and she was at Mount Holyoke. She still remembered Johnny Harris's kisses, those soft fat lips on her mouth. She remembered them the second she kissed Brooke.

*

She had gotten through dinner without a drink, although she and Brooke split an order of lamb and a hot fudge sundae in a flirtatious effort to be bad. Stuart got tired and didn't want to go to Helena's but he didn't want them to go either. He got up to make a phone call, a habit he'd acquired from the boss he didn't respect, and left her alone with Brooke.

'I'm not really into Helena's myself,' she said.

'Me neither . . .' He looked at her expectantly, an eager pupil.

'And I suppose I'm supposed to invite you to follow me and have a joint at my place,' she said.

He smiled, his big horselike teeth, pinkwhite in the pink-white-tableclothed candlelit restaurant. 'Of course you are . . . what a good idea.'

'I'm outta here,' Stuart announced. Cranky. Movin' fast. She used to move fast. When she was doing blow. Did anyone do blow anymore? Sure, they did. But back in the closet, back in the bathroom, in the backseat of the car on the way home from the AA meeting . . . 'Are we outta here?'

'We're gonna go to Helena's,' Brooke said. What a smooth little liar he was. She stood up abruptly and caught her scarf on one of the chair legs. She choked unglamorously and flashed on Isadora Duncan. The scarf was going to look like it had been stepped on. She didn't like near-strangulation. She'd experienced it quite a few times and each incident ran brightly through her mind. Incandescent with psychedelia:

There was the time when she'd held her friend Dominique and her brother above a whirlpool in the ocean off Fire Island as grownups rushed to their aid.

When she was eight her tonsils swelled up overnight, so she awoke gasping for air. She couldn't swallow and she could barely breathe. It was the middle of a blinding winter blizzard. The doctor walked twenty-six blocks through the storm and the snow and performed emergency surgery on the kitchen table. Mostly she remembered the ether – the smell – then the many-colored concentric fish surrounding, and circling into a tiny dot of . . . what? The Void? The doctor kept the tonsils to show her. They were the size of walnuts. They looked a little like walnuts.

Then there was Jeremy*. Breaking through her bedroom door like a gorilla, smacked out of his mind. Powerful hands on her throat squeezing. Her wheezing out *Help!* realizing she wasn't breathing, realizing that she wasn't strong enough to inhibit him even a little. Then him jerking back on the waterbed, rolling and shaking.

She got him out of the house by talking to him loudly and sternly as if he were a large, dangerous dog. He sat down on her front step and wept. She called Michael, he called the police, and they arrived at the same time. Nobody pressed charges. The cops took him home. They told her, 'Look, he is going to try to get in touch with you or see you. If you don't want this to happen again then don't ever see him or speak to him again.'

They were right. He called. He wrote letters. He pressed the button on the call box in her driveway. She spent five grand on a burglar alarm system. Two grand to electrify the gate. He never really went away. Friends would tell her, 'I ran into Jeremy at the Imperial Gardens.' Or, 'I think I saw Jeremy at Fred Segal . . . he looked awful.' Since Jeremy was one of the top five great-looking men she had met in her life that meant he was still slamming . . .

'Hollywood is a funny place,' she said to Brooke as she rolled a perfect joint. 'There are a lot of gorgeous young guys here. Some of them get to be stars and some of them get to be just another beautiful junkie.' She lit the joint and passed it to him. He sucked in the smoke and held it down a long time.

'I wanna be both at the same time,' he exhaled.

'There's that, too, but you won't thank me for it.' They bantered and passed the joint and the time.

She went to the kitchen and got some grapes. He laid his head back against her mattress as if he owned it and dropped grapes into his mouth. 'Nectar,' he sighed. 'Pure nectar.' Twenty minutes later, he was gulping down milk, a home remedy for the violent reaction he was having to the trace of pectin in the grapes.

'But if you knew you were allergic to grapes, why did you

eat them!' She was yelling at him. She barely knew him, but she already cared enough to yell at him.

'They tasted so good . . . couldn't help myself . . .' She tried to remember what it was like to be twenty-five. Was she twenty-five yet?

'You're the biggest kid I know,' Stuart had said with affectionate reassurance during dinner when the conversation moved into age, as it inevitably did with her these days.

When, exactly, had she become middle-aged? Probably the day she knew that she would never ever again do cocaine. That had been eight years ago and she had only been thirty-six. When she'd turned thirty-five someone had sent a telegram that said only HALFWAY HOME, and she, the Caterpillar from Alice in Wonderland sucking on her hookah, laughed 'not a chance' behind a cloud of white, cocaine-laced smoke. Had she given up her youth when she dropped the big C?

For the first three years she dreamed about freebase every night. Whatever short part of it that she slept. Much less dreamed. The shimmering white dust igniting and liquefying into amber, circling down the stem of the pipe to be collected and rewashed into another higher substance later . . . the smoke . . . the taste . . . the high . . . She would wake up sweaty, with her ears ringing, her heart and head and groin pounding with fear and excitement. Gradually the dreams diminished. First the high was gone, then the taste and smell. Finally the dreams themselves.

Sometime in the middle of her fourth cokeless year, she woke up one morning knowing she'd never do it again. She felt angry and stopped eating. Then she got very, very sad. Finally she descended into the kind of deep grief most people experienced with the death of a lover or a friend or a child.

She went in on a wholesale buy of a hundred Lemon Quaaludes and immediately abused herself with her share. She hadn't done any serious drugs for three and a half years and all of a sudden, without any conscious moment of choice, she'd fallen off the wagon. Hard. Two or three quacks and a martini or two. She either got blitzed and then depressed or sick and then depressed.

It was in such a state that she and Richard Baskin went to

see *The Big Chill* and she became suicidal. She never knew if the movie itself got her so extreme or if it was more because Larry Kasdan, who was an ambitious babe when she was a young Hope of Hollywood, was now a Major Film Maker. At any rate, she started to do the long sleeps of depression that she recognized from the period in college just after Michael broke up with her. And to drive very sloppily, which in L.A. increased your chances for death at least a hundredfold.

Finally she went to see Ron Siegel, who had become pretty famous for curing her of freebase.

'I think this could be biochemical,' she told him disconsolately, thinking of her mother's alphabetized medicine cabinet.

'I agree,' he said in his nasally professorial way. 'All the drugs are about you medicating your own depression.'

'At least when I did coke I got to be manic sometimes,' she said wistfully. 'Maybe I need to be thinking about another route.' She sighed, some part of her giving up.

'Look, Julia, there's a guy named Ozzie Janiger I'd like you to see . . .'

'Ah, another great and famous . . .' She recognized his name from Timmy Leary's book, *Flashbacks*.

'He's the one who gave Cary Grant acid so he could be straight . . . he's a true pioneer and a major force in the area of antidepressants.'

'I ain't doin' Lithium,' she said. ''Member Reice Jones, Mr. Langley Porter . . .'

'Yeah, he diagnosed you as suicidal . . .'

'Well, it would've been a self-fulfilling prophecy if I'd let him take care of me: first, take me off the coke that's making me manic, then treat me for mania and get me down as I'm sinking into depression . . .'

Ron Siegel stayed dispassionate and intellectual with her, which was how he'd first gotten her attention. 'Ozzie Janiger was one of the first guys in the thirties into antidepressants. You think this is biochemical. Go see the man who pioneered this shit.' With her halfhearted assenting wave, he called Janiger and made an appointment. The guy was over on La Cienega and San Vicente.

'I'm telling you,' Ron said, as she got up to wend her way

15

to the next great and famous, 'give up smoking and start running. You'll get higher than you ever did on drugs.'

She saw Janiger right away, who put her on Norpramin 25 and 0.5 mil. Xanax. She loved that Xanax was the same spelled forward or backward. Made you feel it had you covered either way. 'Together they make a pretty good pill,' he said. He looked like Ed Begley and smelled stale but he had a pretty good riff.

'This sort of depression isn't rare among Jews from New York,' he started. Well, okay, if he wanted to simplify, but she was pretty sure her mother would be rolling violently in her grave over that one. Deep down neither one of her parents really qualified as what people thought of as New York Jews, but strictly speaking, that's what they were, and she was prepared to go along with that assumption if it was going to prevent her from killing herself.

'First, there's the biochemical predilection,' he continued. Ooh, *predilection*, that was good. He was grabbing her the way Siegel had. Intellectually. 'Then, there's the psychology reinforcing it.' He almost couldn't spit out the end of a pretty good sentence he was so short of breath. She lit a cigarette, probably subconsciously hostile, and hoped he didn't die of emphysema before he stopped her suicidal cravings, let alone this wonderful meeting they were having. Or were they taking this meeting? He had mentioned the Gubers as people that he knew in her business. Whatever the fuck that was . . .

'I just want to get you into the Up Elevator and out of the Basement.' Bravo! It was the use of the word *basement* that got her. This recent acquaintance understood her surroundings. 'Have you had thoughts of suicide?'

'Doesn't everyone?'

'Yes, but some are more serious than others. Jews like passive suicide. Goyim blow their brains out. Jews like to drive into trees.'

'Jews like to plant trees . . .'

'That's so that they're there for them to drive into when they want to die before their time.'

'Well, if they die – even by killing themselves – isn't that their time?'

16

'No, suicide is an aberration . . .'

'I'll try the pills. I like that Xanax is spelled the same backwards and forwards.' She didn't want to have the suicide/ fate discussion right now. For weeks she'd been feeling as if someone or something was fucking with her norepinephrine levels. She was exhausted from the effort to stay alive when she wasn't motivated. Like an involuntary reflex, Kate's face flipped onto the vid-screen she carried at all times in her head. It used to be a movie screen, but that was in the seventies.

It was the don't-kill-yourself-it'll-fuck-her-up-for-life picture. It was always what 'saved' her so she could survive and move to the next level of . . . what? Consciousness? Understanding? Pain? Or was it with consciousness came understanding which led to pain? Really made you want to keep on going.

But in fact the Xanax and Norpramin worked. She gained weight and got constipated, but she also fell asleep around two in the morning and slept till eight, occasionally without interruption. She even dreamed from time to time. Benign, floaty dreams. Everybody told her how glad they were that she was back, that the danger was over, that she wasn't dead. Hell, she'd survived a half an ounce of freebase a day and two homicidal boyfriends. Not to mention the tender care of her mother. What chance did a suicidal depression have with her?

The pills made her tired all the time. And foggy. The cloud over her head drifted inside it. When she looked into her eyes in the mirror, one of her favorite lifetime pastimes, they looked muddy and uninteresting, and she'd turn away. Was this what 'better' was?

Her favorite drug buddy, Mara*, who gave up freebase with her, said one day, 'Maybe you should exercise. You know, they've been doing a lot of studies . . . when you do aerobics or pump iron your body releases natural drugs called endorphins. They're supposed to bliss you out and cheer you up.' Well, she was all for that.

She called the personal trainer Mara's trashy fashion friends all favored, Rebecca Eastman, a handsome six-foot person from a farm in Iowa whose claim to fame was that she had gotten Lily Tomlin into shape for the one-woman show that was now wowing them on Broadway. Rebecca's star was rising with Lily's. Maybe she was good with comeback types.

Rebecca showed up one hot August afternoon with a perfect blond, blue-eyed specimen named Glen three paces behind her. Glen had the wild look in his eyes that was usually sported only by stuntmen and acid casualties. Could he be experiencing an endorphin rush? Maybe there was something to this exercise shit. If she could have his hips, she would take the shoulders, even though she thought them too broad for a woman.

Rebecca was hard-edged and empathetic at the same time. She came equipped with a detailed questionnaire and a tape measure. Rebecca was impressed with her credits, some of her favorite movies, Rebecca said. Mine, too, she thought, but she was more impressed at the moment with her measurements. When it got to hips 38″, she thought, I am doing this just in time.

'Any drugs?' Rebecca asked. She felt like saying, 'Define your terms,' but instead she said, a bit apologetically it seemed to her, 'I do have the occasional drink or joint.'

'I said drugs,' Rebecca said meaningfully.

'Well, just these mood elevators and relaxers . . . I really hate them . . . oh, and birth control pills . . . out of habit, I guess.'

Rebecca stood up, a towering, athletic figure backlit flatteringly by the festering sun.

'Good,' she said briskly. 'It is good when you're starting out this program to set some goals. We want those hips down three or four inches, we want you on the pill for a reason, and we want you off those damn elevators.' Exit Ozzie Janiger, enter Rebecca Eastman. It might be a good idea to get off the elevator and onto a treadmill. It might seem like forward motion.

As she got into the workouts more, she started to feel better. She stopped the pills, but there were some days when she felt all she did was work out. Then what did she do? Close all the doors and look in the mirror?

That was something that she noticed about Brooke. He spent more time looking in the mirror than anyone else she had ever known except herself. She had looked at herself a great deal when she was young, then through herself when she was deep into drugs. Now, even with her improving face and body she still tended to focus on the deterioration: the frown mark between her eyebrows, the coke lines etched on the sides of her mouth, the sagging breasts, the loose belly.

Susan Rice, a screenwriter/friend, had once said to her when they were carefree and in their twenties in New York, 'I used to think that you looked in the mirror all the time because you were vain; now I realize that it's just to check to see that you're still there.' A little of both. Which was why she understood his impulse to check himself at every possible opportunity. Like all beauties, he could also look weird, more like a creature than a person. Probably most of the time he was trying to figure out why he had such a dynamic effect on people.

That first night, after he'd recovered from his allergic attack, smoked another joint, and then drunk some coffee for the drive home, she caught him checking himself out unabashedly in her mirror in the bathroom.

'Look at all these products!' he exclaimed happily. It was true; one hairdresser after another had left more mousse and gel than any straight person she knew had a reason to use. There were the Tenax from her Jose period, the Kamikaze products from her Peter Nagai period, Aveda Spray Gel, compliments of Daley, and always plenty of Paul Mitchell and Sebastian from Victor.

He threw one after another into his hair and pulled it this way and that. In the unforgiving fluorescent light, she noticed for the first time that he had mascara on. She handed him an Andrea Eye-Q and wrapped her arms around him from behind, peeping her face out and tucking it under his armpit.

'Whaddaya think of the couple?' Reilly O'Reilly* had used that line on her more than a decade before and she had used it over and over since then, always to great effect.

'Dunno.' Then he considered them seriously. 'Very andro-gynous, very confusing, very eighties.' He was turning around as he said this, and then they were holding each other very tightly, kissing hard, tongues all over each other's faces and

19

mouths. She could feel his heat and his hard-on against her and her pussy was dripping. What a nice surprise . . .

For a moment, she thought they might fuck right there on the floor in the bathroom. Something she hadn't done in a long time. But he pushed her away. When he did, she found herself face to face with the dozen or so toothbrushes she still kept in a glass on the counter behind him. Tombstones, Michael Brandon, a movie actor in search of a hit TV series, had called them. Some time ago . . .

'Ah, c'mon . . .' she heard herself protesting. Wait a second, was she the guy here?

'No, I think I'm being very adult,' he said, and she could tell from his face that he was cold sober and meaning it.

'In that case, it's late . . .'

'Yeah, I should hit the road . . .'

'Should we exchange phone numbers?' Her voice sounded small and frail and she hated it.

They moved out of the bathroom, and the second they hit the larger space of her oversize bedroom, everything seemed light and cheerful and possible. He pulled her to him and they had a good succulent kiss. This time she broke it and they found a pad and each wrote down their phone numbers. She noticed that when he wrote his name it looked like an autograph. Probably something he had been practicing for years. She started to walk him to the door, and as they passed one of the many mirrors he stopped her and held her there next to him.

'Whaddaya think of the couple?' he drawled. Was he taunting her or did he really want to know?

'Dunno yet.'

'Well, we'll see, won't we?'

They had reached the space between her room and her office, an addition she'd originally built for drugs. The Oscar stood discreetly in the corner facing the wall, in protest, she was fond of telling people, against the state of movies. He bent down and picked it up. Everybody did. It was so tarnished and dusty he had to rub at it with his jacket to see the credits. She watched his lips move as he read the plaque on the base:

ACADEMY AWARD
TO
'THE STING'
BEST PICTURE OF 1973
A UNIVERSAL–BILL/PHILLIPS–
GEORGE ROY HILL FILM PRODUCTION
ZANUCK/BROWN PRESENTATION PRODUCTION, UNIVERSAL
TONY BILL, MICHAEL AND JULIA PHILLIPS PRODUCERS

He replaced it tenderly, and she turned it so it faced the wall again. So many names, so many relationships, so many breakups. She was still the only woman to win for Best Picture.

Every year, when *Who's Who* sent their little bio for updating she'd cross out 'first' and type in 'only,' so she guessed it still counted to her at some level. Out here, that little statue that she had taken to treating so cavalierly ages ago, a lifetime ago, was still what it was all about. Oh, the too-much, too-soonness of it all . . .

She used to take Polaroids of people holding it. For their amusement or hers? She thought of doing it now, then changed her mind. Was she withholding because he didn't want to fuck her? Nah, because it didn't matter to her enough. Nothing did, least of all sex. He started toward the office door.

She let him open it and look for a moment. Quite a treasure trove: stained-glass windows, awards, a bulletin board of the fifties, sixties, seventies, furniture that still bore the burn marks of fires set by propane torches that she kept lit all day, she smoked so much freebase. His eyes seemed to be on fire. She knew he wanted to go into that room and stay there for awhile. Like the instinct to fondle the Oscar, it was something that everyone wanted to do.

'Next time.' She smiled and opened the other door, the one that led outside. 'When will that be? I wonder . . .' She heard the uncertainty in her voice, felt like she was eighteen. She would never voluntarily be a teenager again.

'When it's right, it'll happen.' And he smiled his killer smile, flew down the steps, and started up his car. Peeled out of her driveway, negotiating the hairpin turn without a hitch or a scratch. Escaped, and left her on the landing.

Thinking about it all.

Thinking. The one excitement left. The others – sex drugs money travel clothes jewels art success – living on the edge – had all disappointed her. She was probably lucky they hadn't killed her.

So here she was, disappointed but alive, with thinking as the one pastime that was still fun without too much downside. Unless you counted depression, rage, and anxiety as the downside. If they came only in spurts, like happiness did, you could deal.

If you were determined. She was nothing if not determined. To do what?

Well . . . to think. Cogito, ergo sum, baby . . . Hey, it is what it is.

Incogito, ergo sumbody else. It was what it was.

I think, therefore . . . I yam what I yam . . .

163 Ocean Avenue, Brooklyn, New York
1948

'I hate this Brooklyn,' I tell my mother, and, from the trembling of her lower lip, I can see she agrees. 'I want to go back to my cute little house in the Village,' I add and start to cry. My mother's eyes well up, but she brushes her tears away. My mother is a beautiful cry-er. We are in our new kitchen. It is August in New York at its hot damp worst, and we have just moved from the Village, where my mother and father have enjoyed a glamorous existence, to this Brooklyn place. True, the apartment is big and airy and on the top floor and everyone has his own bedroom, but the neighbors don't seem like my parents' friends in the city.

My mother turns away from me to get busy at the sink. Like

she loves to wash dishes. I hug her from behind and feel her stiffen. She doesn't like it. She disengages herself from my grip and blows her nose loudly into a towel. She reaches into the corner of the lowest shelf of a nearby cabinet and pulls out her extra large medicine bottle with the orange rectangular pills. She unscrews the top and takes one. She swallows it dry.

Lonely, lonely. I run around my room in a desperate attempt to fill it with my presence, but I get tired in the damp heat. I wait for night to fall. Some relief from the heat. I hate this heat. I hate this room. I hate this Brooklyn . . .

My mother was an immigrant.

She came to this country when she was seven, all the way from Russia. With her very old father and his young bride, my mother's mother. My grandfather was a wheat speculator, a wealthy Jewish middle classnik, stuck in the middle of the Russian Revolution. He got his family out one by one. My mother and he and my grandmother were the last. She left Russia when she was four. Long journey.

They wandered around the Balkans for two years and ended up in Greece. My mother's father paid for this wandering with huge quantities of precious jewels. From Greece they went to Italy – I don't know how – and landed in Naples. Her father bribed the Secretary of the U.S. Consul and their application for immigration to the United States rose from the bottom of the pile to the top.

They boarded a Greek ship and thirty days later they disembarked in New York. My mother and her mother both had malaria, but they got in the country anyway. Her father set about getting them cured. He kept saying, I know this disease, I know this disease, but none of the American doctors listened. Finally he scurried my mother in to see one of them while she was having a fit and she was cured. My mother's mother, a frail, beautiful woman to my mother's recollection, didn't fare so well and died. In her little-girl arms.

My mother's father remarried and my mother didn't like her stepmother. They moved to Monticello because my grandfather had tuberculosis. It was the best weather they could afford with the little money they had left. My mother was regaled in her youth with stories of past wealth and memories of drifting through the Balkans with the family jewels sewn inside the head of her doll.

There were no Jews in Monticello except in the summer. My mother, being a native, hated Jews.

My father's family was one-half German and one-half Russian. My grandfather was a Menshevik in the Russian Revolution. My grandmother was beautiful. When he was jailed by the Bolsheviks in 1916 she flirted with a guard and kicked a damaging piece of evidence around the floor, and under a chair, where it remained hidden until two days later when he was released. They fled St. Petersburg (now Leningrad) and walked – *walked* – to Warsaw. Check it out in the atlas. It's a lot of fucking miles. My grandfather and grandmother came to New York City along with all the other Russian Jewish emigres. My grandfather (now Elias Miller – renamed, no doubt, at Ellis Island) was one of the founders of the *Jewish Daily Forward*. His socialism was satisfied by most of the New Deal.

My mother grew up the youngest – by seventeen years – of seven siblings. When her eldest brother died at the age of eighty-five she was in her mid-thirties. My mother was estranged from her family, the offspring of four different wives. She did not tend her stepmother when she was dying. She was a very brilliant anti-Semitic Jew. I don't imagine she ever had a childhood. She made sure I didn't either. Perhaps that was how we developed the habits of introspection – just thinking – early on.

My father was born on the exact birthday of his older brother. His older brother told him he was adopted, a birthday present from his parents. He, the older brother, was the only real Miller son. (One of my brother's children was also born on this particular day – August 12, an exceptionally hard-luck number, for those who play with alternative mythologies.) My father was very smart. He went to Walden and Columbia and graduated at the age of nineteen. He went on in metallurgy. He was a gifted composer and mathematician, but the family was broke. The Depression. He worked on the Manhattan Project nevertheless. He was very, very handsome and not very good at making money.

My mother went to New York University on a scholarship.

Her family (the older brothers and sisters), who were quite well off, would not pay for her tuition as punishment for her not helping her stepmother through death. When Samson (her eldest brother) died she was invited to the funeral, but refused to go on the grounds that she was always invited to the funerals, but never the weddings. I remember her sobbing into the kitchen sink in our large hot apartment in Brooklyn, and saying over and over, 'Always the funerals, never the weddings.' My father tried to hold her vibrating shoulders, but she pushed him away.

My mother and father ran with a pretty fast, eclectic crowd (Judy Holliday, Adolf Green and Betty Comden, Henry and Phoebe Ephron, I. I. Raabe and Salvador Dali to name a few) in the thirties and forties in New York City.

My mother stole my father from her best friend. My father came to visit the friend and my mother was there. They talked and talked. The friend went to sleep. My mother and father stayed up all night and talked and talked and fell in love.

My mother tried to get jobs in the Depression. She wanted to write, but she didn't get the jobs she applied for at *The New Yorker* or *The New York Herald* or *The New Republic*. She ghostwrote some radio plays for awhile. Three years into their marriage I was born. My mother stopped ghostwriting horse operas. She was very fond of telling me that at that time one made a choice between career and motherhood. I became her tragedy. And her creative act.

My mother had a borderline peasant face in that it was broad. Broad brow, broad cheeks, broad jaw (which was exceptionally square and defined) but her black, deep-set eyes and her wide smile cut against the broadness. She had gorgeous legs. She was probably a knockout for ten minutes somewhere between twenty-one and twenty-five. She had a peasant's chubby hands and the high-tone comic timing of an aristocrat. My father, on the other hand, possessed a low brand of humor and the looks of an aristocrat. Handsome and elegant – elegant hands, elegant gestures, elegant piercing blue-gray eyes.

My mother and father lived in New York on West 9th just off Fifth Avenue. In a fourth-floor walkup. My father was a metallurgist. He filled out P-R-O-T instead of J-E-W and got a job running a plantation in Guayaquil, Ecuador.

Heavies went down there between them. The marriage was lucky to survive that year. They got very involved with the workers on the plantation. They understood why the workers were communists. My father told me stories about the handsome young foreman, a Catholic, who was also the head of the local Communist Party. 'The people, they need a leader,' he told my father, 'or they will all go to hell.'

My father and this man had a close bond, as this man almost saved my father's life. My father was caught in a sugar-threshing machine literally by the seat of his pants and the foreman struggled to stop the machine, when my father's pants ripped and dropped him from the jaws of death. It was cheap fiber that saved his life, but my father always gave points for effort, and this foreman and he got tight from then on. They occasionally got drunk together and did guy things without my mother.

My mother was very unhappy in this village. She hated the earthquakes and the rain and the machismo. About a year into this experience my father filled out P-R-O-T instead of J-E-W again and landed a job in Research and Development at Standard Packaging. They returned to NYC and settled in the Village village. Two weeks after they returned, the town they had lived in, the plantation, and all the workers, disappeared during a quake into a ten-foot-wide crack in the earth. Everybody died. 'The people, they need a leader or they will all go to hell.'

My father didn't fight in World War II. Instead: He worked on The Bomb. I got to know duck-and-cover was a crock of shit when I was eight.

Two things I am born with: mobility and insomnia. The ability to move fast and the inability to sleep. The two are linked, I think, because people who don't sleep much don't REM much, so they are doomed to dream during their waking hours. The joyful fantasies and the frightful nightmares live in the real world with you; they tend to make you accelerate.

Or maybe it is just that my mother transmitted her unhappiness and fear of death to me prenatally. In the placental fluids. I can't sleep because I know I am going to die, and I move real fast on the off-chance that I can outrun the big D. At least the gravitational pull of my mother's despair. I am born in motion. I know this from baby pictures of me running, me skipping, me dancing, me struggling out of my mother's arms.

I am a head-banger. A classic symptom of retardation say a number of my legion of doctors. I have a theory about this: I am nearly three and extremely motor-advanced. But I'm not saying a word. No mama, dada, no cat, no dawg – *schtum*. I seem to understand what is said to me, but I make no attempt to communicate verbally. Except to cry loudly when my parents play me a Woody Guthrie record. Years later, my mother tells me that I must have been a very sensitive child, and was crying because I heard his physical suffering in the music. I think it is that I hated his voice.

I start to invent some fairly sophisticated physical entertainment for myself. One rainy afternoon, in a miasma of boredom, I stand up on a rocking chair, just to see what it feels like. I get some pretty powerful back and forth going – I remember the exhilaration of having attained enough speed to create a feeling of air whooshing against my cheeks. Then I crash. The back of my head hits the glass edge of a breakfront – blood is gushing everywhere – then I pitch forward and land head first on the floor, chomping down hard on my front lip with my baby teeth.

My lip can't be repaired and still has a funny bump. My head is sewn back together with forty-nine stitches. And three weeks later I am talking. Not baby talk, but colloquially, idiomatically, and in full sentences. It is as if the bang on the head moves all my neuroceptors two steps up and to the left.

My mother convinces me that I am the sweet, pretty one in the family – by no means as smart as any one of them separately or together. The message seems to be that you are either smart or pretty; if you verge on both, you might be a tough act to follow, but you are also a tough act to take. You'll curry favor and love, and you'll get it, but at some point people will resent loving you and then they will probably hate you.

When I am four, my parents take me to my first dinner at Lefferts, a local seafood restaurant where I try oysters. I make a big face and tell them they feel like snot going down my throat. A pretentious older woman stops at the table to remark how well-behaved I am: 'She seems to really be participating in the conversation,' she says condescendingly. 'What could you all be talking about?'

'Snot,' my father says, and rewards her with his cold blue stare. We are very good at alienating people. This incident gives me the illusion that I can count on my father to defend me. Perhaps from the outside world, but I am really more in danger from my mother. My father is very unreliable where my mother is concerned. They call it love.

This dinner is basically consolation for the traumatic move to Brooklyn: My father, a scientist indentured to Big Biz, is to inflict a few more disruptions before I have control of my own living arrangements; there isn't a single one of them that isn't traumatic, but I don't know that at four. I've already endured the onslaught of my little brother, Matthew, whose premature birth was not only a drama of major proportions in my little life but a dark secret between my parents, revealed in incremental stages of anger throughout my childhood.

He is born prematurely, in a sea of my mother's hemorrhaging blood. When she complains of pain in the morning, my father ignores it, the result of a book he's been reading that advises never to indulge a pregnant woman in imagined problems. The problems are real, though, and end up a hospital emergency: cesarean section, lost blood, tainted blood – the whole catastrophe. While my mother recovers in the hospital, my father takes me out. The highlight is a Burl Ives concert. Burl doesn't make me cry. My father holds me high above his shoulders and I express myself loudly along with Burl: A haint cain't haint a haint, My good old man, A haint cain't haint a haint, My honey my l-a-a-mb . . .

An apparently average family of four, who no longer fit into the hip little walkup on West 9th, we move to the large, airy apartment on Ocean Avenue in Brooklyn. A reverse gesture on my parents' part, but my father doesn't make enough money for us to move to Long Island yet. Besides, my parents pride themselves on marching leftrightleftright while the rest of the world marches rightleftrightleft. Each of us has his own bedroom; mine is painted blue and white to my specifications. No pussy pink for me.

Looking out the window at Prospect Park, I fixate on a hole in the fence. I later learn that the older boys have made it so the little kids can slip through and not have to go around the block to get into the playground. It is dangerous for little kids to have to go around the block – too much traffic and too many hoodlums, some of them from nearby Negro neighborhoods. In the summer months, conversation from the streets about the encroaching *schwartzes* wafts through the open windows.

Although my mother shares these views she doesn't like our neighbors much. They are the very Jews she'd hated all those summers in Monticello. I think my mother is as unhappy as I am to be in this alien place. It is the quintessential AugustinNewYork. I have developed an allergy to my own sweat, and I break out and swell with a mottled rash.

My little brother Matthew is a very angry baby. He coos all day with his big brown eyes and long lashes and dark curls, but he screams all night. He has become the center of attention. I'm not real fond of him. That night I upstage him and develop a raging fever. The next day I wake up with my eyes shut. My pediatrician tells my parents that they have to get me out of the city. Fast.

And that is how they discover Fire Island. They get us the hell out of the city the second the temperature is more than 75 degrees F. for more than three days running (that is when my rash begins). That is usually in May, long before school lets out. And we don't come back until we are forced to by hurricane, which is usually in mid-to late September. We never simply leave Fire Island. We are evacuated. Mostly in a boat provided by the Coast Guard, but every once in awhile by seaplane, the kind with the pontoons instead of landing gear. Once a gale wind comes out of nowhere and my brother, who is four, and I who am seven, try to shut the door against 75 mph winds. Making the effort quells our fear of nature, but we need Mommy's help to get the door closed. We sit on the floor and play Monopoly. Wind and rain pummel the house. Then a magical blue light that looks like a tiara slips under the door, fires across the floor, scattering paper money in its path, then flies up the chimney.

'What was that!?' we exclaim.

'It's called St. Elmo's fire,' my father explains. 'It's a collection of ions in a transitional state . . . it happens during bad storms . . .'

I think my mother is already very disappointed in her life. It is 1953 and she is not about to drink or shrink. She is well into a manic-depressive mode, amplified by an impressive array of uppers and downers and whatevers. Probably what she does most every day is think. I catch her sobbing into the morning dishes from time to time.

Once she explains it away by telling me she is crying because she is an atheist. I get to learn this at about the same time I am grappling with how babies are made and born. Great. First, sex . . . now this. I'm a third-generation atheistic Jew. I look out the window. It's raining. I guess that means galoshes.

'What does not believing in God have to do with crying like this?' I ask.

'Because we don't believe in heaven or hell or an afterlife – it is what it is – You're born, you live, you die – that's it,' she says, blowing her nose, loudly, into a dish towel. She smiles abstractedly at me, somehow cheered by this thought, and rushes me off to school.

I have a nice long walk to P.S. 92 – down Ocean Avenue to Prospect Boulevard – all the way across Lincoln. First big wide blocks, lots of apartment buildings, the park on the other side of the street. Then clothing and food stores. Then nice tree-lined streets with single-family dwellings.

I take my time going to school the morning of this interchange meandering around the concept of the finite quality of life. No doubt at the age of nine I think about death on a pretty regular basis, anyway. Have for quite some years. The way I figure it, you get three good years as a human being and that's when you're a tiny baby. Then at around the age of three or four, a pet, a grandparent, or a parent's friend dies and you have to get the D word explained to you. Having fun? Forget it, you're going to die – to end – to cease – fun isn't as much fun anymore. I march to school avoiding all the cracks in the pavement to the beat of death squish death squish.

On the corner of the last intersection before the school is a candy store. Manny's. I always stop in before facing the school yard. Discuss the Army-McCarthy hearings with tough guys who sip scalding hot coffee without wincing. Buy a bar of chocolate, which I've just discovered. I'd been very resistant to its charms until about a year before. I saunter in. Nestle's Crunch or a Fifth Avenue is what I want.

A hairy, heavyset man comes out of the back door and leaves it ajar, revealing some guys on phones and a lot of smoke. It smells like home.

'Twenty-five on Alphon's Dream in the fifth, Manny,' the hairy guy says on the fly and races out the door. It is ten after nine. Manny squints down at me sternly, 'Why aren't you in school, Julia?'

'It was a nice day . . . what was that guy talking about, Manny?'

'Nothing, you're late for school,' he snorts, reaching for my dollar.

'He was making a bet, Manny.' Not for nothing has my mother schlepped me to a revival of *Guys 'n Dolls*. I laser him with my best imitation of my father's coldest gray-eyed stare. My eyes are a tad lighter. It is very effective. Manny studies his Florsheims – 'So . . .?'

'So I wanna make a bet.'

'Are you kidding?' Manny the bookie actually looks

shocked. I still haven't handed over my dollar. His hand hovers uncertainly over mine.

'No, I'm not.'

He sighs and gets a lot shorter – he is an old Jewish mole – 'So whaddaya wanna bet?'

'I don't know. Show me.' You stoopid doodyhead.

So Manny shows me and I get into betting horses and numbers. I don't get into sports and cards until I get rich much, much later, but I certainly am getting the low-rent juice early enough. You win – you get an adrenaline rush, you lose, your stomach goes into your knees. In either case you get high and it sure beats turning around and around to get dizzy, which at this point is the only other high with which I am acquainted.

The first time I have a really big win, I treat all the kids in my class to ice cream after school. At Manny's. At first, they all want to know where I got the money, but they get distracted by their little sugar rushes. Manny and I exchange a knowing look. I know it is a grown-up, and not a kid, moment, but I feel prepared . . .

DINNER AT MY PARENTS' HOUSE:

The foursome sits around the dinner table. CAMERA three-sixties the assemblage from the POV of the roast that rests in the center of the table.

OMNISCIENT VOICEOVER*: If my mother is sedentary on the couch, she is active at the dinner table. In a sedentary sort of way. Her foot and leg never stop going. Sometimes so hard that the table vibrates and we have to hold our food down. My father is always active. Just now he is jumping up from the table to expostulate freely on the issue of the Van Allen Belt.

CAMERA RISES with DAD. We see him vaguely through a cloud of PUFFAGE emanating from MOM. His index finger pokes holes through the smoke.

DAD: (yelling) We're poking holes through the Van Allen

---

* Hereafter, ovo.

32

Belt! If we don't bury ourselves under a mountain of shit first, we'll suffocate from lack of air or heat prostration!

ovo: My father has been discussing some interesting articles about hot spots around the world in a rational tone to this point. My father makes sudden moves, leaps through time and space. My father, no matter what, is determined to speak the Truth. I squirm in my chair. Not believing in God coupled with this suffocating-under-a-mountain-of-shit-or-sweat concept isn't calculated to make you feel real secure when you're nine. Plus my number didn't come in today . . .

me: This isn't making me happy . . .

mom: (stops vibrating; stops puffing) Happy? What's happy? Cows are happy . . .

I get to pay my dues in the grown-up department right away. There is a girl in my class, pretty in a Sean Young kind of way, who is a little retarded. She has some reading problems. I have a problem too, which is Miss Marlowe, our teacher. She loves the rest of the class – especially Marion Schwartz*, the one with the reading difficulty. The only one she doesn't love is me. She hates me. She takes every opportunity to undercut my apparent confidence and popularity. My mother has already done a pretty thorough job on my ego, but I have also developed overcompensating tendencies and have run for elective office and won a time or two.

I have been taught to blow my nose hard. Postnasal drip, sinus infection, bronchitis – I have the entire upper respiratory catastrophe. At first, Miss Marlowe thinks she can restrain me in class through ridicule. She doesn't seem to understand that no amount of teasing can make a kid beleaguered by snot who wants nothing more than to breathe free blow softly.

Finally, she punishes me for my honky ways. I have to teach Marion Schwartz how to read. The weird part is that I am successful. And the success feels wonderful. It is one of my first deeply moving experiences that has nothing to do with my family. The first time she reads through the second-grade primer – it really did see Dick and Jane run – which is two grades behind where we are, but which is a huge accomplishment for her – we both cry.

After that she reads better and faster and more and more. She also begins to cling to me and to follow me and to idolize me. It is flattering and embarrassing. It makes the other kids laugh. I don't want to hang out with her but I don't want to hurt her feelings or seem rejecting in any way. It might inhibit her reading progress. My ego is already vested in her continued accomplishment. I am a bit like a stage mother. I push her. Hard. And she follows me around even more.

One day I am fooling around with a fountain pen with a bunch of friends. We have figured out a way to make it spurt ink. In my case, it spurts backward – over my shoulder and onto Marion Schwartz's brand-new white silk blouse.

Miss Marlowe accuses me of inking Marion purposely, Marion agrees, and my friends testify against me. It is a totally unfair incident, but I learn some valuable lessons:

1: Something about me invites accusation. Best to be rigidly honest as I am likely to be suspected anyway.
2: Friends will turn on you.
3: Never teach a slow child how to read.

Most important: 'They're trying to put out my fire!' I tell my father after the requisite parent/teacher battle, which he wins. 'And I won't let them!'

My mother takes me to the City just about every Saturday to see the ballet or Jose Greco or a play, if it is appropriate. For my eighth birthday, my mother takes me to see *Mrs McThing* with Helen Hayes and Brandon de Wilde and Jules Munshin. We sit in a box, and in the middle of the first act Jules Munshin winks at us. One Saturday my mother takes me to the Museum of Modern Art. I particularly like the pea soup in the cafeteria and *Guernica*. I sit down and watch it, as if it is a still movie, for a half hour. My mother thinks I am a tired kid. I think I learned everything about War.

Sometimes she takes me shopping. An almost unendurable experience.

My mother is always looking for bargains. Excruciating for

a child to watch her mother fight off other women for a dress, even if it is for me. Dressing rooms like stalls for animals. Women behaving like animals. Store employees treating them like animals. It creates in me a desire to buy retail for the rest of my life.

Maybe the bargain hunting also feeds my gambling fever. By the middle of fifth grade I am into a real rhythm. Leave for school, think about death, hit Manny's, eat chocolate, make a bet. Go to school, race out, pick up the *Daily News* and check 'Li'l Abner' for the winning number. My losses are small but constant, my wins are pretty big and rare.

One day, after a decent win, as I am strolling home, humming to myself with the pleasure of the jingling of coins in my pocket, I see a classmate mowed down by a hit-and-run driver and discover several things about myself. One, I have a photographic memory – I provide the police with the license number of the evil car, and two, I am not much put off by the sight of blood, of which there is plenty, because the kid is hit in the head. My classmate is proclaimed dead a few days later, but I know that when I see the accident.

The third thing I learn is that I might not believe in God, but I sure make some unusual connections. There is no way I can convince myself that my illicit gambling isn't in some way connected to the accident I witness. The wages of sin are death. My sin, his death. Some part of me understands the therefore-do-not-send-to-know-for-whom-the-bell-tollsness of it all. Pretty religious thinking for a miniatheist.

My parents' civil-libertarian views are not always reinforced by their personal behavior. By dint of her upbringing in Monticello, my mother is not only anti-Semitic. She also harbors some outrageous prejudices about black people. I mean, she does go to great lengths to teach us 'Negro' instead of 'colored,' but in her later years, she reverts to 'nigger.' When she was in college, she once tells me, her friends tried to get her over her tendency to think of black people as savages whose brains were smaller by telling her that a guy she was dating, David Levine, was actually half black. I guess they thought that since she was fond of him, it would make her revise her worldview. She dropped him abruptly, instead.

In spite of the fact that my mother doesn't work, she always sees it as her right to have maids. At least from the time we move into the big apartment in Brooklyn. The first maid I really develop an attachment to is Willie, who is light-skinned, twenty-five, and gorgeous, save for a funny gap between her two front teeth, one of which she has embellished with gold. I get to see a lot of the teeth because Willie is always smiling, just one of her many great traits. Willie has spark and energy, and gets done with the cleaning early so she can play with me. I worship Willie and imitate her whenever I can.

'A-a-aggs,' I say one morning to my mother who has just asked me what I want for breakfast. I am trying to sound like Willie. I guess I do a pretty good job, because my mother whips around, shocked, lips pursed, ready to get mad.

'Eggs,' she corrects, sharp but subdued.

'A-a-aggs, a-a-aggs, a-a-aggs,' I la-la happily, my voice rising and falling in a semisong of childishness. Uh-oh, am I in trouble now! My mother raises her hand as if to strike, then laughs, cracks up, in fact, and cracks some eggs into a bowl.

'Eggs, Julia, not a-a-aggs,' she says, and places a perfect omelet in front of me.

'E-a-a-ggs,' I smile and she smiles with me, and lets it go.

One Monday morning it gets to be pretty late and there is no Willie. My mother makes a call. She looks upset, but all she says is, 'Willie's got a cold. Her sister, Emma, is going to be here in a little while.'

Emma is a big fat woman who drinks my father's scotch. My brother cries and screams and says he won't stay alone with her. Why? my mother wants to know. 'B-b-b-be-cause she's black,' he wails.

'Honey,' Emma says, lifting his dirty hand and holding it next to hers, 'you ain't so white yo'self.' My mother and I smile big smiles at each other, and my brother sputters into silence. As far as he is concerned, Emma is queen for a day. Emma is okay, but I miss Willie. I ask her a couple of times to please tell Willie I hope she gets over her cold real fast so she can come back soon, and Emma looks sad every time.

I see her and my mother huddle together in various corners of the house, whispering in an urgent grown-up way to each other, but I never catch any of their conversation, not even bits and pieces. When Emma leaves that night, she says she'll see us Wednesday, a bad sign. That night, when my father gets home, my parents close the door to their room and talk in low voices for a long time.

They come out and start to make noises in the kitchen. My brother plays on the floor of his room. I walk into the kitchen and offer to help set the table.

'Willy was murdered Saturday night,' my mother tells me. Don't candy coat it, Mom! 'Her boyfriend stabbed her with a knife and she bled to death . . .' My mother seems furious. Horrified, I open my mouth to say something, and to my surprise, I laugh. This feeds the horror even more, and escalates to uncontrollable giggling. Oh, the mixed feelings of it all.

In retrospect, in the excruciating ride home from dropping Brooke off, snarled in desperate Saturday-night cruising traffic on Sunset, she chided herself that she should have known that times were such that raw eggs, hurled from another table at her host, was not something outside of the realm of everyday experience.

They landed on his new Maxfield's white linen suit and her thousand-dollar Thierry Mugler quintessential little black Jetsons number. She should have seen it coming. She should have been funnier in the little speech she felt impelled to make. Imagine telling all those assholes that they were assholes. She should have said something about having to depart to change wardrobe. Or that she could go for a little breakfast, but she was too furious to think. Bummer. She knew she hated parties, and this one had been a doozy.

She hated getting hung up on who might have thrown the fucking thing and she hated the way the yolk was already coagulating into the ridges of the silk gabardine of the dress. Later on, she hated obsessing on who hated Alan enough to behave that way at his party. She was glad whoever it was wasn't equipped with a hand grenade.

She assumed that it was a he and there were plenty of them at that table. Pretty boys. Basically Alan's friends were half real people whom he loved for their minds and their souls and half pretty people whom he loved for the obvious. She was sure the perp was a pretty person. The price you pay for having pretty people around. Pretty people did things like throw raw eggs on expensive clothes at Beverly Hills restaurants at private parties.

It was fucked up: this person needed to go to AA or to a shrink or maybe just back to whatever bohunk town he was from. Pretty people still came in droves from bohunk towns in the Midwest to be stars in Hollywood. Some of them did, and no doubt threw eggs at people. That made them difficult or colorful, depending on your taste for blood, but she really resented having egg goop on her as a result of the whims of another up-and-coming asshole without portfolio. She was sorry she had said that, even though ninety percent of the guests fell into that category.

Brooke and she left. She told him she'd give him the money for a cab, but he wanted her to drive him. He took one of the centerpieces, a vase made of pasta. The raw eggs rested precariously in the vaselike structure.

Basically it was the uptown equivalent of a drive-by shooting. She really despised being perceived as a victim in any way, even though in this instance she was. It made her think of death. She was starting to think about death all the time. Just like when she was little. Death had come back as the four-hundred-times-a-day thought. It made her want drugs, not viscerally, but intellectually. A passé palliative, but it made her feel good to think about them as a dismissible option. It made her remember why she had done drugs.

Because people are fucked up, she thought. Because if you did drugs you didn't think about the D word. That wasn't true, but it sounded good.

She remembered Joel Schumacher telling her years ago, 'If a bird shits on you,' he flicked imaginary shit off his shoulder, 'next.' She wondered if anything had ever shit on Joel. Certainly having a raw egg break on your favorite dress was being shat on. It made her furious to think about it. She couldn't remember the last time she'd been this enraged. Was this passion? If it was: she flicked her shoulder – the egg had missed that – next! If this was passion, she remembered why she had given it up at the age of thirty-five.

She took the egg incident as a sign that she shouldn't go out and about. Her Mercedes was in the shop and she was driving around in a rented Rabbit convertible; it made her feel exposed. The Mercedes was like a tank. Safer. Although of course traveling around in L.A. these days without a gun was really not being safe. But then again, what was?

Two days later, it was a birthday party for Roz Heller. Caitlin Buchman had asked her to this party weeks ago; how could she explain to Roz or Caitlin that an anonymous pretty person had yolked her just two days before and she was still in trauma and couldn't come? So she stalled and got there late because Jesse Jackson was giving his speech at the convention and she wanted to see how he played on television.

At the party she shocked the guests by giving the following review: 'Where else do we go? At least he's a nigger. I relate. I am, too. He's a woman I'm a nigger . . . same difference.' She was shocked back the next day when several in attendance called to tell her she was right.

Actually she distrusted Jesse, but as Emily Levine had said at dinner, at least he brought the sex back into politics. Where had it gone? Into the ground with Kennedy.

My mother and father have mixed feelings about money. My mother seems to resent the fact that my father is a genius who can't get rich. On the other hand, her attitudes toward the nouveau riche, especially *galitzier* from Pitkin Avenue, are snobbish. I don't know how she manages to do it, but she inculcates me with the notion that we are somehow superior because my father drives a Plymouth and not a Cadillac. As far as I am concerned, as long as we have enough money for me to buy chocolate, make bets, and go to the movies every Saturday, with my little brother in tow (twenty-five cartoons – twenty-five! – and a double feature for a quarter) we are blessed.

Another special Saturday activity doesn't cost a penny and it is more fun than all the rides in a Cadillac. My father takes my brother and me into the City, lets us hang out in his lab, shows us experiments he is developing. Once, for our amusement, he pours some mercury into a watch glass filled with nitric acid. The reaction, which precipitates alternating positive and negative charges at the perimeter of the mercury, causes it to beat, ba-boom, ba-boom, just like a heart . . .

My father, who takes my brother and me up to the roof of our apartment building in Brooklyn and introduces us to the constellations, doesn't really give a shit about money. My mother can do fearsome things to our minds with her dialogue, but my father brings home some laminated paper that glows in the dark and out of which he makes decorations for our Christmas tree one year.

My parents have complicated standards and values that I don't really appreciate till much later, like Mark Twain and *The King of Marvin Gardens*.

On the one hand, we are Jews, but we are atheists. But we

also have Christmas trees. On another hand, we prize knowledge and ideas, and it is a source of frustration that these are not get-rich-quick, not to mention get-rich-period commodities.

On the third hand, there is the Jewish holiday that my mother makes me go to school because I am not, as an atheist, going to shul. A case of me standing up for her principles. I come home in an ugly mood: 'It was me and the janitor's kid, and you can't make me go tomorrow,' I announce. This makes my parents double over with laughter, which insults me, but I never have to go to school on a Jewish holiday again. Make people laugh and you get your way.

It is always clear to me that my mother and father are different from most of the people surrounding us. When we live in Brooklyn, the whole issue of our basic non-Jewishness weighs heavily on the psyches of our neighbors. The Christmas tree sort of nails it for them, although all the kids do trek up to the apartment to add a decoration and groove on the lights.

The other thing that makes us suspect are all the books. My parents have a huge personal library. My father can't buy a new car, but every day we are deluged by books and periodicals and magazines and newspapers. The library keeps growing. There are shelves everywhere, even the kitchen, and each time we move the enterprise of building the shelves and unpacking the books becomes a more daunting task. Once we are in and out of a house before we unpack the S's.

Having all those books around encourages a kind of haphazard education that infuriates my teachers. They seem to resent my having read some of the books on the syllabus. They don't know that at home my mother derides those who think they are reasonably well-educated by having read the Classics. It is her view that that should be over before one reaches puberty. At which point, one should be discovering the art of the time. Having the good taste and sense to make judgments for yourself. My mother is very strict in this regard. Particularly when it comes to the English language.

I rewrite a paper on China five times before I get a 'that'll do,' from her. Finally, I stand in tears at my parents' bedroom door and accuse them of being like McCarthy. Talk of the

Rosenbergs and McCarthy is background walla throughout my childhood; I am only eight years old, but I have already decided that of all the isms fascism is the most repressive. And that's with Catholicism, communism, and racism in mind. The word *sexism* has yet to be invented.

My parents buy a television set, which they have resisted in spite of the heartfelt imprecations of my brother and me, to be able to see the Army-McCarthy hearings. I am so fascinated by the set I get locked into watching; my parents are rabid anti-McCarthyites even break up with a good friend who loves the guy – so my views are colored by their passion. But as far as I can tell from watching him, they are right. And you don't have to be a TV executive to know that making Joseph Welch cry with his cruel insinuations is a great drama-in-real-life-moment that has to lose McCarthy a lot of support.

At dinner between comic discourse on various bodily functions we discuss the hearings. My brother, who is awfully young, develops a pretty good slapstick essence of McCarthy with dialogue that goes, phonetically, 'Ichy, bichy, ichy, bichy, ichy, etc. . . .' He accompanies it with a snarl that he, a Born-Furious preemie, does with an authority way beyond his years. It is a satire of the thing itself – it is scary, and it is very funny. But we know McCarthy isn't funny, and we root for his reign of terror to be over, if for no other reason than that our parents aren't as much fun while he is around.

It is the habit at P.S. 92 for the teachers to 'elect' the student officers for the class. With all this talk of fascism and repression at home, I get pretty worked up about living in a democracy and having teachers assign the offices of president and vice president at school. In between talk of shit and snot one night at dinner, I ask my mother and father: 'We live in a democracy, right?'

'Right.'

'Then doesn't that mean that officers of the class – like president, vice president – get elected?'

'Right.'

'Well, they assign them at school, and I don't think that's right.'

'It's not . . .' My parents look pissed. My mother has her

mouth pursed in that way that is always a prelude to an outburst. It scares me when she looks like that. She doesn't say anything. I expect her to talk to my father in Yiddish, which they do whenever they don't want us to understand, and which I find very retro, considering.

'Isn't there a thing called a referendum?' I pledge allegiance to the flag . . .

'Well, you would have to get a petition signed by a majority of your classmates in order to have a referendum,' my father says calmly. I love it when my father provides me with information. It always makes so much sense. My brother commences to 'ichybichy' hilariously, and my mother unpurses her mouth. FADE OUT.

FADE UP: Dinner, a day or so later.

'Remember the other night when I told you that the class officials were assigned?'

'Yes . . .'

'Well, I got a petition together, and everybody signed. Mrs. Pressman said that was enough for her, so we had elections – '

'That's wonderful – '

'Don't interrupt!' My mother and I are already at it. 'Well, guess who's president!' And I smile a Cheshire Cat smile. The people, they need a leader, or they will all go to hell.

I provoke my first fight between boys when I am in third grade, looking from one to the other with the old up-from-under-the-lashes whammy, smiling a small secret smile. The boys would find another reason to fight if I am not there, but I am and I make the most of it. They give each other a pretty solid pounding, but nobody really gets hurt.

I have three boyfriends during grade school: Abner Rosenthal: he is beautiful. Richard Hirsch: he is weird looking but has a lot of personality. And Josh Kane: he likes me. He teaches me all the words to the Hitler song: Hitler had one enormous ball, Goering had two but they were small, Himmler, now his were sim'lar, and Goebbels had no balls at

43

all; I give him part of 'Leprosy' back: Lep-rosy, is crawling all o-ver me, There goes my eyeball into your highball, There goes my fing-er-nail into your gin-ger ale, etc.

One day he says to me, 'Have you ever heard of rock 'n' roll?' I'd spent the entire previous summer at Fire Island misrepresenting the words to Bill Haley's 'Shake Rattle 'n' Roll' (I thought they were singing 'shake Marilyn Monroe,' which made perfect sense to me).

'Yeah,' I lie, 'why?'

'Well, there's this big rock 'n' roll show at the Brooklyn Paramount on Saturday – you ever listen to Alan Freed?'

'Yeah,' I lie again, 'why?'

'Well, he's the one who's putting on this show, lots of different acts. It starts at one and goes all day. You think your parents would let you go?'

The Brooklyn Paramount is in a tough neighborhood, but this rock 'n' roll boogie sounds like something I should know about, so I say, 'Yeah, why not?' It never occurs to me that Josh views this adventure as a date and expects to pay for the tickets and transportation, which is a lot of subways. Worried more about the cost than the permission from my parents, I bet my entire allowance with Manny. You never win when you need to.

So altogether these three make one perfect guy: Beauty, Fun, and Caring. I keep them all on a string and never make a choice, but that is because sex isn't a part of our lives yet.

Polio is still an issue in the fifties. Certainly less of an everyday occurrence at Fire Island than in the City. The virus seems to breed and spread in the heat of the City. Something dissipates its force at the beach. One summer, however, there is an outbreak of eight cases in Saltair, the town next door to Fair Harbor, where we stay.

Frantic, my parents call our pediatricians, who have been saving gamma globulin for their own two daughters. We leave Fire Island and take trains, subways, and taxis to Brooklyn. There is no air conditioning. Traveling in, I start to break out in my rash. Gamma globulin requires big, long needles and is a thick serum. I am seven, tne eldest, so I go first. It hurts like hell, first one cheek, then the other. My brother hates shots. Terrified, he runs around the doctor's office, and when we catch him he is so sweaty he is like a greased pig. He tightens up so hard he bends the needle, nearly breaks it off in his cheek. The entire enterprise is a harrowing experience, but we are immunized for six weeks at least, and return to Fire Island the next day. May this house be safe from polio.

Matthew and I are on the upper deck of the ferry. I have made him my human pet, since my mother doesn't like dogs and thinks cats smell. We are drinking Coca-Colas from the bottle. My parents are chatting with a retired military type, who is completely bald, and his wife, who is completely gray, beneath us, on the lower deck. They are sipping martinis out of paper cups, compliments of General Baldy's silver flask.

'I wonder how the Coke would splash if you hit the exact center of his head?' I smile to Matthew and tip my bottle encouragingly. Anxious to please, he follows. I point with my finger to the exact center of the general's pate, and Matthew fires. It splats out in many directions. The grown-ups look up sharply, surprised. My father grins, but my mother's eyes have gone from brown to black, and her lips are pursed in her Restrained Fury expression. The general is angry, but dismissive. I am more afraid of my mother than him anyway . . .

Bored, my brother and I go inside. He decides to sit in a corner by himself for awhile. The man sitting next to me strikes up a conversation. He is almost handsome and very funny. His wife, who is thin and prematurely gray, seems gentle and nice. I chat with them all the way over to Fair Harbor. Just before we dock and my little brother comes over to be led by me to our parents, they invite me to visit them the next day, say five, for drinks.

Next day, I tell my parents I'm going to these people's house for a drink, and my mother says fine, be home by seven. I go to my new friends' house every day for a week, at drink time. Finally, my parents say, gee, we'd like to meet your new friends and can they tag along. And that is how my parents come to be pretty good friends with Tony and Florence Randall.

Tony is the first person I know in real life who has a

recognizable, noticeable, visible show-business success. A year or two after they become friendly, *Mr Peepers* goes on the air and becomes a big hit. Tony ultimately leaves New York and goes to California to play second banana to Rock Hudson. Years later he shows up again in *The Odd Couple*, but he never expresses any desire to socialize. Actually, he had lost interest in me long ago, when I became a teenager. 'I only like 'em when they're very young,' he joked.

Skip likes them young, too. I met him the same summer, when I am seven. Fair Harbor likes to give itself a July Fourth celebration at the Firehouse, which is steps from our house on the bay. I take my brother. We drink the bottoms of people's glasses. I hate the taste of alcohol, so I don't have so much, but Matthew likes it. The goyim raise their glasses and say 'Here's luck,' and put their glasses down and my little brother clutches the glass with his chubby little hands, goes 'luck,' and chugalugs. I try to get him to stop but he wanders off on his own, in search of more luck.

A blond teenager is playing the piano, not bad, so I saunter over to watch. I like music, feel drawn to it. My parents play classical music all the time; I can handle Mozart sonatas in the morning, Beethoven quartets after school, but the symphonies my father favors, conducting wildly, pacing from room to room, make me overwrought. Their 78 collection of the blues is awesome, though, and I discover Bessie Smith, Billie Holiday and Burl Ives all on my own. If I leave them lying around, my brother sits on them and breaks them.

The guy smiles at me, asks if I want to sit next to him. 'I'm Skip,' he says. 'What's your name?' During the course of the evening he teaches me 'Chopsticks' and 'Heart and Soul.' The room has heated up and there is a lot of toasting and flirting and wisecracks. Grown-ups doing their thing.

Suddenly, screaming from the other side. My father has my brother slung over his shoulder and he's powerwalking toward the door. My brother is purple with rage, bellowing, 'More luck, more luck.' My father is laughing but signals with his head that it is time for me to go home, too. I get up and say goodbye. Skip says, 'I'm around the Firehouse all the time if you want to come visit . . . I'll teach you more songs . . .'

46

I can teach a thing or two myself. Reading is my specialty. That summer, for spite, I lay my pedagogical expertise on my annoying little brother. Now I can post missives on my bedroom door like NO DIRTY LITTLE BOYS ALLOWED and drive him up the wall . . .

I sit at the edge of the dock, in the ferry slip at the sunset hour with my recent discovery, Johnny Harmon, who is sixteen and built like a man with mean little pale blue eyes, the gross features of a pig, and white-blond hair. He is as close to an albino as you can get in Real Life. He bothers the shit out of my father. He does wild things like drink beer and then ride around and around the harbor in ever smaller circles with his hydroplane. He also looks at me in a way that makes both me and my father sweat, which leads to the dreaded allergic-reaction rash in my case. My father just smells funky. I think my father is really more worried about Johnny Harmon killing me than he is about him fucking me. Arguably he does both, because Johnny Harmon is the one who teaches me to smoke.

Sitting on the dock, all peaceful and relaxed and drunk, in an unconscious gesture of sex and friendship, he offers me a cigarette. I am curious about this activity my parents do so often, and tell me not to do. Puffing away, doing the old 'do as I say, not as I do' routine that parents still get away with in the fifties. I take it. He has to coach me through getting it lit.

'Suck . . . Suck harder.' How many times would I hear that in my life? What do I know? I'm eleven. The wind is whipping around us as twilight encroaches, and the matches he lights in that toughguy way, with his hands cupping the flame, keep going out.

'Suck harder,' he screams. And I get lit. I like the way the ember looks and the way you can make it bright by sucking harder. I was a bottle-fed celiac baby. 'Now suck it into your lungs and blow it out.' Johnny Harmon is so cool. Okay, I will.

I am so nauseated that I keel over, off the edge of the dock and into the water. If I hadn't hit water, I'd have probably puked all over Johnny Harmon and my rash would've gone away, because in all likelihood Johnny Harmon would have gone away. Unless he was kinky. He *did* have that great Nazi look. This is a look that will appeal to me into my thirties, especially if I am on the rebound from a smart, funny, dark, ethnic guy who seems cute but has broken my heart with cruelty. I come to in the water and swim ashore, completely straight. Johnny Harmon is convulsed with laughter. I am a regular Jerry Lewis as far as he is concerned. I will never get rid of this rash.

Pissed, I make him give me another. I enjoy it. It is love at second sight. There are quite a few drugs that make you puke first and get you to love them later. I never pass out from smoking again.

My parents decide to say bye-bye to Brooklyn.

Their decision is based as much on the fact that I make S.P. as a feeling that it is time to move on. S.P. stands for special progress, an accelerated program for kids with IQs over 135. Basically, it is a way to move students through a school system that is overcrowded, by collapsing seventh, eighth, and ninth grades into two years. I am already young for my grade, and my parents are worried about my moving ahead another year. But also, there is encroaching poverty and violence. My father now earns enough to get us out of there, and our weekends become filled with the search for the perfect house.

We look in Westchester and Long Island. I remember a house that we all really liked in Pelham, but then my parents found out that there were only thirty Jewish families there. First our Jewish neighbors had snubbed us because we were like goyim, now my parents worry the goyim will snub us because we are Jews. My mother's natural instincts keep her favoring just such neighborhoods, but finally ethnicity prevails and in the summer between grade school and junior high, we move to a pleasant, ramshackle colonial in Great Neck Estates, Great Neck, Long Island.

I hook up with a spoiled rich girl down the block named Carol Weinseir, who has a lot of matching cashmere skirts and sweaters and Papagallos and Capezios in her closet. I remember a dinner at her house with her parents where her father, a handsome man who seems too interested in me and Carol, and her mother, a leather-skinned virago, have an argument over which toilet-seat covers to choose in the current redecoration of their bad-taste home. Carol and I keep looking at each other, trying not to crack up, but we are going to splatter food all over everyone with laughter if we don't get out of there. Her parents are so wrapped up in their George-and-Marthaness that they barely notice our lame excuses and wave us away. Carol walks home with me.

'I'm adopted, you know.' This seems to be all we need to hear from each other and we stroll the rest of the way, which is only two blocks, to my house, which is much less grand than hers, needless to say. My family is just finishing their dinner, so we sit down and have coffee with them. They are having a nuclear discussion. My father says, 'You know, the day after we dropped the atom bomb on Hiroshima, your mother had a dream that we all died in a nuclear blast.'

'Sometimes I think we did and we're all living in hell,' my mother cracks.

'I thought if you dream you've died, you really do die – that's why the brain tells you to wake up, so you don't die in your sleep . . .'

'Oh, that's just an old wive's tale,' my little brother opines. Carole Weinsier smiles happily. Now *this* was a dinner conversation you could sink your teeth into. She stays over that night and makes my acceptance by the popular crowd pretty easy. Probably because they like hanging out with my parents.

About the only time I can remember my mother actually creating a life for herself is during the '56 election between Adlai Stevenson and Dwight Eisenhower. My mother adores Adlai. Outside of my father, he is probably the only man who attracts her in a deep emotional way. She does something during his campaign I have never seen her do. She works. She gets up in the morning, inspired, gets us all out of the house, gets herself together, and canvasses one neighbor after another who likes Ike and disdains Adlai. Jews who should be Democrats are going to vote for the benign-looking general. I think my parents understand and accept this awful truth, but it hurts them. Cynical as they are, they have some romantic notions about the basic goodness of mankind. When people behave stupidly, or greedily, or selfishly, they feel betrayed. Child beating and wife beating and violence and murder appall them. They never really get it.

'He says nu-cu-lar . . .' my father says miserably, knowing this does not augur well for the future of mankind.

'He's gonna go to Korea,' my mother hisses through pursed lips.

'What's he gonna fucking do there?' my father says. Something about the fact that Adlai doesn't have a chance makes my mother work even harder for him.

My brother and I resent this deeply. For the first time in our lives, she is not at home when we come home from school, and occasionally she gets home even after my father does. From time to time we eat out, or, worst case, we eat half-done leftovers. My mother has always been one of those women who start her day, and yours, by wanting to know what you fancy for dinner. Which is usually greeted by no response or by hostile response: How should I know what I want for dinner? I haven't even gotten indigestion from breakfast yet!

Now, she isn't even there to ask the questions I disdain and do not answer. One night we gang up on her, complaining about her lack of caring, her nonpresence. She has come in very late, her eyes blazing, her cheeks rosy, hot and bothered from the excitement of knowing that she is working for a cause that is so futile and important. She is genuinely surprised that we feel the way we do, because we have all urged her to go for it, intuitively pushing her out of the house and out of our faces.

Sometime after our move to Great Neck my mother takes up her Naked Maja position lying on her hip, puffing away at her Camel, like some suburban housewife who has ended up in an opium den. From there she pontificates, pronounces, predicts, and occasionally devastates you in an aside. *En passant*. As it were. She reads the *Times* from cover to cover, she reads a lot of books and mags, she is very brilliant. All children think their parents are the three omnis: present, potent, scient. I never outgrow my parents' omniscience. Not only are they both exceedingly well educated and smart, they determinedly keep up with the state of the world. The first time I ever bring home a *Time* magazine they pooh-pooh it.

'Every time I've ever known anything about a particular subject, they've been wrong,' my father says.

'Well, they do always let you know if someone is Jewish, though – "son of a Jewish peddler," "son of a Polish Jew," "son of a Jewish Russian immigrant" – anti-Semitic sons of bitches . . .' from Guess Who?

My best friend in Great Neck is one of maybe four gentiles in the whole school. Her parents hadn't copped gamma globulin for her when it counted and she has a withered leg and arm from polio. She walks with a limp. But she has a cute face and big tits and a big, handsome, wild boyfriend. The three of us go to parties together and he and I dance athletically, while she chats or watches from the sidelines. Then they go home and fuck. And I go to Stefan's, the local hangout, and smoke and flirt with other boys, none of whom has his virile craziness.

We go to rock 'n' roll shows at the Brooklyn Paramount hosted by Alan Freed. Buddy Holly, Joanne Campbell, Jerry Lee Lewis. Sing along with Buddy loudly: 'Faggy sue, faggy sue . . .' Air-piano with Jerry, bambambambam. Once, on a foray to the ladies' room, there are tough-looking older girls smoking funny-smelling homemade cigarettes.

'Marijuana,' my girlfriend says. I ask for a puff from a small, tough-looking tart, and she gives me one. It makes me cough violently, but Buddy Holly never sounded so good. Pretty pretty pretty pretty faggy sue . . . I infuriate my father for a full half-year by responding to his every question with: 'Goodness gracious, great balls of fire.' Thinking of my girlfriend's boyfriend.

One day my mother, seeing me eye him in a naked moment, gives me some unsolicited advice: Don't even think about stealing your best friend's boyfriend, is the gist. I hate her

51

advice, but I know she is right, and I set about finding someone of my own.

Steven Paul Mitchell: he is older and cooler. He drives his own car, a '57 Impala convertible. He has an amazing swimmer's body and a small head. If eyes are the window to the soul Steven's is covered with a layer of dust, furniture in an abandoned house. He is one of the few brown-eyed people I've known who look as stupid as he is. He listens to WBAI. Jocko Henderson. The first rapper. Every night before his show Jocko screams, 'Way up here in the stratosphere, you gotta holler mighty loud and clear – EEtiddlyock, Ho, this is the Jock, and I'm back on the scene with the record machine, saying Oohpoppadoo, and howdoyoudo . . .'

We drive into the city, to a Jocko show at the Apollo: Jackie Wilson, Screamin' Jay Hawkins, Al Hibler, Wicked Pickett. The audience is Oreo-ish: two-thirds black, one-third white. It is tough, but not quite dangerous yet. I go to the ladies' room and girls are snorting white lines of powder up their noses. It looks disgusting and I make a face. Loaded and generous, one of them hands me a rolled-up dollar bill and coaches me through the process, then tells me to rub the excess along my gums. My first freeze . . . I power my way back to my seat and impress Steven Paul with some new dance steps . . .

My mother never stops my cultural education, and occasionally still goes to the city with me. She takes me to see a revival of *The Glass Menagerie* with Helen Hayes. As we walk up the aisle after Laura has blown out her candles, me sobbing, she says, sotto voce: 'It's really too bad you didn't see it with Laurette Taylor . . .'

I am enjoying a pretty happy adolescence, all things considered, and then my father drops a bomb at dinner one night. He tells us he's gotten a job offer that's much better than what he has for more money. Hooray! we all say, but I can tell by his face this is not a hooray type of situation.

'Just one drawback,' he says offhandedly, 'it's in Milwaukee . . .' Well, just how much better a job and how much more money? Define your terms, Dad.

Like all Easterners, we have a prejudice against the Middle

West. Cows. Farms. No all-night diners . . . No New York City . . . No Steven Paul Mitchell . . .

We are all very quiet, then all at once, we are a chorus of support, Let's do it, let's go . . .

Time's Man of the Year is Dwight Eisenhower. Again. It is the end of his era and he warns us about the rise of the military-industrial complex he invented. At least I won't have to listen to my father complain about 'nu-cu-lar' anymore . . .

When I was eight, my parents bought me an English tabby at a cat show, but it shit awful runny stuff for weeks, and finally they gave it away. My mother giveth and taketh away. When we moved to Great Neck, however, a gorgeous, wild, three-month-old male who had been living on the streets adopted me. He followed me home daily for a week, and on the seventh day my mother said okay, especially since he was already an outdoor cat who obviously knew the neighborhood. I named him Caesar, so I could call him Julia's Caesar.

Caesar and I kind of hit adolescence together. While he howls and rests his burning balls on the shady part of the hood of my father's car, I torment my parents with a stream of big-chested pea-brained wonders. It is not an era of neutering, so Caesar walks on the wild side. While I engage in hours of tongue kissing and heavy petting he goes out and gets laid.

The day before we move to Milwaukee, Caesar and I get into a fight and he wins. He holds on to my right hand with his sharp little fangs until he is dragged off. The hand blows up immediately, and the doctor up the street, a South African Jew, gives me massive doses of penicillin, muttering worriedly about cat fever. I ask him what that is and he explains that it attacks your lymphatic system, and everything swells: your groin, your neck, your armpits. Oh please, save me from hanging armpits, I wail, laughing through my tears.

I am in such great physical and emotional pain the next day

that I cry for the whole flight to Milwaukee. Caesar, in his cat box at my feet, howls along in perfect harmony . . .

'Miller, get your ass in that pool!' The gym teacher, Mrs Erdman, has a bad attitude anyway, and I seem to bother her in some way that makes her even more irascible. I am not feeling so hot and she wants me to dive in this pool in the middle of January in Milwaukee, Wisconsin. I haven't felt so hot since getting back from Christmas vacation in Hollywood, Florida.

My extreme claustrophobia was fixed for life by the trip in the confines of a Plymouth traveling from Milwaukee to Florida with my parents. They fought with each other and she fought with me. I don't know how my brother managed to remain *hors de combat*. It seemed to be something he knew from birth. How to keep my parents, particularly my mother, at a distance. The high point of the trip, for me, was somewhere in Alabama, where I spotted a litter of baby pigs. My father stopped and I oohed and aahed over the piglets for awhile.

I hit the pool and feel a tide of dizziness. Serve the bitch right if I puke right here right now in her precious pool. I fight my way to the surface. Little concentric fish like the ones I saw all those many years ago when the doctor gave me ether to remove my tonsils swim before me. I use my last bit of strength to get to the surface. Something's wrong with me, I think, I'm a much stronger swimmer than this. It is an effort to get out of the pool. I know I am going to pass out and I lie down at the side of the pool. My friends laugh. Erdman looms over me, a cartoon character from a nightmare.

'Get back in that pool!' Her face is mottled from anger.

'I can't,' I whisper. My friends howl. Some others giggle. Oh, that Julia, she'll do anything for a laugh. The girls think I am kidding and the gym teacher thinks I am fucking with her. I start to vomit. This comes as such a surprise to me that I am as grossed out as everyone else . . .

A moment for the girls. These are not girls like any that I had known in any of my previous lives, predominantly New

York, Jewish-of-one-sort-or-another, rather sheltered types. No, these girls in Milwaukee all have blond hair and three names and they are wild. In Great Neck, you smoked, gave and got head, and went to rock 'n' roll shows. In Milwaukee, you drank, shot skeet, and got laid.

If you were caught shoplifting so much as a pack of cigs in Great Neck it was a shanda for the neighbors. In Milwaukee they not only ripped off the store, they booby-trapped it with fishing wire so customers tripped over each other and upset bins of underwear and socks and scarves. One thing's the same, though. In Great Neck you went to the City as soon as you had a black turtleneck and an authentic pair of jeans. In Milwaukee, you drove to Chicago.

A lot is going on in the Middle West in the late fifties and early sixties that are cues for the rest of the country. For one thing: there is the emergence of the John Birch Society. The first really legitimate right-wing org. And the story about them breaks in the *Milwaukee Journal*, not *The New York Times*. Another thing: there is a whole bunch of comedians and performers in Chicago at that time that East Coasters aren't aware of. Second City includes Alan Arkin, Barbara Harris, and Shelley Berman. Lenny Bruce plays on Rush Street all the time. My favorite thing about Chicago: Lenny Bruce. He is as irreverent and dirty-mouthed and smart about the world as my own family. But at a distance, which makes him easier to enjoy.

I have adjusted to Milwaukee quite well, considering the initial trauma of the move. It isn't so hard to get into the popular crowd as it was in Great Neck, where it seemed that the rules kept changing according to who you dated and what you wore, although none of the cute Jewish boys ask me out for a year. And I have my first brushes with anti-Semitism. Driving in a car with a bunch of kids one day, cutting out of school during lunchtime, heading for the local hangout, a drive-in called the Pig 'n Whistle, affectionately referred to as the Pig, one of the guys makes a remark about his Jewish nose, then makes a big show of apologizing to me.

'What are you apologizing for? You're the one with the Jewish nose,' I say, and everyone laughs gratefully. A long way from the first day of school for me, when I came home crying, 'I'll never make it here – everyone's blond!' Then one of the star football players gets a crush on me and I am home free, even if I do say 'water fountain' instead of 'bubbler' . . .

Vomiting poolside is clearly a symptom of something, so I am hauled off to the school nurse, who takes one look at me and calls my mother, who is finally located at the hairdresser. She comes to school and picks me up. By then I am green at the gills and in a state of semi-faint, so she takes me right to the doctor. He takes my temperature, which is below normal, looks down my throat and up my nose, and says I have the flu. He gives me a penicillin shot and sends me home to bed. On the way home in the car, I notice that my mother's lips are pursed in that angry expression that has terrified me from birth. I ask her if she is angry about something:

CLOSE UP: MOM, puffing and huffy:

MOM: Oh, I had a fight with Phil, the hairdresser.

ME: Why?

MOM: Oh, he's just one of those inconsequential little pricks who thinks he's better than any woman . . .

When I'm not better a week later and have lost five pounds, they throw me in the hospital for tests. My least favorites are upper and lower GI series, and gall bladder, where they shoot me with dye and make me sit still for almost an hour until they take blood. I am losing weight and feeling pretty weak, but they aren't coming up with a diagnosis. One day my doctor asks me if I like school and I shoot him a filthy look and with the last bit of strength I have, whisper/scream, 'Are you accusing me of malingering?'

Finally my eyes and skin go yellow, and they take some blood, test for jaundice, and discover that I have hepatitis, the kind that is usually a result of undiagnosed mononucleosis. They take some more blood and my white count is very high, too. Hepatitis is not a particularly chic disease in 1959, and

56

about the only prescription for cure is complete bed rest, along with a very restricted diet.

The school drains the pool.

Mrs Erdman gets fired, and shortly thereafter she has a miscarriage.

I don't feel an ounce of pity for her, but I am at an unforgiving age, and feeling pretty sick.

For the first two weeks, I sleep about twenty hours a day, so I don't feel too many pangs of loneliness, but by the middle of the third week I start to get very lonely in my bedroom upstairs. Most of my friends, not to mention my friends' parents, have panicked, so no one is allowed to visit me. Which is how I end up with Michael Smith as a boyfriend. I had been dating him, along with several others, before I got sick. He starts to visit me every day, brings me peace offerings, like Mel Brooks and Carl Reiner's *2,000-year-old Man* – 'don't tear paper' – and so naturally I fall in love with him.

My other entertainment is reading. I start on easy fare: Hemingway's *The Fifth Column and the First Forty-nine Stories*. The year before, my brother had written a very good short story for a creative writing assignment called 'The Cat and the Bridge.' He had only gotten a B and I had always thought he was robbed. I was secretly jealous of the story, though; my brother was supposed to be the scientist, I was the creative one. In my perusal of good ol' Ernest, though, I find the story, 'The Cat and the Bridge.' Same story. It brings color to my cheeks. I run downstairs with the book and find my mother in the kitchen, crying into the sink. I don't bother to ask why, just scream: 'Look at this, look at this . . .'

That night my brother gets busted by my parents and confesses; then everyone has a good laugh about Hemingway getting a B. I think my brother has gotten off pretty easy for plagiarism and wonder how I would've been dealt with; I suppress such negativity by toying with the concept of a think piece for the *Saturday Review* called 'The Day Hemingway Got a B.'

I also read most of Thomas Wolfe and William Faulkner, plus *Mourning Becomes Electra*, by Eugene O'Neill.

Every other week I go to Saint Michael's and a nun takes

blood. Then I am told I am not any better and am sent home to bed.

Wisconsin provides a tutor for any student who misses twenty-one consecutive days of school, a little socialist hold-over from the LaFollette days, and I draw a nice fat lady who starts coming twice a week. I can keep up with English and history, but I am lagging dangerously in math and science. My parents talk to the school, which comes up with an experimental project that the phone company is exploring: basically, it is an intercom system from sickbed to school that travels through the telephone wires. They install one in my house and five in my separate classes.

I have a friend named Penny Lozoff who is in all my classes, so she carries me around in a little box and plugs and unplugs me from class to class. It keeps me relatively current with my grade, which is a relief, because I really don't want to be left back a grade and spend another year with my parents in this cold venue known as the Midwest. There are aspects to the illness, the self-taught education, even the blossoming romance with Michael Smith, that are pretty pleasant, but as I am getting better I am also getting bored. Going to school filled my days, at least.

Outside of being sick with a disease that saps my strength and makes me think that they are lying to me and I really have leukemia, there is another downside to all this time at home. Mommy. I am a prisoner in the house nay, in the bedroom – from morning to night, subject to the ebb and flow of whatever drugs she is administering to herself. Milwaukee is pretty much my mother's Waterloo. She comes face to face with the more powerful enemy: Herself.

She smokes: Camels.

She eats: Cheese and Chocolate.

She swallows pills: Preludin, 25; Miltown, 10; Librium, 25; Codeine, whatever.

She leaves her bathrobe on till noon. She retreats inward, into her mind, which defeats her. But not before she projects as much of her internal dissatisfaction onto me as she can. And here I am, all day, every day, just waiting to be picked on.

One night she rides me so hard that I explode into physical violence. I smack her, hard across the face. The imprint of my hand rises up in angry welts. Like all bullies, she backs off, cries hysterically, and races out of the house into the car, which she backs up so fast and so inexpertly (of course, she's a lousy driver) that she grounds herself in a snowbank across the street.

My father, who isn't around for ninety percent of the harassment of my daily life, races into my room, screaming, 'What did you do? What did you do?' Then he hits me, and my head bangs into the wall. I slump onto my bed. Now I have mono, hep, and a concussion. I hate her. I hate him. I hate this Milwaukee . . .

This is about the only corporal punishment ever dispensed in my household, but it leaves a permanent scar. Of course, everybody apologizes to everybody and life moves on, but I know I have crossed a line forever that I can never recross.

I'm sure the only reason I have gotten into Mount Holyoke and Barnard is that, coming from the Midwest, I fulfill two quotas. A Midwestern Jew. Named Miller. Sometimes I wonder if they've confused me with Miller of Milwaukee, but I'm sure they know everything. I feel I applied to these schools in the first place to fulfill a fantasy of my mother's that she once had for herself. The day I'm accepted, my guidance counselor finds me in detention, writing 'I will not make other classmates feel stupid' a hundred times on the blackboard. I have redone it twice, because I can't make the hundred lines fit. My right arm and wrist are getting very sore. The school knows I've been accepted before I do; I won't get the mail till later in the day. My pal, Penny, is the only other student to apply to Eastern schools. She gets into Wellesley.

My parents are out of town, in San Francisco on a business trip. I call them and they are thrilled. They bring me back a strand of pearls. Penny and I are wired so we go see a late show of Gone With the Wind. It is the second time I have seen it, and I roam the theater, restless . . .

*

I am a freshman at Mount Holyoke College when John Kennedy is selected *Time*'s Man of the Year. It is the only thing that cheers me up in my otherwise dismal surroundings . . .

> *'This is my letter to the World*
> *that never wrote to Me. . .'*
> – Emily Dickinson

When I am at Mount Holyoke College, and Sydney McLean is making sure they don't flunk me out, I fall in love, under her tutelage, with Emily Dickinson. More the legend of Emily than the actual work of Emily. Sydney takes me over to Amherst one afternoon and we go on a tour of the house where Emily Dickinson lived and died. With her stern father and maiden sister.

'And in these drawers,' Sydney is telling me, indicating some dresser drawers in the small room Emily occupied, 'they found all these packets of poems tied up in pink ribbons after she died. She was never published in her own lifetime, and the first set of poems was rewritten . . .' Ooh, tell me more, Sydney, I love this story. 'There were all these poems about an unnamed lover, but now we think that he was just a man she had an unconsummated crush on.'

The little house in Amherst is hot and stuffy. How had Emily written all these poems in this congested little space? 'Diadems drop and doges surrender . . .' Actually, you probably have to be in a tiny little space like this to come up with lines like those.

Thank God for Sydney. I don't think I ever would've made it through without her. And my father. In his beautiful blue suit. I am in serious academic trouble by the end of sophomore year, failing French, failing math . . . *Au secours au secours*. Daddy, and by the way, what is this shit, $e^x = e^x$? I am summoned to the office of Mrs. Rhymers, a slick article in Chanel. She pulls out my SATs and my writing sample. She starts to read my writing sample and has the nerve to ask me if I wrote it myself. Hey, if you thought it was cribbed, why admit me? She says she will have to talk to a parent.

My father has business in the East and drops by. He takes me to dinner at the Yankee Peddlar Inn and comes down so hard on me for so long that I embarrass us both by crying silent ugly tears at the table. He can't bear it, and says not to worry, he is going to put on his beautiful blue suit and charm the pants off her.

The next day he goes off to Mrs. Rhymers and charms her almost out of her Chanel suit. French, well, they'll pass me with a D. Meanwhile, Sydney has told them I'm a talented writer, and they bestow the Katherine McFarland Short Story Award, and the Phi Beta Kappa Award for Creative Writing on me. I make it through. By the next day my father and I are making beautiful-blue-suit jokes. Sydney and my father and I have tea at her house.

It is hard to describe Sydney's impact at first meeting. She is extremely tall – at least six feet, and the size of a ship. She moves like a ship, too, as if she is gliding through water. She lives in a house full of cats with a ladyfriend. We don't care. She is the one thing in this alien environment that inspires me . . .

The school agrees to allow me to make up math during the summer at Marquette University, a Catholic School in Milwaukee. The guy who teaches me calculus that summer passes me with a note: 'Please don't take any more math.' Two years later in the vortex of a homosexual scandal at the school he throws himself from a window. I feel I participated in his suicide because it caused him pain to pass me . . .

The day the market crashed, Stuart and she went to Gladstone's in the middle of the afternoon to commiserate. 'It's over, it's over,' he kept saying, and she thought, it was over a long time ago. Five hundred billion dollars had disappeared in a day. The grandeur of *billion* had been whittled away by Carl Sagan and Bunker Hunt anyway. Five hundred billion isn't what it used to be. When would a trillion isn't-what-it-used-to-be? She laughed to herself.

'Do you ever go around the house talking to yourself?' Stuart asked at the end of a long diatribe about her not going out and not seeing or speaking to many people. He wasn't particularly judgmental about any of this, as he used to be. She had expended a fair amount of energy educating Stuart, and as he was basically the three S's – smart, sweet, and sensitive – he had proved a very adept student. He still did too much party/nightlife in her opinion, but then she was a decade older than he.

Personally she didn't care if she never went to another party in Hollywood again. Have to interact with all those old vampires and young vampires-in-the-making. The assholes, with and without portfolio. Have to say hello to all those old acquaintances. Have to meet all the new ones. Deep down, she didn't ever want to meet a new person again.

Years ago at the Trancas Market, she and Michael had run into Steve McQueen and Ali McGraw. They knew Ali from New York, so she had to stop and say hello. Steve McQueen was wearing a Navy peacoat and Navy hat pulled down over his eyes, but she caught sight of them for a moment. They said: I don't want to meet a new person again.

'Out loud?' she parried. She had developed a hell of an interior monologue over the past couple of years, and felt compelled to speak less and less. Was this just middle age or was it from her particular peaks and valleys? A little of both. Wasn't that always the case? It got harder to sort out when it was more than an Either/Or.

'You see too many sides to an issue,' Marcia Nasitir had complained at lunch when they were at the *Ladies' Home Journal* together. She'd been just a whippersnapper then, and a few of the older women had adopted her because they knew she was a mutated version of them, and that she was going to leap tall men in a single bound, and go way beyond where they even dreamed of going. 'You have a Talmudic mind,'

Marcia continued. 'It could keep you from making decisions fast enough.'

'Not a chance, I have a mother like that. Just 'cause I see all sides of an issue doesn't mean I can't act.' One of her first acts after that had been to split from the *Ladies' Home Journal* for her first movie job, as a story editor at Paramount. Broke the ten-thousand-dollar-a-year barrier on that one.

'Develop a firm handshake and always go where they pay you more money,' her father had told her even though he didn't know how. Basically that was how she got into movies. She drifted in. Because the gig paid more.

Marcia Nasitir had not turned out to be a major supporter. The first clue she got was the morning of her twenty-fifth birthday. Marcia called at seven. 'Quarter of a century is not that old, Julia.'

'You're not putting the best light on it, pal.' Twenty-five seemed younger than quarter of a century, but they both laughed. Years later, after Michael and she had split up, the house where they'd lived – the house where all of prevailing Hollywood had jump-started itself, in its youth, in the seventies – was condemned by the State of California. To be made into a public beach. It was razed to the ground, and the chimney was left standing.

Marcia went to a party at Brian and Jean Moore's, which was on the hillside just above, and took a Polaroid of the lonely chimney surrounded by rubble. 'Dear Julia,' she wrote on the back, 'kind of says it all, doesn't it?' And mailed it. It was on the bulletin board now, the bulletin board that she called her novel, the one that stopped somewhere in 1979.

'Don't you talk to yourself?' she asked Stuart.

''Course I do,' he said matter of factly, but then, his mother was a shrink.

She thought of her conversation with herself as an extended negotiation that had been initiated with her birth and would close with her death.

I know a lot of dead people, she thought.

'I know a lot of dead people,' she said in the shower that night, scrubbing herself hard, as if anxiety could be soaped off. The price you pay for surviving into middle age. The price

63

you pay for seeking out the bad characters. The price you pay for living through the seventies. Hell, sometimes she thought she fucking invented the seventies.

She remembered a production assistant who'd worked on *The Beat*. 'I loved your movies,' he said. 'You made growing up in the seventies worthwhile.'

'Thank you,' she'd beamed. I know. Did I grow up in the seventies? Was it worthwhile?

It took her a couple of years and a couple of mil and a lot of fucking agro to figure out that she wasn't going to do that anymore, but there wasn't any great bad-little-girl trip that interested her instead. While she'd become middle-aged she'd developed into a woman. For the first time in her life she considered the possibility that she ought to be pleasing herself.

The more she thought about that, the longer her Hate List became. I hate men. I hate women. I hate Hollywood. I hate L.A. I hate all the people I know. I hate my life. Every night as she unmade her bed, she'd say derisively, out loud, to herself, 'You made your bed . . .'

Did I go too far? she had to wonder. I fucked with Nirvana and now everything is an anticlimax. A permanent state of intellectual postcoitus. The list got longer. I hate the news. I hate clubs. I hate always having to meet the men in their offices. I hate driving. I hate all the people out there. I hate movies . . .

She realized this one night at Mortons watching Larry Gordon dine with Joel Silver and Scott Rudin. There was a lot of facial hair at that table.

Larry Gordon was a southern Jew from Mississippi who had once been a friend. Somebody she'd really liked. But the other two were his protégés and they were so disgusting they made her want to leave the business. She was half out, anyway; out wouldn't be that far to go. 'When in doubt go further out,' Jack* used to say, but he went from just getting by, dealing drugs, to turning huge profits – merchandising revisionist Vietnam movie posters . . . more in than out, it seemed to her . . . how eighties . . .

These hairy guys also made her rethink her attitude toward Larry; if this poison were the sons he never had then what was he? Joel was a fat slob who liked to decorate his table at Mortons with women who looked like medium-priced hookers (the best ones, a male friend once informed her: they worked hard for the money). Scott was a previously fat slob with little interest in working girls who was going to be fat again judging from the eating pattern he was displaying now. Together they made up what she thought of as the Philistine Front. Or Affront, depending on your point of view.

And face it, Larry was a loudmouth. When she first knew him he'd made some cool pictures that also provided a start to a lot of talented unknowns who were her friends. Anyway they hung out at her house a lot. She respected Larry. He was going to produce *Fear of Flying* for her back when they still were telling her they would let her direct it. Although she had agreed to something they referred to as a 'producer of the first stripe' and the studio had balked at his name.

'You tell him he's not of the first stripe,' she'd told Begelman, and he relented. But that was probably because they had no intention of letting her direct. A lollipop for producing Close Encounters. Suck. Suck harder.

And Larry had called many times, just to leave his name on the service, during her exile from Hollywood. But then, Larry had been the one delegated to come up and see her during the dark days of freebase to see if she wouldn't be interested in relinquishing her rights in a dead project so that a guy who was big in television and wanted to be big in movies could rewrite and direct it under his new Bigtime Studio Deal. One of those guys from the Grady* days, who always breezed in, did a little coke, spread some gloom, then split.

'But that's my idea, my novel, no, you can't have it,' and offered him the pipe, knowing his answer already.

'No, thank you,' he said, more to the pipe than her. 'I love it too much to do any.'

'This is that prick Grady's idea, isn't it?' Larry went real quiet.

'Just do us both a favor, think about it.' Don't be a baby, sell out, as Lenny Bruce once said.

'Okay,' she'd said, because she wanted him out of there. When he left she'd called Norman Garey and said, 'I want it back from Warners. They don't get it, they don't want to do it, they could revert the rights back to me. No way this is happening again, no way I get ripped off.' Norman had gotten it back. Nobody had wanted to touch her or her projects with a ten-foot pole. She still thought it would make a great movie.

Joel and Scott were big successes right now and they were making movies like *Reckless* and *Predator* and *Streets of Fire*. The best they ever did was *Die Hard* and *48 Hours*. Cheap heartthumpers. Same old dick love story – Don Simpson's phrase; Christ, he should know, only his had extended to threesomes, very eighties. Charisma movies.

Jon Milius used to say that you should get a slash on your cheek for every bad movie you made so it was there for all the world to see, and after you had three big ugly scars on your face you shouldn't be allowed to make any movies anymore. Maybe that's why they all had beards. Milius had one, too, come to think of it. After they had shoveled tons of red meat and pasta into the slits in the middle of the hair that they called mouths (did these Big Boys know that sometimes their faces looked like female privates?), Larry ambled over to the table.

'Were your ears burning last night?' he asked her.

'Not that I can remember . . .'

'Michael Douglas stopped by on his way out of Michael's and we got to talking . . . He said, "I think I'm going into business with the wrong Phillips."'

'I bet you say that to all the Phillips women.' Of which there were getting to be quite a few.

'We must have talked about you for an hour. We think you're the only smart woman in the business.'

This was Larry's concept of a compliment and one she'd heard from a lot of guys over the years. She looked around Mortons and then at Larry. 'But I'm not in the business. I just get good tables at these restaurants.' Smiled so he knew it was a joke. Yeah, then what are you doing here? she asked herself. Research, I'm doing research.

'Yeah, well, let me know when you want to direct.'

'Oh, I stopped wanting that years ago.'

Larry looked a little uncomfortable, but then she thought

66

he always looked ill at ease. Maybe that was why he was such a loudmouth. His dinner dates joined him and now all three were hovering. Like a mantra, the word *hirsute* rolled over and over in her mind.

As she was turning back to her dinner partner she sensed a presence at the edge of her peripheral vision. She turned and found herself face to face with Don Simpson. Well, not precisely face to face. The war between his right and left brain had finally moved outside. The sides of his face didn't match. So they were face to faces. As it were. Well, he certainly could afford to fix that. 'What's happenin'?' he grinned at her.

Not you. 'Oh, not much . . .'

Driving home, she got a pain in her stomach – a sharp pain that she used to get when a man she loved was fucking someone else.

She was jealous. She was jealous of those fucks. They were getting to make movies, piece-of-shit movies, and she was getting backhanded compliments from them in restaurants where she paid out of her pocket and they paid out of some studio's pocket.

Christ, she had known her relationship with movies was at an impasse when the article about *Flashdance* had run in *Calendar*. Just about everyone involved had been up-and-comers with her in the seventies. And now, here they were, starting the decade by tripping over their shoelaces and each other for credit on something from which she might have considered having her name removed. That's how out of touch she had become . . .

And when exactly had Michael Phillips absconded with her career? Check that: Not absconded. Picked it up from the middle of the road where she'd carelessly dropped it, she was leaving so fast. Well, he was welcome to it! Years ago, she and a bipolar hyphenate, who she always thought of as The Guys, had dropped by Michael's palace on Gilcrest to pick Kate up for a screening. All evening she could tell he was stewing about something. Both she and Kate were on excellent behavior, so by the time they dropped Kate back at Michael's she was getting pretty angry at him for being pissed off. As he opened the car door for her he looked back through the wrought-iron gate at the house.

'How did he get your money?' Meaning it. The Guys was always very concerned about money. It made him behave against his better self a lot of the time. Literally. She had once adored him, but that ceased when he asked her to marry him.

'We don't fuck before, we have a wedding and then a threeweek honeymoon, and if the sex is great, great, and if not, we have a good marriage anyway,' he said earnestly.

She smiled. 'Could we live in separate houses?'

'We could live in separate states!'

'But why would we want to ruin this significant friendship with marriage?' She laughed, hoping he was kidding, remembering one attempt they'd made at sex which involved him in leather chaps and her eating a forbidden Quaalude.

She threw up fifteen minutes into foreplay and they both knew it wasn't from the lude. He had laughed about it later and pronounced her a 'great little thrower-upper.' Two days after his proposal, he met Someone Else, and they were now living in domestic bliss at least a thousand miles outside L.A. She and The Guys never talked anymore. I know a lot of dead people.

'I hate movies,' she said out loud. The affair she'd had with the movies was over. It was over. And Larry Gordon? Jews sit shivah for those who die and those who marry out of the faith. A typically brutal Jewish custom. They sit and mourn for seven days. I know a lot of dead people. Some of them still walk around but they're dead; it's just that no one's told them yet. She would sit shivah for Larry. And the movies, too, while she was at it. She didn't want a stomach-ache like this again, thank you, not if she could help it.

And besides, with all his dialogue, Larry was the president at Fox who terminated – didn't renew – her deal when she needed it. Push came to shove, they told her how smart she was and how talented, and protected their friends. Male bonding. So damn damn damn Larry. Even though he was a pretty good guy. Whatever the fuck that was. When had she started to terminate people on the basis of what they stood for? When they didn't die soon enough. She had learned that from them.

Mostly, though, the dead people in her life had died too soon. Was it always too soon? Probably.

So she was shocked, but not surprised, when Anne Dollard, who was only thirty-two, fell offa horse and hit her head and died. It was July 2 when she fell; she was dead July 4. Her friend, Scott, a typically nonexpressive male, early thirties, was a close friend of Anne's, so she went to Gladstone's with him to pass the time while they were waiting for Anne to be pronounced dead. She wore a Betsey Johnson print spandex structure and a tan; he wore a red baseball cap and a three-day growth of beard. And sunglasses, to hide his pain.

They drank and talked around the subjects of Anne, sudden death, wearing a helmet while riding, and how many commercials had horses in them. They sat outside, on the breezeway cantilevered over the beach, as if the sandy wind that prickled their skin would blow despair away.

Occasionally they would turn their attention toward a guy in an orange slicker and hat who was posting DO NOT PLAY ON THE BEACH signs every twenty feet or so in honor of the latest toxic booboo.

'Maybe Anne knew something we don't,' she said, and he nodded his head and chortled grimly. She went to the funeral with him, too. It was a big event, all of young Hollywood, looking stricken. Yeah, she wanted to tell them, people die. Personally she thought sudden death might be hell for the survivors, but easier on the die-er. Except for the moment of terror preceding the death . . . Death. The major bummer of Life. Hey, Life's a trip . . . and then you get there.

Lionel Chetwyn began, 'Memory is not chronological . . .' and she let her mind drift through Steven Stills singing off key and ending, 'Well done, Anne' (what well done? dying so soon? well, he was a musician, not so good with words); then Bobby Kennedy, Jr., and finally she heard Corinne Mann say something about July Fourth: 'There will be fireworks,' and people started to get up to leave.

'What a shame,' she overheard one yuppie say to another, 'and she was just about to happen . . .'

'I know a lot. Of. Deadpeopledeadpeopledeadpeople . . .

Sydney MacLean and her creative writing course have saved me from drowning at Mount Holyoke. When I do run off with a couple of awards, my mother takes complete credit.

'I guess it takes two generations to make a writer,' she tells Michael Smith, who is so upset by the statement he repeats it to me.

'I used to think that to be eccentric you had to be rich,' my mother says, summoning a salesman who is looking the other way with a tap from her umbrella, 'but now I discover it's one of the benefits of middle age . . .' In my opinion my mother had passed from eccentric to wacko years ago. And I get to be the product of her vivid imagination. I wish she had written her novel, gone to a shrink, something besides her obsession with me.

We are buying clothes to fit my restored body. I have gained serious weight away at school. And dropped it in six weeks. My mother helps me along with her Preludin 25s and the thought that she has only seen my father cry twice: once when his mother died and once when he saw me get off the plane for Christmas . . . She also doesn't talk to me for a week . . .

'You act like I was a possession,' I cry.

'What do you *think* you are?' she snaps. I am stunned. 'And by the way, it's *were*, not *was*.'

In spite of my basic alienation from the Mount Holyoke Girl, a good group has pulled together for junior year. Grace Tyler, a senior who is head of house, admits to me one day that she was worried about us coming into the dorm together, that she had been told we were 'a vicious, cruel, and demoralizing' group. I tell her that's true, but not where she and her friends are concerned. I am actually elected to Student Council, and I haven't participated in extracurricular at all. Least not at school. Extracurricular means drinking and guys as far as I'm concerned. Basically I'm hanging in because I have no real alternatives. I don't have enough money to go to Europe for a year. I have no inclination to take a secretarial job, no other skills. I figure best to get a college degree.

Nineteen sixty-four: We'd all just had our cherries busted by the Kennedy assassination. The Gulf of Tonkin hadn't happened yet, but the Beatles had. Peace and love hadn't hit, but the Free Speech Movement and Mario Savio made the front page of *The New York Times*. Drugs weren't an everyday necessity, but a group of seniors were denied graduation for spiking the punch at a Sunday mixer with mescaline.

Nineteen sixty-four: At Mount Holyoke College you do chores. Sit bells, which means hanging around the front desk and answering the phone for a couple of hours; wash and/or dry dishes, which is over fast but is intense. You can barter or trade your chore. Or pay to have someone else do it, but that's frowned upon. I'm dating locally, Amherst mostly, so I'm doing someone else's Sunday bells. The luck of the draw.

Michael Phillips and Chuck Coen breeze in looking for one of my best friends, Chris Schillig. I'm wearing what we all currently wear, what we refer to as a doody dress. A smock with an empire line, nipped in under the tits and falling loosely over hips and belly. Sexy in a nonrevealing schoolgirl way. My hair is clean and my legs are shaved. Hell, it's Sunday.

Michael and Chuck are a welcome sight. I've been at play in the fields of the goyim for five years, and not one has really grabbed my heart since Johnny Harris disappointed me by dropping out in his sophomore year. And now, here are these two slick guys, tanned, tall, fit, and wearing blazers with double vents, like their fathers, both in the rag trade. Michael's father does knockoffs and Chuck's father is the money in Evan-Picone.

Michael asks for Chris and I drawl, 'Oh, are you one of her

friends from R-o-o-o-slyn . . .' with a mixture of contempt and interest and an up-from-under-the-lashes look that has always worked. It takes Chris awhile to get downstairs, so Sue White and I entertain the guys. When she makes her entrance it is with full makeup and nicely dressed. Michael kisses her on the cheek and Sue mouths to me, 'He's kissing our Christine . . .' Pristine Christine is what we call her to her face. The 'He's kissing our Christine' line cracks us up for days. Our humor relies heavily on repetition. And we're smart girls.

A few weeks later, Michael and Chuck return and we go out to some bar in the neighborhood. Chuck and his date vacate the car to get us a table inside, and we say we'll join them in a minute. We turn to each other in the half-light as if to speak and start kissing instead, tongue revolving around tongue. It is one hot kiss and it goes on for the rest of the night. We never get out of the backseat of the car. On the way back to my dorm, Michael sings me all the words to 'Louie Louie.' I'm impressed. He writes them down so the gang will be impressed, too. They are, and pronounce that it is definitely okay for me to fall in love with him. Which I had already done.

My initial rebellion against my parents' being too hip for the room is to marry Michael. An insecure, bourgeois choice. And Michael is middle class, which makes the choice that much more of a declaration to my parents.

Also, marriage is the punishment I mete out to Michael for breaking my heart on the phone in college. We were having a pretty hot relationship, and he cut school in the middle of the week to bed down with me at a local motel for forty-eight hours. When we took breaks, we pitched out a major paper he had due. I 'helped' him write it and he gave me magnificent head. A week later, he called me to break up with me on the phone.

He calls on the pay phone outside the room Jane and I share. The only room in the whole dorm with its own bathroom. It is smaller than all the other rooms, but we took it in a flash. At Mount Holyoke, you drew numbers out of a hat for your dorm and room the next year. My freshman and sophomore years, I got to move on three ninety-two out of four hundred.

My junior year, I drew number eight, and fourteen of us moved to Torrey Hall, new and modern, out of Mead, which was one of the first dorms built on the campus. Jane and I, public-school Jews who didn't know from community living, hadn't taken a decent shit since freshman year, so the concept of a private bathroom loomed large in our collective consciousness. The bathroom was good for smoking, too, although the smoker was steps down the hall from us, as was the pay phone, which could be used after the switchboard closed at 10 P.M.

He calls in the middle of a pretty cold day, but by the time he is done with me I've lost three pounds from anxiety-sweat. Poor Michael. He is under pressure from me to get married. Jane is marrying an older guy whom I intuitively know is gay. I actually beg her not to marry him the night before the wedding, in which I serve as a hostile maid of honor. (When he comes out of the closet twelve years and one child later, and she and I have been out of touch for ten years, she tries mightily to find me, but I am exiled on Oahu and do not respond to her imprecations for communication. Hell, if my own mother, who is dying of cancer, can't get hold of me, what chance does a previous best friend have?)

I am very much under the influence of Jane our last year at Mount Holyoke. I really do want to marry Michael. We graduate in 1965. The year Bob Dylan goes electric and gets booed at Newport, but 'Like a Rolling Stone' goes to number one. We are the cross between the beer and mescaline generation. We span Perry Como to the Beatles. We have old and new values. Plus, we are all so traumatized by the Kennedy assassination, we need extra love and security. I really do want to marry Michael; he wants to get laid. When he blows me off by phone, he tells me he doesn't love me anymore.

'I'm not coming down this weekend,' he starts. I can tell by his voice he is saying more than slight change in plans, honey, I'll be there next weekend. I peel back the skin of an orange.

'That's okay,' I say, chirpy. I sound like his mother. Michael had once complained that his mother didn't talk, she sang.

'I'm not coming down anymore. I don't want to see you anymore . . .' My stomach slides out of my body and I start sweating profusely from my head. My bangs sag onto my eyebrows. But while I am getting sad, and trying everything to make him change his mind, I am also thinking, Prick, you used me to get your paper written. I am beyond hurt and angry. I love him and I hate him. I don't accept for weeks that he isn't just going to show up one night. Or write a letter. Or call at some odd hour, like four in the morning. Which I would hear, I wouldn't be sleeping then. I'm not going to sleep ever again. Not until he comes back and tells me what a big mistake he has made. Which he doesn't do.

While everyone is having a blast and being seniors on the brink of graduation, getting their little trainee jobs at Chubb and Bache and Bloomingdale's, I am sinking into my favorite spot: the slough of despond. My studies, marginal at best, are going over the edge into failure. What caps it for me and makes me know I am going to have to make a move is that one morning I make a friend cry by screaming at her to define her terms about something banal, while she is trying to eat breakfast.

I con the dean, who keeps telling me that life is really much simpler if you approach it in the Cartesian manner: one step after another. Orderly. I have no idea how Descartes has any bearing on my nervous breakdown, but I do mention, I think therefore I am . . . unable to think about anything but my man and how he done me wrong. I'm given two weeks off, and a lot of reading and blue books to fill so I can graduate.

I go home to Milwaukee. It isn't really home, but my family still lives there. It isn't ever home to my parents either. Probably the only person in my family who doesn't experience a serious emotional decline in the Midwest is my brother, Matthew, who was moved there at the malleable age of twelve. I help them pack their books. Therapy. They've given up on the heartland and are returning to New York in a month.

My parents are both very supportive. They want to help me get over Michael because they didn't like him and think I am well rid of him. I get better and I go back to school and finish out the year and graduate – the dean actually gives me a smile and says, 'This is a pleasant surprise' as I get me my diploma – but I am pining away inside. As angry as I am, I'd take him back in a second, I know.

This pining isn't helped by the fact that school is out and I don't have a job. I didn't get into a single executive trainee program. I am offered a summer job at *Time* as a researcher, which the personnel lady says could become full time in the fall, but I decide to really hit the streets and find something else. We have our conversation over 'Satisfaction' playing at full blast in the room my parents are letting me occupy in their apartment on 13th Street while I figure out my life.

I have just bought the album and am dancing around when she calls. I think the words influence me against the job. So young and already a victim of media hype, and the media haven't proliferated yet. I turn the music and her down with the same motion. I turn on the radio for a second..Cousin Brucie says, 'And now here's little Bobby Dylan, with "Like a Rolling Stone" . . .' I laugh to myself, wondering how the Master would feel about the intro, then caterwaul plaintively, 'like a complete unknown, with no direction home, like a rolling stone . . .' and flash on Caesar who never adjusted to Milwaukee. Committed suicide on a sharp tree stump in the freezing cold trying to get back to Great Neck.

My other friends from school are bunking with each other, and Jane and David have an apartment in the Gramercy area. I have been away at college for four years, but something in me isn't ready to let go of family life, however poisonous, and they aren't going to make me pay rent until I get a job. My mother, always a dedicated and thorough reader of *The New York Times*, combs the Help Wanteds early in the morning, so by the time I check them out she has the appropriate situations circled already.

It pisses me off that she is always right. I am a liberal arts graduate, with as many credits in poli. sci. as English. When would I ever know as much as she? When would she stop being omniscient, omnipotent, omnipresent? When I marry Michael and move out of the house. When I get a job that pays enough money so I can support myself. Hah! That could be a long time . . .

I have an extremely discouraging June. By the middle of July I am starting to consider calling the lady from *Time* back and taking a chance on the research job. Which is probably no longer available, plum that it is. Then I open the paper and my mother has circled a job for a production assistant at *McCall's* Magazine. I show up at personnel and am sent immediately to meet a pretty, delicate creature named Dorothy Chamberlain. An old maid with white hair and perfect features, she takes to my credentials (Milwaukee, Mount Holyoke). There have been over a hundred applicants for this inconsequential little job. She says she'll let me know by the end of the day, but when I walk out of the building at 230 Park I am pretty sure I have the gig.

I start at eighty bucks a week. Production is just about the shittiest of all magazine departments. The Art Department lines up the front-of-the-book and you do their bidding on all the really creative stuff. You line up the back of the book, all the continued froms and the recipes. Garbage that is beneath the Art Department.

There are four women counting me in Production, and we sit in descending order of title, from Dorothy, to a virago named Alice, who is the hatchet man (she yells at guys in the composing room from morning to night), to a pleasant-faced endomorph named Barbara, to me. Old maids all in a row. Dorothy teaches me diacritical marks, and how many characters to a line, and how to get rid of widows. There is a general look that type has on a page – the forest if you will; then there is ease of reading – the trees.

But the best part of my job is that I have to pick up and deliver stats and photocopies and rewrites from morning to night. I log ten-twenty miles a day. I can interact with any number of different types of people, pick up little tidbits here and there, and I can keep on the move. Me and my little geometric Courrèges knockoffs and little short white boots churning along. Armor, like the false eyelashes I wear. We have the illusion that we are going somewhere.

I hook up with Chris Miller and Mark Meyerson. Chris has

a job I want, at Dancer Fitzgerald, as a copywriter. Mark is still in law school. Sometimes we meet and go to lunch. Even have a drink at lunch. Sometimes. I get a five-dollar raise at Christmas, so I know there isn't much future at *McCall's*. although it is a trip to see my name on the masthead every month. I think that if Mark Meyerson, whom I've known since my first week at Mount Holyoke, would just loosen up a bit, he might serve as a good Michael replacement.

Mark Meyerson and I just never get it together and it comes up again and again for years and years. I start to date him, for real, when I come down to New York.

He likes the theater and old movies and jazz, and we hit those clubs and restaurants and walk too many blocks when it's too cold, and romance seems on the brink of blossoming, but I am still harboring lust for Michael. One night I call information to see if there is a listing and there is. I knew he'd be in the neighborhood because he had planned to go to NYU Law School. To avoid the draft.

No one is against the Vietnam War yet, except me and my mother – the polls show twenty-five percent against the war – but everybody seems to be doing something they don't want to do to get exemptions and not fight the war. Law school, medical school, babies. There he is on 17th Street. It makes me nervous to know he is living this close to me. I don't even think of dialing the number. Hatred boils inside me. He is right here, and he has still made no attempt to reach me.

I see Terry Finkel, an old boyfriend from Great Neck, a few times. One night he takes me to Ondine under the bridge at 60th and First. Girls wearing fringe minidresses bugaloo in cages to 'Like a Rolling Stone.' As little as we had in common in high school we have even less now except that he is handsome and I will overlook all sorts of character defects in favor of handsome. Driving home, I tell him I love him, which guarantees his speedy departure. I don't meet anyone new, but I haven't been in the City that long.

One evening, while I am hacking the hems off minidresses to make them even shorter, the phone rings.

'Hello, Julia . . .' Michael says. I get so nauseated and excited, I think I will lose my cookies right there and then.

'. . . Long time . . .' You can say that again, motherfucker. Not that long in the vast scheme of things – about eight months, seventeen days, and three hours. Just as I was not thinking about you all the time. Well, Michael always did have good timing.

'Hi, Michael.' I hear my voice and it sounds parched. The ensuing phone conversation, which isn't long, is one of my first out-of-body experiences. The gist is that he can't stop thinking about me and will I have dinner on Saturday night. I accept as casually as I can. When the big date arrives, my parents beat it for a local movie theater because they can't stand the fact that I am going on this date or the sight of him. They have seen me suffer, almost not graduate, have a rough time finding a job. They blame Michael for all of this. I blame Jane and David.

We have a long, awkward kiss at the door and our bodies fit perfectly again. I don't want to stay in the apartment and fuck him right then and there, so we take off down the street. Thirteenth is one of those streets in New York replete with restaurants of every ethnic persuasion. Michael is passionate about Chinese food and I am passionate about Michael, so we go to the Mandarin. Both of us get huge headaches, a result, no doubt, not only of the MSG but also of the conversation.

We haven't even ordered drinks and I have already declared, again in that parched out-of-body voice, that if his intentions aren't honorable, I never want to see him again. He cracks up, and I crack up, too. Then I surprise us both with a tears-spring-involuntarily-into-the-eyes-lip-starts-to-tremble-nose-swells moment that we always hope won't happen in public. I am not an especially attractive cryer. I make my body shudder and regain composure.

'How could you break up with me on the phone?'

'It was the only way I could go through with it . . .'

'You told me you didn't love me . . .'

'I was very much in love with you . . . I just felt so . . . pressured . . .'

'Pressured by what?'

'You wanted to get married so badly . . .'

'Isn't that what people wildly in love do?' my imitation-Jane self said. My Menshevik grandfather is yelling at me in my mind from the Other Side in a thick Russian accent 'nonononono.'

'I was just too young, am, just too young . . .'

'Then what are we doing here now . . .?' I am getting anxiety titsweat. It is collecting inside my wool-and-poly gray Courrèges knockoff. I take a sip of my drink and stop breathing.

'I miss you . . . I love you . . .'

We are married the following summer at the St. Moritz Hotel by a judge who costs seventy-five dollars. I have refused a rabbi, I want a nonreligious ceremony. The judge says *God* nine times.

Victor cuts my bangs too short just days before the wedding; probably he agrees with my mother that Michael is not good enough for her. I do everything, including pulling at them, to make them longer. Nothing works. This gives me permission to hate every picture of the event, save two: my father, out on the terrace, with his glasses on, signing checks, and one of me and Michael's father looking right through the camera, like Brian De Palma would instruct me to do a few years later. When people see the picture they always ask who the guy is. Possibly I married the wrong Phillips.

Michael and I honeymoon for three weeks all over Mexico . . .

It is the middle of the night and pouring rain by the time we arrive at Las Brisas, where every room has its own pool, which makes it a big favorite with honeymooners who are still interested enough in each other to want to fuck in warm water. The air conditioning in the hotel room doesn't work and there is no one around to fix it. I make a fuss about the air conditioning, which infuriates Michael, who likes heat. We have a pretty good fight, which consists of me tantruming and the steel door of Michael's psyche slamming shut. Bang. Locked out. We are probably also freaked that we are actually married. We fall asleep with our backs to each other. I watch overripe verdant palm leaves commit suicide against the windows in the driving storm.

The next day there are croissants and fresh fruit. I pop an

Entero-Vioform per instructions to guard against *turista*. There is splashing in the pool and I assume it is Michael, but it's the couple from downstairs who smile and drawl hello in thick southern accents. E-e-e-u-u-u-w, Texans! Michael has similar feelings.

We don't talk much, but we get in our bathing suits and rent a jeep and head into town. The concierge sends a guy to our room to fix our air conditioning. Driving into town, we see a huge empty beach with giant waves. We agree on a swim, and I race out of the jeep pulling clothes off along the way. I crash through the waves. I know it is a mistake the second I hit the water. Powerful forces suck me to the bottom. I swim furiously and break through them somewhat and just as the thought occurs to me that this might be my last thought, a hand comes through and pulls me back. It is Michael . . .

'You were swimming for the bottom,' he screams, dragging me to shore. I can see his veins popping in his temples and arms from the effort of rescuing me. This is a strong fucking current. We throw ourselves on the sand and make out fiercely for a moment. Later in the day, a native tells us this is Hornos, and you don't swim there, you just look at the ocean.

We do all the tourist things in Acapulco: drinks at El Presidente, morning swim, dinner at Armando's, some silver shopping, some beachfront oysters. Then we hit Mexico City, which is only pop. six mil, and isn't the most polluted city in the Western Hemisphere yet. Mexico City is very cosmopolitan and the natives are whiter than in Acapulco. One night Michael picks up a Spanish-language paper and says, 'Oh, Julia, I'm so sorry . . .'

'What?' What could possibly have happened to affect me that would be on the front page of a Spanish newspaper? He hands me the paper. There is a picture of a naked bloated dead guy on the cover. Do I know this person?

'Lenny Bruce O.D.'d . . .'

We go out drinking that night at chic bars, and every time I think of Lenny Bruce and how the forces of the right done him wrong, I start to cry. Michael thinks this is pretty silly and gets tired of it fast. He buries himself in a copy of *Catch-22*. which I have insisted he read if we're to stay together.

Next we go to Cozumel, an island off the Yucatan, more Caribbean in nature than Pacific. The hotel is in an odd phase of midconstruction. We marvel that they have the nerve to take in guests. The floors are naked cement. There are either partially finished walls or no walls at all. The layout is promising, but it is spooky living inside this skeleton. Talk about the barest essentials . . .

The water and the beach are gorgeous, and the hotel turns out to be populated by characters out of a Tennessee Williams play. O-o-o-h, living theater instead of walls . . . how entertaining. There is an Old Salt and his Old Whore, some middle-class Mexicans, doctors and lawyers, a medium-level British diplomat and his French femme fatale wife, also their three bratty blond children, and a University of Chicago professor, an embittered middle-aged drunken pinko, who comes in mighty handy two days into our stay, because I am assaulted by *turista* and he is the only one for miles around with paregoric. My kinda guy . . . I am deathly ill our last day in Cozumel, but by the time we are headed for Merida, I can control my runs with paregoric, not to mention drift onward toward la-la land, my favorite venue.

So many people fall sick from *turista* that paregoric is a nonprescription drug in Mexico. Every morning Michael hits the *farmacia* and brings me my instant cork for the day. There is a power failure every afternoon at three o'clock, which I take personally. Michael has spent his junior year abroad in Spain and has a much more relaxed attitude. He is really into *Catch-22* by now, so between my runs and his reading we blow off the fifty-mile bus ride to the Mayan ruins, although it has been the one part of the trip I have really anticipated.

One night we go to an Elvis movie. It is in English with Spanish subtitles. The crowd adores Elvis. The movie is terrible and gives me a headache, but when we walk out into the night air in the square there is a balmy breeze. In the electric light with a starry night sky as backdrop the square, the foliage, the adobe buildings – even the *mestizos* – are beautiful, a strange tropical painting. Michael and I sort of make up in bed that night, but we're pissed at each other the next morning.

We fly to Miami, where we are to connect with another plane home. When we arrive in Miami we discover that there is a strike and there is no flight home. We end up spending thirteen hours in the Miami airport waiting for a flight, during which time Michael finishes *Catch-22* and we have a nice chat. We go to bar after bar and then into those little booths where you can take four pictures for a quarter.

By the time we fly home and reenter Washington Square Village, Building 1, we are friends again. I know I love him because I keep having nightmares that he is drafted and killed in Vietnam. The dreams usually end on the positive note of me and his mother fighting over whether he should be buried by a rabbi or a judge. Sometimes she leans across the coffin and starts pulling my teeth out. Wherever she pulls one out, the one next to it fills in. By the time I awake sweaty and crying, my mouth is occupied by two giant teeth, one upper and one lower. It hurts . . .

I am getting incredibly bored at *McCall's*. I think of my father's advice, strong handshake and always go where they pay you more money. I look through the Help Wanteds on my own. There is a job at Macmillan as an advertising copywriter for their college book division. A pale, pear-shaped guy named Conrad Squiers interviews me, gives me some books to read, and asks me to write jacket copy. Piece of cake.

He hires me at $110/week, which is twenty-five dollars a week more than I am making at *McCall's*. Macmillan is located in crummy offices downtown with no air conditioning. When the temperature humidity index goes over ninety-two they are required by law to let us off work. There is another girl in the department, a Barnard graduate, couple of years older than I. Her name is Alice Bach, and in spite of the fact that she is a dumpy, bespectacled broad, we make instant friends. She is from Princeton, New Jersey. I get the feeling from serious gentile money.

Our jobs consist mainly of rendering jacket copy for deathly boring textbooks and then cutting and pasting snippets from the original copy for ads. Two-line ads, four-line ads. It becomes very tedious labor and within six months Alice and I are completely burned out on our work and start behaving badly. Long lunches where we drink. Late arrivals.

The boredom is broken only by a move uptown to a spiffy new air-conditioned building and each other. Alice and I crack each other up, particularly by cutting up all our copy and repasting it. We sing a song in the back room: cut-ting and pasting, cut-ting and pasting. Conrad Squiers comes back one afternoon to check on us, and the blood of rage suffuses his fat face. We are both on thin ice. Time to move on. I polish my handshaking skills. Time to move up.

Time chooses 'Youth: 25 and Under' as Man of the Year. David and Jane call to congratulate us. Jane is pregnant. She must feel very old, I think . . .

An acquaintance had cautioned her long before, when it first started coming in, and she had confided how uneasy the money made her. He said, 'There is a saying, who knows from what culture, that people relate to money in one of three ways: one, like blood to nourish; two, like sperm, to create; or three, like shit – to be gotten rid of . . .' They both knew that she stood firmly behind door number three.

Now, fifteen years later, the money was just about all gone. It had taken a hell of a long time to go through all of it. Of course she'd had a lot of help.

First there were all the partners. She knew that nobody liked to think of her as exploited or victimized, least of all herself, but over the years it had occurred to her more than a few times, that other people had really made a great deal of

83

money out of her efforts. If they acknowledged that at all, they resented her. But more often than not, she just became a dead issue in their minds. Sometimes she felt like the Frances Farmer of producers, if they could have found a way to remove her name from the credit blocs, they would have done so years ago.

Then there was the government. Land of the free home of the brave really liked to take its chunk out of the self-made woman. After the Three Mile Island incident, a year when she had paid seven figures in taxes, she began to appreciate the stance of previous rich hippies like Joan Baez. Every time there was a military failure, she felt like she'd personally underwritten it.

She wasn't famous enough to take a stand that would land her anywhere but prison for income tax evasion, and she had a string of business managers who liked to be rigorously honest with the Internal Revenue Service, although there were a few who didn't seem to have held themselves to such high standards when it came to her.

Then there was all the coke and all the jewels and all the furs and all the first-class travel and all the loans – wasted on those who would never pay them back.

And it had taken a long time to go through it because she had so many assets to sell off while she was creating an environment for her comeback. She was optimistic; it didn't seem possible that she wouldn't. Eventually. Even with her tarnished drug rep, she figured if she showed up clean for long enough, somebody would do one of the projects she held dear. Eventually.

But it was a whole new ballgame. Why would 1985 be different in Hollywood than in the rest of the country? It was Reagan time. Even when she did deals with guys who really knew what she could do, who were fans – like Begelman and Hirshfield and Norman Levy – it wasn't the same. Everyone was scared.

Then there were the new guys, the guys who got added into the Rolodex every couple of months. These people were not visionary nor did they like visionaries. They were not gamblers either. They hadn't had the personal experience of working with her on dreams that became big important movies, so they didn't support her new dreams at all. Bit by bit, the guys from her era passed from power and all these new guys were the power.

They were short and they had ratty beards to hide their unimpressive jawlines and often they had eyes that looked in two different directions at once. These eyes saw only if their competition was gaining on them. Oh, and something they called the bottom line. The bottom line, she once told one of them, was that there is no bottom line. His eyes flickered for a moment, then glazed over. These guys kept hours that only made sense if you were shooting a picture, and she was pretty sure that they didn't have any dreams at all. There was no way they would go along with the pictures that formed in her mind and she really had trouble being in the same room with them.

That's when she stopped entertaining at home and started to eat out at restaurants.

She kept selling assets to stay in the game, and when she finally did get a little picture on, *The Beat*, borderline pretentious, but then, so was *Taxi Driver* ten years before, she ended up paying far too much out of pocket, and that really impoverished her. Reagan time. Lee Iacocca and Donald Trump were role models. And Bechtel had several cabinet posts. When Reagan went to China and sold nuclear reactors, Bechtel was going to build them. *Dynasty* was a hit. Shit, she couldn't even stand the clothes. And they were all so rapacious. Sex as money. Money as sex. Boring. It annoyed her that there were so many junctures when she could have said, Fuck it, this ain't happening, I'm gonna cash in my chips and think about it on a beach in the South of France for awhile.

Then Mitch Freedman, her downward-mobility manager of the moment, summoned her to his office. As she'd gotten poorer she'd slid down the scale of business managers in town. Before Mitch, she'd been with Mickey Rutman at Gelfand, Breslauer. Norman Garey had seen to it that she went to him after she'd fired Hank Levine. Some guy named Dick Lauter had filled that in-between by preparing her taxes. She owed $774,000, she remembered, which was exactly how much she'd spent that year: 'I've never seen anyone spend quite so much in one year,' he kept saying. Oh yeah, well, *you* try doing a quarter ounce of freebase a day with a boyfriend who keeps destroying your house.

The first day she went for a meeting at Mickey Rutman's office, she arrived with Fins, to meet Norman in the waiting room. There was this small matter of Rottweiler's* AR-15, which Fins had lifted out of his arms while he slept, postcocaine-crash-style, an hour before. For the last two days, Rottweiler had been terrorizing her household by variously threatening windows, property, and her and her four-year-old daughter Kate.

Nobody wanted the fucking gun; it passed from person to person like the gun in *The King of Marvin Gardens*. Ultimately it ended up in a safe at Abercrombie & Fitch, and Rottweiler reclaimed it. There was still the matter of getting rid of Rottweiler, which Norman hired a private dick named Briscoe to do. This guy thought he was really Robert Mitchum and he ended up scaring her more than Rottweiler had.

She had been so distracted the day of this meeting, that she forgot to be apprehensive of all the squares in the conference room. Mickey Rutman handled both Steven Spielberg and Barbra Streisand, which meant that he was a star business manager at a star firm. At that point, even with the notoriety and the lack of work, her credits were recent enough so that she was a big enough deal to sign on. She knew Gerry Breslauer from the Steven-buying-a-house trip, where she'd personally viewed thirty-two venues with him until he found the house up on Alto Cidro. They walked in and the house was decorated horribly – 'housitosis' Sherry Phillips once called it, referring to flocked wallpaper and everything wrong. The ceilings were all twenty-five feet high, and she'd turned to Steven and said, 'I think with a little work this place could house your ego.' And they'd all laughed and Steven had bought it, to the great relief of Gerry Breslauer.

She was at Gelfand, Breslauer from the time she started to clean up, in 1979, when she was strung out and rich, until shortly after her Fox deal ran out in 1985, when she'd been summoned to Mickey Rutman's office to, in essence, be fired.

'We service rich people,' he'd said, 'and you are no longer a rich person.'

Now another accountant summoned her to his office, less well appointed than Mickey Rutman's, and said, in essence, the same thing. With a tad more warmth. The lower down the scale, she noticed, the more humane accountants were. Why had she ever been with this series of five percenters – of gross – anyway? As far as she could tell, not one of them had ever made her money work for her. Mostly they'd just complained about her department store bills and paid full taxes. She'd stayed with them because she was terrified of her money.

The day Bob Colbert had received their first check for *The Sting*, the check that she and Michael and Tony and David Ward would split four ways (which was funny, because that was pretty much how they were in real life: split four ways) Michael and Tony had been at his office to sign at 9 A.M. She had cruised in from the beach, wacked out on pot and Quaaludes, at about four, which meant they lost the interest on the check for that day. Bob showed her the check: it was for $4.3 million. She tried to calculate the lost interest but couldn't do the arithmetic.

None of it had been about the money for her anyway; she was always telling the guys about how much money they would make, because she understood that was how you had to talk to guys. But the movies, the aggressive pursuit of the career, the striving – hadn't been about the money. She thought it was just about the motion. An old notion, held over from childhood, that if she moved fast enough she would escape death. At the very least, her mother.

She walked to the window of his fifth-floor office, which looked out over Century City. It was a hot September day and smog clung to the sides of the buildings. She was awash in self-pity. If the window hadn't been sealed, she might have contemplated throwing herself out of it. Colbert knew the check was making her feel bad, but he couldn't relate – not even a little bit. Wasn't this what it was all for? Not for me not for me. She sighed deeply: 'This is more responsibility than I can handle,' she said, but she meant, I am afraid I am afraid.

Now she found herself thinking the same: I am afraid I am

afraid. Getting poor was an awesome responsibility, too, and even though she'd once joked to Mickey Rutman that the only thing that thrilled a sicko like her as much as acquisition was divestiture, she'd had enough of those laughs to build her character. And she hadn't acquired in a long time. And she was running out of things to sell. She'd collapsed her pension and profit-sharing plan to stay afloat. That had been dumb because she'd already lost the heart for the new game and the new players. She knew it, but she refused to cop to it: 'Your third eye is always open, you put the blinders on,' her shrink emphasized during one of their phone sessions.

She wished her third eye had been wide open to everything financial from the collapsing of the pension and profit-sharing plan because that was the coda that she really should have avoided. She collapsed the pension and profit-sharing plan, a million or two of past effort, paid two hundred thousand in taxes right away, and basically owed the government six of the eight that remained.

Mommy mommy do I forgive you?

I call a woman named Jean Freeman, whom I have met while Sydney MacLean's protégé at Mount Holyoke, an editor at the *Ladies' Home Journal*. She is a previous protégé of Sydney's. She takes me to lunch at the Brussels, a tony place for publishing types on East 54th. She has a martini at lunch. She is borderline pretty, voluble, southern. She doesn't think there is anything there, but she gives me a couple of short stories and asks me to read and précis them. Short comment at the bottom. Piece of cake.

I send them off to her with little hope, but to my surprise she calls me within days and says if I can get away I should come meet her boss, Wesley Price. I go after work that day.

Wesley Price is a tall sixty-ish curmudgeon who is exactly the kind of cranky teacher I always get along with. There is just the final okay from the publisher, a dapper short guy named John Mack Carter, and within days I am giving notice to Conrad Squiers, who is jealous and relieved at the same time.

This job, with all the interviews, nets out at one-two-five a week. Within six months Jean Freeman is history, quits to write her novel, and I get a promotion. And a raise. To seventy-five hundred a year. I consider this permission to get out of the subways and into cabs, although without help from Michael's parents we wouldn't even be able to afford rent on the apartment.

Michael, meanwhile, has discovered the glories of the stock market and the Thursday night card game. He and two college friends have formed a partnership from card winnings. They invest in options on Syntex, the company that is producing synthetic female hormones for birth control pills. The stock goes bananas. They take their profits and keep going. Michael goes to class, studies, and buys and sells. Every Thursday he plays poker.

One Thursday night he doesn't come home, which freaks me out. He returns the following morning with money oozing from every pocket. A grand. Freddy Gordon has brought his bookie, the Cheese, to the game, and they have gotten involved in killer black-jack. The Cheese has a penchant for cheeseburgers and weighs about three hundred pounds. He is taken to the cleaners by one and all. This goes on for the next couple of weeks, and then the Cheese begins to welch on his losses, and shortly thereafter the game dissolves for good. Years later, the Cheese gets blown away by a loan shark. Karma for welching on his bets with the boys.

I have been eying a little pale blue suede coat in the window of Nina, a shop up the street. Finally I break down and buy it for seventy-five bucks. Michael gets so angry about the expenditure he throws an ashtray at my knee and splits. I call Bernie Raisner, a guy he goes to law school with, panicky, and Bernie finds him on 3rd Street having an ice-cream cone.

He comes home, but by that time I have developed so much anxiety I get a powerful migraine. This infuriates Michael even more, and he moves in with Bernie. I take to my bed for three long days, during which time it is impossible to move without blinding pain. On the fourth day I get out of bed and have some Rice Krispies. Then I get on the scale. I am overjoyed to see the headache has created a five-pound loss. I weigh 103 pounds. I think I look gorgeous. Michael comes back and the only relic of the fight is my exploded knee, which I cover up with pants for a week.

The war is getting worse and worse and Michael is going to graduate from law school soon. All our friends vulnerable to the draft are having babies. I have no desire to have a baby; I want a career. Michael says he understands, but he is furious with me. He starts to search for a reserve unit, and we are beyond thrilled when he finds one in New Jersey that will take him.

He graduates from law school and passes the bar in the summer, but he has already found himself a job with a small portfolio manager named John Rosenthal. Between the bar exams and the beginning of his new job, we take a vacation in Jamaica, the result of a fabulous new set of ads they've been running on TV: it has beaches, it has mountains, it's hot, it's cold, etc.

At the airport, we notice, but do not speak to, two other couples. They eye us, too, but we don't meet until one of the girls gets stranded in the falls at Ocho Rios. They are Long Island types with good weed, and good speed. We hang out constantly in Jamaica, getting high and giggling. Daytime is easy. Sun. Night presents some problems: we travel out to Rose Hall, which is supposed to be haunted, and try to capture the ghosts on infrared film. There is a stirring in the foliage and we flee. We head into town to see a movie. Montego Bay is as scary as 125th and Lenox in New York, and we make a fast pass around the square.

The next day the six of us book ourselves out of Jamaica to Puerto Rico. The plane stops at every island in between. In Haiti, we are actually escorted off the plane by soldiers with mounted bayonets and marched through a gift shop. I buy a statue of a headless, stacked, ebony woman. I am sure if I don't buy something we will never get back on the plane . . .

I start to search for a new job. The *Ladies' Home Journal* is the longest I have stayed in one place since I hit the job market, and I know I'm in a stall. My mentor there, Phyllis Levy, is ensconced as an associate editor, as is Wesley in the senior spot. I have gotten pretty proficient at cutting together a couple of books for our book bonus section, but the job is becoming humdrum and there is no opportunity for advancement. I share my feelings of frustration with Phyllis and one day she comes back from lunch with a lead for me.

There is a guy named Marvin Birdt at Paramount Pictures who is looking for something called a story editor, as his story editor, Barry Beckerman, has just left him for a job with Dino De Laurentiis. Phyllis sets up a meeting, and Marvin and I hit it off immediately. He asks me if I have any experience in the movie business and I say no, but I see a lot of movies. I have no idea how profound this statement is until I actually land the job.

I have a tense weekend awaiting his decision – I know there is a girl from Warner Bros. publicity who is running ahead of me. In the end, Marvin probably chooses me because I come from magazines and have a six-month jump on anyone in movies in terms of seeing material. When I go over there, I take all the coverage I've done in the last year and redo it for him.

This movie job is a barrel of fun in comparison to what I've been doing. First of all, I get my own secretary, an actual professional older-woman type named Phyllis. The Jewish mother I wish I'd had. She is very proud of me and everything I do.

Second, my own office, which is very much in the shape of a bowling alley and tucked away in a corner of the building. The other important aspect of the job is that I finally break the ten-thousand-dollar-a-year barrier. The downside is that I get to work in the funky part of town, on Broadway between 41st and 42nd. Sardi's is around the corner, and I create a relationship with Vincent, and Jimmy the maître d', on my expense account. It amuses them to put me in the horseshoe next to David Merrick, sour faced and expensively dressed, the only other daily diner. This sets an early pattern for me: figure out where you like to eat, where they treat you nice, and buy a relationship that you can call on on a daily basis.

And they are always screening their own movies during the day. Grab a cup of coffee and see *Downhill Racer* at ten in the morning, and get paid for it while the secretary they've given you fields your calls . . .

Michael gets called up for active duty by the reserves. Rosenthal gives him a leave of absence. He is in a reserve unit stationed at Fort Dix. It is filled with guys similar to him: twenty-five-and-a-half years old with careers and nowhere else to go but Vietnam. They are not especially trainable types. The first time he comes home to visit for a weekend I am in shock over his hair. I try to be as loving as possible but it is a difficult hurdle.

With Marvin in the middle of a divorce, and Michael in the reserves, we are good escorts for each other. One night he takes me to a party at Andrea Eastman's that includes Ali McGraw and her boyfriend, Robin, Marty Davidson and his wife, Sandy, and Jane Oliver. Janie and Marty are both hotshot agents at Ashley Famous, one of the myriad precursors of what now stands as ICM. Janie's client, Dustin Hoffman, has just scored big in *The Graduate*. Janie has represented him for ten years.

I allow that I have read *The Graduate*, and I'm a little confused about why anyone got screenplay credit. It's pretty clear to me they just passed out copies of the book on the set. The decibel level rises as the discussion moves to the subject of just how much Charles Webb, who wrote the book, was paid. I have heard twenty grand and he's working in a shoe store in the East Village. Everyone else involved with the movie will make millions.

Jane and Marty get into a screaming fighting match with me over the money netted by the guy who originated the 'full material.' They are philistines, as far as I am concerned. I make a vow in my mind that I will not fuck the writer if I ever get into a position of power. It is my first glimmer of the prevailing show biz attitude toward writers: at once on a pedestal and under the thumb. (I don't find out till years later that women are regarded similarly. Writers and women are the niggers of Hollywood.)

Marvin gives me pretty free rein, and I have far more interesting activities in my working day than I did in magazines. He gives me a script called *Puzzle of a Downfall Child*, by Carole Eastman. It is to be directed by Jerry Shatzberg, a pretentious fashion photographer who aspires to moving pictures. Faye Dunaway, his girlfriend, is committed to the lead. It is a Didionesque look at the fashion world, and I love the writing, but it runs very long.

Since I have only recently been reworking no less a personage than Simone de Beauvoir for a book bonus section for the *Ladies' Home Journal*, I figure it okay at a meeting in Marvin's office to express some ideas for shifting and cutting. Marvin is impressed. Jerry is not. After he departs sullenly, Marvin asks me to write him a lengthy memo commemorating all my ideas. It takes the better part of an afternoon, but it is on his desk – my little eight-page masterpiece – at the end of the day.

Two days later, it comes back to me through interoffice, but it is addressed to Jerry Schatzberg from Marvin Birdt. I am furious that this guy thinks it's all right to put his name to my work, but instinctively I know it is part of the deal. Part of the reason he hired me and I have free reign. Part of the law of the land, and not the first time it will happen to me. I never mention it. Neither does he.

Notwithstanding the first impassioned argument at Andrea's, Janie and Andrea and I become good girlfriends, as much as show business allows. Janie talks me up to her colleagues at Ashley Famous. Andrea, who is credited with casting Ali in *Goodbye Columbus*, tries to protect me from myself in exchange for my writing her memos. I am too honest for my own good. I antagonize Peter Bart in a meeting by not allowing him to nestle condescendingly into his customary role of house intellectual.

The next day I am walking down the hall with Andrea and we see the selfsame Peter walking toward us whilst confabbing sotto voce with a dark curly-haired tan guy in gray slacks, white shirt open below where his chest hair should be, and a tight gold-buttoned navy blazer. He bears an uncanny resemblance to George Hamilton. 'Who's the hairdresser?' I query Andrea, just a bit too audible to be similarly sotto voce'd, as we are passing. He glances in my direction.

'Bob Evans,' she scolds. Oh dear . . .

By the time Michael is out of the reserves and his hair is growing in, Marvin Birdt has been fired from Paramount and moved to Mirisch. He takes me with him. I am still in the funky part of town, Seventh Avenue between 48th and 49th, in an office substantially the same. I now have a powerhouse working for me named Eunice Bellucci. This situation lasts a year, and is the most fun I have in a job like this. Mirisch is now run by the younger brothers – Walter and Marvin – of the dynamic Harold, who has passed from the scene, but they still have a slew of deals with directors: John Sturges, Peter Yates, Pollack and Rydell, Billy Wilder. I actually find a book that Pollack buys.

I promote a trip to the West Coast just as Michael promotes one out of his boss. With a stopover in Las Vegas for the laboratory animal convention. Michael has found a little company called Charles Rivers Mice and Rats, and he's covering the convention. On the plane trip out, I consider the meaning of Life to overcome my fear of flying. I wonder if it's a laboratory, and I'm just another guinea pig. In the vast scheme of things. As it were.

We go to some shows and lose Michael's boss. The next day, he is nowhere to be found. Michael and I change the reservations, and we call the company the boss is supposed to see in L.A. and say he is sick. We find him on the floor, dusty and rumpled, with hundreds spilling out of every pocket and a shit-eating grin on his face.

We get him dressed and on the plane but have a hard time convincing him to get off. We rent a car, start to head for the flat, dusty industrial part of town for the meeting. We stop at a diner to straighten him out. As he pours coffee into himself his hair straightens, his tie ties, and his shirt presses itself. Popeye and his spinach. We have a brief conference and blow out the meeting anyway. We work well together, we tell each other.

We drive into Beverly Hills, to the Beverly Hills Hotel. It is the first time I have ever seen L.A.; I ooh and aah along Sunset. Michael and his boss go off to their business, and I go off to mine with Marvin, meet all the directors and staff. I am the same Julia I always am, but I notice that here in Hollywood it seems to have great impact. It is the late sixties. There are no women in the business but stars, secretaries, and bimbos. High-powered directors flirt with me, and I flirt back, but they seem most impressed by my mouth. Mark Rydell (very pre-*On Golden Pond*) kvells all the way through lunch: she walks, she talks, she spins great tales. I permit myself the thought that I might have a future in this business.

Marvin and I last a year at Mirisch. They are now making movies like *The Return of the Return of the Magnificent Seven* and UA isn't so inclined to maintain their overhead. Walter comes to visit one afternoon, asks if I have any hot tips. I tell him everything I know, then he fires me . . .

Michael and I smoke a joint for the moon landing, turn on our little black-and-white TV and fool around till they land. It looks like a fifties sci-fi movie. The pot gives me a headache . . .

David Begelman is a great laugher, and when he does, his eyes crinkle at you the way Lady Brett's did in *The Sun Also Rises*. I meet him in the summer of '69. I've been out of a job for three months, and Michael, who's secured one with Alan Alan, an investment banker investment banker, just as Mirisch fired me, is getting pissed off at the cab fare to unemployment. I need gainful employment or it's back to the underground for me, and it's the summer.

Several situations come through within a week of each other: Marc Jaffe of Bantam asks me if I'd like to head up his paperback movie tie-in division for seventeen five; and United Artists will replace Maia Gregory with me for $245/week. I'm not thrilled with either job. The first seems like a giant step way out of movies, and I've only just gotten in. The second just doesn't pay enough, and besides, I'd fucked a junior executive there, and I have a cat's distaste for eating and shitting in the same location.

Then, I get a call from Jane Oliver, who's just started with CMA.

'I just came back from lunch with David Begelman,' she says, 'and I think there's something here for you.'

'Ah, Janie, I don't want to be an agent.'

'I don't think that's what it is, Julia.'

'Well, what then?'

'I don't know what they have in mind, but I did my ten-minute commercial on you and he's waiting to hear from you. Call him.'

'If your commercial was really good, he'd be calling me.'

'Men . . .' Janie says. Even then, that's all women need to say to each other by way of explanation. So I call him. Several times. Goodness knows, I'm not real busy. He certainly is. It gets to be an *idée fixe* with me – get through to Begelman get through to Begelman. While friends are urging us to go to Woodstock, I keep saying, 'I can't, I'm on this mission.'

It's so hard to accomplish it gets to be fun, and when I finally do, it is curiously anticlimactic. He's charmingly brusque, acts as if I have made it difficult for him to reach me. We make a date for me to come up at the end of his busy day so he can look me over. I don't know why, but I wear a white cotton dress that is well above my knees. With white socks and shoes. The whole outfit emphasizes my smallness and my youth. I don't know what I'm trying to accomplish, but I get a pretty good gig out of it.

I arrive a few minutes before our six-thirty meeting. Connie, his beautiful red-haired secretary, ushers me in even though he is on the phone. He is dark and sparkly, incredibly well-groomed, even with his jacket off. He has a little *db* embroidered on his shirt just under where his left tit would be if he were human. He crinkles his eyes at me and gestures for me to sit on one of the two oversized chairs opposite his desk.

There's a small desk between them with another phone and

just the listening part of the receiver. This is so that people can listen in on conversations without any telltale breathing heard on the other end. I am fascinated by this device and have to overcome a natural impulse to pick it up.

My only previous experience with David Begelman has been when I submitted a treatment for something from Mirisch to Peter Yates, his ultra-hot-off-*Bullitt* client, and he called me on a speakerphone to turn it down. I told him that my mother said don't say anything but 'fuck communism' on a speakerphone, and he laughed but left me on it with all my disadvantages showing.

'. . . so I'm standing there, with a thousand-dollar bill in my pocket, and the table is hot, and I'm thinking, Yeah, but it's one thirty in the morning and you've got an early plane . . .' Pause, for the other party, which I can't hear because I don't have the chutzpah to pick up the listening device on the table. 'Nah, I passed it by, went to bed, and came home a winner. Yeah yeah you too, bye.'

Now he stands up and extends his hand, which means I have to stand up and walk over to his desk and shake, like a guy, across the abyss. A gambler. A kindred spirit.

I spend a long time with him. He tells me about this company that is Freddie Fields's dream, a company called First Artists, which has been invented out of some of their client list who want more creative control over the movies in which they star. The company consists of Barbra Streisand, Paul Newman, and Sidney Poitier, conceived as a modern version of the original United Artists, also created around stars (Mary Pickford, Douglas Fairbanks, Jr., and Charlie Chaplin).

They have hired Patrick Kelley, the prince of business affairs at Universal, as president, but they're still looking for a 'creative executive.' Preferably a woman, who can be underpaid. Begelman remembers the Peter Yates interchange and remarks that several other of their clients have given me high praise indeed. 'I never met anyone who didn't have a P.R. person who gets the kind of press you get.'

'I'm collecting unemployment right now. I could hardly afford a press agent . . .' I smile. See, I'm harmless in my little white dress and my snotty attitude. Who could be giving me high praise? Probably Mark Rydell and Sydney Pollack. They've fucked me up with a job offer that dematerialized with their breakup. They were both into being guilty Jews, so they further fucked me up by not informing me of the evaporation of my job and their partnership. They disappeared and I read about it in the trades. This is a very Hollywood way to behave. Business by nonresponse. A recommendation for an alternative gig would get them off the hook. Cheap.

I'm starting to get angry at people who are doing me a favor, so I suspend this train of thought. I wish that I had learned from it instead. I pause for a moment and consider a thinkpiece for *Psychology Today*. Tentative title: Men Without Balls. That's why I'm so attracted to Begelman. Here's a man with *cojones*. At least, the appearance of same. (At least then, he did. They might have gotten a little ground down or atrophied once he moved to the West Coast.) When I meet him, he is the quintessence of the Ivy League Jew. East Coast street-guy toughness crossed with Four Hundred polish. Like me.

Begelman says he'll get back to me in a couple of days. In the interim, I get a call from Pat Kelley, nominal president of First Artists. We have a pleasant chat, but he doesn't commit. The next day Begelman calls to ask about my salary at Mirisch. I lie, and he busts me. Well, if you knew, why ask? To see if I'd lie. I haven't perfected lying on the telephone yet. I never perfect lying in person. He asks me what I want.

'I want a thousand dollars for every year of my life,' I joke.
'How old are you?'
'Twenty-five . . .'
'Done,' he says. 'You can start on Monday . . .'

When I report for work, he's On The Coast and has neglected to tell anyone of my arrival. I sit, frustrated, in Jane Oliver's office until we decide it is late enough to call him. He sounds perturbed.

'Well, just use my office,' he snaps. Two minutes later,

Connie comes down to find me and walks me back to his office. I try to feel at home, but I feel ridiculous. Later that afternoon, his wife, Lee, stops by and I feel less ridiculous. Compared to her. She is one of those leather-skinned medium-age ladies who dress too young. She is wearing a black-and-white gingham number with white starched petticoat showing. Matching ribbons tie up two pigtails. She is doing the Showbiz Wife Thing, redecorating his office, and throws down some pillow covers and ashtrays. Surveys the scene, me included, then leaves.

I get moved from office to office, and finally, when I can't stand it anymore, screw up my courage to go see Himself after work. He gives me a closet right next to him and approves thirty-five hundred dollars for redecorating . . .

Michael picks me up from work late one night. We are going to a screening of a movie called *Easy Rider*; a guy named Lee Beaupre has been doing opinion-maker screenings for weeks now. I notice that they're producing a buzz in New York. I am anxious to see the picture, and I've had to move heaven and earth to get my name put on a list. Michael looks great in three-piece pinstripe. I bring him down the hall to introduce him to Begelman. They chat male chat, but they do not bond. As we leave, Michael cackles his Cancer cackle.

'What're you laughing about?'

'He *looks* like a Begelman . . . you know, I was wondering what a guy named Begelman would look like, and he just *looks* like a Begelman . . .'

The screening for *Easy Rider* is packed. I introduce myself to Lee Beaupre, young and gay. The air conditioning is out. I like the opening; Phil Spector playing what everyone thinks Phil Spector is. But I get restless with the movie right away. My head pounds lightly. Some lines, like doing your own thing in your own time, crack me up. I start to think: if Dennis Hopper says 'man' one more time, I'm going to jump into the screen and strangle him. I know they get to die in the end, long before it shocks the audience. Michael loves the movie, but then Michael thinks Bob Dylan is a poet. I tell Lee

Beaupre that I don't like it, but I think it will be a smash. I make an impression, because that is the opposite of what everyone else is telling him.

I am a spotter of trends: the drug paranoia underlying the movie is rampant in the alternative culture that has sprouted. It amazes me that this is not obvious to the people releasing the picture.

Michael and I have accumulated a large circle of friends: friends from school, friends from Roslyn, friends from.work. My work: showbiz. His work: money. I am good at bringing in new people. Michael is good at staying in touch. We start mixing up our get-togethers, à la Lee Beaupre.

An old high-school chum of Michael's finds him. He is classic: the rich kid who never had a summer job. Then his father died leaving him and his helpless mother with nothing but debt and taxes. He is now a speedfreak, living off the streets in the Village. He owns an acoustic guitar and a free pass to the Translux Theaters. He keeps talking about a movie playing at the Translux East, finally calms down enough to insist we smoke a joint and head uptown with him. The movie is *Performance*. It blows us away.

Michael's friend is beautiful and pathetic and dangerous all at the same time. Very appealing. We let him sleep on the couch for a few weeks. It is too close. I have uncomfortable feelings about him that are my demon ruling me. We ask him to leave and he puts up at a state hospital for awhile. By the time he gets out, we have left New York, and I am saved . . .

September '69: New York is unspeakably humid. Sweating-in-the-shower humid. A light mist pervades everything and it brings with it a kind of sewer smell. I am wearing rayon and it has melted and become a part of my skin. Begelman sits ramrod straight and stares ahead into the back of his driver's head. This is my first limo ride and I wish I could enjoy it more, but Begelman is like a stern Jewish father; it takes the fun out of things.

He is escorting me for my first big meeting with Barbra Streisand, up to her apartment on West 96th Street, and I am excited and nervous. I have not been in the movie business that long. The biggest star I personally hang out with is Redford and he is not as big as Barbra Streisand yet. Maybe he never is. It's a tough call. On the other hand, his star is rising and hers has been up there in the show-business heavens for so long that she seems to be from another generation. I have mentioned that thought to Begelman and he has said that he is relying on me to take care of that. I don't know if he's kidding or not.

Barbra's place is the penthouse of a borderline building. It is not a part of town I would live in if I were a big star. The apartment is nice, especially the entryway. Jason, who is about four, is running around with a flyswatter and he takes a swipe at me and Begelman. I take it as a matter of course; Begelman's face twitches nastily and I can see he hates this part of his job. Jason starts to make a return run and we step out of his way.

From another part of the pad, I hear music. Barbra comes out in a pair of rusty corduroy jeans and a matching T-shirt. She is neither thin nor fat, but her eyes do go in two different directions, and it is hard to know which one to address. She ushers us into another room, where a tall guy with curly hair and gigantic teeth is fiddling with dials. He and Begelman acknowledge each other curtly and Barbra introduces me. His name is Richard Perry. I recognize it from album jackets. They are listening to a rough mix of 'Stoney End,' the Laura Nyro song that will be Barbra's only semirock, semi-top-40 hit. It sounds great. I feel better already. Her outfit, the song, even rotten Jason – it all seems accessible.

Richard Perry splits and we have our meeting in a funny little sitting room. She stares at me a lot. I make sure to let her know I'm Jewish, like the first time I met Michael's grandmother, and that pleases her. We spend a long time there. Begelman acts pleased, but on the drive back he never utters a word . . .

*

I am at First Artists for only six months, but I start a remarkable number of projects while I'm there, a delusional process that spoils me for the truth I am to discover, bit by bit, over the next fifteen years.

The greatest triumph is the acquisition of a short story by Isaac Bashevis Singer called 'Yentl the Yeshiva Girl.' Not just because it is such a cool project, but because I can pay Jane Oliver back right away for keeping me out of the ranks of the unemployed. Jane and her husband, Val Sherry, own the rights to 'Yentl.'

We hire Ivan Passer to write and direct. I see the movie in black and white, a daring departure . . .

Joni Evans, who preceded me at *Ladies' Home Journal* and with whom I became instant friends, is now an editor at William Morrow. She gives me a book she loves called *Maiden*. I love it, too. I send it to Barbra. She turns it down. 'The clothes are like Doris,' she says. Huh? It takes me awhile to realize she is referring to the character she played in *The Owl and the Pussycat*. Oh, so that's how it goes . . .

Michael and I combine another West Coast business trip and stop off in Las Vegas to visit Barbra. I bring her a copy of *The Exorcist* in galleys and an Elton John album. I think she should do a cover of 'Amoreena.' We have dinner in her dressing room with her and Marty Erlichman, her manager. He sits, Buddha-like, on a large stuffed pillow.

'Whaddya think of this?' she asks, indicating the bound galleys.

'It's great if you want to play second banana to a kid,' I reply. She smiles appreciatively. Marty shifts in his chair, finally excuses himself. The second he is gone, Barbra wants to discuss with Michael the size of her fees. She is the first person in show business who treats him like a person. Then she has to go do her show. She smokes a joint onstage. Afterward she asks what we thought of a certain song, and we have to admit we don't remember it. She tries to sing a couple of bars, but she's off key.

'Funny thing about that,' she muses, 'I only seem to be able to sing for money . . .'

*

Redford understands claustrophobia. He is telling me a story about traveling cross-country on a train, in a tiny room with a tiny bathroom and a tiny rectangle of a window. He holds up his four fingers and opposable thumbs; it is a movie gesture, something cameramen and directors do all the time on the set and in their minds. 'So there is this minuscule window on the part of the country that is supposed to be the most beautiful and spacious skies, and this weird old couple walk in camera right and peer in at me, and I think, this is not my movie . . .'

'So did you bolt?'

'Nah . . . thought about it, though . . .'

'See, I would've been more freaked by the tiny room than the tiny vista . . . probably because I watch too much television . . .'

'You could always leave the room . . .' Yeah, I bet that's something you're good at. Leave before you're ready to go, Jeremy would say. Leave before you've even been there, I would say back. But not till much later and then only in my mind.

Redford is being charismatic and entertaining because he has managed to be almost an hour late for lunch. I wonder if he has changed jeans numerous times to create this wonderful drag he's in. He is very into incognito so he sports a lot of scarves and mufflers and hats and shades, which only make him look more Redfordish. And he makes me meet him at restaurants that are so off the beaten path and so empty that you know there is a reason. Generally that the food and service are lousy. This is a little omelet place on East 61st. The owner is a smelly, cranky French woman, and her omelets are as rancid as she is.

I've been at First Artists a couple of months, and Barbra has asked me to read Arthur Laurents's treatment for *The Way We Were*, which really is a pretty nifty novella. When I call to impart my reactions, she says, 'Yeah, but it would be working for Ray again . . .' She sounds like this is not her favorite thing to do. I ask her if she knows Redford, who is perfect for the part of Hubble. She doesn't, which surprises me. As in: I thought all famous people knew each other. I mention the project to Redford and he makes a face.

'You've seen it?'

'No . . .'

'So what's the face for . . .?'

'I just can't see her and me in the same movie . . . we're, like, from different generations . . .'

'Have you ever seen her in anything but *Funny Girl*?' He admits he hasn't. 'You should go see *The Owl and the Pussycat* . . . I'll run it for you . . .'

'Are you really serious?'

'Really, this is a great project . . .'

'Tell me about it . . .' By now, with all the jobs I've had précis-ing long form I've gotten very good at the basics. The forties, the setting, the politics, the chemistry, the title . . . Evocative, my mother would call it, all lit. crit. The talent. I get pretty worked up about the whole thing.

'And here's the most important thing,' I say, while he is starting to laugh at my childish enthusiasm. 'It's a tearjerker!' I remember Marvin Birdt saying, while I wiped my tears away after finishing *Love Story*, totally embarrassed that I would fall for such manipulative slop but moved nevertheless, 'They cry they buy . . .'

'I don't believe you just said that . . .' I don't either, but go see the picture . . .

He calls a couple of days later. 'Well, I went to see *The Owl and the Pussycat* . . .'

'I'm right, right?'

'I don't see me and Barbra Strident in a movie together . . .' I laugh. The pun is perfect; it is a performance that is not so much energetic as overwrought. But this broad is one big blob of walking talent. I like the rawness against Redford's gentile pseudointellectuality.

'You're wrong . . . will you read it . . .? it's a good read . . .' I messenger it to him that afternoon. I never press it, though, as I am looking for projects that she will do for First Artists, not Ray Stark. I do mention what I have done to David Begelman. After all, he is her agent. He starts out by being very cross with me. He snaps something about that I shouldn't meddle in anything that's not my business.

'You mean, if she asks me to read something, I'm not supposed to? Or am I supposed to clear it with you first?' My tone is snide, even though he scares me, like a strict teacher, or my father, when he would criticize me, then criticize over the top because he assumed my silence, which was absorption, was really stoic defiance. I would usually have to cry to get him to stop, but it did raise my tolerance for pain.

'Plus, it's not like anyone is getting Redford a job so fast. Am I not supposed to read anything he asks me to? Too!' I have a tendency to get very righteous whenever I feel hurt. Then I never really take the time to feel the pain.

Begelman crinkles his entire face at me. He almost says he's sorry, mutters an inaudible something, which I decide to take as *I'm sorry*. I let him know that even if they ask me to, I won't introduce them to each other. 'But someone should,' I toss over my shoulder as I depart, still feeling a little huffy behind the whole experience.

I hear about Tony Bill a lot. I hear about him from Pollack, and Redford, even Janie Oliver. Everyone keeps saying to me, 'Do you know Tony Bill?' and I tell them no even though I feel I do from his performances in *You're a Big Boy Now* and *Come Blow Your Horn*, movies that made me laugh. Tony had made me laugh, too, which misdirected me. It was his lines that were funny, not Tony. At least, not in the ha-ha sense. People keep asking me if I know Tony Bill because he and I send them the same material. Some of it is fairly arcane. Like *Arkansas Adios* by Earl 'Mac' Rauch, which we messenger Sydney Pollack within hours of each other.

I am at First Artists, nestled in the latest of my many temporary offices, when I finally meet Tony. He's wandering around the halls of CMA, and somebody collars him and says, 'You have to meet Julia.' Turns out that even though I've never appeared on the silver screen, the same people have been asking him the same question for awhile.

Tony Bill is an exceptionally handsome young man, which

he's trying to cover up with dirty, stringy hair, a cowboy hat, and a thin mustache that looks vaguely Puerto Rican. He's produced his first movie, *Deadhead Miles*, starring Alan Arkin, directed by his partner Vernon Zimmerman, from a script by Terry Malick. Paramount has financed the movie, and ultimately they will shelve it, but at the moment Tony is very hot. The movie has just completed principal photography and nobody knows yet that it is incoherent and unreleasable.

He is in the process of packaging an idea about barnstorming with Redford and George Roy Hill and is in town for meetings with Redford. I'm dressed quite nicely because I'm expecting to have lunch with Redford at L'Etoile around the corner. We've barely been introduced when he says sullenly, 'I guess you know Robert isn't going to make lunch . . .' Robert? Who calls him Robert? Not make lunch?

'No,' I reply, not surprised. I ask Deena, my secretary who doesn't type, to call him. Tony sits down in the one chair in the office and eyes me suspiciously from under the brim of his hat. We small-talk until Redford comes on the line.

'I hear you're canceling,' I say, too direct. Now I am interacting with two uneasy men.

'Can't . . . call me later . . .' I take it as a matter of course that even though he's being the rude one, I'm supposed to be doing the calling later. It isn't that I'm thick-skinned or insensitive; it's just that I have endless endurance. Growing up with an abusive mother has rendered me seemingly strong and persistent instead of weak and retiring. Overcompensating and overachieving.

'You're right.' I smile; then, without missing a beat, 'Free for lunch?' What the hell, I have an expense account, and I am curious. He smiles beautifully and accepts.

Once we sit down and Tony gets a little wine in him, he turns out to be very forthcoming. We eat heartily and at length and by the time he walks me back to my office, we feel warmly enough about each other to agree to stay in touch. Which Tony does very well. He checks in often and we become better friends on the phone . . .

*

Time's Man of the Year is 'Middle Americans (A Man and A Woman).' Who *are* these people, I smirk to myself, then wipe the smirk off my face. The people who elected Nixon . . .

Tony and I start to exchange information on a daily basis after we hang out for a little while in New York. He and Andrea Eastman come to dinner in our little apartment in Washington Square Village and for once I make not only an edible, but an excellent dinner. Mussels in white wine garlic sauce with pasta and a salad. Tastes delicious and easy to prepare. All that really matters is that the mussels are fresh. Tony and Michael like each other, and Tony talks about the deliciousness of the meal for months after, clearly more impressed by my culinary abilities than my intellectual ones.

My years in Milwaukee and Mount Holyoke have given me some practice on guys like Tony, but I haven't really interacted with that many guys from California; men brought up in California are different from all other American men. For one thing, they are better looking and in better shape. They also tend to be weak in ways that are very subtle. At least by Eastern standards. It is interesting that Tony, a lapsed Catholic with two alcoholic parents from California, and I, a confused, atheistic Jew with a pill-popping mom and a workaholic father, should find the same material appealing.

Therefore it is not surprising to me that Tony shows up with a tape in my office on his next trip east and says, 'Got time to listen to something?' He takes out his little recorder and puts the tape in, rewinds, and then, on comes David Ward's voice talking out the idea for *The Sting*. Or anyway, talking out some of the basic precepts of *The Sting*. The revenge motive for Hooker is a little more direct: he wants Hooker's brother to be a boxer who doesn't throw a fight, and is killed by an ultra bad guy named Hawk (the prototype being Lee Van Cleef); he describes the switch and the wire, and then kind of indicates that he doesn't want to tell the end, because it is going to be the biggest and best surprise in movies ever.

'Think this is something for Paul Newman?'

'It sure is, but they'll never buy this . . .' I've been at First

Artists just a few months, but I can tell which way the wind is blowing. If John Foreman, an agent from the old school presently running Newman's company, didn't like *The Getaway*, an out-of-print Jim Thompson novel Tony had sent me, he sure isn't going to go for this. And dealing with him is tiresome; he always has a snotty tone with me on the phone. Makes me want to say, Wake up and smell the shit, John, *WUSA* is not where it's at right now.

'Has this guy ever written anything?'

'Yeah, he did this script *Steelyard Blues* for his master's. It's pretty good, pretty quirky characters, nice little antiestablishment theme, lots of good parts for actors . . .' I get up from my chair and close the door.

'Tony, is this something we should buy for ourselves?' Tony and Michael and I had been discussing the concept of going into business with each other for awhile. Since Michael is on Wall Street we think a venture capital company is the way to start. This, as a result of an interesting side trip I have taken with Sydney Pollack. He has a half-written piece by David Rafael that he dearly loves, and Redford is interested, too. Rafael needs five to seven thousand dollars on which to live in order to finish it and Pollack and Redford can't come up with the bread.

'Can you believe it, Michael, Sydney Pollack and Robert Redford can't come up with five grand between them!' I exclaim over Chinese food one night. Michael loves Chinese food, so we eat it about three times a week. I don't care for it much and it gives me headaches to boot. (When Michael and I split up I got far fewer headaches; it's debatable whether that's because of no Michael or no Chinese food, which I never ate again.)

'They're cash poor . . .'

'What's that?'

'Oh, it's something rich people suffer from time to time. They make a lot, but then they pay a lot of taxes, or their cash is all tied up in investments, some of which they make to avoid paying taxes . . .'

'So, isn't this a great idea for a business? We put up small amounts like what Rafael needs in exchange for some equity in the production – should it ever come to pass.' Michael, who is very good at business, thinks it is an excellent idea. We ask Redford if we can use his name if we're successful in putting something together and he says no, but Michael and Tony and I stay committed.

'Tony, do you have a copy of the script?'

'No, but Medavoy does. I'll have him pouch it to you.' Mike Medavoy is a hot young West Coast agent at CMA. I haven't met him yet. Heard of him enough though . . .

'Can you have a copy of the tape made?'

'This is a copy. Take it home.'

I do. Michael and I play it, and I like it even more the second time. Part of it is David Ward's delivery. He sounds like a very cool guy. The script arrives in the pouch the next day, with a note from Medavoy, which is basically a heart with our initials in it. I slip it in my drawer, ever the trophy collector.

Michael reads *Steelyard Blues* first, then I read it. The dialogue is wonderfully well written, but David is young, hence he kills off all the principles in the end. It is Donald Sutherland who asks David to come up with another ending. And he does. And what an ending! Eagle, showing up with the horses. All those misfits riding off into the sunset, the PBY that they had been rebuilding burning to the ground, blocking the evil Frank and the police from pursuit . . .

Michael and Tony and I option *Steelyard Blues* and *The Sting*. It costs us thirty-five hundred dollars in option money, which puts a big dent in our savings. We put up most of the money for a fifty/fifty split with Tony. Nobody at the CMA offices knows I am a partner. They think it is just Michael and Tony. They relate to Michael as if he is just the money guy. Probably they have in mind for me Star Agent. It never occurs to anybody that I might want to go out on my own with the guys . . .

Sam Cohn likes to dribble ashes down his rumpled shirt. He is round and bland-looking and sports his intellectual pretensions as proudly as the holes in his shoes. It is there that any resemblance to Adlai Stevenson ends. He displays a cheerful coldness. Which makes him a wonderful agent. *Steelyard Blues* has become a serious piece of business for Michael and Tony and me. In a very short time, a package that three months ago had merely involved Donald Sutherland in the lead as Veldini has been completed.

We have Peter Boyle, hot off *Joe*, as Eagle, a flashy quickchange artist, and Jane Fonda, the prom queen, has deigned to agree to play Iris, a whore with a heart of gold, how new. David Ward's talents did not yet extend to creating an interesting woman, and I never really blamed Jane for what no doubt stands as the most lackluster performance of her career.

She and Donald are having an affair as a result of their successful teaming on *Klute*, in which she has more accurately portrayed a whore with a heart of stone, and they are touring the country, with Peter and a band of merry pranksters from the Committee, a San Francisco offshoot of Second City, in these FTA shows. FTA stands for Free the Army or Fuck the Army, depending on how inside you are. The director of the show is a nice man with a ponytail named Alan Myerson, and they have all grown quite attached to him. For reasons known only to them, their fondness translates into a commitment to do our movie, if he directs.

Tony should know better; Michael and I are surely innocents in this regard. But God knows we are ambitious to get the fucker made, so we are thrilled. It is a matter of get it made; there is no real thought *what* will get made. The success of *Easy Rider* has made studio types receptive to the idea of first-time directors. Plus Jane and Donald are willing to work at bargain basement prices . . .

Sam Cohn, who's been its driving force, has the *Steelyard Blues* package on the line: Medavoy, Sutherland, Myerson, and Tony on the West Coast, Michael and I from here in his office. I am chewing my gum intensely and I keep snapping it, annoying Sam, and he tells me crossly to stop. I stop for awhile and then start again, half unconsciously, half fucking with him. Sam is running this meeting on the phone. We're very close to setting the picture up with Warner Bros.

Dick Zanuck and David Brown have taken over, and seem inclined to do the picture at a price. It is still possible to do this with a major, with a back-door negative pickup. Also, the work is scarce just now, so the unions are granting a lot of waivers on low-budget projects. This is how Bert Schneider, Bob Rafelson, and Steve Blauner – aka BBS – have been so successful in such a short time.

I snap my gum because I am picking up betrayal vibrations on the phone. Michael and I keep glancing at each other. The conference call is inconclusive. I indicate, Let's get out of Sam's office so that we can talk. On our way home, in a cab, which I insist on, I tell Michael I think he needs to go to California to protect our interests. He does, sleeps in a drawer in Tony's kids' room. When he and Sutherland meet, they have an instant dislike for each other. Sutherland says, 'I hear your wife has Robert Redford's ear . . .'

He, Tony, and Medavoy have a meeting with Frank Wells at Warners. As he leaves, Frank says, 'I hear your wife has Barbra Streisand's ear . . .'

I am still not out of the closet in this partnership. What's the point if the picture doesn't happen? I am a novice at packaging. I don't understand that *Steelyard Blues* is taking very little time to come together. Michael comes back exhausted from Los Angeles. We have another end-of-the-day conference call from Sam's office. We discuss everybody's fees and credits: one hundred thousand dollars each for Jane and Donald with an executive-producer credit for Donald. Seventy-five thousand for Peter Boyle. One hundred thousand for Tony, Michael, and me (who they still don't know about), and thirty-five thousand apiece for Alan Myerson and David Ward.

Sam and Medavoy negotiate in earnest and actually close the deal with Zanuck and Brown at Warners. Yippee!

'It either takes five minutes or five years,' Jane Oliver tells me over drinks, rueful, maybe a little envious, since she and Val have been struggling ever so long on the *Yentl* project.

I have no concept of what producing a movie is, but I think that I should go for a leave of absence from First Artists. Hedge my bet. Michael, more confidently, quits his job and we head to the Coast. Tony picks us up at the airport.

'I don't know what you can do but casting,' he says to me, and it is clear that not one of the men involved in this project, save Michael, has taken my participation seriously.

I have an inconclusive conversation with Pat Kelley, who has endured major root canalwork that day and just wants to take a nap. Michael and I sleep for three days in a trundle bed in Peter Bill's room. We shoot best two-out-of-three odds and evens every night for who has to sleep in the drawer. On the fourth day, we move into the Sunset Marquis.

I call Pat Kelley and he tells me that I don't know it, but I am really out the door already. I take this to mean I'm fired. Deena, my assistant, calls to tell me that she's been fired and they've locked my office and impounded everything in it. The office has finally been decorated. I never spend a day in it.

It is the day before my twenty-sixth birthday. I am totally depressed. I call my mother. She says, 'So, what're you going to end up to be: the producer's wife?' I hang up and get hysterical. Michael calls my mother back and asks her to try to be a little more supportive. (For the longest time I imagined my mother's obsession with me tainted our relationship. Years later, a shrink, the semitalented one, said, in response to one of my innocent 'I-didn't-knows,' probably about some shitheel who broke my heart, 'Oh, yes you did. Your third eye was open but you like to keep blinders on . . .'

He continued: 'Your mother was obsessed with herself. You were ignored, but she managed to be in your face at the same time . . .')

I tell Michael I'm going to walk up to Sunset. There I discover Ben Frank's and Holly's Harp. I cop a gram at Ben's, a long Empirewaisted low-cut pale gray Qiana number at Holly's. All in all I drop three hundred bucks that we don't have, but I feel somewhat better.

*

At Michael's and Tony's urging, I call Barbra to explain my hasty departure. I say I don't want her to think I was using her, that I always liked her and her talent.

'It was probably a little of both,' she replies.

I take Tony's casting suggestion to heart, and devote myself to the finding of 'The Kid.' Alan Myerson has insisted on casting all his Committee friends in the other good parts: Gary Goodrow as Duvall; Howard Hesseman as Donald's brother, Frank, but there's nobody young enough for 'The Kid . . .'

I get Donald to read with Keith Carradine, but he's too threatened by his looks and vetoes him. We are running out of time . . .

Late one afternoon, Jerry Steiner from CMA calls and says he's sending a kid over. We cast him immediately. His name is John Savage.

The day we begin shooting, Tony presents me with a Purple Heart he found after hours of searching at the Rose Bowl Swap Meet . . .

We shoot in and around the San Francisco area for the summer. The worst is Berkeley, which is in the black part of town. One night, twelve of us get in the elevator and it stalls between floors. Gary Goodrow starts to tell running-out-of-oxygen stories, and I, claustrophobic to begin with, have a snit. By the time they get the elevator started, I am a babbling mess in the corner. I don't speak to Gary for days.

Santa Rosa, Wine Country: We are shooting in a deserted hangar/airstrip. Everything takes longer than it should. One weekend, Michael and Peter and Hannah and I go to Geyserville. Natural geysers. Sulfur baths. We strip for the sulfur baths. Just as we are getting ready to leave, a black guy comes in. Hannah won't leave until she gets a gander at his dick. She wants to know if what they say is twoo. It is . . .

Roger Vadim comes to visit Vanessa, his daughter with Jane. He plays with her in the pool. Another little boy takes a toy of hers, and she whacks him hard. I overhear Roger saying to her: 'Why, Vanezza, deedn't your muzzer tich yuuu, zere is no zuch sing as perzonal proberty?'

By the end of the shoot, when Frank Wells asks me, needling, if I know the difference between a grip and a gaffer, I can answer him . . .

We were very tired, we were very merry,
We had gone back and forth all night on the ferry.
– Edna St. Vincent Millay

To me, there has always been chocolate cake and all other kinds of cake, Stanley Kubrick and all other directors, free-base and all other kinds of drugs. There is also the beach and all other places to live.

Like any reasonable person who's been oppressed by claus-trophobia in New York – in the office, in the apartment, in the street, in the subway, in the elevators, in the stores, the markets, the museums, the movies – I am all for blowing our entire fee from *Steelyard Blues* on an oceanfront domicile. Michael, a sun addict himself, agrees. He keeps saying, as the money is running out and *The Sting* hasn't happened yet, 'We'll either make it or we'll have a hell of a two-year run at the beach.' We keep adjusting downward in terms of time, because the beach gets to be very expensive. Basically, we use the venue to further our careers.

We really don't have any idea how very looong it takes to make a movie. When we leave our apartment cat, OJ, with my mother-in-law, we tell her we'll be back for it in a couple of weeks. The cat lurks under the bed hissing and making that deep growl catnoise for ten days, and then Sherry throws her out into the suburban world. By the time we pick up the cat to return to the Coast she is knocked up. She gives birth under our bed within days. One of the litter of four dies right away. Sobbing loudly, I dump it into the incinerator outside our door. The other three and their mother travel on the plane with me. It is an empty flight and people move away because the cats keep pissing and it smells awful. Frankly I am afraid one of the kittens will drown, there is that much urine in the carrier.

Michael has preceded me back to the Coast to set up house in a pretty cool year-round rental we've found way up in

Trancas. When I arrive in L.A. with the urine-drenched cats, he is waiting at the airport. He can't wait to get to the house and show it off to me. It takes about an hour what with baggage claim and all. All the hot air has wafted out to the beach, the result of a baking Santa Ana. The ocean is shallow and still and flat. The house, which had been closed up, is a steambath.

I run around opening windows and making rude remarks about goyim who won't spend the money for air conditioning. Like that's really what you need at the beach ninety-nine percent of the time. I sound exactly like my mother and Michael gets frustrated. We are doomed to go to tropical climes in rooms with no air conditioning. The cuteness of the kittens keeps the fight we are working on in abeyance. When the Santa Ana blows over, I apologize and he accepts . . .

Margot Kidder and Jennifer Salt, who were to be our neighbors on the second move at the beach, the one where our marriage died, throw a party after our return from shooting *Steelyard Blues* in northern California. We are still boarding at the Sunset Marquis, and the drive itself is a refresher. Once we get out there, though, we know *this* is where we have to live. They are just a quarter of a mile away from us. Tony and Antoinette come out to visit with the kids, who run wild on the beach.

'You know, I've seen sunsets in Tahiti that weren't any better . . .' Tony intones wistfully, drink in hand. 'What a great place to entertain . . .'

And so, with little money in our pockets, we start to organize weekend-long soirees. People have such a good time, and are so impressed with who they meet, they bring more interesting people the next week. These enterprises grow and grow and it is possible to see Robert Redford and Liza Minelli, the veteran famous, along with Brian De Palma, Marty Scorsese, and Steven Spielberg, unheralded and barely known, drinking wine, eating steak, walking on the beach. A rare mixture of haves and have-nots.

Plus there is a fascinating beach community: the Dunnes,

the Moores, Katherine Ross and Conrad Hall, Lee Grant and Joey Feury . . . And always, always, talk – grandiose talk – about movies, about the state of movies and how much better they will be when we make them.

Pot is around, some psychedelics, and there is a whole branch that is getting into Arica. The Jake Brackman/Paul Williams crowd. I like them, but I think they are pretentious and snobbish, in a way that reminds me of my mother.

One night, after Jake has his first long talk with Joan Didion, he says, 'She's like a candle flickering on the top of the mountain, and there are winds whipping all around her, but the flame doesn't go out . . .'

'That's because she has John there to protect her . . .'

'I wonder what it's like to be, like, the four-hundredth best living writer, married to the greatest living writer . . .' Jake muses. Prick, arrogant prick . . . my head starts to pound.

'Whoa,' I gasp, standing too suddenly, 'I just got a wicked headache. I gotta get some aspirin . . .'

'Don't take the aspirin yet,' Paul says. 'We just learned this new thing in Arica . . . you gotta let me try it . . .' and he's moving me upstairs, 'we gotta have a darkened room . . .' and the headache is making me sick. I think it is Bob Dylan's relentless whine in the background: 'sad-eyed lady of the lowlands . . .' that is giving me this nauseous headache, but maybe the pot . . .

'Okay,' Paul instructs. 'This is real simple. You lie down flat on the floor, close your eyes, relax. I'm going to touch points up and down your body lightly – nothing kinky – and say, "Feel the pain, feel the pain," and you'll feel all the pain in that spot . . .'

'How long's this gonna be? Before I can take my aspirin, I mean.'

'About twenty minutes.' I have been dutifully getting myself into position, but I open my eyes and start to rise. I must wince with the pain, because he says, 'Please try this . . .' and there is something so intelligent and gentle in his pointy, bespectacled face, that I lie down, close my eyes, and try not to obsess on the hardness of the floor jammed against my coccyx bone or my strong desire that he not touch me in any remotely sexual way . . .

'Feel the pain.' He starts at the top of my head and goes to my toes, on each side, slowly, then more and more quickly until it is all one word, 'feelthepain,' and he is going really fast now, and it is very hard to focus on the pain as quickly as he is moving, and the pain falls behind, further and further, and then it is gone. What's more, I feel as if I've had a good run and a nice hot shower. This is better than drugs . . . well, almost . . .

A core group of beach and close friends starts to form. Heavily skewed toward actors and directors, so a lot of games are played. The actors like a game called 'killer,' which is good to play at a dinner table, during coffee. You draw lots and the short lot is the killer. You kill by winking at someone, without being caught winking by somebody else. When you get killed you have to die, slump in your chair, or fall to the ground.

I am not very good at this game. I am so uncomfortable with being a killer that I tend to machine-gun everybody all at once and get caught right away. Tony and Ken Howard are exceptionally good at it. They can wait a long time, and they can wink just the eye, so that there is no giveaway wink-squoonch on the face. During one of these killer parties, Michael and Janet Margolin slip over to Jennifer and Margot's down the beach to get more records and wine, and right at the dinner table I accuse them of having an affair. The party breaks up before the killer for the evening is caught.

The next day I am so filled with remorse that I have to call every one of the dozen to apologize. People are pretty understanding about it, but Bruce Paltrow gives me a hard time. 'You should have been a star,' he says, 'your mother is such a stage mother . . .' Well, if you get it, feel sorry for me, don't give me such a hard time . . . I had known him in high school in Great Neck, sat next to him in English class, in fact, had known him since 'when she was a virgin' as Bruce had told Sydney Pollack, and then he had turned up in show business, in New York, palling around with a guy who looked like his older brother, Manny Gerard, who was working on a big deal, Bruce told me.

Manny Gerard has been working with Alan Hirschfield and Ted Ashley for a year to put Kinney and Warner Bros. together, and will turn up time and time again. Bruce does, too, showing up again as a friend of Keir Dullea, who is a friend of Janet Margolin's. Actually, it isn't Bruce who is so tight with Keir. It is his wife, Blythe Danner. Blythe and I don't like each other from the start, but we don't have a major falling out for quite some time.

Ultimately we break up very publicly at one of Jennifer and Margot's Sunday get-togethers. Jennifer and her father Waldo, who scripted *Midnight Cowboy*, and I pass a joint among us, somewhat off to the side. Then Blythe, who is always oh-you-big-strong-man-could-you-do-this-for-me-I-don't-know-how, cuts through a desultory conversation about astrology with a hoarse: 'I could never get my chart done; my mother can't remember if I was born ten A.M. or ten P.M.'

'What kind of mother . . .?' Jennifer queries and I reply, too loud, too fast:

'Blythe's mother,' which sends the three of us into pot paroxysms and her flying up the stairs in tears. Bruce never speaks to me again, except when we run into each other in first-class lounges in airports and he can't avoid me.

When I call Janet for the really big apology, she says, 'You know, you don't have to talk all the time . . . sometimes you can just sit quietly in the corner and be beautiful . . .' No, *you* can be beautiful in repose; *I* only work with sound . . .

After awhile, killer gets boring, and we move on to charades. This is great fun for about a month, but it gets more and more competitive. It stops forever one night at our house. Everyone arrives at nine. Brian and Michael get into a dispute on the very first game and the house is empty by nine thirty. Michael and I look at each other, sad for a moment, and then we crack up. No more killer charades . . .

Michael and I have inherited Tony's representation. It's not so bad in the case of the CMA crowd, who perform their tasks in a passable manner, but Wally Wolf, his lawyer, seems more concerned with the perception 'the community' has of him than the protection of our interests.

Tony, via Steve Shagan, comes up with an alternative. At a party Steve's wife, Betty, throws for Zubin Mehta, we are introduced to Norman Garey, who is a rising star at Rosenfeld, Meyer and Sussman, a heavy entertainment law firm. His intelligence, sensitivity, and essential goodness are immediately recognizable in an otherwise pallid visage. We fall for him immediately.

Would you be interested in representing us? we ask shyly and he surprises us by seeming more than thrilled at the prospect. Tony is all for the move, particularly pre-*Sting* peddle-age, but hates the idea of firing Wally. It falls to us to do the dirty deed. Our first enemy in Hollywood . . .

Michael and I form a close bond with Norman, who within a year of our meeting splits from his wife Diane. He becomes a fixture at our beach house. Lotsa pretty girls there. He bunks there so often, he becomes family. Often, late at night, we find ourselves saying to our heavy-hitting, tough-negotiating, suit-wearing attorney, 'Norman, go to your room!' As if he is our pesky little brother.

Tony still maintains an office in Bert Schneider's building, so we get to be familiar faces. One day he asks if we'd like to come to a screening of his movie, *The King of Marvin Gardens*. We are flattered to be invited to a small screening by Bert. Bert and his partners have revolutionized the movie business with *Easy Rider* and they are continuing to do so with pictures like *The Last Picture Show* and *Five Easy Pieces*.

The King of Marvin Gardens is an all-star team: Bruce Dern, Jack Nicholson, and Ellen Burstyn, directed by Bob Rafelson, with a script by Jake Brackman. For the first five minutes, as Jack Nicholson is doing his late-night radio talk show, à la Jean Shepherd, I think I am about to see the greatest movie ever made. But it is so intellectual I disengage. Except for the scene with Nicholson and Scatman Crothers, where Scatman, the bartender, says to Nicholson: 'Now your brother, he thinks you're the artist and he's the businessman, but we know it's the other way around, don't we?'

When we leave the theater, me with a feelthepain headache and Michael ready for a long nap, we travel in the elevator with Bert.

'What did you think?' he asks politely.

'Oooh, I didn't like it . . .' I say, never the soul of tact. He smiles and rests his lanky body easily into the corner of the elevator.

'I don't care,' he replies. 'I love this movie . . .' and we leave the elevator. Good for you! Love the shitty, pretentious movie, stay loyal to your product. I find I admire this attitude. I don't appreciate *The King of Marvin Gardens* till much later, like Mark Twain and my mother . . .

Michael and I focus on our career as producer. While we wait and wait for David Ward to write *The Sting* we go through an extremely discouraging postproduction on *Steelyard Blues*. It is our lesson in movies. We haven't really known enough about the process to evaluate the dailies, although Michael hates Sutherland's performance from the start. The movie is static. Why not? Alan Myerson comes from improv comedy where the stage goes black at the end of a bit so people know when to laugh. Alan leaves too much time between laughs. For movie comedy to work, you can't wait for the laugh. There's always the chance you won't get it. We've had a disastrous screening for the executives at Warner Bros. We've expected it. By now we know this movie is static and unfunny. It is unreleasable.

The movie also makes no sense. One day we walk into our offices and Tony is playing around with a dupe of the work-print on his Steenbeck. He has always been very proud of this piece of equipment, and when Vernon and he split up, he moves it to Warners. In the year we've been out here, I have never seen it used. He has reordered some of the scenes. This opens a delicate matter. We've matriculated at the BBS/ Harold Schneider school of film making. Get the money on the screen, and protect your director. We have dutifully protected Alan a very long time. But the barriers are down the second we see the impact the recutting has had on the movie and we decide to give serious reediting a shot. Who knows, maybe we can make it better.

Tony and I have literary background to rely on. Michael has good sense. We sync the film by eye, because we don't have a sync machine. We ask Alan to take a look. He is defeated enough by now to think there are some very good ideas. Alan has made a bad mistake as director. He has let his politics rule and has acted consistently out of paranoia about the studio. Very little guy versus the big guy. Harold has fed his paranoia. I also wonder if Harold is some kind of twin to my brother from another plane. He throws giant snits over ten-dollar issues. And like my mother, he doesn't edit his dialogue.

Donald, the great executive producer, has taken a powder, so it is left to us to see the picture through. We exchange ideas with Alan for weeks and come up with a new version of *Steelyard Blues*. There is some black leader where new scenes will be added, if Warner's will give us the money. We run the picture for Zanuck and Brown. We actually get a few laughs out of them, although it is clear from the set of Dick's jaw that he still doesn't think it's a good picture. It is hard to tell what David Brown thinks, he is always so perfect in his manners and charming and tactful. This does not make up for the fact that the man has the worst handshake in show business. When you grasp it in greeting it just lies there.

They give us another seventy grand for the new scenes. The movie is now releasable and it gets laughs in screenings. We invite Tony's acting agent, Bill Robinson, to every screening. He has an infectious laugh. It makes the picture seem better than it is.

We run the picture for Jane and Donald. Jane is so upset that she stumbles in the parking lot and breaks her ankle. What goes around comes around; you phone in your performance, you have to look at it one day.

Leo Greenfield, the head of distribution at Warners, has the picture slated for release at the end of September, a time studios traditionally dump their dogs into one-week-action houses. But Dick Lederer, V.P. of Ad/Pub, keeps filling us with Stanley Kubrick stories. They have just released *A Clockwork Orange* and one day he tells me a story about a fancy screening in New York. He calls the story an illustration of 'the things that happen . . .'

The screening is to take place on a Sunday at Cinema I. Cinema I projects their movies onto a white cement wall with no matte. Stanley wants a black matte. They get Rugoff to agree to paint a matte. Stanley has a bad night in London and calls Lederer at six ay-em California time. Please check what they are doing. Lederer sends his lieutenant in charge of publicity, Joe Hyams, to the theater, gets a call from Joe:

'Good thing you sent me over,' Joe crackles over long distance. 'They were painting the matte neon orange . . .' The things that happen . . .

We get Warners to agree to a couple of spill-and-fill previews behind *The Candidate*. We figure the crowd might be simpatico. We do it at the Bruin in Westwood. While the picture is running, Tony, Michael, and I split a stack of cards and fill them out *Good or Excellent* in the bathroom. It doesn't matter. It is a Friday-night UCLA/local high-school crowd. They love it. Actually stand on their feet and applaud the end. Wow! The Warners execs are impressed, but they want to try it again.

They send us to New York with the film, to run the picture after *The Candidate* at the Sutton Theater. When we get on the plane in L.A., it is eighty-five degrees. There is an early New York snap when we arrive. We spend the next three days trying to get warm.

The reaction to the picture in New York is the same. I try to corner Ted Ashley into a promise of a better release at the candy counter, but he puts up his hands and says, 'Don't do this to me . . .' DO. THIS. TO. YOU? Hey, just who's the chairman of the board here?

We fly back in limbo. Two days before the picture is being dumped in theaters where Leo owes favors, they pull it. Reschedule it for winter . . . It feels like a triumph. Over what, I wonder . . .

We celebrate by going to dinner at the Aware Inn with Milius and his wife Renee. When the check arrives, Milius lays his MasterCard on one side of the table and we lay ours on the other. Milius tells the waiter to choose one: 'Let Allah decide,' he says. The waiter chooses his card. Good thing, as we have practically nothing left in our bank account. Way to go, Allah!

'I'm a triple Scorpio!' Simpson exclaims happily at lunch. I'm not deep into alternative theologies, and haven't a clue what he means, but I smile politely. I've noticed him before, in this drugstore across from the executive offices at Warner Bros. We have offices over the courtyard next to the drugstore. The offices come equipped with bathrooms, showers and Murphy beds.

They had been built in a previous decade so that the Warner Bros. could check out of their offices at lunch, walk across the street and get a grilled cheese to go, then walk upstairs and knock off a quick one with a starlet who'd been waiting forty-five minutes to get laid by a dirty old man. I always wonder who got the cheese sandwich. Years later, a guy who was more funny than successful would tell me that he had become a comedy writer in Hollywood just so that he could fuck beautiful women on a regular basis. *Plus ça change, plus c'est la même* bullshit.

Don Simpson has a twinkly presence and a simian physiology: twinkly eyes, twinkly cheeks, even a twinkly beard that is close-shaven, so you can see it is an accoutrement, not camouflage. But he's short, with a large upper body and narrow hips. He reminds me of a wrestler I dated in high school named Richie Carsell. Née Carselli, no doubt. I have a real weakness for apelike men, maybe because I like that physically they always remind me of exactly what I'm dealing with. It's not that they're stupid. It's that nine times out of ten they will go with the right, instead of the left, brain. Just incredibly retro.

Michael and I refer to Don as Ach, Seempson! recalling a dazzled fat hooker's description of the pathetic creature played by Peter Ustinov in *Topkapi*. It renders him mythic – well, taller, anyway. He's more articulate than my high-school boyfriend, but less colorful. It is hard to beat a New York Italian for colorful, although Ach! Seempson certainly does his best.

Warner Bros. still maintains a large ad-pub staff, both in Hollywood and out in the field. Now that we've convinced them to reverse the release pattern on *Steelyard Blues*, and they've pulled the picture, they are feeling their way, with us, toward something new. Don Simpson has made a name for himself being the hot happening young person on their staff; they count on him to relate in a meaningful fashion to films made by people under the age of forty. Ergo, he's been assigned to us. More precisely, me, since I am the only one interested in this part of producing. Michael is in preproduction on *The Sting*, and Tony is drunk.

Several things are going on at once: a new ad, to be rendered by Dick Lederer's favorites, the Gold Brothers; some opinion-maker screenings on both coasts – the direct result of my being so impressed by the work Lee Beaupre did for *Easy Rider*; and the shooting of a short production story film of the sort usually placed at the end of an ABC Movie of the Week.

Simpson and I have reconnoitered at the drugstore to discuss our impending trip to New York, where we will shoot the film with an outfit that specializes in these ten-minute wonders called Professional Films. Additionally we will lean on the Golds, who have yet to come up with a satisfactory graphic, and assemble as many names for screening lists as possible.

Since Peter Boyle plays a quick-change artist named Eagle, we think the best approach to this little public-relations tool will be a fake production story on him and his myriad characters. It is December and it is major New York cold, but I have convinced him it's a smart idea for his career. He's still freaked that he turned down the role of Popeye in *The French Connection*, the part that has made Gene Hackman a star. Anything that will help him in his quest for a part that Hackman turns down is aces with him.

'You're going to have to change in the men's room at the zoo . . .'

'Would Gene Hackman change in the men's room?'

'Before or after *The French Connection*?' Peter laughs, so I think it'll be okay. December can be spectacularly cold in Central Park.

The minute we arrive in New York, me and Simpson have a meeting with the guys from Professional Films. Middle-aged Jewish guys who seem to do an adequate but unenlightened job. One of the things they are unenlightened about is me. They never put it together that I am the producer. They assume I am Simpson's secretary. They throw orders around and look at me lasciviously. Neither Simpson nor I correct them, but when we get back to the hotel, I say to him, 'Learn something,' and send him to his room. He looks at me as if I'm seriously weird. Learn something? Alone? In my room?

I go to my room and call Ernie Grossman, head of publicity at Warner Bros. in Burbank. Ernie and I are particular fans of one another's. He has been dealing with Redford on the release of *Jeremiah Johnson*, and we are just starting preproduction on *The Sting*. Redford has broken his thumb in a skiing mishap. He wears a sling with his thumb encased in plaster of paris, pointing heavenward. I tell him it is an interesting look for him and start referring to him, in conversations with Ernie, as The Thumb. We tell each other Thumb stories. We share a star in common, and form a relationship in the glow his light emanates. Ernie comes right on the line.

'Talk to The Thumb today? I told him you were in New York . . .'

'Nah, but I met some other friends of yours and I don't think I can work with them . . .' I feel Ernie bristling on the phone and it is not at me. 'I don't think the guys at Professional Films have heard of women's lib . . .'

'Whaddid they do?' Ernie is pissed. When I answer I make sure the edge in my voice is more from sorrow than anger.

'They were arrogant, abusive, and rude, but hey, I can take it . . . they think I'm Don Simpson's secretary . . . I think I'll go downstairs and have a drink and think about it all. I'll call ya back in a half hour. Okay?' I hang up, then pick up the phone immediately and dial Don. 'You should order something from room service,' I say. 'You'll be getting some calls you should deal with.'

I have just settled down to vodka and cream, on my bed across from the mirrors that line the closets. I have gotten used to doing phone calls and watching myself in the mirror. There is something forbidden and sexual and dark about the process. I never really get off, but I get off on the concept of getting off and that makes me sharper on the phone. Which I have not been answering since Don left smirking. It has been ringing constantly.

Apparently, Ernie Grossman goes into action right away. I'm pretty angry from the meeting and I throw back the vodka urgently. I pick up the phone to order another drink. There is someone on the other end of the line. Thank God it is Don and not one of the people whom I have been making suffer. He is frightened and impressed.

'Did you call Ernie?'

'Right away . . .'

'What did you say?'

'Guess . . .'

'Ernie fired 'em . . .'

'Good . . .'

'Not so good . . . this is what they do . . . there is nobody else . . .'

'Oh, puh-leeze. . .'

'You just made my job very hard.'

'As in, what a drag, I have to work . . . come up here and have a drink . . . we'll figure it out . . .'

'Only if you tell me what you said . . .'

'I'll tell all the secrets . . .' Nice little flirtation we're having here, as if I didn't have enough on my mind already.

The doorbell rings; it is a bellboy with a dozen red roses. I open the card. It is an apology from Professional Films. I give the bellboy ten dollars and tell him when he takes a break to take the flowers back whence they came and to say the lady refused them. He leaves, a happy Puerto Rican, and I look in the mirrors to see if I am happy, too. My eyes are very sad. Just because you know how to do something well doesn't mean it makes you happy.

The doorbell rings again and it is Don. He skirts past me as if I am radioactive. The phone never stops ringing. Don has the impulse to answer it several times, but I smack his hand away. Women can watch a phone ring and ring. Men always think it is going to be The Call. I call room service and order some more martinis. I get some pot from its hiding place in my night table and roll myself a couple of what Erica Jong will later refer to, in the nasty diatribe she calls her second book, as the tightest joints in the history of middle-class marijuana smoking.

A call comes in where the ringing never stops. Don questions with his eyes, please, can he answer it, and mine reply, Okay, if you must. Ach, Seempson!

'Hello,' he says. Then, huffy, 'Well, who the hell is this?' The answer must be pretty stunning news because Don, who is fairly smooth, stutters, 'Yes, she's here . . . just a moment,' covers the phone and, impressed even though he doesn't want to be, stage whispers, 'It's Redford.' This will be a nice break in what promises to be an otherwise shitty day.

'Hello,' I say into the receiver.

'Look out your window . . .'

I look out the window, and there, kitty-corner from me in front of the Plaza, is a whole umber-coated movie company and Redford's blond hair. It sparkles, nearly white in the sun. That's right! They're finishing *The Way We Were*! Today? Tomorrow?

'I can see you glowing above all the rest . . .' he laughs.

'You busy? Come down and visit . . .' Like, I'm too busy to visit you, Gorgeous Creature. Redford has already committed to *The Sting*. We're just a month away from shooting. Since the day he signed on, we have started to be less tight. I like this invitation but don't answer. 'Barbra's here . . .' he adds aimlessly. Ever since I left First Artists under cloudy circumstances, to produce *Steelyard Blues*, people have been re-fixing me up with Barbra. Redford has already done it, once, when I'm dropping by the Malibu set of *The Way We Were* to pick him up for dinner. I hang out with Barbra and Cis Corman in her trailer while he and Sydney Pollack have a confab. It is very pleasant, but then, so is lying still in the sun.

'Okay, sure, I just gotta wrap up some stuff on this little shoot. I'll be there in fifteen minutes.' I hang up.

'I'm gonna desert you,' I say to Don. 'Look, you wanna hire these guys back, make our lives easier, fine, but just let them know . . .'

'What're you gonna do . . .?' He walks over to the window, and I point out Redford's totally recognizable top of head. 'I'm gonna go visit my star.' I love the way that sounds. Then, just to rub it in, I pick up the copy of *The Sting* that is lying ostentatiously on my nightstand and throw it toward him.

'Read this, you might learn something.' I pull on my coat and gloves and hat and scarves. I feel like one of those Shmoo-shaped Russian babushka-lady dolls. 'You can use my room, my phone . . . oh, and when you talk to Mr. Jay Professional, tell him you talked me into accepting the flowers so he can send them back.' Am I really this snotty, or am I just overcompensating? Sometimes even I don't know. All I know is, it works . . . hey, whatever's good for the project . . .

Before I see Redford or Streisand, as I approach the set, I see a man from behind having what can only be described as a conniption. He is tearing at his hair and screaming. He is wearing jeans and an expensive brown suede bomber jacket. He has a very cute ass, but even from behind one can see that this is a man having a shitfit. Unconsciously I give him a lot of room as I pass. When I glance sideways I am shocked to see Sydney Pollack. He smiles through his anger and greets me, 'They're over there.' Oh, I see, huddled against Bergdorf's. I wave, and Redford waves back cheerily in all his glorious blond whitetoothedness. We hug hello. I wonder if Don is checking out the scene from my window. I hope so. I am trying to seduce him with my impressiveness. I am just into the process of seduction. I have no plans for what I will do with him *if* – or, as Joel Shumacher would say, *when* – I get him.

It is really cold out here and everybody's nose is running. Guys run around me, and I hear a lot of them checking out their missions with an unprepossessing, molelike creature in a brown corduroy car coat. Ray this, Ray that they say, query, or scream, depending on if they are Sydney or not. Redford says, 'You ever meet Ray Stark?'

'That who that is?' I am nonplussed. He looks like a unit

production manager to me. Go know. Redford takes me by the arm and steers me over to the little man who is really the Big Man.

'Hey Ray, I want you to meet Julia Phillips . . .' We shake hands, or rather, gloves. 'Julia's my next producer,' Redford adds. 'From now on I'm working only with producers who don't wear jockstraps.' Ray and I laugh, then Ray turns away.

'You hate him,' I say.

'I hate him,' Redford says.

'Where's Barbra?'

'Oh, she's been real teary . . . you know, end of the picture . . .'

'Pretty sad scene . . .'

'Yeah, but she's supposed to be fine, I'm the one who's lost everything . . .' We are headed back to the Bergdorf's corner. Protection from the wind. I see Barbra. Her face is all puffy from crying. She says hello, but she doesn't want to talk, so I don't. The three of us just stand there in the gray New York cold with the wind whipping around us. I think about poor Peter in Central Park tomorrow. At least it will look good on film. Scenes shot in this overcast gray always look so good on film.

'Hey,' Redford whispers, 'I'm gonna have some people over for dinner tonight . . . wanna come?'

'Can I bring someone?' I figure this will blow Ach! Seempson's doors off.

'Who?'

'Oh, this guy Ernie Grossman gave me to handle this shoot . . . he's a good guy . . .' Redford is beyond protective of his privacy, but I can't blame him. I've walked the streets of New York when people recognize him . . . let's just say they're not always on their best behavior. Once, after a particularly harrowing experience with a bunch of schoolkids, I asked him what would he feel if it all went away and people stopped recognizing him.

'Oh, I'd miss it, of course . . .'

Right now, Redford looks doubtful about me bringing a stranger into his abode, though. 'Oh, pleeze, pleeze . . . it'll be such a nice reward for the crap he's going through with me

. . .' I launch into a brief description of Don's afternoon. Redford laughs and says okay. Then they call him for the scene, the biggie at the end, where they hug outside the Plaza and he does the small wince of pain. In closeup. I don't want to witness this private moment, so I say goodbye, and race kitty-corner back to the warmth and safety of 1409 at the Sherry.

Don is halfway through the script and doesn't even say hello. It is without a doubt the best screenplay I have ever read. I do not know at the time that it is probably the best screenplay I will ever read. I have already noticed that Don gets pretty engrossed in his reading. Once, when we are having dinner in my room, he reads at the table and I give him a small lecture about his manners.

'I grew up in Alaska with a family I hated,' he apologizes, reluctantly ceasing his perusal. I can't relate. I grew up with a family where the high point of the day was dinner conversation. 'This is amazing,' Don says, never looking up.

'Wait'll you finish it . . . everything set for tomorrow?'

'Piece o' cake . . .' He continues to read. I am tempted to say the building's on fire to see if I can get his attention. Instead:

'Wanna go to Redford's for dinner with me tonight?' He looks up. I thought so.

'What time . . .?' Oh, right, like your dance card is filled.

'Dunno, eight, eight thirty . . .'

We arrive at the Fifth Avenue apartment at eight fifteen. In the elevator on the way up, I cannot resist reminding him not to read at the table during dinner, and he laughs, but he grabs my hand while we're waiting outside the apartment door, and it is clammy. I love that he is nervous. I am, too, but not clammy-hands style; I get sweat under my hair at the back of the neck.

It is a very homey scene, very casual, with the possible exception of Richard Schickel, movie critic for *Time*. He is very anxious to let us know that he's known Redford forever. I sip my wine and try to remember what Janet Margolin has told me: sometimes all you have to do is sit in the corner of the room and be beautiful.

Redford asks Simpson if he's read *The Sting* and Simpson says yes, excitedly, and says it's huge, the perfect American movie.

'What do you mean?'

'A dick love story . . .' Simpson is nothing if not concise, a phrasemaker. We are all impressed with this remark. Redford laughs.

'This last one was a dick love story, according to Ray . . .' This is such a provocative remark we all 'do tell' him.

'Well, Ray needed to stir up trouble, so, after the first couple of days, he calls Barbra and tells her the cameraman is lighting her wrong, that she looks like she's got a beard. She goes bananas, calls Sydney and the cameraman. They set up a screening, but meanwhile everyone's running around worrying, "Barbra's got a beard, Barbra's got a beard . . ."'

'So, did she?'

'Well it wasn't the best lighting, they fired the guy, but she didn't look like she had a beard . . .'

'It was his control program, right?' Everyone nods, Right. 'But soooo mean . . .' Everyone giggles, then nods, Right. After dinner, Redford and Don get into a pretty intense conversation about skiing. The evening passes at a reasonable pace, and then it is time to leave . . .

'He's not such a hotshot skiier,' Don says on the way down in the elevator. 'I busted him on the skiing . . .'

'What time do we start tomorrow?'

'Early . . .'

'Good, you go early . . . I wanna go see Victor . . .' I've only recently re-found Victor, who used to cut my mother's hair, and Jane's hair when we were in college. Now he cuts Jennifer Salt's hair and Jill Clayburgh's hair and he's at Cinandre, and I have gotten addicted to Victor haircuts. Nobody in California understands the importance of a good haircut that changes every six months. Everyone seems to be wearing the same old Paul Mitchell shag, which was cool when Jane Fonda had it in *Klute* and is now on everyone and getting more extreme.

When we get back to the hotel, Don is still wired from the Redford evening, so we have a nightcap in my room. We get into some heavy necking, but he is very uptight about my married status. I say something corny, 'Don't make me beg,' but the farthest he ever goes is down on me.

After this quasi-sexual encounter, he feels very free about expressing his preferences, which seem to revolve mainly around turning women over and fucking them in the ass. He talks about angry fucking, and I am grateful we never get to intercourse, because I don't think I'd like it very much his way. We stay tight friends, but it is by silent mutual agreement that there will be no more sex.

I am doing L.A. calls when the first emergency call from Don comes in. Peter is flipping out in the men's room at the zoo. Copping attitude, blowing shit. In short, behaving as if he played Popeye. Don gets him to the phone and he hurls epithets at me for a minute. It is always hard to know which way to go in a situation like this: blow them away, or indulge them. It is even harder to know which way to go by phone. I try to walk the thin line between; when he takes a breath, I ask him in an ironic tone if he feels better now, then soften somewhat with an offer of lunch from room service, delivered personally by me. He takes a deep breath and says, no, everything's fine, he'll finish out the shoot and see me later.

Before he or Don think better of it, I split, go to Victor, get chopped. You take him for the day, I say in my mind, I'll take him for tea. But I worry about both of them; I am so unfocused that it is hard for Victor to hook into a statement. We both could use a change but I don't inspire him. I rush him and race back to the hotel.

Michael calls to tell me that the first part of our *Sting* fee has been paid out. I feel this deserves a celebration. I look through my cards. Yup, there's Saks. Let's go to Revillon and buy a fun fur retail! I suggest to Simpson the luncheon after the day before. He's game. Hanging around with me has not been boring. There's a tinge of *All About Eve* about him. I feel I'm being studied . . .

We hit Saks and I buy a black fox bomber jacket with suede insets on the side. The shoulders are so big I look a little like a gorilla. The weird proportion so diminishes my hips, though,

I can't resist it. It's under five hundred dollars. I wear it out of the store.

Don and I settle into our nice big fat first-class seats. I throw the fox jacket into the overhead. We have done the last of the blow on the way to the airport. We drink.

'I know what you want!' Simpson suddenly says, twinkling. Who asked you? I did.

'Oh yeah, and what's that?'

'More!' He chortles into his drink and I do, too. It's true, of course. It's the drive we share in common, we people who want to make it big in show business.

When we return, we direct our attention to putting together opinion-makers screening lists by intercutting fashion lists, publishing, show biz, Andy Warhol, etc. We do this on the floor of my office with paper and scissors and give ourselves loads of laughs seating Pat Ast and Diana Vreeland next to each other . . .

I am still under the influence of my college friend Jane. She and her husband have visited once or twice with Andrew, their two-year-old, and I start to think, well, with *The Sting* happening, and *Steelyard*'s release revised, we'll be rich enough for a baby and a nanny. I talk this concept over with Dr. Milstein. He says it'll take me a year after the pill to conceive. I talk to Michael about it. He's been wanting a kid for awhile. I go off the pill. And on the road with *Steelyard Blues*. Nobody wants to promote the picture but me. Probably nobody believes in it but me. Ernie Grossman arranges a fourteen-city tour in the same number of days. In January.

I get on a plane at night, meet a new P.R. guy, read my list of interviews for the next day, have dinner, take a Valium, sleep, wake up, have some blow, knock 'em dead, and get on a plane. I go all over the country: New York, Toronto, Chicago, Kansas City, Boston. I get stuck for a weekend in Washington and the P.R. dude thinks part of his job is to fuck me. I have a hard time convincing him it's not. When I finally get rid of him, I call Ernie, depressed. He tells me to go shopping. I go shopping in the Watergate complex, buy some Yves St. Laurent pants and a sweater . . .

I have noticed that my appetite and waist are growing. By the time I hit Boston, my last stop, I am having trouble closing my buttons. The P.R. guy, a nice Catholic man with ten kids, watches me scarf down a bucket of steamers at Anthony's Pier No. 4 and tells me I'd better check with the doctor. He thinks I'm pregnant.

The minute I get home I go to Milstein. I'm pregnant. I have only been off the pill for a month. I'm pissed.

'You're just mad about the timing,' he tells me. Chauvinist pig.

'Well, but what about all these drugs . . .' I say lamely.

'Just don't do anymore . . .'

'But I thought the first trimester . . .'

'Just don't do them anymore. You're only about six weeks pregnant . . .'

'Well, I have to think about this . . .'

'Okay, you can have an abortion, but you need to make your mind up right away . . .'

Michael votes for having the baby, but he says the final decision is up to me. I call my mother, who says she doesn't see any reason why I can't have it all. Very helpful. I chat with Peter about it and he says, 'Poor Michael . . .'

'Why?'

'Well, you'll have the award, the money, the kid . . . bye-bye Michael . . .'

'That's very mean . . .' Still mad you didn't get the part of Popeye?

'You'll see . . .'

The next day there is an earthquake. My first. The epicenter is at Point Magoo, a few miles up the coast. I hope the shaking has dislodged the fetus so I don't have to make a decision . . . It hasn't. I flip a coin. Heads, the baby, tails the abortion. Heads . . . I flip again: best two out of three, I abridge, three out of five, five out of seven . . . It keeps coming up heads . . .

No matter what she thought, Stuart was still impressed with Mike Ovitz. She figured Mike Ovitz, Jeff Katzenberg, and Mark Canton were to blame for the decline of movies. Christ, her Oscar had been facing the wall for six years, in protest against the state of movies, never mind the state of the guys who made movies. She didn't really like looking at all the names in a row anyway. Each one of them had been a fight, a breakup, a moment of sadness.

There was a real poverty of vision abroad in the land. Worse than when she came West, per Horace Greeley, to make her fortune. But Brad Darrach, who was doing a think piece for *Esquire* on the New Hollywood, had mentioned that in an interview with Olivia de Havilland she had said, each vowel elongated the way they had been trained in her era, 'Greed is rampant in the land . . .' Why is he telling me this, she wondered. Am I part of the rampant greed? That seemed to be what he was saying.

It was the beginning of the seventies, they were the junior partners to Tony, who was pretty junior himself, and Brad Darrach was much more interested in talking to him than to her or Michael. She'd been drop-dead hysterical just to grab some attention, and some of her quotes had found their way into the piece, all preceded by a description that found her 'witty and ambitious.' What, no *beautiful*? No *charismatic*? He hated me, she thought.

She'd always thought of men as doing business to each other. Dicks on parade. She had read somewhere that Lyndon Johnson had been fond of opening his fly and whacking his penis on the table to make a point during his escalation of the Vietnam War. She wondered if guys did that in negotiations when she wasn't in the room. No, mine's bigger; no, *mine's* bigger. Who the fuck cared but them?

From gangs to wars, from drug deals to gun deals, from treaties to covert operations, the state of the world was pretty much whose dick was bigger. She wanted to tell them all that size didn't always count, but they wouldn't believe her. As she had gotten older, playing along with the whole dick charade/ parade had turned her off, pissed her off, made her take her ball(s) and go home.

When she was young and lit by some inner fire that came out as ambition she played along with it. Plus the guys she had to tolerate were just a better caliber of scumbag than the guys who were running things now. David Begelman may have been a gambler and an embezzler, but his high-rolling instincts had helped her keep two major movies together. She couldn't think of anyone around who had the courage to do that now. Imagine Josh Donen (Uni) or Billy Gerber (Warners) or David Kirkpatrick (Par, for now) fighting for *Taxi Driver*. She smiled at the thought.

'What are you smiling at?' Stuart was finally calming down. She wished he would relax. How could he? He'd worked Ovitz's desk for years before going out on his own. She shuddered to think what the lessons he learned there might have been. 'Hey,' he said in his defense, divining her inner thoughts, 'when I first started working for Irwin Winkler I was full of creativity, full of ideas, full of hope . . . they were ground out of me . . .' This is the way the world ends this is the way the world ends this is the way the world ends not with a bang but Irv Winkler . . .

SCENE FROM A MOVIE WITHIN A MOVIE:

OVO: I am standing on a chair, having a face-to-face over a glass of wine with Michael Crichton one afternoon at Margot and Jennifer's, early seventies. He and Paul Lazarus are making a movie called *Westworld* over at MGM with Dan Melnick.

HANDHELD CAMERA CIRCLES AND
WEAVES THROUGH YOUNG HOLLYWOOD:

Scorsese, Dreyfuss, Milius, Spielberg, Schrader, etc. A rogues' gallery of nerds. There is not a single guy here I would have dated in high school or college. Outside of Michael Phillips.

Michael Phillips and Michael Crichton know each other from Roslyn. They used to do the circle jerk as Cub Scouts together. Male bonding. It is amazing how many people from Great Neck and Roslyn there are trying to make their way in show biz. A number of them do . . .

ME: So what's it like, making a movie with Dan Melnick?
HE: It's like being bitten to death by ducks . . .

'What do you think of Dan Melnick?' I ask another friend. She thinks for a long time.

'W-e-e-l-l, he dresses nice . . .'

I had met Melnick at the beginning of my movie career, when I was getting restless at First Artists. Arlene Donovan set up the meeting. Melnick was in business with David Susskind – they had established a company called Talent

137

Associates. They seemed to be big in television and wanting to be big in movies. Arlene thought they were looking for a story/development person. They were within walking distance, so I just trotted over there at the end of the day.

Melnick kept me waiting a long tlme, and he kept me there a long time. I got the impression that Dan Melnick found himself very attractive. He was very smooth. In a deep voice he told me loads of John Lindsay stories. It was his way of letting me know he was politically connected.

This kind of stuff did not impress me; Victoria Schuck, the head of the Political Science Department at Mount Holyoke, had been an early supporter of the Kennedys in Massachusetts. She had actually been on the presidential commission regarding a reduced voting age. Needless to say, in the early sixties she was pretty connected, and a trail of Kennedy relatives and assistants made their way to Mary Lyons's bailiwick for the odd lecture or seminar.

I was one of those Democrats who had voted for Lindsay but felt suspicious of him at the same time; when his election caused the subway strike and he couldn't get it together to negotiate with the mean-faced mick who ran the union I lost faith. I walked forty blocks a day to *McCall's*, and I thumbed rides home with beer-drinking types in repair trucks. The traffic was so bad that if a guy picked me up in the fifties, he had to pee real bad by the time he got to my parents' apartment on 13th. I made quite a few friends that way. Call it a polishing of my skills with the common workingman.

Dan Melnick aspired to be involved with the common workingman as little as possible. The very first time I met him little voices and noises and bells spoke and warned and rang in my head, but my heart was swayed by his smoothness. What did I know? I was twenty-five. He called me back twice on the job. It wasn't really a development job. It was better. They were looking for someone to produce their television shows. He kept promising to set a meeting with Susskind and didn't.

Finally he confessed that he didn't think that a bunch of common workingmen were going to take orders from a 'beautiful young woman.' Thanks for the *beautiful*, Big Guy, but I'd rather have the job. Had he thrown in the *beautiful* to take the sting out of denying me a giant step up the ladder? Whatever his reasons, he wasn't gonna hire me, and suddenly his smoothness felt gooey, like grease, his manner unctuous, not polished. Are you gay? I thought. And by the way, I hate John Lindsay. But thanks, Dan, for saving me from a career in TV.

Couple of years later, we've produced *Steelyard Blues*, and we're trotting around Hollywood with *The Sting*, because Zanuck and Brown have told us as 'friends' that they won't go along with David Ward to direct. We say, Fine, we understand, but we hope they understand that we have to test the waters, take a poll, try our best. We all know at the end of the meeting that we'll be back. Our principal agent, Mike Medavoy, now head of the movie department at International Famous Agency, which is daily expanding due to numerous acquisitions, assaults the town with the script. My pal Andrea Eastman, presently one of his star agents, is cozy with Melnick. Melnick is head of production for MGM.

Nobody with a script as good as *The Sting* wants to work with MGM. There is a man named Jim Aubrey who comes out of CBS television and thinks he is a film maker at the helm. There are terrible stories about him. He recuts everyone's movies. Supposedly he is the model for Robin in Jackie Susann's *The Love Machine*. Fewer and fewer people are going there if anyone else wants them. MGM has become the studio of last resort.

Dan Melnick reads *The Sting* and requests a meeting. We say no. He insists. We say no. He begs, and worse yet, Andrea begs. We say okay, but bring Robin French, senior to Andrea at IFA, along for extra protection. It is an exceptionally hot L.A. Friday. Melnick is wearing a purple silk shirt and it has tiny wet stains in the armpits. Like rivulets, they develop into large ponds during the course of the meeting. He does not remember me. *Beautiful*, hunh?

He is charming disarming and obviously loves the screenplay. We ask him if Jim Aubrey will recut the movie. We ask him if he thinks any first-rate talent really wants to work here, his presence notwithstanding. He tries to reassure us, but he is so fucking smooth that everything he says sounds like a lie.

He tries to corner us into negotiating a deal. We say we can't. He says something about two hundred thou for the script, ditto for us. It is 1972 and we are running out of money. We look at Robin, and he asks if Dan can put us someplace where we can talk alone. We are sequestered in a room off his office to talk to Robin. I'm sure it's bugged. We laugh. You can't be paranoid enough, I say. We laugh again, but nobody feels very good about this discussion and we're not even getting David the directing gig.

The room is a private dining room and it has flowered covers on the chairs that match the wallpaper. I start to sneeze; I think I am allergic to all the flowers. We try to reach Zanuck and Brown. They are out of the office and not expected back. It is only three in the afternoon, but I have heard that Zanuck splits for Newport if surf's up. I have an image of him on a surfboard. It is the opposite of Milius on a surfboard. If Milius looks like a bear on a twig, I imagine Zanuck looks like a twig on a surfboard. We are uncomfortable about not reaching them.

Robin is in a funny spot. He cannot really let us look this much money in the face and not say anything. How can we make a deal without making a deal? We ask Robin. He smiles slowly. We are speaking his language. This is something Robin French knows how to do very well. Robin is like an English schoolboy, but he is also a man who fired his father. Robin is ruthless. We are glad he is on our side. He hammers out some nuts and bolts with Frank Davis and leaves so many points open we can blow the deal on Monday.

Everybody shakes hands. Not me. A handshake is my word. In Hollywood, you can kiss the air next to someone's cheek and it counts. I go for that. The figures are exciting, but I have a bad feeling. I don't think Michael and Tony feel so hot about this either. Michael and I are very quiet on the long drive to the beach. When we get home, the phone is ringing.

It is Melnick. He's called Redford in Sundance to tell him the good news. He's excited.

We call Redford who says if it goes at MGM he's out.

Medavoy calls screaming. We have heard that during a tennis game he has promised Zanuck that he will steer us in the right direction. Well, why didn't you come to the meeting with us, we say. He harumphs.

I always like to keep in mind with Medavoy that he didn't start to speak English until he was eighteen and that his real name is Morris. I have felt a kinship with him on this latter point, because for some reason that is my middle name and I hate it. When I was a little girl at P.S. 92 a guy once yelled in the playground, 'Call for Julia Mor-ay-uss!' I made sure he got in trouble with the vice principal, Miss Ryalls, to discourage the name from sticking. (The first time I see the little guy who used to scream out Call for Phillip Mor-ay-uss in the commercials at the Polo Lounge, where he worked as a page until his death, I am afraid Miss Ryalls hasn't spoken to him and he is going to embarrass me.)

The next morning at eight o'clock, not precisely my time of day, the phone rings. Michael doesn't seem to be around, so I pick it up. It is Dick Zanuck and he sounds glum. He is not very articulate, but the general thrust of his dialogue is: How can you do this to me? He says he is so blue he is just sitting in his living room at Newport staring at the waves. I think, That is what I am doing, but you can afford your ocean, and I cannot. I say, 'You know, we're not completely unethical, we did try to reach you yesterday afternoon.'

'I was at a funeral,' he says. I can't help it, now I feel terrible. I tell him, as we have told Medavoy, that nothing is closed. I indicate I will see what I can do. After we hang up, I call Norman. He answers before the phone even rings. Apparently, he was just about to call us.

'What happened yesterday?' he wants to know. It is Rosh Hashanah weekend, but he's been called at home by Rudy Petersdorf, head of business affairs at Universal, where Zanuck and Brown are now ensconced, and been told Lew Wasserman is going to sue our asses and make sure we never work in this town again. I start to laugh.

Couple of months ago, when we needed help getting more

money for *Steelyard*. Zanuck and Brown didn't want to know us. When they left Warners we assumed they would end up executives somewhere and gave them *The Sting* hot off the presses, well in advance of the rest of the town. They emerged as a production entity at Universal, which was something different from what we had in mind, but we stuck with them. We told them we had to look around elsewhere and they said fine. Now we were being sued and blacklisted.

But there is no way to take any of this lightly. It is agreed by all parties that we should have a big meeting Sunday at Robin's. Robin has a compound on Cherokee and I always like going there. So Sunday, instead of having a nice day at the beach, we drive into town. The meeting consists of Norman, Robin, Andrea, Medavoy and Tony, Michael, and me.

Mike and Andrea are intent on who is to blame and Norman and Robin are required to keep the meeting on track. Jesse, Robin's wife, who is a painter, has made a lot of finger food. She is almost as good a cook as Joan Didion. I keep eating it. This is making me very nervous. The consensus seems to be that we shouldn't, under any conditions, go to MGM.

It is pretty clear from the meeting that Medavoy has guaranteed Zanuck delivery and Andrea has done the same with Melnick. Agent ego. As in: you work for them. A codicil: We have bad news for David Ward, and it is pretty clear Michael and I feel worse about it than Tony does. It is also pretty clear, and had been a month ago when Harold Schneider eyeballed the script for us, that David Ward has written himself into a corner in terms of this being his directorial debut.

Period pieces are not an everyday occurrence in movie production in 1972. There's no way to save money and shoot on real locations. Everything would have to be built and that would be expensive. At least two, maybe three million dollars below the line. That is a very expensive price for the time. Nobody's going to spend it on David's directorial debut.

Dick Zanuck and Rudy Petersdorf are prepared to go into a closed-door secret meeting at ICM Monday morning at eight o' clock. My stomach sinks. I will have to be up at six to make that meeting. Maybe if we stop this meeting now, and I go home and smoke a lot of pot, I can get to sleep early enough to wake up early enough . . .

Norman and Robin call Zanuck and Petersdorf at home and tell them in carefully chosen words that without us admitting to having done anything wrong or being in breach of anything, since there is no contract or even understanding, we will be at ICM at eight o'clock ay-em tomorrow to have a chat. By now it is four o'clock in the afternoon. Robin makes a divine pitcher of bloody marys and we all relax.

While I lie wide-eyed, awake in the middle of the night unable to think anything but, 'I am going to die; he is going to die,' staring numbly at the stars knowing that I am but a speck of sand under the fingernail of a larger being who is after all but a speck of sand under the fingernail of a larger being, etc., and that we live in a universe that is either expanding or contracting but is probably random, anyway, Michael tosses and turns, sweating out point definitions and credit blocs and break-evens.

We are both cranky in the morning, and when we arrive at the meeting, we are comforted to see that all the participants are dyspeptic. The air in the room is electric with the kind of excitement and tension that generally precede an exceptional rock 'n' roll show.

Dick Zanuck announces that he has come to make a deal. That he is not leaving – that nobody is leaving – until a deal is hammered out. Tough guy, hunh? I remind myself that he is Darryl Zanuck's son and that he was brought up on dialogue like this. Who knows if he is tough or not? He is a film maker, and there is something about his uptight, short handsomeness that is endearing. Beware the short man, I used to say to Redford. Beware the fat man, he'd say back.

They offer us a lot of money for the screenplay and our services. Urgently. Something's afoot. Casually, Mike Medavoy asks them if any directors have seen it. Rudy Petersdorf says that he has shown it to George Roy Hill, who has a deal at Universal. Business Affairs doesn't usually purvey screenplays, so we assume he's covering for Zanuck and Brown, who, after all, made *Butch Cassidy and the Sundance Kid* with George. So they were sure the kids would come back. I feel the strong desire to self-destruct and tell them, Piss on your money. (Years later, we discover Rudy was indeed the conduit to George. As my dad says: Never assume.)

Tony has History with George Roy Hill. who has absconded with a project about barnstorming that Tony was trying to put together with Redford back when I first met him in New York. Hill is currently developing a screenplay of his own. We tell Tony if he wants us to cease and desist in this negotiation we will. He appreciates our loyalty, but he is smarter than we are.

George Roy Hill is a first-class director, and his inclusion in this package will make for a better chance at a hit. Hollywood is full of people loaded with assets but cash poor. Tony's been in Hollywood longer than us. He can hardly wait to sell out.

We break for lunch. More precisely, we order lunch. No one is leaving this room until Dick Zanuck has his deal. Mike leaves to check his messages and I hit the ladies'. Andrea is there. When she sees me, she juts out her lower lip, baby-style. Then she hugs me and tells me she just wants what's best for us. I tell her MGM isn't best for us, even if we do think Melnick is a smoothie.

The IFA conference room begins to take on the characteristics of an all-night poker game: chips and dip and leftover sandwiches. Smoke and ashtrays filled to the brim. Papers with numbers on them in front of each participant. When Medavoy returns, he tells us that Columbia and Warners are trying to make offers that he is refusing to hear. Zanuck brightens, and we return to the negotiation.

The Hill hurdle vaulted, we get to the issue of points. Zanuck leaves the room to call David Brown in New York, and he comes back with an offer of five extra points from their share. It is clear from this single act that George Roy Hill wants to do the picture. And we already have Redford, just so long as David Ward doesn't direct.

Now comes credits. This turns out to be a learning experience, for though we get the same height as Zanuck Brown, we neglect to negotiate for the same width of the letters of our name. It is agreed that the credit bloc will read A Zanuck/ Brown Presentation of a Bill/Phillips Production of a George Roy Hill Film, Tony Bill and Michael and Julia Phillips, Producers. When the picture comes out, everyone's name is in thick black letters but ours, which are willow thin.

It takes all day, but the deal closes.

Two days later we're in a screening room watching the nineteenth recut of *Steelyard Blues* and Melnick calls me.

'What if I say it's okay for David Ward to direct?' he oozes into my ear, presuming, I guess, that I am the weak link. Liar liar pants on fire.

'It's too late,' I reply, a catch in my voice. He begs this way and that and though I waffle, I maintain a steady no.

Tony runs into Melnick a couple of weeks later and reports to us in a shocked voice: 'He said, "I'll just say to you what John Lindsay used to say to me: Don't get mad, get even . . ."'

George Roy Hill is a tall, mean-faced goy. He started out to be a composer, even studied briefly with Hindemith, whose music always gives me a toothache. He has a habit of banging down the phone at the end of a conversation, even if the call is relatively innocuous. He doesn't see himself as an auteur, but an administrator. That's what he says. Once he is done with David, he bars him from the set. He insists that only one producer be around. Tony, encumbered by Ancient History with George, is out of the question. George chooses Michael.

I disagree; I think it should be me, and I tell that to Zanuck, who reiterates Michael is who George wants. Michael, who's been in law school and on Wall Street? As opposed to me, who's been stomping down the mean streets of movies mags and books for years? Well, okay, but . . . hey, whatever's good for the project . . .

Hill gives the script to Paul Newman, calls us, and says Newman has called to ask him: 'Would I be ruining the movie if I wanted to play Gondorff?' We are young and foolish and answer yes he would without hesitation. We had always hoped Peter Boyle . . .

Hill tells Michael: I know if this were a 'young film maker' there would be a lot of gritty street shots, runny noses in doorways. He says he wants to make a movie that looks like a thirties movie. He runs endless thirties comedies for himself at Newman's house on Heather Drive, which he is renting for the duration. It is a brilliant choice, but it makes David Ward want to cry.

His choice for Lonigan is not such a brilliant choice. He offers the part to Richard Boone, who is such a drunk at that point that he doesn't even respond to the offer. Hill pulls rewrite after rewrite out of David to make Lonigan a stronger and stronger adversary. No matter what, Boone doesn't respond. We keep asking George to think of alternatives and he keeps saying, 'I'll jump off that bridge when I come to it . . .'

It is barely two weeks before shooting, and, finally, Boone responds with a flat no. Hill very nearly hires Steven Boyd, but Michael, with Tony's and my prompting, goes down on his knees and begs him to go for greatness. And what might that be? he sneers. We offer up a list of English actors: Olivier, Griffiths, Shaw.

Newman is shooting *The Mackintosh Man* in Scotland, and he hand-delivers the script to Shaw, who responds the following morning with: Delicious, when do I start? John Gaines, his agent, holds us up for lots of money, and name above the title after Newman and Redford. Probably costs his client a Best Supporting Actor nomination . . .

Two days before shooting, Shaw slips on a handball court at the Beverly Hills Hotel and has to wear a brace for the entire picture. He walks with a limp, which he uses to great effect for his character. One day he tells me, 'You know, this is really the most intellectual performance I've ever done . . .'

I ask Hill what he means by that and he launches into a short lecture on intellectual and visceral actors. He says Redford noodles and noodles about a part and then makes totally instinctive choices; Newman vice versa.

He has a great aphorism: If you can't be first, be best; if you can't be best, be first. Why not both? I think but don't say.

One night, on the set, I chat a little with him about *The World of Henry Orient*. He is feeling benign; the more pregnant I get, the more comfortable he is with me. 'Oh, I had a terrible time with the prop guy on that one,' he allows. 'Every morning on the set, I had to follow him sweeping the street and throw garbage down . . . otherwise it would have looked too clean . . .'

Meanwhile we are having our own problems with Tony. Tony really likes people when they are just starting out, supplicants. David screws up all his courage and says in view of the exalted price we've gotten we should re-cut his deal. We are only on the hook to him for thirty-five grand and two and a half percent of a hundred percent of producer's profits. Michael and I think he has justice on his side. Tony doesn't. We push Tony hard on David's behalf and he caves. In the end, we take cash out of our end, and Tony takes points out of his.

Oh, and by the way, Tony, we don't think that the two of us should be equal to the one of you. We'll stick with it on this one, but we want a third a third a third after that. Tony is newly in touch with his anger. He vents it at me a couple of times.

Inevitably Michael and I split up with Tony halfway through the shoot. We are pretty scared about making it on our own, but we get a deal off the ground with Universal on a TV movie with Marlo Thomas that Jeffrey Fiskin writes. It pays the bills until we get in gear.

All the way through the shoot, Redford complains that he's not acting, just running. When we finish, Hill gives him a sculpture of the roadrunner, made out of nails. The plaque reads: IF YOU CAN'T BE GOOD BE FAST.

Dear Mom and Dad: Some lessons from *The Sting*: If you can't be first, be best. If you can't be best, be first. If you can't be good be fast. Don't get mad, get even. Jump off the bridge when you get to it. And don't forget to throw some garbage on the street on your way down . . .

Love, Julia.

P.S. Remember to negotiate thickness as well as height on the lettering of your name.

'This is making me so nervous . . .' I twitch in my chair.

'Relax, it's only a movie.' Lederer smiles. I am talking informally to Dick and Leo Greenfield about how to get *The Sting* released. These guys are full of knowledge, they love to talk and love me asking them a favor. In Hollywood, I notice, people love it when you ask them this kind of knowledge favor. Particularly if they are the kind of people no one ever listens to. Usually they have been saving up for years waiting for someone to ask the question so that they can pour out everything they know.

In this case: theaters, how wide the release, how much money for a network buy. *The Sting* is coming out right in the middle of a marketing revolution. Up until *The Godfather*, every time you had a picture you thought was going to have reviews and audience appeal, you let it out slowly in a handful of chichi theaters in the major cities, and let it build. Then you went in ever widening waves. But Frank Yablans had released *The Godfather*, and then *Love Story*, as if they were two-week actioners, and now everyone was figuring out that a quality picture could really rake in the dough. Fast and long. Not one or the other.

The revolution has not yet occurred at Universal, which at this point in its career has not decided if it is in the movie business or not. It is definitely in the TV business, but not too many people there are in the movie business. There are George Roy Hill and Steven Spielberg, and Sid Sheinberg and Ned Tanen. Outside of them, nobody at Universal knows that there is a marketing revolution going on.

By the time they release *Jaws* for Steven they will know it and go with a thousand theaters. But just now, they are going with about thirty-five in key markets, and I am checking out with Lederer and Leo, who together form a pretty dynamic

148

marketing duo for Warners, if I should take a stand or not. I have made myself learn a lot about this part of picture-making on *Steelyard Blues*, and I figure I should apply it to *The Sting*.

Lederer and Leo are going blind. They don't know what *The Sting* is. They just know who is in it and who is directing it and that Warners had passed on it. They aren't yet ready to take my word that it will outgross *Butch Cassidy and the Sundance Kid*, at which the head of advertising has gotten on his knees and said, 'Please let it do just as much.'

'You've got no vision.' I smile. I am beginning to feel a lot like Cassandra. Hollywood is still a shock for me: here's where the dreams are created and people Think Big, yet nobody seems to be Thinking Big at all. Because I am young and small, they look at me fondly. Their looks say: You'll see. (Well, I did, but never about shortsighted grosses. I guess it was that I could always see the finished picture in my mind, feel the audience response to it in my heart. I didn't need the empirical evidence. You know. Vision.)

If you can't be first, be best, if you can't be best, be first. George has pulled it off: *The Sting* is both.

'Then get them to do a television buy during the summer, when the rates are reduced, and get enough theaters so they can justify the money spent on TV . . .' Lederer tells me. 'And Julia, watch out for the things that happen . . .'

I attend a meeting in New York with Zanuck and Brown and Hy Martin, head of distribution. I am seven months pregnant. I get to say, 'Hi Hy,' which they think is cute. Zanuck and Brown are trying to keep a picture together with John Avildsen and keep leaving the room for hush-hush phone calls. I tell Hy while they are gone that I will stand in the hall and cry if he doesn't guarantee at least two hundred theaters. He laughs and waves away the concept of a guarantee. Nobody likes to put anything in writing. He says he'll try. Three months later, surprise surprise we get the theaters. A good man of his word is hard to find . . .

*

I am about three weeks overdue during a long Indian summer that September. I give dinner parties in the hope that they will induce labor. I arrange for George Roy Hill to meet the Dunnes, and serve them horribly seasoned overdone chicken. George's wife, Luisa, is in tow. And in tow is how it really is with her; she seems like one of those addled middle-aged gentile ladies, often southern, who've been driven to distraction by their selfish, ungiving husbands.

Kate is born five days before *The Sting* is in answer print. The Gold Brothers, who worked on *Steelyard*, bring me the ads in the hospital. All it takes is a little confidence . . .

I don't think many people read *The New Yorker* the week of November 22, 1963. I did. Force of habit. There was a novella in it by Harold Brodkey called *The Abundant Dreamer*.

It is about a director, Marcus Weil, a thirty-fiveish Jewish expatriate shooting a picture in Italy that stars his current girlfriend, an Italian diva. While he is setting up the opening shot, he is handed a telegram. The telegram tells him that his grandmother is dead, and he flashes back to a summer when he visited her.

There are a pair of cousins, beautiful upper-class goyim, that he runs with. He has an affair with the girl; she is also having an affair with her cousin, who is Weil's pal. His grandmother is one of those German Jews who thinks she should live among these people; she thinks that she is welcome. She is not; she is hated and reviled behind her back in a subterraneanly anti-Semitic way. The girl gets pregnant and blames Marcus. In fact, she is pregnant by her cousin, but they want the smart rich Jew to take the fall. His grandmother wants him to marry the girl; he runs out. He never stops running. Isn't he a director in Italy now? They never speak again.

Back to the present. Marcus Weil is being craned up for the opening shot. He holds the telegram in his hand. He is crying. What's wrong, the cameraman asks. 'My grandmother was

150

such a stupid woman,' Marcus says. Wow! This story knocked me out. Of course, the only person around to discuss such matters with, particularly the week Kennedy was shot, is my mother. She and I – we *feel* this story. We *are* this story.

When *The New Yorker* arrives the week of November 22, 1973, ten years to the day after Kennedy was murdered, I read the issue from cover to cover. In memoriam. As it were. I am not at all in what Californians refer to as a good place. I've just had Kate a month before, I've felt excluded on *The Sting* all along, I've tolerated the experience of being pregnant, but a lot of fucking assumptions were made. My particular favorite was Ray Stark offering me a job as a reader – something to do in my spare time while I sat at the beach with my baby. I turned him down.

'I have this movie coming out – it's called *The Sting*. I have points. I expect to make zillions.' With most people, this usually passes as an explanation for just about anything. Men especially.

'That's all well and good; why continue, then?'

'I expect to make some other movies, some great movies.' My movies, not some dick love story.

Ray laughs softly. I could tell this is a new concept in Hollywood. 'Call me when you decide to be a mother.'

Fuck you. 'I won't change my mind.'

Ray laughs again. Derisive? 'Well, nice chatting with you.'

'Same here.' Fuckyoufuckyoufuckyou. Where has he gotten such an idea? David Begelman, he's said. I thought David really liked me for what I am.

And what is that? The son he never had.

In the aforementioned issue of *The New Yorker*, in the post-Watergate lull of the late fall, waiting for the release of *The Sting*, I read a long review of a book whose title I respond to immediately. The book is called *Fear of Flying*, and John Updike, who wrote the review, raves. I call my friend, Bob Bookman, who is a literary agent at International Creative Management, although that seems like a contradiction in terms.

'Could you find out about a book for me, Bookie?'

'Shoot.'

'It's called *Fear of Flying* and it's written by Erica Yong, I think, I can't tell – J-O-N-G. Published by Holt Rinehart.'

'I'll get back to you – where are you?'

'Beach . . .'

'Don't you think you ought to start coming into town?'

'Don't blow me any shit, Bookie . . .'

'You okay?'

'Probably just postpartum depresh – ' I don't wanna talk about it. Find me the book. Make me laugh. If I do, my stitches will hurt, and I'll know that I'm alive. At least I won't feel so empty.

Basically I'm not getting along with anybody, and the only thing I can think of when I look at Kate, aside from deep involuntary love – which feels disgusting and foreign – is that her shoulder is way up high from resting in one side of my uterus. Mine had been a perfectly blessed pregnancy until two days before her birth when I had bloody show and she still hadn't dropped. The X-ray showed that she was a footling breach.

When I went into labor, the doctors tried to turn her. They hooked me up with wires and Michael and I played hearts for eight hours. Finally her heartbeat got irregular and they performed a cesarean. It was all very sudden, and the last thing I remember, as they wheeled me away to pump drugs in my arm and make a smile across my lower abdomen, was the expression of alarm on Michael's face. When they did open me up they discovered that I had a partial septum in my uterus. Kate had simply squoonched over to one side for the last month or so of her incubation. This baby was determined to be born.

In addition to the tilted shoulder she had one sleepy eye. I had been specifically constrained by the pediatrician from pressing down on her shoulder, or tweaking her eyelid. 'She'll straighten out – don't touch,' he'd said on the fly, talking to me through my favorite fog: Demerol. The only good thing about having a cesarean so far had been the drugs. Oh, and that I wasn't pregnant anymore.

Bookie calls me back pretty quick. He is excited. 'Guess what?'

'You found the book . . .'

'Not just that. I found the book, we represent it, it's available. I've got bound galleys coming to you by rush messenger.'

'I'm impressed.'

'I think you're onto something. This is a Lynn Nesbit book.' Of course it is a Lynn Nesbit book. Good, I can talk to her about it.

'So rush messenger means it'll be here tomorrow?' We live just a mile south of the county line. Remote.

'Please. We're a full-service, same-day delivery agency . . .'

The book arrives all nicely wrapped in the ICM envelope and I read it straight through. I call Bookie at home at seven o'clock the next morning.

'I've got to have this book . . . how do I get this book . . .'

Flustered, Bookie says he will get into it. I transfer over to Ptak, my personal favorite. 'I've got to get this book . . .'

I call Begelman: 'I've got to got to . . .'

Agents talk to each other for about two weeks. Nothing. Finally, John Ptak says, wearily: 'I think you should go to New York and meet the writer . . .'

'You mean, do an audition . . .' The book is getting a lot of attention, a lot of support. From guys like Henry Miller . . . Holt Rinehart has gone with too small a first printing, and they don't seem to be in any hurry to go into a second printing . . . makes me wonder if they are going broke . . .

'Yeah, she wants to meet you . . .' I am still at the age where I travel on the red eye on the grounds that it is the most efficient use of time, and this is the perfect excuse to get away. I kiss Michael, Kate, and Sonya goodbye and I'm out of the house at the beach headed for LAX in a flash . . .

I am blowing my wild hair wildly when Erica and Betty Anne Clark, an ICM junior (who, as it turns out, is her real agent) arrive. Betty Anne is tall and willowy. Erica is short and overweight. When she smiles, broadly, which she does often, she is totally engaging. My first thought, high school to the core, is how interesting it is that dumpy broads give and get head, too.

Betty Anne is one of those fragile white-bread girls who attend schools like Skidmore. Erica, on the other hand, had gone to Barnard. Another Jew who went to an Ivy League school. I can make fun of Mount Holyoke all I want, but I never fail to mention that was where I attended college. White-bread Jews and their silly snobberies. Like, comes the revolution, we don't all get to go to camp. I'm always telling my gentile friends I expect them to hide me and Kate in their galley. They laugh, ha ha, isn't she funny . . .

Erica has cut her finger in the elevator. It is bleeding. We stick it under cold water in the sink and I find a Band-Aid. This seems an auspicious start.

We go downstairs for some eggs benedict and have a whopping good time. I have the dual task of making her love me and of finding some way to love her. Truth is, I am completely disarmed. I tell her she says my words for me, and disarm her back. We spend a long time together, and when they leave, I'm pretty sure I've accomplished my mission . . .

Nessa Hyams calls that night. Nessa is built like a football player: all shoulders and chest and no ass. She has a butch haircut and dissatisfied expression. For a spoiled rich kid from the East Side of Manhattan, she possesses few social graces. She is cold as ice, but for some reason, at the time I meet her, she and I connect.

One day, zipping up and down Rodeo, spending some of my first check at Giorgio's, she looks me deep in the eye and says, 'You are what I have been looking for all my life: a compatriot!' I laugh and we move up the street to Hermès where I buy a hideous purse that looks just like a doctor's bag for five hundred clams. I am thinking, The fuck I am a compatriot. My grandfather isn't S. Hurok Presents, but whatever turns you on.

Nessa never does anything that she hasn't calculated beforehand. While she is a casting lady at Warners, it is bruited about that she's involved in a nowhere affair with a married executive. When the bruit reaches gale force, she is set up at Columbia as a production executive.

This puts her in direct competition with Roz Heller, who is really capable and my friend. Nessa looks down her nose at Roz because Roz came up off the street. Roz feels the same way about Nessa because she's always been handed the things Roz has to struggle for. They put me right in the middle, and I think the smartest way to deal it out is to talk to Roz about *Taxi Driver* and to Nessa about *Fear of Flying*.

Erica has called Nessa to check up on me. Why would she call you? Oh, we've known each other since we were little girls, she says casually. Hmm, I know those girls. Jewish Princesses from Manhattan who go to Seven Sisters schools . . . Not my kind of broads, but hey, whatever's good for the project . . .

'I don't know what he means by it,' I lie, 'but Steven says he wants to do a movie about UFOs and Watergate, and I want to do it with him.' I am leaning on the edge of Begelman's desk, because when you are in his office, it is best to stand. He likes to keep the heat up and the Muzak just at the edge of your consciousness. He likes the vibe soporific. He likes to keep the meetings short and docile.

I like to walk around anyway. It helps me to keep my naturally circuitous thinking patterns linear. I make more points walking, and I slamdunk on the sudden stop or the lean against the desk. Begelman stands up; now he is taller than me again.

'I'm in,' he says. 'Let's go.' Lies work. Just sweep him along on pure excitement.

How am I to explain to D.B. that anyone who has ever dropped acid and looked up at the sky for a while or smoked a joint and watched the Watergate hearings on TV is waiting for this movie? And that it is uniquely this group of people who is going to give it to them? Hubris and youth and the promise of really good drugs fire these ambitions. There is no question in my mind that this group – weak as we are on story and screenplay – can pull it off. It will be like building a city.

Steven and Michael and me wait in the holding area outside Begelman's office. We wait for Begelman, but more to the point, we wait for Guy McElwaine, a star agent at ICM. He represents Steven, so he is going to represent all of us on *Close Encounters*. We offered to do that to guarantee Steven staying in the project. Steven was hanging out with men who were too old for him. Who bet and drank and watched football games on Sunday. Who ran studios and agencies. The group centered around Guy and Alan Ladd, Jr., otherwise known as Laddy, and included such disparate types as Joey Walsh and David Giler, the former more for the betting than the football, the latter more for the drinking than the football. Male bonding.

We got Steven outta Guy's house in the Bev Hills flats, and on to the beach, where people were still discussing art and greatness, and were occasionally smoking a joint. Where the ambient sound was rock 'n' roll, and the house wasn't so decorated that even the inhabitants felt like guests. Steven was the most talented contemporary we knew. He and Michael had become friendly while we were at Universal and we'd seen some dailies of *Sugarland Express*. We wanted to guarantee his staying in, and Guy and ICM tithing us seemed reasonable.

Guy is the most immaculate man in Hollywood. His blondness and his bland perfect features always remind me of Lenny Bruce's description of the white-collar drunk: 'Clean white shirt, good suit, buffed nails – whacked out of his skull.' There is that old-timey thing about him. Too much gold, too much shooting of the cuffs, too many wives. He admits to five, but we know there are more. Probably he omits them because he forgot. Guy is possessed of the Convenient Hollywood Memory. Somehow he represents a substantial portion of the promising young film makers of the time. Weird, because he doesn't seem simpatico at all. I assume that means he is a very good agent. Whatever the fuck that is.

He arrives about fifteen minutes late, a symphony of beiges. Steven checks him out with his disturbed Woody Allen look: 'Guy, you look like a Bentley,' he says, and we are ushered in immediately. If Guy is a Bentley, Begelman is a Rolls; we are Mazdas and Toyotas.

It's funny. The deal is being constructed around this idea in search of a movie, and we are the linchpins, but there is no question in that room of five who is more important. Hey, it is the seventies. Nobody knows how hot Toyotas and Mazdas will be. (And it's not really that different if you consider that today Mike Ovitz is referred to more often, and with greater awe, than his heaviest clients.)

We actually look Begelman dead in the eye during the meeting and agree to a $2.8 million budget below the line. Say anything and close the deal.

George is away shooting *Waldo Pepper* and Robert Surtees has a nasty fall that incapacitates him. It falls to Michael and me to check all the release prints. Plus backups. We take an excruciatingly long time on the one slated for the Cinerama Dome, because we know that's the first place George will go when he comes home for Christmas. They run five prints for us simultaneously. Fast forward. We start looking only at the heads and tails of reels and around optical effects. Everything else gets by us. By the end of the second day I don't care anymore and Michael has to finish the job alone. I don't know about Michael, but I'm pretty sure I'll never want to see this movie again.

We throw a New Year's Party: Steven Spielberg, Marty Scorsese and his girlfriend Sandy Weintraub, Bobby De Niro and Diane Abbott, John and Renee Milius, Schrader and his wife, Geneen, Norman Garey, recently divorced, and Nessa, the Fiskins, Roz Heller, and the Wards.

Jeffrey Fiskin raises his glass near midnight and says, 'Let's all get rich and live forever!' We all drink to that, then Milius fires his gun toward the ocean . . .

*

Michael throws the I Ching one day and is told he will live a
long and happy life and be surrounded by many people who
love him when he dies peacefully at a ripe old age.

'You try it,' he says, and shoves the book over in my
direction. I rifle through it. He tosses me the coins. Party
tricks. They're all out here, great toys. Numerology, astrology,
I Ching, Sufi, which becomes Arica, then est, Lifespring, Self-
Actualization. Actually est is the marriage of the yuppie ethic
with some ancient pop philosophy tossed in. Michael likes the
I Ching. Michael likes anything with coins. I have never
known anyone in my life to whom money is so important. I
am glad he is on my side.

But we are very much not on each other's side. We are
breaking up and it's my fault. I love him and I need him, but I
don't want him anymore, I want to move on, and I'm pushing
for the breakup. I am frightened about it most of the time; I
am hating myself for some incredibly bad behavior that I
choose to do in public, and that is fed by a coterie of fags who
are amused by incredib]y bad behavior.

'What do I do . . .'

'Throw the coins . . .' I jiggle them around in my fist then
throw them like dice. 'Let them fall more – don't throw them
– Let them slide off the side of your palm.' Okay, I get it; laid
back. I let them slide. Michael peers down at them, then grabs
the book and thumbs through the pages quickly. We do this
three times, and on the third time he reads me a long passage
about a lark who leaves all her friends and family behind her
to fly higher and higher, and soar in great loop-the-loops and
skim the tops of the trees only to be caught in a burst of wind
(ancient wind shear?) and fall suddenly to the ground. Moi? I
Ching, therefore I am.

'It's a warning, you know,' Michael says gravely. I can't
help it. I must see what it's like up there. Down there, too, I
suppose. As it were. 'Sometimes I feel like you're a balloon
and I'm the knot, and if the knot comes undone you'll just go

158

phhhht around and around and then fall to the ground . . .'
Balloon, hunh? In that I am round? In that I am full of hot
air, worse yet, helium? You got it right about the knot part
though. Sometimes it is so tight I can't breathe.

She put the house up for sale that winter. Over the past
two years the house had been listed with three real-estate
agents. It had 'sold' five times. It had been in escrow three
and fallen out each time. Meanwhile the house deteriorated,
sort of at the same rate she did. She could aerobicize and work
out *sans* trainer, but if the gate broke down, she needed the
electrician, and the gate person. If a toilet died, she needed
the plumber. If the dryer blew a gasket she needed her lonely
Maytag repairman. She started to notice that the house cost
thousands of dollars just to stay funky.

Why hadn't any of the business managers pointed out to her
that this house was a sieve? She started to hate the house. She
talked to it in her mind, 'I said goodbye years ago; why am I
still here?' she said to the house. Meanwhile she aerobicized
and looked miraculous. As the bank balances diminished from
six to five to four – low four – figures, she got better and better
looking, like the way women do when they are either pregnant
or in love. She was neither. Did this much anxiety agree with
her? Was there some greater meaning to all these financial
straits and tests? Did this mean that there was a God, and that
he wanted to make damn sure that she understood the value
of a dollar? Oh no, was God a mercenary?

She kept walking around the house, noticing the wood
planks in the floors that needed refinishing, the carpet peeling
back from the door in her bedroom, molding sheared off,
brick that needed replacing. The deck was crooked and there
was a giant crack in the flagstone around the swimming pool.

159

Why did this house keep coming unglued? Why couldn't she seem to stay in escrow, never mind close escrow? Was something keeping her here?

She began to believe that she was in someone else's movie. The classic: the actor who doesn't know his lines. How had she gotten in the Victim Role? She began to be afraid to pick up Häagen-Dazs at Gil Turner's on Sunset after midnight. If she was exuding a victim aura, she felt she could be a target for all kinds of things happening to her that she never countenanced before. Had her chances for mugging, rape, murder even, been mysteriously increased by some new victim smell emanating from her?

While Mitch was telling her which bills hadn't been paid for the last three months she kept looking over his shoulder into a mirror hanging on his wall. From a distance she could still be mistaken for being in her late twenties early thirties. How could she look this good and be this poor? And by the way, what kind of a business manager let bills pile up unpaid for three fucking months? Had she been so intimidating to him that he couldn't bring himself to tell her until she was going under for the third time?

He recited this bill and that alternative in his high little voice. When she and her assistant Harlan had first met him, post-Mickey Rutman, she'd wondered aloud if he had a testosterone deficiency; just what she needed – a business manager with no balls and power of attorney. He wasn't so hot for power of attorney now, though, and finally told her that he was reorganizing his office staff and couldn't handle her account anymore. Well, you're going to handle this account a couple more weeks till I find another accountant, she said, because if you leave me in this mess without some sort of cover you will lose sleep for the rest of your life. She pleaded with her eyes, and he agreed. This is not my movie, a little voice kept saying inside, but even that was not her own. She left his office very depressed.

It had always been her theory that it was best not to put off till tomorrow what she could put off till next week. Just now, however, she was going to have to borrow some money and she was going to have to call some creditors. Not to mention find a new business manager, although that job description hardly applied, given her reduced circumstances. In between negotiations with creditors, she put on last year's Alaïa and went off to meet a series of them, knowing she was auditioning for them as much as they were for her. She was feeling so low, it amazed her that anyone still wanted her account.

Her father lent her thirty grand. Michael lent her fifteen, which she guaranteed with a lien on the undeveloped lot next to her house, and on which he charged her interest. Of all the creditors, the only one who wasn't compassionate was Gelsons, an upscale supermarket.

Every morning she would call Mitch's assistant and tell her which checks to cut and for how much. House, utilities, phone, food first. Then doctors and department stores, so they wouldn't turn her over to a collection agency. She could tell from the assistant's voice how much she resented dealing with her, and hated herself for even talking to the cunt. Then she would schlep over to his newly expanded pink-and-gray offices and sit in the conference room with the mountains of checks that all of a sudden he was most anxious she sign herself. He would have pads brought to cover his monstrous new table so that her signature wouldn't scratch it. Fuck, I probably paid for it, why shouldn't I etch my name in it, she thought, but kept it to herself.

The borrowed money that was meant to be a cushion diminished quickly. Oh well, she thought, here today, gone today. That was pretty much how it always was with her and money. When the crisis passed, she allowed herself to succumb to a nasty flu and took to her bed, where she sweated and ached for three days. On the fourth day, she arose and took a long feeling shower.

Going broke wasn't the worst thing. Taking money from her father and Michael was close. From the time she had departed *Close Encounters* she had been educating herself to be totally self-sufficient. Her reconstructed life had been predicated on never never depending on a man; now she had to depend on the two whom she had left behind so long ago. Ah, the ties that bind . . .

She started to bug her broker. She had always made the

house difficult to see; now she made it too available. Hung around for an open house or two, presided over by a depressing Persian gentleman who seemed to attract all the wrong people. Angry, middle-aged couples who wouldn't understand the house if they tried, and they hadn't tried to understand anything in years. Pear-shaped schlemiels, male and female, who looked like lawyers and really wanted a pad at the beach. Underaged starlets whose lives seemed like a fashion statement. Why couldn't they find an eccentric twenty-five-to-thirty-five-year-old self-made man or woman, like she had been when she had bought the house?

How would a broker recognize one anyway? More to the point, she began to wonder if any existed. People that young weren't as spiritual as her crowd had been. People that young didn't look for a refuge anymore. People that young were afraid to be alone. People that young eschewed eccentricity. It was all part of the larger picture: the diminished visions, the bankrupt dreams.

Michael and I are breaking up. I wake up every morning wondering if today one of us will make the move. Torture would be over and misery could begin. I am determined to shake up my life. Witnessing Michael's pain on a daily basis is beginning to affect my looks.

'Are you just waiting until I'm ready?' he asks sadly one night.

'I feel as if we're on the crest of a vast social wave,' he says another.

In New York, during all the sleepless nights worrying about the draft, worrying about Vietnam, I'd only focused on the grief I'd feel at his death. Now, out here in California, I start to obsess about my own. That is how I know I don't feel the same way about him. My own death saddens me more than his.

SCENE FROM A MOVIE I CAN'T WATCH: MOS MONTAGE

THE BEACH – OUR HOUSE, SOON TO BE MY HOUSE.

ovo: An afternoon get-together, but not the usuals. It is skewed toward gay. I am telling a story, loudly, and they are encouraging me, also loudly, about a recent flirtation at an airport bar with Peter Hyams, Nessa's brother, a mediocre director with fierce eyes and extreme baldness. He actually combs his hair forward from the back of his head to cover it. Michael is on the couch with TV Wonderwoman, Deanne Barkley, and baby Kate, trying not to hear . . . DISSOLVE THROUGH TO THE BABY'S ROOM:

Later; a glimmer of setting red sun sneaks through the windows. It gives the surroundings a postnuclear glow. Michael and I are having a fight. The baby lies screaming and shaking with rage on the maid's bed. SOUND UP

MICHAEL: (angry veins bulging) I could kill you for this!

ovo: He grabs me, makes robot moves, he doesn't know what to do . . . me neither. I'm rigid with fear. He puts me down . . .

CAMERA ZOOMS IN on the crying baby. Kate. She never cries CLOSER on the MOUTH, and as we cut to BLACK, we HEAR the ECHO of a SCREAM.

If the bust-up of my marriage is a movie, *Fear of Flying* provides its theme and *Vegas* its characters. Giving birth and winning the award in such rapid succession have created hormonal riot in me already. I'm not prepared for the outrageous success. Nobody is. Not really.

The only way I can justify the sudden visibility to myself is to use it as ante with the town to go on to make better pictures. Not to mention, I love the action. I am so driven, I think I might be overproducing cortisone in my body. Plus,

Hot in Hollywood is about as Hot as it gets. And we are fizzing and steaming and burning up the track.

For our contemporaries, we're the Hope; for those who are older, chicer, more established, we are a ticket to what is young, hip, happening. In 1974, these things matter. *Easy Rider*, Bob Dylan, Watergate . . .

The gatherings at the beach just grow and grow and grow in size, strength . . . *heat*. And there I am, hostess with the mostess, with the beautiful Hollywood baby on my arm. Driven and energetic and smart and arrogant. With and without portfolio, if you can put potential into your portfolio. Metamorphosing into an asshole in front of everybody.

And Michael is right. We are on the crest of a vast social wave, even broader than the comparatively small issue of our marriage: by the time we break up that summer the conversion from the *we* thinking to the *me* thinking is almost complete. Not just in marriage . . . but in America . . . around the globe . . . consideration of anything more cosmic gives me a headache. Oh no, did God have his Me Decade, too? As I look around it would appear so . . .

John Dunne tells me a story about being at a dinner party with Sam Peckinpah in which Peckinpah, after stating that all movies are westerns – 'You put the hare in front of the hounds and let the hounds chase the hare' – adds, 'What I want to do is make a movie about the third man through the door.' When John asks him what he means he explains it roughly:

'In the big shootout, when the good guys break into the bad guys' hideout, there are always three men who come through the door. The first man is the hero, his name's above the title, he wears white, his gun is drawn, and he's firing.

'The second man through the door might be looking the other way, but he's either a youngster on the way up or an oldster who's got respect. His hand is on the holster, he's looking forward, he might get a ding on the arm.

'The third man through the door isn't even a featured player, he's coming in backwards and he's not sure he's in the right movie. He gets to die before titles.'

'Ohh, what a great story . . .' I coo to John.

'I'm working on a book about the third man through the door . . . I've got about forty pages . . . wanna take a look?' I am flattered to be asked and fastbreathe yes.

John Dunne gives me forty-three pages of something he is calling *Vegas*. It starts with a three-page rundown of all the facts about *Vegas*: churches, schools, population, on and on and on. On the fourth page, the book finally begins with the sentence: 'In the summer of my nervous breakdown I went to Las Vegas, Clark County, Nevada.' From there on I am riveted. The book is about the writer, plus a private eye named Buster Mano with a crazy Catholic wife, a black hooker, and a comic named Sammy Shore who calls himself a semi-name. Ooh, I think, I wanna make a development deal on *Vegas*. Ooh, I wanna make a movie about the third man through the door. Even if he's a woman.

I call right away and tell him I love the pages. I give him the tiny suggestion he should take the *Vegas* facts and put them in italics before the book, a prologue, so the book starts, 'In the summer of my nervous breakdown . . .' I am thrilled to blushing when he decides it's a good idea and does it. I ask for a free run to set it up and he gives it to me. I start to look for a writer. Nothing in life comes for free.

Everyone I ask thinks a writer for *Vegas* qualifies only if he's also a compulsive gambler; I guess the theory is that he spends a lot of time there. Two names keep coming up: Reilly O'Reilly and Grady Rabinowitz*. They come to their compulsion from different sides of the California track. Grady is from the Iowah clahsses of Southern California, Reilly the prodigal son of a prominent, aristocratic family from up north.

Grady is big in television. The pecking order goes music television movies, no matter how much money you make, so this gig is a step up for Grady. Grady feels degraded by television and he does his best to degrade the money he makes from it. As in: snorts coke off his Emmy. He's written a script on spec about death, my favorite subject. A kindred spirit. I'm up to my ass in go pictures, so I try to explain I don't really think I can produce/perform on its behalf in the way it deserves.

165

'What about Mel Brooks?'

'He says he wants to do his *own* movie about death.'

'This *is* his movie about death, didn't you tell him that?'

I pass the script on to another producer, who gets it made with a big star, who also directs. It is what Reilly refers to as a directorproof script. ('All but ten directors in the world just cock it up. You try to write a script so good, so complete, that it's directorproof.')

I see my giving the script to a competitor as an act of generosity. Grady sees it as a rejection, a lack of belief in the work. The old half-empty/half-full-glass syndrome. What do I know? I'm still young enough to believe in high aspirations and great movies, even if they're not mine. Grady, a Cancer man, like Michael Phillips, carries silent grudges. Like Michael Phillips. It's a mark against me. A biggie, as Grady would say.

Another is that I'm whistling when he first sees me. He's waiting on the balcony outside my offices at Columbia. I'm coming from a soul-battering production meeting on *Close Encounters*. a daily activity. Whistling away the desire to cry. I take my time traversing the parking lot for a meeting with him about *Vegas*. He will often remind me that this is his first impression of me: an elf whistling and sauntering her way across the parking lot. It makes him think I'm happy. It makes him angry . . .

Reilly, who prefers Really, is one of those guys who shows up just in time to put your marriage in the toilet for good. He had grooved his way through many a Hollywood household that was getting ready to blow. Reilly has always been precocious: played tennis well enough to bet on himself by the time he was eleven; won a violin competition at thirteen; nominated for several book awards. For his first novel. He didn't win any.

His wife committed suicide shortly thereafter. Grief-stricken, he fled to a Caribbean island with a friend, another novelist, who ripped off his half-completed novel. A Hollywood kind of friend.

Reilly was big in the sixties. He lost a million and a half dollars in just a few years, gambling. Married a beautiful descendent of the wonderful folks who brought you the Teapot

Dome Scandal. Ghostwrote screenplays. Legend had it that he and another Famous Junkie Writer were put in a back room at a large independent production company with two typewriters, reams of paper, and unlimited amphetamines and coke.

By the time I meet Reilly in 1974 he is in decline. And still, he is a magical Irish poet. He wears tennis shorts and a sweater and he makes the girls swoon and the men bridle. He tells me that my eyes are hypnotic, which makes Michael furious.

'All you need is some handsome decadent writer to tell you your eyes are hypnotic,' he fumes after our first meeting with Reilly, who is so destitute that he has to have a beach bum named Lance (aren't they always?) drive him to our house . . .

Grady is more cute than handsome, an alternatively attractive and unattractive trait in a man approaching forty. He is also attached to a blond-haired, blue-eyed California Valley girl whom he is proud to have stolen from a major macho moviestar. But he likes flirting, and he sees a liaison with me as a ticket to the next rung on the show-biz ladder. He'd like the gig.

Reilly, on the other hand, who is truly gorgeous, is unattached and dangerous. Within days of our first meeting he tells me he could tell how loaded I was when I won the Academy Award, on TV, and all he kept thinking while I was delivering my line was, Oh, you fool, you fool . . .

While he is telling me this and hurting my feelings, he reaches for my hand and says he is really more interested in me than the job. My ultimate punisher. The more he tells me what a piece of shit I am the more I'm crazy for him. Ah, the relationships we get into just to get out of the ones we are not brave enough to say are over.

I insult Grady by making him perform as my beard once or twice to see Reilly, who develops an exploded testicle and needs to take a short rest at his ex-wife's house. They outfunny each other, a sign of pure male hatred . . . Okay, so it's not two black guys beating the shit out of each other for the world heavyweight title, but it's as close as it gets for me.

Either one of them seems a glamorous alternative to

Michael, although casting one's eyes backward, they just seem symptomatic of an extended postpartum depression.

Vegas blows because no matter how good a definition of holdback Norman gets him, John Dunne isn't satisfied. The real reason, which I don't figure out until years later, is that he wants to use the Buster Mano character as a model for Tom Spellacy in *True Confessions*. I resurrect the project as something called *The Third Man Through the Door*. The Third Man Through the Door. In Hollywood. As it were.

Grady and I commence our pitch around town and get some Classic Wisdom thrown in our faces: hits about Hollywood are rare, is it a comedy or a drama? I don't see it, I don't get this Third Man concept, it's not accessible enough . . . Discouraged, we go to see an old friend of mine who's just landed a new job.

SCENE FROM A MOVIE ABOUT A MOVIE WITHIN A MOVIE TITLE CARD WHITE ON BLACK: *THE PITCH*

OVO: We are ushered in by the first of the English secretaries, a photojournalist between assignments. Huge corner office in a state of de/re-decoration. Male bonding with his space. He is yelling into the phone.

EXEC: Well you tell him to go check out his plot at Forest Lawn 'cause that's where he'll be residing if he doesn't close this fucking deal! . . . WHAT? . . . (he waves us in as we hover uncertainly) . . . Make the client CAVE on that fakaktah point!

OVO: The office is in such disarray it is hard to know where to alight. We settle on an undersized loveseat. Rather closer together than I want. I see I'm gonna have to do this performance on my feet.

EXEC: Okay, okay, close of business tomorrow. Hey, give Sharon my love . . . She did? When? . . . Oh, I'm sorry to hear that. What's that now, four? Just kidding, man. Hey, babe, it's the seventies. What can I tell ya?

OVO: He bangs down the phone and smiles at us graciously.

EXEC: So Spielberg tells me the budget's going north.

ME: Hey, whatever's good for the project.

OVO: We all laugh like we know what I really mean. I introduce Grady and the exec.

EXEC: Can I getcha anything? No? Good. Amanda, hold all calls except for you-know-who's. So tell me this super idea of yours.

OVO: Grady opens his mouth, but I'm already on my feet.

ME: Well we have this idea about a comic version of *La Dolce Vita*. A dark comedy about the making of a movie.

GRADY: (interrupting) With Dom DeLuise as the dead fish at the end.

OVO: Studio Exec laughs. Yeah, right, like he's seen *La Dolce Vita*. Amanda buzzes him.

EXEC: (holds up his index finger in the one-moment-please gesture) I gotta take this call.

OVO: I can tell by the Oh-baby-me-too-but-I'm-in-a-meeting-right-now exchange, this is a personal call. Duh. He can't wait to tell us what it's about.

EXEC: That was (he mentions the name of a famous starlet of the moment). She told me she came so hard last night she couldn't stop.

OVO: She's an actress, man, I think but don't say. I remind myself I'm participating in a deal in the making. Grady shoots me a look. Has he read my mind?

EXEC: Look, I have no idea what you're talking about, but I'll spend fifty, seventy-five grand to find out.

OVO: Sooo easy. Am I wrong to feel cheated? Grady permits himself a sad smile. The pocket calculator he calls his mind is toting up his piece of this deal in search of a story.

EXEC: So have your people get in touch with my people. Always a pleasure.

OVO: He smiles a broad shark smile. (JAWS THEME UNDER) Did he have that many teeth when we came in? Grady and I, just actors in a scene, take our cues and exit. As we wait for the elevator, I say

ME: *Came so hard she couldn't stop?*
GRADY: Hey, baby, she's an actress . . .
ME: When it comes to coming, pal, most women are.
GRADY: (somber) That's funny . . .
OVO: We step into the elevators and the doors close. After three weeks of strenuous negotiation, the deal blows. I consider buying a plot at Forest Lawn. Grady offers to buy one for me . . .

Reilly. He is out of money and strung out most of the time, and he doesn't hang around for very long; he rarely gets a hard-on, but the mind-fuck is really irresistible. Grady, even deal-less, makes out infinitely better than I do. In the vast scheme of things.

Michael finally leaves the house on Nicholas Beach Road on July 29, 1974, two days before our eighth wedding anniversary, the day Cass Elliot dies. He's decided to move into the Sunset Marquis, where we'd first come four years before at the advice of Marcia Nasitir. ('It's cheap and it's central. Very L.A. It's the kind of place where people go to commit suicide. You'll love it.')

While he packs I hide out next door with Margot Kidder (who insists on being called 'Margie,' a fake childhood nickname that I always find hard to utter to such a sex beast) and Michael Sarrazin, with whom she's just done a picture and set up housekeeping. That is her pattern. Work with 'em, sleep with 'em, then bring 'em home to the nice little beach house that she'd originally shared with Jennifer Salt, an infinitely more entertaining roommate than any of the guys, and that included Brian De Palma, even if he did play chess with Michael, make me laugh, and give us *Taxi Driver* because he wanted to direct it.

The phone rings at Margot's. She hands it to me because we both know that it is Michael. He is calling from a pay phone. His voice is wobbly.

'I just heard on the radio that Cass died. She was found

170

dead in bed with a half-eaten ham sandwich.' I guffaw involuntarily. I remember Marvin Birdt telling me about being a pilot in Korea: 'On our first mission the guy next to me was shot down, and you know what I did? I laughed.' Which is what Michael and I are doing now, cracking up, generating instant hysteria through the phone lines. Talk about reach out and touch someone. Margot starts to laugh without knowing why, and somewhere in the distance I can hear Michael Sarrazin's low, drunken chortle.

'Where was she?' For the past three months Cass had been doing gigs around the world. We never knew which faraway place her scratchy voice would come from or from what time zone.

'London. Brian Augur's apartment.' I knew I didn't like his music. That apartment was to be a bad luck venue. Keith Moon died there, too.

'Drugs?' The first question you asked. The second one: 'Murdered?'

'Who knows . . .' Michael starts to cry.

Cass Elliot is the only fat person I ever really loved. I was so crazy about her I didn't notice her obesity. Which was hard for a person with my anorectic-bulimic profile. (Personally I preferred starvation to vomiting, but two pounds over perfect required instant attention, no matter what.) She'd come to the house on Nicholas Beach with an eighth, and a suitcase and a couple of decks of cards and we would get into killer canasta that could last for days – or at least until the blow ran out.

By the time I met her the Mamas and Papas were history, the communal Jeanette MacDonald estate was history, and Cass was in desperate financial straits. She was doing shitty gigs all around the world just to pay back taxes. First, John Phillips fucked her, then ABC Dunhill fucked him, and the government, who fucks everyone, was up her ass for their money. At one point she paid ten grand in back taxes to the state in pennies. Which she had deposited in front of the Federal Building by a dumpster.

It was a costly joke – finding the pennies and the truck large enough to do it cost her another three grand, not to mention being cited by the government for contempt and having to collect the pennies and remove them. All in all she came out about even. That was how it was with Cass. If she broke even, she was having fun.

She had a pretty good attitude about her fatness, too, which is why it made no difference. One foggy day, we decided to walk over to Jennifer and Margot's next door. It was a hazy sunshine kind of day at the beach, but we were all fanatics, so when they didn't answer the phone, we knew they were lying on the beach (no tops for sure, maybe naked – Nicholas Beach was known as a nude beach because of us) and figured, fuck it, the walk will do us good.

Taking a walk with Cass was a bit of a chore because you don't get to weigh three hundred plus pounds and walk briskly. I was still a New Yorker in this respect, so I kept having to stop and wait. We could see them faintly through the mists, but they were all waving wildly. We were easily two hundred yards away.

'I wonder how they knew it was us.' Cass laughed.

It was Margot and Jennifer and Jill Clayburgh and Al Pacino and Steven at the beach and Al was already abusive, so we took off pretty fast with Steven in tow.

'You know what that son of a bitch did?' Steven was upset. 'I didn't recognize him at first so he threw down a movie magazine – I mean threw it at me – and said "Read this, maybe you'll learn something."'

'And his picture was on the cover, right?'

Steven looked at Cass, astonished. Did she have telepathic powers?

'I never had a problem being recognized, but I remember what an asshole you get to be after you've been on a few covers . . . but before you've been on a whole bunch of them . . .'

That settled Steven down right away. Cass was more of a Jewish mother than a rock 'n' roll star. She would have made a great manager.

Her manager was Alan Carr. At the beginning of his Alan Carr-ness. He had bought a house in Benedict Canyon that had been owned by Richard Quine and before he had a stick of furniture in it he was throwing large Alan Carr parties, with lots of young-boy help in togas and candles lining every room, every staircase. The house had a great driveway, one of those driveways that went on forever.

Michael and I went to a dinner party there once. The guests were Andrea and Doug Cramer. Cass. Aaron and Candy Spelling. Altovise Davis arrived before Sammy. I had no idea who she was, but I gathered someone important because Aaron Spelling was obsequious to the point of becoming one giant can of Crisco, he was so oily. Candy Spelling had very red-rimmed eyes and a lot of jewelry.

'She looks like she cries all the time,' Michael whispered.

'She's got nine sets of eyelashes on; she's probably allergic to the glue,' I hissed back, snide as hell because she already had her baby and her figure, and I was six months bloated under my Holly Harp empire-waisted dress. We played Trivia during dinner, because that's what Sammy liked to do.

Cass lived in a house up on Woodrow Wilson Drive, right near Giler and Grady, which was convenient. Her place was a sanctuary on days when I was foolish enough to see them both in the same afternoon. She had a blank, half-painted wall in her living room that guests were supposed to grace with graffiti. You were judged, of course, by ensuing guests, and as this was pretty much a roster of the great, the near-great or the about-to-be-great, everyone tried, probably too hard, to be memorable.

Cass had started it all one night by writing 'Who is Chuck Barris and why is he saying those things about me?' in black magic marker. Over a period of time, as other missives by Jack Nicholson, Michelle Phillips, Robert Towne, and her daughter appeared, she edited it to 'Who is Chuck Barris?' Basically no one could compete with her in the epigram-for-the-seventies department. Except possibly Timmy Leary, whose Turn On, Tune In, Drop Out still cropped up from time to time.

*

And now she is dead. Dead in some faraway place. History. Nessa Hyams and I go to dinner that night at Alice's Restaurant.

'Do you want me to go to the funeral with you?'

'Please – I'm going to meet Michael there, but I don't think I can bear the drive by myself.'

Michael comes with Peter Boyle and we all sit together, sandwiched in between Alan Carr and Carol Burnett. Later I can't remember the particulars of the funeral, because the two of them cried so hard and so loud I couldn't focus on words. They seemed to be expressing the grief we all felt. Let her mascara run, let his eyes get swollen, let me get out of here and have a drink.

We go to the Polo Lounge. At another table sit Michelle Phillips, Jack Nicholson, Harry Gittes. Harry and I check each other out. We exchange looks. The looks say, I'll catch you later. Right now, we are all drinking to the death of Cass.

When I get home, Grady calls to see if I am okay. This is the man who, upon being informed of Michael Dunn's death, said, 'Oh, that's terrible, are they going to bury him three feet under?' Now he asks me, 'Was the casket very large?' In fact, it was, and the effect was enhanced by flowers draped over the coffin. I laugh weakly.

Later, I go through my Rolodex and find her card. I'm not throwing this out, I think, and I line the edges with black Magic Marker like the In Memoriam ads in the trades.

Michael and I go to Disneyland for our eighth anniversary the next day. I pick him up early at the Sunset Marquis in my trusty Mazda. He lets me drive. We have a pretty good time. The day turns out to be a sort of celebration. Of what, I don't know.

Michael hasn't been out of the house for two weeks when Reilly and I take a road trip to Del Mar. He picks me up in a big beautiful white Mercedes 450 SEL, his last rich man's possession, which some bad guy has been holding on to until Reilly pays him something on a longstanding debt.

'How did you ever get this back?' I say.

'Well,' he says through clenched teeth. 'I went to his house with a gun and a crazed expression, unannounced, and I made him understa-a-a-nd what a bad idea it was to keep my car . . .'

While Reilly sweats and loses, I read a script of his that has made the rounds, a thinly veiled autobiographical account of the particulars of his aforementioned biography with a nasty cocaine understory. It is a powerful piece of work and it makes me cry at the end, the female equivalent to coming, Reilly tells me. I tell him I think I can set it up somewhere.

We are hanging out with a sleazebag younger couple who has bought some smack and we snort it in celebration. That night we do a poor imitation of fucking, limp and losing as he is, at the end of which he proclaims, 'That was just like fucking a whole person.' Oh really, that was just like fucking dead zucchini, I think, and force myself to sleep so that I won't say anything.

The next day we run out of money and I cash five hundred dollars on my MasterCard.

Somewhere in the middle of the smack and the coke and the Thai stick rolled in Tampax paper because we've run out of Bambu I start to get sick of the whole thing and want to leave. We pack up my car and head north on the San Diego freeway.

He insists I pull off at San Clemente, on the grounds that the recently resigned Nixon is in more psychic pain than he is. 'I wanna soak up some of that Nixon-pain,' he smiles wearily.

He picks a fight with me as the drugs are wearing off and I pull off the freeway and push him out of the car. He walks away. I pull up next to him and tell him to get into the car, but he gives me the finger and screams Fuck You just in case I don't understa-a-and.

I get back on the freeway and keep myself pretty much together until I get near Los Angeles, at which point Barbra Streisand singing 'The Way We Were' comes on the radio. I pull off the freeway and call Michael from a pay phone in tears. He is groggy and tells me that somebody is with him. I hang up the phone and bawl my way back to Malibu.

There is a message on the service that Margot has called. I call her back, hysterical, and she comes running over. We clear out the back of the car. Thai stick, Tampax, a couple hundred dollars, and Reilly's 'losing pants.' I want to burn it all down on the beach. She talks me out of burning the stick and the money, and we watch Reilly's pants turn to embers.

Monday, Reilly calls, all smiles and apologies. Maybe we should just do business together, I say, a glutton for punishment. By the end of the week, I have Bobby Sherman, who is at Fox, creaming to make a development deal on the script. Desperate for money, Reilly pushes me hard and I push Bobby. The pressure seems to make everyone enjoy the enterprise more, and at five o'clock on Friday, a curious group gathers at the El Padrino Bar in the Beverly Wilshire hotel to make a deal: Mort Smithline, the business affairs guy from Fox, Barry Haldeman, Norman Garey's associate (Norman is out of town), John Ptak, who is Reilly's agent as well as mine, and me and Reilly.

We pound out a step deal that starts out with a down payment of twelve five. It becomes clear that Reilly needs cash that night, which no doubt some bookie or dealer is prepared to break his face over. Smithline has a check made out to him, but there isn't a bank in the world that will cash it at this hour. We are still hammering away at the deal at eight o'clock, which is when Ptak starts to fade, but it seems pointless, since there is no way Reilly will get the cash this night.

Reilly and I excuse ourselves to go downstairs to the bathrooms. That's when he says, 'You could get this money. Get me five grand or I'm out the door.' I pee and then I call Colbert at home and explain the situation. He sounds intrigued and challenged. He says he will see what he can do. A half hour later Colbert comes into the El Padrino with a plain brown bag filled with cash.

'How did you do this?' I ask, genuinely impressed.

'Don't ask . . .' But he is smiling and blushing from ear to ear, genuinely impressed himself. Probably got it from the same guys Reilly has to give it to. I get a side letter from Smithline that Fox would repay me for the cash advance, and we all walk back to Barry's office at Rosenfeld Meyer and Sussman on the corner of Wilshire and Camden to initial and Xerox the deal. Reilly disappears shortly after, to pay his debt, no doubt, and I plow my way back to the beach, vowing to fire Ptak as soon as the right delicate moment arrives.

The next day, Reilly calls and says he needs one more favor. I am beginning to enjoy the feeling of power that the cash in the paper bag gave me. What new mission impossible will Reilly have in store for me today, I wonder as I drive to his apartment to pick him up.

He is bright and chirpy and I say so. He smiles and his lips stick to his teeth. Coke? Meth? He could be recovering from one set of drugs and starting off on another. He does have amazing recuperative powers for the amount of drugs he does and tension he creates. Good genes, my mother would say.

'I just gotta make a phone call . . .' He dials a number and asks to speak to Phil*. 'I wanna come visit my Titian.' He laughs into the phone. 'About an hour . . .' He hangs up the phone and grabs my hand. His palms are very clammy.

'Okay,' he says to me, 'let's go. I'll drive.'

'Who was that?'

'Oh, he's a gangster.' He smiles bitterly. 'Like everyone.'

'Your Titian?'

'I used to have all three. Now, I have only one . . . this guy's holding it for me . . .' Boy, Reilly is into some pretty deep shit. Why does that make him so . . . desirable? We climb into his big fat car and head into town. By the time we are on the Santa Monica freeway it is pretty clear from Reilly's driving that something is interfering with his vision.

He is all over the road and he is doing about eighty. I keep grabbing for the steering wheel and he keeps pushing me away. I am torn between the desire to strap myself in for the impending crash or wresting control of the car from him. The third choice that keeps going over and over in my head like a mantra is to turn the clock back an hour. Why am I in this

177

death-car on this dangerous drive with this crazy person whom I'm not even fucking?

'What drugs do you have coursing through your body right now?' I yell. He has the windows wide open. The roar of the wind is like a tornado crashing through the car. He keeps opening and shutting his eyes for long periods of time, like that is going to bring the world into focus. And going faster. Like the less he can see the faster he has to go.

It occurs to me that maybe his wife didn't kill herself after all. Maybe he killed her. He is cutting across four lanes of traffic without signaling. Cars are beeping and honking and getting the fuck out of the way. He pulls over onto the shoulder and throws the gear into park.

The car lurches to a stop. Sweat is pouring down his face. I am breathing hard, but I manage to yell, 'You could have gotten us killed! Or worse. Arrested. Just what I need in my life right now.' He shrugs his shoulders and laughs. It makes his eyes sad, while his teeth shine brightly below. It is a very sexy look.

'I took a lot of Quaaludes this morning,' he says.

'Why?'

'I got nervous about seeing you. I needed to calm down.'

'How many is a lot? Just curious.'

'Oh, three or four . . .' Good old Rorer 714. I have a T-shirt someone has given me. Black with a white Rorer 714. When I need good luck I wear it. Like an undershirt so no one can see. My little secret. Bad little girl. Three or four, hunh? And driving. What am I doing here? This is not my movie.

'I think you should let me drive, don't you?'

'Absolutely!' He laughs. God, he is gorgeous. Okay, let's press on Life or Death Freeway for the Gorgeous One. We switch seats. His car feels like a boat. I pull back onto the freeway, and before I know it I am going ninety. I am immediately pulled over by a cop and given a ticket. Reilly can't stop laughing. The luck of the Irish. Well, they need it, given their lifestyles. Me, I'm ready to take a cab.

'We're almost there,' he says. 'Press on . . .' We wend our way through Coldwater Canyon, and then he says, make a hard left here, and I think we are going off a cliff but instead we pull into what can only be described as a compound. I can see a big structure in the back. This is not kid stuff. My heart races a little. This place has its own generator.

Like Pavlov's dog, I take this as a sign that it needs to race a little more, and bring out some toot. Dangerous in front of Reilly. Reilly does not do little toots, or even lines. Reilly can do your whole gram if you don't watch out. With one nostril. Reilly has lost all sense of proportion. That is the heart of his appeal. In a couple of years, I would know that Reilly was just another blatant Hollywood casualty. But to my recently opened eyes he is Jack Fucking Nicholson.

When we get inside, there is a good-looking white-haired guy waiting. There is also a Titian in the hallway. Reilly may be mean, but he doesn't lie. Phil and I sit at the bar and chat. Mostly he wants to talk about David Begelman and Freddie Fields. He doesn't like them. I get the feeling they owe him money . . .

'In Hollywood you're supposed to fuck up,' Schrader says. This means fucking someone whose credits are more impressive than yours. As opposed to fucking down. As I've already won an Academy Award, there is a dearth of the former and a glut of the latter.

He looks at me sternly. Drunk and loose and wondering what if but still a Calvinist. He doesn't talk. He lectures. Something about him is very lovable. Maybe his aspirations. Certainly not his preoccupations. Certainly not his screen-plays.

'Oh yeah, and what does that mean – Bob Evans, Warren Beatty?' Neither one of them turns me on. Bob Evans is too tan and Warren, I've heard from my actress girlfriends, is priapic. Those guys were usually rammers. No thank you.

Having just split up with Michael nothing turns me on, certainly not this drunken get-together with Schrader at Moon-shadows. I drink too much and so does he, and pulling out of the parking lot, making that dangerous left onto the Pacific Coast Highway, not one but two cars almost hit us, and I gun it and fishtail into the traffic. Petrified, I turn to Schrader to check him out and he is blissed.

'I'm sorry, Schrader.'

'That's okay – I always wanted to die in a fast car with a beautiful woman.' My heart pounds bambambambam and I know it is just an acceleration of my fright. Schrader always scares me. When we first met him, after Brian De Palma had given us *Taxi Driver*, he was so shy he talked into his armpit. He had a schlivitz, which made understanding him an act of will. On top of that, he pontificated.

After I read the script, I refused to be alone in the house with him. He was following Milius around and had bought his own .45, an act of romantic adulation; I was pretty sure that he liked me enough to rape me with it, given half a chance, so I just didn't hang out with him on a singular basis. He had a sweet, self-effacing laugh, though, and as I got over my prejudices and he got over his crush, we actually became pretty good friends. I still wasn't thrilled with being alone with him, which is why I liked to keep control over our social interaction.

'Ah, Schrader, what a nice thing to say.' Good dog, good dog. We drive to his car in silence and I permit him some extra time in a full-frontal bear hug. Whatever turns you on . . . Does Schrader think that *he* is fucking up?

Guys I am working with are always giving me advice on whom I should fuck. When push comes to shove I always go for looks.

Michael Brown is rich and idle. He's always going to make a movie, but his principal role in life seems to be introducing rich and talented and famous people to each other. It is reputed that the song 'Nowhere Man' by the Beatles is about Michael Brown. Witty and opinionated, he keeps the soirees at the beach going when everyone else is too stoned. I can see why the Beatles might have kept him around, if the story of 'Nowhere Man' is true; he sings for his supper, he hits the right notes, but he is a groupie, nothing more. Really.

He had done the honor of introducing me and Julie Christie

up at Paul Williams's beach house, a dark hovel heavy with the scent of incense. The seventies . . . pot 'n' coke 'n' incense. What a wonderful way to spend a Sunday afternoon: I have a good brain-fucking conversation with Paul, relate to Barbara, the woman he's with, do a hit of this, a taste of that, and interact with Julie Christie. She seems warm and relaxed, if a tad nonverbal. A perfect audience for me.

Years later Warren Beatty says to me at a party that he would have liked to have been there for that meeting, and I, high on a coke joint, reply, 'Well, let me put it this way, I did all the giving and she did all the taking – does that turn you on?'

He says, 'It's interesting,' and walks away. I think it turns him off, because he never attempts seduction and Warren tries to fuck everybody.

A couple of weeks later she calls and says she's up at Paul Williams's place again with some other people, and should they drop by. I am bored, depressed, a little overweight, but very *tan*. I say yes.

She arrives with Michael Brown and Artie Ross, guys on the fringe. And Jeremy, on the fringe of the fringe. 'I've brought you a present,' she whispers, as she brushes past me, and there is Jeremy.

Jeremy, with his dark tousled hair, his unearthly blue-green eyes, his perfect features, his perfect tan, his little white teeth, his height (six-three) – is a fucking vision. I say to him out loud – I guess it is how I win him over – 'You're the handsomest man I've ever met.' Beautiful would be a better word.

Additionally, he has incredible grace. It is absolutely thrilling to a visual person to watch Jeremy do anything. That night what I get to watch is Jeremy snorting a lot of coke and pouring a lot of scotch. He does it so gracefully, so unobtrusively, that it isn't until the next day that I realize he has done a gram of the former and a fifth of the latter.

I never really think much about the quantity. He seems totally normal behind it. 'Course he hasn't said much; besides my perceptions are on hold in favor of his looks. I am listening to the thump, thump, thump of my little heart, and not the data data data in my left brain. It says: Jeremy is a major heavy-duty junkie.

Bit by bit in dribs and drabs Jeremy's story comes out, in that retentive way certain goyim have of giving out information. To them it is giving up information, something that it frightens them to do. Jeremy had been a special child, but when he hit high school, the school districts were gerrymandered to accommodate The Great Society. He ended up in a high school that was half blacks from Palo Alto and half rich white kids from the surrounding 'burbs. The black kids beat up the white kids or they sold them drugs. Jeremy took to smack and was an off-and-on junkie throughout high school. He married his high-school sweetheart and O.D.'d. Brought back to life by a family doctor, he split from everyone, thinking, I'll handle this myself. Maybe a change in scenery. He hadn't been on the road more than a month when he and I met.

'All my friends are dead or in jail,' is his résumé.

That seems pretty sexy to me, but I don't know anything, haven't been anywhere. Not really, even though I am thirty. With the Oscar sadly in place on the mantel. A woman alone with a year-old baby girl. Jeremy is twenty-three. No past no future no prospects. After a hot three-week affair he wants to split, but I am a powerhouse woman producer getting my way all over Hollywood. I don't want him to leave. I tell him it will be pretty hard to get anywhere with me and Kate hanging on to his ankles. He laughs.

'Ours is a great love,' he says, pseudosolemnly. He stays. Poor Jeremy.

My phone starts to ring at seven thirty with business from New York. *Taxi* is going, *Close Encounters* is a closed deal, and I am negotiating for *Fear of Flying*. I say, not meaning it, to impress Jeremy, 'I hate my life!' Jeremy is around the house more than I am, since I am always going into town to do business, so he and Kate develop a pretty close and mystical relationship.

I go to New York and while I am gone he and his best friend pull my house together. This broken-down, condemned

182

fire hazard of a house is as beautiful as it is ever going to get when I get home.

Jeremy tells me the story of his friend Randy*, who was making that one last huge dope deal – 'that big dope deal in the sky' – to get out of the business. Pursued in a high-speed chase by the Canadian Royal Mounties to the end of a pier, he stopped short and let them bust him with three million dollars' worth of cocaine in the trunk of his Porsche.

Danny is in solitary in a jail in Vancouver, and we decide it would be fun to visit him. I have never visited anyone in prison. This is all research as far as I am concerned. Jeremy and I fly to Vancouver, rent a car, and drive for two hours to an ugly government building called a prison. Jeremy's friend Randy is an exceptionally nice, handsome boy. He has been studying Krishnamurti and is planning to visit him in San Luis Obispo when he gets out, which is a few months away. We spend all afternoon with him. When we leave, he stands outside, on the other side of the barbed wire, his hands showing through, just like in the movies.

When he is released, he gets his impounded Porsche to head for the L.A. area, us, Krishnamurti. He is hit by a truck, which leaves the scene of the accident, and he suffers brain damage. I never see him again. All my friends are dead or in jail, Jeremy says, but he doesn't mention that some are both at the same time.

One morning the phone rings really early and it is Andrea. Her voice sounds small and vulnerable. 'I'm in the hospital in Century City. I fell off my horse and it stepped on my leg, and there's a clot . . .'

'Where are you? I'll come see you on the way in . . .' Outside of Jane Oliver, with whom I've lost touch, Andrea Eastman is the only woman in show business that I trust. She has hooked up with Paul Lazarus and it looks like they are going to get married, a relief to all her friends who really care about her. I race to get ready. The toilet overflows, and while I am plunging it I think, I have to get out of here, I have to leave the beach, I can't do this fucking commute anymore. I kiss Kate and Jeremy and Sonya goodbye and speed into town in the trusty Mazda.

Andrea is in tears when I arrive at the hospital. Her leg is in traction and there are a lot of IVs going to and from her arms. I think she's in pain, so I ask if she wants me to get her a nurse. I am one of those people who're good in hospitals. I have spent so much time in them. She sobs and shakes her head. She forces herself to calm down enough to talk.

'Paul and I are getting married . . .'

'That's wonderful. Why are you crying?'

'Because we're going to move to his place, so I rented my place . . .'

'Perfect. Why are you crying?'

'I rented my place to Leslie Ann Warren, and now she's decided she's too poor to afford it and she wants out of the deal . . .' Hollywood. Everybody is always reneging here. A subliminal cut of my overflowing toilet flies through my brain.

'How much?' I ask.

'Eight hundred a month and first, last, and security.' Andrea has a cute little house on Westwanda up in Benedict Canyon. Its only drawback is no pool. Nothing's perfect.

'I'll take it,' I say, fumbling in my purse for my checkbook.

'You're kidding . . .' Andrea stops crying and reaches for a tissue.

'My toilet overflowed this morning,' I explain. 'I can't stand that house anymore . . .'

The day we commence the move to Westwanda Jeremy beats the shit out of his face with the steering wheel of my car, crashing into the wall of a tunnel leading from Pacific Coast Highway to the Santa Monica freeway. It takes me awhile to realize he hasn't showed up and might be dead.

From there, it takes my assistant Pat Dodds the better part of a day to locate him at Santa Monica Receiving. A black nurse tries to keep me from him, but I threaten that I will vault right over her barrier. She lets me through. He is lying on a raised bed. When I look down at his beautiful face I am

184

deeply saddened by the damage. Bloodied, bruised, and swollen as he is, it is only his nose that is broken. Changes his perfect face forever, what a shame. I ask the resident why he hasn't done anything, and he is at a loss. I start to get feisty with the guy.

'Are you implying he's not getting good care here?' No care would be a good way to describe the situation . . .

'*Implying* would be too soft a word . . . *stating* might be more accurate.' This is not calculated to make this guy and me close personal friends. We continue to argue across Jeremy's body, and then I decide to settle it. I pull out my checkbook. I will beat you to death with my money, you prick!

The resident calls a plastic surgeon and I call Jeremy's parents. They say they will hop on the first available flight out of San Francisco.

Bad news travels fast. Jeremy's soon-to-be-ex-wife calls to see if he's okay. Was he loaded? she asks dryly, at which I, dumbo, take umbrage. I am pretty much into taking umbrage wherever I can find it. I move Jeremy into a suite on the top floor. The plastic surgeon arrives, takes more X-rays, does what he can for Jeremy's nose.

By the time Jeremy's parents arrive, he is situated in the only rock 'n' roll suite at Santa Monica Receiving, his nose set, Demerol coursing through the IV into his veins. He's probably happier than he's been in months. It occurs to me that a joint would be a nice thing to have, and that I haven't had any decent pot in a long time . . .

Jeremy is released in my custody from the hospital a couple of days later, and we return to the beach. Immediately he starts complaining about the pain, and by three that afternoon there are several attending doctors at my house. He wants more Demerol. They don't want to give it to him; one of them takes me aside and says the pain can't be as great as he describes. I retort snottily that he must indeed possess extraordinary extrasensory powers, because I would never hazard a guess about the pain someone else is feeling.

Sadly, it seems to me, he writes a prescription for a limited number of pills and cautions Jeremy to use them sparingly.

He looks at me while he tells him this. I am too infatuated with Jeremy to understand the meaning of his words . . .

'He's a man who doesn't understand the waltz of people.' Howard Rosenman is bad-mouthing his partner, Ron Bernstein, behind his back, but so eloquently that I just let it go. We are doing the last of the blow on the little seatback tray table. It's all that's left from the party that Nessa and I gave for Erica. We're winging to Gotham. Erica is in the seat behind us. She has on a greenish mumu with a blue bra underneath. The strap keeps showing. 'With the harlequin glasses, with the dyed-to-match shoes from Miles, I've never met a poetess from New York who doesn't look just like her.' Howard is saying this under his breath and over the roar of the plane at the same time.

I am still high from the party. Streams of names and seminames have come to pay homage. I have done a fair amount of blow with a handsome young thing, heir to a fast-food fortune, in the bathroom, and he has given me this little package for the road. I've driven myself and Erica to the plane, in the Mazda, at breakneck speed. I know enough to travel us first class but I haven't learned limos yet.

Nine days later, when I get home, I have swallowed hash on the plane, and I spend forty-five minutes searching for my little gray Mazda. I have forty-two dollars left to my name, which is exactly what the tab for parking comes to. (Years later, when I read the *Hitchhiker's Guide to the Galaxy* and discovered that the answer was forty-two but we had forgotten the question, I felt I had invented Douglas Adams.)

'This is giving me a very bad case of FFA,' Howard says. I lick the end of my finger and dab at the last few grains of coke on our little tray table, rub it under my tongue. Teensy little freeze. That sour taste. Makes your mouth go *eeeeouououou*. Suck on a slice of lemon. Harder.

'*Qu'est-que c'est* FFA?' I like talking to Howard. He is as smart as any friend I made in college.

'Darling, it's Howard Rosenman's five stages of mankind – you know, Jung has eight, I have five more modern. There's

FFA: free floating anxiety; MAA: massive anxiety attack; NB-ette: nervous breakdown-ette; NB: nervous breakdown; and D and Q: death and quiet . . .'

I crack up. Only a Jew could come up with such stages of man: not one moment's peace in Life. I agree. ('Course after having a child, I want to add PPD: postpartum depression, and that ol' standby PMS, no explanation needed.)

I do a fair amount of running around with Howard in New York. He takes me to a fancy party with a lot of uptown types. Good for my career, he tells me. Hey, what else is there? I talk to his friend, Barry Diller, for a long time. Barry Diller comes on very heavy: business as sex, sex as biz. When we leave I tell Howard I feel like I've been raped, and he harumphs. Not likely. But tell me, Howard, did I have a good time? I can't remember.

We go to the opening of *Equus* with Tony Perkins and his wife Berry Berenson. I think it is a crock of faggot shit. Me and Tony get into a pretty heavy argument about it over snacks at Sardi's after. When we say goodnight, and kiss air, he feels me up. High school high school high school. Six months later he takes over Anthony Hopkins's part in *Equus*. . .

In spite of his friends, Howard and I stay close, if only by rumor. Mostly I see him at Hollywood Parties. To the point where I wonder sometimes (à la *if a tree falls in the forest*) is it really a party if Howard's not there?

We move our belongings to the house on Westwanda incrementally. When Jeremy's nose is sufficiently repaired, we move our bodies there, too. The house is a low-ceilinged affair in the slummy part of Benedict Canyon, but it has its own cuteness. I set about decorating it in far more expensive good taste than it warrants, but I know that essentially this is a transitional stop before I figure out where to live. In the meantime, I practice spending my money.

My favorite acquisition, which stands improbably in the

187

center of the living room, is a beautiful antique Italian pool table. I've just bought it from Goldie Hawn, who is in the process of divesting herself of everything, mostly Bruno, her embarrassing Swedish boyfriend. I'm already full-up on embarrassing boyfriends but I take the pool table off her hands for a mere fifteen hundred dollars. It's a tad undersized, so it makes anyone who plays on it look like Fast Eddie Felson. It's a convenient toy for the boys, and since it's so small, I occasionally look like hot stuff on it, too.

Kate and Sonia and I look just right in this oversized dollhouse; Jeremy looks too large. He has to lower his head to get through doorways, and his cowboy boots and engineer boots and combat boots clomp clomp clomp distressingly on the hardwood floors. He is as glaringly out of place in this house as the pool table, but I am too busy to notice.

Concomitant to the busy-ness, I am developing a nasty pattern of lateness. I am always late. I am a naturally late person who is constantly overbooked. I am a naturally over-worked overbooked person because I am at a time in my life when it is just too fucking hard to look at my real personal situation. I take on more and more responsibility and more and more work. I am a hamster on a wheel. Going Noplace. I work hard to earn the money to buy the coke to work hard to earn the money to buy the coke.

I need to come down.

I need some pot.

I realize one day with a jolt, barreling along the Ventura freeway to the Burbank Studios, that Jeremy and I always have coke, but no pot. Since Michael and I split up, I have had barely any pot. I have a stab of the pain of missing Michael. It was always one of his chores, scoring pot.

I'm not really wonderful at chores, although since I was four I've always made my bed and taken out the garbage. Changed the roll of toilet paper if it was out. But now I have turned myself into a moviemaker savant. I know two things: how to produce movies that reach for the Heavens and how to do drugs that reach for the Underworld.

That's why the money fear is always with me, always there, under the surface of my ready quips and smiles and my meetings and my deals. I'm ashamed to admit even to myself that I miss Michael most viscerally when another *Sting* check arrives. He isn't there to take care of the money, which he understands so well, and I so imperfectly.

Maybe that's why I'm working so hard to make more money, I think as I pull off the freeway and wend to Hollywood Way. I'll just keep making miraculous movies, I tell myself as I pull into my space, and then Kate and I will never have to live in a welfare hotel.

On the other hand, I continue, climbing the stairs to the suite of offices, maybe a little pot would cool me out. Keep the underlying worry – nay panic – at bay. So I call Arnold Stieffel, whom I met at a Joni Evans dinner party in New York. He was the Star of Pee Are at Bantam and had been instrumental in pushing Jackie Susann over the top. Within a year he's out here starting up his own agency. A nervous proposition; naturally he knows more about pot and pot dealers than I do.

'Darling, of course I know who to call.' He laughs. 'I'll call you right back.'

Within minutes, Pat Dodds buzzes me to tell me a very rude person is on line one. Calling per Arnold Stieffel. She is amazed when i pick up. I speak to a sullen, mid-range Joisey street voice, one Jack Spratlin*. He is not a pleasure to talk to, so we arrange to meet at my house in Benedict Canyon at the end of the day with as much alacrity as possible. When I get off the phone, I feel sullied by the call and make a face for Pat indicating same.

When I arrive home, predictably late, Jack Spratlin is playing pool with Jeremy. Predictably. Jeremy is blasting, feinting, subtling his way through a rack, but Jack Spratlin, *sans* finesse, is winning. Bland blond curls and big baby blues notwithstanding, he has a hard face. Humpy body. He is abrupt. I try to engage him in conversation, but he is mainly business.

This interests me after a day of doing more business than he could even imagine. I snap into all business, too. For some reason, this charms him and makes him smile. Suddenly. Just once. It changes his whole face and personality. Bright intelligence sparkles from his eyes and teeth.

Pressing my advantage, I force a laugh out of him. It is the most insane laugh I've ever heard. It knows something I don't. It pisses me off. It makes my pussy wet.

He sits down and rolls a joint, which he lights for himself. Jeremy pours himself a drink. Sits down next to him on the couch. Jack passes Jeremy the joint. Male bonding. I throw some coke into the social mix, which everybody imbibes cheerfully. Jack is impressed, but he has to move on. Places to go. People to see. Money to make. I entertain us both with a brief negotiation, not something I care to do, but I know if I don't he'll think I'm a *wuss* and feel compelled to rip me off. Not his fault. It's a guy thing.

He lets me pay by check, and when he goes into his briefcase to store it, I glimpse a wad of high-end bills: hundreds, fifties, twenties. No tens or fives or ones. All that cash gets me excited for a moment. The fruits of selling the goods to get the bread to make the buy to sell the goods to get the bread to make the buy. Another hamster on a wheel. A kindred spirit. Who appreciates really good drugs.

I ask him casually if he ever gets decent blow. Sometimes, he says, give me your home number. I do. I'll call you, he says. I bet you will. He laughs his crazy laugh and splits.

Jeremy and I argue and fuck later on. In bed, after, I reassure him, He's a lowlife, a fucking dealer, it's business. Who do I think I am here, Don Corleone?

I decide Jeremy needs a job. Michael and I are executive producers on a picture going at Paramount called *The Big Bus*. They've thrown Howard Koch, Sr., on to watch over us. He's a wonderful guy, but his instincts are to flatten everything, be well liked. *The Big Bus*, which started out as an outrageously funny sendup of disaster movies, predating *Airplane* by five or six years, is grinding down into outrageous mediocrity. It will be Michael's and my second failure at comedy.

Robin French had sold the project to himself when he exited

IFA to become an executive at Paramount. Fred Freeman and Larry Cohen, who wrote the script and wanted to produce, with us tagging along as the successful ones, the executive producers, signing our names and keeping arm's length from the process, were incredibly nice guys. We made a terrible mistake going in and extended the studio's right of designation so that the deal could be closed and Fred and Larry could get paid. It would be the film's undoing.

By the time the script is finished, Barry Diller, flush with success as the architect of the *ABC Movie of the Week*, not to mention The Week of the Movie (i.e., *Roots*, etc.), has become the head of Paramount. We go through several disagreeable meetings with him, in which he uses phrases like 'high concept' and 'getting the asses in the seats.' He is never as cordial as he was when I met him at that New York party. In fact, he seems to take pleasure in making me particularly uncomfortable in these large, overstuffed get-togethers.

We come to loggerheads over the issue of a director for this opus. He has just signed a three-pic pact with a pale, possum-like creature named Ken Shapiro, who has a rude, semifunny alternative flick to his credit called *The Groove Tube*. One of the biggest jokes in the movie involves shit coming out of a water faucet. I think the script is sketchy enough without this guy's input. Freeman and Cohen detest him.

When we run the picture with Robin, he laughs out loud at jokes that I know he couldn't possibly find funny. We dutifully meet the guy, who is suspicious and retentive. Oh no, not *Steelyard Blues* again!!! In a moment of clarity I tell Robin that this guy could single-handedly create anti-Semitism if it didn't already exist.

We blow the guy off, but we are running out of time on this right-of-designation issue. The studio and we finally agree on Jim Frawley, whom I always think of as Jim Fraud-ly. His claim to fame is that he failed as an actor and succeeded as the director of most segments of *The Monkees*, an innovative, tricky hit television show of the sixties that provided the foundation for the house Bert Bob and Steve, otherwise known as BBS, built.

191

A great deal of money is spent on sets, and cast. We rush into production. It is clear from the first few days of dailies that this guy has almost no talent. Michael is in New York on *Taxi Driver*, so it falls to me to cover the set for a few weeks, a completely depressing task. At one point, Joe Bologna has the temerity to scream to Frawley, 'What's my motivation?' and I think but don't say, To be funny, motherfucker.

I ask Howard if, in exchange for my forty-minute drive every morning to Paramount, he would oblige me by putting Jeremy in the movie as one of the extras. The background passengers in the bus. Three weeks of work. Of course, he smiles understandingly. Now I can leave this movie that is a sendup of, and a disaster at the same time. Not to mention a boyfriend who I am figuring out falls into pretty much the same category.

Cut across the Cahuenga Pass back to Columbia and work on getting *Fear of Flying* closed, and *Close Encounters* into its next screenplay.

Close Encounters of the Third Kind.

I repeat the title several times. For Koch. For Diller. High concept enough? Will it get the asses in the seats? Even Don Simpson, whom I run into one day. I am delighted that he has finally landed a job. Working for Dick Sylbert, who has replaced Robin as head of production. Pretty soon Sylbert will be out and Katzenberg will be working for Simpson. Things are accelerating in Hollywood. If you can't be good be fast . . .

Victor has cut my hair glamorous and given me a perm. I stand in the steamy bathroom to make it frizz up.

'I think you have to make your brows thinner!' Sandy Harmon is shouting from the bedroom. We are in my suite at the Sherry. I have moved from 1409 to a Fifth-Avenue-but-low-floored suite. It is very blue-and-white Victorian, a great place for little girls to be bad. Erica and I are going to have dinner and Sandy has some free time in the afternoon, so we are hanging out, smoking a joint, talking about business and men, fucking with my new look.

As soon as Sandy leaves, I say to Erica 'Can we close our deal already?' We have been dicking around on being *closed* closed for a long time, and I have already gotten Columbia spending money. Christ, I even helped her with NAL when they wanted to do that shitty Mickey Spillane illustration for the paperback cover . . .

She hasn't answered my question so I look at her. She is thinking it over. It is remarkable how much she looks like Miss Piggy when her face is in repose. The very first thing I'd noticed when I met her was how v-e-e-r-r-r-y flattering her jacket photo had been. Long blond hair and an insouciant broad smile with big beautiful teeth.

Now that my hair has straightened anyway, I indulge in a quick blow-dry. Petty power play. Which she makes a big deal of in a later book, after she has fallen out of love with me.

Probably she never really loved me. She was too busy being in love with herself. It was something we had in common. In the beginning. It was starting to seem like a long time ago. What's the point, I think, feeling my curls deflate.

Erica is splitting from her husband and making a conscious effort to lose weight. I keep giving her diet tips, trying to be supportive; she keeps reminding me that I don't eat enough and I'm too thin. We visit my father before going on to dinner. The next day he says, 'I don't know, Julia, she made me very nervous . . .'

'How?' I want to know. My father has only expressed himself on people in my adult life twice before. Once about Michael, whom he thinks is self-absorbed, once about Tony, whom he thinks has 'no core, no center, no soul . . .'

'Well,' he says, choosing his words carefully, 'she strikes me as very dangerous . . .'

Shampoo is a couple of weeks away from being released and Nessa and I are discussing the possibility of Goldie Hawn playing Isadora Wing. I know that everyone is thinking Barbra Streisand. All I am thinking about that idea is: Over my dead body. I already know Goldie through Steven. *The Sugarland Express* did no business but has reestablished Goldie as a name that is okay to put on a B list of actresses when you are trying to cast a movie. I hate this kind of thinking, but it is a reality of the business. I like projects in which the script and the director are the stars, but it is more often the other way.

'She's a star; she's a star and a major actress.' Nessa sounds real definitive about this. I always listen to Nessa and Andrea on matters of acting. They have been in casting a long time, and they see things I don't. Kind of like going to an Antonioni movie with my friend, Francine, who is an artist. I am the hoi polloi – I'm into basics, like a great story and great characters. I will not like the picture better because it is pretty, but Francine will, so even though Antonioni bores the shit out of me, I will go to his movies with her because I like what she has to say about them afterward.

Goldie is pretty astonishing in *Shampoo*, particularly in her last scene where she makes Warren tell her everything. A thirty-eight-take enterprise, according to Goldie, grabbed after she'd been on hold for hours in the middle of the night. Warren needs a lot of time to work himself up; in the process he wears his costars down. According to Goldie. In her case it worked.

'So should we give her the book?'

'Why not . . . what could it hurt?'

'Well, remember Brenda . . .' Half the actresses I know have already gotten mad at me just because I have informed them in my excitement that I have gotten this book. Brenda Vaccaro is my neighbor on Benedict Canyon and I love her, but the prevailing wisdom is that her time to become a star has already passed. She has iced me haughtily twice at La Scala because I have told her honestly she doesn't have a chance.

I give Goldie the book. She and I have started to hang out from time to time. She is an okay broad. The best thing about her is The Laugh. The worst is that she is borderline dirty, with stringy hair – all the time. One Sunday, Jeremy and I go to the Polo Lounge on the spur of the moment to have some eggs benedict and we gossip indiscreetly about her dirty hair. At the end of lunch I notice that she is confabbing with Stan Kamen, her agent, at the next table. I worry about it all the way home.

'You think she heard?'

'We were outside – maybe the wind blew it in the other direction.' I smile. Jeremy does have his moments. Although they are getting to be fewer and further between. I don't know, or won't allow myself to know, that Jeremy has found heroin again. A lot of people know but don't tell. He disappears in my car for hours, he raids my stash of coke, he goes off on a nod with Kate in his arms and a cigarette burning down to his fingertips. Heroin is not a part of my lexicon. I am still a recreational user; it does not occur to me that the first explanation for Jeremy's strange behavior is addiction. Although Michael has told me somewhat cryptically that his shrink thinks that my being with Jeremy is really me acting out taking care of myself.

I have been accepted to the AFI Women Director's Workshop. I am planning to do the beginning of Reilly's script. I think I have Dreyfuss for the lead, but he develops pneumonia after doing some pickups on *Jaws* in Verna Fields's swimming pool. I cast Jeremy. What a laugh! The character is a compulsive gambler with a coke problem. Jeremy is smacked back. I fill out the cast with some pros. We shoot at my house. I use every trick I know to overcome Jeremy's low energy, but I know he is ruining the piece . . .

Jeremy tells me that he has to clear his head and that he's going up north. I get him to stay a few more days so he can go to a party Goldie is having that is giving me anxiety. He is unhappy about it, but he stays. I know he is looking weird, but smack just doesn't occur to me.

The party at Goldie's is mostly the *Shampoo* crowd: Hal Ashby, Lee Grant, Julie Christie, Jack Warden, Warren. I'm the only one in the room I wouldn't recognize on the front page of a newspaper. I hate the situation, grab a drink and sit with my arms crossed on an overstuffed floral-covered couch in the living room. The party is going on in the dining room. At some point Lee Grant comes over and says I should hear Warren's ideas about *Fear of Flying*.

Warren has already called wanting to know about Erica. I have said, 'Well, she's more Sue Mengers than her photograph on the jacket would indicate,' and give him her number. When I hang up the phone I feel mean and small and petty. Why would I want to hear Warren's ideas? Lee says he thinks it should be a porno movie.

'Yeah with see-through dildos and vibrators . . .' he elaborates when I ask him.

Lee says, 'Can you imagine the casting couch?' and I think, no different from any other . . .

Goldie overhears and we tell her Warren's ideas for *Fear of Flying*. She laughs her tinkly laugh, and in the background, Jack Warden, who jokes that he goes on and off the wagon according to his work schedule (just now he is not working) bursts into a soulful basso profundo: *Some enchanted evening* . . . Everyone laughs. I look around and don't see Jeremy. I start to search; I wander upstairs. He is coming out of the bathroom.

'You should go in there. There's some excellent coke.' He

heads down the stairs. Ah, the seventies. There's the party downstairs, and then there's . . .

THE PARTY IN THE BATHROOM

OVO: I am carrying no stash and would love a toot. But I hate the coke-whore implications. For about a second. Ah, fuck it. I head for the BATHROOM DOOR, reach for the doorknob and it ZOOMS away from me. Horror movie shot. I hate this fucking corny shot. Wait a second, just who's movie is this? I reach for the doorknob, grasp it firmly, and push it open.

The BATHROOM is capacious. Very white. Very Bel-Air. A clean, well-lighted place. In the corner sitting on the closed toilet, a very TAN, very handsome MANAGER (call him TAN MAN) snorts from a large stash. Also very white. His daughter, a MOVIE STAR, leans against the sink, watching him. Love and contempt contort her pretty features. She is twelve.

He offers me a toot. I feel weird about doing it in front of his kid. For about a second. The coke is excellent. I have nothing to talk to them about. I ask him if he's read *Taxi Driver*. I know Marty Scorsese loves Jodie Foster, and she's great, but I've slipped the script to this guy, because there's something about his daughter . . .

TAN MAN: (rather violently) I'm not gonna let her do the part!

ME: (shouting, a combination of conviction and coke. Just now the coke is doing most of the talking) This part's a career maker and the movie's gonna go through the roof!

MOVIE STAR: (clear, direct. A twelve-year-old adult) Tell me about the part.

OVO: I lean against the sink but keep my distance and tell the story of *Taxi Driver* and little Iris Steensma. The MOVIE STAR seems intrigued.

ME: Maybe you'll look at it again . . .

OVO: TAN MAN and the MOVIE STAR exchange a look and I say . . .

ME: Thanks for the coke.

ovo: And leave the party in the bathroom because three's a crowd . . .

When I get downstairs, Jeremy's sitting with his arms across his chest on the couch. He tells me with his eyes, which look weird, almost like a cat's, that we have to go soon. Okay by me. We are the first who leave. That night he reiterates that he has to get out of L.A. for awhile.

I still don't understand the profundity of this statement, so I negotiate one more weekend down here. My parents will be out then, and I have decided that, in lieu of real contact with them, I will throw them a huge party, see how many people they always wanted to meet I can scare up on short notice . . .

Pat Dodds and I throw ourselves into it for a hot three-day period. The enterprise is not dissimilar to producing a movie. She is wonderfully capable and a true friend. We get a hundred seventy-five yesses, a unique blend of the old and the new, the talent and the writers, the stars and the star agents. The night of the party Jeremy wears jeans and a peach-colored T-shirt. It accentuates the unearthly paleness of his skin and the peculiar set of his eyes. His pupils are so tiny that his eyes are more catlike than ever; his behavior is catlike, too. Skittish. I feel no support from him at all. Sometimes I think I keep him around just to make my life more challenging. Taxing, anyway. I look at him again; my little vampire . . . he seems less beautiful . . .

It is a good party I have jammed into Andrea's little house. Noisy, interactive, pretty . . . The food is adequate, but people aren't into eating. They're into getting loaded. I have told anyone who asked that pot is okay, alcohol is okay, nothing else.

Every time I turn around, I hear my father tell Lily Tomlin, 'Now do the cheerleader . . .' 'Now do Edith Ann . . .' My mother chats vivaciously with Dreyfuss. They are having a good time. Jeremy is nowhere. I don't care. I have this party to attend to.

I run out of ice, call Gil Turner's. When the delivery boy

arrives, I give him his tip in blow. He runs back and forth all night, replenishing my party's needs.

Ryan O'Neal pontificates loudly in the corner of the dining room, behind a desk, like anyone cares what an actor thinks about world events . . . that's okay, my parents can tell their friends in New York that they met him . . .

The party goes on till neighbors complain and police break it up. The only casualty is that Steven's wallet seems to have been stolen from the glove compartment of his car. How dumb to leave it there, I think but don't say.

Jeremy, overhearing the news, rushes out of the house and disappears in my car for fourteen hours, in search, he explains when he returns, of Steven's wallet. I flip out. More about the car than anything. In L.A., disappearing with someone's car is equivalent to rape. Jeremy says he should leave. I feel rejected but have no desire to fight him on it. To our mutual astonishment I agree. I get him on a plane that afternoon.

I go out with high-profile friends to high-profile places. Ma Maison for lunch, La Scala for dinner; La Scala for lunch, Ma Maison for dinner. I am addicted to the mussels marinara at La Scala, and I have made close personal friends with George, the maître d', so I get one of the six booths in front whenever I want. Every night. One night Dyan Cannon comes over. She makes me take off my underpants so they don't leave a line. It feels breezy. 'You'll get used to it,' she says. 'I have.' She and I hit La Scala full bore and end up laughing too loud and drinking too much with Guy McElwaine for hours.

Another dinner at La Scala: Me and my famous girlfriend dump the coke on a plate and toot it off the ends of our steak knives. Right out there in the front room. Very pretty. Bad blow and bad vibes, and a whole fucking box of tissues right there at the table. It puts the guy sitting next to me off his food. Oysters, I think.

I fill up my loneliness with activity. I am working hard and now I am playing hard. I hate myself for it, but no matter what I do, I miss Jeremy . . .

Goldie comes over one afternoon late to hang out. She has

been reading *Fear of Flying* and liking it. The phone rings and I pick it up:

'Hey, there, is this Julia?' a cheerful black man's voice says.

'Y-e-e-e-sss.'

'Well, this is Don, up in San Francisco, I'm with a friend of yours . . .'

'Y-e-e-s-s-s.'

'I'll get right to the point. I'm with an organization called Do It Now. We help addicts become ex-addicts . . .' I sit down and I must go pale because Goldie gives me a questioning look. I put my finger over my mouth. I feel sweat on my upper lip. Good old Don continues. 'Jeremy came in here pretty strung out wanting some help. We've been talking all afternoon and I thought it was time to bring you into the picture . . .'

'Strung out?' S.T.R.U.N.G.O.U.T.?!@#¿!

Goldie reaches out and squeezes my hand for a second.

'Jeremy came up here to kick, you know, but he wasn't having any success, so he came to us . . .' KICK?#@!

'I don't know anything about heroin . . . What do I do?' Poor little problem solver. It never occurs to me that there are some things I can't do for Jeremy.

'Well, *he*'s got to do it, but I think he's got a chance. The question is, *where* should he do it . . .? Do you want him back?' Every part of my being wants him back. I can't help myself. He's just so beautiful . . .

Don and I talk a little more. He explains that it would be best for Jeremy to stay in San Francisco and talk to him for a day or so, then he should come back. He tells me there are organizations, Do It Now, AA. Jeremy gets on the phone weak and sad and I tell him how much I love him. Finally, we hang up. I tell Goldie everything.

'But do you want him back? Honey . . .' We go out for a bite and talk some more. I can tell that Goldie is trying to ease me into the concept of not letting Jeremy come back. I keep telling her that love conquers all. We get back to the house on Westwanda late.

'You want me to stay over?' Wow, a real girlfriend. I am

grateful, but I'm exhausted and looking forward to sleeping alone in my own bed.

Couple of days later, Jeremy is back. He looks terrible. He is compelled to show me all the tracks and tell all the secrets. How he didn't want me to know so he had taken to shooting up under the insides of his eyelids, between his fingers, his toes . . .

We go away to Palm Springs for him to really kick. He tosses and turns and sweats in the bed. The weekend is horrible. He is going through physical suffering, but when we return, I tell him he's got to go to his meetings and get a grip because I am really busy. Silly little problem solver . . .

When I split up with Michael, Nessa was right there as an understanding friend, no doubt on the grounds that she could relate to the breaking up of a marriage. We stay pretty tight until the moment when Begelman asks if I will take Nessa on *Fear of Flying*. I am just going through the nastiness of how to stay in business with Michael on *Taxi Driver* and *Close Encounters* without ever running into each other. Heavy Partner Karma.

For some arbitrary reason, Michael decides that he should be on the line for *Taxi*, and I should do the same for *Close Encounters*. The one time I come on the set for *Taxi Driver*, he makes me feel bad about the special treatment I get (why not? we are all friends and no one has seen me, although I speak to the group often, since I'm the one watching dailies with Begelman and having to answer for things like insert shots on magazines shot at four different speeds). I walk off the set at two thirty in the morning in the East Village and cry all the way to 8th Street.

Maybe that is why I am not raped or killed. Maybe even bad guys take pity on a crying woman. By the time I get back to the Sherry there are several messages from Michael. Fuck him. Let him worry I'm a body in some East Village gutter. For the next hour the phone rings incessantly. Fuckyoufuck-you fuckyou.

I take a shower and calm down and by the time he finally

gets through, I don't care. I let him off the hook easy. Guilt dues. I let him off the hook easy on everything because I broke his heart and hurt his pride. Just as we were getting semifamous in Hollywood.

So when Begelman calls from somewhere in the South of France on vacation, I'm not feeling especially charitable about potential partners. I am having so much trouble keeping the present ones in order, the idea of taking on another puts me into an unreasonable state of mind.

'You could do me a big favor,' he says through the static. Great. Just what I need. Another favor to do.

'What, my liege?'

'Take Nessa as a producer on *Fear of Flying* . . .'

'I can't say yes or no on that . . .' Hey, buddy, you're the one who taught me that.

'Well, that's okay, think it over. But, Julia . . .'

'Y-e-e-e-sss . . .'

'You'd be doing me and Columbia an enormous favor . . .' So they want to move Nessa out of the executive ranks. Studio execs aren't racing through a revolving door circa '75. Only the most exalted fly out by Golden Parachutes. So I should be an accommodating good little girl and have her parked onto my project. I wonder if she would go for Associate Producer; maybe Co-Producer on a separate card? Not a chance. No separate card for the granddaughter of S. Hurok Presents!

It is clear from Begelman's suggestion that he thinks anyone can be a producer. Tony once told me that his mentor Leo McCarey told him: You've got to figure out what you want to succeed at out here, because whatever job you succeed at first is the job you keep. I have already begun to suspect that producing will prove deeply ungratifying for me. In Hollywood, the only guys who seem to get their creative ya-yas off are the directors. I want my ya-yas, too.

A radical concept begins to form in my mind . . .

Ever since freebase, the only thing that got her heart really pumping was the news. Or whatever they were telling you was the news. Which could just as easily be all the ads for alcohol and drug dependencies and bankruptcies that punctuated their headlines. The feeling of constant outrage about the state of the world kept her from being preoccupied with her own death. Why did the inevitability of the death of the planet cheer her up? Because she was right?

And now, here were all those ladies, all her former compatriots getting everyone's attention for a nanosecond on a Sunday in April. The fact that the Sunday came two days after the only birthday she had ever chosen to celebrate by staying in bed may have accounted for the moderately hostile feelings she felt welling up in her. There was Jane and Whoopi. She squinted, searching for Roz or Emily or Marilyn, but there was just a mass of mostly women in white reminding the Court that they had the right to abortion and felt like keeping it.

It seemed small to be so absorbed in these earthly concerns. Yeah, she didn't want her daughter to be constrained from any choices about her body, but she felt like there were forces of destruction loosed in the world that went so far beyond abortion, that even if she had still been a member of their group she probably wouldn't have gone. She got out of bed and thought about the Great Attractor, the immutable force in the universe she'd been reading about in *Scientific American*.

As much as the ladies irked her, the rest of the news pissed her off more. She had already gone through shock and surprise. She was still capable of being horrified, like when James Purdy killed the Asian babies in the schoolyard, but she expected to have that sort of thing reported as a daily event.

Lots of Travis Bickles out there. And it wasn't even from the war.

The war, to her, was the Vietnam War. How had we managed to create an entire generation of men suffering from survivor's stress syndrome with no unjust war going on? Boy, only in America. And it was probably the best place on earth to live. If you gave the matter much thought at all, you began to wonder what was so terrible about the death of the human race . . .

So much of the news seemed to be the result of male characteristics. Or deficiencies. Or their fear of deficiency. Christ, she was really beginning to hate men in her middle age. Not that men were the only bad ones. Women were greedy and bellicose now, too. Little imitation men. Looking around the restaurants these days, at all those pear-shaped broads in the same suit, she was sorry she had blazed a trail.

She got so depressed about the whole situation, she went to visit Mara, who had just had oral surgery.

'I think I'm a victim of media hype.' Mara smiled. 'You know, lyin' in bed all the time with this fucking mouth . . .' She pulled her lips to reveal gross packing and stitching and swelling. Wounds. Yech. I'm alive and suffering, save me. 'I've been locked into CNN and I'm starting to worry about a plane falling out of the sky and killing me, or a gang war happening outside my door and a stray bullet hitting me . . .'

'Can you imagine growing up knowing all this shit?' I was a middle-aged two-year-old, she thought. What did that make Kate? 'It's over; don't people get that it's over . . .'

'Yeah, but I think specific . . . you think global . . .'

'. . . Cosmic . . .' The more news she saw the more it fed into the cosmic avoidance she was enduring . . .

'Whatever . . .' Mara smiled again and waved the cosmos away with a beautifully manicured hand. She had her nails wrapped and painted every other week. Let's get down to specifics.

'You'll die of cancer, like everyone . . . you'll die of toxins you know are in the air we breathe the food we eat . . . let's have a joint . . .' And they felt better even though it was true.

David Begelman has a coromandel or a fake coromandel dining-room table in the private dining room off his huge office at Columbia. It is various tones of a muted turquoise, orange, and buff. It isn't as ugly as it sounds. If you have serious shit to discuss with him, and if he likes you, he invites you to come here for lunch. If it is really serious shit, he makes you come to his overheated office. If it is serious but celebratory, sometimes he takes you to a restaurant. I have done all three venues and really prefer this, particularly if I have a lot to talk to him about.

Erica has written a terrible screenplay and a book more timely than important, but I have an obsession with getting *Fear of Flying* made. Why not? I've been right about it all down the line. That it would be a paperback hit, that it would become part of the lexicon of the day, that every major female star would be interested in playing Isadora Wing.

Things are getting heavy with Columbia. *Taxi Driver*, *Close Encounters*, and *Fear of Flying*, all separate deals, are with him. On *Fear of Flying*, he holds up the negotiation a long time trying to cross-collatoralize all three retroactively. I keep saying no, and the constant delays incurred by my nos are getting Erica Jong seriously pissed off. He has put me in deep shit with her with his renegotiation, but I don't care. She is a cunt and he is my liege.

Begelman has cost me her friendship and he has just recently cost me Hal Ashby (who was nixed by Begelman not six weeks before the release of *Shampoo*, brilliantly realized and incredibly successful). Ashby, discouraged by Columbia's dicking around, went off to do *Bound for Glory*. which he'd been prepared to give up for *Fear of Flying*. I am already delivering Begelman two great pictures. I think he should deliver something to me besides my memos with his comments written on them, papers in high school with disappointing grades. Actually, these memos provide me with some good laughs, big exes next to Ashby and Schlesinger.

I play with the turquoise-and-gold inlay in the dining-room table, and think about what I wanna be. When I grow up. In five minutes. Before lunch, if possible. Why the fuck not? Two places are set, but no food has been delivered. I know I won't eat; I have a lot of talking to do. I am nervous and thirsty. Beautiful Connie brings me a Tab, and I trace the pattern with my fingertips over and over so that I can space on them – self-induced drug flashbacks. They put me in an alpha state. They make me clear and charismatic. By the time Begelman makes his entrance I am in my selling groove.

We hug, we kiss air, we make little aren't-you-wonderful noises. I bring him up to date on all the developments on *Close Encounters*. Steven and I are still heavily into testing and rewriting, but *Jaws* has opened, first-carriage talent and department heads are signing on. The picture is beginning to move forward of its own weight. Sort of. Well, actually, every other week for a couple hours in the morning, it moves forward of its own weight.

I have Columbia spending constantly. On tests, on more assistants, on one under-the-table rewrite after another. The Beges has agreed not to read Schrader's first draft, called *Kingdom Come*, because I told him it would make him not want to make the movie. Certainly it was not a screenplay that Steven wanted to direct, although it very much created the Roy Neary character, a man obsessed by something way beyond his intellectual but within his visceral comprehension.

David and I chat about this and that, and he plays absent-mindedly with his roll. Even though we are sitting down for lunch, I never like to waste his time or lose his attention, so I bring up what is on my mind right away.

'I want to talk to you about an idea whose time has come.' I smile. He smiles back, receptive. 'I think you should let me direct *Fear of Flying*. I'll develop the script after *Close Encounters* and I won't think about shooting it until the picture is in answer print. It's the era of the woman. I'm doing this thing for the women director's workshop at AFI. Ashby's gone . . .' Begelman chomps at his roll intensely. He reaches for another.

'Have we exhausted all possibilities?'

'I brought the lists . . .'

'What about Paul Mazursky?' He finishes his roll and takes another. I guess this concept whose time has come is making him nervous. I put my roll, untouched, back in the roll basket, just in case he feels compelled to reach for another one.

'Should we have Connie order more rolls?'

'Good idea,' he says and crinkles his eyes at me. That was a joke, David. He buzzes her and tells her to order more rolls. 'Want anything?' I shake my head no. A cup of gruel. With a martini straight up. And a Quaalude. Thank you. When he finishes, I start to read from the usual list of suspects.

'What about Sydney Pollack?'

'What about Sydney Lumet? He's such a sloppy film maker,' I say, negotiating with myself.

'Yeah, and after his tenth *bubaleh*, he'll turn us down anyway.'

'There's always Sidney Furie. One of the great one-film guys.' *The Ipcress File* is one of my favorite movies, but Furie has been directing some real shit these days. 'David, I think we should take a stand here. There will be no Sidneys directing this movie!' I smack the table with my fist lightly, an emphatic joke. He laughs and smacks the table, too, a bit harder. Crumbs fly everywhere.

'Agreed!' Silence. 'What about Paul Mazursky?'

'Well, I liked *Bob & Carol & Ted & Alice* . . .' Elliott Gould brushing his teeth hysterically while Dyan Cannon, Natalie Wood, and Robert Culp waited in bed together for their orgy-to-be was a truly classic moment. I even liked the next one, the Fellini ripoff.

We discuss some other names and one or the other of us vetoes them. Begelman keeps What-*about*-Paul-Mazurskying me, and I keep What-about-Paul-Mazurskying back.

Connie knocks on the door and arrives with another plate

of rolls. Begelman reaches for one immediately. This is really pretty extreme. Can one O.D. on carbs?

Jane Fonda asks me to be a dance hostess for some event she is throwing to raise money for Tom Hayden. I have already contributed for the fun of it. Once there was a gathering at her father's and Shirley's manse up on Chalon Road in Bel-Air. It was a curious assemblage, given Tom Hayden's politics: James Garner and Tony Curtis were there, but then, so was I and so was Hal Ashby. Sitting on the couch next to each other. After Garner got finished running Tom around the room, I gave a grand along with Hal, who twinkled, 'I love trouble, don't you?'

So probably Jane thinks I will be only too happy to sell dances with myself for her new husband. Nobody in Hollywood has really absorbed that I am basically a very shy person. I can stand up for my convictions. I can make loud noises on behalf of a piece of material, a brilliant director, but these social gatherings that Hollywood people invent for themselves, usually to raise money for the cause of the week, bring out all my shyness. Maybe snobbery, too, because it's pretty funny, all this posturing, from a bunch of people who are predominately street hustlers, most of whom haven't gone to college, let alone graduated from high school. They read moving their lips and they have horrible table manners.

Jeremy and I get all dressed up for this do. Do a couple of lines, and just as we are about to go out the door, I turn to him and say, frightened, 'I can't do this . . .' He starts to untie his bow tie. I call the event and leave a message for Jane that I am sick and can't make it and I hope she'll understand, and then I take off all the clothes and makeup. We smoke a joint.

'Let's go to Imperial Gardens and have sushi and saki,' Jeremy says, and I concur. We are sitting at the bar, alone, working on our first saki, when Dick Sylbert and Susannah Moore come in all duded up. They take the seats farthest away, but we acknowledge each other. Dick is one half of a set of twins; twin production designers. They look exactly alike, but Paul, his brother, is the nicer one. Dick the more talented. Exact as they are, it is easy to tell the difference because Paul's mouth is always turned up in a smile, Dick's down, sulking.

'So are you coming from Jane's event?' I ask.

'We were there for about fifteen minutes,' Dick says sullenly.

'So, how was it?' I am rooting for crowded and hot. A smashing success, with or without me.

'Hot . . . crowded . . . everybody there looked like they were getting a migraine . . .'

That pretty much covered the Gubers' parties, too.

Peter Guber, Columbia's head of production, is somebody I already know and dislike from the salad days in New York. Pre-show business for us both. That far back.

'Try to get along with him,' Begelman said, after another stormy lunch during which Peter ran off at the mouth about *Taxi Driver* being a picture about loneliness, duh. He hadn't eaten anything but half a grapefruit and he talked too fast.

'Heavy amphetamine implications, there,' I kid the Beges and gesture toward Peter's deserted lunch. Begelman crinkles his eyes at me. We both know Peter's drug of choice is ambition. In my book it's the same thing.

'Make friends, he loves *Taxi Driver*, he loves you . . .'

'What do you want me to do, my liege.' I pound my chest, a Viking in a fifties movie.

'Have lunch, talk about the production, make friends . . .' don't tear paper . . .

I keep wondering how Peter has gotten to be in charge of this project when it was my friend, Roz Heller, who wheedled the go-ahead out of Begelman. She calls late, seven maybe. I think we are probably the only two people left on this quiescent lot.

'He still hates the script,' she says, 'but with that talent, he'll do it at a price . . .'

'As in, under a million?' She laughs. 'So tell him $999,999.'

She does and gets the nod. Even though the price goes up, when it's all over, it comes in at only two mil . . .

I go back to my office and call Peter. We make a lunch date for the following week. We go to Musso and Franks, and during lunch he turns the topic to sex.

'You know,' he says, 'if you put Chloraseptic on your cock you can stay hard all night . . .' Nice production meeting we're having here. The last thing I ever want to see is Peter Guber's penis, erect or not, but I say: 'Oh really, all my friends use coke . . .' and order a martini, because this make-friends-with-Peter assignment is going to be tougher on me than I thought.

That afternoon *People* magazine is hanging around, taking pictures of me and Steven. They want one with a studio executive, so I summon my new best friend, Peter Guber. He is there in a flash; we take pictures; everyone but Steven leaves.

'Boy, he came flying over in a hurry,' Steven says.

'I had lunch with him today . . .'

'He acted like a little puppy with you . . .'

'David says I have to be friends with him . . .'

'Doesn't look like that'll be too hard . . .' Well, that all depends on his use of mouthwash, I want to say, but don't. Then Steven says offhandedly, 'Julia, are you going to direct *Fear of Flying*?' Uh-oh . . .

'Well, the Beges hasn't made a decision, and I wouldn't think about it till after *Close Encounters* . . .'

'Why didn't you tell me?'

'As far as I know, it's not official yet . . . what would have been the point?' Because we tell each other everything . . .

Producing *Close Encounters* is beginning to get to me. I have met a couple of 'line' producers, exalted production managers with production manager mentality. Aggressively noncreative money-watching types who are afraid to talk to the director. This is still an era where the producing job isn't so subdivided.

Michael has made it clear he ain't doin' it; he's planning to go around the world in search of the soul he doesn't have. Originally Verna Fields, who edited *Jaws*, was going to be associate producer, but then Steven started to resent all the credit she was giving herself for its success and asked me to kill her off.

Which, to be honest, was fine with me, because I hadn't liked her from the start. She was my mother: angry, bitter, middle-aged, frustrated. Mad at all the kids having their big shots. Being the Big Shots. Once she and I were invited to speak to a convention of Eastman Kodak types in Rochester, New York. I had just done one of those silly commercials for them that appeared in all the *Film Digest* magazines. I had mentioned her in the body of the copy and Steven had cut her out and said, Come up with another woman. I had put Marcia Lucas's name instead.

Verna got a little booze in her and regaled me with stories of Marcia's and George's ineptitude and how she had saved *American Graffiti*. When she did her talk at Rochester she used a piece of film from *Jaws* and kept snapping her fingers to indicate when the next cut should come. She was never really on the beat. I kept thinking of a line of Pearl Bailey's to Skitch Henderson on the old 'Tonight Show,' the one that Jack Paar used to cry on all the time: Honey, Pearl had drawled, how do you keep getting *between* the beat?

So I knocked off Verna, who was never really on, and had a meeting with Bill Sackheim and Tommy Shaw. Sackheim seemed like a Nixon Plumber. A spy, he would be working for the studio, not us. Shaw was a tall, white-haired, red-nosed Irishman who wouldn't get along with me. Michael and Steven said, in essence, You can do it. I was scared, but I figured, okay, I can do it. As it turned out, I was doing it magnificently well. But I was still scared.

'Maybe you'll be executive producer on *Fear of Flying* . . . tell the Beges you'll take it over if I fuck it up . . .' Steven nods, yes, maybe, as long as I understand *Close Encounters* comes first. My life on hold, my dreams on hold . . .

'All great movies are the product of one person's obsession,' he keeps telling me. My obsession, his film. Not a very good deal. But I'm not into deals. I am into one step in front of the other, up the ladder, don't get stuck, stuck here on the ladder of my life . . .

Part of the make-friends-with-Peter assignment means going to a large party he is throwing. Jeremy and I manifest our disdain for the event by showing up in jeans. It is filled with everybody who is anybody of the time. We settle into seats on the floor under a piece of Colombian art. I notice Richard Pryor at the other end of the room and want to talk to him but I am too shy. The only people who do talk to him are the help . . .

Robert Wagner comes over to talk. He bends down to light our cigarettes and when he stands up he hits his head on the bracket holding the art. I giggle. Embarrassed, I get up to make the rounds. Maybe if I leave him alone, Jeremy will go talk to Richard Pryor.

The Gubers' house is decorated from the sets of Columbia pictures. I walk through a white wicker room and a hand touches me on the shoulder. It is Izzy MacPherson*, Grady's friend. We go out into a neon and black-lighted hall and talk for a long time . . .

I am summoned to another roll-filled lunch. I remind myself of something Larry Gordon has said: 'Directing ain't that tough a gig.'

All the Pauls have passed and when Begelman sees which way the wind is blowing, he doesn't bother with the Sydneys. He views my AFI tape and is not blown away, but Jeremy's performance is so comatose he forgives me. Biting down hard on an appropriately bullet-shaped number, he commits to the idea whose time has come. He says, 'You can do it . . . you're a learning machine . . .' All it takes is a little confidence. His.

Goldie commits, although Stan Kamen is having a hard time getting Columbia to close a deal for three hundred thousand

and a few points. I know they are sandbagging me because I have tenaciously resisted every approach Begelman has made to having our three projects at Columbia cross-collateralized. He made his bed, he should lie in it. This for a man who clearly never sleeps.

A pre-pre-production meeting with Doug Trumball about *Close Encounters* goes until at least seven P.M. We chat alone in the offices. He informs me that the effects we want will probably come to three mil. I know if I tell Columbia that now, they will wrap us up and tell us to go away.

'What's the lowest we could make it come in at?' Doug hems and haws, his spoiled fat lips working silently, adding phony figures up to a fake total.

'Probably a hair under a mil . . .'

'Do it.'

'I won't be able to do it for that, you understand.' Duh.

'I'll get you what you need as we go along. Put together a presentable start-up budget . . .' He smiles. He has a truly handsome face when he smiles. One could almost forget the lumpy body, shameful on such a handsome man. His bright blues dance and twinkle.

'Whatever you say, J.P.' This Jay Pee business is beginning to take hold. I know it is a sign of respect so I let people do it. Personally, I prefer Jools, but I haven't been called that since I lived in Brooklyn. I start to pack up my things. Just as we say goodnight, the phone rings sharply. I wonder for a moment if I should pick it up, it is so late. But I am the mother of a child now; I never let a phone just ring and ring anymore. I don't wanna attract any bad karma by worrying *what if*; so I grab it.

'Julia, it's Andrea.' Something's wrong. Andrea's always high-strung, but she sounds unwound. She doesn't pause for pleasantries. 'Look, Jeremy is banging the door outside my house. Robert is there alone and he's terrified he's going to break in. Julia, he says he's acting really weird . . .' Andrea and Paul Lazarus have married and set up a nice life for themselves on Sunset Plaza Drive. Robert is Paul's twelve-year-old son, a

213

handsome kid with a sweet soul. My heart swoops down to my knees, picking up my stomach along the way. 'I'm stuck here at the office and Paul's out of town – ' She's almost crying.

'I'll drive over there right away!' I blurt decisively. I grab my things, call Sonia at Andrea's other house, the one on Westwanda, where I live with my perfect little daughter and her perfect little nanny and this large imperfect beast named Jeremy. Sonia clucks reprovingly; she is an upwardly mobile Hispanic woman who eschews the company of heroin users. She wishes I would get rid of Jeremy. I know this from the silent volumes she speaks with her limpid brown eyes whenever he's around. Which is less and less, come to think of it, preoccupied as he is with his secret drug life.

I power over to Andrea's. Jeremy is on the porch sobbing. I see Robert's frightened face peep around a partially drawn shade inside the house. I signal him I'm taking control, and he lets the shade fall. When I touch Jeremy's shoulder lightly, he bolts upright, hand aloft. Ready to strike. He looks crazed, and for a moment I fear he doesn't recognize me. When he does, he exhales deeply. 'I thought I was being followed by cops,' he says tonelessly, sags, a wilted flower, then pulls himself up, compliments of my outstretched hand. I look deep into his eyes. They say: I am alive and suffering, save me. Ah the weapons of the weak . . .

QUICK CUT:

ovo: MOM, the naked maja on the couch, almost completely invisible behind her cigarette smoke. Only the too-long ash at the end of her butt is clear. It falls to the carpet.

MOM: Sometimes I think we're all dead living in hell, living in hell, living in hell . . .

We drive home in silence, save for Jeremy's crying. When we get home, Sonia and I help him into my bed as if he is an invalid. Kate wants to comfort him, but when she sees him crying, she starts to cry, too, and races from the room. I distract her and myself with tales from *The Cat in the Hat* and

Curious George. Finally, she agrees to bedtime. Sonia turns in shortly after.

I check on Jeremy. He seems to be sleeping. I go to the kitchen, always a comforting room, grab a Tab from the refrigerator and stand over the kitchen sink. I think for a moment, I might cry, à la Mom. I consider my options instead. All of them come up: Get Jeremy out of your house and into a hospital. Second choice: Have his parents take over.

I realize that as usual I have put the cart before the horse and invert my plan.

Before I put myself completely on the hook, I call his father in San Francisco. I run down the situation.

'Throw 'im out,' his father growls. Scumbag goyim, I think. I have no appreciation for how tired they all must be of Jeremy's addiction.

'Look, I don't know how you'll feel if he turns up dead in some scummy hotel room three days from now, but I know how I'll feel . . .' Terrible, guilty, relieved. Silence. 'Look,' I continue, selling hard, 'I have no choice. I don't care if it costs me a fortune. I'm gonna put him in Thalians . . .'

'Just a minute,' his father says, softer now, and covers the receiver for hushed confabs with his beautiful wife, Jeremy's beautiful mother. Maybe if she hadn't been so beautiful . . . He comes back on the line.

'Look, don't do anything, yet. We'll drive down tomorrow.'

I cry tears of relief: thankyouthankyouthankyou. Jeremy is way beyond anything even I – Superjulia – can handle, e.g., Howard Rosenman's fourth stage of man: N.B. Nervous breakdown.

I toss and turn on the tiny wicker sofa in my living room, a speck of sand under the fingernail of a larger being . . .

The following morning I have to rush to a breakfast at the Polo Lounge with Bob Towne to continue this endless discussion we are having about him rewriting *Fear of Flying*. When I leave the house, I tell Jeremy that he should call me there if he is freaked or frightened. He seems pretty shaky. I tell Bob Towne I'm afraid Jeremy will kill himself.

'You know, I had a girlfriend who was always threatening suicide . . .'

'Did she ever attempt it?'

'So many times, I lost count . . .'

'What did you do?'

'Well, in the beginning I used to drop everything and race over to her house to save her . . .'

'Yeah . . .'

'And then one night, I just said, Fuck it, bitch, do it if you want to, I ain't comin' over . . .'

'And . . .'

'Nothing happened . . . she didn't kill herself . . .'

Just then they bring the phone over to my table. It's Jeremy, panicky. I calm him down and tell him I will come home after this meeting. He wants to know when that will be. I get a hard tone in my voice and say, 'When it's over,' and hang up.

'Get out of it,' Towne says, but I don't listen. After our meeting is over, I go home and try to comfort Jeremy. I decide I need some professional help. I call my doctor Al Sellers, and he says I should consult with a colleague of his, one Dr. David Thiele. Stay put, he says, I'll find him. Within minutes Thiele calls. He's doing his rounds at Thalians, the psych ward at Cedars. Could I meet him in the visitors' lounge in fifteen minutes? I could.

Getting into Thalians is not so easy. I have to be buzzed through one set of heavy metal doors after another. They click heavily, ominously, behind me. I am directed to a vacant seat in the visitors' lounge by a professionally cold nurse and instructed to wait for the doctor. I 180 the room. Listless patients allow family members to barrage them with small talk. Some of them loll their heads to one side. This is not my movie, but I wouldn't mind knowing what drugs they're on.

I puff one cigarette after another and I have a screaming headache, but my neuroseptors are in high gear. Talk to me, doc, throw those good medical terms at me, I can understand anything.

'This is a hard case, you know,' Thiele says and sits down on an ottoman facing me. He is a scruffy professorial type, dressed in tweed. He sports bottle glasses that enlarge his rheumy blue eyes into great globes. I look deep into those globes and find no answers.

'This your specialty?'

'Yeah,' he admits tiredly. This line of medicine must be about as rewarding as oncology. 'When I was a resident, a bad thing happened to me.' He smiles. 'I treated an alcoholic and a drug addict, and they both got cured . . .'

'Why is that bad?'

'Well. I was one hundred percent successful . . . that's not an accurate description of the success rate in these cases . . .' He takes a deep breath. 'The fact of the matter is that of all junkies and alcoholics, only about four percent ever seek help, of those four percent who seek help, maybe one in a hundred actually gets cured and stays cured . . .' I gasp. These are very daunting odds, even for Superjulia, problem-solver savant.

'I don't think he's very motivated to get cured . . .'

'Well, at this point he's sick, he's tired, he probably would just as soon die . . .'

'I'm glad his parents are coming down . . .'

'They're probably part of the problem . . .'

'I can't worry about that . . .' I feel as if Goldie is talking for me. Goldie, with the cute face and cute ass and cute laugh and the heart made of stone. I wanna be Goldie when I grow up.

'Listen, go home, get some rest, here's my number . . . Call me when his parents arrive and we'll take it from there . . .' You mean, they'll take it from there.

I go home and hang out with little Kate. I feel better. Goldie calls to see how I am doing. Not so hot, I tell her and she makes clucking understanding noises, then: 'You've gotta let this go, Julia . . .' Tell me about it.

Goldie has a cold, hard streak to her that I really admire. Funny, that's what people think about me; I am constantly telling them that I am a sabra, tough on the outside, marshmallow within. They laugh, isn't she funny? Now, your brother, he thinks you're the artist and he's the businessman, but we know it's the other way around, don't we . . .

Jeremy's parents come and consult with the doctor. They decide, against his advice, to take him to a summer cabin they have in Oregon. Thiele tells me it is not a hopeful situation and I'm best out of it. I know that by now. Jeremy cries when they take off in his parents' car. I tell him I will come and visit as soon as I can. We both know I am lying. He presses his face against the rear window of the car, like a child new to automobile travel.

And then they turn the corner.

And they are gone.

And I am FREEEEEE . . .

To cap the entire situation, Erica launches a lawsuit. She has already asked a number of attorneys in the entertainment business to intercede. Begelman has hung tough with me. We both know I am creative and organized and ambitious enough to pull directing off.

Begelman doesn't like to be crossed. Neither does Erica. She finally finds a schlemiel in the Valley willing to take her case. Norman says, Thank God she's ended up with this guy. I have heard it bruited about that Noel Marshall, whose name is on *The Exorcist* and who looks uncannily like sixteenth-century renditions of the devil, is financing the suit.

I feel the way I did when my jewelry disappeared from the beach. I feel assaulted and misunderstood by somebody whose best interests I carried as close in my heart as I could to my own. Erica has gone through any number of representatives and friends of the project. I think it's too personal, and she never should have sold it. It insults me that she would prefer someone who looks like the devil, whose credits, if he deserves them, aren't as good as mine.

I run into Lederer on the lot one day. I love running into him. He is real. He is sane. He is smart and much older than I. We catch up. He is one of the most supportive men I know. He *kvells* for my success. I tell him about the lawsuit last. I feel it is a mark of shame. He is dismissive: 'With success comes litigation,' he says easily, with a smile.

'Oh, so you wear your lawsuits like a badge?' I say, feisty, and he laughs. Dick Lederer always makes me feel better. Too bad there aren't more of him around . . .

*

I pace back and forth in my suite at the Sherry Netherland. It is summer, 1975. Kate, now three, is out on Long Island with Grandma and Grandpa. Michael is out on the Island, probably Amagansett, with Sandy Harmon. She has become his girlfriend and we have stopped talking. I feel it is expected of me. I miss Sandy more than Michael, but Michael and I have been separated a bit longer. Goldie has called from the airport to say she scored tickets to the Rolling Stones Cocksucker tour that night. Backstage at Madison Square Garden, the whole trip. I order a limo for us from Dav-El.

Michael and Sandy are dropping Kate at the hotel with Jackie, Kate's young English nanny. The Foxy Nanny, we call her. We have arranged the times so that we will not run into each other. I don't want to deal with them, or the confused look Kate gets across her baby brow when she's passed from one clan to the other.

Steven and I are doing some research for *Close Encounters*. We meet with a guy from Con Ed who cues us into how a blackout is dealt with. We create an entire scene shutting the system down, which is ultimately cut from the movie. Unnecessary information. Steven and I are both very taken with the guy who meets us. He is a charismatic Peter Boyle. Or Gene Hackman.

Basically, though, I am here with David Begelman's money babysitting Steven while *Jaws* opens in New York. I have worked long and hard keeping Steven's interest in the project. Today he has gone around the City in a cab with Albert Brooks taking home movies of the lines of people waiting to get in to the theaters. The boyish joy and pleasure he expresses make me, a natural cynic, feel more hopeful. He is so blatant in his excitement for himself that he is adorable. I do not notice for at least a year that this kind of behavior bespeaks a childish self-preoccupation that tends to remove all hope. In the end. Because cynics are hopeless romantics, and they get more disappointed.

Goldie's plane is late, and she arrives dirty and rumpled with only a half hour to go. Goldie favors a dirty, rumpled look, so she elects not to change or wash up or even brush her teeth. E-e-e-u-u-u. Steven and Albert come back to the hotel and Albert makes us all laugh. He walks around the room and picks things up and says funny lines and then moves on. Object humor. Albert is screamingly funny. Q: Why don't I like him? A: I'm tired of screaming. *Dying is easy; comedy is hard*. Comedians even harder.

Goldie is in jeans and a shirt and a flak jacket. Her hair falls in greasy tendrils out of a makeshift ponytail. She looks just right to go to this concert. I don't have concert clothes. So I am wearing a pair of black cotton pants and a black T-shirt with BILLY COBHAM written in yellow. I am carrying a white shirt, in case I need to cover up my body because I get cold. I am always getting cold. My regular temperature is usually below ninety-eight and the coke and the tobacco keep me even colder. I cover up if it goes below seventy-two. Besides, I am verging on Fat Julia and I probably won't want the reveal of the T-shirt and pants on their own.

The car arrives and we say goodbye to the guys who are going out on an evening sojourn that will have nothing to do with the Rolling Stones. Just as I am about to step into the car, Michael and Sandy and baby Kate arrive. They have a similarly stricken look on their faces, as if they have been caught doing something wrong. I am so distressed that I take too large a step into the car and rip my pants all the way up the seam in the ass. We have no time to spare, so this is how I get to go to meet the Rolling Stones. I keep thinking of a poem from the Beat Generation that begins: Little Johnny Nolan has a hole up his ass. Goldie assures me that I look just fine with the shirt over, but I know I look like a middle-class girl trying to be cool.

We are ushered through hordes of fans and escorted by a hostile security guard through the underground workings of Madison Square Garden. Everything is concrete. Even the dressing rooms. Very depressing. We are shown into a particular room. On a high chair there is a small person with a lot of hair. From behind, it is impossible to tell if it is a boy or a girl. It turns its head and it is Mick Jagger in full makeup. Very depressing. He jumps off his chair to greet us. He has a huge head and a little body. A photographer has told me long ago that this is a characteristic of big stars: they have big heads and little bodies. I ask if anybody has a needle and thread and they laugh. Very depressing.

Bianca floats around in the background. She is wearing a sailor suit and cap. Her eyes are dead. There is a smelly Israeli named Freddie who seems to be very important to everybody. He carries two medium-sized bottles filled with rock cocaine. He offers some to Goldie and some to me. Fuck you, Mr. Under-Assistant West Coast Promo Man. We turn him down; I've got my own. I always carry my own stash. It is usually better than whatever anyone else has got. It also establishes the rules. This is not a coke whore, it says. Like these guys really could give a shit. A big, tall conga drummer named Ollie makes a remark about my T-shirt. I ask him if he has a needle and thread. He laughs softly.

Keith Richards breezes in past us. He has body makeup all over and black leather pants and a jacket open to his waist. His skin and teeth are awful, but he has far more charisma down here in this little cement basement room than Mick Jagger has. He glides in about two inches off the floor. His eyes are pinned. Smacked back. He and Jagger laugh at a secret joke and go off somewhere.

'Pregame blow jobs,' I say to Goldie under my breath and she giggles. The best thing about running with Goldie is The Giggle. For a person who is depressed a lot of the time, like I am, this is a major asset. We are introduced to Ronnie Wood, who is making his debut with the Stones on this tour. He is very sweet, but he smells terrible. Why don't the English like to bathe? I wonder, trying to keep in mind that he is a pretty good guitarist. I feel air whooshing up my ass and keep asking people if they have a needle and thread.

When I ask Freddie he offers me some coke again, and I feel I just must check it out. It is in big crystal rocks, but it has a nasty bite. Things are getting rough in the seventies. The middle class has fallen in love with coke and it is getting harder and harder to find anything that hasn't been stepped on. It is even being hit in South America, right there in the kitchens. Even the Rolling Stones are getting screwed. For some reason this cheers me up. I must smile, because Bianca, in passing, smiles back.

We take our leave and go to our seats. There is only one seat for the two of us, but that's okay because we are on our feet the entire time. It is a great concert highlighted by two events: the first is the forty-foot balloon that looks like an erect penis. The second is much better. For the encore, they do a version of 'Sympathy for the Devil' that is preceded by steel drummers coming on the stage in concentric circles. They range in age and size and go from short to tall. This is all done in the dark with candles. It is quite a sight. From where we are in the balcony I can see that there is a five-pointed star in the middle of the stage. The Stones are really into their Satan. Isn't everyone?

There is a party after the concert being held at Earl McGrath's who is working for Ahmet Ertegun. I have met Earl and his wife, a pear-shaped principessa, at the Dunnes'. They are a typical New York couple of the era: they go to a lot of parties, they give a lot of parties. One wonders if they spend time alone with each other at all. They live in a duplex near the Russian Tea Room. Victor tells me it is a hot building the next night when we go pub crawling and I can relax. Before we get to go to the party, we go back to a suite of rooms at the Plaza. Mick Jagger has registered under the name Michael Phillips.

I cannot stand the karma, and I start to hyperventilate in the car. Goldie giggles her Goldie Giggle and it cools me out. We haven't eaten a thing. I feel unpleasantly high. The weather, my outfit, the Stones – they are all getting to me. Plus Ronnie Wood's body odor. We have offered him a ride and he is stinking up the car, it is that strong. He has a feather on a piece of leather around his neck. I admire it and he takes it off and ties it around mine. Uh-oh, does this mean I am going steady with this awful-smelling person? I tip my head down to catch a whiff. Fortunately the feather doesn't smell too bad.

I check my watch, a sign of incipient anxiety. It is already one o'clock. We go up to the suite. There are about twenty various and sundry. Mick and Keith hang pretty tight and speak to each other through their instruments in the bedroom. In the living room there is something like a party. I get a drink and sit down. I am sitting next to Charlie Watts, who gives me a light with his Cartier lighter. I admire the lighter, having little else to say.

'It doesn't mean fuck all,' he snaps. I presume he is referring to the money that buys the nice things, and I want to tell him, Hey, fuck you, I'm rich too. I know it doesn't mean fuck all: I never have a chance, though, because he goes into a kind of it-doesn't-mean-fuck-all chant, and I don't want to interrupt. He is finding a new beat; far be it from me to interfere with him and his muse. I get up and walk away, very conscious that I have a rip up the seam of my ass. It doesn't mean fuck all, Charlie.

I check out some drawers around the suite for little hotel packets of needle and thread. None. I have to wait on line to get into a bathroom. There is none there, either. I pick up a phone and ask for housekeeping. I ask them for a needle and thread, and tell them the suite number. They don't want to come up.

'How about if I meet you at the elevator? I'm a desperate woman . . . my pants . . .'

'O-kay,' is the brisk Jamaican reply. I head out the door and leave the bolt out for easy reentry. I stand at the bank of elevators and space out on watching the numbers light up. I squint to see if it makes it more psychedelic. Nothing is psychedelic about this evening. The housekeeper, a handsome black mountain who could be anywhere from forty-three to seventy-three, hands me needles and thread and a thread cutter. I give her a five and she takes it with a brusque 'T'ank you.' The elevator doors close. A cut in a movie.

So I cut back to the suite where no one has moved since I left. Mick and Keith are between the beds on the floor of the bedroom, strumming guitars and not talking. They form a freaky little unit, right there on the floor, but there is something peaceful about the scene. I calm down long enough to think about repairing my ripped ass. I take up residence in the bathroom, slide my pants off, sit down on the toilet-seat cover and do a nice little backstitch and then a whip stitch for insurance. Too late to change my point of view, but better than before.

When I hit the living room again, I see that Goldie is chatting up a cute roadie. I light a roach and inhale deeply the way they do in *Easy Rider*. Sometimes I think that the reason I never really get high on pot is that I never smoke it correctly. I close my eyes and hold the smoke in my lungs. Then I swallow and exhale through my nose. A college friend and I have done extensive research on how to get highest and have agreed this is the way. The only thing higher is to have a gulp of water instead of a dry swallow.

I open my eyes and big Ollie is a tower of black power in front of me. He is smiling blankly. I hand him the roach and he puffs. Ollie is tall enough to be Watusi. He sure banged the drums good, but I ain't gonna fuck him. I realize it has come to that point in the evening when people are beginning to line up their sex for the night, but it couldn't be further from my mind. Accommodating the rip in my pants has tightened my moves and my body and I don't feel physical at all. Besides, I'm not partial to black men. My mother's influence, no doubt . . .

Then everybody is making leaving noises, so Goldie and me and the cute roadie find our car outside. There is a line of limos. Everybody from the party climbs into one or another of them and heads toward the McGraths'. There is half a party already going and our group fills it out. The McGraths live in a great corner apartment on a high floor. If you stand where the windows meet in a ninety-degree angle you can catch a glimpse of the park a couple of blocks up. The principessa is putting hors d'oeuvres together in the kitchen, which is tiny.

Ahmet Ertegun sits at a breakfast table with a beautiful Chinese girl. The principessa works around him. I know who Ahmet Ertegun is because my friend Mark Meyerson works for Jerry Wexler. I know Jerry, but not Ahmet. I don't introduce myself. I'm too shy.

My host, Earl, kisses my cheek and screams at me: 'I heard you made three million dollars and left your husband!' He reeks of alcohol and garlic and he is extremely sweaty. I pretend I can't hear, and he moves on.

It is clear that this is an Atlantic party. I don't know anyone. I have never been very good at parties. That's why I have gotten so good at giving so many of my own. At least at my own party, I know most of the people. Plus, when you are a host, your mixing and mingling are of a pre/proscribed sort. I find Goldie and camp out.

'Honey, is this all making you uncomfortable?' she says after a while.

'Yes.' I look at my watch. It is well after three. 'I'm gonna go . . . I'll send the car back for you . . .'

'No, we'll come with you . . .' She's still got the roadie in tow. I look around for the host and/or hostess to say thanks and goodbye and as I make a sudden move an arm links smoothly through mine. I follow the arm up and am startled to come upon the mask that is the face of Mick Jagger.

'Leaving so soon . . .?' he says.

'M-m-m-m . . .'

'But we've only just met . . .' he smiles charmingly. I resent being fucked with, but I kind of like the linked-arms bit. I never stop walking to the door. This will be *exactly* the right amount of time to spend with him. This is *per*fect. I *deserve* this. He hesitates, like is it cool to play this out to the elevator? He stops and turns and says goodnight to Goldie. There is something schoolboy courteous in his manner. Very disarming. He walks us to the elevator. He stands unmoving as the doors close. I *like* this shot in my movie.

Goldie and me and the roadie head for the Sherry. Sometime in transit, Goldie decides she doesn't want to sleep with this guy, and they both end up in my suite. I want to go to sleep. We get the bellboy to go to a local coffee shop for rancid English muffins instead . . .

FLASHBACK TO DINNER AT NICK'S FISHMARKET

ME AND THE BEGES. In a booth, laughing.

ovo: Everyone in here looks like he kills people for money. Or can find such a person on short notice. Nick's does, however, serve a decent eastern lobster, and the tables are far away from each other. The Beges requires some reinforcement about this *Close Encounters* endeavor which keeps embarrassing him by getting more expensive, but he is being uncharacteristically relaxed about bringing up the subject. He likes these surroundings . . . so do I. They are familiar to the East Coast part of me that never gets quite used to living in this unchallenging climate all year round. I perform my last ambush . . .

ME: So you think he blames himself at all for his son's suicide?

BEGES: (thinks for a minute) I don't think he's ever had a private thought . . .

OVO: We pick at our food. It's almost halfway through the meal and he hasn't come to the real point of this little get-together . . . I notice the hairs on his head getting more sleek right in front of my eyes, and his suit and shirt kind of press themselves. Uh-oh, here it comes . . .

BEGES: Julia, you said two-point-eight . . .

ME: That was two years ago . . .

BEGES: It was up to nine yesterday . . .

ME: It's gonna go higher . . .

OVO: THE BEGES gives me an exasperated look and picks at his lobster. He looks around the table, presumably for a roll . . .

ME: So whatever it goes to, it'll be worth it . . . it's the marriage of the right director with the right idea. I'm telling you, this guy is going to wipe the floor with all of them. Plus, I'm there to protect ya . . .

OVO: He doesn't get my reference to a line from *Taxi Driver*, but when I smile at him he smiles back. His face smiling is what Happy should look like.

BEGES: (face acrinkle) It is a great idea, isn't it? It'll make a hundred million dollars . . .

OVO: I don't know if he means this or not, but I go with the flow . . .

ME: It's gonna make more money and more history than any other movie . . . ever!

OVO: And we drink to that.

It is significant that I can't remember the first time I met Alan Hirschfield, but I'm sure the Beges threw me at him shortly after dinner at Nick's. We had made a pact: we were gonna make film history. We were gonna make *Close Encounters*. He was gonna throw his best stuff at those whose support he needed, so he threw me at Alan Hirschfield.

Alan was smart, charming, attractive, vulgar, horny, and indecisive. He said things like 'do a deal' and 'neg-o-siation.' I had superfluous knowledge of Wall Street from Michael. Anyway, I understood most of the jargon. We clicked.

So now I'm gonna throw my best stuff at him: Steven. While Goldie wings West, and Albert continues shooting home movies for Steven of people standing in line for *Jaws*, Steven and I walk the few blocks from the Sherry to 711 Fifth Avenue to pick up Alan. Each of them is looking forward to this meeting. I've set that up with rave reviews. The summer heat beats upon my cocaine-drenched skin, sucks it out. I've spent the better part of the morning with ice cubes on my eyes chomping down aspirin. Hey, whatever's good for whatever.

We ride up in the elevator, chatting lightly, and Steven starts to stutter. I can never figure out if this is a sign of nervousness or a manipulative device. Alan comes out, oozing laid-back charm. They are comfortable with each other immediately. Phew.

We go down again in the elevator and I suffer a mild nausea-high buzz. It almost feels good. We get into Alan's limo and head downtown. The air conditioning is too cold, but it jolts me out of the elevator buzz and into the moment.

On the drive, Alan mentions that Herbie Allen is joining us, and this restaurant we're eating at is his choice. The restaurant is a hole in the wall with no name on 14th Street near the Academy of Music, which happens to be the first place I ever saw the Rolling Stones. On their first American tour. With Michael. Before we were married. An eternity ago.

Herbie Allen is a handsome, dapper guy, slight and tight of build, medium height, medium hair. The surprise in his face is bright blue, almond-shaped eyes that exude intelligence and torpor simultaneously. From the moment he orders for us, it is clear he expects to be chairman of the board of the lunch. This suits all the rest of us just fine. The food is excellent.

The conversation turns to deals. Both Steven and I are fascinated by these Wall Street types and egg Herbie into telling a story about the heaviest deal he's pulled off so far. He mentions the name of a business manager who was big in the sixties and is currently bankrupt. He's a guy I've met in my travels on the drug circuit. I say that I've met him, and he seemed tired and old and broken. Herbie's eyes brighten.

'He was something in his time,' he says.

'He's one of that crowd who discovered acid too late . . .' I blurt. Loud guffaws all around, thank goodness, and I am rewarded with a benign aren't-my-kids-wonderful-let's-give-them-the-money-to-make-a-movie-we-don't-understand look from Alan. From his point of view, this lunch is going well.

Herbie tells his story of the biggest deal he's done so far: Back in the sixties he was putting together a two-hundred-fifty-million-dollar deal – a quarter of a billion dollars, he repeats – letting the figure sink in.

Everybody had come from all parts of the country to close this deal. There were a number of principals, but the fulcrum of the deal was this guy. He had just recently found himself through acid and was consequently nowhere to be found. The venue for the closing was a private home, and for some reason a capacious nursery became the holding area for all these heavy hitters.

Herbie Allen's eyes twinkle as he describes men of age and dignity and three-piece-suitedness cramped into children's chairs, on their rocking horses. One napped in a playpen. After many hours and calls to his office, his house, his friend's offices and houses, etc., they decided to send a limo out to his house with two big strong men, just in case he had trouble remembering how important the deal was.

They found him under his house, naked save for a pair of pink, heart-shaped sunglasses. He was in a full lotus position and doing his Oms. They dressed him in a bathing suit, a raincoat, and a pair of Jesus sandals and hurled him into the limo. They were smart enough to leave his love glasses on.

They called ahead from the car and the other principals started signing. When he arrived, seeing God, he could only muster an X where his signature should be. It took an hour to get him to sign – letter by letter. It was the most artistic signature, Herbie Allen laughs, he ever saw on a deal.

Okay, Herbie, you're the star of the lunch!

Everybody leaves liking everybody else. In the car, on the way uptown, Steven surprises me and Hirschfield by expressing a desire to buy a suit. Alan has a tailor in the East Sixties. He insists that after we drop him off we head over there; he'll call ahead. As he steps out of the car he instructs me to be fitted for a woman's suit, his treat. It feels a little hooker/gunmollish, but I also feel I've earned it.

Steven gets a blue pinstripe number and I get fitted for a fourpiece (pants, skirt) taupe gabardine outfit that the tailor tells me will be ready in four weeks, tops.

On the way back to the hotel, again in Alan's car, I figure the lunch has gotten us at least fifteen mil; Steven agrees.

'He reminds me of Michael,' Steven says.

'Why, 'cause they're both Zen Wall Street guys?'

'Kinda . . .' I sing a little song of Oms, and Steven cracks up. Henceforth, I declare, I will pray only to the God of Money, Herbie Allen Hirschfield . . .

Re: the quintessential money man. He is an evolving species. For a long time, he kept himself in shape and his profile low. In the eighties, he gets fat and famous. He wears his weight as an emblem of his success.

He gives a hefty portion of his ill-gotten gains to politicians and charity. He thinks he can buy his way out of anything, including getting old and getting dead. He likes pushing other people around. Power, in his narrow view, is the ability to make other people suffer.

He doesn't believe in therapy, unless it is some chic California lifestyle pop psychology that reinforces his right to be a greedy asshole. Besides, he thinks that he knows everything. He's made a lot of money, hasn't he? Just remember, the quote isn't 'Money is the root of all evil,' it's 'The love of money is the root of all evil.'

And the evil that men do lives long after they're gone . . .

*

We've been back in L.A. for a couple of weeks. Sunday morning. Very early. Goldie calls. She is upset, can I come to the house now? I can tell from the sound of her voice there's trouble, but for some reason I think I am about to help with a personal problem. I pull myself together and speed up Stone Canyon. Goldie is in sweats, huddled into a profusion of pillows on her bed. She looks like she hasn't slept a wink.

'I'm having anxiety about *Fear of Flying*,' she says.

Hey, I'm having anxiety about waking up in the morning, but I say: 'What's the matter?'

'Well, I went to a party at Bob Evans's house last night . . .'

'Mistake number one . . .'

'. . . and I go to the bathroom and Sue Mengers follows me in, and I put my alligator bag on the sink, and try to pee and Sue asks can she borrow my brush, knocks the bag in the sink, and while she's brushing her hair, she talks to me in the mirror and she says, "You know, you're ruining your career committing to Julia" . . . I don't know, the whole thing has made me very nervous . . .'

Damn Begelman and Columbia for not closing her deal! but I say:

'Goldie, I'm your friend . . . I don't want you to do something that will cause you anxiety . . .' and I know I've lost her right there, but I've got to let her go. Damn Damn Damn.

Somebody sets up a meeting with Jane. We meet at my house. It is pleasant; we talk about our kids. Her boy, my girl. She says it doesn't matter how high you've raised your consciousness – boys will be boys. Guns. Fights. Aggressive behavior. Kate la-la's happily on the floor with her doll. Jane says she's sure I can direct, but doesn't feel comfortable doing my first movie. If I pull a gun on you, will you commit? I wonder pointlessly. Balls, said the Queen, if I had them I'd be King Vidor!

I convince Begelman to let me pursue Carly Simon. I visit her at her hideout on Martha's Vineyard. We talk about Jeremy and James. She asks if Jeremy is young and I say yes, surprised. She says, 'There are no old junkies . . . they give it up or they die . . .' I talk her into doing a screen test, but by the time I return to L.A. the whole concept has gotten caught in the mire of negotiation. Her manager, Arlyne Rothman, is nonhelpful in the extreme . . .

After the deal for a test falls apart, Begelman summons me to his office. He wants to know why Goldie fell out. I act out all the parts, especially Sue Menger's Bob Evans Bathroom Bit. 'That cunt!' he explodes.

I have cut a deal with the Burbank Studios to re-edit my AFI tape on their new CRX 50 system. Make it look more professional. My little product reel. They give me free time and an engineer. I will break in the computer. I have been at it for days, and everyone is ragged. The machine keeps making its own cuts and nobody seems to know how to control it. Least of all me. One day, in frustration, I swear at the machine. It makes a belching noise, prints out the title eighty-five times, then stops. The engineer asks us to take a break. Twenty minutes later, he comes outside.

'You know, they always call these machines "she,"' he says, 'but I think we've gotten a "he."'

'So what're you saying?'

'Julia, I think you should go in there and talk to it . . .'

'You're kidding . . .'

'I don t know what else to suggest . . .'

I go into the room and talk to the computer. I apologize. Profusely. It starts up. We go back to work. The phone rings. Sue Mengers. She keeps me on the phone a long time. She never intended to make the picture fall apart, etc. I think in my mind that she is evil, but I tell her if she wants me to say, It's okay, I forgive you, well, okay I forgive you . . . I don't want to talk this long with her. I'll make a mistake, and as my mother used to say, I have a better way of committing suicide than jumping into this woman's mouth. There is a saying of the time: Sisterhood is powerful. Not in Hollywood . . .

*

I am so bummed at the state of *Fear of Flying* that when Roz invites me to dinner with her and Jon Peters, I accept. I've met him a few times, at her wedding, at their ranch, but he is a shit disturber, and always makes trouble for me, principally with Barbra. The two of them come to the house and we smoke a joint. He studies my face.

'I ain't goin' to dinner with a woman whose bangs are so fucked up,' he says, ever the hairdresser. 'Lemme fix 'em.' We go into the bathroom, find a scissors, and he cuts. We go to dinner. He drives. We talk about *Fear of Flying*. He says: 'Times are changing. Men are afraid of women. I know a lot of beautiful women who should be with men, but do you know what they're doing now?'

'What!?' me and Roz want to know.

'Whacking off alone in their beds with vibrators . . .' I have seen the future and it hums . . .

The next day when I look in the mirror, I notice the bangs are uneven. I call him and complain. 'Whaddya want from me?' he laughs. 'I'm a producer now . . .'

I set about looking for a writer to doctor *Fear of Flying*. My first choices are Carole Eastman and Robert Towne. I get to both of them pretty quick, and even though they are both more interested in me than the project, they ultimately turn me down, Carole much more quickly and directly than Towne, who strings me along for six long weeks.

When I tell Harry Gittes, 'I think he wants to do it!' Harry says, 'I think he wants to do you . . .'

'That's a terrible thing to say. I think he's a serious person and he knows this is a serious project!' Actually, Towne strikes me as a dilettante who flirts mournfully with everyone.

'Oh, Julia, don't you get it? Men would fuck mud . . .'

'Really?' I know it and I don't know it.

'Really. And you're not mud . . .' Then Harry tries to backtrack and makes friendly noises about how hot the book is getting and how hot I am (business-ly of course), but I am preoccupied with the mud concept. Nevertheless, I play the entire Towne situation through. Who knows, he could be the exception to prove the rule, and I could end up with a directorproof script. Which is what I figure I need.

Towne is legendary, and I think that both *Shampoo* and *Chinatown* were brilliantly written. Towne tells me his ending to *Chinatown*, which would have made it a much bigger movie, and I want him to write me a brilliant screenplay for my directorial debut more than ever. Instead of Faye Dunaway buying it at the end, they get away – via a stretch of Mulholland that affords the Valley view, filled with orange groves. Their car passes out of frame and the camera freezes over the background. Towne tells me that he has collected seventeen stills, all approximately from the same POV, which cover the intervening years from then to the present. They show the death of the orange groves and the birth of the San Fernando Valley with all the overdeveloped living spaces for humans, trapped in the basin of the mountains. The last couple of stills, he says, were the most damning, because you couldn't even see the ugliness of the development, because the smog obliterated everything. I tell him I love his ending. 'Yeah, well, Roman had some things to work out,' he replies in a long-suffering tone. He has told this story a lot of times, but I don't blame him – it is so much better an ending.

I put up with four o'clock in the morning calls, I listen to his diatribes about the whales (accompanied by that mournful soundtrack that he plays in the background), I sympathize with his endless hypochondriacal litany. He has a bump in the middle of his forehead that he rubs constantly. He is a very annoying and talented Jew. Occasionally I wrest a laugh from him and he reminds me that it isn't my words that are funny, but my delivery . . .

I play it out, even though I know he is going to break my heart. When he does, I am not sure which direction to turn in. I meet Carole Sobieski at her request, but she seems somewhat mordant casting. What about Giler? people keep saying, what about Giler? What about Giler? I think. I've only known him as the Scourge of Nicholas Beach, when he came between Jennifer Salt and Margot Kidder, who shared the house next to ours and damn near broke up over him.

His name came up all over town. I had met him later on,

and was amazed that this unprepossessing fellow with the sharp nose and the glasses was such a cocksman, but I was still into Looks: Very Number One. His personality should be described only in French: *bon vivant*, spouting *bon mots* and he had lots of *joie de vivre*. He had a deep voice and looked from his tight pants to be fairly well hung. But still. He didn't seem awesome enough for Jennifer and Margot to have almost broken up over. In the end, he left them for Michelle Phillips, something he did over and over. He also liked Eurasian girls – had been married to Nancy Kwan or France Nuyen, I could never remember which.

I don't have any other good ideas so I ask him to read the book. We have lunch at La Scala in one of the front booths to talk about it. Giler has a couple of things to say that make me think that maybe he should write the screenplay – or what we are calling a 'rewrite.' He establishes his position up front that this is a write not a rewrite. I agree. Write is right. He drinks quite a bit, and once lubricated he says things like, 'You know, the zipless fuck I could really make work if I could take Adrian down a peg . . .'

'What do you mean?'

'Well, have less talk from Adrian . . .'

'But that's what seduces her . . .'

'But, Julia, the people you like to talk to are not the people you like to fuck . . .'

'Smart women do . . .'

'Right, like Jeremy . . .'

'Well, you can't count me. Paul Lazarus says that my taste is comparable to that of a twenty-five- to thirty-five-year-old self-made Jewish businessman . . .'

'He trivialized you.' Giler, who fucks eighteen-year-old Eurasian beauties. Unreal.

'Is it vice versa, too?'

'What?'

'That the people you like to fuck are not the people you like to talk to?'

'Precisely.' Smiling, like he'd said it himself. This was but one essential expression of a worldview shared by almost every guy I ever met in the business. *Plus ça change* and all that jazz. Then Giler says the thing that makes me think of him as David Be-guiler for the next year or so. 'You know,' he muses in a nearly genuine moment, 'it is very difficult to bring self-pity to the screen in a way that makes it interesting . . .' You're getting closer . . .

'Maybe we should just lose that particular aspect in the translation . . .' I muse back. I have to race across the hill into the Valley. It is picture day at the Burbank Studios. I have a bad perm and my forehead is shiny, but I have a three o'clock date with the Great One in his office and he doesn't like to wait. In the game of Hollywood hardball, he gets to keep you waiting.

When I get there, they have set up a shot in which I am on a director's chair that says *Julia Phillips* in script on the back, and he is hovering over me casuallike on the corner of his desk, handing me a copy of a screenplay that says *Fear of Flying* in print.

The photograph that is the product of these maneuvers (I had to have my head turned *Exorcist*-like toward the camera) is reprinted in a number of mags and newspapers as part of an announcement that David Begelman had decided that it was okay for me to direct *Fear of Flying*. (Later on, during his days of Shame, I am cropped out of the picture and it is just his smiling face accompanying all the stories of misappropriation, embezzlement, and forgery. In the end, I am just a footnote in a larger story.)

September 22, 1975

Marty bobbles around on the bottom of my waterbed. We are watching the news. Sara Jane Moore has tried to shoot Gerald Ford.

'You think this'll hurt the picture?' Marty has his worried look. Please don't wheeze . . .

'Only if she'd killed him . . .' Film makers. Nothing matters but our pictures . . .

I've just moved to this house in Benedict Canyon and Marty

lives on Mulholland. Neighbors. More or less. He's recently back from shooting in New York, and I'm recently ensconced in my house. We are reestablishing our relationship, hanging out before dinner, because we suspect we will have to call on this relationship anytime now . . .

Marty and I split a Quaalude and wash it down with some Dom Perignon. It is around Thanksgiving, 1975, and I haven't discovered Cristal yet. There is not much left. We have been doing this for hours. Locking reels. Marcia Lucas, who is the better – certainly the warmer – half of the *American Graffiti* team, sits perched over us on a stool. She swivels back and forth in a self-comforting motion in front of her Steenbeck. We are on a killer schedule; five editors are working around the clock – four male stars under her supervision. I am sure they are not making life easy for her.

We already know Marty is not easy. He has shot so much footage at so many different speeds we are overwhelmed by too many choices. If you make him feel too cornered or disagree with him too often he bites his hand in that Italian gesture and wheezes. Marty bludgeons us with his asthma. But Marty is endearing and cute and inspirational, so we let him.

So far, it has been more fun to work with Marty than anyone else. We have been going through the ringer on this movie from start to finish. More Michael than me. He's kept it together for four long years. This has been an especially shitty time for me, because Michael really doesn't want me to play on *Taxi Driver* at all. We have agreed that he should be the man in front on *Taxi* and I will be the man in front on *Close Encounters*. The picture is virtually locked, but we are still in a crunch on editing. Michael, burnt out, sapped of four years' worth of energy, bodily fluids in dire need of replenishment, has split for Hawaii. Therefore I am hanging out with Marty in the editing room. Hey, whatever's good . . .

The day after he leaves, which is also the day after Bernie Herrmann, a disagreeable but talented old codger (he scored all the Hitchcock movies), has finished the score, Bernie

Herrmann wakes up dead. It is quite an emergency. His wife freaks out, not the least because she has literally not a penny to her name. John Veitch steps into the breach because I don't want Marty distracted. I tell Marty Bernie died because he made him put a variation of the *Psycho* chords at the end of our picture. Weak laughter, heavy wheezing. Death . . . it makes us work harder.

I wonder if Michael is cleaning up. *Taxi Driver* is a cokey movie. Big pressure, short schedule, and short money, New York in the summer. Night shooting. I have only visited the set once and they are all doing blow. I don't see it. I just know it.

Worse yet, the film has been cut according to Schrader's script and sucks. We have had a rough-cut screening that is a disaster. The movie just never gets to the audience, plus it often doesn't seem to make much sense. Brian De Palma laughs uncontrollably during De Niro's and Cybill's last exchange in the cab: Betsy: How are ya? Travis: Well, I don't get headaches anymore. The rest of the audience follows suit and our powerful ending is drowned out in hilarity. And these are our friends!

I had to agree with Brian. It was pretty funny. Sure, go out, kill a few people – better than Tylenol and codeine. Nevertheless, this little outburst cues us to some other bad laughs in the movie. There is nothing worse for *Taxi Driver* than bad laughs. There is nothing worse for most movies than bad laughs, with the possible exception of *Valley of the Dolls*.

We have recut the picture repeatedly and come up with a pretty sexy cut. Basically we have ignored everything – matching De Niro's myriad wigs, worrying about signs announcing the candidate's impending arrival – in favor of creating a forward-moving story out of too much footage.

We have gone according to De Niro's voiceover, including some false starts, which is where Marty gets the idea to restart the cut, which gives the impression of being in Travis's mind. I, who have never been particularly fond of this script, have gotten extremely fond of this movie.

I think it is a ground-breaker, and I think Travis is someone people should know about. I know he is out there, created by

American culture and etched in stone by the Vietnam War. And the difference between an assassin and a savior is a function of his victims, not his own sparkling personality.

Frozen behind Marcia on the screen is Marty in the back of the cab with De Niro. He is describing what a .45 magnum can do to a woman's pussy. By accident, in one of the takes he says, 'I'm gonna stick that gun up her cunt and blow her brains out!' This is not in the script although I am pretty sure it is an accurate reflection of the way Schrader relates to women. It is the ultimate male retro remark and I am fighting hard to keep it in the movie.

Marty, scion of women's lib, ho ho, is having a hard time seeing himself saying the line. The part of the psycho with the gun sitting outside his ex-wife's new living quarters was originally to be played by George Lemmele, but he totaled himself on another picture trying to do his own stunt. Marty cast himself in the role, which he probably wanted all along, and he is very good. He just has a great deal of trouble with this one line. Marcia has put the line in and taken it out, put it in and taken it out. The rest of the dialogue in the scene is pretty tasty, too.

We have all grown tired of hearing him ask, 'Do you know what a .45 magnum can do to a woman's pussy?' reiterate, 'Now, that is something you should see, what a .45 magnum can do to a woman's pussy,' and exclaim, ''Cause she's a nigger-loving cocksucker!' We keep inserting the stick-it-up-her-cunt-blow-out-her-brains line in between Marty's ponderings about guns and pussy and his thought that she deserves it because she is a nigger-loving cocksucker.

Then Marty hates it and Marcia Lucas jiggles the film this way and that, her deft hands cutting and pasting, and she lines it up and we watch it the other way. Marty raises his expressive eyebrows and makes his eyes more sad, more old, more questioning, and Marsha and I tell him we like it better with the line in. Women will applaud you, we tell him, and I wonder if they are smart enough. They hadn't been with *Carnal Knowledge*, which I felt women greatly misunderstood. Just because it was from the point of view of the misogynistic prick didn't mean that it wasn't a statement on behalf of the liberation of women, however unconscious.

Marty's misogyny was apparent from his casting of Cybill Shepherd as Betsy. We had interviewed just about every blonde on both coasts, and still he kept looking, looking, looking. I liked Farrah Fawcett, her fine bones, her aquiline profile, her big teeth, and her thin body. Marty picked Cybill for her big ass, a retro Italian gesture, I always felt. In the end, he had to give her line readings and De Niro hated her. Watching the dailies with Marcia Lucas of their scene in the restaurant would have been painful if it hadn't been so funny, her with the clip in her hair before each take, De Niro scowling, Marty's line reading off camera, then Action!, which always sounded like ACT! the way Marty said it.

'She can't ACT!' I say on the seventh take, and Marcia and I laugh mordantly. Call it painfully funny. Later, when we're cutting the picture, there is a shot during Travis and Betsy's date where they walk away from camera. Marty had dressed Cybill in a white knit dress, and the shot catches her ass at its widest point, not flattering, from a *Vogue* point of view. I beg Marty to cut it, but he keeps saying, 'I'm Italian, and I love it.' So-o-o-o unattractive . . .

I had found nothing really attractive about Taxi Driver when I first read it, except for its sociology. Travis was a nut case, a valid nut case but a nut case. I thought Schrader was, too. And of course, there is my partner, Tony, who seems so laid back and nice, until a bunch of us play volleyball at the beach one day, and he nearly explodes a vein in his forehead from bad-mannered competitiveness. For two seconds, Tony thinks he wants to direct *Taxi Driver*, which astounds us: how could beautiful California Tony relate to Travis Bickle? Michael and I go through the motions of star submissions and turndowns to convince him this should not be his directing debut. (Flash forward: *My Bodyguard* is, perfect casting.)

The script appeals to a number of up-and-coming and well-established directors and we have a meeting with Irv Kershner, who actually has the nerve to come on to me when we're alone by telling me his wife doesn't understand him. Marcia Nasitir has warned me he has this habit of drawing a sketch of you on a napkin at lunch and then saying the time-honored line. When he takes his pen out at lunch I know what is coming and cough wildly to cover what might become uncontrollable hysterical laughter. Kersh never really materializes as a serious choice, though, because he wants major rewrites, the kind that indicate that he doesn't really want to do *Taxi Driver* at all.

We flirt with Lamont Johnson for two minutes, but he is so morose that I think that he will drive us all to suicide before the picture is over, maybe even before we can set it up.

Milius tells us he would be interested, but we manage to convince him that he is meant to debut with an epic movie, which he does a bit later on – something he writes for himself, *The Wind and the Lion*. I see the movie on the plane with Steven and he tells me that I watch the whole thing raptly with my mouth open like a five-year-old. I actually love the movie, but I am sure that my mouth is open because I have eaten a piece of hash before I get on the plane and I feel the need for oxygen the entire flight.

A year of the false starts passes.

Marty sidles up to me at parties and tells me in his intense undertone how much he wants to do this picture. He is shoulder high and sometimes I find myself talking out of the side of my mouth into the top of his hair. Not a chance. Forget it. Come back when you've done something besides *Boxcar Bertha*. Then Harry Ufland forces us to see the rough cut for *Mean Streets*. I am three months pregnant and peeing constantly. We're prepared to commit after the third reel. With a little hitch. Get us De Niro to play Travis, and it's all yours.

Marty gets De Niro, but this picture is one that just doesn't ever want to start. This is not the sort of script, De Niro's performance in *Godfather II* notwithstanding, that studio types are likely to embrace. We dick around and dick around with John Calley at Warner Bros. A very yesnomaybe enterprise. Finally, *Mean Streets* closes the New York Film Festival, the *Times* raves, and Calley calls us from his shrink's office: Do we think we can make this picture for $750,000? I say yes and immediately go into labor. By the time Kate is born and I am recovered enough to drive, Charlie Greenlaw, the nuts-and-bolts guy Calley uses to turn you down, has figured out no way the picture can be made for under a million. Once again we are out on the street.

We have a thankless meeting with Roger Gimble, who thinks he wants to go into movies, but ultimately succeeds where he belongs: television.

Next, De Niro wants to do *1900* with Bertolucci. We have no choice but to say okay. Marty gets involved developing *Bury My Heart at Wounded Knee* with Marlon Brando. It feels like we will never be able to keep the principals together long enough to shoot the picture. Fortuitously, the Indians behave badly. Get drunk and attempt to rape Sandy, Marty's girlfriend. Marty squiggles out of *Wounded Knee*, and the package comes together. I think of this package as a bowl of Jell-O. It is jumpy and fluid, but it seems to be staying in its bowl.

Steven and I have lunch with David Begelman, who is enamored of *Close Encounters*. I get Steven to rave about *Taxi Driver*, even to go so far as to say if Marty is a bust, he will come in and finish the picture. We all know this is the worst possible directing choice for the movie, and probably a lie, but it keeps the picture going.

Even Begelman has to take a deep breath on that one. He hates the script. He has hated it for years. In the beginning, when we first optioned it from Schrader and gave Brian De Palma his walking papers, one of our Tony submissions was to Begelman for Al Pacino's consideration. We never know if Pacino turns it down because of Tony or the script. But we do know that Begelman detests it, because he has told us so.

We feel so bad about Brian, that after the picture is made we give him a point. (I don't know till years later that Michael has told Brian the news in such a way that he thinks only Michael has given him the point. Gee, Bri, if that's what you think, could I have the part that came out of me back?)

Warners offers Marty *Alice Doesn't Live Here Anymore*, which will star Ellen Burstyn, right after *The Exorcist*. Well, De Niro is off on *1900* anyway. They both swear that they will do our picture right after. Sometimes you've just got to say what the fuck. We get more committed paper out of Harry

Ufland in exchange for being nice, although Marty and I go through a knock-down drag-out fight in the middle of a Santa Ana over *Wounded Knee*.

He is cutting *Alice* and there is really no room on the Burbank lot for him, so they have set up an air-conditioned tent on the edge of the parking lot. Since I smoke, I am not allowed in the tent. He stands just inside the curtain, and I stand puffing away on burning concrete in 104 degrees. I am wearing a wrap-around purple-and-blue Pleasure Dome dress that is sticking to every part of my body. *Alice* isn't even completed, and he is going off with Brando to the Indians. I freak out. I tell him we committed to him, why can't he stay committed to this project that he is supposed to love.

What the fuck am I doing? We are talking Marlon Brando here. I don't have a chance. I do take a cheap shot and make him think this is busting up the friendship. I say, You know, man, we're in Hollywood now, you shouldn't be discarding your real friends so promiscuously. He gets his worried look, and then the editors who have been working feverishly in the background, making a big show of not eavesdropping, summon him to look at another alternative for a scene, and he leaves me.

I am boiling mad and boiling hot and tell him to think about what I've said, toss my curls, and march angrily to my office. Whistling so that I won't feel so blue. When I hit the air conditioning of the office, I collapse. I am pissed that something this dramatic has happened and Marty hasn't seen it. In the end, it is not anything I have done or said to make him be honorable, it is the Indians assaulting Sandy that sends him scurrying into the arms of *Taxi Driver*.

In spite of his disloyalty, or maybe because of it, I am superloyal to him. When he shows the rough cut of *Alice* to Ellen Burstyn and Kristofferson, he asks me to attend and talk to her.

'Whaddya mean, talk to her . . .' Marty starts to wheeze. 'Oh, you mean, the old woman's point of view?'

'Yeah,' he sputters and I can't tell if this is an appreciative chortle or something that he should be treating with Primatene Mist.

'No matter what I think?'

'Yeah . . .'

'Okay, I got it.'

The movie gives me *spielkas* but I sit tight, and when it is over, I race over to Marty, who is sitting next to Herself. I do a steamroller presentation, basically applauding the movie's elevated consciousness. I feel as if I have appeared as Paula Weinstein. On speed. In their movie!

The next day Marty sends a dozen white roses with the note, Thanks, and I get worried about the significance of white. I am always confused about the significance of white or yellow roses from a Sicilian. Finally I call, ostensibly to thank him for the flowers. He tells me what a good job I have done, so I guess I don't have to worry about sleeping with the fishes.

Maybe Marty's consciousness does get raised by doing *Alice*, because in the end, even though he knows it's better, he can't see himself saying the gun/cunt/brains line. Or maybe he is just smart about public perception. It's heavy enough that he is director of this movie. We are just going for the other cut when the phone rings. It is Pat Dodds to tell me that Connie has just called and that Mr. Begelman and Mr. Jaffe are ready to see me and Marty now.

We split another Quaalude and take the long walk across the parking lot from the editing suite to Columbia's executive building. It is dark out. Marty is carrying a notebook and talking nervously to himself. Ostensibly he is addressing me, but he is talking to himself. I feel I am eavesdropping on a personal and confidential conversation.

'Look, Marty,' I interrupt, 'we're just going there to listen, that's all . . .' We already know that the MPAA is going to give us an X for violence. We already know that Columbia is not in a mood to fight it or even back us up fighting it. We are young enough to feel, fine, don't back us, we'll do it ourselves. Before we take that route, though, it seems reasonable to sit down with the guys and find out what their objections are. No agreements made, just listen.

Marty and I sit next to each other on the couch, Begelman

in his favorite chair, and Stanley on a sofa chair. I can tell that this is meant to be an ambush, but I will turn it into a war of attrition and I will win. I am surprised myself that someone as volatile as me has as much patience as I do. With these kinds of guys. In these kinds of wars.

Marty takes a deep breath and opens his notebook, uncaps his pen, and Stanley starts to speak. After he finishes, Begelman says some words, too. Nothing direct. Just noise. The gist of the noise is: change the picture to get an R or we'll change it for you. I know they will never do that, but Marty doesn't. He never writes a word in his little notebook. He closes it quietly and recaps his pen. He holds onto his knees tightly, as if keeping them attached to his legs. The meeting takes about forty minutes. When we leave we promise to think about everything they have said. They say they will, too.

'I know what I have to do,' Marty says grimly as we make our way across the parking lot back to the editing offices. It is pitch black and cold. It is ten o'clock at night. What the fuck am I doing here? I wonder. Protecting your interests, I reply. I am so busy with this internal conversation I don't ever find out what Marty has to do.

Later that night, probably about two in the morning, the phone rings. Again, I am not asleep so I pick it up. It is Marty, to tell me what he has to do. In an intense murmur which sounds like the voiceover for the Harvey Keitel character in *Mean Streets* (which was Marty; he has told me that he did it that way because one's interior voice should sound different from one's speaking voice) he says: 'There's only one way to deal with Stanley Jaffe. I'm gonna go out and buy a gun – a little gun, I'm a little person – and I'm gonna shoot him.' I laugh, but Marty doesn't laugh back.

I wish all these guys would stop hanging out with Milius. Milius, who was paid in part for *Jeremiah Johnson* (née *The Crow Killer*) in antique guns, Milius who fired a gun off into the night one New Year's Eve at my house to signify the coming of 1975, Milius who damn near shot his own wife, Renee, on the roof of their house because he thought she was a prowler. A moot point, since she, too, was armed, and came close to offing him. In the end they got a divorce, which is a bit less final than murder, although probably not as gratifying.

'Marty, what will shooting Stanley Jaffe accomplish?' I sit up in bed and light a cigarette. I puff it defiantly into the receiver. Marty wheezes. Guilty, I tamp it out.

'You're right, I can't shoot him . . . maybe just threaten him . . .'

'Is this with a small or a large gun . . .' Marty makes a noise. I root for this to be laughter but of course it is more wheezing. I decide to go for my strong-producer performance. 'Marty, you just keep cutting it the way you want to . . . let Michael and me deal with Columbia . . .' We are going to be releasing this movie in February and it is December. Not that much time when you consider that we still want to test it ourselves, and have to go through all the other postproduction steps.

There is no preview house, no test screenings with professional teenagers. The guys with no opinions – marketing mavens – haven't completely taken over yet, so we just keep showing it to our friends. We know the movie is working when there is gasping, no laughing. In the scene where the bodega owner beats the dead black guy with the tire iron Steven turns his head away from the screen and onto my shoulder and blurts: 'God, now it's getting ugly . . .' which makes me smirk, because we have done our damnedest to make it pretty ugly *before* this point in the movie.

Marty never threatens Stanley, although Stanley does make a tape of his comments while screening the picture for himself to give us suggestions of what we should cut, which I play on my own little microcassette recorder. We are all using them – the emblem of the mid-seventies. We all have such brilliant thoughts and so many of them and we are all so busy that we record everything. We play our notes on each others' cassette players. Stanley's notes are so insulting – i.e., when De Niro looks into his glass while the Alka Seltzer fizzes, Stanley says in a spoiled high whine, 'What is this, an Alka Seltzer commercial?' – that if I play them for Marty he will kill him with his bare hands.

'We'll make a list,' Marty says in a rare rational moment.

'I know, a very short list, 'cause you're a very short person . . .'

'. . . and we'll give it to them one by one . . . as in one a week . . .' Neither one of us wants to give a thing away. Not the sound of De Niro's zipper in his scene with Jodie, not the excessive tire-iron beating, not the violence of the assassinations at the end.

Marty experiments with de- and re-solarization of color in sixty-five cuts at the end, and the MPAA pronounces it acceptably nonviolent for an R, but there is still the matter of Jodie's age re: the zipper, and the beating of the dead guy.

Marty and I look at the newly colored ending and he cackles: 'Look what it does to Murray's brains . . .'

'Seems more pronounced to me . . .'

'That's right!' Marty chokes joyously. 'Isn't that great?' I cackle, too, mostly at Marty's bent pleasure.

Dreyfuss and I run around for awhile to fill the in-betweens, and besides, he is finally committed to *Close Encounters*.

I really had to scare the hell out of him and his agent, Meyer Mishkin, to close. Ray Stark had a project at Columbia that was never made called *Houdini*. I guess Meyer thought Richard was ready for a raise coming off *American Graffiti* and *Jaws* and for reasons known only to Ray, he extracted a five-hundred-thousand-dollar deal and five gross points from break. Not that they would mean that much since there was this Jewish Santa at Columbia named Eli Horowitz who had invented a real cute deal point called a rolling break. I am not a numbers cruncher so I never really understood much about it except that it was another way for the studio to keep profit participants from getting their money.

Once Meyer established his price on the *Houdini* deal, he thought we should match it. Michael and I had split 2:3 in Steven's favor on fees and points. Our deal, two years old already, called for net profits. We didn't want no gross participants, even if it was Richard. Besides, the request felt unjust. He hadn't been sweating it out through draft after draft. He had been making money on other gigs. Begelman was pissed about it, too, so we devise a plan to break the deadlock.

'I think we should submit it to other guys, let Richard hear about it. Besides, maybe one of them would wanna do it . . . even better.' I had never seen Richard as the perfect Roy Neary anyway, although he was a great actor, and I thought he could probably pull off anything he wanted to. Begelman crinkled his eyes at me. I was a good pupil.

'Like who, for instance . . .'

'Like Jack Nicholson, Gene Hackman, Al Pacino . . .' They were all stars, they were all working-class heroes, they were all preapproved by Steven.

'Those guys'll take more of the gross . . .'

'Maybe . . . but I don't think any of us would feel insane giving it to them . . . Steven's okay with it . . . he's pissed about Richard allowing Meyer to do this to us . . .' Livid, in fact. He said he was pissed about the justice, but it was really the money. Michael and Steven were pissed about the money, but I was getting to go and fight for it. At that point, I had Begelman behind me. I was strong, he was powerful, I'd deal it out with him by my side.

As it turned out, he preferred to have me in front, so I got to beg Norman Garey to give the script to Gene Hackman, friend to friend, while he visited Gene in Mexico on location with *Lucky Lady*, always a wonderful place to be an outsider. When he got home and we asked, Well, well, what'd he say? he looked sad and told us Hackman didn't want to read any script that was going to be shooting away from town for sixteen weeks. He was trying to keep his doomed marriage from failing and thought he should stay around town.

I gave it to Sandy Bressler, Jack Nicholson's agent.

'He said he didn't want to fight the effects, but he'd sure take points anytime.'

'For what? Turning it down?'

'Julia, he's saying it's a hit . . .'

'I know that. I can't believe he's turning it down. He's big enough for the effects.' As in, the best living American actor. Period. Even better than De Niro.

247

'You know this no is final . . .'

'Nothing is final in Hollywood . . .' But death. 'Couldn't you get him to meet with Steven?'

'No,' Sandy laughed. 'Nonononono . . .'

Al Pacino himself called at seven thirty one morning, not my time of day, and seemed angry that I hadn't given the script to Marty Bregman, his manager, but had sent it to him directly instead. I had done this at Begelman's request. He and Marty Bregman had Ancient History and he was worried Bregman wouldn't even pass it on to Pacino. At least that's what he told me. Maybe he was just using the situation, not to mention me, to fuck with Bregman. Who ever knows with these guys? I was sleepy, so I told Pacino the truth, which made him madder. By the end of the conversation he agreed to read the script. Marty Bregman called me to turn it down, but said that Pacino wouldn't mind some points in the movie. I didn't favor him with a response. Boy, the people a girl had to deal with just to make a giganto movie.

I stood at the edge of Begelman's desk and delivered the news. We had to get someone to play Roy Neary, because the production was now moving forward of its own weight. We were set to go in the spring. The distance between winter and spring can be awfully short, particularly in California, where you never know what time of year it is anyway.

'What about Jimmy Caan,' he said doubtfully. I didn't like Jimmy Caan from years ago when I was at First Artists and he had planted himself in my office at CMA and harassed my secretary.

'Bad nose job . . .' The Beges laughed.

'Let's just call William Morris and see if he's available,' Begelman said, buzzing Connie and instructing her to do so. While we're waiting for the call to go through Begelman asked me casually how the *Fear of Flying* lawsuit was going.

'Well, I'm not hanging out in court on a regular basis . . .' I'm looking for Roy Neary. I had showed up for the first day, because Norman and Chris said I had to, thank God the bitch filed in Burbank, but they said I didn't need to be there again until the decision was handed down.

'Who's the judge?' Begelman asked.

248

'Oh, you gonna have it fixed downtown?' I asked, smartass that I am. He looked impatient. Why did he intimidate me? 'Thomas Murphy . . . Thomas J. Murphy . . .' I couldn't believe it, but he wrote the guy's name down on a piece of paper. Connie buzzed us to say Jimmy Caan's agent was gone for the day. Why not? It was almost seven. Wasn't it the Beges who taught me to return calls when you don't want to reach someone at 12:45 and 7:00?

'Lemme run this Jimmy Caan concept by Steven . . .' The other guys had been his ideas. I had no idea what he thought about Jimmy Caan, but I wasn't about to have Begelman casting the picture. Steven said, Screw it, why not? But Jimmy Caan's agent wanted a firm offer of a million dollars and ten percent of gross for his client to read the script. Begelman summoned me to his office to deliver the news. He was furious. I was relieved. We were starting to scrape the bottom of the star barrel and we weren't any closer to casting Roy Neary.

'Julia, it's time for you to go have a talk with Meyer Mishkin . . .'

'Why don't you have a talk with Meyer Mishkin?'

'Because the dialogue will be better coming from you . . .'

'So you want me to go see Meyer and speak from my heart . . .'

'Well, that depends on what your heart might be saying . . .' This from a man who was credited with saying, upon his departure from CMA to Columbia, 'I know I should tell you I'm leaving with a heavy heart, but as you all know I have no heart . . .'

Actually, my heart had been practicing my dialogue for months. It was:

'We have been killing ourselves for two years while you have been gigging around and making money. You don't have near the personal investment. We don't mind you making a lot of money, but you ain't making more money than us.'

I looked Meyer dead in the eye, and he couldn't disagree. He told Richard, and Richard said, Okay, that's fair, and he was Roy Neary.

I had known Dreyfuss off and on since the early days at the

beach, met him at a party at Margot and Jennifer's. Michael and I had seen him Off Broadway in a one-act Horowitz play called *Line* where he was so memorable that that was the first thing I blurted upon meeting him. Needless to say, he had pretty warm feelings about me.

Now he is involved with the project, so we run around from time to time. We have a great night in New York, make a friend take the limo to Harlem at three ay-em to cop an eightball, stay up all night arguing and interrupting and rewriting the screenplay that is our lives. Go to visit Erica and Jonathan (soon-to-be-married-and-divorced) Fast in her suite at the Beverly Hills Hotel. It is during that little gathering, when the talk turns to sex, as it always does around the author of *Fear of Flying*, that Richard gets very worked up about angry fucking. Ah, shades of Don Simpson . . .

'Whaddyou mean, angry fucking?' Erica says, egging him on. She and I exchange an l'll-never-fuck-this-one look. Oh, please. Dreyfuss is a little shorter than me, and has taken to calling me 'boss' as in, 'Hi, boss,' then pecking me, sonlike, chastely on the cheek.

Dreyfuss pulls himself up to his full height, which is not much, and puffs out his chest. He dryhumps the air, his arms around an invisible whore, and as he screams, 'I hate you I hate you I hate you . . .' one hand smacks his phantom lover about the head and shoulders. We crack up, but in my mind he has moved from a maybe to a never.

I am going to New York for some precasting sessions with Richard and Steven. We all agree, even Michael, that I should bring our still unapproved workprint of *Taxi Driver* to New York and show it to a couple of critics. These guys have all been cultivating Pauline Kael, whom I have met at least five times and who never recognizes me. Plus, I think, maybe Martha Duffy at *Time*, Jack Kroll at *Newsweek*. All this without the studio's blessing. This is part of our young-film-maker campaign. We figure if the critics love it they will guide the studio into backing us against the MPAA. Talk about innocent!

I am traveling with Kate and Jackie. Poor Jackie! Amongst me, the boys, and Kate, it is hard for her to know which one of us is her charge. While Steven and Richard and I meet in Juliet Taylor's place every day to torture an endless stream of possible Jillians, I have Lois Smith run the picture for the Big Three at Rizzoli. The studio has not an inkling.

The casting meetings are a bust. When Meryl Streep walks in, Richard and Steven move their chairs away from the table. This move is repeated several times, most pronouncedly when Katherine Walker, an extremely strong presence, is introduced. Steven says he'll test Mary Beth Hurt and some bimbo whom he is fucking, and I let him. Richard gives me a questioning look – the Bimbo? – but I put my finger over my mouth and make a small imperceptible shake of my head. Let the director do his jerk-off tests. I vote for Meryl Streep . . .

Martha Duffy doesn't much like the picture, what a surprise, although she does make some clucking noises on the phone about all those pretty lights at the end – an allusion to *Streetcar Named Desire*. I never hear from Jack Kroll. And Pauline Kael says that she will write an open letter to David Begelman in her column if we need it.

I don't know what I have accomplished with this trip. No Jillian. Worse, the encumbrance of a girlfriend who has to be knocked out of the box. Plus, I personally have to schlep the workprint back. On the morning of my departure, back to L.A., I bend down to cuff my jeans, and on the abrupt rise, impale my forehead on a particularly sharp corner of the TV set. Blood gushes from my head and when Kate sees it, she erupts. The two of us take the limo over to the ear, nose and throat hospital and a doctor in emergency cleans the wound and butterflies it. He says I will have an ambulatory concussion for a couple of days and I should take it easy, but that if I must fly, I can. Miraculously, we make the plane.

The next day, a Monday, I am scheduled for lunch with Stanley in the Blue, née Green (it has been redecorated) Executive Dining Room on the lot. I wear an umber pants-and-coat Brioni outfit and a giant patch on my forehead. I feel flushed and spacey. How spacey is not apparent until I blurt out that Pauline Kael loves the picture. Oh dear, I forgot he wasn't supposed to know. Red anger suffuses His Baldness and he screams the Stanley usual: 'This is a disaster!' Uh-oh. I have blown my own cover. This concussion must be worse than I thought. I pretend that I am going to faint at the table and deflect Stanley's anger for the moment. Deep down Stanley likes me and will come through for me in his own peculiar way. A disaster a disaster, I feel my eyes roll up in my head; nausea takes over my conscious being. I pass out.

When I come to, I am lying in the familiar surroundings of my office. Judy Bornstein hovers. I bolt upright. My head throbs, ba-boom, ba-boom . . .

'Get me Marty!' She does. I tell him about my little slipup. He scuttles the workprint off the lot in the trunk of his car. It takes Columbia two days to realize that the print is not in their possession.

The good news is that the MPAA will R everything but the sound of the zipper in the scene between De Niro and Jodie. That one is finally judged an R, the result of a friendly call from a Power Broker to Dick Hefner, don't ask.

Once the ratings issue is resolved, the recutting of the movie is an automatic endeavor. If we just follow Travis's inner voice, we know which pictures to supply, and by the middle of January, we are ready to cut negative. Happy fucking New Year . . .

Time puts twelve women on its cover (none of them me) and calls them 'Women of the Year.' Balls, said the Queen. If I had them I'd be. . . *Queen?*

'Why don't we just take this,' I pull the card out of the bulletin board that Steven and Grady have set up in the living room of Francis's suite at the Sherry, 'and put it over here?' I walk the card to the end of act two. 'Why can't this be the second-act curtain?'

'Yeah.' Grady starts to smile slowly.

'But we still need a bump.' Steven rubs his chin and creases his brow like a worried dog. His Woody Allen look.

'More of a bump than clouds forming by themselves?'

'Yeah . . .'

'Well, Steven, you can think of a bump to go on top of the bump . . . that's what you're good at . . .' I sound like the Sundance Kid.

'And then Grady can humanize it . . .'

'Make it accessible but funny . . .'

'Not to mention economical . . .'

Grady doesn't think twenty-five grand is enough money to sit in Francis's suite with Steven and learn how to write movies. He complains about the money constantly. I keep him provided with blow, to take his mind off the money, and he complains about that, too. He has actually managed to make me feel like a failure getting him only twenty-five. He should know what it was like getting twenty-five for him from Stanley Jaffe.

When I first asked Stanley for the money he dismissed the request and told me that friends did rewrites for free. I tried to explain that Grady was a friend, but he was also from television, and was routinely paid fifteen hundred bucks just to watch someone else's run-through and write a couple of jokes. I tried working it out with Stanley, teasing cajoling flirting but he was resistant. I kept telling him that this was who Steven wanted and we had already gone through any number of writers for free. We had gone through some writers for money, too. The best ideas were freebies from other film-maker types we were hanging out with. Brian De Palma came up with the implantation of the mountain. I never really knew whose idea was what, not even my own anymore. Steven would call at night sometimes, and chat about ideas. With *Tubular Bells* playing in the background. I never knew if they were his ideas, or Barwood and Robbins'.

'We just need one rewrite to put the family stuff at the beginning in shape,' I tell Stanley over and over, and still he fights me on this twenty-five grand. The budget is now up to $11.8 million and the picture is moving forward. A start date in search of a screenplay. As it were. The happy result of Joe

Alves's need to tell the guys who are making the blacker-than-black velvet backdrops to go ahead with the run.

I get to call Begelman and say, 'David, it's come down to the short hairs, or the cut velvet, if you will . . .' and proceed to explain to him that if we want the velvet in time, we have to tell the company tomorrow. The velvet alone is costly enough so that we need a green light to afford it.

He calls back at the end of the day and says, 'If you can get all your profit participants to agree that Columbia has the right to take a financial partner from this list,' and he reads all the majors plus CIC, 'which will not impact on your profit definition, then you have a go . . . you can call me at home . . .'

I track down Michael, Steven, Dreyfuss, Doug Trumball, and everyone says, of course, surprised. I call Begelman at home at eleven thirty with the news.

The next morning we have a green light and a start date at the end of May. And now there is this one tiny last step. An approved screenplay. It seems pretty penny-wise and pound foolish to fight over twenty-five grand for a ten-day rewrite to get a twelve-million-dollar movie in shape.

I want to say, Don't let the sun go down on me, Stanley, don't leave me stuck here on the ladder of my life . . . but he is such a square, an Elton reference, even from the beginning of what I always thought of as his Vegas period, won't move him, not even a little bit.

The entire debate comes to an ugly head one Saturday night when I actually scream at him on the phone that I'm crazy to try to reason with him, that any man who still washes his children's mouths out with soap for punishment in this day and age is clearly beyond reason. He hangs up on me. I don't blame him. I've definitely gone over the edge. But I can just taste it. I just know what this movie can be, if only I can get it made . . .

I do some deep breathing and call him back to apologize. His manservant answers the phone, tells me to wait, then comes back on the line: 'Mr. Jaffe is indisposed . . .' Ooooh, that mad. Well, let's face it, it was a rotten thing to say, plus Stanley gets mad at everything . . .

'Please tell him that I called him to apologize. I said a horrible thing to him and I didn't mean it . . . please tell him I'm very sorry . . .' The manservant makes clucking noises, like, You terrible girl, you should be sorry, and says he will convey the message.

Monday Stanley approves the twenty-five grand for Grady.

The more I think about it the more I think Grady should be paying me. Sometimes, just for my own amusement, I imagine amortizing the fee that I am sharing with Michael over the amount of time it is taking to make *Close Encounters*. By the end of the picture, it comes to 18.5 grand a year. Good thing I have all this other dough rolling in from *The Sting*. Every time I turn around, there's another huge check. It's hard to think of this ocean of money as finite, something that might get reduced to a river, a lake, a pond, a rivulet . . .

Besides, I know *Taxi Driver* is going to go through the roof. More than *Easy Rider*. Better than *Easy Rider*. The question is, Will the guys at Columbia move fast enough, think big enough? Norman Levy, Charlie Powell, and Buddy Young – the marketing triumvirate like the movie. They have even caused a good ad to be rendered, although they have allowed Michael, or Michael has allowed them, to drop my name a line on the 'produced by' credit.

The ad is a shot of De Niro walking a burnt-out city street with a triple X porno advertised on a marquee in the middle distance, over his head. He is carrying a paper bag with a bottle. His eyes are filled with vacant desperation. The ad line reads: *On every street in every city in this country there's a nobody who dreams of being a somebody*. Kind of a parallax of Peter Guber's loneliness theme.

The other ad is a piece of original art, by Guy Peellaert, the artist who did *Rock Dreams*, which we all greatly loved and admired, although my original English hardcover disappeared long ago. Michael has taken the original art on the grounds that he line produced the movie. I disagree. I think if a movie takes four years, then half a year at the St. Regis in New York does not a producer make. He keeps the Peellaert, but apologizes for the produced-by credit.

By the release of the movie, everybody has calmed down.

We actually all have dinner in my suite the night before it opens. Schrader and Geneen, Marty and Julia, Me and Michael and Bobby and Diane. Long road we have come. The Sherry makes us a dinner party in the standing dining room at the Skouras Suite. It costs five hundred bucks.

It also costs me Pat Dodds. She has been given the assignment of waking me for an early interview the next morning. After the dinner party, however, I hook up with Steven Prince. who plays the gun salesman in the movie. He *is* that guy, and comes to my suite dripping with coke and Quaaludes and desire. In a moment of weakness I go to bed with him, and poor Pat Dodds, bleary eyed, walks in on us. This behavior tears it for her. She is older than me, she has been around the block, she has seen it all. She knows there is no way I would fuck Steven Prince if I weren't loaded. We do not speak for the rest of this eastern sojourn, although she dutifully keeps typing the product of Steven's and Grady's labors. When we return to L.A., she gives me notice, adding, 'I just can't be around that stuff. . .'

Needless to say, Stanley questions the bill a month later. When I tell him what it was for, he smiles and erases his large red question mark. Stanley wants to have good impulses. But he is just so angry. In some ways a kindred spirit. (Years later, over coffee with Susan Grode, I learn that Stanley's mother died suddenly when he was eight years old and away from home at sleep-away camp, and I understand his anger.)

When I first meet Stanley I lobby heavily for his demise. When Columbia finally gets rid of him I am sorry to see him go. Stanley has been curiously supportive and he is a good personal friend to me. What's even more distressing about his departure is that he is going to be replaced by Dan Melnick. Dan Melnick, who didn't get *The Sting* and said: Don't get mad, get even? When Begelman tells me the news, I blurt, 'Oh no, it's curtains for us,' and he says, 'What do you mean?' and I have to admit I don't know. Silly me with my blinders on . . .

*

Steven and Grady are downstairs, in Francis's suite, now that he is gone. Francis has been in town for the first part of the week and we have finally gotten to hang out. I have only hung out with him once before, when we were shooting *Steelyard Blues* in Berkeley, and we were invited with Tony for dinner. He was very Italian majordomo of his surroundings, and throughout dinner he regaled us with Bob Evans's firing-him stories, which were hilarious in their extreme sliminess. He had been fired three times making *The Godfather*, often in roundabout ways that involved friends' betrayals. He just kept pressing on. Way to go, Francis! We all look up to Francis.

Coincident with my arrival, Francis has come to town on this mission called *Apocalypse Now*. I am only familiar with the original, by Jon Milius, which I have always mentally soundtracked with the Beach Boys harmonizing 'Let's go surfin' now, everybody's learnin' how, surfin' in Viet-nammmm.' He is trying to get Al Pacino to commit to the lead, and in between his confabs and my confabs we take walks along Fifth Avenue or sip hot espresso in his kitchen.

Francis knows I have no sexual interest in him, because he has seen Jeremy's picture on the cover of *Playgirl*. He looks at it, turns his lips down, and tosses it dismissively on the coffee table: 'You don't need that . . .' he says. I know, but I want it. He makes snotty remarks about cocaine, and I counter, equally snotty, that forty cups of his homemade espresso a day is not calculated to make one mellow and laid back.

Couple of days before Steven and Grady's arrival we have a very hotsy totsy screening for *Taxi Driver*. Michael and I go to dinner at the French Shack with Marty and Julia Cameron, who came for an interview and never left. We do Quaaludes and wine at the table, which gets me blitzed. Marty and Julia get into a fight, then tell us that Julia is pregnant. We all drink to that.

By the time we hit the screening, I am halfway between high and nauseated, kind of a nitrous buzz. My parents are there and lots of various-and-sundry New York types. I am in a Kenzo jumpsuit, Ferragamo boots, and Andrea Eastman's mink. I have very high color in my cheeks and white light in my eyes from the drugs. Marty tells me I look beautiful. Even with his Mephisophelean beard his face looks open and young for the first time since I've ever known him. I kiss his head, profoundly moved.

Francis arrives at the screening with Al Pacino in movie-star incognito drag: Why do all these guys like to wrap their heads and faces in scarves? Thank God it's at night or he'd have his sunglasses on, too. Real low profile, Al. Francis doesn't like the movie, but doesn't say; jealous, I think, but don't say back. Francis is pretty absorbed in this mission he's on, which includes being attached to Al Pacino's hip, so when Al wants to leave the après-screening party, Francis has to go, too. I tell him I'll find him later.

The screening, with the exception of Francis, has gone very well and adds to a feeling among all the principals that we should forget our differences (these being mainly between Michael and me) and bask in the glow of the promise of great reviews and big business. Since the beginning, I have been telling Begelman, You'll get ten million out of the big cities in the first two weeks if you play it right. I've had a few battles about the release.

Once, while we are having a meeting with Norman Levy in Michael's office, he gets me so upset that I swallow my coffee the wrong way, my glottis doesn't close, and I start wheezing. It takes a full thirty seconds till I start to turn blue and Michael performs the Heimlich maneuver. While I have been gasping for air Norman is screaming, red-faced, 'Look at the lengths she'll go to. This woman will do anything to get her way!'

Actually, Norman had no idea how far. We were all very distressed over the Westwood theater in which *Taxi Driver* was opening. The Plaza, an art house off the beaten path. I asked Stanley to have dinner with me in Westwood and I'd drive him past the theater. Stanley liked the idea of us going out and me driving. I had to. Stanley had broken his leg in a skiing accident and had a giant cast up his right leg. I drove fast around corners and bumped his cast against the door, hoping to hear him say, 'Uncle, uncle, I'll make Norman get you another theater in Westwood,' but he just winced in pain and asked me to slow down . . .

After the screening, I head for Francis's suite. The combination of drugs, alcohol, and triumph in front of my mother makes me very high. I walk back to the Sherry along Fifth Avenue and the cold New York air gets me higher. The ride in the elevator puts me on the queasy side, but I straighten up in the mirror before I ring Francis's doorbell. He opens the door and I say Hi! too loud for the hour, and his expression changes to quizzical as I feel all the features on my face disassemble and reassemble, and I pass out in his foyer . . .

I awaken the next morning in Francis's bed, still in my Kenzo jumpsuit. My feet are aflame and they feel like they will explode in my boots. Andrea's mink is flung over me. I look left and then right and there is Francis, fully clothed and wide awake, lying beside me. Oh no.

He smiles at the question in my eyes: 'I didn't want you to be uncomfortable when you woke up so I wore my clothes all night, too.' His beard smells stale. The whole situation smells stale. I don't even want to hazard a guess as to how those exploding feet might smell. I wonder for a moment if I'll be able to walk on them.

'My feet are killing me . . .' I am suddenly awake and realize that I am experiencing major pain in my feet. Tears spring to my eyes . . . 'Francis, we gotta get my feet out of these boots . . .' This is no small feat and takes the combined mechanical skills of both of us. Finally we do it. My feet have become the center of my universe. They throb with pain and relief. Feelthepainfeelthepain . . . I try to concentrate the pain away, but now that the boots are off, they hurt more. Francis gets up and makes his antifreeze coffee. We discuss the concept of sending me back to my suite in the dumbwaiter. I tell him my feet couldn't stand it. I limp my way to the elevator and leave.

I get my act together. Francis is leaving town and Steven and Grady are moving to his suite. The entire move is effectuated before teatime. I go to see them. I am wearing the most comfortable shoes I can find short of bedroom slippers. Steven knows Kenzo, the boots, the mink, and I have slept in the same bed as Francis, as I have told him. I tell Steven everything, like a brother. He tells a lot, but not everything.

Men don't. I ease myself painfully onto the couch and Steven exclaims: 'E-e-e-u-u-w . . . Jul-ee-a . . .' I realize that he thinks I am making a reference to my previous night's activity. There is no way he thinks I just had an alcoholic blackout. Why, that dirty little boy, he thinks Francis fucked me in the . . .

'Steven!'

'Sorry . . .' he cackles.

Taxi Driver opens February 8, 1976, in the Cinema I. After an interview that Michael and Marty and I do together, we walk across town to catch the noon show, the first show. People are lined up around the block and we punch each other in the arms with excitement. We stand in the back of the theater. See it with the paying customer, get to know if we have been right. When Travis says, upon returning the cab to the garage, 'Sometimes when I clean out the backseat there's come, sometimes blood . . .' the audience gasps. Ya-hoo. People applaud at the end. This is as good as it gets, we tell each other. When we come out into the bright sunny day, there is a bigger line . . .

Late in the afternoon the next day, Steven and I take the limo up Third Avenue to check out the lines again. They are very long and comprised mostly of pale young men in flak jackets who look like Travis Bickle. Along the way we hit some stores on Madison Avenue and buy each other presents. I get him a clear phone through which you can see all the inner workings and which folds up to the size of a fat wallet. He buys me a deerskin jacket that still has the bullet holes . . .

Grady and Grady's wife and Steven and I go to a taping of *Saturday Night Live* because Peter Boyle is guest hosting. He does 'Dueling Brandos' with Belushi. Up to this point, Peter has been the best Brando I've ever seen, but Belushi vanquishes him, easy. I feel bad for Peter . . . There's always someone better, prettier, richer, smarter, younger. . . Life. . .

I have a thing for Chevy Chase. When he does the news,

our eyes lock for a moment and Grady's wife leans over and says, 'You can have him if you want him.' She should know. When we walk onto the set after, I see Herb Sargent, and think, Yup, it's still the old pros who do the real punching up.

We are invited to the party downtown after. Grady's wife and Steven go, Grady and I head back to the hotel to finish up the blow. We sit at a gaming table with a checkerboard on it. Chop and rechop the product until it fluffs up into a considerable pile. We are both tired and depressed. This sojourn is nearly over. At one point in the endless coke discussion of what could really make two sullen Jews like us happier I say, 'Maybe nature . . .'

Grady laughs and says, 'I once suggested that to my partner, and you know what he said?'

'What . . .'

'He said, "The only flowers I ever want to see growing are the ones on my color television set . . ."'

When we come back from New York, we have a draft of *Close Encounters* that I won't have to beg Begelman not to read. We have warm family interaction in the beginning and Dreyfuss's first encounters; we have a second-act bump that incorporates effects and family drama; we have an 'experience' that is now written shot for shot. The 'experience' reads dry because it will never exist until it is projected in a hushed theater on a big screen with the right lamplight. One of the challenging aspects of movies.

We have another hotsy totsy screening for *Taxi Driver* in L.A. At the Directors' Guild. *Women's Wear* runs a picture of me and my new haircut with a freaked-out looking Bob Towne and suave Bert Schneider. Michael is cropped out of the shot. Serves him right for dropping my name a line on the credits. What goes around comes around. But what if it arrives and I'm not there?

Neither Towne nor Schneider likes the picture. I try to get Bert to tell me on the phone, and he keeps saying, 'This is the kind of conversation friends should have in person, so they can touch each other if one of them gets mad . . .' I think he hates it because I didn't like *The King of Marvin Gardens*, at least, not when I first saw it . . . It doesn't get me mad if people I respect don't like the picture. A little voice keeps going inside, I don't care. Want to know why? I know you don't but I'll tell you anyway. Because I'm right and you're wrong . . .

(Years later, after Hinckley shoots Reagan and blames *Taxi Driver* I run into Bert at one of Mike Gruskoff's international soirees. 'See, it wasn't such a bad movie . . .' I smile, and Bert says, 'If it was really great he would've killed him . . .')

It's been six months since Alan Hirschfield caused me to be fitted for a custom-made tan gab suit. One day I get into a giant snit about Life and Death, the cruel joke of the stop-and-startedness, the green/flashing-amber light of it all, and notice I've never received it. Kendall places the call, and when he doesn't come on immediately, I insist on leaving a message with his secretary. The gist is: Where's my suit, pisher! Then I leave to have a long freeway-madness drive to the beach, my favorite sanctuary.

Kendall calls me at home later. She is cheerful. 'I have a message for you. The suit's on its way. Alan Hirschfield is not a pisher.'

Dreyfuss and I are slated to go to the premiere of *Lenny* together. That day I suffer a baby-sitter crisis. I ask Michael for a hand, and to my surprise he says sure. I drop Kate at Michael's. I am to pick her up after the screening. The screening is in Westwood. We know it is a great movie, but it isn't about the Lenny any of us wants to see. The film puts us in a foul mood, and a group of us reconnoiter at a bar in the neighborhood to bitch about the movie. Grady Rabinowitz and his wife, and Harvey Miller, whom Grady once described to me as the 'only man who swaggers into a room on his knees' and who has a giant picture of Lenny Bruce in the tiny airless room where he manufactures funny lines out of context. Me. Dreyfuss. We cheer each other up by doing other Lenny Bruce routines that were funny, the ones Fosse has chosen not to put in the movie . . .

I arrive late at Michael's. He's wired.

'Wanna try a new drug?' he asks me. Hell, yes, I've just seen a movie that has taken away my will to live. He produces a gram bottle with white powder. Same old shit. I make a face.

'No, this is something new. It's not coke, it's called "green."'

'Doesn't look green to me,' I say, nostrils at the ready. We sit on the floor. I take a toot, and immediately my heart and ears start to pound. I feel frightened, but there is nothing here to be afraid of. Michael. Little Kate sleeping soundly in the other room . . .1 try to stand up, and my legs buckle. I sit down again. 'You like this stuff?' I say in my critical Jewish yenta voice. My mind is racing. This is more like crank than coke. 'What's in this stuff?'

'Homemade mixture,' Michael mutters, but his eyes dance brightly. Michael usually exudes an aura of laid-back aloofness. For some reason, this drug makes him alive. I am usually lively, nay, high-strung. This drug is exacerbating the high-strung part. I feel I'm on the line between Life and Death. It is hard to keep my balance.

'You know what I always felt bad about?' Michael says. Did I ask a question here?

'No. . . what?'

'I always felt bad that we split up before the first big check came in, that we never really got to be rich together . . .'

'We'd have had fights about the money, you know . . .' We always did. Michael mulls this over for a second.

'Probably . . .' he says.

'I think I have to throw up,' I announce, and stumble to the bathroom. When I put my head into the toilet, I feel it separate from my body. I look at my head in the toilet and wonder if I should just finish it all now and flush. The combination of the movie, Michael, our little baby asleep innocently in another room while we, two smart New York Jews, are imbibing a homemade mixture, makes me want to snuff it. Just end it all right the fuck here. Right now. My head jumps back onto my body and my nausea passes. My heart is thumping and my mind is racing, but I feel less out of control . . .

When I go back to the living room, Michael is pacing. Bob Dylan, his favorite, sings 'Lay Lady Lay' in the background. He sounds like Vic Damone.

'Got any downs?' I ask. We split a Valium. 'I don't think I should drive, do you?'

'You can stay here . . .' He gives me a pajama top, and I change, chastely, in the bathroom, wash my face, brush my teeth. My heart will not stop pounding. And my head keeps expanding and contracting. We check on Kate together. She is sleeping peacefully, our little beauty. There is a delicate strand of dribble coming out of the side of her mouth onto the pillow. We both reach down at the same time to brush it away. Our hands touch. I feel a brief electric charge, and then our hands remember we're divorced and separate. It is a very sad moment. We get into bed, back to back, just like when we were married. Scratch that, just like the last days we were married . . .

'What're we doing?' Michael says miserably, and I don't answer because I don't know . . .

When I tell Grady about my evening with Michael, because basically Grady and I are in an endless contest over who is more unhappy, he says, 'I think you should meet my friend Izzy . . .'

'I know Izzy. I talked to him a long time one night at one of those awful Guber parties . . .'

'I know. He likes you . . .'

'Doesn't he have a girlfriend?'

'They're breaking up . . . listen, he's cute, he's remarkably well-hung . . .'

'Oh, well, then how can I possibly refuse . . .'

'I'm gonna have him call you, okay?'

'This is very interesting . . . we have this dryhump, never-happen flirtation, so now you're going to fix me up with your best friend?'

'Hey, Hollywood . . .'

'What do you think this drug, green, was?'

'Ketamine, John Lilly's toy . . .'

'You knew about this drug and never told me?'

'Hey, there's a lot I don't tell you . . .' Men. The old need-toknow basis. Sometimes they're not sure *they* need to know . . .

Izzy MacPherson calls me later that day and we make a date for that night. It has reached the point with me that nobody ever shows up empty-handed in the drug department, so I am put off when he shows up with but half a gram of coke and one paltry Quaalude.

In one of Life's Great Coincidences, Judge Thomas J. Murphy hands down his decision in the *Fear of Flying* case on St. Patrick's Day. I wear a long green skirt with a green-and-pale-gray shirt. When I show up, we are all wearing green. Chris Cuddy is half-Oriental, the rest of us are:

'Jews in green,' I laugh. The ruling's already been written. In my favor. She's used the court in an attempt to wrest her property from my directorial clutches. For an instant, the thought crosses my mind that Begelman has bought the decision. But I dismiss it just as instantly; it was a spurious suit to begin with. I feel more relief than victory.

Even though Erica's been a cunt, plotting against me all along, I feel sorry for her. As Newman says to Redford in *The Sting*: 'Revenge? I been griftin' thirty years and never got any . . .' Chris, under the rules of discovery, has unearthed a datebook that proved that Erica, contrary to her self-portrait as a naïf, was a sophisticated businesswoman. Writers . . . they have to put everything down . . .

'No, no, Clark, tell him to hang a U-ey here!' I have been smoking a joint in the van that is hauling me and Steven and Vilmos and Clark Paylow around Mobile, and Joe O'Hare, white trash and stupid to the core, with his long sideburns and fat ass, has gotten a contact high. Now we are lost and losing precious time and everyone is getting pissed. Joe hangs a hard left onto an empty dirt lot with a small green-and-white building of indeterminate use.

There is a guy standing on the corner, big, with a fat belly hanging over too-blue jeans. He is sipping a beer and he has a mean, hard expression around his mouth. His eyes are hidden by reflector sunglasses, the kind worn by Cool Hand Luke's executioner, and he is reaching for something under his belt. Joe continues his hard left, so he can U-turn around the building and go back the other way under the freeway, to Jillian's house.

The guy is obstructed from my view by the house, but instinctively I move away from the window. He is pulling a gun out of his belt! Joe spins the wheels in the dirt, he panics so bad. Don't get so scared, scumbag, you're our ticket out in these parts, just like Peter Boyle had been the ultimate antibust companion after *Joe*. You could walk down the street with him smoking a joint, and cops would smile and wave and turn the other way . . .

I had arrived the night before with nothing but jeans and a duffel bag. Very free spirit. It is to cover the state of trauma I'm in over lack of cast. Dreyfuss is in, Teri Garr has been cast as his wife, but no kids, no Jillian, no Jillian's little boy. We've locked into the hangar because it is the only space large enough to accommodate physical production and special-effects requirements. We've even purchased a house in a development nearby for the Nearys to live in. We're doing a one-day stopover to check on the progress of the building of the rocks at the base of Devil's Tower in the hangar, the railroad crossing, Jillian's house. Everything is in a start-up state, but I don't believe we'll *ever* make our start date in May.

We finally get to Jillian's house. Nobody has bothered, yet, to make it look like a set for a movie. Unless we were remaking *Psycho*. It is the kind of deserted backwoods place where retarded children conceived by incest live in fear of their fathers.

'Ghosts live here,' I say to Steven as we walk along a muddy road to the front door, which is hanging from one hinge. We both brush away giant cobwebs drooping from sorry-looking weeping willows, but they catch in our hair. I keep thinking, Maybe if I check out what he has in mind for Jillian's house then I'll have a clue what he has in mind for Jillian. The only thing I know about Jillian is that she is an artist who lives with her son, and he is abducted by aliens. Steven's met everybody and rejected everybody. I'll know her when I see her, he keeps saying. The part's not written, I keep saying back, and pray he has something in mind. I look around the house, expecting low moans and apparitions. Nothing but funkiness and disrepair.

'Shari'll be getting back just as we are,' Steven says hopefully. Shari Rhodes has been on the road for months shooting videotape of children whom we can cast locally for Dreyfuss and Teri's family. The most critical casting is Jillian's son. And Jillian.

When we get back to L.A., I'm ready for a long snooze, but Steven calls, very excited, and tells me I'd better hotfoot it to Universal. I make it there in twelve minutes. No shortcuts. He has me look at some tape. It is black-and-white, very low resolution. He acts excited, so I do, too. We fly some kids in, cast two of them for Neary's family. Dreyfuss asks us to hire his cousin, Justin, for the third. We do . . .

Steven flies in two little boys for the part of Jillian's son. I keep wondering why we are casting the kid before the parent, but don't say. One of the kids, Zak, is fearsomely precocious. Steven adores him. One drawback: he looks like a troll. More so on film. The other is a sweet-faced child who looks a little like the drawings of extraterrestrials Alan Hyneck has been sending us. Steven wants to bring them both to Mobile, shoot the first scene, then decide. It seems a cruel thing to do to a child, but hey, whatever's good for the project . . .

We get a tip on an actress named Melinda Dillon who plays David Carradine's wife in *Bound for Glory*, the project Hal Ashby dumped *Fear of Flying* to do. Movie Irony. His picture is done, *Fear of Flying* isn't even slated for takeoff. Hal cuts together a reel of her scenes for us from his workprint. Maybe she is wonderful, maybe we are desperate, but we hug each other wildly in the projection room: We've found Jillian! Not a moment too soon. Shooting starts in two weeks. We don't pay her much, so when she insists on having her hair cut and colored by Carrie White, we say sure, anything . . .

I wait at Grady's while Izzy breaks up with his girlfriend. I don't think he'll have the nerve. But he does. Who knows? We might've lasted if he hadn't been so self-absorbed and I hadn't left to shoot *Close Encounters*. A couple of days before my birthday I come home late and find him relaxing in my tub: Jacuzzi, candles, the smells of pot and incense interlacing with bubble bath.

'Hi.' I smile, pissed at his relaxed annexation of my most private space. He looks up at me, depressed.

'I don't know who I am . . .' Who Izzy? This provides me with the first belly laugh I've had in months, but it doesn't do much for the rest of the evening . . .

Izzy gives me two presents for my birthday: first, a beautiful antique white satin gown from the Crystal Palace. Unfortunately it was made for a woman with huge boobs and no hips. I put it on and it looks ridiculous on me. I stand in front of the mirror, slouching and sticking my stomach out. Real attractive.

'Got me confused with the last one, huh?'

Flustered, he hands me a small box. I open it to find a silver heart attached to a key chain. The inscription reads: Ours is a great love . . . a line I stole from Jeremy and used on him in an emergency. I laugh and cry at the same time. I take to my bed, thinking of Henry Miller serving Erica and me dinner in his tan bathrobe. Maybe he's right. Maybe depression is a sickness and if you go to bed, it passes, like a fever breaking.

But I have a speaking engagement at San Francisco State College (a misnomer, since it is really a Catholic school) on April 9. Worse, I have insisted on an honorarium. I have the check for fifteen hundred dollars tacked up on my bulletin board. It reminds me of my folly. I am up at five in the morning. I call Norman Garey.

'You gotta get me out of this,' I say into his sleepy ear with a trembly voice. He wakes up immediately.

'Is something wrong?'

I burst into tears.

'I'm having postbirthday blues and I'm afraid to get on a plane . . .' That covers it. I turn Izzy's heart over and over in my palm like a rosary. Worry beads.

'You just have stage fright . . .'

'Get me out of it!'

'Okay, okay, I'll try . . .' I crawl back into my bed and pretend I am alone. Izzy's an early riser. Maybe he'll vacate soon and I can have a morning nap. He reaches out to hug, but I turn my back on him and sniffle into my pillow. He gets up. He brings me coffee. He tells me jokes. He passes me a morning joint. I wave it away. I will just stay in my bed and keep this wall around me . . . I doze.

Now there is Mrs. Grady Rabinowitz standing at the end of the bed with a late birthday present. I open it. White satin and lace. A nightgown slit to the waist, with pants. I try it on. Closer, but still not flattering. I sag in the mirror. I'm determined to look as ugly as I feel. I hop back into bed. Grady comes over.

'You're not really going to stand these people up, are you?' he chides, smiling gently, but with that invisible na na na index finger waggling vigorously.

Norman arrives. He is cloaked in false jocularity. 'I can get you out of it, but you'll be leaving the woman who organized this, Mary Anne Sweeney, pretty far out in the cold. You're their speaker – I think this is some kind of precommencement deal – and it's jammed.' This is not calculated to make me feel more convivial about the project. They hover around the bed. I sit up and the waterbed jiggles. It reinforces my feeling that I'm at sea. They are peering in at me, through the porthole. Friends. Concerned.

'Do you know that it has been so long since I got my legs waxed that if I rub them together, I'll probably start a fire. Which would be convenient since I'm sitting on all this water . . .' I push the covers back to show them and their faces brighten. 'Nah, I can't . . .' I lie down again. This is dumb.

I'm good at public speaking. I've been knocking them dead at seminars, even pretty packed auditoriums for years. It's all to make up for Herb Fox beating me for president in ninth grade even though my speech was better.

'This is dumb,' Norman says, saying my words for me. 'You're good at this. It is not good to be a no-show . . .'

'I know that. Can't we just say it was all a bad mistake, that I'm an artist, not a businessman . . .' Now, your brother, he thinks that he's the businessman and you're the artist, but he's got it backwards . . .

'Do you know that the only reasons artists are artists are for fame, fortune, and beautiful lovers . . . that's what Erica says in *Fear of Flying* . . .'

'I'll go with you!' Izzy explodes.

'That's big,' Grady and I say at the same time. Izzy is more afraid of flying than I am. Maybe two fearful people could lean on each other and be brave. Besides, I know I have to go. I'm cutting it real fine. Time has marched into late afternoon. Izzy calls the office to change reservations, Grady, Grady's wife and Norman, relieved, split. I take a shower and pull myself together. Something in black-and-white. I have a little coke, and we smoke a joint in the back of the limo on the way to the airport.

Tom Stout races us through and we get on a United flight to San Francisco. God forbid I should travel on a commuter flight with no first class. They close the doors behind us. I have a mimosa and half a Quaalude. Izzy is white under his beard. The perpetual intellect/fear expression that he sports on his borderline-attractive face has metamorphosed into pure animal/fear. I offer him the other half as the engines start up.

We start to roar down the runway, and he clutches at the inside of my thigh. His hand tightens into a claw during takeoff and I worry about my circulation. Christ, I'll never walk again, I think, as I try to pry his fingers loose. This is unseemly fear, I yell at him in my mind, You're pissing me off! Finally, when we're aloft, he loosens up. I check my stocking for runs. I light up a cigarette and ignore him. Gee thanks for coming along for support.

Mary Anne Sweeney is a dumpy little person with glasses

like bottlecaps. She is so grateful to see me she almost cries on the spot. I don't know why I think it's necessary, but I feel compelled to inform her immediately that I have taken every drug known to man to combat my nervousness. Actually I'm feeling pretty smooth. She says it doesn't matter, she's driving.

She drives recklessly on the freeway, probably to show off how cool she is to me and Izzy, and at one point she tries to change lanes right into another car. Izzy is so relieved to be on the ground that he doesn't seem to notice, but it gives me pause, so I tell her in my stern producer's voice that I am the one who is loaded, and she should please drive like the nice Catholic-school girl that she is.

Miraculously, we arrive all in one piece at the backstage entrance to a medium-sized lecture hall. I peek in and my heart does a little t-prime, u-prime tick. There are a lot of people and there are more filtering in, but they also look like they have been sitting here awhile and they are on the verge of getting restless. I'm gonna have to win them over. My favorite situation, like running for the plane. Ba-boom ba-boom goes my little heart.

'You'd better introduce me . . . Izzy, could you sit somewhere I can see you in case I get lost?' I talk extemporaneously for almost two hours. Show business . . . everybody loves it. Two seconds after I'm done, I don't remember a thing I've said, but I can see from the smiles and the applause I've been a crowd-pleaser. Mary Anne Sweeney beams. I don't feel so bad about taking their money now. I call Dav-El in San Francisco to take us to the airport over her protestation. No way I'm letting her drive me anywhere again. We hug and kiss goodbye and Izzy and I wend our way back to L.A. (Many years later, Mary Anne Sweeney turns up as Paula Weinstein's assistant during Paula's brief tenure as president of UA. Always be nice to people on the way up, you will for sure meet them on the way down . . .)

The day after I fulfill my obligation to speak, I get a surprise package from Norman. It is delivered with some ceremony by messenger. It is a beautiful tortoiseshell Dunhill lighter. The note says: 'This is to light your path to fame, fortune and beautiful lovers, not necessarily in that order . . .'

The lighter, which is the perfect weight in my hand, becomes a good-luck amulet, an object to clutch in my hot little hand when things get tense. We go through a lot together for a long time, like me and Norman . . . I don't lose them, back to back, as it were, for years . . .

Of all the dead people I know François Truffaut wins the prick award hands down.

I was so proud and happy when he committed to the part of Lacombe. It was a coup, no doubt about that, and a score at seventy-five grand and no points. That should have been a clue as to how he felt about the project, but Steven and I were so excited it didn't occur to us that he might just be doing research. He wrote a fab letter accepting:

Dear Julia,

I remember you very well, the night of the Oscar, April 1974 when you came onstage to receive a Award (many of them) for *The Sting*. You whore a beautiful black dress, I thockt [think at the past]: 'If I make one day a film in Hollywood it will be with Julia Phillips'! But in my spirite it wasn't as actor but director! Anyway, I was happy receiving your letter, maybe I will play Lacombe, maybe I won't. Its depend on my schedule about my next picture. If Steven Spielberg is able to make me free during August it will be possible to me to accept this nice part of Lacombe.

I am wondering if you understand my very special English, which I hope you (may) can!

If I play Lacombe, I would like my friend Louis C. Blau [to] arrange my contract with your company. O.K.? Are you agreed with that? Louis C. Blau is a very nice man working for Kubrick and few others from his office 9777 Wilshire Blvd. Her wife is a very good painter they live in Bel Air of course.

Dear Julia, I have to say, I love Los Angeles very much. Each time I come I go as soon as possible for to visit Jean Renoir at home or to the bookshop of Larry

Edmunds on Hollywood Blv., the best movies bookshop on the world.

Before I say goodbye, I have to say frankly: I speak English WORST I write it.

I suppose to hear from you soon,

Sincerely,
François Truffaut

The *whore* for *wore* was also a dead giveaway, but we all thought it was cute and French. I remembered the smell of the theater where my mother first took me to see *The 400 Blows*, the feel of the seats. Me crying after the end, my mother ignoring me, intent as she was on getting a cab in the New York drizzle.

He saw a role in our picture as research for a book he was doing on acting or actors. It was never clear which. I personally never believed his English was as bad as he pretended, just like I didn't think he was hard of hearing in his left ear. I thought he had gone a little over the top in *Day for Night*, making himself lame as well as hard of hearing. I loved the movie, like all movie people did.

François came to town. I was prepared to adore him. We were all prepared to adore him. The dénouement of a recurring nightmare in *Day for Night* was seeing the poster for *Citizen Kane*. If François Truffaut had been inspired to make great pictures because of *Citizen Kane*, as I had, then he was aces with me.

It was immediately apparent that François didn't – or chose not to – speak English very well. We gave him Sally Dennison, blonde, blue-eyed, skinny with a more interesting than pretty look, to translate, and this seemed to please him. He was also given a suite at the Bel-Air Hotel, a car and driver at his disposal, and any other amenities we could provide. But he was an arrogant, famous French director and I couldn't help but feel that he was fucking with us all the time.

I was convinced that the well-known-deaf-in-the-left-ear legend (with a hearing aid as a prop, if you please) was a ploy, like not speaking English, to keep the world at bay and for his own private amusement. Having worked with Donald Sutherland, a top-ten brain fucker, as well as Paul Newman, who was seriously weird (he once said hello to the back of my head and took umbrage when I didn't respond. When I asked George Roy Hill for some advice on the subject he said that the thing to remember about Newman was that he had holes in his head) I thought I could detect the aura of a private dancer in Truffaut.

Still, I addressed myself to making him feel comfortable, revered, safe. That was my specialty. Also my job. But deep down I knew he was a prick and it was making me defiant. Fuck him. I wanted my own private amusement.

'Steven, I'm telling you that left-ear shit is as authentic as the gimp.' A couple of sentences per day were devoted to this subject.

'He's deaf.' Steven laughed. 'He makes me repeat everything several times, even with Sally translating.' It didn't occur to Steven that he was being pimped. People as manipulative as Steven never think that they could be just players in other people's mind games.

'Making you repeat stuff could be any number of things,' I pushed. 'He could be trying to understand his part, which is the nice interpretation. Or he could be pulling a power play. Making you repeat yourself too many times for you to be the boss.' Silence. It was either too easy or too hard to get Steven Spielberg's attention. That's why he was such a great director: for him it had to be perfect small moments between people or Barnum & Bailey. Lots of directors were doing small moments but no one was doing the circus quite so well. 'Anyway it doesn't have to be because he is hard of hearing. Kendall is deaf in her left ear and she is always leaning into you or turning her head if you are on her left side. He doesn't do that.'

'Well, he's not totally deaf and he wears a hearing aid so it's not the same . . . But I'll watch him. Did you look at that test from the computer guys?'

'Which computer guys?' There were three or four outfits taking our money and spending them on tests for our spec f/x that didn't look like much. It was artistically discouraging, but at this point I was encouraging Columbia to spend money, so they served a purpose. I was just getting antsy to see something halfway promising.

'The geeks from Boston.'

'I'm about to.' The test had been sitting in the projection booth all day, but I was so busy I was forty-five minutes late on everything and long overdue for a bathroom visit. If I didn't see it right away, though, Steven would think I didn't care. And if I didn't care enough he might commit to another picture. I had once written in lipstick on his bathroom mirror, 'Stop me before I make another deal,' and he'd laughed but he continued to read scripts. It created underlying pressure at all times and it gave me a big headache every night at about six thirty.

'I'd like to see them with you again. What time are you running them?'

'Right now, I just said . . .'

'Change it to the end of the day. We can go to dinner with François together.'

'That's tonight?'

'Yeah, and Sally is excited to go to La Scala.'

'Our place . . . Hey, I've got an idea . . .'

'I can tell from the tone of your voice it's a wicked idea . . .'

'I'll bet you a hun that François isn't deaf and we can find out at dinner.'

'You're not going to ask him?' This question was not completely out of line. I almost always went the direct route. Maybe too direct for directing, but it worked for me in my present capacity.

'No. I'll make this fun. We'll sit at dinner, me to François's left, then Sally to his right, and you to Sally's right. I know you won't like the seating arrangement, but it makes sense. It fulfills the boy-girl, boy-girl concept as well as the translating requirement. At some point during dinner I'll whisper his name and we'll see if he turns toward me. If he does he ain't deaf and I win. If he doesn't he is deaf and you win.'

'Why can't I sit to his left and whisper his name?'

'Two reasons. One – it makes sense for Sally to sit between you two and that has to be on his right assuming the hearing aid has a purpose at all, and Two – I think any man, especially a Frenchman, would respond to a woman's whisper more than a man's.'

'I love it when you talk like that. Okay, you're on. Change the screening. We can talk about it on the drive to dinner.'

'Ah, the perfect onejoint drive . . .'

'Better that than the other stuff . . .'

'You stop eating Twinkies, and I'll give up toot.' Fat chance. That was easy.

'I'll swing by about five – five thirty.'

'We're not going to dinner till seven thirty. Which is ridiculously early to be taking a Frenchman out to dinner. Maybe we should make it six and tell him it's a late lunch.'

'Six thirty, then.'

'We'll be screening the test in golden time –'

'I love it when you talk like that . . . besides, you're the one who's always saying "Keep 'em spending . . ."'

'You're right. I'll ask for Frank*.' Frank was a pot-smoking projectionist. Maybe if I rolled him a bomber laced with a little coke he would fudge the time. It was the small challenges that kept me going.

I could look forward to the entire enterprise now: the screening at straight time, the computer-image test, the discussion of the test, the joint, the mussels marinara, and most of all – da dah – *the bet*. Making small talk with a luminary through an amateur translator, while on display at a front banquette at La Scala would've been a nervous proposition. Boring, in an odd way, too. The bet would provide an edge to the evening as good as smoking coke at the end of a cigarette in a public place.

The test ran a total of a minute and a half and we ran it about six times until the film broke. Black screen. From the vanishing point, a speck of light speeds forward. It springs this way and that, in a nonballistic fashion, at radical angles until it is dominant foreground, a huge white globe. It was very exciting, but it wasn't the real shit. I knew it before Steven said a word.

'I want the glare, the hotness of the light. I wanna cover myself if the hardware doesn't work.'

'Agreed; then why do we continue to be fucked around by Colin Cantwell?'

'He hasn't spent that much yet. He worked on *2001*. If half of what he says he can do is true, we've got some major problems solved.'

'What I'm starting to find out is that everyone worked on *2001*, that they all take the credit, and that most of them don't know dick. I'm working our way up the special-effects ladder to Doug Trumball, even if I hear he fucked John Whitney over.' And then got fucked over like everyone else, by Kubrick. Why did they think his name was above the title? 'Anyway, Colin never washes his hair. I hate these jerk-off meetings and then we spend more money and he comes up with nothing, and he gives off animal-smell to boot.'

Steven laughed. Best defense with me . . . So we drove off to dinner together in Steven's rattly little Mercedes 280, which meant we'd have to drive back after to Burbank to get my car. Inefficient, but we were into spending a lot of time together. As far as I was concerned, I was protecting my interests.

Halfway through dinner I whispered 'François' and he turned minutely in my direction. Of course, Steven argued that it was an inconclusive gesture, and he welched on the bet. I know I won because it earned me François's eternal enmity.

When the dinner was over and we had all said our good-nights, we got back into Steven's car. We sat in silence for a moment while the car warmed up. We turned to each other. For no particular reason, I put my arms around his neck and stuck my tongue in his mouth. We had a good long kiss. He pulled away. His glasses were tilted at a ridiculous angle; he looked frightened.

'Jul-ee-a, that was a real kiss . . .' Treasure it, pal, it's the one and only. More silence during the drive to Burbank and I patted his hand in a comforting gesture before I got out of his car and into mine. I drove home very fast and brushed my teeth twice before I went to bed. The things a girl will do just to make a great movie . . .

*

'I hate my driver,' I say to Clark Paylow, who is ruddy with psoriasis, and has more important things to deal with. Like find the only cherry picker within a hundred-mile radius, because Steven has redesigned a shot for the reveal of Devil's Tower. It is only the third day of shooting in Wyoming and already we have Stanley Jaffe en route from L.A. to upset everybody.

We are out on a long straight road with nothing but sky and clouds and land. I'm sure the farmers who live here, twenty miles from each other, don't have much social life and probably beat their wives and rape their daughters on Saturday night when they have too much Wild Turkey, but outside this does look like God's country. If there was a God, he'd hang out here.

'I don't see why I can't drive my own car and come and go as I please . . .' I study my Frye boot drawing a figure eight in the dusty ground. Maybe infinity.

'Fine, take the car, drive the car, race the car if you want to.' I can see little patches of irritation erupting on Clark's face, but I know he's not angry with me. I am going to make him a rich man. I believe it. Sometimes he does, too. Greatness, I tell the crew all the time. Two years from now you'll be bragging about working on this movie, I tell the crew, later, in Mobile, Alabama, in the Neary house, where it is 120 degrees with no air conditioning and people speak with murder in their voices.

'Gimme the keys, and dump the driver.' The driver is a hostile brick shithouse who favors flannel and does not understand the vicissitudes of a woman producing a movie with her daughter and her daughter's nanny in tow. In Caspar, Wyoming. There is not much for Kate and Jackie to do but go to the set. This woman does not understand, and she is making me feel uncomfortable in my own car. In my space. Christ, I've got shitty boyfriends for that. No way I am ever sleeping with this woman. She is lucky I am not firing her. I am saving that for craft service.

The next day I drive Kate and Jackie and myself to a new location. Kate is fussy. Grow up, Kate, you're three. You can handle it. It is an hour-and-a-half drive. First through the outskirts of Caspar, which is lined with cricketlike structures sucking oil out of the ground. Pretty dismal. Then, God's country. There is a herd of cattle meandering along the road. A couple of genuine cowboys corral them lackadaisically. Instinctively I know I will get shot if I honk, so I sidle up to one of them, smile, and look up from under my lashes.

'Help . . . I'm a city girl. How do I get through?'

He flashes his choppers back at me, and his weathered face crinkles pleasantly. 'Just go slow and try not to hit any of 'em.' Is this a trick answer? I follow his advice and to my surprise the cattle sense the car and get out of its way. It takes all my self-control to maintain the necessary fifteen-mile-per-hour pace. It takes ten minutes to thread my way through all this brown-and-white flesh. Which I feed on.

'O-o-o-h, cows,' Kate keeps saying, like the first time she ever stood up in the back of a limo headed toward New York through Harlem at night. 'O-o-o-h, people,' she kept saying, as we passed street corner after street corner of dealers and their customers, a deprived California child thrilled to see humans – any humans – instead of automobiles. Perhaps she was still too young to make those distinctions.

She did seem just as happy with the cows as the people. We get through the herd and I punch it. The big American gas guzzler sputters and lurches forward. I watch the speedometer struggle its way up. Forty fifty seventy-five . . . ahhh, goin' ninety. (Goin' ninety, an ancient hippie once told me, is the perfect puff on the perfect joint in a perfect car soaring along a perfect road on a perfect day.)

Kate starts to fuss, again. 'Weaw ahw the cows?' She starts to cry. All the way to the set. I turn her toward me and give her a good talking to. She does that snurfle toddlers do and puts on a brave face.

'Wanna come to the set with Mommy?' She snurfles yes. I pick her up and we head to the set. Melinda and Richard are climbing up an embankment to a fence, Devil's Tower rising up before them. They are right in the middle of a shot as we approach. I tiptoe forward. I'm not sure if there is dialogue, but I see Gene Cantamesa, crackerjack sound man, with his headphones on. I stop in my tracks and watch the cherry picker rise. Kate starts to cry.

I rush away from the set and while I'm kissing her forehead, I put my hand over her mouth. When the shot is over, I hand her to Jackie and walk over to Gene. 'So?' I ask.

'Oh, I never get the sounds of the producer's children.' He smiles and I know I have ruined the shot. I am humiliated. I look over to Kate and Jackie. Kate is investigating flowers on the ground in an unperturbed, deliberate fashion. I hope I haven't suppressed her ability to express herself by muzzling her. Steven calls out to me to get on the cherry picker so I can see the shot. With the exception of Melinda stumbling every time on her walk up the hill, it looks very wonderful through the camera. He is a genius, no question about it. He is very generous with his knowledge. Just so long as they never print any photos of me looking through the camera.

Actually the fight with Ms. Driver happens right away. Coming down from Devil's Tower one night at magic hour, I hear the rattlesnakes for the first time. The helicopters have already wrapped so there is much less noise. Every day we climb up farther on the rock pile at the base of Devil's Tower. The boulders are huge and far apart from each other. I am not in great shape and my legs are killing me from the morning climb. They're vibrating like sewing machines going down.

'Help!' I scream. I'm not shy. Nick McLean is carrying the camera down. He looks like he might set it aside for me. Nice. A big blond football player. Oh, I forgot. I have a boyfriend. In L.A. Wait a second. I'm here and you're there and there's nothing you can do about it. Now, here comes the stunt gaffer extraordinaire. He of the wild glass-doorknob blue eyes and the blond hair and the crisscrossed perfect white teeth. He helps me down. By the end of the climb I'm in love. Scratch that, I'm in lust.

I give him a ride in my car and he walks me to the door of my shabby motel room. 'So, you wanna hang out later?' he smiles and pushes up against me, face to face, belly to belly.

'You're just about my height,' I say back. Beware the short man. He cracks up and moves in closer.

'Just think where that puts everything,' he says. O-o-o-h,

bay-bay. He is wearing a necklace made of eighteen-carat puka shells. It glints at me lasciviously.

'Sure, I'll hang out with you . . .'

There isn't any place to hang out, not even a neighborhood bar. The evening doesn't start out great. I decide I should have dinner with Kate and Jackie in what passes for the dining room. Kate starts playing with the ketchup bottle. The more I Kate-put-that-down, the more she brandishes it this way and that, and finally she spurts ketchup all over my favorite sweater.

Her eyes and mouth form shocked little o's. Furious, I jump up from the table and march outside. When I get there, I realize there is no place to go. After a moment, I walk back inside to the table, where Kate and her face are still in the same shocked position. This cracks me up, then Jackie, finally Kate. My little trooper! We enjoy a full-frontal snuggle. Then I hustle them off to their room so I can have my date with Mr Fearless*.

He comes prepared with any number of aids and drugs. We have a bottle of cheap champagne, a couple of quays, and a hit or two of blow. We indulge in some very athletic sex, but all the drugs and positions in the world are no cover for the fact that he has a tiny dick. I don't wanna sleep in a bed with him so I give him my car. The next morning Ms. Driver goes on a rampage in search of the car, and blows my cover. The only way to equalize the situation in the respect department: blow her off.

Clark has found a gym to set up a projector to run our dailies. Trumball brings down his first test for the clouds. Even though you can see some of the connections for the light, it is amazing.

'How'd you do that?' I want to know.

'Salt water on top of fresh water to create the horizon, and a funnel pumping in our special mixture – mainly tempera – and a grain of wheat light . . .' He smiles a thick smile, well pleased with himself. Among the other dailies are shots of the helicopters circling Devil's Tower at the tail end of magic hour, when it's dark. If there were no sound they would look like UFOs. I point this out to Steven. As in: maybe we shouldn't be doing the expensive effects, maybe we should just do this, and he puts his finger over his mouth, shhh . . .

I have lent Izzy my white Mercedes 450 SL. Two days after I leave it is stolen. He calls while I am negotiating some rattlesnake-infested rocks at the foot of Devil's Tower, Wyoming. I can barely hear him over the mobile phone, but do absorb right away that I have left my other baby in his care and now it's gone.

'What are you feeling?' he has the nerve to ask.

'It reminds me of Jeremy . . .' Jeremy the Beautiful Junkie, Jeremy the Mistake . . . I watch Melinda Dillon stumble on her run and feel a warning in my stomach. 'Listen, fuck the car, talk to Kendall, I gotta go,' and I hang up to deal with the more compelling problem of Melinda's broken ankle. The great thing about show biz: there's always something more important going on than real life.

I don't really have time for these interludes anyway, because I have Stanley to deal with. Stanley has chosen this late moment to be worried about the abduction of Jillian's little boy at the end of Act Two. The bump on top of the bump, if you will. Of course, it isn't clear that this is what's irking him until he gets to Caspar. He is in his 'this is a disaster' mode, and it takes some patience to extract from him that he is really only upset about the abduction.

We compromise. We will shoot it the other way, too: i.e., with her pulling him back in. Steven looks at me: Are you crazy? and I look back: Let's deal with this later. The Stanley snit actually makes us think the abduction through more carefully and I finally say to Steven:

'It wouldn't hurt to have her run after him . . .' which then expands to her running after the lights as they retreat behind the clouds, a tiny figure in a huge field.

I dictate the deal, and have Judy make copies and circulate

it to the crew. They are impressed with my ability to communicate, but they also know which shot will end up in the
movie. At least it makes Stanley happy and abbreviates his
stay. I make sure the still photographer takes a lot of pictures
of him with Steven and Truffaut. Quelled, and really bored by
Caspar, he splits.

Begelman has been nowhere during this conflagration. He
conveys a message to me when I turn to him for help that he
is 'shocked.' He and Michael are in Cannes. Michael calls me
at five thirty the morning we are traveling from Caspar to
Mobile to tell me that we have won first prize, the Palme
d'Or, for *Taxi Driver*. On the plane, the pilot makes the
announcement and everybody cheers. The combination of
leaving Caspar and the award puts everyone in good spirlts.

The Stuntman comes over to congratulate me. He unscrews
the catch on his necklace and holds it out for me to see.

'I want you to wear this while we're shooting,' he says. 'I
want it to be your good luck for the picture.'

'But I have the lighter,' I say. The lighter is already the butt
of crew jokes. I keep misplacing it and freaking out that I
have lost it.

'Well, this screws on, so you'll never lose it,' he says
solemnly and puts it on my neck. He takes my hands and puts
them on the catch so I can screw it. The necklace is heavy.

'I can't keep this . . .' I protest, a tad on the feeble side. It
really is a beautiful necklace.

'Just for the picture . . . I want you to have it . . .'

'You know, the other night . . .'

'A great memory. This necklace has no strings attached . . .'

I look down at the guy's hands. He is missing varying degrees
of two fingers on his left hand and almost a whole one on his
right.

'Those related to flying?' I ask sardonically.

'Okay, you can start to taxi now,' he guffaws, and I lurch us
down the runway. This is my third flying lesson. Well, we are
shooting in a hangar, aren't we? A lot of people cope with
their fear of flying by learning to fly. I had bought Erica's

book for its title. I am having more fear of Erica Jong than fear of flying right now. She has sued and lost, but in the process she has killed my desire to direct, so there's nothing I'd rather do than produce *Close Encounters*.

Steven has bought a scooter and gone off driving on it during lunch hour. He has a Jewish nerd's touch with wheels. He is a lousy biker, and I start going along for the ride, although what I think I can accomplish more than to get two people killed instead of one, I don't understand. I can scream *Slow down* in his ear, and hope he will listen. I do, after all, as they like to say, have his ear. It is actually remarkable, considering, how far I seem to be going by having someone's ear. Redford. Streisand. Steven. No power of my own, just the power to have someone's ear.

I have always loved motorcycles. And their drivers. Starting with Bob Dattila in high school. When my mother decreed, in the summer of my fourteenth year, that I should go to summer school to learn to type (so that I could 'compose at the typewriter') I punished her and my entire neighborhood by commuting on the back of his Harley every day. This was especially troubling to my next-door neighbor, Mrs. Hecht, who was a cranky, middle-aged tutor. When Bob and I were coming and going, not too much learning got done, particularly since most of her clients were our contemporaries. My bedroom window looked almost directly into the study where she taught big-chested football players math and English. When I got bored, I found various ways to distract them. Nuff said. She hated me already.

I had even hung out with a dorky, bad-breathed guy in Milwaukee named Dick Glazner, just because he had a motor scooter. When he tipped us over into a ditch at moderate speed and I walked away with scratches, I stopped for awhile, but I got back into them when Michael and I were first married because they were the only transportation we could afford. This ended with a nasty fight over a freezing Labor Day weekend on the New York Thruway, when I flipped out, but that may have had as much to do with the fact that we had spent an entire weekend with Larry and Penny Bernstein.

Larry was okay, but Penny drove me nuts. She had long red

hair and was a dance therapist. She had a lot of jargon at her disposal, but it didn't cover her basic stupidity. Whenever she felt threatened by the conversation because it was beyond the reach of her tiny intellectual powers, she would go off in a corner and dance, throwing that hair around expressively.

I finally broke up with them when she intoned in a particularly smug voice that I was clearly a product of what she referred to as a 'cold-titted mother.' Of course she was right, but I was not to acknowledge that to myself until thousands of hours and dollars spent on therapy. Besides, I operated on the theory that it was okay for me to call my mother names, but nobody else could. The highlight of this endless weekend we had spent with them was that we went soaring in gliders somewhere in Sullivan County.

I had gone first, squeezed tightly behind the pilot. We caught a particularly dynamic thermal and slid around the sky about eight hundred feet above cows and county fairs and farms for twenty-five minutes. Halfway through the ride I got nauseated, and had to exercise the greatest control over my innards just not to puke on his head. When we finally landed, I rushed to the bathroom and dry-heaved for another twenty.

By the time Michael and I got on his trusty BMW 600 I was in a fury. Mainly with him, because they were his friends. As it got colder and colder on the Thruway I got madder and madder until just outside New York City I started pounding him and delivering nasty little kidney punches. He pulled over and we had it out right there. Impetuously, I stuck out my thumb and got a ride with a gray-haired doyenne in a Rolls. I didn't go back to our Greenwich Village apartment for three days.

Nick McLean, who is now my location boyfriend, has found the pilot, the planes, and the lessons. I, who pride myself on my intuitions about spatial relationships, show no real aptitude for driving a plane. In fact, there really is a lot to learn, and I am surprised I am having trouble with it. Am I into these flying lessons to show myself my own limits? Basically I am taking these lessons to frighten Steven into not driving on the dumb motorcycle. The first time I took off, I could see him and Clark Paylow watching me, looking worried. Christ, all that would happen probably is that Steven would continue to ride the schmucky bike, and Clark would get terminal psoriasis.

Even on the teeny-weeny little Cessna 150, there is a lot of instrumentation, and instruction. The guy never stops talking. He gestures with his hands a lot, so I get to check out those semi-fingers often. Why don't missing parts bother me? Have I made an intellectual decision long ago to overcome morbidity?

It is the coke.

The coke to make me braver than I already am. I am making decisions daily that should terrify me. And every time they do, I take a little toot and I am ten feet tall. That is really all you need to do to be a good producer; you have to convince them that you are ten feet tall all the time. And that you can do something a little crazy. So they better watch it.

The Neary house is a temper tester. No air conditioning, blacks encasing the house so we can shoot day for night. We seem to be getting hung up on the mashed potatoes and the mountain. Every time the mountain gets bigger, Dreyfuss taps on it and yells, 'Victoria, Victoria Principal, are you in there?' Steven ran with her for awhile, somewhere between Sara Miles and the Bimbo. Steven's taste in women is on a par with my taste in men. As in, not so hot.

The crew hates Justin, who is a brat. His brattiness exacerbates an already egregious situation. The heat is overpowering. No amount of Seabreeze in a neckerchief works. Steven gets so depressed between setups, he takes up residence in the playpen. One day I hear the dolly grip complain, 'This place is tighter than a bull's ass . . .'

'I have two words for you, Clark,' I say. 'Air conditioning.' Clark improvises, installs large fans that blow over dry ice. It is marginally better. He worries out loud that he should change his name from Paylow to Payhigh . . .

*

Grady decides that he should come visit. He has become a major distraction. He pays my black maid twenty-five dollars to give him a blow job and then feels compelled to tell me about it. We have a fight and I end up in the bathroom in tears. Grady follows. And then we're on the floor . . . coke and ludes and a hot summer night in Mobile, Rosemary with the Devil, going, Ohmygod this is really happening.

When he leaves, we are both glad to see him go. I make him promise that if he has any inclination to tell his wife or Izzy about it he should call me first . . .

When I replug into the picture, I see that we have been at the Neary house too long, and I wrap us up quickly, reminding Steven that he has a whole second camera crew who can pick up anything he wants: mounds of dirt being thrown through windows, mounds of mashed potatoes, anything he wants, just let's get the fuck out of here . . .

We have only been shooting a couple of months and it is beginning to feel like forever. Now we are going to entertain a whole bunch of guys. Bankers, Stanley, bankers, Begelman, bankers, Hirschfield, bankers, Veitch. We are going to need a lot more money and they already know it. They are coming to check up on us. On the kids. Personally, I think we are all doing a brilliant job. Except maybe Vilmos. And the craft service guy. Steven refuses to fire Vilmos, and by now we have shot enough to have to be committed to him, but I am just waiting for the craft service guy to fuck up so I can have the pleasure of putting him on the next plane back to L.A.

Meanwhile, though, I have to focus on the planes coming in. From all coasts. Checking up. On the kids. I kiss the ground when we return to the strip from my flying lesson, a little ritual with me. We make a date for the end of the week. I run up the stairs at the back of the building and manage to just make it behind my desk before there is the Steven knock at the door accompanied by the Steven 'Jul-ee-a,' and the Steven burst through the door. Ahhh, my little prince! He is nervous. Guys like bankers make him nervous. Christ, guys like David Begelman make him nervous.

'Look, I'll entertain them most of the time . . . you just have to have this little dinner with them . . .' He makes a face, then brightens somewhat.

'If you pick me up a little early I'll play you the five tones . . . I got a little electric piano . . .' Another toy. Steven's and Richard's offices are filling up with toys. Pong! Tank! Precursors of the video explosion. Games at which I'm only barely adequate. On the other hand, I'm pretty good at the game of Banker! And then somebody is looking for Steven on the radio they have given me, the one that has a gold JP glued to its holder . . . Steven tells me it's a big gesture when the production staff gives the producer her own radiomike, and he is off . . .

David Begelman is carrying a wheel of Pete Turner special-effects stills. I take him and Alan Hirschfield down to the big set, and pass them off to Doug Trumball. When I leave, he's dazzling them with the basic principles of the motion-control camera. We have just tested it a few nights ago. First, Nick McLean rides the camera in a simple dolly shot. He steps off. Doug pushes some buttons on the computer to which the camera is hooked up. Then he pushes another button and the riderless dolly moves in an exact duplication of Nick's move. It is spooky. I have seen the future and it belongs to Doug Trumball.

This process will allow a single piece of film to duplicate the same move eight times. That means one special effect laid over another over another over another, times eight. It also means that not every special effect will have to be shot with the camera locked down, which is the way it's been up until now. David, whose attention span is just a tad short of Kate's, loses interest quickly; Alan, on the other hand, is mesmerized and asks Doug to repeat the process several times.

Then he sidles over to me. 'You need somebody older,' he whispers, catching me in a naked lovestare at the humpy camera operator. Not you . . .

'Yeah, but Aristotle Onassis is dead.'

'I'm going to visit one of our offshore rigs in the gulf

tomorrow,' he continues. 'Want to take a short helicopter ride with me?' Horny bastard. I keep trying to figure out what Steven sees in Alan that reminds him of Michael. Besides Om. Secrets. That's it! They keep secrets. Other people have secrets; they *keep* secrets. A game they play with the world. With themselves . . .

The tooth that I think of as my *Close Encounters* tooth starts to throb.

Why does Alan always give me a toothache? This is the second time it's acted up since we've arrived in Mobile. The first was at the Neary house, when Grady was in town. I dealt with it then with cloves and coke and too much activity. I rub at my cheek for a second, then:

'J.P., J.P.,' Chuck Myers screams over the radiomike, 'Kendall needs you upstairs. Urgent . . .' I excuse myself without favoring Alan with a reply, and I race across the set, up the stairs, down the hall, around the bend. Kendall is holding the receiver in her hand.

'It's Dick Uricich. He just talked to the lab and he thinks there's a scratch on some sixty-five.' Oh no, not the shots that we robbed the other night, the whole company moving into rain-soaked fields around Jillian's house in forty minutes, charging through a horde of mosquitoes and gnats and flying roaches the size of golfballs, shots this way and that from all POVS for drivebys, for the abduction scene, for whatever we might think of later. Shots that were *essential*.

'Hello?' I pant into the phone.

'We've got a little problem here,' Uricich says, master of the understatement. He proceeds to explain to me that some-where in the middle of the reel the film has been perforated. He's already spoken to Vilmos, to the lab, to Eastman Kodak . . .

'Perforated? As in, a giant hole?' Dick grunts yes, right in the middle of the reel. Tooth pain bangs away at my conscious-ness. I put it on hold. 'Well, just a second, if something physical happened to the film, it happened in the camera, or in the lab, right?' Probably on a reel, being cranked from one bath to another. I am the daughter of a scientist, and even if I like to torment him with disbelief in the existence of the atom, I have a fair understanding of these sorts of things.

'Well, we could always say so . . .' I have every intention of saying so, in four-part harmony if necessary. Vilmos and Nick have edged into the periphery of my phone-pacing space. Kendall gets the lab and I regale the guy with a short speech I develop on my feet: if something is perforated in the middle of the reel, it's mechanical. My cameraman is standing here and will swear it didn't go into the camera that way and it didn't come out that way . . . I give the same speech to the guy at Eastman Kodak . . . I get pretty worked up about this perforation.

My blood is on that film, I want to tell them, how dare you fuck with my bodily fluids this way. In between, I rub some coke on my malevolent molar. Now Richard and Steven are eavesdropping in the hall. When I get off the second call, everyone applauds. My performances are for such small rooms. I hold up my hands, like any decent lounge act.

'No applause until we see if it worked . . .' I hope none of the bankers or studio guys have heard any of this. They don't need to know that every time we turn around there's another tragedy, another mistake, another fuckup. They need to know that everything is just hunky dory. Later that afternoon, the lab and Eastman Kodak say they will pay for everything, including crew time. Also, Eastman Kodak decides it would be a nice gesture to lay some free sixty-five on us.

I get this news just as Kendall and I are firming up reservations for the big dinner at Russo's that night. Russo's is a decent fish house near the harbor, and they'll do a big table in the back. And I'm making everyone show up for this: Richard, Truffaut for star power, Clark for responsibility power, Doug for baffling bullshit, me, Steven, Kendall.

I stop off early at Steven's and he plays me the five tones, da-da-da-DA-da . . . I have trouble duplicating them until Steven explains that the fourth note is the same as the first an octave lower. It's still hard to do. I tell myself these five notes are worth every penny of the fifty plus thousand I have had to pay John Williams. In fact I have had to pay John Williams his fee times two, since we ran out of time on the previous deal.

Steven shows me the corresponding Kodaly method hand gestures. They're great! Thank you, Doug Trumball: he's the one who told us about this method for teaching deaf kids music. Kendall has done the deal for 250 by telegram . . . Steven drives us over. Steven is a good driver, as long as he's not on a two-wheeled vehicle. My tooth is killing me.

That afternoon we have taken up a collection of painkillers for Julia's tooth. Dreyfuss says, as he eyes my handful of Percodan, Empirin and codeine, and one beautiful Talwin jealously, 'I have two words for you: root canal . . .' Horrifying thought. I of the perfect teeth. I ain't trusting no southern dentist with my mouth, I retort, and he laughs in my face . . . As Steven and I drive, I think of all the times we have traveled to a big occasion together: biz, social, location . . . now bankers. This was a newie, even for me. I'd be looking forward to it if my fucking tooth were't blazing. My gums are exploding beneath it. I've scared up some antibiotics, too, and blasted myself with everything forty-five minutes ago. One little martini, and I'd be fine . . .

The bankers are easy. The guy from Manufacturers Hanover Trust seems mainly interested in signing our personal accounts on. Something Alan Hirschfield approves of. He's always complaining to me about West Coast business managers. He'd much rather my money be managed in New York. I nod intently like I'm really listening but mostly I am involved with my tooth. Feelthepain, feelthepain, a high-school cheer, boomalacka, boomalacka, boomBOOMalacka . . .

The next day, both Steven and Nick give me T-shirts. Steven's is yellow with sparkles and Bullwinkle the Moose. It borders on hideous. Nick's is black with a single white line of type. Very tasty. The saying emblazoned front and back on the diametrically opposite T-shirts is the same: IF YOU CAN'T DAZZLE THEM WITH BRILLIANCE BAFFLE THEM WITH BULLSHIT . . . I know these are high compliments, so in spite of the heat, I put one over the other.

I am informed on my mike that I need to see Joe Alves and Doug Trumball on Crescendo Summit right away. I have been on their cases for a week to check out Crescendo Summit per Doug's needs. Especially re: stereo plates, which Doug has sworn he can make work, in spite of the fact that everybody before us has tried and failed and resorted to bluescreen in the end.

Each of them is too busy for the other, so I have made a date for the three of us to go up in a cherry picker and make sure it's okay. Doug and Joe have been at odds since the beginning. Joe is the production designer and has worked with Steven before on *Jaws*. He is getting to play with a lot of money and design on this one. Also, he's short with what I would guess is a club foot, almost to the point of deformity. He has extreme Mediterranean features and sports a beard. I always expect when he speaks that he will be speaking in tongues, but his inflection is straight Southern Cal with a touch of gayness. Very precise. Keeps his upper body in shape. Kendall thinks he's humpy.

I think that's pushing it, but he's talented and dedicated, and that's good enough for me. I have a personal fondness for Doug and an appreciation for his mind, but I don't trust him. I think he's a self-promoter and possibly a *gonif*, but he's *my* self-promoting *gonif*. I'm determined to make all these noxious relationships work. I am always keeping my eye, as my father likes to say, on the prize. So I dash off to Crescendo Summit to confab in a small basket forty, fifty feet in the air about stereo plates and structural bumps.

Because that is pretty much what the conversation revolves around up in the air. There is a bump, it has developed, that will interfere with the angle required for Doug's stereo plates. I want to know why they didn't communicate often or well enough to have avoided what seems like an obvious error. Silly question. This is all about men and their need-to-know basis. Most of the time they aren't sure they need to know, so they don't even tell themselves necessary information. I am so pissed off I keep saying, 'A beump, a beump?' like Inspector Clouseau, and they laugh.

'Why can't we lose the beump?' I ask, and am immediately

reminded it is structural. As in: Everything falls down if you fuck with it.

'Can we shave it enough to accommodate Doug's needs?' I already know the answer but am compelled to be thorough. We're talking seventy-two grand spent on this set. I wonder if Doug will tell me what his plates really cost . . . I start to shift on my feet and I make the cherry picker swing precariously in the air.

'So you guys are telling me we can't use the stereo plates . . .' Silence. They hold on to the sides of the basket and look off in different directions. Blasé. I have a temptation to swing the basket more and make them confess, but it is a waste of time, so I signal the Valley guy at the controls to bring us down . . .

'I want a production meeting in Steven's office after work, all heads of departments,' I growl at Kendall when I get back upstairs. I collapse into my chair and enjoy the air conditioning for a moment. I rub cloves on my tooth. Dreyfuss walks in and pours an eight-ounce glass of gin. He drinks it down in my face, bye-boss's me, and exits. Hey babe, I'm impressed. A Jew who can drink.

'You think he's heaving in his bathroom?' I ask Kendall.

'Who cares?' I check my watch. Pretty soon Stanley and Alan and David and the bankers will be dropping by to say goodbye. I check my looks in the mirrored frames of the Rosamond pictures Phil Abramson has hung on my walls. Yuck.

Stanley and Veitch have settled for a moment in Steven's office. I call him off the floor. Stanley wants to go over cost. I want to say, Hey babe, in for a penny, in for a pound. We start adding figures. It keeps coming up fifteen million. We're only budgeted for twelve. Now Stanley makes a bad move. Bad for him, great for me. He calls Begelman and Hirschfield off the floor to join the confabs and gives me an opening to tell them fifteen and going north.

They don't want to be in a confrontation like this. They're not supposed to be in this meeting the way Herbie Allen isn't down here in Mobile. A matter of keeping the money and the movie maker as far apart from each other as possible. Alan and David look at their shoes. David's face twitches on the left side. Anger. Veitch gets everyone off the hook by holding out the possibility that we will hold to schedule on the big set.

I want to say, We are never getting off the big set, but I let him get us off the hook. Stanley's red in the face, literally and figuratively, and these guys are going on their planes. Scratch that, Alan is going on his helicopter. To his offshore nature-fucking oil rig. He doesn't bother to ask me again if I'd like to join him. Nobody wants to give me an opportunity to tell them the truth. Fine, I'll go the Cartesian way, one step at a time.

'They're going to react to this news by sending you down here to watch us,' I say to Veitch in the hall, as they're departing. I don't mind. I like his company. He's the only one who thinks I'm a major film maker. 'I hope you don't collapse jogging in the heat . . .' He laughs a mordant laugh, takes one long look back over his shoulder at the camera platforms high in the air. 'Not afraid of heights, are you?' I needle, because I am. So's Steven. He won't go up without me. High is high – everybody hates it. It's not something you get used to . . .

We decide we'd better check some of our sixty-five that looks dicey. The closest 70mm theater is in New Orleans. Steven and Doug and I and the camera crew hop a chartered Lear for the twenty-five-minute trip. I take a Valium, or I'll never get on the plane. When we run it, we all see a visible scratch.

'It's commercial,' Trumball says.

'What?'

'Acceptable, it's acceptable . . . you'll never see it with all the other effects laid on . . .'

'Hell, you don't recognize the film five days after it's been in the theaters, there's so much positive dirt,' Steven says gamely, but I know he's disappointed. I take everyone to Antoine's to ease the pain . . .

'I don't believe I have to do this . . .' I look plaintively at Clark. I'd like to lie down. The Bankers has been an enervating experience. I'm juggling a lot of people. All these employees. All these bosses. Kate and Jackie. Cast. Extras. A lot of fucking people. I'm getting very manipulative. With them. With myself. The drugs enhance this. My replacement for the observing ego. Now Clark Paylow thinks we should have a P.R. kind of a tour on the catwalk with electricians. It is 135 feet in the air. I don't wanna go, I don't wanna go . . .

I sing this little refrain all the way up. We are guided by Earl the Head Gaffer, who, handsome as he is, has no respect for women, me in particular. And he has shamed himself at the train crossing, insisted on snoots over 10Ks in a basket instead of using the HMI spots that Vilmos wanted. The dailies reveal the score at Vilmos: 1, Earl: 0. Cost me heavy overtime. We have laughed over the location stills that progress from morning to night, me yelling up at him, him aloft in his basket, disdaining or deflecting my queries. As in, how much more time, motherfucker! I send him a case of beer when he gets it right. He is a little nicer.

His guys are complaining loud and long about all the lights and no fire extinguishers. I traverse the entire catwalk, introducing myself. They are all fat and smell of B.O. and beer.

'How much is my per diem?' I ask Clark.

'Fifteen hundred a week . . .' even here, others are doing my banking and money for me . . . bad habit . . .

'So how much do extinguishers cost . . .?'

'Couple of hundred per, for decent ones . . .'

'So spend my per diem and get them their fucking extinguishers. I want one every three feet! With big red ribbons!'

'Oh, we don't have to spend your per diem for that . . .'

'Well, let's oblige these guys . . .' I tell them they are getting their extinguishers and try not to look down as I work my way back to the floor. Joe Alves is waiting for me, wanting to apologize about the beump, reminding me what an arrogant prick Trumball is.

'But he's our arrogant prick, and I need you to get along with him!' I snap. A prime case of saying the truth indelicately. Fortunately for me, Joe has an IQ over room temperature and is dedicated at heart, and he cracks a smile. We pat each other on the back.

*

Melinda confides in a panicky voice she's afraid her ex-husband will show up without warning and frighten her withdrawn son. I post a guard outside their hotel suite. She brings me a flower and a poem. I wish I liked her more. Dreyfuss makes an incendiary statement about the Ku Klux Klan. I post a guard outside his house.

Izzy is petrified to fly. Something we have in common. But I do it. He doesn't. He calls, plans to visit, then cancels at the last minute. By telegram. Sometimes the telegrams are so incoherent I wonder why he has decided to be a writer. I tape one to the camera. It is the day we're shooting the scene where Dreyfuss jumps on the hood of Teri's car. It is a steal from Izzy's real life. Grady wrote it, but then we both promised him we wouldn't use it. Steven, too. But that day, Izzy has hurt my feelings and canceled again. Fuck 'im, we say, and shoot a scene from Izzy's life for our movie.

Grady has come and gone, as it were, spilled the beans, so now Izzy is real anxious to visit. He overcomes his fear of flying to visit over July Fourth weekend. Amy Irving comes down for a visit with Steven, too. They've been an item since they met at a fancy screening Brian threw for *Carrie*. 'I met a real heartbreaker last night,' Steven told me at breakfast the next morning.

Steven and I escape them by going to Jillian's house to check out every gag with Roy Arbogast, who is in charge of mechanical effects. Mobile in the summer. Water hangs thick in the ninety-five-degree air. It's noon, but a five o'clock sky hangs ominously overhead. Monday we'll be in Jillian's house: the abduction scene, the house going crazy, Cary Guffey opening the door to let in a shaft of Nuclear Sky.

'I feel weird about Izzy,' I confide to Steven as we watch a flower grow by itself and the screws in the grating unwind.

'Same here. I wish she hadn't come . . .' In the distance, thunder. 'She keeps crying and I keep wanting to say, "Don't you understand, I'm fucking my movie . . ."' The crew has given him the control for a cue light that he's taken to carrying with him everywhere. He plays with the switch nervously.

Doug Trumball and I have dubbed it his whacking-off instrument. Smoke blows out from the grate, but it doesn't move. Roy and his assistant stoop to investigate. Steven sniffs at the air, like a dog. The thunder is getting closer. I shiver.

'Ghosts definitely live here,' I say. Steven smiles my favorite smile, the smile of a precocious seven-year-old.

'I know, isn't it great?'

Knives hurl themselves from their holder on the wall in the kitchen and the house shakes with a thunderclap that seems as if it's breaking right overhead. Torrents of rain smash at the roof. The men look pale and frozen in basic fight-or-flight positions. Steven and I walk onto the porch in the back of the house. It opens onto a field rimmed with a thick line of trees. Lightening cracks the sky open again, and one of the trees catches fire for a moment.

'Me and Izzy,' I say.

'Me and Amy,' he says.

Elvis is making his comeback tour through Mobile. I promote twenty tickets or so. The audience is fat, middle-aged, tired, just like Elvis. He is in the White Leather Suit and he weighs 250–300 pounds. He looks like a freaky Orson Welles, who also peaked early. There is a little guy following him around the stage with liquid refreshment that he imbibes often, and scarves, which he wraps around his neck then tosses listlessly to the overweight, overwrought harpies down front.

'If I look like that when I'm forty, take me out in back and shoot me,' Nick says, sourly. Elvis is depressing him. I won't know you when you're forty, I think. I probably won't know you three weeks after we get back to Los Angeles.

'Okay,' I say, 'if you look like that when you're forty, it'll be my pleasure to shoot you . . .' He rewards me with a nice big bear hug. Football player. Keep drinking that beer and you might look more like Elvis than you expect . . .

I have been cast in *New York New York* as a Rich Bitch. I am allowed to leave Mobile and return in two days. I report to the set and get hair-ed and make-upped. I get to wear a long black dress by Adrienne. I am the only one on the set allowed to smoke. They even give me a fancy cigarette holder. I am in the first scene in which Liza and De Niro meet. He gives me a light and I tell him, 'You're cute, just stay off the drugs and you'll go far . . .' Since the line is repeated throughout the movie, I figure I have a chance to not end up on the cutting-room floor. The day wears on. Pat Kingsley, super publicist, comes to visit. Lois Smith's partner. I have always loved Lois and distrusted Pat.

'So you're going to be a triple threat,' she says unctuously. I guess she's referring to producer, director, bit player.

De Niro is the strong, silent type: I have a seven-minute conversation with him with lots of pauses. A record for me. I tell Marty. He is impressed. Morning turns into afternoon. They have made me look very glamorous, so I don't mind. The dress looks good. The still man takes a few shots of Marty and me. I am in character, not only as Rich Bitch, but as a previous producer of Marty's.

The production staff calls me at lunch and I can tell from their voices things are not going well. Steven calls wanting to know when I'm coming back. Stanley calls to tell me I have to be on a plane that night. I tell Marty. He looks frustrated. 'I've never had a bit with a "stop date,"' he says.

Afternoon moves into evening, and I am getting nervous about making my plane. My car is waiting. Finally, Marty sets me and De Niro up, and Laszlo grabs everything on a creep. We do about seven or eight takes. No way I will make it into this picture.

I tell Irwin Winkler how much I like the dress. I figure he'll give it to me. 'It cost six hundred dollars,' he says. Fuck me? Fuck you. I write the check and change clothes . . .

Cary Guffey gets constipated on the third day at Jillian's house. Christ, he's only four. I tell Steven, Let's think of some other shots to grab, maybe some locked-down sixty-five in the back of the house, for the clouds. I'll call Veitch, it'll be perfect. He goes with the plan. I call Veitch from the car.

'Cary Guffey is constipated . . . we're gonna shoot some sixty-five . . .'

'You think he'll be able to work tomorrow?'

'Sure . . . he's a trooper . . . we got him Ex-Lax and prune juice . . .' We're on half day half night. Hell, everybody's constipated.

I drive back to the house. They are setting up in back. I walk over to the craft service table. It is filled with: congealed sandwich meats, melted chocolate chip cookies, mayonnaise bubbling through a rancid egg salad, and lots and lots of Coca-Cola. Not a Tab in sight.

'You know, I haven't had a decent bowel movement since we got here, the schedule's so bad,' the craft service guy tells me. Who asked? Who cares? Doesn't he know I'm thinking? He repeats it louder and gets some laughs from the loungers, crew who aren't hustling.

The air is thick with humidity and the promise of random violence.

They seem to me to be closing in.

'Well, then maybe you should go back to L.A.,' I hear myself saying. 'Maybe you'll be able to take a decent shit once you're home . . .' This guy is presenting me with a possibility, just like Stanley did with Alan and David.

'What are you saying?' the guy says, advancing slightly.

'I'm saying you're fired,' I reply, and advance back. Fuck you and your bowels. 'You can go anytime,' I say and advance some more. Some part of me is loving the guy for presenting himself as a target for ventilation of my stress, some other part is going, I don't wanna do this anymore, I don't wanna do this anymore. There are tears in the guy's eyes. I will think of this moment every time I threaten Norman Levy with the line, 'I can make grown men cry . . .'

Some of the crew express their displeasure. I tell them I'm real sorry and they all know how concerned I am for their well-being while on location, but I draw the line at shit. I don't notice too much lounging, though. I wish they responded to nice, but they don't. Not crew. Crew understands fear.

Being a prick takes a lot of energy, but it's very effective.

Trouble is, it feeds on itself, and it is not so easy to turn off at will . . .

Everyone wants to go to the dog races. Joe O'Hare says he can get fifty people in if I walk the winner of the first race around the track. Like I'm a celebrity. Actually, down here for the last two weeks I have been, because our production has been commended in the state legislature and we've gotten an award. George Wallace presents the award at some dumbass ceremony at a local hotel. Dreyfuss and Steven don't want to go, but we all know somebody has to show, so Kendall brings a skirt in the car, and I race off the set and downtown for a forty-five-minute photo sesh/little speech with the Guv. I'm curious, anyway.

They set me up on a table next to George. He is pasty gray and wheezy in his wheelchair. His lower body looks wilted. His head lolls to one side. I suppress an instinct toward pity and focus on what a son of a bitch he was. Schrader has always maintained the inspiration for Travis Bickle was Arthur Bremmer, the guy who stalked, but did not kill, George. I feel curiously connected to him. He wants to discuss civil rights, since I'm a northerner. An outsider. Who is pumping almost fifteen million dollars into his poor state.

I thank him for the award; I think he should be thanking me. It is at the point I have this thought that all the cameras go off. I am on the cover of both local papers the next day, and I look like a wiseass. Not only that, but in one shot I think I can make out my nipples under my sweaty T-shirt. Why didn't somebody tell me . . .

Walking the dogs around the tracks is not easy. First of all, these dogs, these greyhounds and whippets, are weird-looking, high-strung dogs. I am not a dog person, anyway, and these dogs are like deer. They drag me around a funky track strewn with dogshit. I am grateful they haven't dragged me face down. My platform shoes are ruined, though. I don't know if I can bear to be in them for the rest of the evening.

The races are fixed. Joe brags he has a line on the winners, a local tipster, and tells us what to bet on. We win. I stop betting. I don't like to gamble anymore. Besides, winning on a sure thing isn't any fun. I go to the ladies' room, see if I can get rid of the dogshit. The water makes it smell worse. I go to the bar in the turf club and order a martini. I hold it up to my nose, get rid of the shit smell. The vodka has a fresh clean smell. I take a deep breath, close my eyes. I imagine I'm in Hawaii . . .

Every time I walk down to the big set I feel I'm making a descent into hell. The longer we shoot there, the more like hell it seems. Hot lights, smoke that's giving everyone the runs. Heat. Every time there is a storm our extension blows away and the guys have to sew it up. Sometimes they can't do it fast enough, overnight, and we have to reverse the camera. Extras. Cubicles. Equipment. We are up on the camera platform for weeks while Crescendo Summit, *sans* stereo plates, is completed.

I have convinced Steven that he should let Mike Shapiro and his crew shoot some footage of the production. At some point we will need to make a product reel. We're certainly not going to have a film to show them, let's at least have a product reel. Pat Kingsley comes with them, bearing a plaque from Bert Schneider. It says: WHEN YOU'VE GOT THEM BY THE BALLS THEIR HEARTS AND MINDS WILL SOON FOLLOW . . .

I am quite used to being able to charm just about anyone if I try, but François and I never connect. My sense of humor is idiomatic and his English is formal. I never see any evidence of a sense of humor. Once he realizes what it will entail to act in this particular movie, he is not very happy about the gig. He waits at the foot of Devil's Tower for ten days before we get to his critical scene, and the set, closed in behind polyurethane, is stifling. Wyoming is no particular fun for anyone. I'm sure that François blames me for everything. There are all these pictures from the production at the time. In every one where Steven and François are alone, François has his warm,

301

brown-eyed expression. In all the pictures with me and François alone, he is shaking his finger at me, as if scolding a recalcitrant child.

Once we are ensconced in Mobile, Truffaut gets a little happier, possibly because we put him up in a suite at the Sheraton, down the hall from Teri Garr. I deal with him as little as possible and hope he is having a good time. One night halfway through the shoot, we are rained out of an exterior location. The bitch of the production all along has been that we have very little cover for such events. Once we commit to moving to the Big Set, as we called the airplane hangar, an exact replication of the foot of Devil's Tower with all the spaceship paraphernalia, we can't move, and it will not be ready until late July.

It is three o'clock in the morning on a half-day/half-night shoot; we have several hours left. We have set up the double for the room where Dreyfuss is interrogated by Balaban and Truffaut, culminating in Dreyfuss's infuriated query: 'Who are you people?' The actors haven't rehearsed at all, and have built up a great deal of anxiety about the scene, but it is the only cover we have.

Steven, Clark Paylow, Jimmy Bloom, and I have a conference. Chicken coops have been preset above, so there will be minimal lighting time, a Vilmos First. Steven says he can do the whole scene in two shots; a slow creep from one angle and then a matching slow creep from the opposite angle. François will be speaking in French with Balaban 'translating.' Steven is resistant, but he doesn't want to lose time.

'Steven, can you do this in three hours?' I ask.

'I can try. The shooting isn't difficult, if Jerry* isn't drunk.' Jerry is the guy who will be moving the dolly on the creep, and I wrapped him hours ago. Who knows if he's started on his evening cocktails?

'I read somewhere that sometimes it's good for the actors not to rehearse on a scene like this,' I lie. Steven smiles. I don't know if that means he believes me or appreciates the lie. 'We've really got no choice,' I say. 'Let's go for it, leave the set standing, and if it's shit we'll do it again.'

So we pick up Truffaut and Balaban, but no one can find

Dreyfuss. Finally, I go upstairs to his office. He is sleeping something off on his couch. One never knows with Dreyfuss these days what that might be. God knows, he and I have done our share of blow together over the past several years. I've had some trouble with him on this production, though. In fact, he collapsed on the set one day at the Neary house and I had to get a local doctor to fudge a report that he was suffering from heat prostration. He and I locked eyes in a meaningful fashion on the drive home and I told him I thought he should let me hold his stash for him.

'You mean put me on a dole?' he squeaked.

'Well, I wouldn't call it that . . .'

'I won't accept a fucking dole!'

'Okay,' I said, shooting him that cold, gray-eyed stare I had learned from my father. 'What would you suggest? You and I both know what happened today. Today was a cheap day. It was only a fifty-thousand-dollar day, and John Veitch is going to have a fit. Not to mention God knows what Steven is doing there on his own.'

'Insurance will cover it.'

'Maybe yes, maybe no. Maybe a little . . .'

'He's probably shooting more angles on the mountain . . .'

'I'll bet you real money he's shooting the dirt coming in the window – something I really want the whole crew to stand around for . . .'

'Inserts on a hand making the mashed potato mountain!' Fuck it, it was too absurd. We started to laugh. Everybody was pretty fried. The situation was worsened by Vilmos fiddling with the lights on every shot. Plus, Steven was getting very hung up on implantation clues that were beginning to seem ridiculous. The mashed potatoes especially, which were taking forever because nothing that looked like mashed potatoes was viscous enough to create a mountain.

'Well, we're almost back now . . .' I said. 'I need to know that this isn't going to happen again. For myself, for the picture, for you . . .' I tried to look concerned, but my facial muscles felt like they were scowling.

'I'll watch it, I promise . . .'

'Okay, but if it's not working, or if this happens again, I ain't covering for you . . .'

'Fine.' Great, now he was pissed.

'Richard . . .'

'Yes.'

'Remember to take salt pills and drink a lot of water. It helps.' It wouldn't hurt to lose thirty pounds, either. Without drugs. Lotsa luck . . .

After that conversation, and especially after we moved to the Big Set, Dreyfuss would come into my office and pour himself eight ounces of vodka, then drink them down, all in one gulp. In my face. And just now, he is probably taking an eight-hour nap, because he is not being cooperative about waking up. I look at my watch. It is three fifteen.

'Gettup GETtup GETTUP!' I scream in his ear, and he opens his eyes. I give him a casual kiss on his forehead. 'We've gotta shoot the interrogation scene, should I send them up here to do you?'

'We can't do that scene. We haven't rehearsed.' He is wide awake now.

'We have to shoot that scene. We don't have any other cover. It's raining outside, the extension fell down in the wind, and it'll take the rest of the night to reverse. I'm sending Anabel and Bobby up here, and I'm coming back in fifteen minutes to get you . . .' I sound awfully definitive for someone who's quaking inside. Dreyfuss decides to take me seriously.

'No, I'm coming with you.' Way to go, big boy. You can be my King for a Day. All the way down the corridors and the stairs Dreyfuss talks to himself, jacking himself up, like Melinda getting herself into a hysterical fit off camera during the Jillian's-house-going-crazy scene. Watching her prepare for each take while Steven preoccupied himself with vascillating lights outside the window and Roy Arbogast reset each gag was the first time I ever had a sincere appreciation of what it is that actors do, particularly movie actors. For the rest of the shoot, no matter what kind of a pain in the ass Melinda is, I oblige her.

Now Dreyfuss is making me love him because I know he is going to pull off this scene. 'Want a toot?' I am feeling charitable. He waves the suggestion away with his hand. My hero. Of the three of them, Truffaut is the most nervous. I don't want him to blow the scene, but there is a part of me that likes him sweating. The atmosphere on the set is thick with Mobile humidity and leftover smoke from the Big Set. The lights in the chicken coops are turned on. It is very quiet, as if the entire crew were concentrating on making the scene brilliant in under three hours.

'Gordon Villis lighting zat you like zo much,' Vilmos snorts contemptuously and gestures overhead. 'Wery zimple really.'

There is so much in this movie that is 'to come' that I have to carry envisioning equipment in my head all the time. As the scene starts to roll, I feel my mind relax and my viscera take over. Just three people in a room, each with his own agenda, each having gone through great turmoil and over great distance to get to this place. It is very quiet in this area off the Big Set where this mockup with flyaway walls has been built.

'Have you heard a ringing, a pleasant sensation? Do these pictures mean anything to you? Have you ever had a . . . close encounter . . .?'

'Who are you people?' Dreyfuss bellows, and I feel my heart leap and tears spring out in my eyes. He does it several ways, emphasizing a different word in the sentence each time.

We finish the scene in under three hours and cheer ourselves. Two days later, the dailies bear us out. I turn to Steven when the lights come up and he is smiling. 'Pretty hot scene . . .'

'Yeah, it's a good thing they didn't rehearse; it would never have seemed so real . . . I'm glad it's over . . .'

That was about the last time Steven smiled.

I'm not sure if I ever really said so long to François, although I made damned sure he understood I was getting the money for the India sequence and he should be prepared to travel to that part of the world in early '77. I don't think he believed me, and I really had to move on to thinking about matters more immediate and pressing.

*

Steven and I have a fight while he is shooting on the Notch, a duplication of part of Devil's Tower, the last portion of Roy's and Jillian's break-in. He won't come down to talk to me. When shooting is over, I corner him.

'Why are you so pissed?'

'I need more time here . . .'

'I can't get you any more time . . . Veitch has taken up permanent residence at the Sheraton . . . I'll bring back anything you need . . . How can you be like this with me . . . We're friends . . .' We kiss and make up.

The next day he sends roses. The note says: Friends . . .

We end up leaving Mobile right before Labor Day. We sneak out like thieves in the middle of the night. Nick cops attitude about Izzy in L.A. and Mr. Fearless's necklace. I give the necklace back. Mr. Fearless doesn't want to take it. He knows it is severing a connection. I call Izzy and break up with him on the phone, just like Michael did to me in college . . .

There is always a second-act curtain in a relationship, an event that signals that the end is near. With Izzy it was the car more than the cancellations; with Nick it was the necklace more than Izzy . . .

We have only been home a few weeks and I am just getting my I'm-in-Burbank-again-and-glad-to-be-here legs back. It is about six o'clock on a Thursday and people are packing up to go home. I am observing decent hours for the staff for the time being because I know it is going to get hard again. I am on my way to the bathroom for a precautionary whiz for the drive home when the phone rings. I pick it up myself.

'Julia,' I hear Connie's voice, 'I have Mr. Begelman for you.' He comes on immediately. I can tell from his voice this is not a good call.

'I need to read something to you. This is going to be in the Arts and Leisure section of the Sunday *New York Times* . . . "Truffaut said it was not difficult to work for another director because, knowing the problems of handling actors, 'I try to be the perfect actor. I never make a suggestion. I never ask a question.' Truffaut, who plays a French scientist in *Close Encounters*, said that the production of the film was badly organized. 'The picture started with a budget of $11 million and now I think it is up to $15 million, but that is not Spielberg's fault. It is the fault of the producer, Julia Phillips. She is incompetent. Unprofessional. You can write that. She knows I feel this way. Sometimes it was so disorganized that they had me show up and then do nothing for five days . . .'"'

What? What?! 'Did you know he felt this way?' Begelman asks in a low voice.

'No, I didn't know he felt this way, and if you want to talk about unprofessional . . .' He must have been really pissed about getting busted for not being deaf is the only thing I can think of. All that waiting at the foot of Devil's Tower must have gotten to him. God knows, I had fallen over backwards . . . maybe when I did I was supposed to spread my legs and service him . . . maybe that was it. I mean, he had written *whore* for *wore* in his letter . . .

'Look, I don't know what this is from, I'll call Louis Blau. Maybe he can shed some light . . .'

'Call me back.' Begelman is sounding awfully grim. It couldn't have come at a worse time, this little venting of François's. We are just about to ask the parent company for some more money. I call Louis Blau without permitting myself a moment to go in the bathroom and cry. Not to mention by now I really have to pee. He is very distressed by the news, and apologetic. I tell him I wouldn't mind knowing what François had in mind when he said such lousy things in print. I am starting to get really angry. 'I think I should call him right now, wake that prick up and find out what he had in his little frog mind . . .'

'No, don't call him. I'll call.'

'Well, do let me know . . . you might want to give Begelman a call, too.' It is now almost seven. I can't believe that I have to deal with this at the end of a day at the end of a week. This is going to be in the goddamned Sunday *New York Times*. too. This will be what everyone, including Mommy and

Daddy, are going to get to know about me and *Close Encounters*. After all this amazing work, all this herculean effort. 'This is really not fair,' I mutter to myself. Right. Like Life was fair. I call Begelman back and tell him Louis Blau is getting into it and I am going home to see Kate before she leaves for college. He laughs. Neither one of us thinks it is funny.

The next day, Louis calls and says he can't get anything out of François, not an explanation, not an apology . . . nothing.

'I presume that means I can't count on a retraction,' I say. He laughs. These guys all have great gallows humor. I am beginning to resent the time I have to spend on this endeavor. Of course, I have to tell Steven. I don't need to read it. The words have pretty much emblazoned themselves on my memory. He sounds shocked and upset. Probably more about getting the money than about how I might be feeling. I tell him that I am counting on him to write a letter to the editor. He says he will. I call Mommy and Daddy to warn them. My father laughs. My mother wants to know if I am incompetent and unprofessional. I call Peter Silberman, our publicity guy at Columbia and Pat Kingsley from Pickwick. Let her earn some of that five grand a month I got them over Veitch's strenuous objection. Pat and Peter arrive after lunch to commiserate and come up with a plan of action.

'The good news is that it's not on the first page. It's on page thirty-six, continued on, as it were,' Peter says.

'We need to have Steven write a letter – I'll see if maybe Redford will, too,' Pat volunteers.

'Steven said he would write a letter . . . I don't know what good asking Redford is . . .'

'He's your friend, I'm sure he'll be glad to . . .'

A few days after the piece runs, I get the flu, what a surprise. Alan Hirschfield tracks me down and calls me at home.

'You sound terrible,' he says.

'I'm sick.'

'What's wrong?' Like you don't know.

'Oh, I've got a bad case of Truffaut.' Big laughs.

'Want to go to the opening of *The Front*?'

'When?'

'Next week. If you've recovered from Truffaut.'

'I don't think I'll ever recover . . .' This, too, shall pass.

As it turns out, Steven's letter is weaker than I would have hoped, and at least forty other people, including Redford, write letters defending my competence and professionalism, but the *Times* is pretty recalcitrant about printing any of them. It takes relentless pressure from Pat Kingsley and Lois Smith to get Steven's letter printed a month after François's interview runs. What does *The New York Times* have against me? I wonder, remembering Guy Flately's piece in which I was referred to as 'exasperatingly thin-lipped,' whatever the fuck that was. Maybe that I didn't have the requisite equipment for giving good head.

Not too many people who weren't looking for it see the piece, and Begelman does get the extra money. Alan and I have a pretty good time at the movie, depressing as it is. I guess being criticized by a biggie makes me some kind of a biggie, too, because lots of people want to say hello at the screening. It is a show of support, I suppose.

I have François's letter and a blowup of the nasty quote on me backed and framed identically and hang them in my office where I can see them at all times. Whenever somebody asks me how I really feel about show business, I direct them to those two items. I never take them off the wall, because some dead people are better than others . . .

Kendall looks unhappy at the prospect of telling me what has just transpired on the phone with Bob Colbert.

'They found your car . . .'

'They what?' I had said goodbye to my car two months ago when Izzy called. Goodbye to Izzy, too, though neither one of us knew it at the time.

There is an insurance law in California that the car has to stay stolen sixty days to be stolen. So on the fifty-ninth day, literally, the cops find my car four blocks from where it disappeared. Please. Some kids took a joyride. Pretty pretty please. But at some level I'm thrilled to be reunited with my baby. It takes it about a month to have a complete nervous breakdown, which it does, on the way to the Valley on an exceptionally hot day. Coming down Beverly Glen the car shifts to fifteen miles an hour, makes horrible choking noises, and spews so much pitch-black smoke that it is hard to see where I'm going. I pull into the Texaco station at the corner of Ventura and Beverly Glen. The gas jockey waves frantically for me to stop. He wants about as much to do with this car as I do. I jump out of the car. Thick, unbreathable air bounces at me from the pavement, from my car.

'This is a park-and-lock situation!' I yell over my baby's protesting wheezes. The car is completely enveloped in black smoke. I lean in and turn off the engine. I do not wish to blow myself up in the Valley. The guy indicates a safe place close by. We push it into a space together. It is so hot and I am so tense, I think for a moment that I will faint. I pass on that idea. Places to go, people to see. I call Kendall at the office:

'My car exploded in the Valley, call Colbert and tell him to have them tow it to Beverly Hills Mercedes, and please come and get me.' Kendall's car isn't air conditioned. I lean against the back of my car, which is hot, but not from whatever machine ailment is killing it. I say goodbye to my car for the second time. I refuse to set eyes on it again.

I hit the dealership with Nick and we organize a deal with a guy named Larry Anish. He loves *Taxi Driver*. I have a one-sheet messengered as we speak. We trade the baby in for blue-book value plus five, fine by me; I am going for the baby's older sister. Black on black. Outside I watch a girl named Debbie hand paint a racing stripe on another car. Too much? Definitely. I want a red one of those. They let me take the car.

I have an accident on the way home, with a mailbox. I drive it back. 'We'll fix it for you while she pinstripes,' Larry says. He has the *Taxi Driver* poster on his wall. The benefits of seminamedom.

The next night I go out with Mr. Fearless. I haven't seen him in awhile. He slaps a black-and-gold STUNTZ 4 EVER* decal on my black merc's ass, and gives me a giant gold belt buckle with the same emblem. It is hideous and expensive. I am wearing jeans, cowboy boots, and a fun fur.

'I think people just get mad 'cause you're having such a good time.' He smiles as we get into the car. I know I get people mad. But I think they love me so much that they get over it. I don't know that if you get people mad often enough that love turns to hate.

'Flash and trash!' I proclaim, all bluster, and he peels out of my driveway. He's going to teach me how to hit someone's bumper on the freeway and not make a dent.

The year we started shooting *Close Encounters*, 1976, *Time* magazine ran a black cover with the question IS GOD DEAD? Not a question to ask me; IS GOD ALIVE? was more to the point, and then, looking around at the state of the world I'd add, AND WHY IS HE SO MEAN? Nah, he/she/it had never existed.

'If God is dead, why not UFOs?' reads a quote of mine in the *Washington Post*. This makes Steven furious, not because I have offended his personal beliefs, but because he worries that I might have cut into the commerciality of the project. Who had time for these God permutations? *Me*, I needed a logo.

My brother, the mathematician/scientist, had once set himself the task of reproving a basic theorem with what he called a simple but elegant proof. I want to do the same thing with a symbol for the movie. I have convinced Begelman, Hirschfield, etc., that we should spend a great deal of money a year before the release of the picture to popularize the expression 'close encounters of the third kind,' make the prospective audience familiar with it. Develop ads that will use first-, second-, and third-kind examples, plus a single logo that will express everything relevant in a simple, elegant way.

First we need to acquire the rights to the expressions, which had been coined by a sweet wacko named Alan Hyneck in a primer called *The UFO Experience*. Hyneck had once been the head of a government project called Project Blue Book, a secret study under the aegis of the Air Force designed to debunk reported UFO sightings, which had increased dramatically in postwar America. I always figured these were sightings of machinery we were testing secretly. Who'd want to visit us? I wondered.

He resigned the position, he tells us, because there were just too many sightings by reputable people that were impossible to discount or explain away. He had opened the Center for UFO Studies at Northwestern University and broken sightings down into three oddly poetic phrases: close encounter of the first kind: sighting of a UFO; close encounter of the second kind: physical evidence of a UFO; close encounter of the third kind: contact with a being from a UFO.

Actually his descriptions were wordier, and the simple, elegant poetry came later, mostly as a result of cutting-and-pasting skills I had acquired in a number of publishing jobs. I am lucky to get art and copy as clean as I do into those first double truck ads in the winter of '76. They are less the product of talent and concept and more the end of a lengthy negotiation, but they aren't half-bad and they do start to get the point across.

Bit by bit the Trifid Nebula is edged out and the road with the glow is featured, and bit by bit overwrought, verbose copy, so characteristic of movie advertising, which runs an easy fifteen years behind state of the art, is simplified. But I have to go through a series of battles and negotiations to get it right. This involves a lot of late-night transcontinental travel, which is starting to wear me down.

First there is the matter of acquiring the rights to Hyneck's phrases, which we do by acquiring the nonexclusive, in-perpetuity rights to the book in which they appeared. No matter how strongly I emphasize the importance of the phrases, nobody in Columbia's business affairs seems to have the time to handle a negotiation, so it falls to Norman Garey to deal it out. (Years later we are sued anyway by a small publishing company that has acquired the book from its original publisher. In looking over all their deals with authors they discovered that the rights were not Hyneck's to sell. But at the time, blissful in our ignorance, we think they are ours to exploit.)

312

Pete Turner has been hired at great expense ($185,000 by the time he is done) to shoot special photographs and help us develop a logo. All during the shoot down in Mobile, one person or another, usually from Lois Smith's outfit, brings us pictures that he has developed. Dreyfuss's face in the middle of the mother ship, across a starfield, etc., etc. All corny and overdone. Steven looks at me disconsolately and says, I hate this, I hate that, and he is right. I think of Pete Turner and say, I hate you, I hate you . . .

It falls to me to tell Pete Turner, who was hired principally because Steven and I were attracted to a very famous photograph of his, taken, grabbed really, between locations a long time ago on a clear stretch of midwestern highway. Foreground was a road with the center dividing line running to the vanishing point. The picture must have been taken very low to the ground. The road stretches to infinity, up against a mountain range. Hanging over the range is a fiercely clear blue sky replete with puffy white clouds. Turner had made the photo monochromatic – in blue, in green, in yellow, in red.

An outfit named Don Smollen is handling the rendering of ads for us in New York, and one day, with nothing lighting up over their heads, they take the road, black out the sky, shine a couple of bright lights at the end, and stick some corny copy along the left-hand side. Far too long, but the last line, WE ARE NOT ALONE, brilliant in its obviousness. Probably it hurts his pride that after all the fancyshmancy work he's done, the only thing we really want to use is the same twelve-year-old picture that everyone wants. Hey, I want to say, Orson Welles peaked early, too.

I fly back and forth on red eyes, often in tourist, just to get it looking right for a presentation that will coincide with a Columbia board of directors meeting in L.A . . . Hirschfield, Matty Rosenhouse, Joe Fischer. Guys who don't know dick about show biz but guys who have the money to commit to a huge buy in Sunday papers a year before the opening of the picture.

John Connelly, ace copywriter, has a fierce headache the day we are meeting to do a final cut and paste. Not for nothing have I spent all those hours reading Mary McCarthy and cutting eighty-thousand-word novels to fifteen for the *Ladies' Home Journal*. We cut each description, we clean up the ad. I call Steven in California and read it to him. We all agree something is missing.

'Stay put, I'll call you back . . .' I hang up the phone and look at Connelly.

'I gotta rest,' John says.

'Here, take one of these,' I say, and offer him a Fiorinal, another wonder drug I know about compliments of my mother. Developed by Montefiore Hospital (hence the name) for the ultimate unbearable headache, it also imparts a delicious alphalike high. His headache is so bad, he'll try anything. I urge him to chase it with a cup of coffee. Open the capillaries, get those drugs pumping through. I go for a walk. Twenty minutes and I'm back. He's on his feet, pacing, smiling. His cheeks are pink with excitement. He's waving a piece of paper around, and every time he looks at it, he cracks up.

'This is the clearest I've been in days – what's the name of that pill?' I write it down on a piece of paper. He takes the paper and hands me his. 'Here is the line.' WEARENOTALONE. I flip and call Steven. We love it. Connelly's people do a paste-up for me, and I race to the airport to get it back to L.A. in time . . .

'It looks like headlights,' Begelman pronounces the next day.

'Well, we'll make it more mysterious – it's just the rough. I like it, Steven likes it . . .'

'Well, let's hope Alan Hirschfield likes it.'

The wish being father to the thought, the board files into Begelman's office just then. I am wearing the suit Alan has caused to be made for me. They smile and wave. They are in a hurry to get to lunch. 'Whaddya think?' I smile back, the corners of my mouth turned up but tense. It still isn't a simple but elegant proof, like *Shampoo*, the woman's hair spelling out the title, but it is getting closer. Everybody glances at it, then Hirschfield says:

'I hate it – it looks like headlights . . . The copy's okay, though.' Rude motherfucker. The copy's okay. You come up with a bunch of sentences in a row that will grab people, and explain without boring . . . I shoot Begelman a look and he shoots one back that says, Say no more, I'll take it from here. Yeah, but I'm the one on the red eyes. With the red eyes . . . 'May I say a few words here?' Alan smiles, as in, this oughtta be good.

'Sure . . .' I am still holding the pasted-up double truck ad in front of me. I feel like a talking blackboard, so I rest it against Begelman's desk. This way I can use my hands and *really* talk.

'Well, this is a big picture with a title that has essential meaning. But it's not presold like a bestselling book or a Broadway musical. We have an opportunity to familiarize the public with the title, which also explains what the movie is about. The graphic isn't finished yet, but it's a strong hook, and it will reproduce very nicely in black-and-white. The idea is to buy a lot of double truck ads in Sunday papers around Christmas, so people will be just panting to see this piece of shit next Christmas.'

'Easter . . .' they all say. Right, in your dreams. We'll never make Easter.

'Right, Easter . . .' Not bad, kid. At least Begelman looks pleased, Matty Rosenhouse, a key player on the board of the parent company, looks interested, and Hirschfield lets me finish with no interruption. My job here is done. They ask me to leave the pasted-up graphic. Yeah, right, like they're going to pore over it at lunch. I do.

I give them a long time for lunch; then I call Begelman. He sounds peppy.

'I think we should punish Hirschfield and take out the ad in all thirty-five markets,' I joke.

'Listen, I'm president of this fucking company and what I say goes, or they can get themselves another boy.' Oh dear, didn't you guys have a nice lunch? Clearly this is not a direct response to anything I've said, and I don't think he is addressing Alan's rudeness, or even all the effort I've expended.

'What do you mean?'

'I'm going with the buy in all markets. Just fix the glow at the end of the road so it doesn't look like headlights . . . and Julia . . .'

'Yes, my liege . . .'

'Lose the nebula . . .' Oh, no, not another plane trip . . .

'Couldn't we do that on the final art . . . we can use starfields from the picture . . .' I know he is right, but we won't have time unless I personally escort the proof.

'Let's get as much as we can out now . . .' Hey, the guy is committing a half a mil. What's another sleepless night in the vast scheme of things . . . I wonder if out there in an alternative universe there is another mogul saying, 'Lose the nebula . . .'

'Okay . . . maybe while I'm there you could arrange for me to get together with some of these merchandising people you've been hiding in New York . . .' I have been hocking everyone about merchandising possibilities on this movie. They smile and ignore me. I am still operating in that Stone Age where people don't know that a single movie is a cottage industry, where ancillary rights are still regarded as 'boilerplate' . . .

'Let's worry about the picture first . . .'

'I've never been worried about that . . .' My liege laughs, and wishes me a safe trip. Suck. Suck harder.

I do so much blow with Grady Rabinowitz that night, who rushes me to the plane, that I get bumped from my seat in first class for Hugh Hefner. I hug the paste-up to my chest and doze against the shoulder of a Third World person. He smells of rancid alcohol and B.O. . . . I don't bother to sleep the next day, racing the proof back to Smollen in time, racing to the hotel, collect messages – good, Vincent Alati, Merchandising, 10 ay-em the next day, lunch with Hirschfield – return phone calls.

I take a shower and unpack my clothes for the next day and then, of course, find myself wide awake. I flip television channels, order magazines. I search through my pills and pockets and find zero downers. I wonder if I should try to stay up for another full day. The very thought knocks me out and finally, I collapse into the arms of Morpheus.

I am awakened the next morning by an angry Vincent Alati,

who wants to know where the fuck I am. I get it together in a half hour (thanks, Victor, for the perm) and walk over to the Columbia Building. Vincent Alati is borderline New York Italian attractive, but really from the lowah clahsses. He's pretty preoccupied with my lateness, and who can blame him – it is eleven, not ten – but warms up a tad after I apologize profusely and explain about the ad. He stores his anger for a later time. I tell him briefly about the picture, about the hardware, mostly about the extraterrestrial.

'Well, if you want to get any toys out, you have to have your prototypes ready by the toy show in February . . .'

'Well, half our effects aren't even done, and the ET hasn't been built yet . . .' Alati frowns, a real I'm-not-an-artist-I'm-a-businessman type.

'Then you won't make the toy show . . .'

He is ready to chat all day, I have turned out to be so charming, but after an hour of education, I tell him I have another meeting . . . I wander down to Hirschfield's office and browbeat him into taking me to Côte Basque downstairs so I can look at all the clothes and jewelry. I thank him for coming across on the ad.

'I think we should advertise the movie as costing twenty million dollars,' he says, pronouncing 'movie' 'm-u-u-vie,' which comes from originating in Oklahoma. Beware the middle western Jew, he could be your brother.

'That's exactly where it will be,' I shoot back, grateful for the opportunity to tell him the truth, 'and I can assure you we'll have more to advertise than its cost . . .' Alan laughs charitably. Best defense with me. He can tell I'm in a rush and assumes it is something to do with the picture.

I don't think it's necessary to tell him that I'm going to the furriers' building on Seventh Avenue with my mother and a friend of hers to find a mink. It is entirely antithetical to my ethical upbringing and value system, but I am spending half my time in New York, and feel myself more chilled-to-the-bone than ever, now that California blood courses through me. Christ knows, I have the bread.

My mother's friend is tall, dark, and slender, antithetical to my mother, as it were, and her name is Helen. She is completely au courant on the burning issues of male versus female, dark versus light, horizontal versus vertical. I just don't want to look like a linebacker for the Green Bay Packers. Victor has said, think lynx, think fox, but they seem overwhelming to me. Besides, I reasoned, I could get one of those later. Seems to me your first fur should be mink. Also, I like little foxes and lynxes and I detest mink, nasty little rodents, not adorable woodland creatures. Helen concurs.

We go up and down in the elevator from showroom to showroom and I find a Norell at Michael Forrest that looks like a bathrobe and retails for ten grand. Helen gets him down to fifty-five hundred and I shake on it. I put him on the phone with Colbert and they work out payment. I tell him I'm leaving for California that afternoon. He turns to me, flushed, and says he'll embroider my name inside, freshen it up a bit, and bring it over to the hotel that afternoon. Yay! Instant gratification!

'I've never seen anyone make a decision this fast,' he says. That's because you deal with rich yentas spending their husband's money. You would think since this money is mine, earned by me, that that would make me more careful, but for some reason, it is provoking sicko extravagance all the way around. Erica Jong has told me repeatedly that I overtip, that overtipping is a sign of insecurity. So's overwriting, I want to say, but don't.

'Comes with the territory.' I smile. I turn to my mother. 'Now it's your turn!' Please, please. Enjoy this money that you always wanted so much. She's already returned a bauble or two that I'd gotten her at Tiffany's. No, not returned – exchanged. Same thing.

'I'd never wear it . . .'

'Oh, please, pleeeeze . . .'

'No . . .' Cunt.

'Well, I got a meeting back at the hotel . . .' I turn to Michael Forrest, shake his hand, with strong pressure, again, like he really needs to be reminded who he is dealing with. 'C'mon girls, let's go . . .'

On my way to the elevator my mother grabs my arm to hold me back. 'I have to talk to you,' she whispers urgently. Helen senses something and says she's going to hit some department stores. We go down in the elevator in silence. Helen and I kiss goodbye, and I thank her again. She hails a cab. My mother and I hail another and head for the Sherry. I look at my watch and pray that the proof, redone, is waiting at the concierge's desk for me, and that my limo is there. I'll just have time to catch the 6 P.M. American flight.

'Your father is going blind,' she says dully. What?@#!

When I glance over at her she is brushing small fake tears from the corners of her eyes and her lips are trembling. Brief and to the point. The Queen of Pith. And I am the Clown Princess.

'Your father is losing sight in his left eye . . .' My father, like me, makes sudden moves. You get a lot of bruises on your legs that way, but come to think of it, he has been bumping into more furniture than usual.

'Has he been to a doctor?'

'Yes . . . two . . . they say he has something called a macular degeneration of the retina . . .' Sounds like a Doug Trumball special effect. My mother looks at me with pleading eyes. Boy, talk about I coulda been a contender . . . I am tempted to ask, in a voice dripping with the irony I learned from her, what she expects me to do with this information. I remind myself that I love my daddy, and I should think of something.

When I get to the hotel, I call Steven immediately, tell him about the ad, the merchandising meeting, gossip about Alan Hirschfield for a moment:

'He mentioned *Close Encounters* and twenty mil in the same sentence today . . . but he really is a horny bastard. You know he sent me a book called *Blue Movie* with a note that said he was available for a reenactment of any and all fantasies . . .' Steven laughs. Best defense with me; as in, she can't really be saying this, she's making a joke . . . 'Y'know, it's really boring flirting with this guy for your money . . .'

'He reminds me of Michael . . .'

'How?' This seems farfetched to me, but I love to hear Steven's opinions. He is remarkably intuitive for someone so cut off.

'Dunno . . . just that calm, quiet type . . .' Alan is heavily into TM; I wonder for a moment if Michael is, too, and if they have the same mantra . . .

'As in, he's made a career of being underestimated?'

'Sorta . . .'

Moment of silence, enough time to broach the real reason for my call. I drop the news about my father.

'Steven, you think Jules Stein might know of something to do? Someone to see?' Isn't this the Wunderkind of Universal, founded by Jules Stein, Eye Maven of the Western World?

'Lemme talk to Sid . . .'

'Will you do it right away?'

'My next phone call . . . when're you coming back?'

'Now . . .'

'Good, I'll call you later . . .'

The doorbell rings and it is Michael Forrest with my coat. He shows me my embroidered name inside. Oh, bay-bay . . . And I'm outta there, sign the bill, to be magically picked up by someone else, duke 'em all, then climb in the limo with the carry-on luggage, and fly to the airport. I smoke my last joint on the way. The flight before the flight. As it were. I wonder if every driver for the last two years has been having contact highs with me in the back, puffing away like the Caterpillar . . .

Steven calls Sid, Sid calls Jules, and within a week my father sees a retired great and famous named Arthur Davoe who takes one look at him and says, 'You do not have a macular degeneration of the retina.' X-rays and CAT scans reveal a large, gelatinous tumor on his pituitary gland. It is resting on the cranial nerve and causing blindness. Nobody wants to hazard a guess whether it is benign or cancerous, but there is little disagreement that it has to come out. Brain surgery? This sounds worse to me than losing the sight in your left eye.

You come in through one great and famous, he leads you to another. I find my father in the care of a brain surgeon named Hausepian, and an endocrinologist named Holub. They are both at Columbia Presbyterian. Hausepian has performed a rare surgery in which entry to the brain is accomplished through the nasal cavity, with gases and backlighting, as opposed to the lifting from the rear. Less chance, we are informed, of becoming a vegetable.

That's nice . . . They will excise the tumor, bombard the area with radiation, and replenish his depleted hormones with medication. The more I hear about the surgery the more it makes me think of Doug Trumball's effects: with my father's brain the mother ship and his nasal cavity a vast starfield . . .

The surgery is scheduled for a week before Thanksgiving, and I worry about the care he will get during a holiday season. I fly back to New York again, this time with Richard and Steven for some premature confabs with Lois Smith about P.R. for the picture. They're spending money on ads and fees for P.R. outfits, but we still don't have most of our effects, the ET, or India.

TRUFFAUT: Where are the sounds coming from, Julia?

ME: India, I swear.

Columbia is still on the brink of financial ruin, and I have to figure out how to continue the flow of cash. The flirtation with Hirschfield can't work forever.

The day before my father's surgery, the *Close Encounters* tooth explodes. I am in excruciating pain and my face is swollen. No painkiller, no coke eases it at all. I know it is a physical manifestation of my psychic pain. I am very preoccupied with my daddy's brain surgery. My father is defined, most of all, by his intelligence and learning. Plus, he lives by his wits. The thought of this being altered in any way frightens me. I have funneled all the fear into my tooth.

My mother gets in touch with her Park Avenue dentist. A medical Alan Hirschfield, if you will. He isn't available, but his assistant, a rigid, Germanic type, fills in.

Big mistake. The assistant breaks an instrument off in one of the roots and the procedure takes longer with more deleterious aftereffects. I go back to my hotel with my Percodan and my ice pack and lie on my bed, in tears, for the night. I arrange to have a limo pick me up at the hotel in the morning, pick up my mother, so we can go up to Columbia Presbyterian before my father is sedated and wheeled off. In the back of my mind I am thinking, This might be the last time you see him.

I am in a nasty mood. I have toot with my coffee, then a perc. When we arrive in my father's room, he is already floating off to la-la land. I scoot into the bathroom and rub coke on the gum all around the tooth. My brother is there, too, but we barely acknowledge each other, no small feat in a room which is, charitably, eight by ten.

I have the chills from the lack of sleep and shock to my mouth and I never take off the mink coat. Something in me knows that it is making my brother hate me more. I bask in his hate and grind my teeth, which sends slivers of pain to parts of my brain that have been dormant until now.

One of the doctors comes up before surgery to tell us we should get out of the hospital for the next three hours or so. My mother wants to plant herself in the lounge down the hall. Smoke and read *The New York Times*. Keep up the vigil. Jews . . . My brother and I find something to agree on: Let's get the fuck outta here for awhile.

We go down in the elevator in silence, and actually get out the door before something between me and my brother erupts and we start screaming insults at each other. We are on the corner of 168th Street and Amsterdam. Not such a hot place to pause for an altercation. The limo driver pulls up. My brother, still holding my mother's arm, starts to head in the opposite direction toward his car. I grab her other arm. My brother and I are screaming at each other and insisting that she leave with one or the other.

Matthew and I have only come to blows twice before in our lives. I viewed my brother pretty much as my personal pet during childhood and tortured him for ten years. My father kept saying, Julia, he's going to get bigger than you and be very mad. My brother did have the most awesome temper I've ever seen, mine included, and that's saying something. So finally when he was ten and I was thirteen he practically broke off my arm. My father stopped him and my brother has often told me that if he'd allowed him to break my arm I would have been a better person.

Different, I always say, because I am now old enough to

have learned the lessons the arm would have taught me then, and the arm might have caused me to be cowardly. We had an equally vicious fight the day before I took off for Mount Holyoke to leave him solo with my parents in Milwaukee, but I've always thought that was separation anxiety.

Now, with no Solomon around, we are getting ready to rip my mother in half, crazed Dr. Doolittles and my mother a human Pushmepullyou. This is not my movie, my mind keeps saying, but my tooth eggs me on: it is it is it is. And by the way, what if we're as good as it gets? What if WE ARE ALL ALONE . . . who cares . . .

'Let her do this for me!' my mother shouts. My mother is always characterizing these acts as Let her do this for me Let her pay for this for me . . . My brother and I go totally silent. We are both shocked that she has chosen to go with me. Probably it would have been better for her to keep the vigil upstairs . . .

My father – what a trooper – doesn't require any assistance to survive. He is up and coherent by the next day. They will have to amplify his missing endocrines with pills, but he seems pretty much himself, which is more than I can say for me . . .

I fall in love with Jack Spratlin because he saves me from Tower of Power. It starts out a beautiful Sunday. Kate is visiting with Michael. Nick has stayed over. Birds chirp. Sun shines. We eat breakfast in silence. Within an hour of our first words to each other, Nick leaves for the last time. Location romances. I do the last of the toot I have, I'm so torn up about it, and I call Jack for some more. He says he'll deliver. Well, at least something is going my way.

I go to the front hall closet, which is hidden in the wall and works on a spring, and I put Jeremy's Tower of Power on Jeremy's eight track. I've kept quite a few of Jeremy's possessions for a long time; the conditions of his departure seem to call for some payment.

I dance around to Tower of Power, strength and energy coursing through me. Antsy on the blow, I bop up the steps to the pool. Jump in. Position myself in front of the water whooshing in and will myself to an intense orgasm. Fuck you, Nick. Lonely lonely. Feeling thirsty, I bounce down the stairs. I freeze mid-bounce between steps twenty-two and twenty-three.

The same Tower of Power cut is blaring out of every orifice of my house, and it's suddenly very annoying. I zip downstairs to the hidden closet, waiting for it to spring open, and it sticks. I start to sweat. Tower of Power would have banged its way into anyone's consciousness, but I have snorted coke. Tower of Power has zoomed into unbearable thirty seconds ago. I try and try the door. Every thirty seconds that I can't change that cut is five minutes. Jesus, they're loud. Five minutes stretches into eternity. Stop. I'll tell all the secrets. I have to get away from this cacophony.

I run around closing up the house, then I grab some cigarettes and kitchen matches, and walk down my driveway to the street. I can hear the din down here. I hope a neighbor doesn't complain to the police. My mother, Russian to the core, trained me when I was too young to disagree that all cops were cossacks. I'd hate to deal with cossacks on this wonderful Sunday I'm having. Actually, the cops might be a convenience. They could shoot the door down and kill Tower of Power.

But nobody in this neighborhood ever complains. We're all shut away from each other behind our electric gates. Very civilized. (Years later, standing on the deck with Harlan one October day at the magic hour, throwing grapes under the wheels of passing cars just to hear them squish, I turn to him and say, 'You can hear a guy farting three blocks away in this canyon. You mean to tell me you couldn't hear them screaming that night?' He looks at me, frightened and knowing. Deep in the subconscious of every transplanted Californian lies a memory of That Labor Day Weekend. The way things are going now, of course, Charlie Manson could end up being a lobbyist for the psycho-murderers. Probably a hardcore twenty percent of the voting population, skewed heavily toward the South and West, where the money and the weather are. Reagan Democrats.

I hear Jack's Porsche before I can see it, not a fancy one,

but the dinky 914 that makes a tinny noise like an old MG. He absorbs my situation and hears Tower of Power simultaneously. He laughs his crazy laugh and speeds past me up the driveway. Like a puppy in training, I run behind him, tongue hanging out.

'I have a little emergency here.'

'ADR?' A movie term for additional dialogue recording which I use as a code with all dealers for awful dreaded runout.

'Worse, my door is stuck and so is Tower of Power. You have to break into my closet or Tower of Power will never stop.' It's starting to burn into my brain. I am dizzy from aggravation. I open the front door, and Jack jumps back from the aural assault.

'This really is a job for Clark Kent, isn't it?' he cracks. 'What kind of tools do we have?' He smacks the door a couple of times, just to see if I'm lying. By now, the door is listing a bit to one side. This job is getting more onerous by the minute. I point to the door.

'They're in there . . . could we have a little toot first?'

'Ah yes, first things first.' He tosses me a Baggie of white shit and paces back and forth in front of the door, sizing up the opponent.

While I play with my drugs, he finds the kitchen. He returns, wielding the kind of knife found only in slasher movies and my kitchen. Another consequence of Jeremy. I'm opposed to having a gun in the house because Kate is small and curious, not to mention me, because I'm small and dangerous, but after his murderous attack, I'm into some sort of major weaponry. The butcher knife can be used on food as well as people, so practical and lethal at the same time. It comforts me on dark lonely nights when the power goes out in the Canyon, as it so often does, and it can carve a turkey or two till the next assailant stops by on his way to the Valley.

Jack tries repeatedly to pry the door open with the knife. He does it with such force that the door moves a bit, but the knife flies out of his hand. Twice. Scares the shit out of both of us. He leaves it lying on the floor after the second misfire, and has some blow. Takes off his shirt. He's sweating. Ooh, nice chest. Well shaped, well defined, just the right amount of hair. He turns around. Ooh, even better. Very nice back and shoulders, *sans* fur. Maybe if I just gaze at this for a while I won't go crazy. Not a chance.

'Jack, I'm going to kill myself . . .'

He reaches for the knife, hands it to me. 'Help yourself.' Cold shot, but I laugh. So does he. God, I love his face when he laughs. He circles around the door a few times. 'When will World War Two be over,' he asks himself out of the side of his mouth. He checks his watch. Places to go, people to see. All the desperate junkies waiting for the magic man on a Sunday afternoon.

'Time flies when you're having fun,' I say, holding the knife at my side.

'We need a new tool . . .' Fine with me, pal. Take off your pants and let's see if it works. Better yet, let's see how fast you get a hard-on and we'll pry the door open with your dick. 'Get me a wire hanger. I've got an idea . . .' I give him a doleful look. 'Don't tell me. They're all in there.'

I take off quick, combing all closets in the house for a wire hanger. Finally, deep in the recesses of my compulsive-shopper closet, I find some unconstructed linen just back from the cleaners, throw it on the floor and come running back with the hanger. Jack unbends it impatiently, leaving a half-hook at the end.

I can't imagine why he thinks this will work when the knife has been such a dud. He pushes and sweats and strains, and I worry a vein in his neck will explode before my door, but *blam!* the door falls open. Jack attacks the eight track, and in a millisecond the house goes dead quiet. I miss the noise now that it's gone, but I clap my hands and fill the void with my applause. Jack appears well pleased with himself. Is that a blush or the strain of his mission accomplished?

'My hero,' I coo, meaning it for the moment. Now he blushes. Touching in someone so cold. I like him better just cold. It's sexier. Touching is like Jeremy or Izzy. Michael. Tony. Pussies every one. Guys who disappointed me, guys who let me down, guys who don't turn me on anymore. Jack pulls his shirt on abruptly, making little leaving noises with his tongue. Don't leave yet, this could be love. But he's packing up and moving toward the door. Always leave before it's time to go, Jeremy had said. And then stayed too long. Jack Spratlin has his pride and he will never overstay his welcome.

Kate sits propped up in bed eating her peas and pretending to watch Walter Cronkite with me. I find Walter soothing. Walter is my mantra. I am preparing India and presiding over an extremely trying postproduction on *Close Encounters*. The disturbing pattern of two steps forward and sixteen steps upside-down and sideways, to keep the various departments at the studio from fucking up is emerging. In every possible way. Beyond imagination.

Which is what three-year-old Kate Phillips wants to discuss tonight. Walter is reporting a UFO sighting (what's good for the picture is good for the Jews, I think) and Kate says: 'You know what I discovered you can do if you're a child?'

'What?'

'Well, if you concentrate, and angle your head right, you can project' pronounced pwo-jeck 'your way into the television.' I don't say anything, so she explains, 'Like if you were curious to meet Walter . . .'

'I've already met Walter . . .' Actually Walter is one of the few big stars I have met who wasn't a disappointment. He'd been gracious enough to meet me and Steven in the hooker-laden bar at the Sherry Netherland to talk about the remote possibility of playing the anchorman reporting the nerve-gas derailment/coverup on the network news. Why not?

He had been an everyday fan/observer in Martha's Vineyard while Steven was shooting *Jaws* and besides, we'd gotten Truffaut for Lacombe, Dreyfuss for net points, Trumball was on board, John Williams was doing the music, and Vilmos was the cinematographer. Why the fuck not Walter fucking Cronkite?

Mainly, he explained, because CBS newsmen were specifically constrained from doing movie gigs. It was frowned upon for newsmen to appear as actors. This was, after all, 1975. Although there were indications . . .

'ABC is the only one who lets them take parts,' Walter said gently.

'So that's why Howard K. Smith – ' I started, the lightbulb going on in a balloon over my head.

'I wanted to avoid Howard K. Smith for that very reason,' said Steven, wistful to the last syllable.

'When are you shooting?'

'We don't really know – sort of from the spring until the fall . . .'

'Because here's an interesting thing. My contract with them is up June thirtieth . . .' Walter smiled and Steven perked up.

'You have a window of time there?' I asked.

'Well, it does come up right against July 4. I could probably create a little space in there where I'm technically not under contract to CBS . . .' Walter smiled pleasantly, just like on TV. 'I think this movie is a good idea. I sure loved *Jaws* . . . and *The Sting*, too, of course.' Hey, you can like his movie more than my movie, just so you do *our* movie . . .

'So, did you project your way into the television?' I ask my daughter, bored with Walter, who hadn't done our movie (Howard K. Smith had), and fascinated by her tale.

'I did, Mommy. I went right into the scene on Crescendo Summit in *Close Encounters* and there was a spaceship . . .'

'Go on . . .'

'The door opened and the ugliest little being came out and he said, "Hello, pretty," and I said, "Hello, ugly" – because he really was ugly, Mommy – and he said, "Want some candy?" and gave me some.'

'I told you no candy from strangers.'

'Oh, he had it in his hand, I didn't go in the ship . . .'

'Then what . . .?'

'Oh, I wanted to come back here, so I projected myself back into bed. I'm not too good at it, though. I think I hit my head on the way back.' And there it is, a welt on her forehead. 'I've got a little headache now, but it was worth it . . .'

'I wish I could do that . . .'

'Oh, you could when you were a child. You outgrow it, I think . . .' And make movies, instead.

*

Time's Man of the Year is Jimmy Carter. He says he believes in UFOs. What a country . . .

So, Ted Bundy was finally going to get to die. Was there any significance to the fact that it was going to be on Michael Des Barres's birthday? Like Elvis bought the farm on Mighty Mo's*? Like everyone else, especially being the mother of a beautiful brown-eyed, dark-haired teenaged girl, she thought the motherfucker should die, her views on capital punishment notwithstanding.

Viz. *Performance:* What would you do with a mad dog, Moody?

Why I'd kill it, of course.

But it was weird to see the crowds of fans gathering outside and hear the cheers when the exterior lights dimmed. Bread and circuses, hunh? Are they going to be televising these from inside next? In between sporting events. College basketball was the next big TV fodder, *The New York Times* said. And now, ladies and gentlemen, we'll take a short break from this exciting Little League Pro-Am series, to bring you the administration of the fatal drugs to Richard Ramirez . . .

Michael Des Barres just kept missing stardom, and she had the feeling that it was because he hadn't found his medium yet. Truth was, though, that he was getting older all the time, and he needed to find it soon. She suspected TV, when it was ready for him. If it didn't pass him by first. She liked a lot about Michael Des Barres, but that was because he was a seventies ex-junkie, which meant shared experience, if not precisely with each other. She had never bumped into him on that trail, and since she was only a fellow-traveler to AA, she hadn't met him there, either. For the longest time, she couldn't remember when or where she'd met him. He just seemed to be someone she knew. Then she remembered . . .

Funnily enough, she met him at the after-concert party for Power Station, when he replaced Robert Palmer singing lead. She thought the band had been just dreadful, thought the group, even with Palmer, was borderline anyway. Beyond that, the evening was an all-time top ten of weird.

She had arrived, by limo, with the following crew: David Debin, Steve Reuther, Paul Mones, Stuart Griffen, John Tarnoff, and Mones's Shmoo-shaped friend, Chris, who didn't fit in with the rest of them, but was thrilled to be along for the ride.

She had informed them all that they could come and go as they pleased, but that they all knew she liked to make sudden moves, and that if for any reason the limo was not available for a quick getaway, well . . . needless to say, the ride in the car had been a little uptight, unaccustomed as these dudes were to being one-sixth of a date. She'd smoked a joint that gave them all, even Mones and Reuther, who were totally straight, a contact high.

It made the music better, which was about the most you could expect from a joint, not to mention that the music needed all the help it could get. She couldn't wait to get out of there and to the party, that's how bad the music was. Reuther, who was a pal of Des Barres's, said that when they started to sing 'Obsession,' which Des Barres had penned with Holly Knight, that was the time to go, but she wasn't sure she could make it that long. She surveyed the audience, as she always did when she was bored.

People rocked out, but in a way that made her know that they were bored, too. The entire audience couldn't wait for the concert to end. How many rock concerts had she been to and why was she still going, she wondered. She liked the fake energy. The longer she lived in L.A., where there was no energy, the more she liked gatherings such as this . . . lots of people lots of sweat lots of noise. A temporary fake city.

The party was at Tramps, a tacky club for the wanna-be hip

over-thirty crowd that had the distinction of being the only club in L.A. situated in a parking structure. She never went there, too many Persians, too many fumes.

She looked around, feeling out the crowd. Lots of leather. Lots of bimbos. Did these guys know that their predilection for bimbos was a sure sign to her that they were gay, or at least what she always thought of as half-a-fag?

Now Reuther was bringing Michael Des Barres to the table. AA buddies. Steven had warned her he would be doing this intro. 'Please be nice,' he whispered. 'He's dying to meet you.' Why, she thought, he already died. Onstage. In front of thousands of people. But Michael Des Barres turned out to be a funny little Cockney in antiquated drag, and even though his mascara was running into his dripping pancake, she actually connected with him, loved his humor . . .

Over the years, bit by bit, they had actually become friends, actually witnessed change in each other's lives, all for the better, and now she was taking him out to Mortons to celebrate his getting a two-week bad-guy part in a Clint Eastwood movie. He arrived all done up in black leather, but who was she to make a comment, donned as she was in the selfsame Friday night maybe-we'll-hit-Helena's-later outfit? Which was to say. Black. Leather. At least she was the only one at the table wearing mascara.

She ordered a drink – spite maybe, maybe just fun – and his eyes flew past her this way and that. It was Mortons on a Friday night. Everyone's eyes always flitted onto her date, the one who got to see the people on their way in and do the front-door interaction with the maître d'. From time to time his eyes slid over to Frankie, the new girl at the door. She was always in competition for the men's attention with the girl at the door. Lisa or Leslie, now Frankie. It made her spout very *bon mots* and it made her contemplate plastic surgery, a hazard of being tight with the Leafs, anyway.

They went to Helena's afterward at his insistence. The crowd had changed. In the beginning it had been empty, then Helena opened her doors and it had become *the* Friday night place to be. Then the doors stayed open too long, and the crowd got mixed. But Helena would be closing for good soon and it seemed loyal to show up for the end. Michael took off like a shot, hustling this one and that.

She danced one lindy with Freddy De Mann and remembered the fifties, one dance with Brooke and Michelle and remembered the nineties. She took up a post at the bar for awhile, so she could find the right moment to hit the bathroom. Helena had gone very nouvelle bathroom, i.e., one stall. She kept telling Helena, I'm gonna open a rival club, no dance floor, but forty stalls for the ladies . . .

When there was a lull she hit the Ladies', ran into Linda Obst. Linda admired her leather and she said it was old . . .

'Ah, the closets of the formerly rich . . .' Linda mused and smiled her mean little ferret smile.

She left Michael to his devices and split for the solace of home. It took him two days to figure out she was annoyed with him.

'You know, Michael,' she heard herself say in a righteous tone, 'you can be clean and sober and still have bad manners . . .' i.e., behave like a sleaze. He apologized, but she was sure he had no idea what she meant.

Re: the quintessential star/celeb. An evolving species. In the eighties, compliments of *People* magazine and *Entertainment Tonight*, the definition blurs. In the eighties, a star is pretty, packaged, and marginally talented, but still works for a living. It doesn't do anything really well, but it looks good doing it.

A celebrity has no visible means of support. It is famous for being famous. It doesn't do anything at all, but it looks great not doing it. If the star is everything we would be, the celebrity is everything we are. The I-could-be-that-if-only . . . But more. Our shiniest self-image.

Trouble is, when we look in the mirror, there is no reflection . . .

After the Tower of Power incident, I don't interact with Jack Spratlin again until I score a quarter of primo coke, surfer coke, from him. Starting in '75, when it was getting really popular, cocaine began to change. No more beautiful opalescent butterflies from Peru, where the competitive Colombians were setting the kitchens on fire. Now it is this reconstituted Colombia-via-Miami shit.

Ricky*, who went to school with Michael, but has somehow developed into my friend, is having dinner at my house when the doorbell rings. It is Jack, purveyor of the aforementioned Colombian product, and he is smiling and laughing.

'I brought you some blow that you can't say no to.' He smiles crazily, and breezes right in.

'I like people to call first,' I say huffily, wondering who's left the gate open. Without preamble, he settles himself at the small dining-room table, takes out a piece of rose-colored marble, and dumps white powder on it. It glistens under the light of the chandelier overhead. This is an unfamiliar sight. I stick my pinky in and lick it. It tastes right, with just an undercurrent of something that makes your mouth tighten, and it doesn't give too profound a freeze too fast.

'Lemme show you a better test.' He smiles and licks the end of a cigarette, dabs some of the sample product on it, then lights it ceremoniously with a wooden match. The ash turns white. 'If there was any cut, it'd burn black or brown, and it would smell like shit,' he brags. 'I'm telling you, Julia, this is *da kine*, and you should buy a lot, because there's only eight pounds of this stuff in all of L.A., and it's the last.'

'Okay, I'll take an eighth.'

Jack laughs contemptuously. 'This is primo coke, smuggled in from Peru by surfers who ain't gonna do this no more. Don't be a piker.'

'Okay, what then – ?'

'Buy an ounce, you can afford it – you've got two hit movies and a third on the way – ' Did I hear a tinge of admiration in his voice? Probably just jealousy.

'No, I don't want to have that much around – '

'I'm telling you, as a friend – '

Now I laugh contemptuously. A friend? 'No, I'll take a quarter, that's it.'

'Please, listen to me, when you call next week for more, I'll be out, or I'll be hitting it – '

'End of discussion.'

'Okay, but don't say I didn't – '

'Want something to eat, Jack, while Ricky fills up his nose?' Ricky has been enjoying the procedure, but I can tell he wouldn't mind partaking of some of the goods.

'Nah, thanks, got places to go – '

'People to string out – '

He laughs and takes out a nice-looking quarter bag, only slightly less high-grade than the sample that still lies on the marble slab. 'On consignment.' He smiles, knowing I will have the cash to him by messenger in the morning, and packs up to leave, dumping the sample coke from marble to maple for Ricky to figure out how to snort.

A week later I dump Jack's surfer coke into Grady Rabinowitz's carpet.

Notwithstanding our location indiscretion and our lack of studio deal, we are committed to the greatness of *The Third Man Through the Door* and we are still meeting on a regular basis to pitch out the story on spec. I want many-layered and complex; Grady wants funny. I love leaving the Burbank lot, where Michael and I still share a suite of offices, to the general discomfort of us and our ever-increasing staff, to come to Grady's where it is easier to work and toot.

I need to pick up an ounce of Hawaiian pot from him anyway, and I want to lay some of this surfer coke, which I am carrying in a Valium bottle – there is so much of it – on him. I share my drugs. It is one of the reasons I have a drug rep. In the same way that very few studios are saying no to my ideas or requests, very few people say no to my drugs.

334

SCENE FROM A MOVIE CALLED *HOW TO WRITE A MOVIE*

OVO: Grady greets me in the driveway. I think it is because he is glad to see me, but it is more because he is glad to see my coke. We repair to his office where I extract a Valium bottle filled with opalescent product. I lay some out on one of his many disco deco mirrors. We chat about a friend of mine, a gambler losing everything . . .

HE: I used to be a gambler, a sicko gambler. Know how I got over it?

ME: How?

HE: Well, I went to Vegas with some acid . . .

ME: Oh, the old give-up-one-for-the-other routine . . .

HE: (impatient) No, listen . . .I played blackjack for three days, off and on, high on acid . . .

OVO: I gasp, fiddle nervously with the Valium bottle, which I still clasp in my hot little hand.

HE: (continuing, on a roll) . . . I won forty-eight thousand bucks, lost half of it back, cashed in my chips, and walked away . . .

OVO: I make one of my sudden moves . . .

HE: . . . forever. . .

OVO: THE VALIUM BOTTLE, childproof top unfastened, flies from my hand. In EXTREME SLOW MOTION it pitches end over end in an arc, spewing little white flakes into the air. It lands in the CARPET. So does most of the coke.

ME: Oh dear . . .

OVO: He grabs a MATCHBOOK, drops to his knees. He tries to scoop the spilled coke onto the matchbook. His efforts only seem to make it sink deeper into the carpet. He lifts the matchbook to his nose with a shaking hand. There is some dust, some dirty coke, some carpet furth, a dead fly. He peers into this mess closely.

CU: THE FLY. Is it still alive, or is his heavy breathing making it flutter?

CU: HIS NOSE, coming into FRAME. Bulbous; capillaries red from bursting and black hairs fight for space. This nose has been around.

CU: THE FLY, still fluttering.

CU: THE NOSE, closing in on the fly.

OVO: I have to do something or he is going to snort that fly!

ME: (blowing it away, snuffing candles on a birthday cake) This is beneath us.

OVO: Still genuflecting to the coke-filled carpet, he starts to wail like the old Jew he truly is.

ME: There there . . .

OVO: Why am I comforting him? It's my coke.

ME: Don't you think it's time to get up off the floor?

HE: Think we could snort it right out of the carpet?

ME: (softer) Don't cry over spilt coke.

HE: (reluctantly standing) Honey, you are the most arrogant cunt . . .

ME: Don't ever call me honey again . . .

HE: (mournfully) That's funny . . .

Re: the quintessential comedy writer. He is probably older than he looks. He makes a lot of money for doing his job. Making other people look good, he will constantly remind you. But he never feels really successful. When success does come, it is too late. No matter what, he carries the smell of failure on him.

He steals everybody's lines and thinks they're his own. Sometimes you'll find your dinner conversation in a book or a screenplay or another dinner conversation. If you say something that makes him laugh, he will turn his mouth down and scowl. That's funny, he will say in a funereal voice, like somebody just died. If you make him laugh more than once, so he knows it isn't by accident, he will hate you behind your back for as long as you both shall live . . .

'Let's see if Jack Spratlin has anything, and I'll have Kendall pick it up,' I say. This suggestion brightens Grady's spirits somewhat even though we both know that Jack Spratlin and his horrible girlfriend do a lot of coke and he has a tendency to hit the product he sells to others a little too hard. Word is he also hits the girlfriend a little too hard from time to time. But any port in a storm, and this definitely qualifies as an emergency. I call Kendall; she puts me on hold to call Jack, comes back on real quick. 'I'm on my way to do the dirty deed. I'll be there in an hour.' I report the good news to Grady.

Kendall was brought up in Hollywood; she knows everybody and she knows just how to deal with them. She does a good imitation of her brother David's snappy patter, and best of all, she is completely deaf in one ear, so she only hears half my insults and the rest of them don't seem to ruffle her at all. She is pretty much unflappable, and, as *Close Encounters* is a set of insoluble problems every day, with a new set coming up tomorrow that needed to be solved by the close of business yesterday, her mere presence feels reassuring, not to mention helpful.

She is half Jewish, half gentile, and the gentile has prevailed. Dreyfuss calls her the *shiksa* goddess, and she is, particularly with her long red Lady Godiva hair and big tits, the perfect counterpart for my Little Lord Fauntleroy act. If it has to be an all-girl band, which, right now, it is, despite all the names on the credit bloc. For the first time, for a number of reasons, I am getting to run the show. I think my graph goes nowhere but up. Suck. Suck harder.

Just now, however, Kendall is very upset, and needs to sit down immediately. Her hands are quivering, and when she speaks, her voice shakes: 'Don't ever make me go to that place again,' she says as she hands over the bag of goodies. Grady is looking for a new idea fast, so he just takes the bag with the coke out, and starts spreading and chopping.

'Shit,' he says, but takes a couple of large snorts anyway. I know that he'll be in the bathroom momentarily because I can see the sparkle is mannite. I lick the end of a cigarette, dab it in the coke, light it with a match. Shit. It burns black and stinks. For the first time, I feel pain for the loss of the surfer coke. Here today, gone today. Kendall slumps in the chair, looking weak.

'What happened?'

'The atmosphere in that place is so heavy, I thought I'd choke on it.'

I grin, lean in closer. I am starting to feel curious about Jack Spratlin. 'Do tell.'

'The whole fucking place is dark, he's got this weird girlfriend, an obvious whore cocoa-nut, who's dressed in a bunch of what-looks-like scarves, and she's got bruises on her face, and she's telling me about the colors in my aura . . .' Kendall pauses briefly, to turn down, with a wave of her beautifully manicured hand, a toot of this awful stuff Grady has laid out. In fact, it is his hand proffering it. Grady can be real quiet on his little cat feet when he wants. How much has he heard? All of it, based on his contribution to the conversation:

'You know, I called over there once, and I think the phone was knocked off the hook, because nobody picked up but suddenly I could hear a woman screaming and the sound of slaps and Jack's voice saying, "How's that, bitch?" and I started going hello hello and someone hung up. It gave me a creepy feeling . . .'

'Then why are you smiling like that? You love telling us this, don't you? So Jack Spratlin hits his girlfriend . . . that goes with the coke. I bet she likes it. I bet that's the only thing that turns her on.'

'How do you know so much about it . . .?'

'Instinct . . .'

Kendall and Grady look concerned. 'Honey, you don't want to hang out with a guy who hits women . . .' Grady starts. That's what Artie Ross had said about Reilly O'Reilly. Artie Ross had died with a mask over his nose and a tank of nitrous oxide by his side; Reilly is still dysfunctionally alive. Somewhere Out There.

'Oh please, that's what some people said about Reilly O'Reilly, and he never laid a hand on me.' I thought about facing him down, squinty-eyed, naked in the shower, with shampoo running out of my hair and burning my eyes. Him, fully clothed, standing outside the shower, furious, with his hand raised, then shrugging and laughing. And leaving me unscathed. To rush back to the track to place another losing bet. It had been no contest. I'm not scared of Jack Spratlin. Not one little bit. Hasn't he given me this horrible coke on consignment?

Kendall stands up, feeling better. 'You know, I don't think I want to do this anymore.'

'The blow? The delivery?'

'Both,' she says definitely, smiles formally, then: 'Steven wants you to call, Guy wants you to call when you have a chance, Andrea said don't forget she's having dinner at your house, she wants to see Kate – Jesus, I've got to get back – I'll call you from the office . . .'

After Kendall leaves, Grady and I get down to the serious business of dividing up our Hawaiian pot, taking out some coke for work, and pitching out our story. The coke is so bad that I reach into the bottom of my cigarette case where I have a little silver gram bottle that Michael, who's given up coke for the last time, had just given me with a note that said, 'Have a White Christmas.' There is just a dash of the surfer coke left, and I split it with Grady, who really isn't a connoisseur and doesn't know the difference.

We don't finish up till about seven, which means I will be very late for Andrea. We stash all the drugs, which are now two ounces of pot and a quarter of mannite laced with a bit of cocaine, into an envelope addressed to *Third Man Through the Door Productions* and head to my car, a black Mercedes 450 SL with a red pinstripe, which Steven has pronounced redundant. He also refers to the car as the Black Mariah behind my back.

I light a joint and ease my way onto Mulholland Drive. A beautiful twilight is amplified by the sun caught in various levels of smog that hang over the Valley. I am so absorbed in this sight that I almost wrong-turn down Coldwater Canyon and have to veer left sharply to continue on Mulholland. Red and blue lights fire up in my rearview mirror, and my stomach sinks to my knees.

I remember Michael once telling me, 'Always hold the thought that nine out of ten cops are younger than you are . . .' But he was talking about getting caught speeding. I glance at the *TMTTD* envelope to see if it is closed. Then there is a flashlight shining on me, and I lower the window. The cop is young and blond with a broad, flat head. A cossack.

Involuntarily I grab my cigarette case and clutch it in my hand as he asks for my license and registration. Then the smell of the pot hits him, and he asks me to step out of the car. Now the other cop ambles over. He is dark and has a mustache and looks like he probably smokes marijuana on the weekends.

The cossack asks for my cigarette case and I give it to him. No doubt he is searching for a joint, but the whole fucking pack falls into his hands and Michael's silver coke bottle falls onto the ground. 'We've got coke here!' he exclaims excitedly to his partner, who seems reluctant to go on. Even I know this is going to turn out to be a bad bust – a roach and the remnants of the surfer coke is not any sort of amount. But then, there is that envelope in the passenger seat. I try not to look at it. I think about Andrea waiting for me at my house, and I wonder if there are people I know passing me in the traffic that flies by. Mulholland is a favorite shortcut for executives from Universal, Warners, and Columbia who live in Bel-Air.

The cops have a long dispute with each other about whether they should bust me; they call for someone to get my car. Then they handcuff me. I think, I will never do this for fun again; this is not fun. They chat with me on the way to the station, trying to figure out who I am. When they do figure it out, the dark one with the mustache says, 'You can call a bondsman from the stationhouse.'

When we get to the cop shop, they uncuff me immediately and take me to a phone. I call Jackie. I tell her not to tell Andrea what has happened. Then I give her a list of names to call to come get me out. Grady is at the top of the list. I give her the name of a bondsman and tell her to call him. It never occurs to me to call Norman Garey because I am mainly preoccupied with my *TMTTD* envelope stuffed with stash. Sooner or later, if me and my car hang around long enough, they are going to look in that envelope, and then I will get to stay in this wonderful place overnight.

I have three hundred dollars in cash with me, which is enough to post a fifteen-hundred-dollar bond. The guy who books me barely grazes my hand in ink for fingerprinting. It is a dumb bust; they all know it. I start to get some of my authoritativeness back, tell them I don't want to have to go out front because I know all the gossip types keep stringers around police stations. Several cops come over to tell me that they love *The Sting*. One of them even remembers my acceptance speech, my brief moment in the sun. The bondsman and Grady arrive at the same time and take care of the details.

'Follow me home, okay? I'm really nervous.' Then I jump in my car and drive at fairly high speed back to my house, as if I were trying to lose Grady, who follows tight on my ass in his shit-brown version of the same Mercedes. I pull my car into my garage and sit in it until Grady walks over.

'Boy, for someone who's nervous, you sure drive fast.'

'Come inside, let's have a joint.'

'Honey, it's two o'clock in the morning.' This is way past Grady's bedtime. He keeps the hours of a grandfather, up at six, asleep at ten. I wonder if he has hot water with lemon every morning, as my grandfather had, to stay regular. I explode out of the car, clutching the *TMTTD* envelope tightly.

'It's all your fault – everything – all of it – your fault!'

'You're the one who made the peculiar turn. You're the one who spilled the coke. You're the one who got busted – and I'm the one who showed up!'

'You're the one who insisted on coming to location, you're the one who paid my black maid twenty-five bucks to give you a blow job in my house, you're the one who distracted me from the Neary house so we went over two hundred fifty grand in ten days – ' I am running out of breath. We walk in angry silence up the steps. In the distance, a dog barks. Just like in the movies. I open the door and we tiptoe in. Jackie is still awake and makes us some tea. England's answer to chicken soup. It feels soothing and I hate tea. Grady rolls a joint.

'Are you all right, Julia?' Jackie asks, looking as if she isn't.

'Well, I'm not in jail and I still have all my drugs . . .' Grady passes me the joint, always a conciliatory gesture, and I take a long, unsatisfying pull that makes me cough. 'I really hate pot,' I exhale, and we all laugh.

*

The day after, I vomit all day. In between trips to the bathroom I call Andrea, Norman, and Steven. Andrea clucks sympathy and disapproval. Norman and Steven fly over. By that time I am under my covers with a bucket at the side of my bed. Linda Wickstrom, a fulsome California girl with artistic aspirations who fills in for Jackie on weekends, calls Cedars emergency room to see if there are some home remedies for uncontrollable vomiting. I tell her to go in Kate's medicine cabinet and get me whichever elixir applies. She comes back with a bottle of Bentyl, Phenergan elixir, and Children's Tylenol. An overmedicator by nature, I slug all three.

'Why didn't you call me from the police station?' Norman yells. He is very upset.

'Because I was holding. It was in an envelope, but I was very intent on getting my car and myself out of there.'

'Very stupid. Now you're booked. Now I'm gonna have to chase it down. This could be real trouble . . .' I can see his mind at work behind his glasses.

'Ah, c'mon, Norman, you know it's a bad bust . . . besides, we can always buy our way out of the situation . . .'

Steven throws himself on the waterbed and I start to heave. 'Sorry,' he says, and tries to settle its undulations.

'I'm gonna make some calls,' Norman says, kisses the top of my head, and leaves.

Steven and I hang out for a little while watching television. 'I hope Rona Barrett doesn't get hold of this,' he says. 'You know, she's been asking a lot of questions about you and the drugs. You gotta stop for a while . . .'

'No shit. Listen, thanks for coming over. But now it's time to go. I'm gonna be sick.' He seems relieved to be dismissed. After he leaves I fall asleep. I sleep through Sunday and wake up Monday morning to Rona Barrett reporting news of my arrest. Within minutes the phone starts to ring. Dick Sylbert, Mike Nichols, Michael, John Dunne. Interesting group to be watching Rona. I call Norman.

'I've been chasing this down all day. The good news is there was hardly enough quantity to justify the arrest.' Dust sticking to the sides of the vial is all I remember. Probably just cut.

342

'Will it be on my record, or will it be expunged?'

'That's a conversation I still have to have.'

'Okay, lemme know.'

That afternoon the arrest is expunged, compliments of Norman's oratory skills. He ain't heavy, he's my lawyer.

Okay, so I won't get raped at Sybil Brand, but I know that the real damage has come from Rona. It crosses my mind that Steven, and not a stringer at the station, has passed the information, but I dismiss it. We are far too tight for him to do that to me.

Oh, your third eye is open, the shrink said, but you put blinders on . . .

Jack Spratlin is a middle-echelon Hollywood drug dealer. He services middle-echelon Hollywood types, sells middle-echelon quantities of dope to them, and the drugs he sells are very mid-ech: no smack, no opium, no dilaudid. Of course, if a batch of Percodan or Preludin or Quaaludes comes his way, he turns them over.

Jack Spratlin is an acid casualty. He was meant to be one thing – an upwardly mobile street Jew from New York who came to Hollywood to be an agent and a luminary – but he became another because of drugs.

He apprenticed at William Morris in New York in the mailroom and then as a secretary. He was in the mailroom with guys who all became luminaries: Wally Amos, Jerry Brandt, Jeff Wald, David Geffen, Barry Diller . . .

One day, hanging out with Grady and Grady's wife, he calls, and when I talk to him, I find myself making a sort of a date with him, kind of I'll be in the neighborhood, oh drop by.

'Honey, did you just make a date with the dealer?' Grady needles, a snob, like all those who claw their way up from the lowah clahsses.

'Fuck you, Jack Spratlin is smarter and cooler than most of the people we hang out with,' I shoot back, surprised that I actually am saying what I mean.

'I didn't know you were into S and M,' Grady continues.

'I hang out with you, don't I?'

343

Grady lights a joint and passes it to me, a gesture of friendship. I puff away angrily, not even wanting any. 'So you think he'll show up with good, free coke?' I ask, taunting him with the possibility.

'He wouldn't dare show up without it,' Grady's wife states flatly. She does no drugs, but that's probably because she grew up in California. Her quota for drugs was probably up by the age of seventeen.

'Well, that's something to look forward to . . .' The price of coke is skyrocketing, going ever higher on a weekly basis. Lots of demand, very short supply. No more surfer's. No more Peruvian. Mostly this reconstituted yellow rock. Burns like shit. Add the hit to that and all it does is make you grind your teeth. Not your basic ecstatic experience.

I leave Grady's a bit later, and I drive home very carefully. Every time I pass a corner or a driveway now I reflexively look into my rearview mirror waiting for a flashing blue-and-red light. C'mon out, you dirty coppers, come after me, I dare you. There's not even a roach in this car.

I am doing long hard days, and when Jack Spratlin hasn't arrived by midnight, I take a Valium and go to sleep. I have a violent dream, a face, looming closer, hands on my neck, oh no, not Jeremy, go away go away . . .

'I just got here . . .' It is one o'clock, the burglar alarm is clanging and Jack Spratlin is peering into my face. I jump out of bed and turn off the alarm. I run to the other side of the house to tell Jackie and Kate that everything is okay. Count on Jack Spratlin to arrive with bells on. I am wide awake, my heart pounding with remembered fear and anticipation. Kate and Jackie haven't even stirred. When I get back to my room, Jack is turning on lights, setting down his things.

'I'm sorry I'm so late – things didn't happen on time. They never do when the moon is in void . . .'

'What?' I am smiling. Something about Jack Spratlin makes me smile.

'The void . . . it's an astrological term. Nothing ever comes together, everything's delayed, people misunderstand each other . . . it's a good time to get your hair cut.'

'What a splendid time for our first date . . .' He indulges

344

me with his crazy laugh. He continues to set his belongings down. So many briefcases. He opens one and I see a lot of cash. 'How much is in there?'

''Bout twenty grand . . .' He moves his hand this way and that inside the suitcase and pulls out a Baggie of reconstituted Miami shit. He studies it, thinks about what to do with it. 'You got a sunlamp, by any chance?' Of course I do. It's California in the seventies and we all want to be George Hamilton when we grow up. Jack feels around in his suitcase and comes up with a bottle of some liquid. 'Acetone.' He smiles. 'I'm gonna entertain you with a little coke theater . . .'

We repair to the bathroom. Jack sends me to the kitchen to bring back a Pyrex custard dish. He plugs in the sunlamp, pours product into the custard dish, then some acetone. He sticks it under the sunlamp. 'Wanna help me count my money while we wait for this little reaction?' No, I wanna stay here. And watch . . .

'Okay . . .' We go back into my room and Jack turns the bag of bills onto the bed. For a second it turns me on. I'm torn, then I remember it's my house. 'Let's count the money *after* I see the reaction . . .'

'You must never get too attached,' Jack says solemnly.

'Well, we're just too attached to different things,' I parry, eying him and then his money. He laughs. I go back to the bathroom. The product and the acetone are bubbling gently, a little cocaine stew. Jack comes in. We watch some more. Then he takes the custard dish from under the sunlamp and pours out the yellow goo. Off-white paste remains. He puts it back under the sunlamp.

'Is that for drying purposes?' I ask.

'Yeah . . .' I can see the product hardening slowly into opalescent crystals.

'Lemme try something,' I say and take the custard dish. I set my blowdryer on LOW and hold the dish about a foot away. I turn it on. I check out Jack's expression in the mirror. He hasn't flinched. Cool. The dryer is pretty effective, although one flat plane of coke flies into my left eye. It gets me high immediately. I also see more clearly from it than I have since I was five.

We turn off the sunlamp, scrape the product onto a mirror, and go back to the bedroom. Jack puts a Jackson Browne tape on a ghetto blaster nearby. God forbid I shouldn't have access to immediate sound. As I look around my bedroom I see lots of cigarettes, tissues, and sound-emitting technology.

We count the money: nineteen seven. We put it in neat stacks at the end of the bed. We do some more blow. We throw the money all around the bed and later on we fuck in it. 'Say a prayer for the pretender . . .' Jackson wails and I do in my mind . . .

Jack really courts me, brings me presents, calls a lot of times a day, makes an effort with Kate. He just has this unfortunate occupation. I overrule my business self in favor of my personal self and Jack moves in. Sometimes he deals to people I know in another context from my house. Sometimes he brings new people, whom I don't like, into my house. I stamp my foot and stand up for my rights. The money from *The Sting* and *Taxi Driver* is just pouring in. I insist he retire, but the label 'dealer' sticks. Besides, he keeps his oar in a little, or how would we score wholesale product?

Ariel*, née Amy Schwarzenberg, says, 'April seventh, hunh . . . and Kate's October seventh?'

'Yes . . .'

'That makes you polar opposites. That's a heavy mother-daughter relationship . . .'

Well, shit, I know that. I don't need a fat-assed astrologer/gemologist to tell me that. Ariel is a friend of Jack's. She is a nice Jewish girl from Louisiana who knows quite a bit about antiques. She is married to a guy named Clyde* who cuts hair. They are a quintessential New York couple – he gay, she gay – who are in California by mistake. I am beginning to think everyone in California is here by mistake. Dregs, pushed westward by the tides of change to the Pacific Coast Highway, as Joan Didion once said.

Ariel has arrived with a beautifully colored, highly detailed, precisely defined chart for my horoscope and Kate's. Sometimes Clyde comes, too, and you can have your fortune told and your hair cut at the same time. Something to do when the moon is in void, because Jack is right: nothing else really gets going when the moon is in void. If Clyde doesn't smoke too much pot, he gives an okay haircut, but after all, nothing can compare to Victor.

Ariel, on the other hand, is quite an act, and quite good. She tells the future in my life. She is generally off in time, but she is uncannily accurate. Ariel is my first experience that convinces me that there are those much vaunted, much maligned Forces We Don't Understand at work in the world. She makes two very specific predictions:

First, she tells me that I have rented or bought a place at the beach, and that for unforeseen reasons I will not be able to take occupancy when I expect to. This is true. In a feeble attempt to stay together as one happy family, Nick McLean and I have rented Edie Adams's house on Broad Beach Road. The house is infested by fleas and it takes a month of haggling to establish that she was responsible for defesting the place. By that time, Nick and I have been exterminated, with extreme prejudice, too. But I've signed the lease; and the place is nice enough for weekends, or little expeditions in the middle of the week.

The second prediction she makes with a squoonched-up face, and she seems very perturbed about it. 'I know this will upset you, but I see the price of Columbia Pictures stock plummeting right about the time *Close Encounters* is released . . . does that make any sense?'

'Only if Doug Trumball can't deliver on the effects . . .'

The Dunnes turn out to be the only married couple who stay friends with me after Michael and I split up. Very loyal friends, too. When Erica forgets that the way she knew them was through me and sends an advance copy of *How to Save Your Own Life* to Joan for a quote, Joan gets on her high horse, not easy for a woman who weighs maybe ninety pounds, and reminds Erica through the publisher that I am a good friend of hers, and she wouldn't think of giving the book a quote.

The whole drama of the impending publication of Erica's book comes and goes pretty quickly. But that is because I underestimate its impact. First off, none of my dear, dear friends in publishing ever sneaks me the book. It is Deena Kramer, my assistant from First Artists, who has disappeared back into Brooklyn to become a consultant for a number of soaps, who gives me a copy. Norman and Michael and I read it the same night.

The character who is supposed to be based on me is named Britt Goldstein, and is described as having no talent, no charm, no intelligence, just enormous amounts of chutzpah. At one point, she has me in bed with two Mafia guys and at another she describes my nipples as looking like wrinkled raisins. Hey, maybe I had a chill. Michael calls the next morning, laughing. 'Wrinkled raisins?' he says, and I laugh, too.

Norman gives me the usual lawyer riff about the cure being worse than the disease. But he doesn't need to, because I have decided not to sue. If I do, I'll just bring her more attention. Who needs to make her shitty book a hit? The only other people as greatly maligned as me are Anne Sexton and Henry Miller, not bad company to be in, even if both of them are dead people.

Giler and I bear down hard on getting a *Fear of Flying* rewrite into Columbia before I have to leave for India, and we decide to meet out at the beach house. Giler and I work hard and then head to the Dunnes'. Dinner at the Dunnes', but not a drop to drink. I call ahead of time and say we are on our way.

'You sound a little down,' John says.

'Ah, I read Erica's masterpiece last night . . .'

When Giler and I arrive, John is waiting at the door, drink in hand. 'Be grateful it was Erica,' he says, 'we would've really made you bleed . . .'

'Oh, I feel pretty wounded . . . I think it's the wrinkled raisins that's gotten to me . . .' But the truth is, I think it is a lousy book wrought from bile and I can't imagine it will have any consequence for me. I forget, of course, that everyone even remotely in The Business, most of whom move their lips while reading, will gobble it up and take it as Gospel. One way or another, Erica continues to cause me pain long after I have any hopes of *Fear of Flying* becoming a wonderful, ground-breaking movie.

Giler absconds with one hundred thousand dollars for a rewrite and a polish. At a certain point he comes to me, and tells me in an edgy voice that he's been up for days problem-solving, but it is running long. Long! It is over two hundred pages. In the history of movies, I don't think there has ever been a comedy that stayed funny for two hundred pages. We decide that I will help him cut it out at the offices he shares with Gordon Carroll at Fox. I bring along an eighth. Gordon and Joey Walsh are working in the other office. Every once in awhile, they run in for a little pick-me-up. The energy emanating out of the offices starts to snowball and by three in the morning, Giler and I have cut a good fifty pages out of the script. Still long, but submittable. I want to get it in before I take off for India.

'You know, this last act is not as developed as the other two,' I say. It is little more than a series of montages. But that was the problem with the book. No ending . . .

'I can't do any more,' Giler says crossly, and gets a stern schoolteacher expression on his face. 'And you can't hand it in until I get my check . . .' Look at you, laying down the rules, but I, ever the writer's pal, say:

'Of course I wouldn't do that, but will you see about making this ending a little less montage-y?' At three thirty in the morning this seems like a good deal to both of us.

Giler must stay up because I get an extremely cross call from him of the where's-my-money variety the next day. Either that or lifestyle has caught up with him and he has pressing needs. He wants thirty-five grand or he won't give me the script, not even for retyping. I call David Marks, Columbia's head of business affairs.

'He won't give me the screenplay without his check! What's

holding up this fucking check!?' My concept of relationship/ business dialogue. Marks starts to get legal. I hang up on him. I call the Beges, explain the situation to Connie. I hear her typing, word for word, over the phone. Ten minutes later, Marks calls me back.

'I got you the check,' he says, nervous. Hating me. He should hate Giler, but he hates me. 'What do you want me to do with it?' I'm gonna let that pass.

'Bring it here . . .' I call Giler. 'Bring the script to my office. Now. And David Marks is going to take that long walk across the parking lot to give you your check . . .' Giler laughs mordantly, appreciating the situation. They arrive at the same time. Giler is shaking, Marks is quaking. Giler hands me the script, the longest comedy in the history of movies, and Marks hands him the check. Handshakes. Nobody wants to stay for tea.

'You still owe me polish,' I tell Giler when Marks leaves first. 'And you really should take a shower . . .'

I was not one of my generation to have any spiritual interest in the Near and Far East. I thought of them as homes for the great unwashed, more backward than fundamentalist. I expected to wake up one morning and hear on the news, 'The Third World caught fire today. Africa, where it started, has burned to the ground.' I just assumed that that part of the world was home to people of color living in medieval squalor. Therefore I did not travel to India to find inner knowledge. I went there for blocked rupees.

I haven't hung around Michael and Alan Hirschfield for nothing. Years before *Close Encounters* I read *The Money Game* and figured out a way to string a couple of stories together for the *Ladies' Home Journal* Book Bonus section. I learned a great deal about money men while I was at it – not money, never money, but money men, which is almost the same thing. Especially if all you need is capitalization.

I know what blocked funds are because I often see them referred to on my quarterly statements as money I won't be receiving from *The Sting*. People in the movie business talk about using blocked funds in India constantly. It is a movie-going country, and when Indira Gandhi nationalized the currency in 1969, the majors were caught with a lot of rupees and no way to spend them except in India.

As Lacombe developed from a device (commander of what I referred to as the 'shock shots') to a character, the shots became little scenes, and soon he had his own story, which played contrapuntally with the suburban morass in which Dreyfuss's character, Roy Neary, was engulfed.

It is important to the movie that the two stories interlace, and we want the audience to feel the enormity of coming events, the global – dare I say universal – aspects of Lacombe's search. Here in the desert, there in Morocco, now in India. Anyway, I get kind of preoccupied with the blocked rupees and how I can use them for the Where are the sounds coming from? scene.

The first scene, where the planes from Flight 19 are discovered, and the sequence in India, are items negotiated with a legion of studio executives and Wall Street types throughout the development and principal photography of the picture. It is easier to get the money for the India sequence than the first six minutes – the crucial setup – of the picture. It probably appeals to Herbie Allen's and Alan Hirschfield's Wallstreetness to use funds that would otherwise just sit there without even earning interest.

François refuses to go through the ordeal of getting his shots until he knows that I am getting them. Steven keeps calling him and telling him it is okay, but even though François hates me, and has hated me in public, he knows the dreams aren't reality until I act as if they are. Cholera, typhus, yellow fever – yellow fever I have to go to the board of health downtown, for Christ's sake, no private doctors carry it. I keep thinking, Boy this is some fucking place we're going to. I am also given a production manager, very connected, named Baba Sheek, who has the lowlife air of an Arab white slaver, but does a first-class job organizing the shoot.

We are by now attracting some of the best photographic talents in the business. Everyone shoots something on this picture, even though Vilmos, whom I begged Steven to fire early in the shoot, ultimately receives an Academy Award (for which he thanked Czechoslovakia, by the way. I was so furious that I sent him a telegram the next day from my exile in Hawaii that said, 'You're welcome.'). I do everything in my power to let the world know how he sandbagged us, by the credits.

Separate cards go to Fraker, who shoots the opening sequence and the ET, and Doug Slocombe, who shoots India. Matt Uricich for sixty-five photography. Plus we had a card for Steve Poster, Laszlo Kovacs, and John Alonzo for shooting 'inserts,' which are not your basic 'CU hand coming into frame.' Anyone even remotely in the know has to recognize that many names means something. (Apparently not his peers, because it is the Directors of Photography who nominate him after all.) Sometimes, though, on a bad night, I can still see a scene being shot, with Vilmos walking into it, and telling his crew that we just need 'vun leetle inky-dinky over here.'

We organize our India shoot for February, 1977. We have been shooting the picture, off and on, since May '76. Steven and I and Jim Bloom will go from Los Angeles to New York, lay over in New York. New York to London, where we will pick up our English camera and sound crew. Then London to Bombay, where we hook up with Balaban and Truffaut. Baba Sheek will meet us there, where he will have assembled our India crew and our Indian extras, of which there are to be thousands. Steven and I are permitted to fly Pan Am. Everyone else travels on Air India, compliments of the blocked rupees. I wonder if we'll ever see them again.

When we arrive in New York, I dump Steven at the Sherry Netherland and hightail over to my parents' condo on 64th and First. My mother has developed some undiagnosed symptoms. I don't want to go – it has gotten to the point with us that I never really want to see her – but my father has sounded upset the last couple of times I have spoken to him. When he opens the door I understand why. She had blown up in her midsection; basically she looks like she is about seven months pregnant, a very disturbing look on a sixty-year-old woman.

The rest of her looks drained, as if she were fodder for a vampire. Cancer, I think. My mother has cancer . . .

I know that they are both as worried and scared as I am. We make smalltalk, at first, over dinner. Then i take off, flee with a promise to call from all my ports of call. I cry in big sobs on the short ride back to the hotel. I don't sleep a wink that night, but since I am compounding my congenital insomnia with an ever-increasing daily dose of blow, I have come to view such sleeplessness as my lot. Have fun with it, I think, and instead of sheep count the number of gunshots I can hear coming out of Central Park.

The only benefit of sleepless travel for me is I don't have to be really conscious when I get on the plane. Not for nothing have I been the one to be so attracted to *Fear of Flying*. It is a concept I relate to on a deep emotional level. Sometimes I cope with my fear by stalling and stalling until the last minute to take off for the airport so my anxiety will be concentrated on whether I'll make the flight. If I do, then I am so spent by the time I take my seat that I fall asleep. Others, I go for being in a foggy state, so that it won't really matter to me if the plane crashes and I die. It pretty much depends on which drugs I take before.

Steven insists we resist the urge to sleep. He says it is the only way we will turn around Over There. Since he is far more traveled, having gone around the world with each new opening of *Jaws* the previous summer and fall, I decide to go his way. Besides, he needs a playmate, and that is me. has been for a couple of years now. His wish is pretty much my command. So we dump our bags at the Dorchester and hop back in our car. The driver takes us to Windsor Castle, and then, because it is so cold, to the actual mile-square old city of London.

'They put the heads of their enemies on stakes outside the city as an example,' he says, as we step out of the car near the gate. I stop at a headstone. It says: *Here lies Sir Rupert, most fearfully betrayed and murdered on this spot by his fellows. 1585.* I read it twice. I look at Steven.

'Most fearfully betrayed . . .' I say, and he smiles. The winds are really whipping around us now, so we get back in the car. 'Is it teatime yet?' I ask. I want to taste a scone and rid myself of an embryonic FFA, with its aura of a migraine coming on.

We return to the hotel and order scones and tea and coffee and hot chocolate. Too intimidated by my too-recent bust to carry drugs, I have been deprived of coke for almost two days so I am ravenous. When the food arrives, I scarf it down quickly. Since Steven hasn't seen me eat like this for months, he smiles like a proud Jewish mother. The scones are a disappointment, just undercooked, unhalved English muffins. But the cream is divine. I think about ordering a great deal and taking a bath in it. Close my eyes. Just for a minute. Mommy Mommy . . .

'Don't go to sleep!' Steven yells.

'Maybe just open a window,' I say woozily. I light a cigarette, carry the lighter in my hand, Norman's lighter, the one to light my way to fame, fortune, beautiful lovers . . . India. The windows are stuck. I push. They open suddenly and for one horrible instant, I think I am going out and over and down.

'Look out below,' I scream, and watch my lighter plummet to the street, thinking of Arlene Francis's dumbbells that fell off the terrace of her apartment and through the skull of a passerby. A stockbroker. Fifty-two. Family man. Here today, gone today. I don't think I can face becoming an involuntary murderer. People look up and scatter. Minutes later the doorman comes up and presents me with the lighter. I am so preoccupied with a perusal of his English doorman's drag that I just turn it over and over again in my hand, feeling its friendly weight. He gestures for me to try it. I do, and it lights right away. Dunhill, man. Sometimes you get what you pay for. More precisely, what Norman paid for.

I squint my eyes meaningfully at Steven. 'I think you should let me go to sleep now,' I say. He shakes his head, no. Should, too, should not, should too, should not. In the end, of course, he sleeps like an innocent child, and I, burdened by the karma of previous lives, sleep not at all. *Sir Rupert, most fearfully betrayed, betrayed, betrayed* . . . I collapse on the plane,

354

commencing the natural separation Steven and I are supposed to have for this endeavor.

We arrive in Bombay just before dawn, drive toward the city as the sun is rising. Hordes of malnourished-looking people are sleeping on the street. Official-looking dudes wake them roughly. Once in a while a body doesn't move.

Then there are the half-finished buildings, a feeble attempt at low- and mid-income housing that the government lost its taste for in mid-construction. They are already half-decomposed and nobody has ever set up house in them. People live instead in the shanty towns surrounding the concrete skeletons. The sun shines brightly, but I am depressed already, and we have been in India less than two hours. I have been carrying my mink over my arm, and I am developing a river of sweat underneath it.

Our hotel, the Taj Mahal, looks out over Victoria's Gate, over the harbor. It is an exact replication of the real Taj Mahal, and is actually quite beautiful in the rising sun. The scene outside is not beautiful. Little children in tattered clothes hold out their twisted little arms begging.

'Their parents break their arms and legs, so they will get more money,' Baba Sheek says matter-of-factly, and signals for a bellhop. I check the mink into the hotel safe and feel ten pounds lighter. A necessity against the chill of New York and London, it is a burdensome embarrassment in this hot, *poor* country. I am deposited, with all due dispatch, in the Neptune Suite, a four-room, two-bath affair, which seems sinfully opulent with all its turquoise and purple throw pillows and delicately striped silk covers. I look out over the harbor. Really quite beautiful. I unpack my summer things because it is hot, and go to Steven's suite, kitty-corner from mine, to harass him into getting on the road.

We are going to check out our location, a village about thirty-five miles outside of Bombay. We collect our crew, Dougie Slocum and his guys, John Mitchell, the sound man, Jimmy Bloom, and get in two cars. The drive is like Mr. Toad's Wild Ride at Disneyland. Driving in Third World countries seems conceptually linked more to the honking of the horn than brakes, accelerator, or steering. We pass a few terrible-looking accidents, including an overturned bus, with several pairs of skinny limp legs sticking out from underneath the still-smoking metal. There are also sacred cows and oxen on the road, but not one of them is honked or hit. It takes at least two hours to get to the village.

By then it is past noon and boiling hot. Tropical hot. The village is very poor. Lots of scraggly children with torn bright clothing and perfect white smiles. We walk up the incline to look out over a basin in which our extras will be positioned.

I start to suss out the physical aspects of the village. I have learned, from so much outdoor shooting, that the first thing one needs to find is a private place for bathroom requirements. Down a dip and up another rise, away from the village, is a small, enclosed structure. I do not find out until I have peed there twice that it is a temple. I comfort myself with the thought that this is probably where many of the locals relieve themselves, too. It is not as if we will have a legion of honeywagons here.

Groups of little children follow me everywhere. They are pretty and shy. Everything I do is a scream to them. I want to make friends, so I go back to our car and get out a bag of crackers. The children gather round, and I start to hand them out. Suddenly they are all over me, a swarm of insect-children. They are pulling and tearing at me to get at the crackers, which are turning to dust in my hands. A couple of the men from the village pull them off me. Very *Suddenly Last Summer*. I feel greatly chastened.

We hang around the village and set up as much as we can, and then, by silent agreement, as in, none of us can stand to be here anymore, we leave. Baba Sheek has arranged for some interviews back at the hotel. He has me figured pretty well. 'Don't say anything controversial,' he has cautioned me, not Steven or Balaban or Truffaut. I smile back and say that I have been practicing for a week what I will say if I am asked about Indira Gandhi.

'What will you say?'

'I will say . . . Indira Gandhi . . . wonderful woman . . .'

Outside the hotel, our car knifes through crippled children offering cocaine and hash. Jimmy Bloom, whom we all call J.B., and I look at each other meaningfully. I wouldn't want to take a chance on what an Indian child might sell as coke, but the hash part sounds tempting. We are, after all, in the middle of hash territory. We are dropped at the front door and J.B. and I have a little confab. I think it's time for Baba to cop some hash for me. He thinks I should put up the cash and he should make the request. I give him a fifty and tell him to do his thing.

I have noticed that there are quite a few interesting shops in the lobby of the hotel, and as there is plenty of time until the press arrives, I feel I should take one little pass through the only place I will have a chance to spend money while I'm in this funky town. I ask Steven if he wants to join me, although I am pretty sure he is going to want to relate to his actors and crew; he surprises me by saying yes.

There are jewelry and silk shops, usually my kinds of places, but I am most drawn to the Indian rug stores, of which there are three. I must look like a live one, because the proprietors almost take me by the arm to lead me into their stores. For the next forty-five minutes, I ooh and aah and get a basic education in rugs. They are woven on a forty-five-degree angle, which means that there is what is called a dark side and a light side. They are fifty percent wool and fifty percent silk. The silk gives off a sheen, particularly from the light side. All the rugs are copies of famous patterns. They are thousands of dollars, but they are also negotiable. Steven thinks I should bring Baba Sheek to negotiate for me, and I give him a cold gray stare, as in, I got us this far, surely I can handle a few fucking rugs. He has other things on his mind and looks away.

Nobody from the press asks us at all about their leaders. They really want to know about Robert Redford and Jane Fonda, and how Steven got the girl in the beginning of *Jaws* to go this way and that so violently in the water. (Fearless stuntwoman, ten men, ten harnesses, pushpullpushpull, lacerations and bruises for years to come, don't ask.) François and I touch eyes only once and he looks away first. Steven has dinner with the actors and I take the rest of the guys to a

357

restaurant downstairs. We have preagreed that I am going to stay as far from François as possible, which is easy, because this happens to be a very capacious venue.

J.B. comes to pick me up in my suite. He has a shit-eating grin on his face. He produces forty dollars and a round ball that is the color and consistency of baby doody. It is an ounce of hash at white people's prices. He did it himself. I pull out my Swiss Army knife and scrape off a nice chunk. It is so soft that it is hard to keep it on the end of the knife. I mold it like clay around the knife point. We light it, take a couple of hits each, giggle, and scamper down the stairs to join the English, but not before I stash what is left among my winter clothes in a bag, which I lock after me.

Robin Vidgin, the focus-puller, is complaining about Customs. Customs? Trouble? I get straight real fast. There goes my lovely hash high. He answers my unasked question: 'We're having trouble getting the film and the camera equipment out of Customs . . .'

'Is Baba Sheek gonna have to pay someone off?' The English smile at my ability to get to the bottom line so quickly. I can see them thinking: Oh, you American girls!

'Not yet. I'm determined to try the red-tape method . . .' I remind him that we need film and cameras day after tomorrow. He shoots me a look: you don't need to remind me . . .

'But red tape can take days, weeks . . .'

'Oh, believe me, if it doesn't work right away, we'll go for greased palms. Let me cope . . .' I love these English. They adore the adventure, the distance from Western civilization. They have all been in tropical locations, they have all contracted malaria, been bitten by large poisonous insects and snakes. They are undaunted, which gives me some odd confidence that they will come through. I understand why they were the ones to expand their empire. Isn't there a Victoria Something in every one of these countries? After dinner, we walk off the meal around the street of shops in the lobby and I show them the rugs.

'Maybe you should have Baba Sheek negotiate for you,' Dougie Slocum says. I'm beginning to think these guys think

I'm here for decorative purposes. I frown and vow no way Baba negotiates this for me. Maybe just a little conversation with him ahead of time about the general parameters of Indian haggling.

The next day we go on a tour of the city, which reveals even more to be depressed about than dead bodies being swept off the streets at sunrise and little children's arms and legs being broken at birth so that they can fetch more money begging. We are driven deep into the bazaar, where there are women in cages. For sale. The air conditioning in the car isn't very strong so I open the window. My arm is resting on the side of the car, and when our driver slows down for impassable street traffic, an Indian man slaps it. Hard. I am outraged. Baba suggests I roll the window up again. Which is okay by me, because I am not turned on by the slaps of strangers. I keep checking my arm for bugs.

We have a six-thirty call the following morning, and Steven tells the whole crew there is not a chance I will make it. Baba says he will leave a car for me, but I am afraid of this place, and I have no desire to make the trip to the village alone. In a car with a Third World driver. I, who love to come and go as I please, make a determination that I will make this call. When I arrive in the coffee shop at 6:29, I get a standing ovation. Even François smiles.

When we arrive at our village, the scene is very different from two days ago. The villagers are completely out of sight. Where the basin was once empty it is now filled with a sea of Indian men in saffron robes. There is a natives-are-getting-restless tension in the air. The extras chatter quietly with each other, but there are twenty-five hundred of them, so they sound like the waves of a small ocean. Steven sniffs the air apprehensively; there is a flicker of revulsion around his mouth.

'How long have these guys been here?' I ask Baba Sheek.

'Since last night . . .'

'They seem kind of restless . . .' We follow Steven, who is discussing his first shot with Chick Waterston, Slocum's camera operator. Steven has explained to me before that this is why English cameramen are called lighting cameramen. The big guy does the lighting. The operator works out the moves of the shot with the director. In America the cameraman does both, although, I bet Nick McLean, Vilmos's operator, would have a thing or two to say about that.

'Of course they are restless. They have been sitting here since last night . . .' Baba Sheek repeats. I get the feeling this is how he deals with White Westerners. The way we do with people of color. Like they are stupid children who need every piece of information repeated. The thought makes me smile. The quiet yammering of the extras is beginning to be a roar. Steven looks anxiously over at me and Baba Sheek. I wave his concern away in a gesture with my hand, as in, let me deal with the slave trader; you work out the shot.

The camera truck is nowhere in sight. It will be difficult to get this shot without our equipment. It has taken Robin the better part of three days to extricate the equipment and film from customs; it would be a shame for all that effort to be vitiated in a single Third World collision on the road. Ever since Jeremy beat the shit out of his face on the steering wheel of my Mazda, I worry that people who don't show up have been in an accident. In this case, based on my previous travels, it seems like a good bet, not at all a remote possibility.

Steven and Chick hold their hands up making little squares, moving, traveling, trucking and tracking their shots. Steven has a marvelous ability to stay unaware, unaffected, by everything around him. Everybody thinks this is because of his powers of concentration; I think it is because he doesn't care about anything but the movie he is working on. Even I take time off for Kate and family problems.

It has been hard to maintain contact with my father; it is a miracle that I can hear anything he tells me anyway, given the scars on his vocal cords and the nature of the phone system in both India and New York, but the gist is: many tests, no diagnosis. My mother will be under the knife within a day or two of my reentry to New York. Something to look forward to.

I stand on the bluff and look over the extras. I squint, as if the effort will bring my camera truck to me. Steven comes over to my vantage point on the bluff.

'You're going to have to call John Veitch and get us more rupees,' he says out of the corner of his mouth, looking fretful. 'Even if the camera truck gets here now, we're going to need more time.'

'Let's take one thing at a time,' I say calmly, but fear pierces my heart and I am subsumed with nausea. More rupees? Is he fucking kidding? Sometimes I think he doesn't understand how hard it's been to oblige his endless requests. I have made it seem too effortless and fun. Not to mention, I have had to hang out with any number of boring lechers. The longer the picture goes on, the more lechers I have accumulated. Standing on this precipice, I wonder if New York magazine would be interested in a think piece called 'Men Who Stuck Their Tongues in My Mouth When All I Wanted Was a Deal.' I give myself a little chuckle and Steven thinks I am laughing at our situation. First he is angry and then he laughs, too. There is a roar from the crowd.

'What're they so upset about?' Steven asks Baba. 'All they're doing is sitting there . . .'

'They are sitting in their own shit!' Baba explodes.

'This whole country is sitting in its shit,' I tell Baba, and he permits himself a reluctant smile.

As if on cue, the camera truck arrives. The equipment is unloaded and set up. We are able to use European equipment instead of American and I am amazed to watch the guys set up steelpole dolly tracks in forty-five minutes with a little spider crab for the camera. This is some big difference from the usual American wooden track with its wooden wedges and the five guys needed to set it up and straighten it out after each shot. And still the camera jiggles. Not here, in this godforsaken town in India.

One of the extras right in the front row has glasses on. They seem incongruous to me and I say something to Steven, who gets huffy and says he likes them. Every time I see the shot later on, I disagree in my mind, but just now I am exhausted. I sit under a tree and think about the meaning of life. Life is shit. And I'm the fly. Helllpmee, Helllpmeeee. And still I try. Why? Well, because.

I look around. François looks a little green at the gills. Wait a second: I think, therefore –

François passes out. We have him carried to a tent. Steven doesn't want me near him, but on the other hand, nobody else wants to deal with the ashen Frenchman either. I get some bottled water and salt and go to his side. He flutters his eyes at me.

'I em zo zorry . . .' he whispers, meaning all of it, the quote, the bad blood, the time he was costing us . . . I choose to take him literally.

'François, I am going to give you some salt, and some bottled water. It is going to taste terrible, but it will make you better immediately.' I prop him up and he opens his mouth like a child. I toss the salt in and hand him the bottle. He takes a swig, and within ten minutes he has his color back. A half hour later, he is back on the set. We never exchange another word.

The day goes well, with the exception of François's heat prostration.

At the end of the day, Chick Waterston, the camera operator, hits his head on a truck and blood gushes forth. He pours expensive Scotch whiskey on it and it stops. Useful first aid, compliments of the English. I give Slocum a ride back to the hotel and ask him a lot of questions about all the pushing and flashing Vilmos likes to do to the film. He says he never does any of that, just lights the shots right and makes sure he's shooting on top-quality film.

'If you have excellent steak, why screw it up with sauce?' he says. This makes me hate Vilmos more.

That night, after my shower, I look carefully in the mirror, squinting this way and that to see if I'm still there. Even with my hair wet I can see that my bangs are going white. I have not smoked any of the J.B. hash, so this is not a drug-induced psychedelic episode. I've already had that today: We're gonna need more blocked rupees; and then, François, frog prick extraordinaire – fainting, and nobody but me to deal with it . . . the phone rings and it's my father's dim voice reporting again that there's no change in Mommy's condition . . .

I find my stash and a knife to cut the fruit the hotel sends up every day. In my dreams I partake of the fruit, in real life I smoke the hash. I put on some light clothing and mascara and a smile, grab my American Express card, and wander down to my rugs . . . no Baba, no J.B., no Steven. Just me and the rug man working out a deal. He has informed me that you can put half the amount on American Express, make the other half COD on American Express, thus circumventing Customs.

'The rugs will be delivered right to your door,' he says jubilantly and eyes me expectantly, as in, do I have any contraband I'd like to include in this little package to myself? I think about the babydoody hash for a moment then shake my head no. We go around and around on price and finally agree on thirty-five hundred for three rugs. One is about ten by twelve, a knockoff of a pattern Queen Victoria favored, which incorporates the top thirty-nine colors and gradations of colors rugs can have. Then two smaller ones about four by six that match. All the rugs have strong colors blended with pastels. The yin and the yang of it all. For my floors. He takes the imprint of my card and we shake on the deal.

As I leave his shop, I look in a mirror. Now that my hair is dry it is even whiter. I look like my mother. But thin. I wanna go home I wanna go home . . . Then I wonder just exactly where that is: with Kate in L.A., with Mom in N.Y., with this movie? In India? I decide whither my rugs goest, I follow . . .

The next day I go to the set again, and J.B. gets assaulted by a Third World insect that provokes a major allergic reaction. When his eyes start rolling up into his head and he is shaking from chills in the fetid hundred-degree air, I decide I'd better get him back to Bombay, to the hotel, to a doctor. The picture is rolling along now; Steven, Baba, and Dougie have it well under control . . . It takes forever to get back to the hotel and J.B.'s reaction has almost passed, but the hotel orders up a doctor who administers the usual, Benadryl and cortisone.

We leave India in the middle of the night. We try to give our Indian crew the ends of our film rolls, but the government makes us take everything out that we brought in. Exactly.

Earlier that evening, Steven has stood over me and made me flush my hash down the toilet. He says there is a master list of people who have been busted in the last six months at every port of entry in the U.S. What if there was a fuckup and I was never really expunged? He has a point, but I weep over the flush. I almost forget to take my mink out of the safe. J.B. reminds me, and at the airport we are all so hot to get the fuck out of town that I leave it on the counter and the focus puller, Robin Vidgin, rescues it for me.

'Boy,' Steven laughs, 'you really want to get out of here . . .'

'No, you do, and you're going so fast I'm afraid you'll leave without me . . .' It's true. Everywhere we go, he moves so fast and so pointedly. Never as fast as when he's walking off a set and he doesn't want to talk, but still, we're talking Bombay, India, here. He smiles and slows down.

'What have you done to your hair?' he says, and actually takes my coat and throws it over his arm. Steven Nice.

'I've gone white overnight . . . I'm going to end up looking just like my mother . . .'

'Never,' he says – Steven Encouraging – and we step off the bus with our boarding passes and climb up the steps to Pan Am First Class Out of Here. Back to England, the Dorchester, back to New York. We arrive at six in the morning and Customs just waves us through. I give Steven major shit about my hash all the way into the city. Into the Sherry. Into my bed . . .

I have lunch with Brian De Palma, and then Alan Hirschfield comes over to visit. It is about three in the afternoon, but I stopped knowing what time or place it was days ago. The phone rings and I pick it up in my bedroom. It is the call I've been waiting for. It is my father. From the hospital.

'Well?' I ask/say.

'The news couldn't be worse. Mommy has cancer, cancer everywhere – her lungs, her spleen . . . they don't even know the origin, but they suspect gynecological . . .' He is talking in his scientist voice, telling me what I knew weeks ago, when I first saw her distended belly . . .

'Is that what she blew up from?' an aimless, stupid question. I am stalling for time. Time for what? I don't know . . .

'It's a fluid given off by the cancer cells, something called escides . . .'

'Do you want me to stay?' I ask in a voice heavy with say no . . .

'What're you gonna do here . . .'

'Nothing. I should go home, see Kate, get this picture in order, then come back . . .' I still have to get more money for Doug Trumball; then there is the small matter of the opening of the picture – the Gift in the Desert – 'I'm gonna go home . . .' Well, at least I know where that is now. L.A., where Kate and the movie are. Two out of three wins. 'I'll call from there tomorrow . . .'

Alan and Brian have been chatting in the other room. I lay my news on them. They both look at their shoes and say they're sorry. They can't wait to get out of there, but feel obliged to hang around. I feel numb. I call Kendall. She says she's sorry. I tell her to let everyone know, because I want to deal out what I can and then get back on a plane and come east. Like hell I do . . .

Brian and Alan leave, cold men together, and I burst into tears. I am very frustrated with my mother for dying too soon. I throw cold water on my face, cold coke up my nose, and puff on a hot cigarette. Steven knocks at the door. Brian has told him. He gives me a hug. I break it quickly. I don't want sympathy. The car is downstairs, he'll understand if I don't want to go back. I tell him I've been packed for hours, and I leave New York, leave my father, leave the cancer. I don't forget my mink . . .

Jon Peters is on the plane going back. He is shooting *The Eyes of Laura Mars* with Faye Dunaway in New York. He looks like I feel. Spent.

'I don't know what kind of life she leads, but it takes hours to light her eyes so you don't see the baggage underneath,' he says, depressed.

*

Hanging out with Melnick, the third head of production during the making of the film, I tell him the François story.

'I would've held the salt back,' he smiles, 'until he guaranteed a public retraction.' Kidding on the square. Yeah, that's the difference between you and me, I think, feeling superior. The point is, he wouldn't have dared to say any of those things about you. The point is, if he had, he would've retracted, because somewhere you would have some damaging tape on him. The point is, life is not fair.

Oh, your third eye is open, the shrink would say, but you put blinders on. Yeah, so I can run faster, like a racehorse.

'It was way past the point where it mattered anymore,' I say.

My reentry into L.A. is a pressure cooker. I immediately start a campaign on two fronts: 1) secure a million more from Columbia for Doug Trumball's spec f/x; and 2) convince them we are still in need of an opening for the picture. We've designed a sequence involving the discovery of the missing planes from Flight 19 – a famous Bermuda Triangle occurrence. Who knows how much that'll cost?

I am thrilled to have this overdrive activity. I don't have to think about my mother's cancer. I do a twenty-page memo on my feet that explains everything to everybody; I actually address it to: ALL SHIPS AT SEA. My middle-aged, straight secretary starts to run out of steam midway through my dictation, so Kendall gives her some blow. We finish in record time. Starved for activity, she proceeds to rearrange all the files, as well. She keeps saying, 'I don't feel anything different. I don't feel different at all,' while looking for other chores. Kendall and I crack up with our hands over our mouths, so she won't hear.

Begelman calls to congratulate me on the memo, a first, and informs me that the parent company is sending Joe Fischer, its treasurer, out for a meaningful discussion. It is decided that he and I will run in front, and we'll bring in Steven and Doug at the end for substantiation. Doug and Steven are reluctant; they are looking at some tests. I say fine, breeze in for coffee, full of excitement about the tests, and then explain or even better, agree with what I have already explained.

I do two things in preparation for this big lunch, to which I wear a black Brioni pantsuit with a white chiffon tuxedo shirt unbuttoned to my waist and a matching white chiffon scarf doubled around my throat so it just gives glimpses of tan in March; I watch *The Wild Bunch* the night before, because it always fires me up; and I let Jack Spratlin fuck me from behind in the closet in front of the mirror just before I leave for the meeting. An impulsive thing, standing in my closet naked waiting for the right outfit to say yes.

Talk about fired up! Fischer is smart. The memo has prepared him. Plus, I do not lie. I have only lied twice during the whole picture. Once about Trumball's budget, and once about being on the Neary set when Steven shot mashed potatoes for four hours. I was running around with Grady Rabinowitz. I actually cop to the latter while charming Joe Fischer at lunch. Every time I shift I feel mung in my pants and it inspires me. I've got Joe Fischer agreeing to everything by the time the boys – flushed with success and rushing – arrive.

Doug seems mainly determined to not be impugned as a bad guy, so he harps on my encouraging him to lie about his original budget. Doug, man, water under the bridge. This is not that kind of meeting.

'You lied about his original budget?' David sounds alarmed. This, from the Great Prevaricator. From the very beginning, Steven has fretted about David Begelman being a 'pathological liar . . .'

'Of course I lied. How could we know? We were shooting in the dark, pissing in the wind . . .' swinging gently in the breeze . . . 'Uncharted territory . . . you would've canceled it. Aren't you glad you didn't cancel it?' They still have nothing to go on, really, but what we tell them. Oh, we've cut together a product reel, over Steven's strenuous objections (he actually made me drive to the editing room in the Marina and instruct Mike Kahn to cut in six preagreed wedges in preagreed places, while he stood there silent and brooding, the integrity-filled artist overcome by the drive of the businessman. Unfair, unfair, I told him in my mind, but didn't say).

They've seen that. And nothing else but my girlish enthusiasm. Pretty soon, I keep telling Steven, we are going to have to show somebody something. Either for the effects, or the opening sequence.

Doug is getting ready to throw Joe Fischer figures. He is also putting a piece of paper in everybody's hand, a memo to his files. Beware the fat. Man. Redford said. 'Okay,' I throw up my hands. 'I did it! I made him shave six hundred thousand dollars. But that was when it was at a million and a half. Now, it's going to be three . . . four if Doug makes any more mistakes . . .' Take that, you fat fuck!

Everybody gets very quiet. Joe Fischer clears his throat. Tentative. 'What about this opening sequence?' he says.

'The Gift in the Desert? Who knows until we start scouting locations?'

'Are you prepared to do that right away?' Sure, why not? I'll tell my mother to put her cancer on hold . . .

'Yes,' Steven pipes up, 'we could do that right away . . .'

'. . . because I'd really like to have the total figure together before I ask them to commit any more money . . .'

'That won't work, Joe,' I say, and everybody looks at me as if I'm Linda Blair in *The Exorcist*.

'Why not?'

'Because we need the revised effects budget approved now, or we don't have a picture, period. I personally feel the same way about the opening, but I can understand your wanting to wait on that . . .' Gimme the money for the effects now, you bald-headed twerp!

Steven and I go to the Golden Globes together. We sit at a table with Marty and Julia and Liza and Jack Haley. Liza is wearing emerald earrings so replete with stones they are making her earlobes a new shape. She seems extremely depressed. Marty is standing at the opposite side of the table with another bearded guy who is staring and staring at me. Do I know you?

Marty makes a big show of tittering behind the hand over his mouth. I lean over to Steven, who is staring at Sophia

Loren, sitting at the next table. When she entered, just awhile ago, I thought, She is the most beautiful woman in this room, on earth, but as she gets closer, I can see a line across her forehead where her wig is not set right.

'Steven, who's the guy with Marty . . . do I know him?' Steven looks, and he laughs in my face.

'It's Francis!' he says. I look again. Francis is a lot thinner. The Philippines will do that to you.

'Francis, you've lost a whole person!' I get up to kiss him hello, but find, after a warm salutation, there isn't really much else to talk about. I'm sorry I got up. I go back to my seat. Liza looks so sad . . .

'Wanna go to the bathroom?' I ask meaningfully, and she bolts out of the chair. The ceremonies are going to start any time, lights are dimming, but she and I hit the ladies'. It is empty. We pass a gram bottle back and forth under the stall, then stand in front of the mirror and fuck with our hair. Checking out ourselves and each other. We have nothing in common. Well, movies. We have movies in common. Which covers a lot of territory. Like heart disease. And this little gram bottle, which we pass back and forth one more time, out in the open, because nobody else is here. Then we head back to the table. Steven gives me a disapproving look, then turns his attention to the ceremonies. I turn around to watch and find myself face to face with the back of Sophia Loren's head, or more precisely, her wig. I'm buzzed, so I start to fixate on it. I can feel myself dividing the strands of hair, moving through them, me on a *Fantastic Voyage* . . .

Taxi Driver has been nominated in several categories, in both the Golden Globes and the Academy Awards, which is a few weeks after the Golden Globes. Of all awards, the Golden Globes is the most fraudulent. Please. The Hollywood foreign press corps, nominators and voters, are maybe seventy-five to a hundred people. But it is good to show up for these pretentious gatherings. Besides, Jodie Foster wins . . .

Steven escorts me to the Academy Awards. We sit right in the front row. When Warren presents the Best Picture award, he winks at us. The next day, hustling Amy, he tells her that Steven and I looked cozy together. Uh-oh. More trouble. But it's good to show up for these dos. Besides, Jodie Foster wins . . .

'I hate music,' Irving Azoff says and clutches his Samoyed to his tiny chest. Irving has arrived early for a meeting it has taken us weeks to arrange. He comes in through the back door of my bedroom sporting Jesus sandals, little white boxer shorts, and a matching white Samoyed resting across his crook'd arms. The dog and Irving are about the same size, so with the backlighting they look like an icon for a man-and-dog kind of Christianity. Maybe just a plus sign.

'You don't hate music.' I smile. 'You hate the music business . . .' Me, projecting again. Doesn't everyone think like me? They don't.

'No, no, I l-o-o-o-ve the business,' Irving says offhandedly and smiles sweetly. He rocks back and forth in my wicker chair, his feet barely grazing the floor. The dog rests benignly on his lap. I wonder if it is sedated. People are regularly dosing their pets with Quaaludes to keep them from barking. I don't like to ply my pets with drugs, the result of a relationship I'd enjoyed with a cat at the beach who was crazed from being fed too much acid by an actress whose name was as wacko as her pet-rearing skills.

It is hard not to notice that Irving is short. He has a casually friendly manner, but you can't be that short and not be mad about it all the time. Little Irving is a dangerous and powerful man, and he is just starting. I met with him at Ma Maison for lunch about a month before about a deal in search of a story concept I had for *The Third Man Through the Door*. The deal part involved his clients, the Eagles. The story would be provided by me and Grady.

'So,' Irving smiles charmingly, 'you think they're the Beatles?' I'm determined to be charming back. I smile a broad smile and try to keep from bouncing my foot under the table.

'They're the Beagles . . .' Nobody's the Beatles. Not even the Beatles anymore. Everything that rises must break up . . .

I do my develop-movie-develop-music riff on him. He looks confused. I'm afraid he doesn't like it. I open my mouth to start again. He holds up his hand.

'I don't have the vaguest idea what you have in mind, but you seem like a crazy creative person. Let me put this together . . .'

Like everyone else who thought they were young, decadent, and rich in the seventies, I love the Eagles. I especially love *Hotel California*. There is a song called 'Life in the Fast Lane' that I think of as the short version of one aspect of *TMTTD*, which has grown in scope since John Dunne gave me the first forty pages of *Vegas*. Couple of years have gone by, and I want the movie to be right on time. The longer we stay in development the bigger it gets, the more stories there are. It is getting to be a very complicated movie, and it will benefit greatly from a unifying soundtrack.

I am looking at the credits on the back of the album jacket while I am chatting with Steven one day. We are in postproduction on *Close Encounters* and people are starting to figure out that it might really be something. Steven has insisted on total secrecy from the start: closed set, closed dailies, locked doors whenever possible. We are still cloaked in secrecy, but it is hard to have that many people in your employ trying to do that many things that have never been done before without being visible.

Plus, he and I have made it a point to show up for certain things: David Begelman's wedding to Gladyce, held at Ray Stark's pad, out on the lawn among the Moore sculptures; the Oscars, the Golden Globes, etc., not to mention our posts at Ma Maison, La Scala, and the Imperial Gardens. You run into pretty much everybody in town that way.

The problem with showing up at these events with Steven is Amy. She didn't like us going to the Oscars and the Golden Globes together on all those *Taxi Driver* nominations. I would've been happy to take someone else, but Steven and I are tight as can be, and it makes good business sense to show up together. I had made the mistake of bringing Jack to Dan

Melnick's coming-out party. It isn't smart to appear in public with him, even if people are already gossiping about the fact that I am living with a dealer. Hey, cut out the middleman . . .

When Dick Sylbert expressed a desire to meet Steven, I arranged a dinner as a foursome. Maybe Amy wouldn't get pissed off that way, I figured. We dine at Dominick's and I'm the last one there. Steven's mouth twitches with annoyance. At some point the guys get it on, and Amy and I repair to the bathroom. I pee; she fucks with her hair. She pees; I fuck with my hair. Wash hands. Good little girls. Share a secret – well, maybe two. Bad little girls. And I think, Well, now we share secrets, we're pals. Fat chance. Every time Amy is afraid she's losing Steven, she opts for a tearful confession. Bad enough to blow your cover, bitch, tacky to blow mine . . . I think she's retaliating for the Oscars and the Golden Globes.

Steven starts to complain about her . . . he's nervous that he's let her move into the house, the house I told him to buy . . .

'Maybe you should talk to her, Ju-lee-a,' he stutters. Steven stutters a lot. He also repeats whatever you just said to him back to you. It reminds me of my father, when he had his clinical depression. In the beginning of our mission to make *Close Encounters*, these personality traits seemed endearing, now they bore me. And I know he is at the end of his rope on my drugs and lateness. Still we're tight enough for him to imply that it would be a nice producerial gesture on my part to move her out of his house. I laugh in his face. In your earhole, man.

'Are you suggesting . . .' He interrupts me with laughter. Best defense with me.

'Forget it . . .'

I have been tuning out on the conversation and just for a nanosecond, my eye, which has been traveling across the publishing company credits on the back of the album, sees an interesting phrase in a tiny parenthesis. *Copyright in dispute*, it says.

'Steven, can I call you back?'

'What. Something wrong?' People ask these questions since the Jeremy Incident.

'No, I just remembered I gotta take care of something, I'll call you right back.' Go make Amy come, go – whatever. Resolve your differences. Me, I've gotta call my lawyer.

I dial Norman at home. He answers the phone with his mouth full.

'Sorry to interrupt you at dinnertime,' I say insincerely, 'but I just noticed something very interesting on this album by the Eagles . . .'

'What's that?' Norman is unperturbed. He is production counsel on *Close Encounters*, for a measly fifteen-thousand-dollar fee. Considering the amount of shit he has to do . . . sometimes actually, I think of Norman as my coproducer, not Michael, who has spent a good part of the last year traveling to Third World countries in search of his soul. If you really had one, you wouldn't have to look so hard. You would have one right here in L.A. Not easy, but possible.

'There's a line with all the publishing credits, and then in parentheses it says, "Copyright in dispute." Does that mean that Warners and the Eagles are fighting over the publishing?'

'Yes, and they can't resolve it. Why would they release it . . .'

'Because the Eagles are getting so fucking hot nobody wants to blow the money . . . does that make any sense?'

'You coulda been a lawyer . . .'

'. . . a contender . . . Chawlie . . .'

'Soooo . . . what's the point?' Norman starts munching again, just in case I've forgotten that I've interrupted his dinner.

'Well, the point is . . . I've always wanted to do a movie where the music was integral to the movie . . . you know, incorporate the musical talent with the writing talent at the very beginning, and *TMTTD* is about a lot of the stuff these guys are writing about, and I think it would be interesting, since Warner Bros. is financing the development of *TMTTD* to see if these guys are interested in going into partnership on *TMTTD* and settling their lawsuit . . .' Norman stops munching.

'That's a brilliant idea!'

'The true marriage of art and commerce, right?'

So Norman found Irving, and Irving and I found each other, and I laid this idea of developing a movie to music. Music to a movie. I let Frank Wells know about it, too.

'A truly brilliant solution . . .' he said after I did my riff.

Irving, of course, doesn't want to talk as much about the settlement of the suit as about the music movie, and he doesn't want to talk about that too much either without his clients around.

So now it is Don Henley and Glen Frey, from the Eagles, Grady, me, and Irving and his dog. Jack hovers in and out of the background. Jack, in fact, makes the most important contribution to the meeting. The ounce of blow, only moderately stepped on. Everyone but Irving partakes throughout.

I do my riff. Grady is funny. Don Henley seems bright and responsive. I get kind of hung up on his ears, though, which stick out. A recalcitrant Glen Frey does a lot of blow and seems angry about it. I don't know how to tell Irving, but I don't think they're the Beatles. No star power. They seem sparked by the idea, but by then everyone except Irving is pretty lit from the blow. They agree to think about it.

I report to Norman and Frank, then slip back to Columbia. I have a meeting with John Veitch about dubbing. Dubbing time, actually.

He is armed with his lieutenant of postproduction, Tom McCarthy. An ambush. It has reached the point where even friends, and John Veitch is certainly a friend, are adversaries. Funny how that happens when a lot of money is on the table and the stakes are getting higher all the time.

They take the tack that I don't know how easy dubbing requirements are. Not when you're trying to boldly go where no one else has, I counter. Pleasantries are brushed aside quickly and we start to holler. I am wearing a tight choker and as I yell louder I cut off circulation; I almost knock myself off yelling at them.

'This woman will do anything to get her way,' I hear McCarthy aside to Veitch as I am coming to . . .

*

'I love these shots . . . what's wrong with these shots . . .' I hear the aggressive speediness in my voice and want to keep it down, because this ampiness has prompted him to dub me the Madwoman of Beverly Hills, but Steven is frustrating me. Why have I gone to all this trouble to get immigration papers for Carlos Rimbaldi and quite a few of his minions to construct this wondrous toy? This creation that can do eighteen or so things with just one side of its face? This . . . ET? We called the extraterrestrials ETs. We acronym everything. I still think of *Close Encounters* as CE3K, which I had printed in inch-high white letters on black, for the crew T-shirts. Very tasty.

ET, or Puck, as we call him, has been here for quite some time. Carlos Rimbaldi has done one of the most complicated tasks for the picture and he is the only guy who has delivered on time and on budget. Puck sits on a stage waiting for key crew to be available and I can't convince either David Begelman or Dan Melnick to go over and take a look.

By now there is no way the picture ain't going to twenty mil, and neither one of them has the time to check out one of the nine million things in the movie that make or break us? Finally I embarrass Melnick into going over and checking out what Rimbaldi can make Puck do. He says that it is more expressive than ninety percent of the women he's dated. I say ninety-five. And then I worry that maybe the model isn't quite real enough.

I have gotten Steven a great deal of money to shoot the ET. Columbia, and all the bankers and the Herbie Allens, and Alan Hirschfields and Joe Fischers and David Begelmans, etc., have gone down the whole road with us. Not always happily, sometimes reluctantly, but they have stuck with us. And they haven't seen dick. And they aren't going to for quite some time, because we need the extraterrestrial to find focus for the 'experience,' as Verna Fields once dubbed it. For the last twenty, maybe even thirty, minutes of the movie.

Every time I walk on the set, Michael is working one of the controls for the ET. He is desperately searching for a role to play on the picture, now that he's back from his soulsearch and has an inkling of what *Close Encounters* is. I think he looks ridiculous and I am unbeatable. I am wrong.

At the end of two weeks, I have to force Steven to wrap the ET, or we'll never get the amount of time he wants on the dubbing stage. We have a fight instead of a party. Clark Paylow calls me later to tell me that he and Michael have told Steven he can keep shooting and Steven has said, 'Julia says I can't shoot anymore. Without Julia there would be no *Close Encounters* . . .' I guess Clark is telling me this story to make me feel better. I am at the point where nothing makes me feel better.

Michael and I have gone to a screening and gotten into a fight before the film starts to roll. As the lights go down he says, under his breath so Mike Kahn won't hear, 'I hate you.' Tears shoot out of my eyes and I split. I go into a three-sixty spin at the corner of Schuyler and scare myself half to death. Steven calls, enraged, about my leaving the screening and I tell him the story. They run the picture for me the next day but I know I am not forgiven . . .

'Jul-ee-a,' Steven says on the phone, so that my name has three syllables. The only other person who has ever done that in my life is Miss Wismer, my guidance counselor in junior high school in Great Neck. Miss Wismer was an original Ms. Great trim figure, chic hair, great suits, and she wanted me to be excellent. I was in seventh grade the first time my stumbling block with math came up, and she gave me a black star and told me that if I didn't fix it I would never get into a good eastern school. Something about the three instead of two syllables in my name always made me think of her expectations of me. Unconsciously I straighten my shoulders while I shift the phone.

'I want to talk about the opening credits,' Steven says. He has already made me pressure every writer who made a contribution to the script. When the Writers' Guild insists on an arbitration, I get Schrader and Grady to back off their right to credits. When his lawyer, Bruce Ramer, a nice guy who wants to stay that way, also backs off from the issue, Norman and I step into the breach. Steven is going to get a 'written and directed by' credit, compliments of us. Now he wants to make sure it's in front. I do some fast thinking.

'So that means our production credit is in front, too?'

'Yes, how do you want it?'

'A Julia Phillips and Michael Phillips Production, same height, same width, first after you at the end as well,' I say, although I have never thought about credits before now. I pat myself on the back for my business acumen . . . I will get to pay some heavy dues for this credit . . .

'Agreed,' he says, faster than a speeding bullet. Now, your brother, yadda yadda yadda . . .

Steven and I sit in a dark room out at Trumball's operation in the Marina and watch seven points of light travel through a twinkling star field, and converge, nonballistically, to become the Big Dipper.

'I've been waiting to see that shot all my life,' Steven says, pleased. And I got it for you. We have a great deal of the footage for the end of the movie, and we have reached the point where it is smarter to put it together and then see what effects we need, than to create the effects and then cut them together. I don't want to waste any of the money that is getting harder and harder to squeeze out of Columbia.

One day Steven calls from the editing room at the Marina and tells me to drop everything and get over there. The only other time he has ever done that was with the discovery of Cary Guffy, so I drop everything.

'What's going on?' I ask Judy. She will know, because I have gotten her husband, Charlie, a job as assistant editor.

'I don't know, but Mike Kahn's been in the editing room all night. He called Charlie at three in the morning . . .' Mike Kahn is hardly a night person. He must have had an inspiration . . .

Excited, I Mario Andretti to the Marina. There is a palpable charge in the room when I arrive. Mike threads the film on the Kem and pulls the shades. The entire third act of the movie – the experience – flows before me. All that disparate footage, pulled together. Even without a good percentage of the effects it is coherent, beautiful, uplifting . . . they've nailed it! Hugs and kisses all around. I depart elated. I think I am one of maybe three people who knows how huge this picture is . . .

The Gift in the Desert comes shortly after I schmooze the money out of Joe Fischer for Doug Trumball. Now that I've won the last two campaigns in the endless war to make this picture great, I start to think grandiose. Album. Board games. Toys. If *Close Encounters* is a hit it could be a cottage industry. Scratch that. *When Close Encounters* is a hit it *will* be a cottage industry. Great. A cottage industry and no piece for me and mine, encumbered as we are by a-three-year-old deal. Back in 1974 the studios weren't giving up so much of the ancillaries. Not that they were worth much, since their own studio mavens handled them incompetently. Gotta renegotiate the backend. Uh-oh. More campaigns. And once I get our share of these rights back, I ain't entrusting it to nobody.

I have always tried to be the conduit between church and state. I have a horror of them talking to each other. But after I get the money for Doug, I have to put church, Steven, with state, now embodied by Dan Melnick. There are reasons the Founding Fathers, in their wisdom, kept them apart.

We start out well with Melnick. He wants us to know he's a film maker, committed to film makers. We hang out at his house and Melnick and I share a joint of this terrific Maui Wowie I've just gotten from Grady. Next day Melnick asks me to get him an ounce. I do, but I don't have a good feeling about it. Couple of times on the phone, he tries to induce me to talk about drugs, but I know already that this is the guy with all the tapes. I know I am no match for this evil fuck, but I am not entirely naïve. And he does seem to be getting along with us. I assemble a crew to suss out the situation in the desert so Clark and Veitch can come up with a real figure for what it will cost.

I tell Melnick I want to go to New York to see my mother. He says if I let Steven go to the desert with no one but Clark he will come back wanting two thousand extras and four hundred fifty stallions. I let the remark go right to my ego and cancel my New York trip. We go to Lake Mirage. The desert is in bloom, plus I have been imbibing some evil reconstituted Miami shit and I get a violent case of the sneezes. I know it pisses Steven off, but between sneezes I am still nailing the particulars down for him and anticipating his needs.

When we drive back through the desert, night falls in front of our eyes, first wrapping the hills in a purple blue. And then thousands of stars, crisp, clear, not like in L.A., blaze in the midnight-blue sky and the hills are black against it, and we both remember what we're trying to do with this picture and we're friends again . . .

I book another flight for New York. It is now close to my birthday. Not that it will be great for me, but maybe it will cheer my mother up for us to celebrate in New York. The budget for the Gift in the Desert comes up at $585,000 which astonishes everyone, and Melnick orders me to stay in town. Jack gets a quarter, which we clean with acetone and end up with only two grams.

Between my parents in New York, Melnick and Steven here, and the short yield, I get very constipated. Melnick schedules a production meeting with me and Steven and him for lunch at his office, which he has his cook prepare and bring in. It is the day of my birthday and I haven't gone number two in days. Shit presses against my rectum from the inside out while we review the artistic/ commercial/business realities over some sort of lobster in thick sauce . . .

Later in the day Begelman calls and tells me he's going to need me to run the film for Herbie Allen at ten o'clock the next morning. I know that this is the final step to the money for the Gift. I cancel another flight to New York. I obsess on this giant turd that is forming inside of me. I'm pretty sure I won't get any relief until I know I have the money for the opening of the picture.

Me and Mike Kahn pace outside the room at Todd-AO. Herbie Allen arrives fifteen minutes late with a blond beauty. I am furious he's brought his squeeze to a secret screening of this picture, but I just smile and explain that where major effects are missing I will try to describe what will be where now only black leader resides. I will try not to be too obtrusive, I continue, and launch into some rhetoric about what they should imagine is at the beginning of the picture. It is the longest two and a half hours I ever spend anywhere.

I know that Herbie Allen is on his way to a meeting with Begelman. He tries to split superquick with his date, but I corner him outside the ladies' room.

'What about the money for The Gift, The Gift in the Desert?' I ask directly, mimicking François's line in the movie he has just seen. No preamble, no social graces, edges out, like a slip peeping from beneath a hem.

'Don't do this to me,' he says, and his almond-shaped eyes tilt down a notch more.

'Do this to you? Do this to you?' I am outraged.

'I'll deal with it right away . . . I'm not discussing this in the hall with you now . . .' But you are, I want to say: I don't press it. Let Begelman close this fucker. That's what he's good at. Besides, if everyone vacates this building right now I think I can go to the bathroom. But I call Begelman to report in. He thanks me and says he'll take care of everything. I hit the ladies' room and experience the first gratifying interlude I've had in a month . . .

Steven calls later to complain about me yelling out effects in the screening. Great. Now Mike Kahn is a spy. It's reached the point that I don't know who is an adversary when there are too many elements in the room.

'Well, how else you want me to get the money for it?' I explode. 'I even made up some extra ones, for the overages that will surely occur . . .' The things that happen . . .

He backs off. Later that day, going over some ADR requirements with Kendall, whom I have put in charge, Steven says, 'Just tell her I know she's calling me L.P. for Little Putz, not Little Prince . . .'

I don't hear from anyone I need to hear from for two days. Then Melnick calls. 'Well, I got you the money,' he says . . .

'Thank you-u-u,' I ooze through clenched teeth. I. Got. You. The. Money!@#? Then why didn't *you* run the picture for Herbie Allen while I visited my cancer-ridden mother in New York?!@# I get off the phone and feed my anger with more blow. I have taken to storing it in plain sight, hanging from a Baggie in the middle of the bulletin board. Coke Theater.

Now the plan is to shoot in the desert in May, come back and shoot the ET and any inserts we need. It is a year since we started principal photography at Devil's Tower. I convince my parents they should come out here. My mother has responded well to chemotherapy and is in remission. Remission, a friend of mine says: a word that should be outlawed.

I have to start pushing on campaign three: release, marketing, renegotiating.

The whole conception of the release is a holdover from the days when the picture was opening Easter. Now that it has settled in at Christmas, I feel I need to go over everything again. I actually make a team of people do charts and maps and dates on the kind of cardboard Kate uses for her school projects.

Steven and I have a marketing meeting late one night with Melnick and Begelman. I bring my visual aids and rest them on the corner of Begelman's desk. I walk them through the plan: Magazine covers starting in early November. November release in New York and L.A., November 17, a concession to Norman Levy's requirements, which seem mainly to be that he promised the picture to the Walter Reade Organization. Record release at the same time, so that it can be climbing the charts in time for a wider release before Christmas.

We go over and over it. Norman wants the picture wider in November. It is a dead time of year between Thanksgiving and Christmas. We'll take the New York and L.A. release, that's it. I do most of the talking, and I have made a point of no drugs for the day. I maintain a calm veneer, no matter how many times I have to go over the same speech. They all know I have no patience. I think they are making me reiterate for their amusement. I don't care. I'm on a mission.

It is a very long meeting. They say they will think about it, but when Steven and I leave the building, I'm pretty sure they're convinced. I am nothing if not convincing. Particularly when I'm on a mission. It is cold and dark outside and we huddle on the steps together, just to get our bearings. He hugs me, starts to say something, but I blurt his words before he gets to say them.

'I know, I know, it's the old Julia, right?'

Ariel comes to the house one night to update my chart. She asks how everything on the picture is going and I tell her great, in fact, I'm renegotiating for some rights, it's going to be so huge. She furrows her brow over her bottle-cap glasses.

'Is this a new set of issues?' she drawls in her Louisiana accent, but her face is a mask of worry.

'Yup . . .'

'Not good . . . Mercury's in retrograde . . .'

'*Quest-ce que c'est* Mercury in retrograde?' I ask politely, knowing already it must pertain to matters astrological.

'When Mercury goes retrograde it is not a good time to start anything new. It's a time of small car accidents, lovers' quarrels, misconnections in business . . .'

Great, now she tells me . . .

Meco's cover of the theme from *Star Wars* stays at the top of the charts for weeks. I get devoted to the concept of a ten-inch disco hit for our five tones. John Eastman offers Paul McCartney, but McCartney wants to do his own music. I keep telling John that the tones are a lock, but he doesn't seem to understand. I pass. Something in me loves passing on McCartney. John Lennon's my favorite, anyway.

I am invited to a cozy lunch with David and Norman to go over release plans one more time. They are warm, friendly, like we're all just a bunch of tired old dicks having a casual poker game. I overplay my hand by telling David snidely about Dan Melnick 'getting me the money.' They laugh and poke each other in the ribs, but I see a trace of – call it concern – in their eyes. Who are they afraid of? He? Me?

When I get back to my office, Alan Hirschfield is on the line. I make it a point to chat and flirt with him as often as possible. Feeling loose, he tells me that he has been showing the product reel at small luncheons on Wall Street. Whose product reel? I ask, all hyperalert antennae. David's copy, he tells me, bragging.

I start to check Columbia stock on a daily basis and notice that the trading is heavy and the price is going up. Is Alan doing something illegal? Does showing the product reel constitute a misuse of insider information? Or is it just so close to the edge that it's open to interpretation? By creating the reel am I an accomplice to something illegal? Most important, could I go to jail?

My brief experience with the law on Mulholland Drive has reinforced all the negative feelings I have about police, police stations, jail . . . These are the kinds of too-smart questions I keep asking myself as I shovel more shitty-reconstituted-Miami-product-cleaned-with-acetone up my nose at two in the morning, wearing myself down exponentially in the process . . .

I keep working in town when Steven goes to the desert. Nick phones repeatedly to tell me I should get my ass down to location. Michael is there. I see a production still. He and Steven on board the nose of one of the planes. Matching hats. Matching beards. There are a year's worth of stills of me on location. The one with Michael of the matching beard is the only one that will be used . . .

Clive Davis, head of Arista, and Alan Hirschfield's new best friend, insists that Steven and I meet him at the rock 'n' roll Bungalow at the Beverly Hills Hotel and listen to the Alan Parsons Project. He plays it full blast and moves his head around to the music. Roger Birnbaum, his assistant, fields the phone, which rings constantly. It is quite a sight, Clive Davis bopping in his chair, with his tight English-looking mouth, his protégé in constant flight around us.

Steven is here under duress and resents the entire enterprise. He shoots me filthy looks constantly, like this is my idea. I remind myself that Clive Davis was responsible for the *Taxi Driver* album, a crappy enterprise, the only Bernie Herrmann soundtrack never to go gold, and after the requisite forty-five minutes, we tell him we'll think about it, we really must go . . .

We explode out of the bungalow, naughty children released from detention hall, and laugh our heads off all the way to our cars . . .

I blow him off in a week . . .

I'm becoming aware that there is a tension, a pull, between Alan and David, and hope I don't have to decide which one is my ally . . . I don't stop for a moment to realize the Clive Davis gesture already looks like a decision. I am so absorbed in the picture, I don't even think about what might be on all these executives' hidden agendas. It doesn't occur to me that the time is very near when they won't need me anymore. I do not see them, lined up in a row outside David's offices, pointing impatiently at their wristwatches . . .

I start searching for someone to do the ten-inch record. Jack sets up a meeting with George Clinton. What a good idea! We could call it CE3funK. Clinton arrives for a meeting at my house with his white girlfriend and a Baggie with an ounce of blow. He's the only one who's ever brought his own. I'm impressed.

I call Jon Peters to find out how to handle this album negotiation. He tells me that they went for a dollar a record on *A Star Is Born*. But that was Barbra. Try it, he suggests. Also, you should meet the Scotti Brothers.

'What's a Scotti Brother?' I ask.

'They get them played . . .' he says in a sinister voice.

Tony Scotti turns out to be the guy from *Valley of the Dolls* who was married to Sharon Tate. I tell him he is a great die-er and he laughs. I tell him my plans for the album. He's impressed. He takes me and Jack to dinner at the St. Germain. I ask him if he would be interested in watching the ticket count opening week. He laughs and says sure. I ask him if he's certain he can get the record played. This time he doesn't laugh. Sure, he says.

When I get a bid from him, he asks for two hundred grand, a small price to pay, particularly if we are going to get an enlarged piece of everything. David, more harassed than usual, says he'll take it under advisement. Norman Levy seems insulted by the concept of the Scottis counting tickets sold. Whatsa matter, I needle him in my mind, cutting into your kickbacks, am I?

I have a meeting with Begelman. I wear Ronnie Wood's feather and a T-shirt with Alan Hirschfeld's suit. We sit knee to knee across from his desk. It is the closest to sex we ever come. He is beginning to believe in my cottage industry concept.

'What do you need?' he wants to know. A piece of these rights I think, but I say:

'A selling tool . . .'

'Like what?'

'I'd like to fix up the product reel, but use the five tones as the hook . . .' He gives me approval. He'll give me a week with Mike Shapiro and Andy Keane, and then we show the reel to Steven, then to the record companies.

'You should get that product reel back from Alan,' I mention casually. 'You know, with this new version, with our own music, we don't need that other one out . . .' with music cues borrowed from *Taxi Driver*, with Alan Hirschfeld and his little stock-manipulating lunches, I think but don't say.

I ask Frank Warner, star sound-effects editor, to supply me with different versions of the five tones, from the first squelch over the sighting on Air Traffic Control radar to the Mother Ship booms. He cuts them into the reel.

'For the first time,' he says, 'I understand what this movie is about . . .'

*

As the reel metamorphoses, I let some heads of record companies sneak a peek. I've been told they object to the word *auction*, but I'm determined to have them bidding against each other. I have a friend do a mockup of the road with the glow folding out from an album cover. I keep it in the trunk of my car, and impress both Jerry Moss and Artie Mogul with it. Artie Mogul calls me at home one morning and offers a million dollars. I laugh and take another toot . . .

Too late, Columbia decides that I have been right about merchandising. At the last minute, they decide they want me to take a trip to San Francisco for some sort of convention with David Marks, who's the head of business affairs, which is as far away from albums, board games, toys as you can get and still be in the same country. I am coming down with a cold and I don't wanna go. They take this as another example of bad behavior. It is at this point that Vincent Alati complains loudly about the hour I was late for a meeting with him . . . how long ago? six months? a year?

Steven is on the dubbing stage and cannot make it to the Cinerama Dome to check lenses. I am informed I am his replacement at eight in the morning for a nine o'clock appointment. I am forty-five minutes late, and I don't know dick about lenses, but somehow Veitch and I pick the right one . . .

Another marketing meeting; I am spent. I throw the blow right out on the table. I have become so arrogant. It is the worst public behavior I ever indulge in, and all the time I play out this scene I am thinking: What are you doing? This is not your movie . . .

*

I get a nervous call from Steven. You're not showing this reel without my approval, is the gist. I lie and tell him I wouldn't think of it. I haven't perfected lying, not even on the phone. He hears right through me, but lets it pass. It's almost done, we'll all be watching it in a couple of days, I steamroll forward, after I have this one last meeting with Begelman . . .

Just fucking nail down this fucking ENDless BACKfucking-END renegotiAtion . . .

I wake up sweating from leftover flu and a nightmare. When I bolt out of bed, I upset a mirror with at least a gram of coke spread out from last night. Jack is in the corner flagellating himself with the cords from my blinds. This is a morning ritual with him. At first, it was just another wacky, hilarious thing about Jack; now it is getting to be a satire of the thing itself, like Rod Steiger's acting.

I dive after the mirror, but the coke flies into the carpet. I already know from the Grady experience that carpet consumes coke the way black holes consume nebulae. I look at the spot on the carpet that used to be my morning heartstarter, and I cry over spilt coke. I am on my knees, crying, when Jack stops beating the shit out of his chest and comes over to touch my shoulder gently. I look up at him.

'This is going to be a very bad day,' I say.

It is September 13, 1977.

It is the worst day of my life.

I check in with Kendall. 'You'd better get over to Todd-AO,' she says. 'Steven's been on the phone all morning with Dan Melnick . . .'

Nauseated, I throw myself into an ungratifying two-minute shower. No time for negative ions today. I dress quickly: Maxfield top, black Brioni pantsuit, mascara, lip gloss, gram of coke. I take off in the limo that has been provided for the last week, I'm on such a tight schedule and I'm such a bad driver. Jack comes along for the ride.

*

I meet Norman at the dubbing stage. I go in to talk to Steven. He sees Jack and his mouth twitches.

'I'm going to this meeting this afternoon,' he declares. Uh-oh. I wanna see the Beges alone . . .

'Steven, I don't think that's a good idea . . .'

'I'm just gonna go and listen to everyone . . .'

'Steven, I'm asking you, please, don't go . . .'

'I'm going . . .' *Here lies Sir Rupert* . . .

'You know, you may be a great director, but you're a lousy businessman,' I say, feeling earth going to dust beneath my feet. I didn't mean that. Human being. I meant human being. Now your brother, he thinks you're the artist . . .

Norman and I go to lunch scheduled long ago with Frank Wells and Paula Weinstein at Le Serre to talk about *The Third Man Through the Door*. Window seat in the front room. Airless but pretty. With all the coke I do, restaurants are a hazard. They are filled with plants and the windows are sealed. The recirculated air with the pollen, plus the perpetually itchy nose, often lead to a colossal sneezing fit. Feeds the bad rumors.

My third eye does not see: This is it, babe. Your last lunch in *this* town . . .

I have to tell them that the Eagles have fallen out. Henley is in a hospital with an ulcer attack and Frey has gone to Colorado to build a house. I wonder if they're breaking up. Paula and Frank act like it doesn't matter, but we all know that's not true.

Jack splits with the car and brings back presents. One of them is a silver pin of a cupid, whose ass has been wiped for luck so many times that it is a bronze color. I put it on my lapel.

We go to the Burbank lot. There is a message from Connie that Steven, Melnick, and Norman Levy will all be joining us. I haven't a clue who's been cast as First and Second, but I know I get to be the Third Man Through the Door. Fuck them! I instruct Norman to go over instead, tell them I won't attend a stacked meeting. Unless they want to close the renegotiation first. Never give up the product, Jack has reminded relentlessly, until you get the money. I wait in my office for a call from him. They need me . . .

They tell him that I can 'retreat to the standard position of producer' or walk. He calls and tells me this news. I am stunned. There's been nothing standard about this producing gig so far. Why start now?

I know I should stand up for myself. Go to the meeting, beard the lions in their den. But the coke, which has amplified my courage for so long, turns on me and makes me weepy. I have overplayed my hand and I have lost.

I know that I am being betrayed by the only partners who have mattered: Michael. Steven. Begelman . . . *most fearfully betrayed* . . . I call Michael at Todd-AO, where he's been hanging out. I tell him he's got it all, I'm going home. He worries out loud that we might be sued.

I mention to him he might want to pursue the Artie Mogul offer. When he does, Artie denies ever having made it.

I take the car home. I get one last burst of energy for a telegram that I send to Herbie Allen Hirschfield. It says: BELIEVE YOU ARE BLOWING A BILLION. NO ONE KNOWS HOW HUGE CE3K IS.

I get no response.

Rona announces the following day that I am no longer the captain of the ship of *Close Encounters*. Since the picture is about to go to negative cutting, and therefore in the dock, there is no way to respond.

Nobody but Frank Warner calls.

Two days later, Grady calls. I think he is calling to comfort me, but it is a you-fucked-it-up call instead. Kendall says he's been waiting a year to make that call . . . *and murdered on this spot* . . .

Randy Fields brings me a final proof of the ad. I cut all the exclamation points and excise the period after WE ARE NOT ALONE.

*

The answer print is run for me at Todd-AO. I sit alone in a darkened room, pad and pen with light in hand. 'The experience' seems a tad leaden, cut between the beat. As it were. The effects stay on too long, congratulating themselves. I write heads and tails cuts furiously. When the lights come up, I sigh deeply and tear them up. Who cares . . .?

L'affaire Begelman breaks . . . he's in, he's out. Columbia stock is suspended from trading for a day. How did Ariel know that? I weep for my picture. With me gone and him gone, and the power struggles and ego confrontations that will surely ensue, I know the release will be half-assed. I feel like four years of my life have slipped through the cracks. When his case comes up in Burbank, Judge Thomas J. Murphy presiding, he gets a five-thousand-dollar fine and community service . . . Less than me . . .

I half sink into drugs. I show up for the screenings in New York and L.A. A press conference has been arranged after the one in New York. I have been placed half off to the side, between Alan Hyneck and Doug Trumball, far away from Steven, which hurts me deeply. I am late and disgrace myself even further by slurring my words while answering a question. Not the best public speaking.

After the screening in L.A., Dan Melnick sends me a huge floral arrangement with a note that says: 'The triumph will be remembered long after the pain is forgotten.' Who writes your dialogue?

I make Kendall find a Venus fly trap. I send it to him with a note that says: 'Don't get mad . . . get even . . .' I send his lackey, Bill Tennant, thirty dead flies for plant food. Empty gestures, nothing will comfort me . . . *by his fellows* . . .

I go into a deep state of mourning.

I do not come out of it for a decade . . .

Some say the world will end in fire,
Some say in ice

> *From what I've tasted of desire*
> *I hold with those who favor fire.*
> *But if it had to perish twice,*
> *I think I know enough of hate*
> *To say that for destruction ice*
> *Is also great*
> *And would suffice.*
>
> — Robert Frost

Here's my theory, she thought, we *are* the missing link. We are halfway between our animal selves and wherever it is that we're going. Our minds are good enough to invent nuclear weapons, dioxin, and cluster bombs, but our animal selves find these things beyond our maintenance abilities. Besides, we need our space. The soul was invented as an arbiter between the two, and drugs could be very helpful in spiritual and territorial terms.

We're smart enough to know we need to live in groups to survive, but we're still animals and we need lots of room. In the case of the male of the species we also probably need that-guy-over-there's space. And his wife and cow, too.

People have a drink to loosen up a business dinner, celebrate an award, or a nuclear disarmament treaty. They have a joint to hear the music, or have sex, or chat with themselves on a sunny afternoon.

That was how it used to be, before Operation Intercept, when Reagan wiped out marijuana. A grower from northern California had told her at the beginning of the eighties that Operation Intercept was a Republican plot to get everyone back onto Valium and alcohol. So they dried up the pot and brought in the blow . . . made a smokable version to replace weed.

Now all the drugs were drugs of despair. Fucking mean Republican machine. Sent all those planes with guns to South America; what did they think, that something else wouldn't come back? Never send an empty mode of transport, Fins said, and no, smugglers didn't make distinctions among contraband: guns, cash, drugs, they were all the same. Illegal. Profitable. She couldn't get over the feeling that there were straight-looking Republicans with a lot of cocaine money in their savings and loans. Inevitably coke had slipped down the scale: not chic, not expensive, just sex and violence.

Now smack was the chic drug. She hated going out these days. The clubs were filled with rich kids and young actors who had just thrown up on their shoes in the bathroom and then took up space in the bar nodding out.

And somewhere in dark corners of the land, there were freaked-out chemists and Hell's Angels grinding out designer speed for the middle class. What was left of it . . .

When she had been at MGM she had noticed a sign in a window that said: THE END IS HERE. Right the fuck on. What she wanted to know was who had the tickets on the bus for Planet Z? And how would they know when it was time to board?

Now George was going to wage war on the casual user. What about treatment? What about curing social ills? How long ago had it been that she had told her parents that drugs were going to be the big issue . . . 1961 or so? And when had she known about the Colombians – mid-seventies, even before that good Peruvian surfer coke . . .

'Hey, we're not performing brain surgery here,' guys like Mort Engelberg always said. A smart guy who had made and kept a fortune from such offerings as *Hot Stuff* and *Smokey and The Bandit I* and *II*. If you please.

And she would always counter with the same old argument. Of course we were: we were shaping the dreams, the fantasies, the aspirations of the next generation. Why was everybody so surprised that fourteen-year-olds were gunning each other down with automatic weapons? No public funds, no Head Start, and just enough change in their pockets to see an afternoon showing of *Rambo*.

I look out at the sea, sitting cross-legged on my bed, and floss with a vengeance. Jack sits cross-legged on the other bed and does the same. Ozzie and Harriet on blow, ripping and tearing at their gums because the cut from the coke last night is living somewhere between tooth and gum; when they finally bleed you get some relief from that itchpain that never gets you high and never goes away. This beachfront room, in the annex that juts away from the main building of the hotel, has its finger on the pulse of paradise.

Suddenly there is a pale, pear-shaped guy right outside the room, peering in, beaming at me. 'I'm so happy to see you flossing,' he kvells. Oh God, a dentist from Long Island, there's the wife right behind him, a little broad in the hip, highlighted hair, nose job, the whole trip. What are they doing here in Hawaii at the Kahala Hilton peering into this beach-front room? I'll let you be in my movie if you'll let me be in yours. But I don't want you in my movie – don't I even get to choose that? Ah, fuck it, Who cares? I'll let you be in my movie if you let me be in yours.

Jack and I grimace at the pain, and the dentist and his wife take this to be a social gesture. If you step into my room, I'll kill you in my mind, I think. They stand uncertainly before us, blocking our view of the ocean. Then they take the hint and move on. We've been here a week. I'm in the slough of despond and not getting any better.

I have not started out too well; in fact, I've created a major ugly incident that has been blown over by Kay Aherne, the woman who takes care of VIPs. We had arrived late at night, put Kate and Jackie to bed, and done an incredible amount of drugs. Jack had finally fallen asleep, but apparently I had gone off on a little wander. The last thing I could personally remember was walking out onto the beach.

From there, I had walked around to the side of the hotel that abutted the golf course, and let myself into someone else's room, locked all the doors, and gone to sleep in their bed. They couldn't get into their own room, because I double locked everything, and security came and took me back to my own room, although they had a hard time figuring out who I was because I kept telling them my name was Nancy Miller – an alias from a past life, no doubt.

The person whom I had barred from his room turned out to be Peter Lawford, and he made a hell of a stink, wanting to know who had been eating his porridge. Kay Aherne stepped into the breach and when things got really nasty, she kicked him out.

I find it amusing that she has chosen to regard me as more important than him, but then, he's in one of the golf course rooms, which are not the priciest.

She doesn't know I'm a disgrace, en route to show-biz oblivion. All she knows is that there's a major motion picture that has just opened in the best theater in downtown Honolulu with my name above the title.

So two huge security guards carry me back to my room, wake up Jack, who doesn't even know I'm missing, and put me to bed. I sleep for a day, and when I wake up, Jack tells me the whole story, laughing all the time. I can't remember a single thing. I have never blacked out before, and I get scared. Jack laughs a bit more, and then he goes very quiet, too.

'Ah, it's all just a rehearsal, anyway,' he says, a Jack aphorism.

'Seems like a major reality cookie to me,' I say back, another Jack aphorism. 'Do we have any drugs left?'

'Lotta blow, no pot. I was thinking of looking over the beach boys . . . see if one of them looked like he'd get us some Maui Wowie . . . long as we're here.' He laughs his crazy laugh and pulls back the covers I've been holding up to my throat.

I'm dressed in the same clothes I traveled in. How many days ago? Two? Three? I stand up. How do I feel? More important, how do I smell? Not bad, considering. Good enough to pick a beach boy out for Jack.

I walk out the front of the room and survey the scene. Fat Jews on towels, couple of Japanese businessmen, Princess Grace incognito under the tree at the end of the beach swathed in clothes and hat and sunglasses. Just another day at the Kahala Hilton.

I watch the beach boys hustle. An angry white boy with white hair and zinc oxide on his nose, some Orientals, working their way through school, no doubt. Hustle bustle. Not a pothead among them. Then, down the beach, a mixed blood with streaked hair, taking his time between assignments, checking out the waves. 'There's our boy.' I wink and Jack saunters off in his direction.

By the middle of the afternoon, we have psychedelic pot, and a genuine Hawaiian in our care. He is possessed of an unpronounceable Hawaiian name, so I christen him Sir Mauie Wowie. I can see girls going wild for him. He has a distinctly Polynesian face and streaked blond hair. He's rather medium in build and height. Too slight for my taste. He drives us around the island to the North Shore, where he keeps our car safe from the brothers. Tough dudes who don't like white people. Like all paradises, underneath the sun and the breeze there is a heavy current of racial tension. The possibility of random violence lurks under every palm tree.

We sit down on Sunset Beach and smoke a great big fat one while Sir Wowie surfs. This is no over-the-hill gang, like the Lances that John Milius used to schlep out to Nicholas Beach in a sorry attempt to impress me and Margot. Milius, decked out in his wetsuit, struggling to stay afloat on an antiquated red board.

I loved Milius's writing, and even his bluster, it was basically so harmless, but he had awful yellow teeth that surely he could afford to have fixed. And he smiled and snarled a lot. I got pretty hung-up on his teeth. Me and Milius ended up not being friends. While we were making *Close Encounters*. Steven, to whom I had introduced Milius, kept telling me stories about the terrible things Milius was saying about me.

What for? What'd I do to him? What could he possibly be

pissed at me about? Maybe it was my use of drugs, Milius being as straight as he was, maybe I was supposed to fuck him and didn't understand. Maybe it was just another Hollywood Thing. Beautiful people doing beautiful things, as David Debin said.

Just about every morning that I ever lived on Nicholas Beach, I watched the real California surfers, the kids who waited in a row at Point Zero on Nicholas Beach, out past the Bad Vibe Roy Ashe house that jutted out and cut off the view of Santa Monica. They looked like ducks on a pond. Milius was so far behind them he was beneath last.

And Wowie puts them all to shame. I am actually getting high on Hawaiian pot and watching a master.

'All he ever hears is the sounds of the buds opening and the waves rising,' Jack says, and pulls a reluctant smile from me. I'm starting to feel a little better, if not about Life, then at least about Last Night. My face feels weird smiling. Christ, it's been a long time.

Walking off *Close Encounters*. Two months and ten pounds ago. An eternity . . .

I didn't even attend the Dallas preview. Pat Kingsley and Pat Newcombe argued with me all day that I should go, but I didn't want to. I was doing tons of blow in a suite at the Mayfair Regency that I hated. My parents were around me and so was Jack. Jackie and Kate, me barely in touch with them at all.

I was drowning.

I went back to L.A. that night instead of to Dallas. I couldn't bear oversleeping in that overdone suite another day.

Years later, Hirschfield tells me that they held the plane, he and Veitch, so sure were they that I would show up for my own preview. How could I explain, you took it away from me, you betrayed me, it will never feel good again to think about this movie?

It's taken me a long time to get to Hawaii. I have to pay some more humiliation dues. And see my mother, who is enduring chemotherapy. And my father, who's incarcerated himself in a prison called 'clinical depression' and taking Tofranil.

We move from the Kahala Hilton to a house on Black Point. On a spit of land that juts into the sea. Trade winds pummel the house all day. It is rumored that Richard Boone lived here once. The electric garage opens and shuts by itself. Haunted. *A haint cain't haint a haint . . .*

A perfect venue for me and my ghosts . . . I sit on the deck and watch the sea and peruse myriad screenplays for a project I have in mind. Working title: *Close Encounters of the Third Man Through the Door*. I keep firing writers and hiring new ones. Each one of them is me. I demand rewrite after rewrite and tire myself out. I hate the ending . . .

Real estate is to Oahu what show biz is to L.A. I start to look for a house. I find one, a bullshit, at-one-with-nature house. I buy it, mostly for paper.

Hank Levine, my business manager, comes over for the closing. When everything is signed, I turn to Jack and blurt, 'Michael, isn't this great?' Everyone goes quiet. Whaddya say: Just kidding?

We return to the Mainland for a brief spell. It is comforting to be back in good old Benedict Canyon. I sift through mail that has piled up, idly puffing on a joint. There is a confirmation slip for the sale of my fourteen thousand shares of Columbia stock. Sale?! I have been holding on to that stock, which has been going down steadily, just for the pleasure of being able to attend the next shareholders' meeting and ask Herbie Allen Hirschfield why Norman Levy has kept the picture idling in the Ziegfeld three months after release without another Manhattan theater. More than one way to skin a gangster, I figure.

I start calling people at home. It turns out that Michael has sold my stock, under an old and invalid power of attorney.

Seems he wants to buy himself a palace in Coldwater Canyon and needs the cash. He tells me plaintively that I asked him before I left not to let me take a bath on the stock. It's been hurtling downward. I don't remember.

The next day, various and sundry representatives attend a meeting around my pool table in the living room. I make them all stay on their feet, because I have built up a serious rage over this stock sale. For me it is the morning after the sleepless night before. Larry Kartiganer informs me that I don't have to honor the sale.

'What does that mean?' I brighten at the glimmer of hope.

'Well, Michael would have to come up with the stock . . .' My shoulders slump automatically.

'You know, if I was one of those ruthless Melnicks or Begelmans or Fieldses whose names you intone with so much respect, I'd stiff him . . .' I sputter ineffectually.

'You do not have to honor this sale,' Kartiganer reiterates. I think I'm being challenged. No way I can leave Michael holding the bag. I am so weakened by my sense of loss and drug intake, I wuss out again. It seems one defeat leads inexorably to another . . .

I attend the Golden Globes. Freddie Fields is sitting at my table. He doesn't want to acknowledge me, but I plant myself in his eyeline. He barely says hello, finds another table. And it's so much fun to be snubbed by somebody beneath me . . .

'If it's reached the point where I'm being snubbed by scumbags, I'm leaving . . .' I say later that night, but Norman talks me into a meeting here and there. Ned Tanen. Jerry Moss. Ned wants right of designation twenty-six weeks before principal photography on any picture I would make under an overall deal. Jerry pulls his back out and lands in the hospital. What's wrong, Jer, bad case of Julia?

'There's nothing for me here,' I tell Jack, and he agrees . . .

We fly back to Hawaii the next day, and we sit out escrow at the Kahala Hilton.

I run into Joan Didion one morning. She is wearing huge sunglasses and a scarf. We agree to have breakfast. Jack and I arrive late, and Joan and John are picking at rolls. They try to be warm and supportive and the meal goes pretty well, but when we stand up, the eighth Jack has been carrying in his pocket slips out, rolls along the carpet, coming to rest on John's sandal. We all laugh, ha ha, and Jack retrieves it casually, but they don't seek my company again . . .

Kate is spending three weeks with Michael back in Los Angeles and somewhere in the middle of the second week she develops the kind of ear infection that only a three-year-old who misses her mommy comes up with. Michael calls, frantic, and when I speak to her she uses her tiny voice. She sounds like Minnie Mouse. I think it is pretty peculiar that even though I am supposed to be the whacked-out crazy one, I am also the one who always gets to be the parent in these situations.

Returning from Hawaii is pretty much like coming back from Fire Island: I am not precisely evacuated, but I don't leave of my own free will. I make it back approximately when I said I would; that is, I miss only one flight. It is hard to be doing a lot of drugs and make a flight on time.

I am in the free-floating mode of a person who is making a lot of money from past effort but has nothing to do. If I'm not precisely on a blacklist, I am still on most everybody's shit list, so the phone isn't ringing off the hook with hot business proposals or invitations. Jack is busier than I am, and I guess he thinks it is time to put some of the money to work. One day he says, 'Don't you think it's time to fix the deck? It'll improve the property and it'll make a great place to hang out.'

This is all pretty reasonable, but seems a step toward the Beverly Hills Housewife Syndrome: have a facial, have a nose job, have lunch, decorate the house, fix the deck. 'Why don't you handle it?' I am passing off as much responsiblity for anything as I can afford. Which is a lot.

'Why don't you do it?' he shoots back. 'I'm busy.' The unkindest cut of all.

'I wouldn't even know where to begin . . .'

'I've got someone in mind . . . he's talented . . . a little crazy, but you work well with guys like that.'

'Who is it?' This is the most interested I've been in anything in six, maybe eight months. Going from too much work all the time, to no work at all can wreak havoc with your biochemical balance. I am pretty lethargic. I understand why air traffic controllers who retire die suddenly of heart attacks. I am worried about my health. I am still in mourning.

'His name is Rottweiler. You know Prince Albert's* bathroom that you like so much? He did it.'

'So get him to come over and he can look at the pool and give me a bid.'

Jack arranges the meeting. Rottweiler is handsome, notwithstanding an impressive array of facial scars, the result of an adolescent motorcycle accident. Funny, too. He takes the job and starts to be around a lot of the time . . .

One day Jack and I have a fight that precipitates his speedy departure in the middle of the night. I run after him, knock myself solidly into the retaining wall. The next day my right side is swollen to twice the size of my left side. Rottweiler and I have dinner and drugs together. It is inevitable that we end up in bed.

ovo: And did we have fun?

me: I can't remember . . .

Two days later, Jack calls from Oregon, where he has gone to visit his daughters. 'We're a family, you and I,' he says. I look at Rottweiler eating popcorn on the bed. I don't think so . . .

When Jack comes home, Rottweiler splits so I can end it with Jack in person. He tries to convince me it's just a stage I'm going through, but I blow him off definitively.

He's right. It is a stage, a downward stage, freebase turning liquid in the stem of the pipe and melting into the dirty water . . .

*

While Rottweiler is designing an office, to be constructed where the garage is, he comes up with the bright idea of a cactus garden, marry the indoors with the outdoors. Very Hawaiian. I have a friend in need of an urgent hemorrhoid operation who's in possession of a mutant peyote cactus. It looks like a brain. She wants two grand, but her ass is more painful daily. I get it for fifteen hundred dollars and her two faggot assistants show up that afternoon with plants and dirt. Rottweiler digs out a space in the garage. Basically he ends up building the room around the cactus.

Sometimes, when the water from the pipe is too dirty to recycle, I throw it into the dirt in which the cactus lives. The cactus grows some offshoots. One looks like a pair of sagging breasts. I think of that offshoot as the female part of the plant. Then the plant starts to grow straight up, a giant dick. Right here, right in this office/drug room, right in my face. A personal affront that threatens to break through the ceiling . . .

The seductive thing about freebase, for me anyway, is that at first I have the illusion that I am doing substantially less cocaine than if I toot it. My nose is very sore most of the time, and this pipe-smoking seems like a convenient method of intake.

More important, the high is substantially more dynamic.

I learn a rough recipe from a nice Jewish dealer in the Valley that involves dissolving the raw product in water, mixing it with a small amount of any household cleaner that has ammonia in it, then drying and rolling it around in a Melita coffee filter. It makes hard little rocks and we smoke it in water pipes or bongs.

We light it with whatever is around. Matches, a butane lighter. The problem with this method is that the yield is pretty low and it burns the shit out of your lungs. Also, you can tell that you are getting as high from the ammonia fumes as the coke.

*

In one of his many alcoholic wanders, Rottweiler finds a fucked-up chemist from northern California who comes over one morning while Rottweiler sleeps off a colossal bender and teaches me how to make elegant crystals that grow up to the sky. This is partially due to the fact that we use my product, reconstituted Miami shit – horrible to toot, but quite pure. Ergo: big yield. But it is also because Walter's* method of production is quite different from what I already know.

Walter's recipe is much more complicated than the one I already know. He tells me that making the rock with household ammonia is very dangerous and can give you lesions on your lungs. This makes me fall over with laughter. Imagine these two freaks discussing anything that is bad for your health while we are batching up this noxious brew?

He laughs, too, and reveals horrible dog teeth. (I don't see such bad teeth on an American person again until Oliver North brightens up one day during the Iran Contra hearings on TV.) Walter bears a disturbing resemblance to Tony Bill, actually. A freaked-out, junked-out, weirder, dirtier Tony Bill, if that is possible.

Walter is very serious about this batching up of freebase. Which is the thing that reminds me most about Tony. He is so serious he takes the joy out of basing, which is not dissimilar from the way Tony made me feel about movies.

Walter is into the ceremony and the ritual of the making of the freebase. Extreme Coke Theater. Maybe he is trying to show me he isn't attached. Me, I've always been a results-oriented type. If you're going to fuck, come; if you're going to improve drugs, do it fast. Get to them before you're bored.

Walter sets his gear up in the office on the table that Rottweiler had made out of a sawblade. He has one of those kids' fold-out chemistry sets, with all the test tubes lined up in a wooden holder. I had a friend in college who kept all his pot in such a manner. An anal retentive hedonist, he also kept all his Marvel comic books in files, alphabetized and cross-referenced by subject, month, and year. His pot was labeled by dealer, year copped, and country of origin. It was a measure of how much he liked you, whether you got the Albanian '69 or the Moroccan '72.

402

Walter takes me through the steps for his method. First dilute the coke in water, a sad moment for me, because I am pretty sure it will never come back. Then add an equal amount of anhydrous ether. Oooh the smell: I have always been fond of ether smell and ether high. It makes a small horizon, like salt water over fresh water. Then the tiniest bit of ammonium hydroxide, to precipitate a reaction. It makes a thin, bright white line that separates the cocaine water from the ether. It reminds me for a second of the way Doug Trumball created the clouds forming over Jillian's house. Just salt over fresh water with some tempera shot through.

Now screw on the cap, and shake it up. He shows me what the mix looks like. Thick, like lamb placenta. Big fat bubbles gurgling around in slow motion.

He unscrews the cap, and the mixture fizzes and rushes to spill over, champagne for coconuts. Hastily he screws the cap on. 'This is why you need these screw-on caps. There's another kind with rubber caps, but they blow out and you lose everything.' He unscrews and rescrews the top several times, until there is no more fizz and the white line is gone. 'Now you just take this dropper and put the liquid above the water line into this petri dish, and let it dry.'

He blows on it lightly and spins the concave disk around on the glass-covered sawblade. Luminescent crystals start to grow. When everything turns white on the plate, and Walter pronounces it dry, he scrapes it with an industrial razor and produces a pipe. This pipe has nine thousand screens in it, to keep the base from melting down the stem when lit. He also produces a propane torch; it will burn cleaner, he proclaims, and lights it for me.

Freebase does not induce good manners, so I am kind of surprised he offers the pipe to me first, even though the product is mine. He holds on to the pipe, like he needs to have it the minute I am done, which adds an unnecessary element of urgency to the entire enterprise. It is already feeling urgent enough.

'Don't suck it so hard,' he says sharply. Whoa, this is a new one. He pulls the pipe away. 'Like this,' he inhales long and slow. The bowl fills with white smoke (there are those clouds again) and he passes the pipe to me. This time I take a nice long yoga breath, and he holds the torch for me. I can see that this is not a traveling kind of a drug. Bummer.

'Hold the smoke as long as you can and let it out slowly through your nose . . .' Hey, just a minute, buster, who do you think you're dealing with here, Rebecca of Sunnybrook Farm? But I go along with his instructions anyway. Heyyyyyy noooowwwww. This is definitely better than that Melita crap. Makes that stuff like a toy. Ohhhh, bay-bay.

Bells go off in my ears, and UFOs dance in my peripheral vision. I have an impulse to stand up and lie down at the same time. I freeze. My heart is pounding the way it did when I inhaled Freon from a Baggie, and I wonder briefly if this is going to be the Big One. The Ultimate. Death. Trip. I wait . . . Nothing. Except . . .

This is just about the highest I've been, I think, and look around. Weird to move. Little bells keep going off in my legs, which feel as if they have been painted by Salvador Dali. Puffs of sensation ebb and flow, and here is the real attraction – they all seem in sync with the ebb and flow of the universe, the macro and micro of it all – the heartbeat of the cosmos in concert with mine.

I stand up and the room goes spinning. I spin with it. Since this spinning is not accompanied by nausea, it is a completely pleasant experience.

'Wait. Wait . . .' Walter's voice comes from far away but clear as a bell. Is he kidding? I'm not going anywhere. Oh, I get it. The pipe. I am still holding the pipe. Walter pulls out a balloon and blows his smoke into it. 'You must always recycle,' he says. I bend down and blow my smoke into his mouth. There's your cheap thrill. He hands me the balloon. 'Let it whoosh into your lungs,' he instructs.

I exhale all the air out of my mouth and suck on the balloon. If I could just figure out how to make this into a traveling light show, I would be sooooo happy. I am getting too little fresh air behind freebase. It is giving me headaches and making me feed on my soul. Couple of years later, when I found Ron Siegel, he told me this was called the Kindling Effect. The fire in your brain.

Walter and I smoke up the product and then he shows me how to burn the residue out of the pipe stem. It comes out gooey amber. Same procedure, only now the crystals are the color of topaz. Cleaner. Stronger. Better tasting. Am I going to have to have someone smoke my product first, a cat tasting food for the emperor, so I can have this niftier buzz? Well, there is always Rottweiler, whom I can hear stirring in the other room. What fresh hell will this be, I wonder, and puff, and do not care . . .

I am burning the residue from the stem of the pipe and recycling cocaine-laced water when Ray Stark calls. David Parks, who has agreed to be my assistant only if I take a movie career seriously, squints at me. His squint says, If you don't take this call, I'm leaving.

'Hi, Ray,' I chirp, and his secretary says, 'I'll put Mr. Stark on.' It's always the same old shit, secretaries outwaiting each other, or putting both their bosses on at the same time; pecking-order bullshit, but I'm not attached. By the time he gets on the phone, I am shaking the cocaine water and the brown residue from the pipe in a little screw-top test tube.

'Hello, Julia,' Ray purrs. Since he usually likes to call me Laurie, I feel the conversation is going well. I add some anhydrous ether and take a whiff. What a great high, the ether. Some dealer has told me that in the late fifties, when Lord Buckley was big out here, and Lenny Bruce was doing bad impressions in strip joints, there was a circle of comedians, mostly, who were ether heads. They'd soak a towel with it and put the towel over their faces until the second before they passed out. Dr. Jekyll and Mr. Hyde.

The great thing about ether is that it whomps you and then it goes away with no perceptible side effects, although Reice Jones informs me years later that there is a high incidence of spontaneous abortion among nurses who work regularly in operating theaters.

'Hi, Ray. Long time no speak . . .'

'Well, not because your name doesn't come up from time to time . . .' Yeah, as in, That bitch still alive?

'What can I do for you? I'm a little tied up right now . . .' I add some ammonium hydrochloride, just enough to make a little white rim between the drugged-out water and the soon to be drug-rich ether.

'Well, what are you doing with yourself right now?'

'Taking a breather . . .' I screw on the cap and shake it over my head, backup in a corny salsa band.

'I just think you're allowing yourself to be a wasted talent.' Ah, there's that phrase again.

'I think I was a wasted talent when I was doing it all . . .'

'How's your health?' You mean: still doing drugs? I watch the fat little bubbles and unscrew the cap gently. The mixture fizzes, and I close the cap again. Open close open close until it settles down. I find an eyedropper and a petri dish and start extracting my favorite brew.

'Never better,' I lie. I cover the mouthpiece and blow on the petri dish. Little amber crystals start to sprout. Ooh, I really love the chemistry of this drug . . .

'I have a little business idea I'd like to discuss with you. Want to come see me?' Is he summoning me? Fuck me . . . fuck you . . .

'I'm never going to Burbank again.' I smile. 'It fucks up my respiratory system for days . . .'

Ray laughs. 'Okay, how about if I come to see you?' Well, this *is* serious. I wonder what he has in mind.

'Okay,' I say, lying again. Ray Stark in my house? Too weird. Too funny not to try, though.

'When . . .'

'Well, I'm on my way out . . . how are you tomorrow?' There is always tomorrow.

'That'd be fine. Say two thirty, three? Right after lunch?' Hey, babe, I don't eat anymore, but whatever turns you on . . .

'I'll look forward to it, then . . .'

'See you tomorrow . . .'

'Tomorrow . . .' He hangs up. Also part of the pecking order, who hangs up more abruptly. Who's busier. Hey, no contest here.

I look at the receiver, fall inside one of the holes in the

mouthpiece for a moment, meander through a billion empty soundbites, return, and then I hang up, too. Hey, a billion isn't what it used to be . . .

'He's coming to see me tomorrow,' I tell David's questioning eyes. 'Phew, that wore me out . . .'

I check my crystals, my little babies. Ready! I find a clean pipe and some Evian, and get ready for the best hit of my life. 'Course, it's only the first hit that's the best hit. All the others are just chasing the memory of the first. The Chinese, whose brains are larger, call it chasing the dragon. For me, it opens up a number of possibilities, most of which lead to chaos. Not a bad place to be if one is contemplating an impending meeting with Ray Stark, who has the insulting proclivity for calling me Laurie when it suits him.

When Ray arrives promptly at two forty-five the next day, I keep him waiting, not out of power games, but because I am still taking that one last hit for the road in my bathroom. When I finally make my entrance, I find him seated in the cramped little anteroom between the kitchen and my bedroom on a far too cute and small wicker sofa. He is dressed a decade behind the times: plaid shirt, jeans, a cowboy belt with a huge turquoise buckle. He looks like a sad old queen.

Further, his jeans are too blue. I fixate on them for a moment, communing with the tightly woven blue-and-white threads. They start to separate and slink around on his thighs. Little snakes on Big Daddy Snake. I close my eyes and take a deep breath and wave them away in my mind. When I open my eyes, they wave back. I sit next to him on the matching wicker rocking chair. As he talks, I start to rock.

'Miss making movies?' Always . . .

'I make them in my mind . . .' Ray permits himself an imperceptible upturning of his mouth. I notice all these things, because my brain is goin' ninety.

'I'll get right to the point . . .' Busy busy Ray. Places to go, people to see. I wonder what Jack is doing right now.

'Please . . .'

'How would you feel about coming to work for me . . .'

'Ray, you've been offering me a job since before *The Sting*. I'm not into a job . . .'

'What then . . .'

'What about a partnership . . .' That oughtta get him outta here quick. 'You know, with exclusions of previous projects . . . a startup situation . . .' the whole catastrophe . . .

'That'd be fine with me . . .' What?! Moving along to Plan B, eh? I don't wanna be in business with anyone, least of all Ray, but it might structure my time. I have been noticing that I am spending more and more of it sucking freebase in my little basement room. On the in-between days, it bothers me. I show more enthusiasm for this concept than I really mean.

'Really? We could call it Ruthless and Ray . . .'

'Not really . . . there is just one condition,' he says, leaning forward and putting his hand on my knee in a gesture that is fatherly and salacious at the same time, 'just don't embarrass me in public . . .' I take his hand off my knee and replace it on his own. I smile.

'Fine, as long as you don't embarrass me in private . . .' Slamdunk for the white girl! Ray laughs. He looks more feral than ever. Jagged, yellowing teeth emphasize the molelike aspects of his demeanor. How do these people make all this money and never straighten their teeth? In Ray's case, caps would be a better choice. I laugh back and set off little jingles of high-ness in every pore. It feels good, sitting and laughing and rocking with Ray.

The rest we do from memory. My people will call his people. In the pecking order my people make the first call. Ray leaves, ostensibly a happy man. I'm happy, too. Ostensibly. I power back to the basement room and puff away. I call Norman. He is delirious to make the first call.

'Norman, I need an office with an attached bathroom,' I add to his list of deal points, thinking ahead. I will need some place private to smoke my drugs. Norman assumes I want Ray to grant me important-person status and thinks it will be no problem. Suck. Suck harder. Be a good girl. Swallow, and try not to bite the dick that feeds you.

David Parks is jubilant. It is the first time in a month his cheeks have any color to them . . . he isn't even bothered by

Rottweiler hulking, lurking, waiting for me to pass the pipe . . .

'Whaddya think is really going on?' he says, posing the question I've been asking myself. Has he been sent by Herbie Allen Hirschfield to neutralize me? Or were they all sitting around one day wondering out loud if it was time to kill me, and Ray raised his hand like that annoying kid with glasses in the first row in third grade, and said: I'll do it, I'll do it? Jesus, this drug feeds the paranoia. While I sleep, I have the occasional rational flash; it says: You are not that important to them. Probably Ray thinks he is doing me a favor. When I am smoking freebase, I flash: nobody does favors for free in Hollywood . . .

Word of this impending deal gets out. Suddenly there is a string of show-biz types pilgrimaging to the house on the hill. Hanging out. Smoking my product, because they're curious. I get to witness some pretty interesting behavior behind this newly active social life. One night, a friend of a friend, smelly French trash, pushes my panic button on the burglar alarm, thinking it is a light switch. Twenty minutes later there are four plainclothes police climbing over my retaining walls and a helicopter with a spotlight on the house fifty feet overhead. Everyone panics. I get my driver's license and a hundred-dollar bill and greet them charmingly in my driveway. On the way down the steps, I catch a rush of ether and wonder if I can get them to go quietly. I apologize for the inconvenience, flash my I.D., and throw my money at them. It takes seconds for them to leave, and my performance makes me think I can handle Hollywood again.

An agent from the good old days gets a tape of *Performance*, one of my all-time favorite movies, and brings it to me personally. He stays for four hours till I'm down to the bottom of visible stash.

'You know what your problem is,' he says, pulling ferociously on the pipe and getting nothing, 'you smoke too much of this stuff.' An audacious remark, even for an agent.

Rottweiler and I exchange a look. It will be a line we will call back to each other for days. Mordant junkie humor.

The same agent decides it will be good for me to show up at the AFI do honoring François Truffaut. Good ol' she-is-incompetent-unprofessional-I-em-zo-zorry François. The irony of the entire endeavor is what gets me there. I wear a bright red Alpha Cubic pantaloon-and-jacket number with a white tuxedo weskit. I am so thin everything hangs.

We are not seated at a particularly chic table; the other up-andcomers in our party make rude remarks about me and my famous drug habit in stage whispers to each other. I defend myself with an interior litany of others who were precocious and peaked early: Orson Welles, Philip Roth, fuck it, go for the biggie – Alexander the Great: conquered the world, died at thirty-three. This thought stops me cold: I'm thirty-five . . .

CUT FROM A MOVIE:

OVO: My mother, lying Naked Maja position on the couch, obfuscated somewhat by the cloud of smoke she creates by puffing furiously on a Camel. CAMERA TRUCKS IN and she says, over and over IN SLOW MOTION
MOM: Sometimes I think we all died and we're living in hell, living in hell, living in hell, hell, hell, hell . . .

I pan the gathering with my camera I and notice another irony: there are more people lined up to do their little tooties in the bathrooms, which are close by, than at any of the tables, ours included. I disdain toot now that I have discovered freebase, which has replaced everything: food, sex, love, work – even tobacco. During this endless evening, however, I go through a pack of Marlboros, a distraction from the freebase crash, the lassitude of which could end with me taking a nap in my soup . . .

The deal is going along nicely, Ray agreeing to some important points – Norman's points more than mine – quickly. It is still an era where the negotiating process is cut short if people really want to make a deal. Every day that Norman calls to report another triumph, I ask about the office with the attached bathroom. I get an I'll-get-back-to-you-on-that brush-off. I start to notice I'm getting no answer.

What I don't know is that the only offices with attached baths are the corner offices. Since my previous experience on the Burbank lot was in a corner suite, I have no idea that the middle sections of these Bates Motel-like structures are bathroomless. Pecking-order bullshit. Ray and Norman have been trying to work out the bathroom issue, but all the corner offices in Ray's building are occupied by people already ensconced in one Rastar, or Ray Stark, project/organization, or another.

When I am finally informed of this unhappy impasse, the deal, in its significant particulars, is closed. There's been a front-page announcement of our joint venture in the trades, David Parks has been paid two weeks salary by Rastar, and I have been doing round-the-clockers thinking of new twists on old movies. That's been Ray's first assignment. How original. How challenging. Think of old movies to remake. Ray wants me on the lot, and I don't want to go. I cop major attitude and say there is no deal.

Ray begs Norman to make me come look at some alternatives; Norman begs me. Parks drives. It is as close as he will come to begging. It is a fetid Santa Ana day. Poison winds with too many positive ions assault my soul as the car crests over Mulholland toward the Valley. I haven't taken a drive in this direction in nearly two years. It has all gotten worse.

By the time we get to Burbank my mood is as rancid as the air. Ray humph-humphs his way through explanation, then tells me he's come up with a solution. He will give me an office next to the ladies' room on the ground floor and break through the wall so I can have a private entrance. He walks me through it, like a child. First the office: large, with a large reception area. Like I care about the fucking office. Where's the bathroom . . .

I find myself cornered in the ladies' room with him. Our voices echo around us as he outlines his plans for renovation.

411

If you hadn't disgraced yourself in Hollywood, you wouldn't have to be here, a wicked little interior voice sings. Involuntarily, I start to back away from Ray, who misunderstands and comes toward me.

'I don't wanna do this,' the little voice says out loud, and now I am backpedaling wildly, almost slipping on the tile, reverb from four sentences ago playing backward in my ears, and I am out the door and actually in my car before an astonished Ray bursts from the ladies' room, waving for me to stop.

'Drive,' I spit at Parks. When he hesitates, I lunge for the wheel and remind him I'll drive if he won't. David would rather be unemployed than dead, so he drives. When I get home, I have my business manager send a reimbursement check to Ray for David's wages. By messenger. It is returned, ripped in half. By messenger. I puff. I laugh. I tack it on the bulletin board, next to a recent pair of concerned love letters from Andrea Eastman and Phyllis Levy begging me to seek professional help for my cocaine addiction . . .

One morning Rottweiler wakes up in a bad mood. We've run out of blow the night before and he's downed himself out with Quaaludes. I melt down all the residue from every pipe, extract leftovers from all the dirty water, make some beautiful amber crystals, and take a shower. When he wakes up and sees me puffing away in the corner of the bedroom he goes from sleep to rage in seconds. He might be having a jealous reaction to my cleanliness as well as my high-ness.

Like all male junkies he takes dope usage as a reason not to bathe. Like all Jewish girls, there is nothing in the world to keep me from a daily shower and shampoo. Not even freebase. Not even Rottweiler. He slams into things and breaks a ten-foot board lying at the foot of the bed into many pieces with his foot. Tears of pain stick out from his eyes.

'You know, just because you're doing some add-ons to the house doesn't mean you have permission to break them every time you get mad.' I always think Rottweiler has gone into construction to atone for his propensity to ravage his surroundings, no matter who they belong to.

'Pigfucker,' he mutters. This is something new and he's mumbled, so I ask him to repeat it distinctly.

'Pigfucker,' he says, in the dulcet tones of the upper class.

'And what does that make you?' Stoopid doodyhead. I puff, watching the base ignite, look up, and pierce him with my icy silver-gray eyes; the eyes always the color of the sky. Today it is gray clouds with silver linings, caused by backlighting from the sun. I know how distracting that look can be. First my father had done it to me, then I'd done it to myself in the mirror for years. I can turn it on the world with predictable effect.

At first, I used it. I had seen it make grown men weep. It didn't make me their particular favorite. Sometimes it just flew out before I could stop it. It said, why, you contemptible little prick (or, piece of shit, or asshole, depending) how dare you be so stupid/rude/suggestive/greedy/presumptuous, etc. This has tended to work against me over the long haul. In time I learned to keep it to myself. I got to study my shoes quite a lot concealing it.

But Rottweiler decides not to stay mad. He wants to get at that pipe, so he gives me an affectionate hug. It is, after all, the day before the day before Christmas. He even takes a shower.

'Let's go Christmas shopping,' he yells over the sound of the blow-dryer. Boy oh boy, this really is a big occasion.

We hit Giorgio's. I get presents for all my family, all his family, and two dozen business associates. It takes hours. I'm over forty grand, when Gale says, 'Aren't you getting anything for yourself?' She hands me a long red fox coat. I put it on.

'How much?'

'For you, seven . . .' I take it. I've spent fifty thousand on Christmas. It brings some weird form of relief.

Psycho Killer, qu'est-ce que c'est? Fafafafafafafafafafa . . .

By New Year's me and Rottweiler are on the outs. Kate and I spend New Year's Eve with Mike Maday (a Vietnam vet who is a classic case of the survivor's syndrome and very talented with stained glass), but I pass out, which makes Kate hysterical. I get the bright idea that he should hold my stash for me. The net effect is that I stampede his house at all hours needing coke and he gets more strung out. New Year's day, as I am taking a shower, there is an earthquake. I feel it is an omen. I've gotta give this shit up. Yeah, next week for sure . . .

The biggest pain Erica ever caused me was her pathetic attempt to apologize for all the previous pain. She calls while she is staying at a friend's nearby, looking for a conciliatory lunch. Her place of course. Her turf. I accept because I am on the way up, cresting in the middle of the second day of a three-day binge. It's quite something to get out of the house even approximately on time, since I keep taking that one last hit for the road, but I finally arrive about a half hour late.

I'm crashing by the time I arrive, which puts the two of us on pretty much the same plane. She's depressed. I remind her of the dinner we had at Henry Miller's place, where she asked him what he did about depression, and he said he took to his bed, till the fever broke. She smiles wanly.

At some point during lunch, she bursts into tears and says she's sorry she wasn't a good friend. I am so eager to get away from her and back to my drugs I accept the apology. I know I won't respect myself in the morning. I never do anymore, anyway . . .

I get seriously ill with an upper respiratory infection, what a surprise. My father calls to tell me that my mother is dying. He doesn't think she'll last a week . . . I book myself on a flight, but I don't wanna I don't wanna. I spike a fever of 102. I cancel my flight. I call my father. It is October seventeenth. Nineteen seventy-eight.

'Mommy died at four-thirty this afternoon. I took her to the hospital, I think she was paralyzed, the doctor came out and told me she was dead . . .'

'Are you okay?' I ask through a fog of snot and drugs and

guilt and antibiotic. Would that the medication could relieve this terrible pain in my chest. Is this grief? Or rage . . .

'I went into the room to see her . . . I said goodbye . . .' Goodbye goodbye. Mommy Mommy do I . . . Mommy Mommy do you . . .

I don't make it to my mother's funeral, either. I let Rottweiler beat me up the night before, after a long day of martinis and coke, and I oversleep. Something in me couldn't make it. She had wanted me and my brother to speak, and the only thing I could think of to say was that we had been bitter enemies all our lives, and that I would miss her more than any of her friends would. Mine anomie grows older . . . but not older enough . . .

My mother, who was rarely sick while I was growing up and living at home, developed one serious malady after another from the moment Michael and I moved to the Coast. I have such a distorted view of her power that I truly think she willed herself to have heart attacks, thromboembolisms, and even cancer as a way of getting to me for moving three thousand miles away. A strange view, but I am truly a product of this self-obsessed crazy person, so I tend to take a rather self-centered worldview myself.

I make it to the party after; my father is forgiving, my brother tight-lipped. Rottweiler shows up later, tears in his eyes. Men can be such good criers when they want . . .

'Here's a rule about smuggling,' Finslander says. 'You never send an empty mode of transport either way.' Finslander is a medium-sized smuggler who really wants to direct. Probably everyone around Hollywood was like that in the sixties heyday when anybody under thirty and over twenty-two with a light meter around his neck could get a development deal from John Calley at Warners. At least. Sometimes they got to direct. Finslander's fame and fortune crested in the sixties when he went off to Mexico to create the perfect hybrid marijuana and came up with sensimillia. I remember a surfer selling me some all the way back in '74. Purple seedless, he called it. If you held it under a light it did look purple.

Finslander shipped it back in great quantities in iceberg lettuce freezer bags, so a lot of people called it iceberg lettuce, and quite a few developed the habit of keeping the product in the freezer. Thus do myths begin. He also married a Wayne sister, I can never remember if it was Nina or Carol. Probably he and Reilly O'Reilly traveled in some of the same circles, although Reilly was never a particular herbal enthusiast. Probably they had the same taste in women.

Prince Albert financed Finslander's operations from time to time. When I first met Prince Albert in 1971, he was blowing coke down Ringo Starr's throat. He did this for five hours so I'm pretty sure it was his job. He was one of those coke dealers who got his thrills from the star-fucking aspects of the trip.

Ringo put it bluntly: 'Prince Albert will provide me with anything I want because I'm a star. He doesn't even expect the stardom to rub off on him, he just likes to be around it. He provides the drugs and I provide the stardom. It's one of the most honest and satisfactory relationships I've ever had.'

Prince Albert isn't in it for the money. He is to the manor born, the heir apparent to a toxin-producing-fertilizer fortune. When I meet him he is thirty-five and he has never really worked, unless you count all that blowing of coke down the throats of the great and near-great work.

There are certain requisite paraphernalia to the coke dealer's lifestyle. I'm not speaking of the obvious ones: the apothecary scales, the Deering strainers, the onionskin paper, the Baggies, the bottles, the mannite, the mannitol, procaine, lidocaine, sugar, and all manner of cuts.

I'm referring to more exalted toys. Prince Albert has them all: the fifty-thousand-dollar remodeled bathroom, with the best and quietest Jacuzzi in town, which periodically breaks down because in the words of his Hispanic maid, 'There are too many spermas,' the closed-circuit TV, mirrors and tooters, along with the Bose speakers of the highest quality and all the bootleg Dylan, Stones, and Jimi Hendrix tapes the ear can stand.

416

Prince Albert drives a Jaguar of that good English racing-green-color variety. He buys his clothes at Bijan and his accoutrements at Gucci. He has a beeper of the type that doctors carry and he has a sort of benign, somewhat remote veneer that keeps his house safe from desperate junkies, rip-off artists, and cops.

Rich people and great people and talented people and famous people take him to dinners and concerts and villas in the south of France and curry his favor. And Prince Albert treats them all like what they are: coke whores.

One of the reasons probably that Prince Albert lives in the safety of a noncommitted existence and never gets busted or robbed or slaughtered, is that he never overuses. He never overextends either. He is not so eager to hang out that he is willing to make deliveries or front large quantities of dope. No favors from the Prince. His theater is one of total self-involvement and self-protection.

My theater is one where I never take gifts and I always pay in cash. I have established this snobbery of never letting any of my dealers feed my nose out of their stash. If such a thing is possible, I command their respect. My theater is not unlike theirs. Over the years, the Prince gets to like me. And over the years I get him to make the occasional delivery.

The Prince comes over one day with a rather large delivery and I suppose if he had thought about it he might say that that day was the beginning of the end for him, because that is the day that I turn him on to freebase for the very first time. He sucks it in, he holds it down, he exhales languorously, and his eyes glaze over in junkie ecstasy. He is seeing Nirvana. 'Wow,' he says. Which is a lot, since the Prince is not only a man of very few words, but also a man who is penurious with his praise.

Once Prince Albert insisted on being able to participate personally in a small marijuana smuggling venture Fins was running or he wouldn't put up the money. A case of my ball, my rules – or more precisely, my balls, I rule. He was a terrible candidate for anything as physical as hauling great bails of pot onto a small fast boat and/or as dangerous as outrunning Federales, should they appear. Finslander tried to dissuade him from such a silly notion, but the Prince got more tenacious the more Fins protested. Finslander acquiesced and the Prince went along for the long ride to and from Mexico.

They were pursued by Federales. Finslander, who had done this many times before, was prepared to outrun and/or outshoot them. Albert, the Jewish Prince/Pussy, started throwing the hefty bags full of boo overboard. Finslander was immobilized for a tiny moment, stunned at the sight of the Prince throwing away his money. Then in a rage, he threw the Prince overboard and left him for the Federales.

They didn't speak for nearly three years, but when they reconciled, the Prince told Finslander he could introduce him to the person who really made *Close Encounters*, one of Finslander's favorite movies. I didn't see anybody old or meet anybody new, save a few dealers who would make house calls. I was deep into suffering with Rottweiler and this freebase jones at the same time. I had heard some famous Finslander stories, so I was just as intrigued to meet him.

The deal is the Prince will provide product and I will cook and share, and chat up old Finslander. Okay. Fine with me. When will you be here? Is right now too soon? Right now is fine, because the Prince doesn't know how to cook freebase yet. He wants me to teach him. If I do, I won't get these nice little deliveries. But sharing, you run out so much quicker. I am going through cash on this shit at a terrific pace, but I am with the wrong business manager, and he doesn't say boo to me, he is so intimidated.

The sheer hell of life with Rottweiler under the roof is almost too much even for a pain junkie like me. When he buys an AR-15, I tell myself it's for our protection, but I start to fear for the lives of me and Kate and Jackie. Rottweiler has gotten incredibly violent a few times.

He has totally taken the fun out of freebase and yet I know that, somehow, he comes along with it. We are coming to the end of a terrifying time, and it is getting downright ugly. I can throw him out at any time, but somehow I have become the victim in my own domain; heavy drug use has debilitated me emotionally. Finslander becomes my cheerleader, and accelerates the long-overdue split.

For starters, he hasn't been into freebase for six months, so he looks a lot better than Rottweiler, who is a basically handsome man. Finslander has a deep voice and a great smile and a long, lean, muscular body. I have been living indoors for almost eight months. I need new furniture. Finslander turns out to be good company. When he leaves, he practically breaks my back, he hugs me so hard. Which makes Rottweiler furious. Just like Michael, years before, when Reilly O'Reilly told me that my eyes were hypnotic.

The Prince brings Ringo around, too. One night, Rottweiler has a snit in front of them and, huffy, I carry the pipe and the product into my room. They sit with him for a moment, male bonding, then fuck that off and come find me. The power of the pipe. This is dangerous turf. I am almost at the point where I don't love the danger so much anymore. Inside every animal is the will to survive.

Finslander visits regularly. I have the feeling he'd like to get out of the business, but can't. He's been on the outside so long there is no way back in.

Finally our friendship freaks Rottweiler out and he holds the loaded AR-15 on me and Kate at five o'clock one morning.

I race back to Jackie's room and lock us in. He storms down the hall and bangs heavily on the door. Then he retreats. Back into the 'office,' the drug room. Kate and I are huddled in each other's arms on the bed. Linda the weekend nanny is trembling. All three of us are sobbing. He buzzes me on the intercom.

'I'm calm. Come down here and talk to me . . .'

'Not with a gun . . .'

'I just wanna talk . . .'

'Not with a gun . . .' I have my woman producer voice.

'It's not loaded . . .' He sobs a loud sob, but he doesn't cry.

'Okay, I'm coming down . . .' You fool you fool. I unwrap myself from Kate and grab a tissue. I blow my nose loudly – fuck you, Miss Marlowe! – dry my eyes. Kate sits up in the bed and I pick her up in my arms. 'Linda, get your act together; you're going to Michael's early . . .' They are due for a visit in the late afternoon. It is currently late morning. 'Go out this door, don't say goodbye.'

Linda is smart, gets that this is the correct course for the situation. She begins to pack Kate's things. Kate starts to cry. She burbles that she won't leave until I come back to the room. Kate is smart, too, and wants to reconfirm in her baby mind that Mommy didn't get killed trying to get Rottweiler out of the house.

I'm frustrated, worried for their personal safety, but I say okay. I signal to Linda with my dead eyes to keep getting ready for an earlier departure. Maybe this won't be as tough as I fear. Fear . . . I hate this feeling.

I'll do anything to overcome this feeling, even face Rotten Rottweiler with a gun.

I hand Kate to Linda. They look so worried. I start to walk away from them to my Destiny, and Kate calls after me, 'Don't forget to come back . . .'

The door to the office is closed. I feel like I am approaching the door to the bedroom in *The Exorcist*. I blast through.

Rottweiler is half in the bag, flopped across a pillow chair. The gun rests across his lap.

'I want you the fuck out of here,' I start. I don't think this situation calls for a preamble. I keep on the move, back and forth in front of the stained glass. All six panels are complete and installed. I love the window. Although I had said, 'I want from the desert to the mountains to the sea, to all of southern California . . .' and everything was there but sea.

'Where's my water; what if I want to move into this scenario . . .'

'Oh, it's there, an oasis behind that panel,' Mike Maday had replied, and he pointed to the black wood panel holding two sections together . . .

Rottweiler points the gun somewhere in the vicinity of the hidden oasis. It is hard to tell if he intends to wreak havoc on my window or my person. I am so whacked out they seem one and the same to me. I squint my eyes.

'What're you doing, assassinating the window! The one beautiful thing in this whole fucking room?!@#'

He squeezes off a shot and I duck. It makes a tiny puncture in the window, right in the neck of a mountain lion Maday has resting on a mesa.

420

'I want a settlement . . . I want money!' he cries.

'Anything, anything, just get the fuck out of here . . .' He starts to say something, falls asleep in the middle of the sentence. I run out of the office and lock him inside. I call Finslander at Albert's. Thank God for Finslander, the man who loves danger. I fly back to Kate and Linda and convince them I have the situation in hand, they should leave. As they do, Fins arrives.

We creep into the office. Rottweiler is asleep, the gun cradled in his lap like a babe. Finslander grabs the gun. Rottweiler stirs but doesn't wake. We go in my bedroom. I call Norman. He hires me a detective and we start packing up Rottweiler's belongings, most of which are presents from me.

The detective, Jim Briscoe, arrives. He's a gangster, like everyone. He and Fins exchange tough-guy stories. They go into the office and wake Rottweiler sharply. They walk him to his packed car. They don't want me to talk to him, but I go over to the window on the driver's side. I hand him some hundreds. He has tears in his eyes . . .

Three weeks after his departure, I am sure I am pregnant. I go to Milstein to confirm. I have an image of a rat growing within me, the Rottweiler Rat, but I have been so busy smoking coke I have ignored it. I am already showing. I figure I'm three, four months pregnant, but Milstein says no, it's less, but let's deal with it now. He books me into the eighth floor, the VIP floor, at Cedars.

Throughout the entire sexual revolution I've never had an unwanted pregnancy, but I had decided on my thirty-fifth birthday that I would have a lot of trouble getting pregnant and that birth control pills, which I'd been taking all my adult life with no noticeable effect, were bad for my health. I actually smoke freebase in the hospital, right up until the abortion. Talk about bad for your health. It takes the combined efforts of Mighty Mo, Mike, and Marcia to get me checked in.

I sleep eight long hours after the operation, and wake up to a black dude named Toute de Suite, who looks like Chuck

Berry, hovering, wheelchair at the ready. He seems in an unnecessary rush to wheel me out, but then, it is I, over Milstein's objection, who have decreed that I should leave on the same day. In-and-out abortion. I know I can't be away from my drugs overnight. When I get home, I am so depleted I sleep another three days, which is just as well, since I can't really move my legs . . .

When I wake up, Kate is hanging out in my bed, watching cartoons. She's propped up against a bolster, with her long wavy hair strewn out from her angel face, looking like a little princess. Except for the black, almond-shaped eyes, one a little sleepier than the other, which makes her disturbingly ancient and sexy. An ad featuring baby pictures of Shirley Temple comes on the screen.

'Hi, Mommy.' Kate smiles beatifically and speaks in a high peepy voice with just a trace of an English accent.

'Hey,' I say, noticing that my legs hurt and they don't move very well. I pull myself into a sitting position.

'Mommy, is that the child star I'm supposed to look like?' She indicates Shirley Temple, who is singing 'The Good Ship Lollipop.' Kate likes the rhythm, so she sings along. It makes the resemblance more obvious. Sure, even Kate could see it; God knows, she spends enough time in front of the mirrored sliding doors outside her room. Just like Mommy.

'That's her . . .' I wiggle my toes under the covers and pain shoots up my legs into the deepest of my female sector. I feel like shit and I don't know if I can walk over to the armoire where I keep my stash.

'Mommy, is she still a child star?'

'Well, no, she grew up . . .' then a two-minute dissertation on Shirley's marriages and careers, including the U.N. post and the mastectomy. The cartoons are back on so I presume my daughter's silence is mindlock with the TV.

'Mommy . . .'

'. . . Yessss. . .'

'Were you a star?' Pronounced *stahhww*. Count on Kate to

ask the deep philosophical question while I'm trying to figure out if I'm paralyzed or not.

'Why do you ask that?'

'Well, I was thinking of all the pictures in the office . . . they look like the pictures in the ad . . .'

'Well, I was what is known as a behind-the-scenes star . . . kind of a seminame, as it were . . .' Why am I doing this, and can I walk? I will my legs to move and they do. Get out of bed and over to the armoire. Painumb, painumb, painumb. Need more numb here. Stash on one side, works on the other. Welcome to my nightmare.

'Mommy . . .'

'Y-e-e-s-s-s . . .'

'Are you still a behind-the-scenes star?' No, darling, I'm a junkie.

'Well, I'm on hiatus . . .' Sort of between pictures, as it were. Between money. Between a rock and a hard place. As it were. I open the armoire. Between stash, too. Not much left. *Quel* drag. Well, enough for one respectable batch . . . Half leaning against the counter for support, I make up a batch in the bathroom, shuffle back to bed. Kate flicks channels while I light a torch.

'Religion,' she says, watching *Lenny* on Z. He is reading from his court transcripts. He is not funny.

'That's a movie . . .'

'No, religion . . . see . . .' She switches the channels and there is Gene Scott, reading from the Bible. She switches back and forth, turns to me and smiles widely. 'See . . . Religion . . .' I laugh behind my puffage, then:

'Oh, Mommy is so funny . . .' *What?* 'Mommy will do anything to make Kate laugh . . .' What what what? 'Look Mommy . . .' And I follow her little finger to where she is pointing. I have set fire to Pete Turner's dye print of the road. A *Close Encounters* present. Flames are shooting out from the road. I tamp them out with my pillow.

Jesus, I gotta give this shit up, soon. Yeah, next week for sure . . .

*

I miss seven flights from Los Angeles to Rochester, Minnesota, between October 12 and October 15, 1979. I am checking myself into the Alcohol and Drug Dependencies Unit (ADDU, as in *adieu* – to all those fun things) at the Mayo Clinic for not less than one month, hoping against hope I can rid myself of a horrendous, all pervasive cocaine addiction. I figure if I don't, someone might convince my father that the only thing to do with me is to commit me to a hospital. Ever the control freak, I'll beat them all and commit myself. *Them all* has by this time been reduced to maybe half a dozen people in the whole world who still care about me, much less even wonder if I am still alive.

At least if you sign yourself in, you can sign yourself out. And it is ADDU, not Psychiatric, and it is sure as hell not like being committed by anyone else. In my paranoid fantasies it seems that nothing could be worse than to relinquish control of my life to that extent. I have diminished to ninety-three pounds. I have strained my large but not unending resources to the point where I am going to have to dip into principal, which it has been some fucking struggle for a string of semiadequate business managers to keep me from spending entirely, not just on coke but on all the other grandiose expressions of consumption that coke inspires: cars, jewelry, furs, trips, houses, presents, and messengers. Messengers to buy the coke, messengers to bring the coke to the house when you get too tired to go out at all, or too paranoid about transporting the quantity necessary to keep you from getting depressed, never mind getting high.

The first plane or two I miss sheerly out of spite – the kind of spite only a junkie can understand – spite born out of the fear and frustration that my tool, my crutch, my reason for living, is going to be taken away from me. What will I do without it? Smoking freebase has pretty much been my job for the past year. I have already sent Kate and Jackie to Michael's house. They have bought me my very own Snoopy to take with me and left me with hugs and kisses and a great deal of hope.

I am to leave the next day – afternoon, of course, because I am never up in the morning, unless, of course, I have been up for days. And I have been up for days because I've decided that I am going to finish up my habit with a bang, not a whimper. With everyone gone, I decide it will be an interesting experience to smoke my base in every room in the house – even Kate's. What a violation! So I miss the first plane because I'm still taking that one last hit for the road. I arrive at the airport just a hair later than the plane's departure.

The second plane I miss because I'm doing a fastidious and unnecessary inventory of my jewelry. Needless to say, this can take a considerable amount of time when you have been up for three days.

The third and fourth planes I sleep through.

The fifth plane I miss because I'm waiting for another delivery of cocaine. I am in such a frenzy of overconsumption that David Parks, my assistant and only real friend at the time, is afraid I am going to have a nervous breakdown before I ever get to the Mayo Clinic. He tries everything: reasoning, cajoling, screaming, freaking out, and books another flight.

I can't even remember now why I missed it. Probably I was taking a nap. The nap of someone coming down from base usually lasts about twenty-four hours.

The seventh I sleep through again.

Finally David tells me that he will not book another flight unless I swear to him that I'll make it. And that Tom Stout, my travel agent, will never book another flight for me again in my life. That seems reasonable enough, and I am ready to go at least three hours before it is time for me to leave my house.

So we get into the limousine, me and David Parks and Mike Maday and all my many bags and two fur coats because it is cold in Minnesota, and a pipe and a propane tank and the last of my stash – an eighth in a Baggie, and a bag of Famous Amos cookies. Maybe it's the fumes, or maybe the anxiety, but halfway to the airport David's face goes ashen and he has to throw up into my Famous Amos cookies.

We are greeted like royalty curbside, which is a good thing, because there is no way I am going to make it under my own power from check-in to takeoff. Tom Stout drives us in a VIP golf cart to an elevator that takes us to the first-class lounge. By the time the plane is boarding, I am so weak, David and

Tom have to carry me onto the plane. David and I buckle our seatbelts and look at each other grimly.

'Oh, David,' I say plaintively, 'how did we ever get here?' Meaning all of it. The missed flights, the missed steps, the missed chances.

'By limo,' he says.

I smoke freebase on the ends of my cigarettes all the way to Rochester, Minnesota. David freaks out each time, like we're going to get busted on the plane. I have to light them with the trusty tortoiseshell Dunhill Norman gave me all those years ago to light my way to 'fame, fortune, and beautiful lovers, not necessarily in that order,' so I lose half a hit each time I light up and it burns brown. It smells like stale Gauloises, i.e., dirty feet.

We are picked up by probably the only limo in a five-hundred-mile radius and arrive at admissions after midnight, which seems appropriate. A series of gay nurses take charge of me. I particularly like the wheelchair ride from curbside through the maze of tunnels that connect all the hospitals. Somewhere very close to the end of the journey, I catch a whiff of ether, and I think I must remember this location for when things get rough.

They let David, who is booked into the Kaylor Hotel for however long I need him to stay, come up to the floor where ADDU is located, but finally a moment for parting is ordained by the night nurse on duty. Big. Tough. With a heart of gold. There's a reason for clichés: they're true. I start to cry. It is one o'clock in the morning, but easily half of the twenty-four patients on this floor are awake, mostly in the common room watching television and smoking. But it is very still, like a cancer floor. Terminal junkies in limbo, waiting for the next bus to come. My crying gets very loud and David shushes me, like we are disturbing people. I don't care, I figure if ever there were a group of strangers who understood, these would.

Big Nurse gives me a Librium 25 and puts me to bed. I insist on staying in my fox coat. I am very cold. I know mascara has run down my face, but I don't wash it. I shiver, my California blood in shock from the chill of October in Minnesota. I fall asleep. When I wake up my head is jammed under the sheet at the foot of the bed. I struggle, but I'm making it worse, like fighting the tide instead of waiting for the next big wave. Someone is saying, Don't worry, I'll have you out of there in a jiffy, but I'm hacking away at those sheets. I feel like air is being sucked out of me. Then a gush of cold air, and a pudgy freckled pretty face peering into my cave.

'Hi, I'm Debbie*. I'm your roommate.' Her smile reveals crooked chipped teeth. I am in the Middle West, no doubt about it. I push and she pulls and the sheets are off my face.

'I kept asking the nurse if we should turn you around.'

'And what did she have to say about that?'

'She kept saying, "Oh, they do that when they first get here." I didn't do that when I first got here.'

'How long have I been here?'

'Three days.' Panic. Have I peed in my bed? I check. Nope. Just a lot of mascara. Has David left? Nah, he would want to make sure I'm really ensconced, or I might fly the coop. I stick my hand deep into the pockets of my coat. The Baggie with the freebase is still there. It feels like at least a gram plus. My heart makes a little leap in my chest, like in a cartoon. I can feel my face heat up and my ears start to ring.

'Are you okay?' Debbie moves forward and helps me steady myself. I am queasy, and a headache from deep background starts to bang. Just then, another nurse pops her head in the door. This one is young and blond and trim – Big Nurse's girlfriend? My mouth feels like an army has marched through it, and my expensive cashmere dress is sticking to me. How bad do I smell under this coat? Instinctively I pull it tightly around me, snuggling my secret packet of drugs.

'Oh good, you're finally up. We need you to unpack and you need to meet Dr. Morse and Dr. Volker.' Dr. Morse is the head honcho, the guy Howard Koch had called to get me in quick. Howard had had multi-bypass surgery here and made a substantial contribution in return for his life. I'd called him in desperation a month before:

'Howard, I know you have a weak heart, but I need a rather large favor.' I'd worked with Howard on *The Big Bus*, and he'd become a kind of a grandfather to me. He seemed to be impressed mainly with my having shot a card game in my AFI Women Directors' tape without ever fucking up the eyeline.

'Shoot,' he said, clearly unaware of my drug problem.

'Well, Howard, for the past year of my life, I've been living in one room in my house, smoking freebase –'

'What's that?'

'It's a smokable version of cocaine. I'm doing about a half an ounce a day –'

'Jesus,' he said with a gasp. I hoped my story didn't kill him before he could help me.

' – I weigh ninety pounds, I don't eat, I'm strung out –'

'Stop. Stop. What do you want me to do?'

'Well, I'm wondering if the Mayo Clinic has a rehab center. I figure if they do, it's got to be the very best . . .'

'Don't go anywhere or do anything. I'll get into it right away.' This was obviously a man who didn't know much about junk, although I suspected that his son, with a junior tagged at the end of his name, might. I wasn't going anywhere or doing anything. This phone call would probably be my major activity of the day. I started to cry, partly with gratitude, and partly because I was at the point where I was smoking freebase the way I smoked cigarettes. I smoked about three packs of cigarettes a day before freebase. Now I only smoked a cigarette if I ran out of coke. I liked the taste better than tobacco. Just now I needed a hit, which is not easy to do without repelling the person on the other end of the phone, as waterpipes make a great deal of noise. I was glad the phone call was over.

Howard called within an hour and told me that he'd talked to Robert Morse about a space that would be coming up in three weeks. My first reaction was why was an undersize actor running the show, but I laughed only to myself. 'Book it,' I said and promised to call the guy in fifteen minutes. An hour later, just as Kate came in to say hello after school, I was on the phone working out details. 'October fifth? Okay, I'll see you October fifth,' I concluded and hung up the phone. I was very excited to tell Kate the news, as she had been the inspiration for this move.

428

Just the week before, I had been swinging her around wildly to the Rolling Stones singing 'Miss You,' extra-strong from a powerful hit, and I had looked down at her beautiful little face. She was smiling up at me, adoring me with her eyes, and I thought, I would really like to be worthy of this unconditional love. I stopped swinging her and said, 'This has got to stop, this has got to stop right here.' My mother with her pills and discontent, me with my coke and insecurity, next it would be her, probably just plugging herself right into an electrical socket. Thinking that it was the swinging that had to stop, Kate did what any reasonable five-year-old would do – she sobbed.

And she was sobbing now, which was a disheartening reaction, considering that I was committing myself to a trip to the Midwest in the fall, not to mention relinquishing a drug that was the best boyfriend I ever had. 'What's the matter, don't you think it's time for Mommy to give up drugs?'

'But what about my birthday?' October 7, 1973. My polar opposite. The *Sting* baby. The New Hollywood Baby. My Baby.

'Omigod, you're right. I was so intent on getting into this program, I didn't think. Don't cry, I'll go after your birthday.' Morse wasn't thrilled, but he was amenable. For some arbitrary reason, new patients were only admitted on a weekly basis, so my foray into sobriety would be postponed for a week.

'I really wouldn't put it off too much longer,' he admonished. I concurred. I was spending fifteen grand a week on drugs and having convulsions from smoking hits that were at least three-quarters of a gram.

And now, I am going to meet the big man himself. Before that is to take place, however, I get to meet the psych assistant, Dr. Volker, a flushed, open-faced, smug resident, whom I hate on sight. I think he must hate me too, but this is probably more a reaction to my appearance than anything. I haven't bothered to remove three days of smudged mascara from my face before our meeting. Also, I am wrapped in this giant red fox coat. To be perfectly honest, my skin and its color aren't particularly attractive, either.

Plus, he knows who I am and there is a natural tendency for midwesterners to dislike and distrust anyone from either coast. Deeply. I am from both. We get into a fight right away. He wants me to check my coat into a safe downstairs. Orders me, in fact. I remind myself he is younger than me, the little prick, and say no fucking way. He raises his voice, a bad policy with someone who grew up in a house of yellers, where interruption was a craft perfected at the dinner table. I raise the ante, and pretty soon patients are eavesdropping and Big Nurse is approaching me in a threatening manner.

But I have faced off a series of violent boyfriends in the past and have learned that standing your ground is pretty menacing to most bullies. She stops just short of invading my required two feet of territorial space, suspended, waiting for some direction from a superior. Volker, predictably, is on his feet, red-faced and screaming. What a dick. What a movie. What a waste. I feel despair cut through my rage. These people are not going to help me. I instruct my shoulders not to slump, because if they do, these two will be subduing me within seconds. Just now, they are scared.

'What's going on here?' A bespectacled, sweet-faced fat guy stands at the door, smoking his pipe in a casual way. He is wearing a large brown suit and a mantle of confidence. I am glad he is here. He offers his hand, 'Hi, I'm Ray Island.' Beware the short man, I said. And the fat man, Redford said back. I shake his hand, hard, just like Daddy taught me.

'Julia Phillips.'

'Ah, the new kid . . .' he smiles. Oh, so that's it. Am I ever going to get out of high school? And when will World War II be over. Already. 'What's going on in here?' There is a nice little edge to his voice. Maybe he doesn't like Volker either. Big Nurse moves out of the room and down the hall in a millisecond; Volker adjusts his glasses and takes a deep breath.

'You know our policy, Ray. She can't keep the fur coat up here.'

'Look, Ray, I come from California – you know, sunshine,

warm air' – I haven't been outside during the day for a year, but what does he know? – 'I'm gonna freeze my ass off here without the coat. I didn't bring a cloth one.'

'Well, you don't get to go out for a week, but I can see your point . . .'

'Well then, fuck it, I'm leaving . . .' I know my rights! I look toward the door, but I don't make a move.

'You can keep the coat,' Ray says, 'just give the program a chance.' Give the pogrom a chance? Give me a fucking break.

'Well, this isn't a particularly propitious start,' I say, facing him, with my back to Volker. 'Are you a doctor?'

'No, I'm a recovered alcoholic. Come with me, I'd like you to meet Dr. Morse.' He steers me out of the room, and I can tell from the angle of his head that he is signaling with his eyes to the shrink. Who do they think they are dealing with here? I have been up long enough now so that I am starting to think about having some drugs. I put my hands back into my pockets. With all this body heat, my stash will probably melt before I can get to it.

Now I am in the office next door meeting the first guy who looks like a real doctor. More glasses – doesn't anybody here see 20/20? Medium height, decent tweed suit, kindly manner. This has to be Dr. Morse!

'Ah, you're awake!' He smiles warmly. 'How do you feel?' This is the first time anyone has asked me that question. I think about it for a moment.

'Better than I expected,' I say, surprised.

'We're going to keep you on these Librium 25s for another day or two. Help you over some rough spots.'

'How many of these Librium 25s per day, exactly?'

'One every three hours.'

'That's a hundred fifty milligrams a day,' I exclaim, outraged. I have perused a lot of *PDR*s in my time, shopping for drugs I might want to try some day. One hundred fifty mils of Librium a day is a hefty dose. As in, enough to subdue a horse, never mind a ninety-three-pound weakling. Ah-h-h, fuck it, give the program a chance. Take the downers. You'll need them . . . You haven't died yet . . . Okay guys, give it your best shot . . . 'I'm exhausted,' I say, 'and I could use a shower . . .'

They let me go back to my little room. Debbie the room-mate is hanging out. My two giant bags stuffed with too many clothes take up half our room. I check out the closet space . . . ridiculous. Good thing I've thrown everything on hangers, like Nick McLean taught me to do on location.

Debbie and I heft one of the suitcases up on my bed and I open it. What a paean to conspicuous consumption! Three years of drowning my sorrows at Charles Gallay. Debbie helps me unpack, oohing and aahing the entire time. How nice for her that I am living up to the prejudices civilians have about the people in the business of show.

'Listen, hon,' she says, 'you really need a shower . . . why don't I unpack these for you . . .' I squint at this apparently honest, open face. Is she going to scurry off with some Zoran cashmere? I inhale deeply. She is right, I need a shower and I don't care if she holds up a few dresses across her robust frame. I peel down, which shocks her. 'My god, you're so thin!' I look in the mirror. At least my hair is growing in. A good inch all the way around.

It had taken me three solid days to cut all my hair off. I had actually come up with some interesting dos along the way. I had certainly hung out with Victor long enough to have picked up some of the principles. Even a bit of the craft. But I got cocaine compulsive midway through and just kept cutting and cutting until my hair was a half an inch all around. With the ninety-pound body, and the huge eyes, made huger by the complete lack of hair, I looked a lot like the ET from *Close Encounters*. My skin tone was similar, too. I thought I looked gorgeous. When Finslander came to visit later in the day, he took one look and said, 'Julia hates herself!' and we both laughed. Drug humor, if there is any, is generally of the gallows variety.

Halfway through my shower, which feels wonderful and prickly at the same time, I remember my stash in the coat pocket. I hope Debbie isn't going through my things. Fuck it, she won't know what it is anyway. Middle western. Alcohol and pills, no doubt.

She has actually hung up a good portion of the most useful clothing in one closet, and is folding the Zorans into one little chest. 'Y'know, we could make lunch if you want . . .' I feel shy, but I'm also starved. And by the way, where's my Librium? 'We can get the Librium at the nurses' station,' Debbie says.

I get dressed quickly in some Harriet Selwyn Fragments pull-on pants/tights and a metallic Krizia sweater with over-the-knee boots, pull at my hair. If I hit it with the blow-dryer for a millisecond, I can make it stand straight up. I do it. I have to . . .

I meet some people at lunch. They are all ages and types, but there are a lot more men than women. Good. I get into a conversation with a cherubic guy named Tim*. He's an alcoholic, has been since he was twelve. I ask him how old he is. Twenty-three. I have a moment of feeling middle-aged. Well, I am. Halfway home. He tells me he's been in and out of treatment programs and halfway houses since he was fifteen . . . I remember when I was fifteen and marvel at how time has marched on.

'When I was fifteen they put me in a halfway house, and I tried to kill myself. I tried to off myself by throwing a blow-dryer into a bath I was sitting in. I must have blacked out and come to, but I thought I'd died and I was in hell. The first thing that happened was that two wetbrains asked me for a light . . . it took me a half an hour to realize I was still alive in the halfway house . . . I was very disappointed . . .' He laughs at his own irony, very Sam Levenson, and I laugh along with him.

'What's a wetbrain?'

'A drunk . . .' Ooh, more lingo.

Ray Island is married to a handsome white-haired woman named Mary Jane. She has been sober for nine years. I ask her if she knows her name is a nickname for marijuana. She likes me in spite of myself.

*

Every couple of days I play with the Baggie with the stash. I don't go into it, but I don't throw it away. Like an ex-smoker who carries a pack. Just in case . . .

I go to my first group session. There are about eight of us. Sitting opposite me is a handsome doctor who is getting over a Ritalin addiction. I cross my legs Indian style, and he accuses me of making an overt sexual gesture toward him. In your dreams, babe. I review my history. At the end of it, he says, 'You sound like the coke did everything, not you.' Food for thought . . .

There is a one-armed Viet vet southern amphetamine freak. We hate each other on sight. One day he can't stop talking about how much he misses his drugs. I break out in a cold sweat, missing mine more. Knock it off, I say, in my stern woman producer's voice. This provokes a fight, which I win. We both cry. Call it a draw. We become buddies . . . He shows me Polaroids of his dogs, whippets and greyhounds. I wonder if he raced them at the track in Mobile . . .

After a week, I get let out. I run with Tim. It exhausts me. That night we go to an AA meeting. When I stand up I say, 'My name is Julia and I'm a junkie.' Volker, who is sitting in front of me, turns around and beams . . .

It is my turn to speak to the group. I wring their hearts out by telling them I was brought up an atheist and I have trouble with this Higher Power concept. They applaud. The people, they need a leader . . .

I call Kate at Michael's. He gets on the phone, wanting to be supportive. We have a fight about whether our producing partnership was really fifty/fifty.

'Sixty/forty,' I shout, 'that's my highest offer!' He tells me I cut off his balls. 'I had to look pretty hard to find them,' I retort. Is this what getting better is?

Toward the end of my stay, I decide I want to put something back into the system and I have Norman call all the studios where I made pictures and get them to contribute a sixteen-millimeter version of each film to the Unit.

Tim gets out before me. I fuck him in a room at the Kaylor Hotel. For spite.

My visitors are: My father, Lois Smith, John Ptak, Mighty Mo . . .

All campaigns have slogans. My favorite from drug school is the acronym: HALT! Which stands for: Never Get: too Hungry too Angry too Lonely too Tired. Which is all just too too. Too hungry is the simplest to address so:

I scarf Snickers instead of blow coke. I gain twenty pounds. Which makes me look almost normal.

I have never spent a longer thirty days in my life . . . When I put on my coat to leave, I find the stash in the pocket. Confident, I toss it into the toilet. It is now the saddest flush of my life . . .

I get home from the Mayo Clinic exactly one month after I left. I have done no drugs in thirty days for the first time since I was eleven years old. I have never flown on a plane straight, and when I arrive, my car isn't there. That is because it was picking Mike Maday up on the way, and he was probably having that one last hit for the road.

The car finally arrives, and when I get home Kate and Jackie and Amy and David Parks are all there to meet me.

Everybody is so happy to see me looking so healthy and being so clear. I walk around the house. Home. I hit the office. I hit the ceiling. My peyote plant is gone! I race out into the kitchen.

'Where's my plant????'

'Oh, it sta'ted to tu'n brown, so I pull' it,' Amy, my Jamaican cook, smiles broadly. You. Pull'. My. Plant?@#*!

Life takes a rapid descent from there. It is November 1979, and there are very few treatment centers or AA programs familiar with freebase, let alone cocaine.

I have no friends left in show business except Norman, and I try to avoid my drug friends.

I am dirty within a week of my return.

I would say, in fact, I experience one of the all-time colossal slips short of death. From November until the end of January, I spend $120,000 on cocaine. Paid for by a piece of my piece of *Close Encounters*, which gives me no peace.

I feel doomed.

I don't talk much to what remains of my very small family for a long time after my mother dies. I talk to my father once in awhile, to my brother not at all. My father wants to come and visit me. Check up on me, would be a better way of putting it. He has tried this once before, but I have made myself completely unavailable.

'I'm a terrible person,' I say to Mighty Mo, sucking on the pipe, watching the white puffy smoke fill the bowl. *Some say the world will end with Quaalude / Others say with base . . .* Cover the hole, blast it into your lungs. *From what I've sampled of the prelude / I hold with Quaalude . . .* Bwong-ong-ong. *But base has grace . . .* Ear-ringing ecstasy infusing all nerve endings. *And will deface.* Who the fuck cares if I'm a terrible person? I pass the pipe to Mighty Mo. 'Do you think I'm a terrible person not to see my father?'

Mo has to take his hit before he answers. He deserves it; he's had a terrible day. I understand. He awakened this morning to find his girlfriend vacuuming and when he made a comment about it, she attacked him with a kitchen knife. Ah, the perils of the pipe. His cheeks are blown out like Dizzy Gillespie's, holding in that hit for maximum overdrive, and he is shaking his head no. He lets out a long, slow exhale and his clear blue eyes go psychotic/stuntman for a moment. 'No, I think you're just being honest . . .' I must shoot him a look that says that this is behavior outside that of normal Jewish children of Jewish parents never mind how hip they are, and he says, 'Okay, very honest, brutally frank . . .'

I can't help it, even through this happy freebase oblivion, I feel I have gone over the top here re: being a bad child. I have gone over the top not going to my mother's funeral. I cannot bear to acknowledge that she is gone. Sometimes I think that the effects of the freebase on me are like the effects of cancer/ chemotherapy on her, and that I am duplicating the process she went through to die. What a sick fuck you are, I say out loud inside. I rest on my side. Way down here, on the floor, so that the ceiling is high enough and the air is cool.

My father persists – who can explain the insane love a parent can have for a child? – and when I finally do see him I mince no words. He is standing on the steps up to the pool. The house is deep in reconstruction repairing Rottweiler's reconstruction. Thank God he isn't around anymore, and I say, 'Look, you might as well know, I'm doing freebase again, I'm going through incredible money, and I have no hope anyone knows how to cure me . . .'

'Jesus Christ,' he mutters, pushing his hand hard over his half-bald pate, the way Robert Duvall does in *Network*, and for just a second, I think, poor Daddy . . .

'What about a hospital?'

'I'm giving it serious thought . . .' I'm not giving serious thought to anything except when my father will leave, so I can get back to my pipe.

My brother has probably written me off for dead. Probably buried me when he buried my mother. We have been drifting apart ever since the day before I left for college. We'd been tight up until that time, even though in high school I ran with the popular crowd and he was a nerd. I can't remember what initiated the fight – I'm sure it was somewhat sexual (I was seventeen and he was fourteen) and somewhat separation anxiety – but I remember the fight itself. When my brother was little and used to try to hit me back, I'd put my hand on his chest and laugh while his tiny little arms flailed away but never reached their mark: i.e., me.

He would always say, when he finally exhausted himself, 'Wait till I'm older . . . and bigger than you . . .' but by the time he was big enough to beat the shit out of me, he wasn't interested. He whacked tennis balls instead. For hours against the garage door. *Bam! Bam! Bam!* My friend Chicky Balistreri was the only one who could beat him. She was an incredibly strong tennis player to begin with but after her mother hanged herself, she was unbeatable.

My parents had taught us that men and women were equal, so we were all kind of surprised that Matthew took it so hard when Chicky beat him in straight sets. 'Equal is okay, I can live with that,' he said, his face and extraordinarily large ears beet red with anger and effort. 'But better? Better doesn't work for me at all.' Oh, so that's how you really feel. Do you hate her, too?

My mother always maintained that he had been so hot to avoid marrying a Jewish Princess that he had ended up with a Chinese Empress instead. Personally, I liked Mae, felt she had a soothing effect on my brother. I remember them visiting me, trying to put me together with my dying mother. On a mission. As it were. Me chopping and rechopping the coke on the mirror for hours. Mae, sitting primly . . . I bludgeoned her with gifts of jewelry she didn't want to take.

Now, my brother is checking up on my father's visit. Calling me. I ask him what he's doing. He's working for NASA now, I think. I stopped understanding what he did for a living years ago. Science . . .

'Oh, I'm just watching 192 varieties of crystals grow . . .' he says matter-of-factly. I blow lightly on my batch on my petri dish.

'Me, too . . .' I say.

*

I keep this giganto slip in the closet for at least a month, during which time David Begelman becomes president of MGM/UA. Bounces back in a big way. Parks shows me the announcement in the trades and urges me to call him. I am functional, so I do. He takes the call immediately, and when he comes on the line, he says: 'It's time to do it again!' We set a lunch date for which I am almost a half hour late, but somehow I am maintaining in public, and we finish off with him convinced I am clean and together and still smart and creative. Norman goes into negotiation with him within days for an overall deal.

The negotiation goes along, refining itself and moving closer and closer to closure. It is to commence May 1, 1980, and last for two years. It will provide offices and secretaries and take care of me and David pretty decently. It is a place to start. Unfortunately, I am re-forming a serious habit again, doing greater and greater quantities more and more of the day. By May first, I might turn into one of the dead people I know so many of.

Ayatollah Khomeini is Man of the Year for 1979. I wonder why I should get straight. To see more clearly how beyond-horrible the world is becoming?

David and I decide we have to take matters in hand. I get an appointment with a great and famous named Reice Jones, who is the head of the psychiatric/drug ward at Langley Porter in San Francisco. I can't risk traveling with the quantity necessary to see the day through, but I have the number of a friend of a friend I can cop from in San Francisco. David has to hold me up as we walk through the airport. I am literally falling asleep on my feet. The first call I make is to the connection, and when we get there, he has made up an eighth for me. It gets me up for the next stop.

Reice Jones takes blood and looks at the freebase – he is fascinated by it, peers at it, shakes it in the bottle. Takes a sample for analysis. He tells me I will have to check myself

439

into the psych ward for a month and shows me around. It is a depressing little place with single beds in sparse green rooms. He tells me that he will put me on lithium immediately. I tell him I'll be in touch.

When we get home I look up lithium in my *PDR*. It is used for manic-depressives and has a number of contraindications. It seems to me that I am more depressed than manic, that it is the coke that is creating mania. So if he takes me off the coke and then gives me lithium, he might smooth me out so much that I'll be a lump. Worse yet, maybe so down that I'll become suicidal. I thought the idea here was to *save* my life.

My gray hairs are starting to look like snakes to me, and one night I see bugs coming out of my cunt. Meanwhile, I am talking to the leaves on the trees and they are talking back. I lie in bed sobbing and feel a pain crawl up my left arm and into my chest. I'm having a heart attack, I think, and decide not to call 911. Let Allah decide . . .

The next morning I am alive, so I go to see a doctor who is supposed to know about getting people off cocaine. I smoke freebase all the way to his office. He takes my blood pressure and says, 'Now, if you were all coked up it would be much higher.' He prescribes Haldol, Ativan, and Halcion. I fill the prescriptions, but when I look them up in *PDR* I decide he is trying to kill me. I call Al Sellers.

I see him the next day and brief him on my up-shit's-creek-in-serious-trouble quandary and show him the array of downers the quack has given me. Doctors don't say much, particularly about other doctors, but Al Sellers's face speaks volumes. I see him copy the guy's name off one of the labels on a piece of paper. 'Whaddya think?' I ask.

'To say that these meds are redundant is to be charitable,' he replies. Grimly, he takes a lot of blood and performs a number of tests. Then he calls me into his office. Behind closed doors he shows me the printout from my EKG and says that I have a t and a u prime beat; an extra tick on the way in and an extra one on the way out. He also tells me my pulse is going at one-oh-eight beats a minute.

I remember from Biology in high school that seventy-two is normal. My white count is high and so am I. How am I still alive? I wonder out loud. He says he can't imagine why. There is no earthly reason why I should be. I switch gears and give him a raft of shit about what a charlatan the coke-doctor is.

'I hear a lot of contempt in your voice,' he says.

'Well, that prick took my money and got my hopes up . . .'

'No, I mean for yourself.' No. Really? Am I supposed to feel pride about this?

'I'm scared, Al. I mean, it's not like I don't want to stop. I went to the Mayo Clinic. I was doing it again in three days . . . I'm at my wits' end . . .'

'There's a guy at UCLA named Sid Cohen who I'm going to try to get you in to see . . .' Sid Cohen, he explains, is a drug expert at UCLA who specializes in cocaine dependency.

'This isn't just cocaine, Al, this is freebase . . .' but he is already on the phone with Sid. Sid Cohen is too busy to see me right away; he tells Sellers all cocaine dependency is the same. Great, another guy who doesn't know what this drug is.

He refers me to a shrink named Teitelman who specializes in drug cases. Mostly marijuana. I laugh, but I figure, fuck, I'm a desperate woman, so Sellers sets an appointment for that afternoon. I go home and make a batch, but I manage to just chip away at it so I won't be late. David drives me to UCLA where Teitelman keeps an office.

He is a weird-looking guy with those kind of glasses that are so thick his eyes are the size of the model ET's on *Close Encounters*. He has a rug with a lot of specks in it and I get preoccupied with counting them. Then this schmuck actually has the nerve to say: 'Look at you. You're a beautiful woman with a beautiful daughter and a great career and a lot of money and you're all fucked up!' Oh really? What keen powers of observation. I'm so glad I drove all the way here and didn't stay in my little room with the door that locks from the inside with a key so I can get high without anyone walking in.

I stand up. 'I don't think that you can help me,' I say. I am tired. Here's your $125, just let me go. I leave. I cry all the way home, and then lock myself in my room. I am trying to keep my 'slip' a secret. Kate has to bang on the door for me to come out.

'I smell ether,' she says. Poor little baby. I start to cry and she tries to wrap her tiny arms around me. We hug each other very tightly. What am I going to do? Who will help me?

The next day, David Parks and I drive to the UCLA psych ward for a preadmittance tour. Everyone seems real anxious for me to check in, but I sense that they know nothing about freebase, and every time I try to find out how much they do know, they ask me more questions. I am supposed to be their education. Hey, Life's an experiment, and I am the laboratory. But I ain't *your* fucking guinea pig! What's the use . . .

I am doomed, I am doomed, I think, and I go home and lock myself in my cave again. This room I had built for drugs is on the same level as the rest of the house, and it is maybe the tastiest room in the house, but I have started to regard it as my lonely basement room – My little cocaine hell.

The next morning, David Parks shows me an article in the L.A. *Times* about one Ron Siegel, an associate professor of psychopharmacology at UCLA who is doing research on a new drug called freebase. Bingo! We get an appointment for that afternoon. 'If this guy tells me that I'm all fucked up I'm killing myself,' I say to David and we laugh. It is the first time we have laughed in weeks.

Ron Siegel lives and works in a modest little townhouse in Westwood with a bad parking situation. David lets me off and says he will just drive around until he finds a space. I am seized by fear. I can't face this alone. Fortunately somebody pulls out of a spot right in front of Siegel's building. Celebrity parking. A positive omen.

Ron Siegel is a thin, intense person whose eyes, behind Lennon-like glasses, are almost exactly the color of mine. His mouth is thin, too. His hair is the thinnest of all, long and wispy; he combs it from above his ear to cover full frontal balding. When he speaks his voice sounds like it belongs in a cartoon.

But when he speaks, his silly voice says intelligent things. I respond to him immediately and I can tell by the way he looks at me that he is enraptured. Which is a good thing, because I am pretty sure we never could have cured me if he didn't have a big crush. It was not an easy endeavor.

I get the other inspiration for cure almost straightaway, when we go into his office with its negative ion machine and his Peruvian and Colombian art, most of which centers around huge erect penises – a fair representation of a central cocaine preoccupation.

He eases me into trusting him by asking me a series of questions that indicate he has some familiarity with freebase. He asks about hallucinations, convulsions, retinal flashing, ear ringing. *Monsieur Neary, have you had a pleasant – a ringing – sensation in your ears?* He asks about sleep patterns, depression, psychotic episodes. He asks about intake, and gasps when I tell him.

He tells me he has been working with a number of dealers in the last year who have ended up in jail, usually because they have tried to kill their girlfriends. In some cases, they have succeeded, often in a gruesome manner. I tell him about the Mayo Clinic, and the previous doctor-disappointments, about being an atheist who couldn't get past step one in the AA program. I tell him that I am at the point where I am smoking freebase, not to get off – that had passed long ago – but just not to feel bad. I tell him that I feel like I have failed in all my attempts at drug treatment.

No, he says, those programs failed you. It's moot, I say back. The point is, I'm still smoking freebase. David Parks has told me that George Blumenthal, a friend of Michael's from Dartmouth days, had asked Kate what Mommy was doing, meaning in her career, and Kate had said: Mommy makes base. I tell Ron the story. I start to cry.

'Are you wildly in love with your child?' Ron asks in a soothing way. Yes, I say; I think that covers it.

'Well, I think you should know that a lawyer representing Michael Phillips came here this morning to ask me all about freebase . . .' Shocked, I stop midsob. 'Needless to say, when your assistant called shortly after this guy left, I knew I was onto a research opportunity. He was a custody lawyer, Julia. Michael's going to sue you for custody.'

A pain goes through me so great I spring from my chair and bolt out of the office into the larger living room, where David is perusing a medical journal. I sob out the news. He makes a wry face.

'I'm surprised he waited this long,' he says. He is right, of course. Trust Michael to move now, as I am cleaning up. Wait a second, who am I kidding? I have never cleaned up except for my thirty-day stay at the Mayo Clinic. Yeah, well, fuck it, I'm cleaning up now, and this skinny weirdo in the other room is gonna help me. I dry my eyes, and blow my nose. Honk honk. I take a deep breath and go back into the room with all the erections.

'Have you ever cured anybody?' I ask.

'A few . . . not many . . . but a few . . . I think you're an exceptionally good candidate for a complete cure.'

'Well, I'm highly motivated . . .'

'You're smart, too . . .'

'That doesn't have anything to do with anything . . .'

'Yes, it does. Just remember, intelligence is a survival tool.'

'Yeah, look how far it's gotten me . . .'

'I think the key to your cure is through intelligence. Look, I'm not a drug rehab program. I'm a drug researcher. I'll take you on as a research patient, and we'll figure it out together . . .' I am beginning to feel subsumed by exhaustion. When you are strung out on freebase, you cannot stay alert and awake without it for very long. I ask if I can smoke some. He says not while I come to see him, but he understands the physiological effects of the drug and he knows I am getting tired. He says he has coffee and Coca-Cola in his kitchen. Kid stuff, but I have some of both anyway. 'Look, Julia, as far as I'm concerned, we're in an emergency mode. I think you should come in every day for a double session.'

'Two hours in a row? I don't know if I can handle it . . .' Kate's face pops into mind. 'Okay,' I agree. Anything to get out of here and home to my pipe.

Ron Siegel decides on an educative approach with me. He checks with Reice Jones and informs me that he has diagnosed me suicidal. I retort, That's a self-fulfilling prophecy if I go on lithium. To my surprise, Siegel agrees. He tells me about some research going on with chimpanzees and freebase.

Apparently chimps will not voluntarily smoke anything – not pot, tobacco, angel dust – but freebase. And once they start, they don't stop. Chimpanzees make families, have mates, live in communities. He shows me a series of pictures of a male chimp that had been into freebase. Taken on a Hawaiian island with palm trees.

The chimp moves away from the group and then just huddles with his mate. Then he starts to climb one of the palms. His mate follows but he shoos her. She tries again and he attacks her. She retreats.

The chimp keeps climbing up the tree until he is at the very top. In the last shot, the chimp is high atop the palm, his friends and family way below in extreme background. He is in extreme closeup in the foreground. He is hanging on for dear life. His mouth is frozen in a grimace of pain and his eyes are filled with terror.

'He probably just ran out of stash,' I joke and Siegel laughs. 'I'm that monkey,' I say.

'Yes, you are, but you are not entirely up the tree, as it were,' he says, and he tells a few more dealer stories.

When we take the first of many coffee breaks, I say, 'Listen, this is all real interesting, but I think we need to come up with a plan.'

'Well, what do you think . . . you want to set a date? Cold turkey?'

'No, I did that once, and it didn't work . . . whaddya think about halving the dose every day until it's down to nothing, then stop?'

'Whatever you think will work, but sooner or later it'll effectively be cold turkey. How's your MGM deal going . . .'

'It's going to close . . .'

'See, this is a good shot for you. You can stop in your own environment, you have something to go right into . . .'

'Yeah, a custody battle . . .'

'Well, the sooner you clean up, the better off you'll be. You should find a good lawyer, though.' Let David Parks find the custody lawyer. I have to give up drugs. It is going to be a full-time job. I am doing so much a day that halving the dose will take a good week to get down to a gram.

Three days into the process, Ron asks how I feel about him coming over and getting rid of some paraphernalia. We fill two giant trashbags with pipes and torches and petri dishes and giant cans of anhydrous ether. He wants me to give up some stash. I say no. What about some finished product? Let me have it analyzed for you.

Ron has been filling me with information about all the fake caines that the dealers are hitting the coke with if they know the client is a baseballer. Lido-, pro-, pseudo-, all with flashpoints close enough to go through the process. Not too healthy to smoke. Like it is healthy to smoke the coke. Okay, I say, and whip up a batch.

Just like everyone, he is transfixed by the process. Théâtre de la Cocaine! I have the touch, no question about it. In another life, I probably would've made a decent chemist. I walk him down to his car, wondering: is he going to dump all this stuff or if he is going to keep it? Is he really having my stash analyzed or is he going to try it? I asked him in the beginning if he had ever tried freebase and he had been evasive. Nah, deep down he is a square. That's why I trust him enough to continue with this eccentric cure.

Next session, I ask him what my stash came out to be, and he tells me lidocaine. It did look a little discolored; I'm not surprised. By now, most of the guys I'm copping from are smoking freebase. Hell, I taught most of them how to cook it. They need more of their product for themselves . . .

'Man, I'm paying almost seven hundred dollars for a quarter of lidocaine,' I say, exasperated. Ron smiles approvingly; well, I've always been a quick study.

'Whaddya say we try cold turkey this weekend,' he suggests.

'You just like to move right along . . .'

'Why not? You're only smoking lidocaine . . .'

'Okay . . .'

That weekend I score one gram after another. Just that one more gram. David Parks calls repeatedly. Norman, too. Ron about every hour on the hour. I let the phone ring and ring. I tell the service not to bother ringing through. I am out.

When David Parks shows up on Monday, his eyes are almost swollen shut. 'You know,' he says, 'I got very sad this weekend. You're going to lose all your money and your deal and worst of all your child. I'm beginning to agree with you. There is no hope for you.'

After all the treatment programs, all the failures, all the false hopes and false starts, something in this simple diatribe touches me. Resolutely I turn on my heel, find a phone, and dial Ron Siegel's number. I tell him that I have been unable to let go this weekend, but that if he hasn't given up on me I am prepared to surrender my stash. He comes over immediately and takes everything that is left.

For the next two weeks, I do a pretty fine imitation of a turnip. I sleep about twenty hours a day and wake up crying and in a state of terror. There are no evil violent boyfriends around to hurt me, so I bump into things and hurt myself. I pull all my courage together and call Michael during one of these awful awake times. It turns into a negotiation over custody of Kate.

'But she NEEDS me . . .' I wail.

'No, I think you need her . . .' he says uncomfortably. I become so overwrought and emotional he starts to there-there me. By the end of the call, we have agreed to joint physical custody, papers to follow. When I get off the phone, I feel like I could sleep for a week, but I continue to sob through my relief.

Ron, David, and Jackie take turns watching over me and keeping me company when I am awake. Jackie makes simple food, like scrambled eggs, and for the first couple of meals, I mostly wear it on my face, because often I fall asleep mid-bite. Ron tries to get me into a running program, but I can't stick with the wonders of jockdom.

Nevertheless, at the end of three weeks, I am not in terror, I am functional, I am amazed most of the time how easy it has been. Physiologically speaking. My dues haven't begun to be paid, postcoke, not by a long shot. The weight and the self-esteem and the other drugs are still to come.

For three years after I stop, I dream graphically of smoking freebase every night. Occasionally, at a traffic light, I get some retinal flashing and it is like a UFO landing on my hood. After awhile I stop having the cravings, and then one day it is really not a part of my life.

But sometimes, on rainy afternoons particularly, I think of how I would stir up a batch in weather like this, and smoke, and listen to the rain, divine each raindrop and talk to it, feel its essence, commune with it, and I feel sad. Sad like you feel for a lover from long ago, and I mourn its passing, as I've mourned for friends who died too young.

I know a lot of dead people, and one of them is me.

Guy McElwaine and I sit in the front table at La Scala. He has been married to Leigh Taylor-Young for about six months, which is about how long I have been cocaine-free. I am starting to gain weight, beyond the requisite ten or twenty pounds that you wear like a badge: DRUG FREE, DRUG FREE, DO BUSINESS WITH ME . . . Guy is telling me in a delicate way to watch it, that you can balloon from giving up drugs and alcohol. I am fending him off with a litany of world events.

'You know, Leigh is very spiritual . . .' Guy actually sprouts tears under his glasses. 'She's into Edgar Cayce, those guys . . .'

'And . . .'

'And . . . all the prophets say the eighties will be a decade of natural disasters: earthquakes, floods, tornadoes, monsoons . . .'

'I got the picture . . .'

'. . . and the nineties will be a decade of war . . .'

'So, Kate, whaddya wanna talk about tonight?' It is the beginning of joint custody and she is at Michael's house. It is the opposite parent's dinner night out. Wednesday to be exact. Off to Mr. Chow's, in the gray Mercedes SLC expressly for the backseat, with Mike Maday driving, for support.

'Tonight,' Kate says, 'I want to talk about war,' pronounced *wahww*, because Kate is six.

'Why!' I gasp in unison with Mike Maday. Mike is a genuine Vietnam veteran, a nice Polish Catholic boy from Chicago who enlisted with his best friend right out of high school when they were nineteen. They arrived in Vietnam on the same day the Tet offensive began. He was the man on point for 365 days and survived his entire platoon including his best friend. He came home with nary a scratch on his body and lacerations across his soul that were so deep I don't think he ever recovered.

Who knows how he ended up in Hollywood? He was a wonderful guy with an identity problem who lived in Laurel Canyon. Dealer City. I met him through Mac, another wonderful guy who'd come to Hollywood to be a star, had married Karen Valentine at the peak of her cuteness, and retreated into carpentry when the inevitable split-up occurred. Mike Maday was reconstructing his life with detailed labor; he was etching his problems in stained glass. I sensed he needed to hone his craft when I first met him, and I made him duplicate a pattern on the bathroom tile already installed by the previous owner for three windows in a row in the front of the house. He was very cranky about the lack of creative control, but I was real clear with him that it would be in his best interest to do the job well because creative ya-yas could always be just around the corner with me. Remember Marty . . . remember Steven . . .

'Because I was watching the news and it was all about Iwaq and Iwan and I got interested in those countries . . .'

'War is a pretty big subject,' I say in a neutral tone, but secretly excited that I have produced a child who did this dialogue.

The white-haired scientist could have been her father. He said her words for her: 'After the bomb went off in Hiroshima – everything changed. The planet could be wiped out – like that!' He snapped his fingers. 'And we chose to approach this fact with old ideas.' The shrink told her that worrying about the cosmos was a way of avoiding the problems in her own little life. Bullshit. She had passed that point years ago . . .

My MGM deal starts sometime in the middle of May 1980. I develop six screenplays right out of the box. Taken together they form a mini-slate: a biggie, *Ghost Town*, which combines aspects of horror, old West, and cosmic reincarnation; three off-beat comedies – *Doctors in Hollywood*, a mean-spirited but hilarious account of a plastic-surgery patient who sets three lifelong friends, all doctors, against each other; *The Fling*, an older-woman/younger-man romance set against the backdrop of a disintegrating New York City with a Busby Berkeley nuclear holocaust finale; *The Lady and the Hunk*, a love story in which a girl's school English teacher turns race-car driver and steals the thunder from the Leader of the Pack; *Short Strokes*, an ambitious, convoluted satire – *Giant*, if you will, from a *Network* point of view – starring a hurricane that predominated the third act; and a Sybil Adelman-Martin Sage (stars in TV) untitled comedy.

Jimmy Wiatt, an ex-politico who neatly segued into ICM and now heads its movie division, wants to do me a good turn and simultaneously get Michael Kane (aka 'Killer') off his back with a job. He sends him over to me, just as I am starting my MGM deal. I think I inspire sympathy because I am wearing my cleanliness on my physique. As in, anyone this fat can't be doing blow. I've gained fifty pounds from giving up freebase, and I haven't gotten sufficiently revolted by it to take action. I'm buying expensive *schmattes* at Giorgio instead, all of which have to be let out.

'Vell, at least your hips are two inches smaller than Zsa Zsa's,' the alterations lady had said. I peered over my girth to check out the tape measure. It was in the forties. I could feel tears forming in my eyes and nose and willed them away. Gale Hayman hovered.

'You'll drop it, don't worry,' she said sympathetically, no doubt counting her revenue while I went up and down, and handed me the receipt to sign. This one would probably send Mickey Rutman into shock. My department-store bills are as large as my coke bills had been. I tell myself it is worth it. At least I have a job now, something I can do right away to fill the void. I *guess* I'm lucky.

I meet Michael Kane that afternoon, and in spite of the bitterness engraved in his features, I like him and his ideas. Impressions, really. He shows me a collection of photographs of abandoned mines and then he shows me a Cub Scout uniform. The beginning of *Ghost Town*.

Next, he tells me about a raucous French comedy called *Pardon Mon Affaire*; he calls it *Doctor, Doctor, Doctor*. He wants to do a wild comedy about Beverly Hills doctors.

'Well, what if I want to develop both at the same time? Would you be willing to supervise one and write the other?' I need to get as much into development that I even remotely like as soon as possible. I am partial, still, to epic, visionary, cosmic (as in, lots of sky), or funny. The funny is a frustration of mine. I have never done a comedy that I was happy with or that was a hit.

Steelyard Blues had its moments, just as *The Big Bus* did, but they were both too inept to be as funny as the scripts had been. The audience, in its wisdom, stayed away in droves, although *Steelyard Blues* did have one hot weekend. A brief, misleading moment. So I am kind of hung up on a hit comedy.

Michael Kane, always greedy because of his gambling, jumps at the chance for two fees: one big, for writing *Ghost Town*, the other too big for what it is, which is a payoff to leave *Doctors x 3* and let someone funny write it.

I start a search for a drop-dead hysterical writer who isn't too successful, or Grady Rabinowitz, or any friend of Grady Rabinowitz's.

Mike Rosenfeld is a guy I had known before I went away, and now he is showing up as a hotshot founder of a place called CAA, which has taken over Hollywood in the three years I've been gone. We go to lunch at La Scala. He keeps flashing a Rolex that his partners have bought him for his birthday. It is the one with the works revealed and actually seems like the most hideous version of a Rolex you can buy, but it cost many thousands of dollars and he is very proud of it. I admire it as best I can, and I ask him if he has any fabulous ideas for a writer for this *Doctor x 3* comedy.

'Gail Parent,' he says without hesitation. What a good idea, Mikey. I sort of know Gail Parent, and I have always thought she is very funny. I practically go down on that ugly Rolex, it is such a good idea. He arranges a meeting for us immediately.

We have lunch at Mr. Chow's. I wear one of the expensive silk mumus I had just bought from Fred and Gale Hayman.

She smiles when she sees me, probably because I am so huge she looks like Peter Pan by comparison. We have a really wonderful lunch, and I tell her the idea and how much I like her work. She says the same back and it isn't until coffee that I bring up an issue that has been gnawing at me.

'I don't know how to say this but bluntly . . .'

'Just say . . .'

'Well, my only other experience with a woman writer was with Erica. It ended up being very painful . . . I just don't

452

want that particular experience again . . .' Gail laughs her soft laugh, as if to say, silly thing.

I take her at her laugh and proceed. First, Gail and I and Michael Kane watch *Pardon Mon Affaire*, truly hysterical but small. Then Gail and I gross out Michael Kane at a few meetings and he stops coming. He and I are getting into *Ghost Town* and it is absorbing his energies.

Throughout this process, I am still in negotiation with Mike Rosenfeld for Gail's services and Jimmy Wiatt for Michael's services. Or more precisely, Business Affairs at MGM is negotiating for their services. An arduous process. In the seventies *The New York Times* had run a story about a glut of law school graduates. I am beginning to think they all moved west to be in Show Business. Just to make my life more miserable. If such a thing were possible.

I start to get depressed. Danger danger. HALT! Or in my case, FALT. As in: too fat too angry too lonely too tired. I can't tell if it's the negotiating that is wearing me down or the fact that I am lugging around fifty pounds of additional person. I decide I must do something about the weight, over which I have some control, and find Leslie Dornfeld and Optifast. I like the fast. It releases enormous anxiety, which translates into energy. I stay on it for eleven weeks. By the time I am a shadow of my present self, i.e., my former self, the deals are closed and half the scripts are in . . .

Ed Limato is an old friend. He thinks it would be a good idea to put me and Richard Gere together. I have already met Richard through Schrader twice, both times when I am at the high end of my postcoke weight, and therefore feeling at a disadvantage with His Handsomeness. Makes it harder to bust his chops and spar with him. Ed arranges a little get-together at the Polo Lounge. Sunday brunch. I am three-quarters through my Optifast program.

I'm the first one there. There is a crowd of people trying to get in and get out. I find myself jammed up against Peter Guber, who is exiting. He is wearing a blue blazer that has *Midnight Express* embroidered in red on the pocket. Jesus.

453

He tries to avoid eye contact, no easy task when you are belly to belly. He finally acknowledges me by name then bolts.

When Ed and Richard and a strange woman arrive they pass me by. I signal them, and Richard gives me an approving look. 'You look like the woman from *American Gigolo*,' he smiles, backhand complimenting himself and me at the same time. During lunch he complains bitterly about the price of stardom, the fans, the autograph hounds. Sylvia, his Brazilian artist/model/whatever girlfriend replies, mouth turned downward, 'Oh, Reechard, you and your eggo . . .' I flash on Peter Guber: leggo your eggo . . .

I am still fasting.

I go to The Palm with Don Simpson for lunch. The last time we made a lunch date I was deep in my slip and deep in my late pattern. He had left already, deliberately neglecting to so inform the maître d'. It took me half an hour to figure out he was gone.

His graph is ascending. He is running Paramount now. It is hard to put this brusque, preoccupied, unhealthy-looking presence with good old twinkly-simian-I'm-a-triple-Scorpio Ach! Seempson. I can't decide if I feel worse for him or me. He orders a salad, I order a double espresso. In answer to his scowl, I say, Nothing serious, just fasting. He says, remarking on my weight loss: Well, at least maybe you'll get laid. Yuck! Seempson! Suffice it to say, neither one of us bangs down the other's door in desperate search of an encore . . .

I discover that if I want to stay straight I have to lose all my drug buddies, but I see Finslander once or twice. The second time I see him, he tells me he has gotten so crazy from freebase that he has actually broken his dick.

'What?'

'Well, I wanted to see what a flying fuck was and I missed,' he says. I am tempted to make him show me, he is such a teller of tall tales, but don't.

A month later I get a collect call. He is in the Oklahoma

City jail. I don't wanna I don't wanna . . . In a small voice I tell him please don't call me anymore. I don't want my friends to be dead or in jail . . .

Steven takes a tentative puff on my joint, coughs, and passes it back to me. We haven't spoken in four years, but we have run into each other on the MGM lot, where he is directing *Poltergeist*. He is supposed to be producing it, but Tobe Hooper, the director, it is whispered, has lost his cookies and Steven has had to step in. I wonder if Steven has been the first to whisper the Hooper rumors. It would fit his m.o. We are acting as if nothing bad ever happened between us, and Steven has walked back to my set of offices with me, the ex-offices of Louis B. Mayer, which I have defiled with acres of chintz.

Steven has asked for the joint, which surprises me, he is such a straightnik. Maybe it is his way of getting along with me on my terms. We hang out for a considerable period, and I am furious the entire time. I don't indicate this externally at all, so I am working on a hell of a stomach ache. Thank God there is no Sara Lee anything around.

'Yup, all hell is gonna break loose in this room,' Steven says. 'We're gonna rotate the whole room day after tomorrow . . .' Oh yeah, I got a better idea of something you should rotate. And where you should rotate it.

'You love doing that sort of stuff,' I reply instead, thinking of Dreyfuss in the cab of the truck, Nick McLean, the camera operator, turning in a 360-degree circle right along with him so that all the papers and ashtray stuff appeared to be rising and floating, the result of the powerful beam emanating from the spaceship above and off camera. They did it twice until Nick was hurled from the heavy straps that held him in.

We'd only gotten two takes, but that was enough, and both guys were green at the gills, ready to puke their guts out, anyway. Steven, oblivious, wanted another take. Nick looked like he was ready to barf all over him, something he wanted to do anyway, just so he'd get the point. Nick had great respect for Steven on the one hand, but called him Speelnuts on the other. Steven intuitively backed down.

'You should come by and see it . . .' he says now.

'Yeah, sure,' I say, coughing violently on the pot and my lie. I will never be on another set with you again. And being on a set with you was probably the most fun I ever had. Which gives you an idea of how much fun I've had in my life. We have been talking about Michael and me breaking up and the effect it had on all our pals.

'It was like Mommy and Daddy breaking up and we were all your children . . . it was scary,' he says.

'Yeah, but we made all those calls . . . we told you we'd make the business part work . . . we *did* make the business part work . . .' So weird, split up and keep all those projects together. Hey, but not as weird as Harry Ufland or Bob Bookman splitting with their wives and subdividing their houses so the children wouldn't freak out. But that was business, too.

'Yeah, but it was like we had to choose . . .' Ah, Steven, do we really wanna pursue this? Nah . . . but I say:

'That was in your head, not in ours . . .'

'You know who I saw not long ago,' Steven says, changing the subject. Hey, you're the director.

'Who . . .' We are both pacing around in my office. We pretty much always had our conversations on our feet.

'Jeremy . . .' The name sends my stomach down that fear-and-loathing elevator to my ankles. 'He was scary . . .' You're tellin' me. 'I'm in some sushi bar and I get a tap on my shoulder and a soft hello, and before I turned around I knew who it was . . .'

'How'd he look?'

'Terrible, with a mangy beard and pimples . . .' I set the joint down in the ashtray.

'So how come you never came to my coming-out party . . .' I have thrown a big party at Jimmy's, a heard-you-missed-me-well-I'm-back shindig.

'Oh, Goldie and I discussed it – '

'I saw you together on the awards . . .'

'We just agreed we weren't sure . . .' So much for friendship in Hollywood. I had gone, after all, to a fancy screening of *Ordinary People* with Craig Baumgarten and gotten some rude awakenings. I was particularly fragile because I was halfway through my Leslie Dornfeld fast, weighing in at maybe 125, not fat not slim. Craig wanted me to meet him there, so I drove myself to the Paramount lot. When I got out of my car, the first person I saw was Barry Diller. He could barely mask his displeasure at my survival. I went to the commissary where I was to meet Craig and bumped into Redford, who seemed warm and friendly.

'How's the baby?' he asked.

'She's great . . . she's seven . . .'

'God, time flies . . .' The last time he'd seen her was when she was a baby. 'Got a picture?'

'Sure,' I said, pleased, and looked deep into the recesses of my purse, fumbled through my wallet, extracted a two-year-old snap, 'Here . . .' I held it out for him to see, but he was gone . . .

The screening was very fancy-shmancy; the movie, too. The tragedies of the uptight midwestern goyim. When it was over, I leaned into Craig's ear and said. 'And they wouldn't let me direct *Fear of Flying* . . .' and got a huge, rude laugh. I knew I did it because Redford had slighted me. Uh-oh, shades of the Old Julia, or anyway, the part of the Old Julia nobody seemed to like much . . .

'Jul-ee-a . . .' Steven says. Have I been drifting?

'Y-e-e-s-s-s . . .'

'I'm sorry I wasn't a good friend . . .' I can't believe I am hearing this. It doesn't suffice, not in the least, but I say:

'Oh, that's okay . . . nobody was . . .'

DIALOGUE FROM SOMEONE ELSE'S MOVIE TENTATIVE TITLE: HOLLYWOOD FRIENDS

OVO: In the Executive Offices of a Major Motion Picture Company, two men look out the window of a large, well-appointed corner office. Silence for a moment while they study the smog.

ME: I know I didn't come out publicly in your favor after you were convicted, but I really need your friendship now . . .

HE: Let me think it over and I'll get back to you by the close of business Thursday . . .

I am just beginning to eat real food, realimenting, Dornfeld calls it, when I get a call from Rob Cohen and Richard Gere. They are involved in a project with Don March at CBS Films called *Marco and His Brothers*. March has said with a rewrite, Richard, and a strong producer, they'll make the picture with Rob directing. They want me to read it and have a meeting with March over the coming weekend. Comeback City! I receive the script by messenger that afternoon.

Fifty pages in, I find I am completely offended by this sheath of pages that passes for a script. When March calls to arrange a time and place, I tell him, not necessary, unsalvageable, not interested. I tell him I will call Richard and Rob, but find by Monday I don't have the will to make the call.

Blowing these guys off in a charming way would have been a piece of cake for the Old Julia. The New Julia rehearses and rehearses and still can't find the words. I never make the call. It is the first time I offend Richard Gere. Leggo my eggo . . .

I will always have a special place in my heart for Mr. Wald, because he was the one, sitting on the beach in Hawaii after I had cleaned up and he had been kicked out by Helen Reddy, his wife and principal client, who made me answer the question, 'Isn't there just one person you always wanted to meet, just one more thing you wanted to do?' The truth is that I am just starting up in movies again, and I think I want to do them for awhile. I haven't been discouraged out of the business, yet. I am just starting the process, which is to take a lo-o-o-ng time.

'I've always wanted to meet Arthur C. Clarke,' I say suddenly, reflexively mixing business and pleasure again. I have already met enough of my idols to know that it is better not to meet them, but Arthur C. Clarke could be a very cool choice for *Ghost Town*. Cool and indisputable, if anything is these days. I was a little girl when I first read *Childhood's*

End. My little brother and I spent a week up on the roof of the apartment house in Brooklyn trying to turn the moon around with our minds before we could accept it as fiction.

Mr. Wald is experiencing great pain in Hawaii. He has not yet accepted that he is addicted to cocaine and marijuana, but he does know that his life is in disorder and that he and Helen have managed to spend most of the $40 million that they have earned. For most people that would be irrefutable proof that something is fucked up, but Mr. Wald is very smart and uses all his considerable intellectual powers to convince himself that it is the world, and not he, that needs to change. Semi-clean as I am, something in his desperate need to fall in love with me touches me, and I respond by participating in some of the most boring sex that I've ever endured. But that is how sex, *sans* drugs, is getting to be with me, anyway. The excitement comes with the principle of love as opposed to the love itself.

Mr. Wald had actually been a childhood acquaintance of Michael's. Their mothers had gone to camp together as teenagers and kept in touch for all their adult lives, something I could never relate to, but perhaps that is because I moved so many times I never kept friends, just made new ones. Jeff and Helen were successful in show business before Michael and I were, and they never invited us to their house until we absconded with the Academy Award for *The Sting*. After that particular event we were invited any number of places, including the Walds', and finally we accepted.

There were four couples at dinner: Jeff and Helen, Susan Harris (who was later to become very famous in TV for such offerings as *Soap* and *The Golden Girls* but was just then a struggling writer with fierce blue eyes and an overly bobbed nose) and a gay agent at ICM who hadn't pranced out of the closet yet, and Neil and Marsha Diamond (he a big if somewhat mainstream star and she a woman who had broken my college friend Chris Miller's heart in a previous life).

Dinner was a gut grinder, since Jeff and Helen indulged in a George and Martha routine revolving around who was the bigger star in the star/manager relationship, the star or the manager. The argument was ostensibly about Diana Ross and

Berry Gordy, but you didn't have to be a genius to figure out that the argument was really about Jeff and Helen. I found Helen cold and Jeff vulgar, and vowed never to see them again.

Which I didn't, much, because to tell the truth, the others I was hanging out with at the time were not much impressed with their enormous success and dollars, but found them as tacky and uninviting as I did. Then Michael and I broke up and I ran into the Walds from time to time at the Kahala Hilton. For reasons unknown to me, Jeff savaged me in public, which he later confessed was to defend Michael against gossip in certain quarters that I was the brains of the outfit.

One of the first things Mr. Wald wants to know when we hook up in Hawaii is how I could be nice to him when he had been so cruel about me. 'Revenge is for suckers,' I say, quoting a line from *The Sting* because I don't really know the answer. Probably because I am bored and need something to fill the in-betweens.

I have just started a little something with Mickey Rafael, the harmonica player in Willie Nelson's band (the cute one with the beard is the way he is generally described) but I know he is another one of those guys who is there but not there and will disappoint me in the end. He has already disappointed me, in fact, by asking me to get in touch with Prince Albert so he can cop some blow. I had met him at Andrea Eastman's Christmas Eve party, where I dumped Hart Bochner so that I could hook up with him later on.

We had watched *Fiddler on the Roof*; and he had played to me on his harmonica, but I hadn't fucked him. I was not into fucking too carelessly. It is 1981, and I have always had a gift for seeing into the future: sex is not so easy for me now that I don't do so many drugs. I am still entangled in relationships with two younger guys (call them Yuppie #1 and #2), both of them the result of losing all the postcoke weight, neither of them any good. Yuppie #1, who is more interesting sexually, which isn't saying much considering the Yuppie predilection for self-love, is living with a friend of mine and afraid to leave, and Yuppie #2 has a tiny dick and comes too fast.

Why I am accumulating all these insufficient men is beyond

me. Very Queen of the Prom. It probably has something to do with not making movies and not doing drugs, but it seems a duplication of a pattern from childhood: all three of them don't make one satisfying guy. So when I meet Mr. Wald, it is, fuck it, the more the merrier. Or the more the sadder. As it were. I dump Yuppie #1 for Yuppie #2 and Yuppie #2 for Mickey – call him Yuppie #3 with stage presence. And then Mickey isn't around and Mr. Wald is. The old I'm-here-and-you're-there-and-you-can't-do-anything-about-it policy.

The dumping of Yuppie #2 had been unceremonious and cruel. He had taken me and Kate out for New Year's Eve, first to a Beach Boys concert with little Kate exclaiming, 'Look at all the people look at all the people,' then dropping Kate off with Michael and on to Fiona Lewis's and Bill Hayward's New Year's party where I faced several distressing moments. One was seeing the daughter of a friend outside the house, puking over the side of the entrance from too much pot and booze, her father shielding her from concerned questions. How old was she? Fifteen, sixteen? I'd known her since she was five. The other was chatting with Michelle Phillips. The Other Mrs. Phillips.

'I've had quite a few alcoholic blackouts,' Michelle said casually.

'Well, are you doing anything about it?'

'Yes, I'm taking pictures of everything, so I'll have a record of where I've been and what I've done.' And with that, Michelle produced a camera and a flash went off.

Which had been the most exciting moment of the party for me, since everyone else there was a drunk. So I made Yup #2 take me home and wouldn't fuck him and wouldn't let him stay, and finally, in desperation, indicated that I never wanted to fuck him again, and that this relationship was not working out. It had been better on the phone. Finally, slump-shouldered and nerdy, he slinked away to his black Jeep and took off. I just had time to shower and change and take off for the airport to pick up Mickey.

Given that life wasn't filled with too many little jolts these days, the drive to the airport early on New Year's Day sufficed. I made it in under twenty minutes, going ninety all the way.

461

No other drivers, no cops, no trucks. The end of the world, and then there was Mickey carrying his clothes on his shoulder, saying, 'Hi, honey, I'm home.'

Mr. Wald isn't really out the door with Helen, though, which becomes clear when we get home. I'm not real good at the other-woman role, so just to remind him who is really who, I take off for Vegas to see Mickey perform at Caesar's Palace. Patrick Terrail comes along as a beard. Just to keep the power struggle on an even keel, Mr. Wald proffers his private Lear for us to travel in. Altogether a satisfactory way to go, although the pilots start it off badly by referring to me as 'Dale.' No, I'm not that bimbo, I tell them, and they look at me cold and blank, like, Well, which bimbo are you? You better be nice, guys, if you want to see Willie Nelson for free tonight.

When we get to Caesar's, I check into a suite with a mirror over the bed (oh goody) and find Mickey in Willie Nelson's suite, a two-storied, terraced affair that probably cost several hundred thou to decorate in the worst possible taste. I have brought an ounce of Hawaiian pot as a peace offering for Willie; he smokes most of it that afternoon.

'That kind of consumption would definitely account for his lack of charisma onstage,' I whisper into Mickey's ear. He laughs uncomfortably.

'I take care of the charisma part,' he whispers back. Me and Patrick gamble and go to the show. They slam some bigwigs into the booth with us, and I cop attitude. The maître d' makes Mickey keep me backstage on bass and drums for the next show. Mickey performs his little heart out, down on his knees in my direction, fat-assed women in the crowd gasping, but Patrick ruins the moment by saying: 'How many times in how many towns has he done this – for how many girls?' After that Patrick and I separate, me to play the slots with Mickey, Patrick to scour the premises in search of the perfect Eurasian beauty. We see him squiring a promising number toward the elevator banks at about 3:30 A.M.

Mickey and I split whatever pills and pot we can find and go up to that mirrored bed. At noon the next day, the phone starts to ring every five minutes. Mr. Wald, getting me out of bed and on the plane. After the sixth call, I get up. I am into a quick escape, and Patrick helps me sweep all my toiletries into my bag. Mickey rolls over in bed, unable to believe I am splitting.

'Well, how long do you think I should stay?'

'How 'bout till June?' For some reason, the private jet home seems more appealing. I call Mr. Wald and tell him, Hold the plane, I'm on my way to the airport. One for the short guys.

After I get home, though, I ask for my key and gate opener and put his clothes in large Hefty bags, just as Helen had done when he returned from Hawaii. Whatever the status of our personal relationship, which is really better when we aren't pretending to have sex, we do have a blast going around the world.

All the executives at MGM tell me *Ghost Town* is schizophrenic. That it should be horror or cosmic reincarnation. I keep saying, 'Doesn't anyone get synthesis here? Haven't you ever seen a movie that started out being about one thing, then moved into being about another, but the two were really intertwined?'

They look at me sternly but finance a rewrite with Michael Kane, which is pretty fucking wonderful, even if he does drive me crazy. There was a reason Wiatt called him Killer. Especially in story meetings when he would say, 'So what's the next line?'

Mr. Wald inspires me to take a stand, especially since he will accompany me as my agent, attorney, and general protector. I am going to ask them to send me with my assistant, David Parks. On my way to see David Begelman. I wonder how Mr. Wald will relate to traveling as Mr. Parks. I have Parks drive me over in my gray Mercedes and I make him park right in front of the Thalberg Building.

'Keep it idling.' It is a dismal, sixty-degree, humid day, so the car spumes considerable exhaust.

I use every good argument at my disposal, particularly that

463

MGM made *2001* and wouldn't it be interesting if Arthur C. Clarke wanted to design a sequel.

'C'mon, don't you remember when we sat at Nick's Fishmarket and talked about *Close Encounters* and you said a hundred mil and I said more? It wasn't even a decent script yet. C'mon, don't you remember how I had to beg you to make *Taxi Driver* and I told you up front ten mil out of the cities in the first two weeks – ?'

'You lied . . . it made twenty . . .' I see the shadow of a crinkle pass across his face.

'C'mon, be a guy. Let me go. And pay for David Parks to travel with me. I don't wanna go to that part of the world alone . . .' Well, yes, he remembers, but now is now, and things are different.

'But you gotta give me a shot. I believe in this, I know it's totally original, it's a big fucking movie – '

'I'd love to, but – ' The son of a bitch is going to say no. I walk him over to the window; the gray car, blanketed by exhaust, fumes below.

'See that car?' I say. 'That's my car, and you turn me down I'm going downstairs, get in that car, drive off the lot and never come back . . .' Please, Beges, don't turn me down. Don't turn me away. Don't turn me off. '. . . And I'll tell everyone you never really gave me a chance, that you turned me down on Arthur C. Clarke doing a rewrite.'

He crinkles his eyes at me, possibly relieved that I have some spirit left. 'Okay, you can go, but nix on the kid.'

'I'm not thrilled, but I'll take it. Thanks.'

I make Parks take off fast, just in case Begelman has stood, Citizen Kane-like, watching to see what I'll do. Mr. Wald isn't thrilled with having to pay his own way, but he comes along for the ride anyway.

The Arthur C. Clarke part of the trip is for three days. He greets us at the airport holding a sad-faced picture of me from the press kit for *Close Encounters*. 'If you didn't recognize me,' he reasons, 'I figured you would recognize yourself.' Well, not always and not really, but okay. On the way from the airport to our hotel, he ticks off his list of rules. No staying up past nine, no major socializing, no drinking. Oh, really. Dialogue like this is a challenge for me. I flash on my days at Mount Holyoke, before everything changed, when there was no smoking in the rooms, no men, no booze. I read the list and broke the rules one by one.

By the kind of sheerest coincidence that I have come to expect as the way my life is mapped out, Michael's parents, Sherry and Larry, are staying at the same hotel on their way back from the Far East. Larry Phillips has always been inspirational to me, because he had truly changed his career midlife. He had a ne'er-do-well brother and an obese sister who shared equally in his prosperous knockoff dress business while he was the brains and the force. He and Sherry started to be interested in Far Eastern *objets*. They started by importing Thai drums, which were pricey and made excellent end tables. They got better and better and more and more knowledgeable and finally, one day, Larry said fuck it to the rag trade and became a dealer in Far Eastern decorative pieces. They learned more and more and started dealing antiquities to museums and collectors. They always liked to stop in Sri Lanka and stay at the Oberai on their way back to New York. And here they are. And here I am. With Mr. Wald, who has not yet been divorced by Helen. As we hang out in the pool, Sherry keeps poking me in the arm and saying: 'You little devil . . .'

'Don't tell Jeff's mother,' I warn. Am I ever going to graduate from high school?

'I won't,' she says, a schoolgirl who can't wait to blow my cover, and proceeds to explain a big festival that is being observed that night. Perahera it is called, and she says they dress the elephants in gold – and silver-threaded batik and stick lights on them and parade them through town. 'You haven't seen anything until you've seen an elephant's thing.' She giggled.

'Down to the ground?'

'Down to the ground . . .' Ah, the league of women, I think, and I immediately flash on elephant shit and how huge that must be. I call Arthur and ask him if he wants to have dinner at the hotel and catch a little of Perahera. Mr. Wald keeps calling it *kinahora*, which flies right past Arthur. I order champagne at dinner. Fuck you, Arthur, I'm gonna get you drunk and make you stay up past nine. You'll be talkin' about it for years.

While we hang around waiting for Perahera to start, I can see from the deference shown to him by the natives that Arthur is really the white raj. He keeps readjusting his sarong, a discreet flasher. I ignore him and think: Never meet your idols. I am just getting over the disturbing glimpse I'd had of Marvin Gaye while me and Mr. Wald were in London.

We had traveled from Los Angeles to New York, where Mr. Wald developed a terrible head cold (probably a reaction to the coke booger that was even then starting to form). The most he could do was sit up in bed long enough for Victor to give him a haircut. While he slept me and Victor went out pub crawling. Pyramid. Danceteria. Crisco Disco. The next day, we took off on the Concorde for London. Mr. Wald wanted to sign Marvin Gaye, and it gave me a chance to visit with 'arriet* and 'enry*, a trashy cockney couple I met in Hawaii. Very rich with no visible business. Smugglers? One could only hope.

Anyway, they knew how to have a good time, and I liked the way 'arriet dressed. My concept of visiting a place was to spend money there, something Mr. Wald was watching. So while he nursed his cold in the presidential suite of the Intercontinental and called his son, Jordan, every three hours to prove his love, 'arriet and I took off in the Daimler Benz with David the driver and saw the sights. Mainly South Moulton Street, where I dropped a few grand in an hour. This sweater, that jumpsuit, couple of those shoes.

When I got back to the hotel and so informed Mr. Wald, he got a stricken look on his face and said we had to stop at Marvin Gaye's first. He'd been busted. He needed money. I felt bad for Mr. Wald that he was giving up his meager spending money for Marvin to squander – probably on drugs. But Mr. Wald was into his comeback. He wanted to sign Marvin, and if it took a little greasing of the old chocolate-colored palm, well, that was fine with him. Okay, okay, man,

I'll go see Mr. What's Goin' On, even if he did kill Tammy Terrell by beating her head in with a hammer. Or so the rock 'n' roll gossip went. But let's bring 'arriet and 'enry with us, just in case I want to make a speedy departure. So I got all dressed up in my dynamic jumpsuit and diamond earrings and trusty mink, and we took off to a black part of town. When we arrived we were kept waiting in a sparsely furnished living room by a snotty Indian girl. Finally Marvin graced us with his presence.

He was very, very handsome, but he was wearing only a dirty tan terrycloth bathrobe. 'Hello, hello,' he said all around, flashing a beautiful smile. 'Forgive the wait, but it's been a devastating day . . .' He decided he wanted to go back into his bedroom and we followed. He threw himself under the covers and started talking, aimlessly masturbating underneath. Poor Marvin! I shot Mr. Wald a look, as in I don't have to deal with this, I'll see ya later, grabbed my mink, and said, 'I'm going to Crocker's. I'll send the car back for you.'

Mr. Wald told me later that he never saw anyone move so fast, but that was because he'd never produced a movie and run after a furious director stomping off a set.

And now, here we are in Sri Lanka hanging out with one of the great minds of the second half of the twentieth century, and he is just another egotistical wanker. I am determined to be charming. The more I dislike him, the more I want to convince him to do a rewrite on *Ghost Town*. The marriage of horror and cosmic hypothesis interests me. Arthur is interested only in the concept of cosmic reincarnation. He thinks the story of the six little Cub Scouts in jeopardy trivializes the piece. I try an argument in favor of the trivial and the grand – i.e., big commercial movie – but he is having none of it. It becomes clear after awhile that he has really been more interested in meeting me than in doing any sort of work on my project. In the end, he turns me down but offers a month of free notes and all the consultation I want as long as it takes place on his island.

I have read some of the jacket copy to his more recent books on various legs of the trip so far. Not only has he come up with the theory of synchronous orbiting, upon which all satellite technology is based, for which he got nothing, save the forty-five dollars from the scientific journal in which he first published it, but he has also done some serious treasure hunting – and at the age of thirty-nine, he had a major score. There are giant mounds of silver and gold holding the doors in the square-block-size mansion in which he is situated. It once belonged to the governor general of Sri Lanka, née Ceylon. Now Arthur lives there in his splendid isolation. One white raj replaced by another.

Arthur, the jacket copy reveals, turned his back on the Western World and moved here right after his find. Divorced the wife and moved lock, stock, and barrel to this remote, semiprimitive island in the Indian Ocean. The best description of the population comes from my mother-in-law: 'They are a gentle but easily distracted people . . .' as in if you ordered a Coca-Cola from a waitress and she ran into her cousin on the way to the fountain, she would get involved in chatting, forget the order, and you would go thirsty.

Neither Mr. Wald nor I are psychologically suited to the city of Colombo, in Sri Lanka, especially Perahera night when the air is rife with the smell of elephant shit and opium. Mr. Wald goes on a strenuous campaign to buy some opium, but the little boys keep thinking he is approaching them for homosexual purposes. That is the drug sold here.

But the spectacle of the elephants dressed in sari silk, tiny little Christmas lights threaded across their heads and shoulders, hundreds of them parading through the tiny streets in this small city, preceded by wildly dancing natives, over-whelms even Mr. Wald. This is the sort of thing that ugly Americans pack their duffel bags and travel around the world to see. It is magical, like watching an owl take flight in broad daylight. It is a rare occasion. It doesn't make me like our accommodations any better, or like Arthur any better, but I would rather have seen it than not.

We commence flying all over Sri Lanka with Arthur. At one point, the pilot forgets to switch over from the empty fuel tank to the full one, so preoccupied is he with delivering the basic communist diatribe endemic to all Third World countries: the people they need a leader, or they will all go to hell. When we finally arrive, somewhere near the ocean, to visit what Arthur refers to as his villa, a dirty shack surrounded by water that makes me glad to have had a cholera shot, and sit down to lunch at a reasonably clean restaurant table, Mr. Wald abruptly starts to laugh his brutal laugh. He sounds like he is barking.

'What's he doing?' Arthur sounds alarmed.

'He's laughing,' I say, translating.

'Why?' Arthur, the scientist, genuinely wants to know. Nobody has said anything funny. No one has said anything at all, preoccupied as they are with reading the barely literate menus.

'Oh, he's just glad to be alive.' I grin, perplexing Arthur, and making Mr. Wald double over with paroxysms. How can Arthur know that back in the days when Jeff and Helen were making so much money they flew by private Lear to the bathroom they'd once fallen twenty-one thousand feet to the ground? And survived? How he even gets into a plane is beyond me. Well, if you are loaded all the time, it is easier to take these acts of faith.

Cambodian schoolchildren wait patiently in line for a plane. If one of them breaks rank, he is whipped into shape by Catholic nuns with switches. From the moment we depart Sri Lanka and head toward Hong Kong that is all we see.

'Look what we've done to this part of the world,' Mr. Wald says as we hurry through the Bangkok airport to connect from Singapore to Thai airlines for Hong Kong.

'Hey, get off the train at 125th Street and you can see the same thing,' I shoot back. I am getting tired of people's consciousness getting elevated to where mine was at . . . what? Three? Four? I can never decide if I am glad with my parents for being so well-informed and cynical. Or mad. At least I haven't come into the world with too many illusions.

Then why have I done it? Why have I worked and strived and do things like try to get Arthur C. Clarke to rewrite *Ghost Town*? Probably just to structure my time. Heaven knows, I don't *believe* the way I used to. But I don't disbelieve either.

And when it develops, through the endless ass-kissing I indulge in with Arthur, that he has actually set down a treatment for a sequel to *2001* called *2010*, I go on a campaign of charm and force to get my hands on it. First Arthur lets me read it in his study, confessing before he does that he has already sent it to Stanley Kubrick.

Mr. Wald says I should tempt him with money. Mr. Wald says that there isn't a person in the world who isn't tempted by money. Mr. Wald says I should pick a figure and write it on a piece of paper and give it to Arthur. I write $250,000 against a mil, and place a side bet with God that Arthur will laugh in my face. Arthur looks at the piece of paper and folds it up and puts it in his pocket. He hands me a copy of the treatment to take back to MGM, who, after all, has financed this cozy little meeting. Not to mention they have the rights. Mr. Wald and I have a small dispute over whether my charm or his paper trick have yielded us this great reward.

I am contrary with Mr. Wald at this point in our trip anyway. I have actually picked a fight with him at the Paris airport about the way he treats the little people. I told him he was a snob and a bully, and if he didn't watch it, I'd tell Customs about those eighty-six joints he had tucked into his socks. Under his boots.

'I am not,' he sniffed, genuinely offended.

'Are, too,' I huffed, dragging my luggage wearily.

'Am not.'

'Are, too . . .' Amnotaretooamnotaretoo, right up to the Georges Cinq Hotel.

For Mr. Wald to feel anything for the plight of the Cambodian refugees strikes me as odd, considering what a plunderer he is. Actually his politics are fairly correct. He's certainly spent a lot of money putting Jerry Brown in office. Hundreds of thousands just to see what it would be like to smoke a joint in the governor's mansion, and then Jerry chose not to live there. People in Hollywood are always donating money to politics and causes. As if to expiate the sin of getting too rich and too famous too fast.

Hong Kong: more opium smell. We are equally unsuccessful

at copping any. Ensconce ourselves Marco Polo Suite, Peninsula Hotel. Tasty and plush. Complete with its own houseboy. Which really bothers me. Another fight about the little people. I sink a low blow. Remind him of his own diminutive stature. He stomps into his bedroom. Fond of this separate-bedroom routine. Last time in bed next to him he had a nightmare and called me Helen. Which gave me nightmares.

Victoria's Peak: Listen to the cacophony of human voices rising from the city below. Shop in bazaars and jewelry stores.

Tokyo: Lay over for a flight to Hawaii. Night. Wish I had a taste for video games. Airport clean. Hit standup bar for a martini. Watch the planes, the flashing lights, the coming and going of it all. Try to absorb the meaning of this trip. Sure not a romantic interlude with Mr. Wald. Arthur wanted to know if he was my bodyguard. No. He is . . . My manager. My Mr. Agent-without-Portfolio. My No-really-we're-just-good-friends.

Hawaii: dressed in the same clothes from Hong Kong, me schlepping 'that fucking mink' over my arm. Airport steamy, jammed with people. Welcome to the US of A. Customs goes through every item. Check the serial number on my Cartier watch. Mr. Wald says they are fucking with us because they recognize him and see that he is traveling with a female person other than Helen. I tell him he has some fucking ego.

After an hour and a half Customs waves us through.

To the Kahala! To the delicate thin pancakes! Yay! Kay Aherne is standing at the doorway to the hotel.

'This is a bad sign, Mr. Wald . . .'

'I'm hip . . .'

'The last thing you are is hip . . .' Arenotamtoo, etc.

'Your suite isn't ready . . . don't get upset . . . I'm rushing them . . .'

We are put in a dingy room on the second floor of the main building, the kind of room I imagine the guys back at Customs would've liked to have taken us into if they could have unearthed any of what was left of those eighty-six joints in Mr. Wald's socks. It isn't even air conditioned.

Mr. Wald and I aren't on the best of terms by now. If

there's one thing fixed dead center in the middle of my mind it is that I wanna get the fuck out of here and into my bed in Benedict Canyon as soon as possible. Poor Kay Aherne . . . hard enough to deal with either one of us on our own, but together . . . I wouldn't wanna do it. Cranky, jet-lagged, overheated Type A's. Once Rod Stewart hadn't vacated the rock 'n' roll suite fast enough for Mr. Wald and when he finally did, Jeff coldcocked him in the lobby. Right there in front of reservations. I am rooting for one little repeat performance. Just so I can get out of my jeans and cowboy boots, both of which are beginning to feel painted on.

A drink. Nothing tropical. Too angry for tropical. Nice American vodka martini. On the rocks. With a twist, thank you. Mr. Wald paces. Calls Kay Aherne.

Mr. Wald thinks it would be a good idea for him to take a walk down the beach. I concur. I sip my martini and stare at my boots, as if I can magically teletransport them off my feet. I have never gotten over *Childhood's End*. He comes racing back to report that Goldie is on the beach, but the more significant report is the one from Kay Aherne that she can move us into our suite.

Main building: Straight-out view of the ocean. Sun blazing. Undress, put on a bathing suit. Hit raft. Mr. Wald reminds me about Goldie, escorts me down the beach.

She is in a yellow bathing suit with a stain on the front. Little Oliver is nearby, whining. He looks frail. Goldie looks dirty as always. She is not especially happy to see me. After we hello each other we both realize that outside of lying and saying how great we each look there is no more conversation to make. This is the way the girls end this is the way the girls end . . . I head back to my raft. Obladi, oblada, life goes on . . .

The next day we are on a plane back to L.A. I reread *2010* on the plane and realize that it is not so hot, but at least I have something to show for my around-the-world-in-fourteen-days-with-two-Type-A's . . .

*

There is really nothing to do after going around the world with each other in two weeks but create distance once we return to L.A. Plus, I am not doing blow and Mr. Wald is. I don't hang out anymore with people I know are doing blow. Just not a smart choice for me, plus now that I don't do it, I hate being around people who do. They talk too fast, they grind their teeth, and they always shake their legs nervously. I used to do that all the time. When I did blow.

Mr. Wald and I attend a couple of political events upon our return, the most notable of which is a heavy-hitter Democratic do at the Beverly Hills Hotel, starring Ted Kennedy. We sit at his table, which also houses:

Georgia Frontieri and her husband, the guy who writes terrible soundtracks;

Bob Evans, who never eats anything and keeps jumping up from the table to whisper secrets in Kennedy's ear, with;

Cathy Lee Crosby, who never stops sniffing a single rose she has brought to dinner with her; and

Angie Dickinson, who is Kennedy's date, and upon meeting me asks: 'Oh, are you Mrs. *Sting*?' I want to say, No, we divorced, but just smile and converse about small stupidities.

When I leave the table for a moment to go to the bathroom, my Dunhill cigarette case and lighter disappear. The rip-off feels like a symbol for the whole fucking enterprise. I survey the room and think, they all look like they have a migraine . . .

Nobody at MGM wants to deal with *2010* and I become so frustrated I insist on meeting with Begelman, who is becoming less and less accessible, but then, Xeroxes of *Indecent Exposure* are all over town. It has yet to sink in these are the final bells tolling for him.

'I bring back this thing that he's already done, and I can tell I'm being sandbagged on it,' I complain.

'You are . . .'

'But why?' I am truly dumbfounded.

'Nobody wants to talk to Stanley Kubrick.'

'I'll talk to Stanley Kubrick. I don't have a problem talking to brilliant, egotistical directors. Don't you remember? It's what I'm good at . . .' Not a crinkle in sight.

'Don't. Tell me about the rewrite.'

'I don't think he really wants to do it, but he said he'd give me a month of free notes on cosmic reincarnation or that he would work with another writer, if they can do it in Sri Lanka.'

Dear Beges: You promised, 'It's time to do it again!' I got the time if you got the nerve . . .

Mike Ovitz keeps his office cold. Probably it keeps him alert and his meetings short. Years ago, a friend in the business had said of a twenty-six-year-old Jeff Berg, 'He's a very good agent. I think that's a terrible thing to say about someone in his twenties.' Cold was what she meant. Jeff Berg was a caring person compared to this motherfucker.

'Ivan Reitman is very interested in *Doctors in Hollywood*.' He says this in a breathless manner, as if it were very good news.

'That's nice,' I say politely. 'Who's Ivan Reitman?' Mike Ovitz makes a face, like I've farted into the air conditioning.

'He directed *Stripes*, *Meatballs*. Frank Price will do anything he wants to do.' Frank Price, the man who put *ET* into turnaround? This guy is better than Steven Spielberg?

'Sorry, I haven't seen either one of those movies. Heard of them, though . . .' From Kate. She thought they were funny. Kate is eight. 'Plus Frank Price runs Columbia. I've got an overall deal at MGM . . .' Mike Ovitz doesn't respond. He's trying to figure out if I can possibly be addressing him.

Rosenfeld steps into the breach. 'Why don't we set up a meeting, off the lot, for you guys, go from there . . .' Why not? What's another meeting between friends?

Ivan Reitman. He is the silliest-looking person I've ever met. Droopy eyes, buck teeth, pear-shaped body. I am not confused at all about this one: he is a businessman not an artist. No wonder movies are getting so . . . unsatisfying. He suggests, all business, that we work together under the table, and if he still wants to do it when we're done, we'll jump off that bridge, as George Roy Hill (another businessman impersonating an artist) used to say.

I talk the concept over with Gail and we take a look at his movies. We're not overly impressed, but we know this guy will get it made. At this point, getting it made is all that counts. What, exactly, we're getting made, seems beside the point. The eighties. I remind Gail that this is under the table and she won't be getting paid. She brushes this injunction aside . . .

'When I first met you, you were so much bigger than me, and now you're getting so much . . . thinner,' Gail says, pinching my upper arm affectionately. Years before, I'd gotten off to a wrong start with Sue Mengers, who was pulling her pantyhose up over her fat thighs in the halls of ICM when I raced in from a meeting. 'Oh, you're so thin!' she said. Dialogue like this is always a warning.

'Oh, you see it,' my shrink had said, the shrink who'd dated Gail, 'but you put blinders on your third eye.' Just now all my third eye could imagine was his head stuck between her fleshy white thighs. More than enough reason for blinders, I'd say. Dark sunglasses at least.

We work with Ivan for months. He keeps saying he'll do the picture, per casting and script. When it's done, he goes to New York to give it to Bill Murray. Gail and I send him into the cold with a cashmere sweater from Neiman's.

Bill Murray's wife declares the script sexist and he passes. Ivan says that's okay, he'll go with Chevy Chase (in another part). I spend the better part of two weeks trying to arrange a meeting via Stan Kamen, Jim Crabbe, and John Ptak. Finally, Ptak tells me that the client doesn't think the director is talented enough. Talk about pots and kettles!

Frank Price isn't that fond of the Doctors project. I have encumbered it with a codicil: settle with us on *Close Encounters*. Columbia is screwing us on television money. When Steven did the 'special edition' another two mil was spent. For what I'll never know. Byzantine Accounting 101 (circa 1982): One of the top ten grossers of all time has ceased to break even. With Columbia on the brink of merging into Coca-Cola, Price seems more amenable to settling on old business than initiating new . . .

At first Begelman asks for a coproduction. Price says no. I arrange a lunch with Begelman. The morning of the big meet, I Waterpik a bridge out of my mouth and have to race to the dentist to get it glued in. I talk funny at lunch, but I manage to get the gist across: I need some relief from you on this issue, David, it could be a million-dollar issue. He doesn't want to, but he says okay.

In the end, Frank Price settles on *Close Encounters* and torpedoes *Doctors in Hollywood*, which has evaporated into nothing more than a nine-month detour. In all the machinations, Gail Parent decides her script has made me money and gets furious. I keep trying to tell her that the money I'm getting from Columbia is for past effort, but she doesn't hear anything but the beat of her own greedy heart.

Michael and I get our money, but I have no picture and I have lost a friend. It seems a wasteful trade, but hey, whatever . . .

Re: the quintessential lady writer. She was fat in high school. Whether she is still fat doesn't matter. It has already colored her point of view and made her very mad. She will always be fat inside. She beats you to death with her brains, but you don't know you're being killed because you're laughing so hard. Try to remember all humor starts with hostility (cf., comedy writer).

She goes through a lot of therapy. Trying to get in touch with all those feelings nestled beneath all that fat. When she gets to them, and discovers she is as hideous on the inside as the outside, she becomes truly furious. The finding of these feelings gives her total permission to forget about yours.

She makes serious money with some clever writing. But money is more often the scorecard for men. Sex is her scorecard, critical to her self-image, probably because she was laid so infrequently when it was first coming on . . . Now lots of men who eschewed her company in high school sleep with her to curry favor but she never knows if they love her for herself or her one-liners. Too afraid to find out, she sharpens her skills, often on other women . . .

Deep down, she just wants to be a cheerleader and fuck the quarterback . . . who just wants to fuck the tight end . . .

The Fling dies during the actors/writers strike of 1981.

Nobody ever gets *Short Strokes*, which is superseded by *Dynasty*, anyway.

Discouraged over the death of *The Fling*, Emily and I never really finish *The Lady and the Hunk*.

The Adelman/Sage comedy never gets off the ground.

Slow, painful fade on my MGM deal . . .

There were always so many sides to a question that sometimes she got hung up, but on the issue of her own continued existence she was real clear. The positive side was that if Mick Jagger could still get up every morning so could she. Who the fuck was she to feel so jaded? Yeah, but Mick promised not to jump around on a stage singing 'Satisfaction' when he was forty and then he did.

And every once in awhile, it was fun to think, Well, but what about the suicides? What about Inger Stevens, and Jim Hutton, and the guy who played Sam's husband on *Bewitched*? What about Norman?

What about Connie Hipwell? Connie Hipwell was to her like Snowden was to Yossarian. A stranger who died and then became a symbol for the bigger picture. Connie Hipwell was a pretty, moonfaced girl from the Middle West who played at being a development girl before there was such a creature in

Hollywood. What she really was was Freddie Fields's tormented tootsie.

She had only touched eyes with Connie Hipwell once, across the room at Sardi's, but from time to time she was haunted by that image and the story with it. Freddie got bored. Maybe she was becoming an embarrassment. He moved her to the New York office of CMA, where the only friend she made was a screamer called Lance. Finally she was fired. Lance lent her his apartment, because he was going to catch some sun in the Bahamas. In the cab on the way to the airport, he got a bad feeling in his stomach and turned around.

When he got home, he found her half-dead from an overdose of household cleaner, and rushed her to a hospital to get her stomach pumped. They brought her back from the dead, and she went home to the Midwest, and then to Menninger's for a year. They let her out to visit her parents and she hanged herself the first night she was home, in her childhood room. And in her parents' faces. End of story.

Where are the Connie Hipwells of yesteryear, she thought, checking out the vast array of beautiful women waiting to get into the one bathroom at Helena's. *Où sont les Connie Hipwells de hier?* Do they know something I don't? she always wondered when she heard of someone offing themselves. Gary Weis, once a *Saturday Night Live* short-film maker, had a collection of suicide notes. None of which she ever saw, but he mentioned them a lot.

Everyone always quoted the George Saunders note: 'I'm bored,' but her personal favorite was a note pinned to a raincoat on a guy who had hanged himself in Boston. It had been an exceptionally stormy month in the Northeast and he had written: 'Too much rain . . .' Mones had once called her the Queen of Pith. Face it, her favorite poem was 'I . . . Why?' Well, Because. That was pretty much what she had come up with over the years. The answer is that there is no answer. The bottom line is that there is no bottom line. The quintessence is that there is nothing quintessential, only penultimate . . . *quel drag . . .*

Why? Because. She had felt freer to think this way in the old days, when she lived at the beach. Nothing like a vast

478

ocean to remind you how puny you are. Why did thinking of herself as small make her feel better?

What had she told the shrink when he asked her what she wanted out of her therapy?

Sublime indifference she had said.

When she left she told him serene neutrality.

Who knew if she'd really had the ability or if her parents had imbued her with so much information and drive by the time she was four, that her course was predestined? I really didn't start growing up until my mother died, she thought. What a shame! And even now, when she tried to forgive through understanding, she still got angry.

Mommy Mommy the money's all gone. Do you forgive me?

Two days after my MGM deal is up I have lunch with Alan Hirschfield and Norman Levy at Fox. Rumors of Sherry's departure have been rife almost since the time she'd started as president of the company, the bitchiest snipe being, 'She gives new meaning to the words *production head*,' so I'm not really surprised when they ask how I feel about the job. This lunch is heavy duty. I haven't seen either one of them since I walked off *Close Encounters*.

There are two things I'm supposed to be at this lunch: Clean and Neutral. I'm clean by my newly revised standards. I'm tan and slim. I look clean, and that's all that's really important. The be-neutral part is a little harder. I'm climbing up a mountain of rebuilding and forgiveness, and the top isn't even in sight. But if I want to get anything out of them, I have to appear neutral. IthinkIcanIthinkIcan . . . I . . . Why?

Who knows if these guys have enough sense to feel even the least bit guilty about my sudden departure from a picture that has my blood on every frame? Which I nurtured for four long years, fighting them valiantly inch by long inch? Until one fateful day I allowed them to betray me? They exhausted me out of show business, and I had given them my very best. The film doesn't suck, either. I'm still mad as hell, but I'm pretty sure I can fake it for as long as lunch takes.

'It'd be fine if you wanted to go from noon till midnight. From my bed.' I've given up drugs but I'm still an asshole.

'Well, what did you have in mind?'

'I wanna be Ray Stark. I wanna be a film-making entity within a larger entity.' This is exactly what I want, having gone through the intense disappointment of my overall deal at MGM.

So I tell Alan and Norman that I will put on a dog-and-pony show for them and all their executives, but that I don't want to end up with an overall development deal, that I want to be a film-making unit with the protection of their huge studio behind me. They look doubtful, but they book the meeting anyway.

'So, how's your love life?'

'What is it with you guys that you always want to know about my love life?' Beep Wrong Answer. Not a neutral response. 'Listen, I know it's just conversation with you and you have this fantasy that it's more happening for me, but guess what, it's the eighties. I'm fucked out. I don't want to get a disease and I don't want to be in a relationship. I'm the wave of the future. But I do still wanna make movies. Let me fuck some movies.' Beep Good Answer. I used to get serious money from these dudes in the seventies doing this act.

Relieved, they start to tell me about Marvin Davis, the oilman who owns the studio. 'He's very emotional,' Norman says. 'Y'know, we brought George Lucas in to meet him, and this guy is just huge – '

'What's huge, Norman?'

'Julia, he makes me svelte and Alan short. Anyway, at the end of the meeting, he picks George up and hugs him . . .'

'That must've just thrilled George.' Although I have only a passing acquaintance with George, he is one of the most exceptionally reserved people I've ever met. Cold might be a better word.

480

'Oh, he turned red, white, and blue.' Norman laughs. 'He's gonna love you . . .'

'Who? Marvin or George . . .' Laughs and chuckles all around. All in all a productive lunch.

Two nights before the big show, I have the whole crew over to my house to run them through order of presentation. It is a pretty good up-and-coming Hollywood party; there are about thirty people, including David Debin and Emily Levine, Marc Abraham, Jeff Wald, Gail Parent, my assistant Harlan and his assistant, Celia, Kenny Friedman. Norman and Barbara Garey are there, too, and it is their anniversary, so they have to leave early to celebrate at Adriano's.

At the door, Norman and I remind each other that we're going to have lunch the day after tomorrow, before I go into Fox. The meeting is set for three and we decide we should go to Orsini's even if the food is too heavy because we'll have the most time together. Norman has stuck with me through everything, and I hope that now I can repay his belief. There were times when he had been the only friend I had, a big brother, someone who took the job of caring for me seriously. We hug warmly at the door, and when he pulls away, his glasses are misty.

'This reminds me of the glory days at the beach.' He smiles.

'Well, let's do it again . . .'

'We will . . .'

'Have a swell and meaningful anniversary . . .' They walk off, with their arms around each other. I have been feeling worried about Norman. He doesn't look right to me. Twice that year, I've blurted to Debin and Harlan that I'm trying to adjust to Norman's death. I feel he is carrying a fatal secret. I presume it is cancer and that he isn't saying anything because it would be bad for business. I'd even had a confrontation with him about it, but he told me nothing was wrong.

'You'd tell me, right?' I pushed.

'I'd tell you,' he said, but I still had a vague feeling of unease about Norman's health.

The next day, Harlan, Celia, and I push hard, creating an

agenda that can be passed out for everyone, book a couple of limos to shuttle people back and forth. Fox is giving me a green room downstairs and the conference room upstairs and everybody – theirs and mine – is going to attend. At least I could demonstrate my ability to create an event. The three of us decide to stay in for lunch, and we're just in the middle of ham and bologna sandwiches when the phone rings. It is Susan, Chris Cuddy's secretary. Chris, my personal favorite during the entire *Fear of Flying* fiasco, had left Rosenfeld, Meyer, and Sussman with Barry Haldeman and Joe Peckerman when Norman went into partnership with John Mason.

Susan is hysterical, crying and gulping and making terrible noises. 'Norman Garey is dead,' she sobs. How many times in my life would I be shocked but not surprised? I feel nauseous, nauseous like smack nauseous, nauseous like getting-busted nauseous, nauseous like 'somebody died' nauseous.

'Where's Barbara? Is she okay?' Norman's second wife is a fragile, dependent woman who can't possibly cope with this.

'She's sedated. Joe Peckerman is with her.' She blubbers something about a heart attack, and I ask her where Chris and Barry are. 'Up at the house, there are police there and everything – '

'Police?' Police? 'Have one of them call if they come back.'

'I will.' We don't say goodbye, we just hang up at the same time.

'Norman Garey is dead . . . Heart attack, Susan said. I don't think so.' What would give relief right now? My mind races through drug possibilities: a drink? a lude? a joint? I decide on all three. 'I think I'm gonna faint.' I feel my knees start to go out and I order them back. Control. Over what? Life, that little speck of sand under the fingernail of a larger being, etc., in a universe that is either expanding or contracting but certainly random, on a planet that is committing suicide . . . My mind stops short on that and I lower myself onto a stool. 'Well,' I say, 'I guess he won't be making lunch.'

The next morning, Barry and Chris call early. I have the cold calm of someone in a rage who is getting ready for the performance of a lifetime. No way I am canceling this. I am so angry, I am starting to look forward to it. I've been hearing some nasty shit about Fox. Yesterday afternoon, thinking about Norman, I'd been reviewing some of the current gossip about Dan Melnick's departure. Norman represented Dan . . .

'He killed himself, didn't he?' I say, and they say yes, he killed himself. He took a gun out of the top drawer of his desk in his office at home. Sometime around noon, twelve thirty, and shot himself through his left eye. I wonder if he left his glasses on.

I've dressed carefully for this meeting, and I am a vision in summer white. White T-shirt, white Claude Montana linen shorts, with a matching white linen bigshirt, white sandals. And a dark summer tan with pink nails and pink lips.

The Fox meeting includes Norman Levy and Alan Hirschfield, and Sherry, David Field, Bob Cort, and that prick Dan Rissner. My troops are gonna do it for me, and I am gonna do it for Norman. I know that everyone knows he died, but not many know he committed suicide. I start the meeting by informing them of this fact, with an apology for being a little off, and check around the table for reaction. Bob Cort and David Field look truly alarmed, and Alan says, 'Jesus' under his breath. Sherry knows already. Of course. I don't linger. I stand up; I like doing these things on my feet.

Harlan directs traffic, and we move people in and out of that room, and I shift gears from project to project, and make beautiful transitions between things that have no relationship to each other. I shine. Everybody shines. The room begins to take on an inspired energy and I can see they are all – except for Dan Rissner – caught up in it. Harlan tells me later that there were people gathering outside the doors eavesdropping.

Sherry has to leave at five for a meeting, but I know it doesn't matter, and I move on. The meeting takes three hours and I could go on and they could stay, but there are some very shady-looking characters in fifteen-hundred-dollar suits who have been waiting for Alan for an hour. Finally, one of them comes in. He is short and dapper, but his eyes are dead. He is wearing a neck brace, and when he speaks, his voice is so gruff that I wonder if he has it on too tight. 'Alan, we gotta talk,' he says, and the meeting is over. Alan and Norman say they will call in the morning, and Harlan and I beat it out of there to meet the others at the house.

'J.P., you are amazing,' Harlan says, puffing on a big fat one as we drive home, and I know it has gone as well as I thought.

'Well, with any luck, we'll get a callback tomorrow, and I get to meet the big man himself . . . I've been thinking about Norman.'

'We've all been thinking about Norman . . .'

'You think this whole Dan Melnick-Fox boogie had anything to do with Norman killing himself?'

'Whaddyou think?' If it were in a movie it would, and this is Hollywood. We laugh. Norman's father had lost his fortune at the age of forty-six. Norman was forty-six. I've read articles about the Anniversary Syndrome. But Norman's father had just gone broke, he hadn't killed himself. I look at my nails. ('Make them the color of the tablecloths at Mortons,' I had told the manicurist, like she would know. She did.) Searching for the Answer. I . . . Why? Well . . . because . . .

The next morning, The Call comes from Norman Levy. He is excited and ebullient on the phone.

'So you liked my projects, huh?'

'I liked *you*! It was the Old Julia, you were fantastic. Can you come in at three?'

'You bet . . .'

'It'll be just me and you and Marvin.'

'What about Alan?'

'Oh yeah, and Alan.'

'That's fine.'

'And, Julia . . .'

'Yes, Norman . . .'

'Wear the same thing, okay?'

'Are you kidding, the exact same thing? Norman, it's summer, it's white, get my meaning . . .'

'Wear the same thing, let's not make any mistakes . . .'

Amy washes the funky T-shirt and dabs bleach on the spots and pressed and dried. When I put on my clothes, I smell like a drycleaning establishment, so I throw on a little extra Chlöe. Everything feels a tad damp, too, which gives me something to focus on besides my quiescent nerves about the upcoming meeting, not to mention the funeral tomorrow. Then Schrader's I'm Back party tomorrow night. Hot tickets for the weekend: Norman's funeral and Schrader's party.

Harlan wants to stay connected, so he drives me over to the meeting; it is weird being driven in my own car. He'll be driving it tomorrow, too, to go to the funeral. Harry Ufland and David Debin are coming with me, too. That ought to be enough protection. No, I think, there is no protection; your protector put a bullet into his eye. To be sure he was successful . . .

Marvin Davis has to be seen to be believed, and even though Norman Levy had said 'huge' at lunch, it wasn't sufficient preparation for the being that looms behind the giant desk. Now I know the image George Lucas had when he conceived Jabba the Hutt. He is joshing on the phone with Henry Kissinger. I am ushered in, and he stands up to shake hands. I know he's in oil, but does that mean he has to look like a derrick? He is six foot seven, easy, and at least four hundred pounds. When he clasps my hand in greeting, I feel engulfed. Like by The Blob.

There are three chairs arranged in a semicircle facing him. Norman and Alan are on either side; I'm in the middle. He asks me to tell him about myself. His corrupt eyes slide back and forth, lizardlike, sucking us in. I can't get rid of the Jabba image. Don't say anything.

'Mind if I stand? I'm best on my feet.' That way we are approximately eye to eye. I do a wittily concise twenty-minute version. My performances are for such small rooms. I am sweaty when I am done, but I know I have him. We discuss various concepts for a deal, the four of us, and after another hour, he is ready for us to leave. Big fat rich man who has the world brought to him on Friday afternoons, hors d'oeuvres on a plate. Beware the fat man, Redford had said. We all stand up to say goodbye.

'So, let's make a deal,' Marvin says, coming around his desk.

485

'Well, I don't know if they told you, but I'm kind of unrepresented right now . . .'

He smiles, cold as ice. 'You're free to avail yourself of house counsel.' I've noticed Mickey Rudin's name on a door; Edward Bennett Williams, too.

'Nah, just give me a week to make some decisions . . .' He is looming toward me and I know what is going to happen next, so I stand my ground and try not to look frightened. Then he picks me up and hugs me, brutally tight, a sadistic father throwing his baby too high in the air.

'Let's just make a deal and get started. Let's make some pictures.'

'A film-making entity, right. Ray Stark City, right?'

'Right.' A glorious end to a fucked-up week and I am glad it is coming to a close.

It is a beautiful day for a funeral; winds sweep across the valleys and clear out the bad air and the sun is bright. I wear a black linen Gianfranco Ferre shirt and skirt. It is packed. I can see Brando and Hackman and Tony and Michael and Liv. Is Melnick here? Ah, there he is in purple. I wonder if he is wearing socks – he favors the Gucci-shoes-with-no-socks look. The funeral is very sad. Norman's daughters speak, and Bo Goldman, too; the family had originally asked me to speak, and I am relieved to be replaced by this calming, unprepossessing man who is a Bigger Name. All I could think of was the Edwin Arlington Robinson poem about Richard Cory, the man who had everything and went home one night to put a bullet through his head.

Walking up to the front door to Norman's house after the funeral, I notice a sign that says, WESTEC SECURITY, ARMED RESPONSE. It bothers me, that sign. There are a lot of people here. Sid Sheinberg says, 'If I were to make a list of five hundred people who might do this, Norman would have been number five-oh-one.' Liv keeps crying. Harry Ufland's ass is in an uproar over Norman's shrink. Apparently, Norman was on some new antidepressant. Well, it sure hadn't worked. Apparently the shrink had pronounced Norman nonsuicidal.

486

David Debin and I split a lude and decide that we should definitely go to Schrader's party that night. The other side of Hollywood.

'You know what Norman said to me,' Barbara Garey, who looks heavily drugged, tells me. 'He said, the other night at your house, while we were walking to the car, "They'll never let me negotiate this deal . . ." What could that mean, Julia?'

'I don't know . . .' Something has gone down with Norman and Melnick and Fox. The name Buddy Monash keeps coming up; Marvin's buddy, the divorce attorney from New York. The one who does the hatchet work. Buddy is negotiating Frank Yablans's departure although it is very hush hush.

I've already told Alan and Norman that if I come to Fox I want Dan Melnick's building. Alan said that could be a problem; Frank wanted it, he said. I pouted and stamped my foot.

'Oh, c'mon, Julia, he's been here seven years, he's got seniority.'

'Yeah, well, why don't you focus on his *Monsignor*-ity,' I punned.

I get the offices, eventually, but I bet that joke costs me *2010*. When Frank leaves Fox, he becomes the head of MGM production, and wrests the project from the $1.2 mil offer Alan and Marvin authorize for me to buy it. At the same time, Fox approaches Columbia to buy *Fear of Flying*. Alan, ever the horny Jew, still likes the project.

When Herbie Allen finds out that Alan is the one looking to buy, he stacks up all the interest charges that have been accruing since the book was first purchased in 1974. I know that Herbie and Alan have broken up, actually read an article in *The New York Times* years ago where Herbie described Alan as a standard 'executive for hire with a $700,000 screening room in his home in Scarsdale.'

There are too many zeros in the figure for anyone to stay serious about *Fear of Flying* for very long. I am disappointed, but hardly devastated.

I am still enjoying a brief honeymoon period with Fox. It is early December, and I'm invited to go to New York with the Big Boys for the opening of *The Verdict*. Victor and I break into his shop in the middle of the night and give my hair a body perm, then cut it short with a long spike in front.

Victor is my date the next night for the premiere. We dress in our matching Armani tuxedos and go in a car with Alan Hirschfield and his wife, Bert, and his best friend, Don Zacharia, who has written an extraordinary first novel, published by my pal Joni Evans, called *The Match Trick*.

They pick me up at 200 Central Park South, where I am getting in a little therapy session with my long-distance shrink. When he opens the door to the apartment to let me in, he pales out. I think it's because I look so great. Later he tells me it is because I look just like a little boy . . .

The movie depresses the shit out of us, and we barely make it through dinner without falling asleep in our soup. The major fun is tormenting Alan by flirting with Don. Victor and I drop them off at the Ritz Carlton, where Alan has insisted I stay, too.

'Take the car,' Alan says, eying us enviously, the kids, going out on the town. Victor and I hit Heartbreak and get into a tug of war over a bisexual bartender. Neither one of us wins, although I score a hockey player whom I then can't get rid of. We have oatmeal in the Jockey Club in our tuxedos.

Alan and Marvin are both in town and encourage me to visit Scott Meredith, Clarke's agent, in his lair. I extend the offer we have discussed and he accepts. I pass it off to Leon Brackman at Fox. Everyone keeps telling me that I am like the Old Julia, even Zacharia, who never knew the Old Julia, but like everyone, gets very turned on by someone creating so much AC-TION . . .

It develops, over the next couple of weeks, that Clarke really doesn't have the rights to sell, and that Freddy Fields is coming up with an offer. Hirschfield tells me that Frank Rosenfeld, Freddy's boss, has referred to me in an angry conversation, as 'that girl.'

In the end, just so I can't do it, Frank Yablans gives it to Peter Hyams. Peter approaches Michael Phillips to produce it, which sends me over the top. I make it very clear to Michael

I'll think he's a worm if he does it and he passes. I don't let it go without a fight. I even go to Marvin.

'C'mon, Marvin, surely you can create a coproduction, you're the greatest tummeler there is . . .'

He stands up and looks at his feet. 'Well, Julia, you tummel and you tummel, and then you don't tummel anymore . . . by the way, do you know Joe Wizan?' And he foists me off on his new president, who sits benignly with his hands covering his dick while we chat about my projects. He isn't interested in doing any movies but those he's developed for himself as an independent producer, *Rhinestone*, for example.

When I leave his office, I know that my relationship with Fox, already diluted through the miraculous efforts of my new attorney, Barry Hirsch, into a standard development arrangement, is going to be another disappointment. Disappointment, discouragement, and finally despair. Maybe Norman knew something I didn't.

One day, I rifle through my Rolodex and find his card. I line the edges with black Magic Marker. 'You son of a bitch,' I start to cry, really cry, like I never cry. I pull his card from the Rolodex and tear it into little pieces. I start talking to the card: 'I'm sorry, I'm so sorry,' I say, and I try to tape it back together. Finally I just type out a new one, and line it in black Magic Marker.

There isn't a day that goes by that I don't think of him.

'Do you think he knew he was going to do it the night before?' I ask Harlan.

'Yeah, I think that's why he was so happy while he was saying goodbye to everyone – you know, shaking hands and thinking, So long, fucker, I don't have to worry about you anymore . . .'

I remember the kind of serenity that enshrouded my mother, a volatile personality to say the least, when she first found out she had inoperable cancer. She had been beatific the way Norman had been at my house that night. That's why I thought Norman had cancer. Well, he did, in a way. Of the soul.

Jesus, I know a lot of dead people.

> *Suddenly, out of the strange,*
> *still dusk,*
> *a white moth flew.*
> *Why am I grown so cold?*
>   – Adelaide Crapsey

I am deep into my I'm-not-doing-freebase-but-I'm-eating-Quaaludes-nobody's-letting-me-do-a-movie nervous break-downette when Timmy Leary calls one afternoon and tells me that his friend Gordon, with whom he's been doing a college tour, is in town. Timmy says, 'I told him you were the best date in Hollywood. Come to dinner with us at Spago.'

'A-a-a-hhh . . .'

'We'll even provide the limo . . .'

'Yeah, but I'm having a big depression . . . I don't think I can deliver on this billing you've given me . . .'

I've seen Alan Rudolph's *Return Engagement*, which is a filmed diary of the Timothy Leary/Gordon Liddy traveling debate-and-chicanery divertissement playing in colleges around the country. I have to admit Gordon Liddy is an awfully compelling prospect to be turning down. He seems intelligent, or at least he has pretensions to intelligence. He wants to be a right-wing intellectual; like Buckley or Jeanne Kirkpatrick, and he has mastered his hyperbole pretty well. Plus there is something about his eyes and the stories of the willfulness that came out during the Watergate hearings; he is a creature – a self-created icon to macho. The ultimate man you love to hate. Given my politics.

But is it worth getting out of this stupor, never mind my bed? I decide it is and call Timmy back. 'I'm in,' I proclaim.

'Splendid!' he proclaims back. Timmy is always talking in exclamations and proclamations. He tends to think in eons. He is the cheeriest person I have ever known, and, contrary to popular opinion, his brain doesn't seem particularly scrambled. He seems more addled than anything, and the stuttering is probably a cover, like Ray Stark's senile harumphing and blubbering. I always presume he is a sprite who happens to be preoccupied with the Big Picture. Who likes drugs. A kindred spirit.

490

As I get out of bed I wonder if he has ever turned Gordon Liddy on. And to what? Gordon and Timmy on acid? Now, there is something to play with while I change my sheets. I have been crying and sweating in my cradle for a couple of days. A favorite pastime . . .

I light a joint with my black-and-gold lighter, and I look at myself in the mirror. Terrible. I am gaunt and thin and the color of my white stucco walls. Under the makeup my skin is about as mottled, too. I inhale deeply, something I rarely do. I smoke joints like they are cigarettes and never really get high. Maybe that's why the rolling of joints has become the basic fun to marijuana. Seems like I ought to be bent in some way for this evening.

I wear purple Missoni jodhpurs and a purple-and-blue hand-made sweater I've bought from Mara with the purple leather Jean Muir jacket and the boots that exactly match, which Kenny Friedman and I found in Houston. All that purple makes me look even more sallow. Well, pale and wan could work. Gordon looks like the type who could be charmed by a frail-looking stranger.

I am bummed by the pearly whiteness of the limo. I like only black in limos. Pearly whiteness is pimps and dealers. Well, I am going to Spago with Timmy and Gordon. I stay committed to my joint in the car, which everyone turns down. Barbara looks glamorous/silly with her nighttime sunglasses, and Timmy wears his orthopedic shoes that look like Reeboks from afar. Gordon wears his demented Charlie Manson eyes. And tweed. He is very gracious and courtly.

When we get out of the car, I notice that he is not very tall. But solid. The paparazzi gather, and Barbara and I move forward so they can get a clean shot of Timmy and Gordon. They take a lot of pictures. I turn around to take a picture of these two icons in my mind. They are smiling and they have their arms around each other. Only in America . . .

There is the usual lineup of stars waiting to be seated at the entrance. Gordon and Timmy join us. Barbara and Timmy link arms, and Gordon offers me his arm. I take it. Macho movie stars step aside hastily so Gordon can pass. With me on his arm.

'Please, please, can I take you to lunch at the Fox commissary on Friday?'

'Why?'

'Because that's when Marvin Davis eats there . . .' I want to see if Gordon will have an effect on Marvin Davis. If he does, maybe I can play cards with the Big Guy with a much hotter hand than I've been dealt. Yuck . . . yuck harder?

'If I'm here on Friday, I'll be glad to come to lunch . . .' Bernard, the maître d', whom I've known since his busboy days at Ma Maison, shows us to a window table right away. I take out a cigarette and Gordon lights it. He is one of those guys who light every cigarette. With your lighter. We order drinks. I have a choice right now: get bombed and cheer up temporarily, then depressed, or get bombed and go directly to depression. Hard to tell which way I'll go, even though it is clear that it is okay to feel safe, surrounded as I am with a benign sprite and a cold killer. My bodyguards, Messrs. Yin and Yang. We discuss my depression during dinner and Gordon suggests the Cartesian approach, one step at a time, then asks if I'd be interested in reading his novel, *Out of Control*. Maybe make a movie out of it. I tell him I'll make a movie out of his book if he'll make lunch on Friday. He laughs grimly.

I ask him what he's doing in L.A. and he says, mysterioso, he's protecting a potentate from assassination. He's a gangster . . . like everyone . . . I wonder if the potentate is Marvin Davis.

He never makes lunch and I never finish the book, but even now, when I think of him, I add, to myself, Hey, I'll let you be in my movie, if I can be in yours . . .

I break up with pretty much everyone I know on New Year's Day, 1984. I never had an easy time with New Year's anyway, and in a pre-epiphanal moment, I just sort of stalk out of everyone's lives and hop a plane for Hawaii. Well, not really Hawaii. Really, I hop a plane for the Kahala Hilton. I take a suite in the main building. I am traveling *sans famille* and who needs the rock 'n' roll suite to myself. Besides, it is a different POV for me, and even the Kahala is getting stale. Kilauhea is erupting, so I book a helicopter to fly over and check it out. I relate to the volcano, but I can't seem to erupt myself.

Celia Cotelo, the assistant to the assistant of the moment. presses a paperback of *Interview with the Vampire* into my freezing-cold hand before I depart and tells me timorously that I might enjoy it. I like the cover art and the title, so I bring it with me. I attempt some of it on the plane, but I am not into a basic reading mode, and the flowery prose puts me off. I put it down on page sixty-five.

When I arrive in the early evening, I check in with Bertha, the head of room service, and she sends up my delicate thin pancakes right away with extra maple butter on the side. This is a dish that only a child or a junkie could love. The pancakes are the perfect blend of flakey and rubbery, and the maple butter is a very good substitute for the I've-died-and-gone-to-heaven aural high I always seem to crave upon arrival in Hawaii.

I roll a great big fat one and hang out on my terrace watching the sky fill up with stars and satellites. If the lighting is right I can catch the Soviet and American satellites crisscrossing in the sky. Always a mystical moment for me. Détente. I wonder if they take pictures of all the people lighting up great big fat ones and looking heavenward. I hope so. I unpack. I order a drink – a bullshit tropical one even though I know it will make me queasy. I go to bed early.

The next morning, I call Bobby, who runs the pool, and tell him I want my raft in a half hour. I go downstairs to spread the usual two hundred bucks around the pool: Bobby, a hundred; Lloyd, the head of the beach boys, fifty; and another fifty for extraneous slaves and bargirls. I buy some of Bobby's grease, which is still the best suntan oil on earth, get some towels, and head out to my raft. It is eight thirty in the morning. The sun burns down hot and sweet. The trade winds waft overhead. Clouds change shape every ten seconds; I light up a joint. Ah, Hawaii . . .

Suddenly, the sky gets dangerous. The next second it goes

black and rain pours down, extinguishing the joint and all my efforts at a beautiful suntan. I tough it out in the bar for the length of one drink, during which time not one, but two, Japanese businessmen with bermudas and short black socks try to pick me up. Disgruntled, I go upstairs.

It rains for the next day and a half, and, imprisoned, I read *Interview with the Vampire*. Straight through with no time off for anything but basic bodily functions. I feel like I am coming down with the flu, feverish and a little spacey, when I finish. By then the sun is shining, and I take up my post on my raft with my joints and my Bobby's grease and my delicate thins and my coco heads. I am getting tanner and tanner, and I am getting up earlier and earlier, but in my mind, I am yearning to be a vampire . . . and in my heart, I am a vampire.

Harlan calls. David Debin calls. One of the guys walks to the ocean's edge to tell me who is on the phone; I puff at my joint, like I'm really thinking about it, then wave the message away. I close my eyes against the intense light, squeeze them shut so that when I open them little points of opalescent light dance in the particles in front of me. I think of Louis and Lestat and Claudia. I start to dream a movie, a movie I really want to make, a movie I really want to see. I return Harlan's call:

'Listen, I read this book Celia gave me. Find out about the rights . . .' By now Harlan knows how to do that. How to call the head of subsidiary rights of the publishing company to get the name of the author's agent, how to call the author's agent and inquire about the rights. How to mention my name when it will help, or not mention it if mystery is the key to the information. If the agent is a man, use mystery, a woman, use your own judgment. Harlan calls back very quickly. A bad sign.

'Lynn Nesbit's the agent.' There is that name again. 'And Paramount has owned it since it first came out.'

'That was a long time ago.'

'Try 1976.' How did I miss it when it came out? I wasn't reading. I was doing *Close Encounters*. I wasn't doing anything but *Close Encounters*. Christ, I didn't even vote.

'Well, call Lynn. Tell her I'm away. Tell her you're calling about this vampire book. Get the skinny on what Paramount is doing . . .'

The only person I can bear to have in my sphere in my particular state is Emily Levine. She is really going to Maui and stopping over for a couple of days. We planned this a long time ago, way before I broke up with everyone. She is arriving late that afternoon and I am switching over to the rock 'n' roll suite in her honor. What a rip. It has gone from $550 to $660 to $770. Mr. Wald loved to remind me that when he started coming it went for ninety-eight dollars a night. No one could be that old, I'd say, never letting him one-up me.

I send a Silver Cloud and a bottle of Cristal, since I want to stay on the raft and think about what an amazing movie *Interview with the Vampire* will be if I make it. Emily arrives with half a bottle downed laughing to herself as she comes down the hall. Being with Emily is like being alone. Except if you want company. The next morning, chatting easily in the burning sun, each of us on our separate rafts, Emily says, in the normal course of conversation, 'Well, face it, Julia, you do have a lot of trouble with intimacy,' and I am just holding my hand to my chest in protestation – who doesn't? I would say – when the rafts, which have been touching, drift apart. Just another moment in a true movie. A reality cookie as Jack would say. Emily and I crack up.

Emily has brought a psychological thriller about a woman brought up by a crazy mother. I can relate, but it doesn't shed any new light. I am much more into this vampire book. I am looking forward to meeting the person who invented this cosmology. Never meet your idols, I remind myself.

Emily leaves Hawaii a few days later, and I follow suit within the week. When I come back, I call Jeff Katzenberg, then president of Paramount. I ask him what it would take to get the book.

'Three fifty and it's yours . . .'

I call Mike Levy. He and I had never known each other in all our previous incarnations, even though we'd been around at the same time, but he has found me at Fox and told me to call when I have something really special. He is a good friend of Joe Wizan's, part of that circle, so I think, why not have a partner on this Vampire enterprise?

'They'll love it – a Michael and Julia combination, they'll feel comfortable with it . . .' Levy laughs softly.

'You know I was the agent on it when it first sold . . .'

We become partners. On something we don't own. Only in Hollywood . . . The guys at Fox don't go for it, which means we're free to go elsewhere. We make the rounds. Mark Canton at Warners goes for it. I call Jeff. He says fine, great, but then the next day, Helene Hahn, in Business Affairs, calls to inform me that with interest charges, the cost is over eight hundred thousand dollars. All I know about her is what Harry Ufland has told me re: his negotiation with her on *The Last Temptation of Christ*, back when Paramount was going to do it. Apparently she was concerned about sequel rights. When Harry Ufland told me the story, he acted out all the parts:

'So then I said to her, "This is not the next to the last temptation of Christ. This is not the penultimate temptation of Christ. This is it. The last. There are no sequels . . ."'

The deal falls apart.

It is pretty clear by the spring of 1984 that Joe Wizan isn't going to let me do anything more creative than decorate my offices. This I have done at great expense to Fox: seventy-five to a hundred grand. A pittance by Hollywood standards, but a whole lot more than they wanted to spend on me. I have obviated every last gray tile of Dan Melnick's by having a spray-paint artist replicate Georgia O'Keeffe's *Sky above Clouds* ad infinitum. Then I've laid vast expanses of sandy white carpet and matching sectional couches.

When Timmy and Barbara Leary come bearing gifts (an edible bikini, for one, which freaks me out) they pronounce it desertlike. I had first seen a reproduction of Georgia O'Keeffe's last painting, the result of her first plane trip (she was eighty), on the wall of the Dunnes' beach house. It was side by side with a giant black-and-white photograph of some stark wasteland with a roadside telling you how many miles it was from Sacramento, which was Joan's home. I think I knew that as far as these new guys were concerned, my head was in the clouds. It gives me peace – the sky the clouds the space. Maybe that's why Joan had it next to the photo – a case of where you're from and where you're going.

I have taken over nine offices in the building upstairs and downstairs and installed a number of talented people to write, to think, to exchange ideas. These are all the people who had reminded Norman of the days at the beach, back in the seventies – that curious mixture of haves and have-nots who came together while Michael and I were coming apart.

To be perfectly honest, though, I don't think my eighties batch holds a candle to the seventies, and I'm starting to be convinced that that was a unique group, not easily duplicated. The times are running against it, anyway.

In the seventies, even the guys who were to become greedy and selfish didn't start out that way. They really did give each other major ideas that showed up in major ways in each other's movies. Now, everyone is so worried about getting their ideas ripped off (often by those very people who hung out with each other on my couch and exchanged ideas) that they never discuss them with other talented people and they never really get them any further than half baked. So in the end, they don't produce anything that I can run the distance with. The entire comeback trail seems fraught with more and more potholes day by day.

'Is it possible to outgrow show business?' I ask the shrink one day. And then Sue Mengers the next, but only in my mind. We are smoking a joint on Barbra Streisand's tennis court. Barbra had been Sue's client for years, but they'd broken up badly, mainly because Sue had put Barbra and Gene Hackman in a dog that her husband, Jean-Claude Tramont, whom John Dunne insisted was named Johnny Shapiro and came from Brooklyn, was determined to direct. *All Night Long*. Boy, there were a lot of jokes about that one.

The circumstances for this exchange are bizarre to begin with, as we are both guests at a coming-out party that Barbra is throwing for herself and Richard Baskin. Since Richard is one of the semitalents who has a nice office, compliments of me, I am a guest of the groom. Sue, of the bride's, although she does say later on at the barbecue that she is the only one who could traverse both groups.

I get up from the groom's table and go over to the married table, the Diamonds – Neil and Marsha, the Bergmans – Marilyn and Alan, the Joneses – Quincy and Peggy. I know them all, but I have very little to say to them, except to notice that they are all married – e-e-e-e-e-u-u-u-w – it doesn't come out funny, so I leave that table and come back to talk to Colin Higgins, with whom Richard has a development deal at Universal.

Talking to Colin, I find out that years ago, when I gave him back a script that Goldie and I were trying to buy, called *Killing Lydia* (which ultimately became *Foul Play*) he thought it was because he wanted to direct it. Actually I was up to my hips in *Close Encounters*, and didn't think I could devote the energy that he deserved. I never questioned his ability to direct, I tell him. I thought I was doing you a solid, I say.

He smiles politely, like he's accepted the apology, but doesn't believe it. Same as the Grady situation. People are so conditioned to the Hollywood way of doing things that it doesn't occur to them that you might be doing something generous. It's because you don't believe in them.

But that afternoon on the tennis court, Sue and I discuss who was more betrayed. Me by Steven or her by Barbra? Colin Higgins walks by and Sue says, Look at the state of things: there's the best comedy director in Hollywood and he can't get a picture made. He's got a development deal at Universal.

Yeah, I think, me, too.

I have lunch with Sue at Le Dome shortly thereafter. She is so bitterly depressed she makes me seem like Mary Richards. Sue, who had never given a moment of thought to the woman question, had suddenly woken up. Fewer women execs than ever before, etc., etc., etc.

'Sherry ruined it for all of us . . .' she pronounces. Yeah, and you. Me, too. I know there are a lot of people who think

I have blown it for women. Bullshit. I blazed the trail. I blew it for myself. Which seems a lot worse to me. From my point of view. As. It. Were.

Sometime between the vestiges of winter and the promise of spring in '84, I am invited to a dinner that my political counsel, Emily Levine, says we should attend. Basically it is a dinner to get some women in show business upset that the California chapter of NOW is about to go under because of insufficient funds.

'How much do you need?' Barbara Corday, who is big in television, asks.

'Couple of grand,' Sandra Farha, president of the California Chapter of NOW, replies.

'That's easy,' I say, relieved it is so little. 'We'll throw you a brunch.'

The women around the table who aren't in the business look at me as if I'm crazy. I press on. 'You know, mailgrams, Mary Macucci, Christopher Rogers, my front lawn . . .' Barbara and Emily smile. The other women look alarmed.

'Look, in Hollywood, the guys have their poker games and their big political contributions. We'll do a brunch. Sunday afternoon. Invite fifty heavy-hitter women. If there are that many. Maybe half will come. Sandra, you'll give a speech and then we'll pass the hat . . .' I don't have anything else to sell, so I kind of fall in love with the idea while I'm pitching it. All the women I know hate Reagan, the election is coming up. Why not buy some entree into the Democratic Party. Guys like Lew Wasserman and Jeff Wald had been doing it for years.

So the brunch goes down, and women like Marilyn Bergman and Anthea Sylbert and Barbara Corday come. We pass a flower basket around that afternoon and collect almost four thousand dollars. Sandra's eyes fill with tears.

The next day Paula Weinstein calls. 'I want to do this with you,' she says. Do what? I've known Paula and Marilyn for years and years. They are people who are highly therapized and social and never deal with you in a direct manner. I've always felt out of rhythm with them, and they distrust me.

'Well, what should we do?' I ask.

'We should organize . . . I heard about the brunch . . . you got something going . . .'

'I can't afford to give another brunch, but I've got these terrific offices . . .'

A short while later, fifty women come to the Sky above Clouds venue for an early evening chat about how to organize. Being an epic thinker, I'm for putting on a major event. selling tables, entertainment. It takes months, but we get Sherry Lansing and Jane Fonda to be co-chairmen for the event, we get Melissa Manchester and Whoopi Goldberg to be the entertainment, we sell tables to everyone in Hollywood for fifteen hundred a pop.

Most of the women are shy about selling tables. I decide to inspire them, do a fine imitation of a UJA fundraiser. Yablans signs up, so does Mr. Wald. I take a deep breath and call Jon Peters. He comes on the line right away. I explain the organization and the event, tiptoeing between the goodness of the cause and the goodness showing up will do for his career. Like he needs help from me.

'I gotta do this, right?' he says offhandedly.

'You gotta do this . . .' Way to go, Jon! Never will anyone hear a snotty hairdresser quip from these lips.

I'm elected president, Paula vice president. We call ourselves the Hollywood Women's Coalition. The event gets so complicated we hire a professional fundraiser with the improbable name of Hope Boonshaft. To me, she represents the rising tide of younger women who have MBAs and power suits and know nothing really about doing business. I think her Reaganesque. She becomes a scapegoat for everything that goes wrong.

We end up throwing the party at the Hollywood Palace. The event has become such a hot ticket that people are jammed together, the tables barely half a foot apart. Marilyn Bergman, at a table presided over by Barbra Streisand, is in a particularly awkward spot, where waiters need to come and go. The sight of that city of flesh pulling herself tightly into the

500

table or standing up to let people pass makes me sad and hysterical at the same time.

I've hired a limo to transport my assistant, Kiki Morris, and me, Paula, and Marilyn to the Palace about an hour before show time. As president and vice president, both Paula and I are going to speak. I haven't been president of anything since my senior year in high school when I got the Student Council to dissolve itself on the grounds that it was just a mouthpiece for the faculty.

They are all very warm and encouraging in the car. Oh dear, am I, the pariah, the outlaw, about to have massive acceptance? I feel a knot start to form in my throat. I run my speech down to them – basically the personal view of things, the old turning away from the process in the seventies to tend my own garden. And now, it is 1984, and Reagan is president, and life feels like it is about to get bleak, yadda yadda yadda. They like it.

Everything would have gone according to plan but for two small things that happen right before I go on: one is that a woman who is a friend of Paula's hands me a two-page list of celebrities in attendance who I am supposed to acknowledge – if I read the whole list, I'll have no time for my speech; two is that I run down my speech one more time with Bobby Walden, whom I have known forever, but whom I have temporarily forgotten is a short, angry, destructive prick.

I complain to him about this list of stars, and I start to develop a line to cover it all. The line turns out to be, 'It is at this point that I am supposed to introduce the stars to the starfuckers in the audience. Let me assure you that you are both here in profusion and we are grateful for your attendance and support.'

I incorporate the line in the speech, which provokes laughter and fury at the same time. For all the looking in the mirror that goes on in Hollywood, there is very little real seeing of oneself. And hell, it's the eighties. Nobody has a sense of humor anymore.

I end up having to apologize to the other women for behaving like Julia, instead of president. Everyone accepts the apology, but it is like throwing coke into the middle of the marketing meeting years ago. It is one of those unacceptable acts that will be held against me forever. My back goes up, too. Fuck me? Fuck you. If I hadn't yelled at you all at this brunch you would never have understood how truly powerful you really can be.

But mainly, everyone gets carried away with the glow of the success of the evening, and the National Democratic Party, in the person of Tony Coelho, approaches us right away. We organize something called the Hollywood Women's Political Committee, and another event supporting Mondale and Ferraro starts to be planned. Now there is a core group of lady lawyers like Susan Grode and Bonnie Reiss, along with the Paula-Marilyn-Anthea-ness of it all.

But Barbra is going with my friend, Richard, and is feeling warmly toward me, so one summer afternoon, me and Paula and Marilyn go over to the Carolwood house to talk about her singing for our event. She hasn't sung in public since McGovern in '73. She has developed a complete hysteria about being on a stage, being, I guess, in a live situation that she can't control. I can relate. We are pretty amazing, the three of us, in terms of the pitch. From the heart – me, from the head – Paula, from the gut – Marilyn. When we leave, I feel we have a better than fifty-fifty shot with her. Marilyn says, in the driveway, flush with the sheer effort, 'We could do anything we wanted, if we put our minds to it . . .'

Probably true, but Barbra turns us down. I'm not that surprised. This is the woman who never acknowledged Jane, who died of cancer, and Val, who died three months later of a broken heart, on *Yentl*. She dedicated the film to her father instead . . .

Meetings take five hours and are filled with the kind of female backbiting that I always deny takes place when I'm asked by men. Business by indirection. They act like they want me to be part of the core, but I am already turned off and so are they, so I resign. By the time I rethink it, they tell me not to come back. Hey, I've invented bigger and better and walked, I think, but my feelings are hurt.

Ah hell, some people, they need a leader, and some people they would rather be in hell.

One Christmas in the early eighties, one of the myriad mistakes who passed for a boyfriend-for-a-minute brought her two paintings by a local artist whose name even she recognized. She had just lent him three grand and she was pretty sure this final offering accounted for at least half of it. They were large, collage-y, violent. She didn't like them much, but they were the right colors, so she let him hammer some nails into the brick wall in her living room to hang them, far from her real space, where she wouldn't have to see them much.

'Do they have names?' she asked politely. He smiled broadly.

'They're called *Sex* and *Death*,' he said; 'naturally, I thought of you . . .'

'Naturally, I'm just ahead of my time,' she snapped back. 'Like always . . .'

'I don't even know why I go to these memorials anymore,' Victor said on the phone one day. 'I don't know anyone anymore. They're friends of my real friends . . . those guys are all dead . . .' She made clucking noises. 'Why am I still here? Is it to cut hair?'

'Well, it's definitely to cut my hair!' And they cracked up, ha ha . . .

Daley said at dinner: 'So many of them die alone . . . they go into hiding, retreat into shame. Fuck it, if I'm diagnosed, I'm shouting it from the roof tops. I want support to die . . .'

*

Howard called from the car one day. He'd produced *Common Threads*, a documentary on the AIDS quilt, and at the end, all the people involved with the movie were going to read the names of people they knew who were on the quilt . . . 'Eighty-five names, Julia,' he shrieked. She couldn't tell if he was screaming over the traffic or if he was freaked out . . . it hardly mattered. It was a lot of names. For all at once.

She was pretty sure she knew a lot more dead people than Howard. She hadn't counted them in a long time. Someday, she was going to be just another name on other peoples' dead-people lists. If she wasn't there already. Dead covered so many possibilities in Hollywood, very few of which referred to breathing dirt forever. Probably the secretaries revised them, along with their Rolodexes, biannually, then threw them out . . .

When the AIDS pamphlet came, she made Kate read it – as if they weren't all being barraged with information and reassurances enough already. Kate, fifteen, with ripe breasts and that sleepy eye, asked, 'What do you think about safe sex, Mommy?'

'For me or for you?'

Smiling. 'Both.'

'Well, for you, I advocate it. For me – well, I'd rather read a magazine.' She didn't think it was necessary to add that all sex felt that way to her. Had she gotten to the point that she hated men so much that the thought of letting one of them enter her made her want to puke? Kate laughed and looked as though she understood, but those almond-shaped eyes had given her a look of inner knowledge since birth, and she didn't want to overrate appearances. Then Brooke called and the conversation had remained unfinished.

Ah, Brooke. From time to time he made her breathe a little faster, but she could never sustain the impulse. For one thing, he had acquired a girlfriend, a tall pretty girl named Michelle. In the beginning, his affair with her had been an annoyance,

504

like a yeast infection that wouldn't respond to Monistat. Now it was just another fact, and it didn't really affect her very much. Once she let go, she started, in truth, to like Michelle more than Brooke. The league of women, and all that jazz.

Sex with him hadn't been a real possibility after that first night anyway. For starters, it terrified him, and then, there was all that data – all those disappointments and mistakes – all those previous *men* in her life – that made her not want it either. She should've known that from the very first. Why had she not seen? 'You can always see it,' the shrink had said, 'you just like to put blinders on your third eye.'

Besides, there was something about being on the cusp of wanting but not getting that was profoundly exciting. She used to use that to make movies; now it had become a kind of self-diddling device.

Every once in a while, in the first couple of months, it had seemed as if they might complete the *pas de deux* they had started that first night. The memory of those hot wet kisses tweaked her for a long time. She felt that sometimes he wanted it, but not really, and then one day she didn't want it either.

Sex was never really the same for her after drugs – and even then, toward the end, it had always been best alone. Or essentially masturbatory: two gorgeous guys, one dark one blond, eating her everywhere, their hair and shoulders grazing each other in their travels, the entire ballet performed in front of a mirror while she sucked the ultimate hit of freebase with a little opium oil poured on top. Butterscotch over vanilla ice cream: the drugs and the guys. Suck Suck harder.

You fucked with Nirvana and now it's all an anticlimax.

It had been her experience that past a certain point no fuck could possibly live up to that much anticipation. Actually, it had been her experience not to expect too much out of fucking; unless, of course, you wanted to use up your kundalini showing *them* a good time. As with her ideas, she had become more protective of those energies as she'd gotten older.

She also knew how to quickly revise a male-female dance if it wasn't to be sexual, so now they had become something else, and while it made her feel better most of the time, it also made her sad, made her feel a sense of loss that was symbolic of all the loss she felt in the male-female department.

Bit by bit, fucking had simply passed from her life. She still required self-gratification from time to time, but she viewed these intervals as times to get off in the truest sense, much the way she ran to get off. Orgasm had become literal for her, another mechanism to let off steam; it was certainly an unwanted metaphor for intimacy. Relief was what she sought, if she sought at all, not ecstasy.

I got to know my cunt pretty well behind freebase, she thought, but nothing in her stirred. She remembered Ron Siegel showing her pictures of ancient coke-inspired art: the phalluses were predominant, huge and erect. Her clitoris had become like that for her. Her vagina had become the center of her being, until she started to hallucinate that hordes of little black bugs were crawling out of it, and she'd sought his counsel . . .

'Oh, Mr. Wald,' Kate beams, 'Mr. Wald makes Mommy look like a K mart shopper.' We all laugh. We are in a nice restaurant after our first day of skiing over Christmas in Sun Valley. It is me, Kate, Jackie and Steve Reuther, and there is a whole gang up here. Richard Baskin and Barbra, Kenny Sylk and Michael Brandon.

My semi-friendship feelings toward Barbra have been aroused by her nicely developing relationship with Richard, and we hang out from time to time. The first day we arrive, she meets us at a local eatery and gives me and Kate bubble bath bought from a local store as token Christmas gifts. The price tags are still on the bottles, and I wonder why she has bothered. When you are as rich as Barbra, you can go for more expensive tokens, is the way I look at it, but who am I to make judgments about how people spend their money? For myself, I would rather spend too much, not too little, a habit I will break only by diminishing my funds to poverty level. Something that will be accelerated by little jaunts like this.

I have rented a private ski instructor for Kate, since she is much more advanced than Jackie and I, at two hundred per, another for me and Jackie, same rate. Jackie and I have each burst into tears trying to learn and execute skiing basics several times during our first day. She orders wine and I order a martini.

We have been discussing how much this trip is costing us. Kate is being very precise and I thank God that she has gotten this quality from Michael. Her eyes are widening with each calculated expense, and I have said in my defense that at least I am not spending the way Mr. Wald would, as we have driven from Salt Lake City, not flown by private plane, and then Kate does her K mart shopper quip, and we move on to something else, which gives me an opportunity to obsess on my new addiction to colossal mistakes. Check that. Expensive. Colossal. Mistakes.

Men.

They are not as much fun without drugs. We are well into the eighties and sex is getting . . . well . . . difficult. It is definitely not as much fun without drugs; the more men I know, and the more I know them, the less I think they are good for anything *but* sex. Little clues have gone down along the way.

I sleep with Michael Brandon, but I do a taste of this and that as sexual aids. Basically, I mix Quaaludes and Ativan and pot – kind of a preforeplay cocktail. Upon awakening the next morning I look at him, and he is cute, but I surprise both of us by bursting into terrible heaving sob/tears. Being Jewish and funny, Michael defends himself with some pretty good jokes, but it is not the sort of event you can cover up. What do you say, Just Kidding?

These are not tears that stop right away either. I am so stunned at my crying, that it kind of feeds the desire to cry and so I cry some more. It feels shitty to do it in front of

Michael Brandon. I keep saying I'm sorry, but I am probably saying that as much to myself as to him. Needless to say, things are never the same as they were the night before again. No matter how many drugs. Several weeks later, I hear myself saying, in a kind of yenta voice, 'So, are you gonna tie me up or what?' and I know it is over even though we spend Christmas together. He brings a bottle of Cristal and we get drunk. He gives me a gray T-shirt with white lettering. It says: LIFE IS HARD THEN YOU DIE. I laugh. It sounds like something Jack Spratlin would say. Probably he made the T-shirt.

Reuther and I have a brief fling, and he tells me he wants to be my friend, that's it. I consider plastic surgery for the first time. It is not good for my self-esteem to continue as his friend. He is a user. I know the type. He is in AA, an ex-slammer. Over our first dinner with friends, between sushi and tempura, he told us he was the pride of William Morris until he went on the nod in the middle of his own pitch at a staff meeting. They waited two weeks till they fired him. He went to AA and told everyone he was sober for a year and a half before he went totally straight. But he is a sleaze at heart, anyway. I always tell these guys, You know, you can be an ex-junkie and still be a bad person. A sober sleaze. They always laugh, like I am making a joke. Reuther has just gotten a job and I have lent him some money and let him charge three thousand dollars on my Giorgio account to dress for success.

By the third day in Sun Valley, I am beginning to wonder why I am not in Hawaii lying on my raft and drinking coco heads, instead of freezing my ass off in this picturesque town surrounded by people who make me grind my teeth. Hollywood East. Every night when I hear the snow blowers maintaining the slopes on the mountain behind us, it reminds me of the sound of the waves rolling onto shore. There is an ad for a package deal to Hawaii on the tube, and I sniffle quiet tears, so no one will hear.

The big social event in Sun Valley is a New Year's party thrown by Richard and Barbra. I have a big problem with

New Year's anyway so I take an unnaturally long time to get ready and am not at all pleased with the result. It is hard to put together a casually chic outfit around snowboots, but I pull it together the best I can. When I study my face in the unforgiving fluorescent light in the bathroom, I notice that my eyes look like a sick cat's. Kate looks adorable in a little black leather skirt and black-and-pink angora sweater.

Jackie doesn't want to go, but I force her, on the grounds that I cannot bear for her to be alone in this cabin, and it will ruin my time because I will be thinking about her. Probably I just want her moral support. How much I need it is immediately apparent the second we arrive.

I am slipping and sliding my way into the house and the first people I see are Mr. and Mrs. Grady Rabinowitz. Oh great. *That* sort of New Year's Eve. There are all kinds of couples there besides Richard and Barbra. Alan Greisman and Sally Field, who have just been married. Jamie Lee Curtis and Christopher Guest, who have just been married. And the aforementioned Rabinowitz duo.

Jamie Lee Curtis tells me that I have saved her life. Years ago, in answer to an hysterical one ay-em phone call, I gave her Ron Siegel's number. And I thought it was for her father . . . I am shocked. Christopher Guest follows her around mutely like a large pet.

I go over to the snug-as-a-bug-in-rug set and say obligatory hellos. They are all pretty cold but they acknowledge my presence. I introduce Kate and they are marginally warmer to her. She starts to play Ghost with Harvey and Cis Corman. I head for the kitchen, but I can see that Steve Reuther is having a flirtatious conversation with Ronee Blakley. He is sitting on the counter, just as he does at my house, and he is laughing. I freeze and turn away simultaneously, surprised that I am wounded.

The next day, I send everyone off to go skiing so that I can be alone. When the blowers go off on the mountain, and the ad for Hawaii comes on again, I burst into loud, hysterical sobbing. I think I am having an NB-ette and, still sobbing, call my shrink in New York. I have never been hysterical with him on the phone. He tells me to get the fuck out of there. Go to Hawaii if I want to. My shrink, who doesn't often give advice, can be exceptionally protective when my center is not holding. I think that he is dispensing karma, making up for all the times he has treated women like shit.

Reuther checks in during lunch and I tell him I have to leave pronto. I have to be out of the cold, in a place with luxuriously running hot water, far away from him. I tell him he can stay in the house, the rent's paid up anyway. With a sigh – relief? tristesse? – he gets out the phone book, makes a call, and books me on a private plane the next morning.

When Kate and Jackie see the Cessna 350 and the wizened lady pilot, they know they're going to die, and they fall into a hard sleep. I stay resolutely alert at the controls and watch her every move.

As we approach Salt Lake City, there is a thick black layer hanging overhead. I express surprise at the pollution and she says offhandedly that it is a basin in the middle of mountains, just like L.A. Oh, do Mormons drive, I say, and she cracks up. The plane is light enough for me to feel the bounce of her laughter.

God, if we land, I'll try to believe in you. Every other day, fifty-fifty. As it were. Okay sixty-forty, my best offer. Take it or leave it. I'll give you 'til the close of business today . . .

Time's Man of the Year is Peter Ueberroth, for the Olympics. One night in Westwood while they're going on, a crazy person mows down twenty people coming out of *Purple Rain* with his car . . .

She went driving with Kate and let her stop off at all her friends' houses in Westwood. More of a neighborhood here than where they were up on the hill, as her friends called it. Up in Benedict Canyon where your cat could be killed on one side by the coyotes and on the other side by a car. Where the neighbors were far away from each other. Where there were lots of small woodland animals and very few people. What instinct had made her smart enough, back when she was still sociable, to capture this house and land?

She had aerobicized for forty-five minutes in the morning because she wanted to be mellow for this drive, which she had promised her daughter a week ago. They ended up at the Polo Lounge at two thirty for some heavy tipping and some eggs benedict, and just as her Stoli Cristal on the rocks with some plain tomato juice and splash of lime had arrived, two over-aged bimbos, reasonably well fixed but bad-taste and trashy, had come in out of the garden on their way to the exit, tipped the maître d', and left.

Kate looked over to her with a smirk, waiting for a zinger, and they just laughed instead. 'You always act like you know people's whole life story,' Kate said, irrelevantly to the point.

'Well, some people's whole life story is in their hairdo,' she retorted, and they laughed again. She sank into the cushion of the booth and sipped at her drink. Oh, God, I love this kid . . .

FLASH FORWARD TO AN AS-YET-UNDEVEL-OPED MOVIE TENTATIVE TITLES:

... ABOUT THE HAIRDO

SHAMPOO II

THAT WAS NO HAIRDO THAT WAS MY WIFE

ovo: Raking shot: Roxbury on a Friday night. Now, about the hairdo. It is streaked and blond, and one variation or another of the mane that Jose Ebert created for Farrah Fawcett back in the mid-seventies. It is frozen in time, and in L.A. it is universal. Boys have it, too. It is the shag on angel dust, and it is trashy trashy trashy. What's more, it is ugly. It is the epitome of the eighties. It makes Victor split a gut.

HE: (leaning against the bar, sourly surveying the scene) Fuck it, why should I care? Look around you. People don't care about their haircuts anymore . . .

ME: People don't care about anything anymore. Except money. They know that the end is here and they hope they can buy their way out of it . . .

HE: You ever get the feeling that there's just a whole lot of jerking off around Hollywood?

ME: (laughing) Always. But it's the eighties, now, so they don't come . . .

ovo: Yeah, they can buy their orgasms later . . .

Kathleen Turner is dressed in a red wool two-piece number and her hair is streaked and bobbed. The effect is certainly more sophisticated than when I first met her at a meeting in

New York some months before and made one of the all-time bad impressions of my career.

She wasn't so hot either, but that may have been because she was dubbing *Peggy Sue Got Married*, which meant she was not only dealing with Francis but seeing an exceptionally unattractive version of herself while listening for her cues. Neither one of us were knocked out by the other. But Gary Devore, my writer, and David Guc, her agent, have arranged this return engagement and we are both determined to make it work. Not to mention, she is committed to my project. Whether she likes me any better after dinner or not.

Her features are rather more pug than they register on film, and her top teeth are done badly. The big distraction from my mission to charm her is that her nose is running. I can see the snot dripping from her right nostril; it shines in the flickering light of the candle in the center of my table at Le Dome.

A-a-a-h-c-h-o-o! Kathleen has to excuse herself from the table for the second time in half an hour. I am running to the bathroom, too, because Dr. Leslie Dornfeld has inculcated me with the ten-glasses-of-water-a-day routine, but I make a point of leaving my bag on the table, so that people won't assume I am doing blow again.

I have to pee right now, and I have a temptation to follow her down to the ladies' room but I resist it. Don't wanna be alone with her. Why take a chance, particularly since she has committed to this incredible script of Gary's called *Wish You Were Here*, Vietnam horror story featuring a photojournalist and a thirteen-year-old-kid searching for his MIA father? The woman in the story, the photojournalist, has lost all control of her life in the horror that is Vietnam. The very least I can do in support of this unpopular project is to exercise some bladder control.

We picked Le Dome as a place to have dinner, because it is infinitely more low profile for dinner than Spago or Mortons. Lots o' Eurotrash and rock 'n' roll here at night. Besides, the food is better. Gary and I come early, so I would get my regular chair at my regular table, back to the wall, surveying all that pass before me. It's the outfits and the surgery I love to see. Bad taste, round pointy breasts, and tight faces.

Kathleen and her ex-boyfriend, but still-agent, David Guc, a repulsively pale fatso with one pierced ear, which doesn't make him any cooler, arrive only a little bit late. David Guc reminds me of Ken Shapiro, the director I had nixed on *The Big Bus* on the grounds that if anti-Semitism didn't already exist, he would create it. Thus, David Guc.

Gary and I had met the husband, a reptile named Jay who owned slums and second-string clubs on Long Island, only once, and had decided that Kathleen must not have looked in the mirror much; Gary thought she must be psychotic to look like that and be with these slimeballs.

Kathleen is a big star right now, and she is out here to talk to all the studios. She goes to meetings and they say, 'What would you like to do next?' and she says, '*Wish You Were Here*,' and they say, 'Can we see it, is it available?' and she says, 'Yes,' and I messenger over a copy.

The second they find out it is about Vietnam, they say to her, 'What else would you like to do?' Dawn Steele, turning it down, referred to *Full Metal Jacket*. 'I think Mr. Kubrick is going to say everything left to say about Vietnam.' Oh really. Hey, he's my favorite director, too, but Jesus . . .

Personally, having lived through the whole fucking era and having been against the war from the Gulf of Tonkin resolution on, I don't think you can say enough about the war. But that is like thinking you can't say enough about the Bomb. Not a popular concept in a Hollywood that has no more art, only commerce.

In the script, the kid figures out that his father was fragged by his men, and wreaks a horrifying vengeance upon them. People like Dawn Steele have a problem with that. They don't think it is realistic for a thirteen-year-old kid to be shooting off an M-16. Yo, check out the news on any given day, I want to say, but don't. What is the point? I'm not even getting my ya-yas off being right all the time.

Kathleen has this habit of making her eyes go from wide to wider, like William F. Buckley, but this gesture isn't in sync with what she is saying. More between- than off-beat. As the evening progresses she does it more. Maybe she really is

514

psychotic. Hell, go with the flow, I think,.you need a picture . . .

How many times in the past – in the past, hell, in the day – have I hated where I was and who I was with, but there was a project I loved hanging in the balance? It seems like forever. I am glad that Gary is seated next to her. He can make conversation. He does it very well. Two disconnected people talking to each other.

Dinner comes and goes, and when we leave there are paparazzi waiting for her outside. She handles it nicely, gives them a clean shot for about a minute. And then David Guc does his manager routine and pushes them away, ushers her into his rented Mercedes, and waves goodbye.

Wish You Were Here is turned down by everyone, even with Kathleen Turner attached. We don't stay in touch.

Couple of months later, I am at Helena's on a Friday night, when that is what I still do on a Friday night. Gary Weis and I are having dinner with Larry Mark and Madeline Kahn, and then they leave and all of a sudden there is a sweaty David Guc and loud-mouthed Jay, infusing themselves onto my table, because the place is packed, and they are exhausted from dancing.

Jay is one of those guys who yells over the music into your ears, but aside from saying hello, he is much more intent on talking to David Guc than me or Gary. I'm a stranger in my own space, I think, my skin crawling, and I crush my body up against the wall for protection. Gary shoots meaningful looks but does nothing to alleviate the situation. Wrong, Gary, I think, and wish Devore were here . . .

Every time David Debin goes off with Gary Devore he comes back the worse for wear. It takes me awhile to understand that they are the kind of guys who regard drinking as an activity, like golf or backgammon. Living in Los Angeles tends to reinforce this view.

When Michael and I first moved to L.A. in 1970, and all

our friends were Tony's friends, Artha Kass, Jerry's wife, had proclaimed at dinner one night that in L.A. there were only three things to do: work, drugs, and have a nervous breakdown. In my case the work was for the drugs and the drugs were for the work, and then when there was no work at all I had the nervous breakdown.

In my book, Jews don't drink, they tend to womanize. A bit of philosophy handed down to me by my mother. Although I have known quite a few who gambled, too. But the colossal drinkers? Definitely not Jewish. David and Gary, however, both Jews of a sort, break the mold.

They are spiritual twins in some odd way: David speaks in an eastern whine in a voice laced heavy with *weltschmerz*, Gary with a western twang in a voice laced heavy with testosterone, but they are both talented writers who feel they haven't gotten their due, and they are marching into middle age with bitterness and rancor. They seem to work it out by exercising heavily and drinking heavily: Zen and the art of motorcycle maintenance, as it were.

Once David shows up at my house after carousing with Gary for two days. He goes into my compulsive shopper closet and finds all the clothes that still have tags on them and moves them to the front, decreeing that I should henceforth only wear the clothes with price tags. Then he hangs out on my bed for a while and paints each of his ten fingers with a different nail polish. When he decides that he should leave, I give him some nail polish remover and cotton balls. The next morning he calls freaked out at his acid-flashback fingernails, and I remind him that he has the remover in his jeep.

'I'll call you back,' he says, 'when I've dealt with my nails.' By the time he does, he is in much better humor. I am very jealous of his recuperative powers. Years later, when I was the one who had started to go out drinking with Gary Devore because David, unable to deal with L.A., had moved back east to Woodstock and Gary needed a new partner, I had to space my carousing, or I would puke my guts out for about an equal amount of time to that which I had spent drinking.

I should have learned years ago from my various Friday afternoons at Ma Maison with David Giler that I could not keep up with these guys. While Sidney Beckerman and Victor Drai and David Begelman repaired to the upstairs room for Friday afternoon poker, Giler and I would continue drinking in the fake garden downstairs, which Patrick had surrounded by a wall of polyethylene, never real conducive to a healthy flow of fresh air. I once came home from drinking with Giler at five in the afternoon so sick that I had to keep a bucket next to my bed, because I was too weak to make the required twenty paces to my bathroom.

I have a brief affair with Gary. He says it is our way of becoming tight friends. I think it is more because he has written two lines that I really admire. One is from *Trax*, a sendup of Rambo consciousness, which in the hands of Stanley Kubrick might have been brilliant, but in the hands of Jerry Garey would turn out to be unreleasable. It is: Garbage you dump, trash you kill. The other is from *Wish You Were Here*. It is: Death isn't the worst that can happen, just the most.

Gary and I slide comfortably from lovers to friends. Three ay-em one morning, unable to sleep with a stranger in my bed, I wake him and say, 'Let's not do this boyfriend girlfriend pretend shit anymore . . .' Bleary-eyed, he gets up, gets dressed, and leaves. The next morning, at the decent hour of eleven, he calls to say that is fine with him.

Gary takes a job at DEG as the head of production and the first thing he gets going is *Trax*. With me producing.

Jim Wiatt, president of ICM, and Bob Wallerstein, of Armstrong and Hirsch, grew up in Beverly Hills together. Which explains a lot. There is a deep spoiledness about each of them. Which might explain why they do such a lousy job for me on *Trax*. Devore, a star client of Wiatt's, has convinced Dino and Rafaela that they should do this movie. I will get to be a producer-for-hire by this Italian scumbag, who has made movies that I've detested for as long as I've been noticing credits.

For starters, Wiatt sends me in to meet with Dino et al. Alone. Never have I been so aware that I need protectlon. I am dressed in Alaïa and high heels, something I never wear, but I feel I need to tower over them. Gary and I go in to see Dino; we chat; he turns to his right arm, Fred Sidewater, a greasy-looking number with a giant gap between his teeth. I notice the gap because he keeps favoring me with an insincere smile. Sidewinder. Fred Sidewinder, I think. Not original, I find out later. Everyone calls him Sidewinder.

Dino has a brief exchange with this person in Italian, which I know is a ploy. Like François's deafness, Ray Stark's forgetfulness, a manipulative ploy. It puts me on guard. If this goes down, I'm going to Berlitz, I flash.

'Why doesn't-a the beootifool leddy go eento dis-a udder room,' Dino says, 'end-a discuss terms . . .'

'I'm not going to negotiate my deal,' I say, alarmed. 'I have an agent and an attorney for that . . .'

'Just some broad strokes, see if we're thinking along the same lines . . .' Sidewinder says.

'I was into thinking rewrite and director,' I say, hoping I am being charming and stern at the same time. Dino frowns. Dino has never been crossed by anyone, it seems to me. People are always saying Dino this and Dino that, always calling him by his first name, but in hushed, reverential terms. Dino is always flying to and from Amsterdam, a city known for its drugs/prostitution/understanding banks.

And he is rich and I am running out of money. Needing this deal. Needing this producer-for-hire deal. IthinkIcanIthink-Ican. Yuu-u-ch. Sidewinder is showing me the door that leads to the conference room off Dino's office.

Dino decorates in direct opposition to CAA. Everything there is small and compact and modern. Everything here is large and wood and oversized. With red carpet. Dino is the old school and he is going to be replaced soon. By CAA. What is the world coming to? I wonder, allowing myself to be ushered into the conference room and shaking Dino's hand in fond farewell. What it always was, I comfort myself, but more. And worse.

The conference room turns out to be a much less constraining venue. I tell the guys that I have another picture going with Vestron, that everyone wants exclusivity, which I have never given before, and that they can have it if they pay enough for it. Like two fifty pay and play.

This is not my movie, this is the Jim Wiatt/Bob Wallerstein movie.

E-e-e-eu-u-uw I hate this movie.

Don't walk, don't walk, stay put and look them dead in the eye.

Shoulda asked for three.

They take everything under advisement, and I walk Gary back to his office, where I call Wiatt to bring him up to date. It is one of the few times he takes my call right away, but that is because he knows I am calling him from Gary Devore's office, and Gary has been making serious money for him lately. Or maybe it's because Andrea's stepson, Robert Lazarus, grown up now, working Wiatt's desk, wants to return a favor. I did, after all, save him from Jeremy years ago.

I made serious money for ICM while Wiatt was still working for John Tunney, but it is a real case of what-have-you-done-for-me-lately; Gary wins hands down in the lately department. And not one of his screenplays, however well written, has ever been a good movie. Well, maybe *Dogs of War*. Some have been really lousy, like *Raw Deal*, but that's what happens when you go only for the money. Push comes to shove, David and Gary, they go for the money. Most of this town. And who am I to talk, sitting here as I am with the gap-toothed Sidewinder?

He has insisted upon exclusivity as a condition for negotiating, and talked very very poor. I have told him that I assume they have asked to see me because they are going to try something new: i.e., working with a classy producer. I see a frown flicker across Gary's perpetually furrowed brow. Fuck it, I don't care.

I tell Wiatt on the phone that I have done Dino and Sidewater, that I expect him to finish the rest, and that I am going home to take a shower, because I feel slimy. He chuckles as if I meant to be funny, and says, 'I'll do it!' It has not been my experience that he does do it! when he says he'll do it!, but I hope he will because this will get me out of a financial jam large, and what's a year in my life if it'll save the homestead?

I give Gary a warm hug and kiss and get the fuck out of that building.

Wiatt, of course, doesn't do it! He passes it off! to Jack Gilardi! On the grounds that Jack has a better relationship with Dino than he does.

Gilardi gets me pay or play and gets paper generated, but the paper is sent to Wallerstein for review. He leaves the papers, unread, on his desk for three weeks while he goes on vacation. By the time he returns, Rafaela and I have experienced creative differences, what a surprise. I talk to her rudely, I am taped, and I am canned.

I get no money. No signed paper.

Gary caves . . .

I am pissed at Wallerstein, but philosophical. I don't think I ever expected much of him. But Gary disappoints me. He takes me to Mortons so we can talk. I tell him I'm not surprised his great scripts turn into shitty movies, if this is all the balls he has. I actually find myself calling him a pigfucker. He looks so stricken, I back off.

In the end, DEG goes belly up, Gary produces an unreleasable version of *Trax*, and I go to New York to suffer through *The Beat*. Wiatt and Wallerstein get large raises and promotions. Question: What is truth what is truth? Answer: Failing up failing up . . .

DINNER AT CHASENS:

ovo: At a front booth, six people of varying ages pretend to have fun. Couple of young actors, him handsome in the extreme, her extremely buxom, a middle-aged highly successful manager, who looks like a Mr. Hyde version of George Bush, the young lawyer who works for him, the mid-level lady agent who is the manager's mistress, and ME. I have been coerced into attendance by the Lady Agent, who purports to be my girlfriend. I try to avoid these gatherings.

CAMERA PANS THE GUESTS AS IT FOLLOWS THE CAPTAIN pouring antique Lafitte Rothschild into each glass. The wine is from the manager's personal stash.

520

I have a girlfriend in show business who has a taste for powerful fuckers . . .

CAMERA SETTLES on the Lady Agent.

Just now she is with a dude who is known for doing samovars of cocaine and beating up his women . . .

CAMERA SETTLES on the Middle-Aged Manager.

I am a little worried about her well-being, so I come along to this birthday party he's throwing for her at a restaurant favored by the Older Crowd. I never come to this restaurant; I am sure that if I do I will have to perform CPR on one of its patrons . . .

MIDDLE-AGED MANAGER: (leaning toward me) You know I was financed by the Mafia . . .

OVO: He likes me . . .

ME: Excuse me?

MIDDLE-AGED MANAGER: Hey, rock 'n' roll . . .

OVO: He really really likes me . . . I mention the name of a mainstream client of his and remind him that anyone representing such a person should not use the words rock 'n' roll. He throws his head back and laughs. I can see a giant coke booger lodged high up in his left nostril . . . he's a gangster, like everyone . . .

AA people will tell you that every junkie is the same. That every drug is the same. That there are rules, principles, steps that everyone who is addicted to something can take that will help to stop the addiction. I know a lot of people, alive as well as dead, who have cleaned up behind AA. They do seem to get somewhat addicted to AA, but over the years, I have decided that this is quibbling . . .

I do really have a problem with the 'same' concept. If every junkie is the same, that is essentially saying that every human being is the same. That denies our specialness, our uniqueness. AA aficionados will tell you that you haven't really 'gotten it' if you don't surrender to the concept of sameness. You're the same as the wino on skid row. I'm the same as you if I love coke and you love smack, but those choices bespeak antithetical highs, antithetical personalities. AA will tell you that you don't want to feel real feelings, so you take drugs to avoid them, but I think that is discounting a whole bunch of drugs that do take you further. Inside. Outside. Upside and Downside. In the feeling department. In the thinking department. In the sensation department. As it were.

As a third-generation atheist I have serious trouble with the Higher Power precept upon which AA so heavily relies. See, I think that you take more responsibility for yourself if you don't believe in God than if you do. The I'm-one-of-God's-children-He-will-forgive-me concept has become so much more popular than the I-am-unique-and-possibly-alone-therefore-accountable-for-myself-and-my-behavior school that it really should not be surprising to us that we have become so greedy and unethical and immoral.

People who don't believe in God are stuck with believing in Mankind. As they get older, if they have an IQ over 120, they come to realize what a colossal waste of time that is. Also as they get older, more and more of their friends die. They start to believe in Mankind less. They then go one of two ways: either they get better with themselves or they go back to God. I get better with myself. And worse with Mankind. But I am forty-four and have smoked all my life, not to mention all those dangerous drugs.

And fuck it, I am just a speck of sand under the fingernail of a larger being, who is just a speck of sand under the fingernail of a larger being, etc., in a universe that is either expanding or contracting and is probably random.

'Christ, it's beginning to feel like an alternative religion,' I say to Brooke one day, complaining.

What was it with these kids anyway? I want to tell them, Fuck, I got to shoot off a pretty good wad, professionally speaking, before I decided to retire into drugs full time. Where do you get offshooting smack behind three episodes of *McGyver*?

'Please, in Hollywood it's a dating service . . .'

'It's certainly a career step . . .'

'Betty Ford is better for that . . .'

'But more expensive . . .'

'It'd be worth it just to see Liz making her own bed.'

When I first got back from the Mayo Clinic I looked around for an AA meeting that seemed simpatico, but at that time it hadn't gotten so chic, and there were mostly drunks from the old school, like Dick Van Dyke. So I pretty much struggled on my own, and assembled this legion of specialists, and tried to move toward adulthood and something called moderation, an extremely difficult concept for me. I didn't really interact in a major way with anyone who was in AA until I hung out with Steve Reuther, and then for some reason, AA-ers were ubiquitous, the Moonies of the late eighties.

They all seemed to be around clubs a lot. Drive to 'em on their Harleys. Just take the straight line to the Ultimate. Death comes quicker on a Harley. And at these clubs, none of which is as nice as Helena's or as charged as Power Tools, I notice the bars are pretty active. Not a lot of Perriers being served. Personally, I think the drugs just went back in the closet. Kind of like tie one on Saturday night, go to church on Sunday. Now it's party all night, go to AA tomorrow. Make sure a lot of people see you there; they'll return your calls on Monday.

Mr. Wald is not that great-looking to begin with and this operation he had two days ago is wreaking havoc with his face. For starters, they have pinned his left eye pretty much back onto his face; I can see that it is held together with the kind of pins you use to do up a hem – with little colored balls at the end to make them easy to remove. Just now he is sporting orange and blue, which give a Modern Art cast to his head.

I'm not squeamish, but I am awfully glad I gave up coke before it came to this. His mouth is already fixed in a permanent snarl because of childhood polio. He could end up with his facial features looking like a Picasso. Now if he just had his glasses askew like Jeff Berg did before he got contacts he could hang himself on the wall and be the piece of art he always wanted to be.

He is bossing Hazel, the black nurse assigned to him on the eighth floor at Cedars, like he is running a company. Ah, the eighth floor at Cedars. The VIP floor. The last time I was here was for the excision of the Rottweiler Rat, smoking coke. But that was then and this is now, and I don't smoke coke anymore, just pot. Just pot.

I look at Mr. Wald again, and I can feel tears well up, the kind that only make your nose runny. I had gotten a hysterical call from his daughter, Traci, the day before, telling me in brief that he had woken up two days ago with his face exploded and his eyes bugging out of his head and that he had been in surgery for six hours before they could cut out the pustule that had traveled from his nasal cavity into his brain . . .

'I did so much blow I tore the tissue away,' he is explaining to me now, talking about himself not in, but as if he were, the third person. 'Jordan found me, bicycled all over the colony until he could find someone to help.' Jordan had found Ali, and Ali had taken Jeff to Malibu Emergency. They took one look at him and said no thank you, so she took him to Cedars. They didn't want to deal with him either, but he had donated so much money, he might as well have his own wing, probably even his own doctors, so they had to take him.

He likes that part, I can tell, because he snarls a little more. That means he is smiling. Even in the hospital, post near-Death, Mr. Wald can dominate a conversation. Outside of Marty Scorsese, Mr. Wald is the only extremely short man I know who can exude a constant aura of power. Oh, and maybe Dick Zanuck, but only sitting down.

He talks and talks, maybe to keep his anxiety at bay. I have had a busy week pitching projects to unfeeling yuppies, so I let his chatter wash over me, wanting a joint. I wonder if he ever listens. I wonder if I should stop smoking pot. It seems, somehow, to be an act of disloyalty to be visiting him in these circumstances and wanting a joint so badly.

Even with his face pinned together and a morphine drip in his arm, he is smoking furiously and telling me about someone who is about to have a new asshole ripped. Mr. Wald is always ripping someone a new asshole or tearing off someone's head to shit in his neck.

Once, he threatened a six-year-old at the Kahala Hilton beach with such invective for stealing Jordan's favorite beach ball. Eliot Roberts said, 'That's okay, Jeff, he's six, he's old enough for nightmares,' and that had made him laugh. Which is to say, stopped him cold.

Just now, Mr. Wald isn't ripping and tearing at anything but his stitches, of which there are quite a few. And he isn't laughing, either. But there is something in him that is enjoying it. Maybe he is just loaded, and grateful to be alive.

Mr. Wald and I have drifted apart. And then the call from Traci. After I see Mr. Wald in the hospital, I talk to Traci again, and she tells me that Irving Azoff and Norm Pattiz have been urging Mr. Wald to check into Betty Ford. He is lobbying heavily that he is on the brink of re-signing Stallone and can't go out of town. Denial, denial, denial, I think, a good little ex-drug student. Traci sounds desperate. Mr. Wald is a force. If he doesn't want to move, nothing will make him.

When I go to see him the next day, he is bragging about a call from Betty Ford the night before telling him she will clear a bed for him at the clinic that bears her name. There is nothing in Hollywood, including near-Death, that doesn't have a credit.

'So, why don't you do it?' I ask, innocently enough.

'I could go to St. John's outpatient deal . . .' I personally think Mr. Wald needs to be shackled to a bed at Betty Ford, but do not argue. I have stopped smoking pot and drinking in honor of Mr. Wald, and am feeling a bit on the dyspeptic side myself.

That night Traci calls me again and this time she is frantic. Irving and Norm feel he is slipping away. We orchestrate an intervention that involves me and Michael Phillips together after Norm and Irving leave the following day. We figure that if Mr. Wald sees us together, he will know that we think he is in deep shit.

By now the room is filled with flowers and good wishes, even magnums of Dom. Not to mention oodles and oodles of celebrity guests. When I arrive, Michael is already there, along with: Leonard and Wendy Goldberg, Ingrid Boulting, and Jerry Moss. Mr. Wald manipulates them all, including Michael, with his I'm-about-to-sign-Sly-I-can't-leave-town riff.

Michael says, 'Well, that's important . . . maybe you should go to St. John's . . .' Jerry Moss agrees, and it occurs to me again how similar they are. Wendy and Leonard sit on the couch, wordless, but I can tell from her eyes that she is studying me, very All About Eve.

I plant my feet in the ground, like a Mexican fighter, and argue passionately with him. I tell him he is a seriously addicted person and he needs serious care, the kind of care Betty Ford has so graciously offered to provide. I tell him if Sly is a real possibility, he will have respect for what Mr. Wald is doing for himself and will wait. I remind him that Sly is not looking for a dead manager. I tell him it is not easy to stop.

I take my moment, look around the room, point my finger at my own chest and tell him that I'm the only one standing here who knows that.

I tell him he can fool himself, he can fool them, but he can't fool me. There is no one else in the room backing me up. He is getting angrier and angrier, I can tell by the pins twitching around his eye. At one point, Ingrid says, 'Oh, why are you being so mean to Mr. Wald?' and I consider killing her, but decide I don't care about anyone enough, not even Mr. Wald, to do serious time. I used to do this kind of arguing for movies, now it is for sobriety. I wonder if there is any money in it.

I am wearing a polyester Yohji Yamamoto jumpsuit, and it is making me pour sweat inside. Mr. Wald and I run each other around the room for a good two hours. Everybody else looks exhausted, except me and Mr. Wald. He is pumped up with fury, I with righteousness. They all get up to go. I say, 'Think about what I said,' and leave with Michael.

In the garage, he says I reminded him of the Old Julia in the room. I figure that means he hates me. I already know Mr. Wald hates me. I sit behind the wheel of my car and cry uncontrollably for five minutes after he leaves. The crying probably has nothing to do with Mr. Wald.

I go out to dinner with Gary Weis, Ileen Maisel, and David Schiff and Lucinda. It is pouring rain. I wonder if God cries from tense days, too. When I get home there are four messages on my machine from Mr. Wald. They start out angry and they progress to love and thanks. He is going to Betty

Ford, please call whenever I get in. I do, and he tells me that I was brilliant, I was the Old Julia, he loves me.

He's going to AA on Sunday with Carrie Fisher and he's going directly from the hospital to Betty Ford. He tells me that Leonard and Wendy called later to say that I was right, repeating phrases they had learned from me that afternoon in the hospital room. He tells me that Jerry Moss is going to pay the rent on his house in Malibu for a few months while he gets straight.

He tells me that the capper was Norman Brokaw arriving that night to visit, taking off his jacket neatly and saying, 'You know, they don't have WATS lines at Forest Lawn.' Well, Norman's a closer, I say. I'm just a creative type. He tells me there's serious money in supervising an intervention. I can't help it, I have to know how much.

'Fifteen hundred a pop,' he replies, and I think, yeah, same thing as punching up a teevee show . . .

Lynn Nesbit calls out of the blue and tells me that Anne Rice has written a sequel to *Interview*, it's available, would I like to see it. Hell yes, I say, and read *The Vampire Lestat* in a day. It is better, for movie purposes, than the first. I call Levy, and he reads it just as fast. We make the rounds. Nobody wants it. Craig Baumgarten at Lorimar gives me a lecture on what makes a hit movie, and tells me, fake kindness in his voice, that I should be thinking miniseries. Sure, what the fuck do I know about hit movies? I think, but don't say.

Ileen Maisel has just landed herself a job at CBS Pictures, working under Alan Levin and Bernie Safronsky. I go deep into the Valley for a meeting, which I consider a major gesture. At one point, Alan Levin expresses worry about Paramount still owning *Interview*. There is some gossip around that they're going to do it as a TV movie, a perfect Hollywood gesture: trivialize that which is epic, try to make an epic out of a tiny story.

'What do you care what they do with it . . . it has nothing to do with the movie that could be made out of this book . . .'

527

He worries some more. The whole scene, these two smoothies from television, the Valley, all of it reminds me of *Network*.

'You know why you're worried? Because you're from television.' Dummy. 'There's a big difference between television and movies!' I'm on my feet.

'And what is that?'

'The size of the fucking screen!' We talk some more. I think he should be convinced and go for it right now. He says he needs a day. I walk to Ileen's office with her and call Harlan.

'Call Mark Rosenberg at Warner's. I wanna know if he can see me in fifteen minutes for fifteen minutes . . .' Harlan puts me on hold, cames back on the line. When I write my autobiography, I will call it *My Life on Hold* . . .

'He's waiting . . .'

Ileen, slouching in defeat, walks me to the bathroom so I can freshen up for a meeting with Paula Weinstein's tub-of-goo husband. Fat and smokes. And with a beard. Every time I get really mad at Paula, I remind myself that she sleeps with Lucca Brazzi. I wonder if I will have to close my eyes to pitch this to him.

'I don't believe you set up that appointment in front of me . . .' Ileen complains, but she is smiling. Ileen always smiles. To cover her anger. It's tough being smart and fat in Hollywood.

'I know. I could've done it from the car, but I don't want to drive around in the Valley any more than I have to.' Ileen smiles some more. I drive to Rosenberg, he says sure, fine, he'll buy it, calls one of his minions in Business Affairs, right in front of me, to call Berg and work out a deal.

That night I get flowers from Ileen addressed to Benedict Arnold. Please.

The next day CBS closes the deal.

Months later they're out of business and we're on the street again. With Ileen. She leaves a message on my machine, 'We're history, we're toast.' From then on, I call her Toast. The night that CBS closes its doors, I get a phone call from Anne Rice. It is the beginning of the best friendship I've ever had with a woman. I think that is probably because we meet as adults. I ask her to please hang in. We will set it up elsewhere. She does.

Ileen lands a job at Taft Barish, working as a production executive for my old friend Rob Cohen. When Rob Cohen first started, a hotshot twenty-three-year-old Harvard graduate running Motown's film division, Michael and I were nice to him when nobody else was. I've always thought it had to do with his looks. Homely boy. But now he is middle-aged, and his homeliness has more authority. He sort of blends in. Although over the years he has developed a nasty predilection toward abusive and arrogant behavior. Which also blends in.

I suck up to this behavior at lunch, glorious lunch, at Le Dome. Same old table year after year, kitty-corner from Mario Kassar and Andy Vanya, next to Wallis Annenberg, across from the big round table that Giler favors. And Sherry sometimes. Bruce Ramer. By the end of lunch I have a deal. On *Lestat*.

So much time has gone by that Paramount's ownership of *Interview* is running out. They ask Anne for an extension.

'Don't give it to them . . . they're just gonna make a shitty TV movie out of it . . .' She doesn't give them the extension.

I have another lunch with Rob. I wear my green Alaïa leather suit. With a skirt, if you please.

'*Interview* is going to be available soon,' I tell him, flirting in my voice.

'Sooooo. . .'

'Look, the reason this never made it onto the screen is the two guys and the little girl. Agreed?'

'Agreed.' Rob smiles fondly. I wish I could say it made him better looking.

'But you know where that would play really well?'

'Please don't say television . . .' Duh.

'No, silly. Broadway . . . a Broadway musical with two gay guys and a five-year-old child. My answer to *Annie*.' Rob's eyes sparkle. Come to think of it, he does have pretty eyes. Hazel.

'What a good idea . . .' Sounds like a deal in search of a story to me, but what the hell.

Taft Barish enters into negotiation on *Interview* for the purpose of making a Broadway musical. Ileen is nothing if not ambitious and effective, and immediately sets up a meeting with Sting. The meeting is to take place in his suite at the Chateau Marmont with Keith Addis, his manager, who started out in show business as Michael Phillips's gofer on *Taxi Driver*.

We are ushered in right away. 'Hello, Julia,' I hear, and there is Natalie Zimmerman, an eyeglasses-model extraordinaire who is ubiquitous. Natalie is from the new breed of girls around town. When I first came to California, the girls around town had pretensions to careers other than actress/model/ whatever: Priscilla English wrote think pieces for the L.A. *Times* about directors who squired her . . . well, around, as did Fiona Lewis; Susannah Moore was a 'designer.' But the new breed, which has bigger tits and fatter lips, from which hardly ever a clever word is uttered, seems content to be on somebody's arm and under his thumb.

There is some pretty nice girl's underwear draped over the complimentary fruit that sits on the table between me and Sting. Moments like this always present alternatives. I ignore it, although I wonder for the next half hour if it is intended as set decoration. It is across this landscape that I do my pitch, impersonal but dynamic, and he says yes, with the caveat that he is not a Broadway show kind of person, and he will need a collaborator.

The Beat had been the kind of struggle that could become an addiction. All the way along there were little warning signs that it would not be a healthy experience for me, from the dingbats I had to deal with on a daily basis at Vestron (the new breed, arrogance without portfolio – extremely dangerous because they scare s-o-o-o easily), to the shortness of money to produce and to live on, to the extreme ambition of my partners, all younger than me.

Ambitious, I keep telling myself, but not basically greedy, an important distinction, particularly when applied to people who are thirtysomething. Mones. Kilik. Wechsler. Any one of 'em coulda been my brother. As in: He ain't heavy, he's my brother.

It is a full ten years since the *Close Encounters* debacle, a great deal of which probably emanated from the desire of so many individuals involved with the picture to see their names, with an apostrophe *s*, above the title. Alan Hirschfield's CE3K, Steven Spielberg's CE3K, David Begelman's CE3K, Herbie Allen's CE3K, Michael Phillips's CE3K, etc., etc. These partners seem like they can share a success. I don't know at the time how much they can't share in the cost of a failure. I don't think failure.

Ah, fuck it, I figure, what can it hurt? My partners are talented and cool, I like the movie and the vision, the guys at Vestron are handleable if I can keep contempt out of my voice. God knows, studio people aren't beating a path to my door, not even on the vampire books. There is so much time between each deal, Anne Rice writes another book, so the project keeps getting bigger and bigger. Too big for this fucking town. Time for a change. Time, already, to do a movie. Christ, I would've done *Trax* just to get my chops going. Maybe I can get them up doing this little one. This down-and-dirty one. I can learn something. I am over forty. I can deal. I walk in with my third eye open.

It is the accident that makes me put the old blinders on again. Because of flu, I don't make it to New York until the picture has been shooting a couple of days. I think getting the flu is some kind of premonition. Don't go, don't go, my immune system is saying. But I chalk it up to my usual fear of flying, exacerbated by the fact that I haven't been on a plane in awhile.

I also know but don't tell myself that this picture will end up costing me money. I end up spending a lot more than I want to, because I get stuck in the process I dragged Columbia through to make *Close Encounters*. Once they get me spending out of pocket to keep it going, my tendency is to spend more out of pocket to protect what I've already spent out of pocket. That is the downside of the experience. The upside is that it makes up my mind that I never want to do it again. And I've been taking a long time to come to that decision.

Let's face it, the producer is the only guy on the set who doesn't have a specific job. How good he really gets to be is entirely dependent on almost everyone else's moods and inclinations. The creative people like to think of him as the money guy. The money guys like to think he's the guy who talks to the creative people. Almost no one else thinks he is talented. He never gets his ya-yas off, unless all he cares about is money, which would explain why there are so many really rich scumbags in Hollywood now – going along with the greedy tendencies of the eighties.

More so out here, where they were for Reagan before he was invented. The story they always told me when I was just a girl in the early seventies was that when a senile Jack Warner was informed they were going to run Reagan for governor of California he said, 'No, Jimmy Stewart for governor. Reagan for campaign manager.'

I met Jack Warner when we both appeared as guests on *Kup's Show*. which was being taped out here. One of the early we're-going-to-Hollywood-to-tell-you-how-it-really-is excursions. And it was the middle of winter and cold in Chicago. He yelled at me on-camera for promoting a movie with Jane Fonda starring, because she was a communist. He said that on the air. I wasn't a real old hand at any of this stuff.

I was doing the promo because I felt shut out of *The Sting* and nobody else wanted to promote *Steelyard Blues*. I told him I was only there to promote my movie, which I loved and in which she had performed. I told him he should address his political remarks to her. Then they stopped taping for some commercials. Kupcinet and Charlton Heston, who was the third guest, both leaned in to me and told me I was handling myself very well.

I asked Heston if he planned to run for the office of God soon, and he settled back in his chair.

I thought *they* should be handling this mad dog called Jack Warner, one of the giants in the industry, instead of kissing his ass and letting him eviscerate me on camera. Jack leaned over and touched my knee. What is it with these guys and knees, anyway? He apologized.

Now I was feeling very confused, but I actually had the

chutzpah to tell him he should save dialogue like that for when we were on the air. When we came back on, Kupcinet wisely moved on to good ol' Chuck. I don't think either Jack Warner or I said another word except smile-goodbye-thank you . . .

When a job comes up on the set that no one else has to do, according to job definition, the producer gets to do it. This comes up on a regular basis, usually because someone else didn't do his job, didn't do his job well, or didn't think of the job in the first place. It tends to be intense, generally shitty work, but every once in awhile, it is awful. I go from shitty to awful in a day.

My first chore is to close a deal with a group called the Cro-Mags, who are to be the Iron Skulls of Death, a fictional speed metal band, for a three-minute concert scene that we are staging the next day downtown at the Ritz.

I close the deal in the back of a limo in some scummy part of Brooklyn and it is a bad deal and far too expensive, but we are shooting the next day. I am way out of date on this kind of deal, and I am interacting with a small smart outfit called Profile Records. As scuzzy as the music business is, these guys are a little bit scuzzier.

I can't understand why Nick Wechsler hasn't done this already. Isn't he the rock 'n' roll manager? I know it is a handle he is trying to leave behind, but why not after he closes on the Cro-Mags? Nick advises but doesn't close, and it infuriates me. I am jet lagged, physically debilitated, generally pissed off, and not at all up to speed.

I get up to speed real quick the next day.

In order to film this scene we put on a free concert for the mousse-and-gel set. They sign releases, take a dollar, and are immortalized on celluloid. All along I have had a bad feeling about this enterprise. I had gone to a speed metal concert during the summer and I had not wanted to stay on the floor for more than two seconds, the smell of alcohol and violence was so heavy. So I ran up the stairs to the balcony that surrounded the floor, and from a safe distance I surveyed all before me.

As far as I was concerned the guys on the stage who were spitting beer in great arcs at the audience were just making noise. In front of them, sitting on the speakers, were five of the largest bouncers I'd ever seen anywhere. They were in different haircuts, colors, and drag, but they all grimaced exactly like the crazed Hell's Angel who offed the black dude at the Stones concert at Altamont. In the Maysles film *Gimme Shelter* they cut to quite a few closeups of this guy getting off on his anger. It was one of those faces you don't forget. Ever. And there it was times five.

Their purpose was to hurl kids who jumped up on the stage into the audience. If one of the roughnecks didn't throw them off the stage, they dove themselves. Most of the time the audience caught them. How sweet, I thought. They're not so tough. At least they catch each other.

A little farther back in the crowd the slammers and bashers variously danced, shoved, tussled, and beat the shit out of each other. Behind them, there was a kind of demilitarized zone, and then there were the silent drinkers. They lurked in the shadows, brushing shoulders with junkies on the nod. Upstairs where I was, it was a lot of press and guys from labels and promo men. They didn't wanna go down there either.

Altogether a very interesting scene, and for the first time I understood why Mones was adamant about keeping it in the movie. We had all been trying to get him to cut it for production reasons. For me, it was also, hey, baby, we've all seen concert footage. It's never as exciting as being there. By now, being there had ceased to be exciting, too, but I have to admit, speed metal in the East Village at one in the morning on a hot summer night got my heart started.

Fear will do that, no matter how jaded you are.

I don't know what makes me wear my tightest Alaïa dress the next day. Probably because I know this will be one of our few indoor days until we get to the classroom, and I figure fuckit, I brought it, might as well use it now before the jeans and long underwear. I tend to wear tight clothes when I know I have to pay attention. I will keep a room too cold for the same effect. Little bracers for the brain, because I am middle-aged now and more and more I go on automatic pilot. Denim Alaïa is hardly location wear, but I am glad I have it on. Big shoulders, lots of authority. We have cameras set up everywhere, and it seems like the crowd, gnarly-looking as it is, is under control.

The Cro-Mags have bare chests and tattoos everywhere they have skin. They also sport a profusion of freckles. Not real attractive, although their muscles are nicely cut and built. Working out instead of doing smack, no doubt. They love me once they find out I produced *Taxi Driver*. No matter what brand of rock 'n' roll, that's the one they always love me for. Is it Travis or the sax solo?

I see that the five tough guys aren't on the stage, but don't notice it. Not very thorough for a producer. The Cro-Mags begin to perform and the kids begin to go wild. Over and over, take after take. Some of them jump up on the stage and dive. I watch, matter-of-factly, from my post in the balcony. Above the hoi polloi.

I never really see the accident. On a set, I always keep my eyes on the director, so I see Mones go nuts and move fast. When he races downstairs, I race right after him. The second I hit the floor, I sense that something is wrong. Kids mill around, but there is a big crowd forming at the front of the hall, stage left.

Me and my shoulders push through the crowd. I am right behind Mones. A guy in a flak jacket and a shaved head is lying on the ground. He looks like Travis Bickle. One of our production assistants is cradling his head. Blood is trickling out of the corners of his eyes. I think: Jesus, blood is coming from his eyes. His mouth is working, but he isn't saying anything. I think: This is serious. Blood is coming from his eyes.

Then the paramedics arrive and get him on a stretcher fast. The production assistant, a huge endomorph named Vern, volunteers to go to St. Vincent's with him. I tell him to call me from there. I need to deal with Mones and I need to find my lawyer. I see Mones's back move swiftly across the floor and up some backstage stairs. I take off after him. That's a producer's job, I think, for the hundredth time, flashing on my various pursuits of Steven. Chasing back. I am in cowboy boots, and the distance between me and Mones is widening.

Clunk clunk clunk I go after him, pursue him up some back stairs, and find him huddled in a dark little room, off the balcony. Where the groups' managers hang out with the girls during shows.

Mones's body is shuddering. He isn't crying but he wants to.

'We don't know what it is yet . . .'

'I feel like John Landis . . .' Ah, the *Twilight Zone* accident. It is the specter hanging over every production. Film makers giving the people what they want. More excitement. More thrills. Take them where they've never been before. No bread and lots of circus for the fall of the Human Empire. I've done it myself. No way Steven wasn't there, I think for a moment, he's always been so fond of the pyrotechnics.

'Great. And what does that make me, George Folsey?' Silence. 'Jr.?'

Mones laughs. He has to. 'I can't go back down there . . .'

'You can take some time to recover, but if you don't go down there, we may as well stop shooting, because the picture will be over . . . You have to go back down there . . .'

'I know . . .' Good old Mones. Mournful, cynical, realistic. Pretty, too.

'Wanna have some time alone?'

'Yeah . . .'

'Good. I'm gonna go out there and deal . . .' I round up Kilik and Nick and we pitch tent in the Ritz manager's office. Neither one of them made it downstairs. I flashed for a moment on an accident long ago, during a pickup for *Close Encounters* the cops going over an enbankment in pursuit of three mysterious lights hugging the road, and then going off into space.

It was a scene shot outside of L.A. during the winter after we had completed principal photography in Mobile. A cop car had to go real fast, then break through a fence and drop thirty feet into a clearing. Mr. Fearless gaffed the stunt, with the ramp just so at a certain angle, but he didn't want to do the drive. Craig Baxley, the youngest son from a stuntman family, did the drive. He angled the ramp higher and he drove too fast. Maybe it was because he knew that there was so much

536

brass there that night. Stanley . . . Alan . . . Michael . . . Maybe he was just a young showoff. It took a long time to hear the word *action*, and then the moment with all five cameras rolling flew by. Just like that. But I could tell by the inactivity from Craig's cop car that something was amiss. I was dressed in the mink, it was that cold. Me and my mink went skittling down the embankment to see what was wrong.

It wasn't clear immediately that his heel was crushed in forty places, because the paramedic and the other guys seemed more concerned with his head. They eased the helmet off and we were all relieved to see that there was no blood, but we could see from his eyes that he was hurt and that he was going into shock. Keep talking to him, I remembered, from other accidents I had witnessed. I knelt over him and talked. He kept asking me if we got the shot, and if Steven was pleased. Michael came down off the hill and talked to him, and while he did, I ran back up to Steven. The paramedic ran off in the other direction to call for an amubulance.

'I don't wanna go down there,' Steven said, huddling close to Stanley and Alan.

'Just for a second, just tell him what a great stunt it was, and that all five cameras got the shot . . .'

I guess he decided he would look pussy in front of the big guys if he didn't go, although they sure weren't making any moves in that direction, because he eased down the slope and said a few kind words to Craig, who at that point was vaguing in and out of consciousness. I dismissed Steven and Michael and I kept talking. Craig looked shivery, so I flung my coat over him. I could tell the other stunt guys felt conflicted about the gesture. Well, it was a little Lady Bountiful, but it sure beat the rest of the Jews who were standing at the edge of the precipice looking, but not coming, down. Elders from an ancient tribe, looking down on some human sacrifice. A shot in a movie. Truth be told, I did retrieve the mink when the ambulance arrived a full hour later. At least in this current situation, St. Vincent's was a stone's throw from location, and the injured party is removed from the scene almost immediately.

Kilik and Wechsler are hardly Jaffe and Hirschfield, but in

my script they are stand-ins, and while we are all performing, I feel a feeling I get too often: I am being deserted and left alone. I call Bob Wallerstein first and Vestron second. Freeze frame: blood coming out of the guy's eyes and I wonder if he is going to live. How do I feel about that? Bad. Inconvenienced. Jesus. The soul of the picture maker. Which is to say . . . No soul. Yeah, Steven had been there for sure, I bet. And Landis. That little megalomaniacal prick. I had been coming off a plane from Hawaii and he was shooting that dog, *Into the Night*, with Jeff Goldblum. He stopped the whole production in the middle of a shot to say hello. Little prick.

Too bad. He hadn't started out that way. Like Simpson, he had started out a movie lover and a movie believer, if somewhat neuro/psychotic. Michael and I met him when he first came to L.A., with Donald Sutherland committed to *An American Werewolf in London*, and some prints of his first movie, Schlock, under his arm. He had an articulate enthusiasm about him that made him childlike enough to seem like a prodigy. Michael and I were so impressed that when Steven was on the brink of hiring Tracey Keenan Wynn (at Guy's urging) for the fifth rewrite of *Close Encounters*, Michael schlepped Landis up for a weekend to meet him.

Steven hated him, although Michael and I always wondered if he felt threatened, Landis being so child-prodigy and all, Steven pretty much feeling he had the corner on that arena. There's always someone younger than you. Landis didn't get the gig, but hung around Martha's Vineyard for the summer and made serious bread as an extra in *Jaws*. They got to be big pals long after I had departed the scene.

Landis was the guy who brought me an original one-sheet for *Stella Dallas* with a note on White House stationery saying that he wasn't sure that this was the right title for *The Julia Phillips Story* and could Stanwyck play Jewish, with a cc: to Bebe Rebozo? What had Stella Dallas done that ruined her life? was the gist of the copy. Was this a warning? Landis was always going out of his way to make you laugh for days. What had happened to him? Steven? Me? Why hadn't I heeded his warning? If I hadn't designed my own downfall, my financial imperative, would I have become the same kind of self-centered pieces of shit they appeared to have become? Was I?

Was this accident in any way remotely like the *Twilight Zone*? I store the question, because I can't think about it now. Later. To everyone's credit, they react quickly and their advice is good. I don't know until much later that Wallerstein has never made sure that I have liability insurance and that every time he puts me on hold he is trying to reach Mitch Freedman, my business manager, who had.

I also don't know at the time that there are a series of production company deals funneling through Ruthless to Vestron, some of which are signed and some of which aren't. Nick isn't mentioned anywhere, and Mones and Kilik are covered by a VOORHAS production company deal. Mitch saves my ass on this one, and my partners would have left me swinging gently in the breeze. Meanwhile, the cops shut us down for a couple of hours. Somehow or other, we manage to shoot out the rest of the day, and at dinner break I find myself in the vestibule in front of the Ritz with Nick.

'I'm depressed,' he says. You're depressed? 'Let's go check out Barney's . . .' We hop into my car and have the driver, a tough, self-assured Italian buck whom I will drive to a nervous breakdown three weeks hence, drop us off at Barney's. I leave Nick in the mens' department agonizing over cashmere gloves, and I go to the back of the first floor in search of boots. Then some scarves. Some hose. Small items. I spend about three grand just getting it together to go back and talk to the cast and crew about the mishap we had today. Nick buys nothing, but he helps me carry my shopping bags, laughing all the way.

As I walk up the stairs to the dance floor I slip on my own *agita* and give myself a nasty bloody knee. A small price to pay. The family has gathered at St. Vincent's and they are not letting out any information. I tell the cast and crew that if any news of the accident leaks out and any journalists or lawyers asked them questions to say that they haven't seen it and to refer all questions to me or to Vestron. I gotta hire a publicist soon, I think. Just to keep a lid on this.

I have been going back and forth on this issue with Vestron, principally Larry Kasinoff, who is the titular head of the low-budget end of Vestron, a peculiar distinction, since everything seems low budget there. Lower budget, is how I always think of him. He is the quintessential Jewish nerd, and Mones is constantly threatening to beat the shit out of him. He has a high, nasal delivery and is occasionally very funny, but that does not make up for his lack of expertise. He is always giving me the kind of fight that those who don't truly understand the business they're supposed to be doing give you. An amateur in movie executive's clothing. Correction. An even more amateur-than-usual in executive's clothing.

One of the few benefits of shooting in New York is New York. Anyway, the kind of New York I am afforded living at the Ritz Carlton. Right across the hall from Warren. I don't run into him for at least a week of shooting, and by then I am into the odd-hour mode of shooting a movie. By the time I bump into him again at Columbus we have taken on some modest characteristics of neighbors.

He tries to get me moved out of my suite for a weekend visit from Isabel Adjani (why move me when it's just for appearances – why worry about appearances when you're Warren Beatty and have gone to all this trouble to get this cocksman rep?) and when Ellie Peters, a motherly VIP-tender, who sees it as her pleasure to make my life unmiserable, refuses, he gets even more cordial.

Nick and I have blown into Columbus from our location, Carl Schurz Park, for a little aperitif. Warren stands up to say hello, turning away from his table and almost blocking my view of his companions.

'Who you with?' he asks.

'Partner. Hustler . . .' Nick isn't around to be introduced. He has fled to our table. 'You?'

'Couple a hustlers.' I peer around his chest and see Molly Ringwald's fat mouth. How does this guy avoid jail?

'Well, I better go hang with Nick . . . see ya . . .' He waves goodbye. I'm beginning to think Warren is nice, mellow in his old age. God knows he can still command attention in a room. I sit down.

'If you want to be introduced, you should hang around . . .'

'I don't care about meeting Warren Beatty . . .' Nick says curtly then smiles. His smile is so wide, his lips catch on his perpetually dry teeth. All the girls like Nick (né Norman), but frankly, I don't get it. He is what my mother would have called *galitzianer*. Pale, freckled skin. Rheumy blue eyes. Strawberry-blond hair. Makes me wanna ask: It's 10 P.M., do you know where your eyebrows are?

I like Nick's intelligence, even if I do think his behavior erratic: Hey, rock 'n' roll. He'll be fine fine fine and then he'll disappear for three days and cancel meetings. When he emerges, his skin is gray and his nose is stuffy. Couple a years ago, Mones and Kenny Friedman convince me I should talk to Nick about it. I do, on the phone, and he freaks out, yells at me for twenty minutes about how he's been suffering from this bad rap for ten years, and that he has a lot of allergies and tics. He's right on the tics, for sure. His face dances and jumps in discreet moves at all times, Oscar Levant City. It makes him entertaining even when he isn't talking.

Talking is better; Nick has a good mind . . . his best line ever was after calling me to report on *Platoon*. How was it, I ask, and he says: If *Apocalypse Now* was a supernova, *Platoon* is a . . . light bulb.

I light a cigarette and he frowns. We order drinks and look outside. We are in the un-chic part in front, which I love. Street traffic. I keep my coat on. It is cold. Drinks come and we toast each other, I guess because we haven't been sued yet. Nick starts to talk about his mom. His mom was sick for years, and when she died he didn't tell any of us.

'Don't you think your friends might have wanted to be there for you?' I ask.

'I stood graveside. I cried . . . I had my catharsis . . .' he protests too much and I envy him. I didn't even go to her funeral. Mommy, Mommy, do I forgive you?

Now he is telling me about her jewels, her furs, her red nails, the streak in the front of her side-parted hairdo . . .

'Nick, do I remind you of your mom?'

'Totally . . . she was very trusting, lost all her money . . . lent it to a relative . . .'

'And never got paid back?'

'She lent him eight million dollars, he paid her back five hundred thousand . . .'

While I'm in New York, Ileen sets up some meetings for possible Sting collaborators re: *Interview with the Vampire*. Tim Rice. Barry Gibb. Always in fancy restaurants. Rice is a pro who is worried about his ex-partner, Andrew Lloyd Webber, doing *Phantom of the Opera*. Gibb is one of those music guys with a large collection of books on the occult.

I also see Ridley Scott, the perfect director for *Vampire*, any number of times. In restaurants. On street corners of locations for his movie, *Someone to Watch Over Me*, or mine. No deal is ever closed. I am starting to worry Taft Barish isn't serious . . .

Victor cuts my hair, and I race down to the Jockey Club for a bite. Warren Beatty is sitting in his banquette, going over promo plans for *Ishtar* with Lois Smith, whom I would love to handle my picture. They wave for me to join them.

'So tell me, Julia, don't you ever have an inclination to knock on my door late at night?' Warren teases.

'Not in the least. Not ever.'

'Well, what would you do if I knocked on your door?'

'I'd send you away . . .'

Lois asks how Kate is.

'Oh, you have a daughter?'

'Yes, she's just about fourteen . . .'

'Well, what about you and me and your daughter . . .' Am I really supposed to answer this?

'We're both too old for you . . .'

In the end, Lois doesn't handle the picture, neither Kate nor I sleep with Warren, and *The Beat* doesn't turn into *Taxi Driver*. But I knew all that then, right after the accident. The guy severed his spine. He collects $3 million in settlement money, one-third from me. Most of my money, but *all* of his life. The

542

picture was under enough bad stars to begin with, but the accident puts the final hex on it . . .

'I don't want to do this anymore,' Melanie says sadly on the morning of the third Sunday I am shooting *The Beat* in New York.

'You don't want to do what anymore,' I say, stomach descending on an elevator to my knees. I haven't thought elevator in years. I have been shooting nights in New York. I wanna go home I wanna go home.

'I don't want to change reservations, and FedEx documents . . . I've taken another job . . .'

'What?' But I've known that already. I feel like the life raft has just let go of me. Melanie is the first really good assistant I've had in a long time. Probably since David Parks. That's a lot of assistants ago.

'I want to leave next week . . .'

'Where are you going?'

'I'm going to be an agent . . .' Graduation. So soon?

'I said where are you going, not what are you doing. I would've assumed agent . . .' Well, quick studies graduate fast.

'I'm going to work for Ellen Fuchs . . .' Her voice dipped quite low on the name. Ellen Fuchs?! Ellen Fuchs#@*?! Talk about someone having her foot in your door! First Michael, then Gary Devore, even little Mike Levy. Now Melanie. While I'm on location, far away. Behind my back!! Nice behavior from Melanie, too.

'You've got to give me more notice. I can't possibly cope without your being there to hold down the fort . . .' I can't believe I have to tell you this. After all those nice bottles of champagne I brought to your birthday party? You remember, the one where I came with your friend Harley Peyton, all done up in his hip Ben Franklin disguise, and the big name was Bruce Willis who arrived far too late with Sherry Riviera?

I called him an asshole-without-portfolio, chatting up Harley and Mitch just as the background din died down for a moment. Are you leaving because I offended your close personal friend Bruce Willis? Well, he's not that cute and he sure can't sing . . .

'Let me talk to Ellen . . .' Yo, let *me* talk to Ellen. Not an easy task. This was one of those wide-eyed bimbos who sucked in your soul with lack of comprehension while you talked too much, just to ease the boredom . . . I'm dancin' with my-se-elf. oh omma dancin' with my-se-elf.

'Fine, you talk to Ellen and make her understa-a-and that she's waited this long for you, she can wait another three weeks . . . I'll pay you, of course . . .' How the fuck am I going to find another assistant in L.A. from here in New York? I look at my watch. I have to get ready to go all the way downstairs, to the comfortable Jockey Club, have a nice ladylike brunch with Joni Evans. Have a nice Stoli and tomato juice, little Rose's Lime. Sunset at dawn . . .

'I know of a few people looking for this kind of job . . . want me to call them?'

'That'd be nice . . .'

Later, sitting in a nice comfortable booth in a semi-off hour, waiting for Joni, I think, I don't wanna do this anymore, I don't wanna do this . . . and then she is there, all bubbling enthusiasm, white teeth, blazing blue eyes, and I am very happy to see her, to see a grown-up, not-show-business, sane person, even if she was born on Hitler's birthday . . .

'So, when are you going to write me this book?' Joni challenges.

'How about I write you two hundred pages that sing, and you take forty-eight hours to decide if you want it?' I reply precisely, surprised. And if you don't go for it, I'll sell it to Dick. He'd probably buy it out of spite. What am I doing here? I haven't written anything. Just that Academy Award chapter from years ago . . .

'Write me a movie,' Joni says, sparkly, and then we drop the subject and move on to the biggies: clothes, hair, nails, men . . .

It seemed like everywhere she looked there was burnout. Job burnout, school burnout, life burnout. Burned-out buildings. Meaningless lives. Sometimes when the smog was really heavy and the heat brutal, she imagined planet burnout. Was this middle age or knowledge? 'It was ever thus,' her father said. He also said, 'This, too, shall pass,' and, 'You can't be paranoid enough,' her personal favorite.

Burnout. Burnout everywhere. And the great unwashed turned away from knowledge. Moved to the right. Worldwide, it seemed. Intellectual burnout. She felt sometimes that she was witnessing the end of the human race. Of the planet. She felt certain about it and would have been okay about it for herself. Mehitabel the cat: i have lived i have lived. But she was pissed for her kid, and that made her pissed for all the kids.

Guilt, guilt, too. I *was* the seventies. I turned to making my fortune, getting off on my dreams, Christ, I didn't even vote in '76, she thought, as she watched George Bush pledge allegiance to the altered states of America on the evening news.

She used to like to watch the news while she was loaded. Bunker Hunt telling the investigative Senate committee that a billion dollars wasn't what it used to be. She had knocked her pipe over on that one, almost set fire to the bedspread with the upset propane tank, she had laughed so hard. Right the fuck on, Bunker, tell 'em, bro.

Now, in fact, with CNN you could have news around the clock. She noticed that a lot of people watched the news all day long while they were cleaning up. She would get calls from them in the middle of the day with a bulletin.

She herself got riveted to China. So, if you want to win just use force. Since China was all over television, she assumed children were seeing it, too. What they were going to learn is that if you want to win, use force. Bring in the big guns and kill and maim people. Why was everybody so surprised about the violence in the world? There was this new learning tool, television. And the whole world was watching. Like the kids said at Chicago.

But Abbie Hoffman committed suicide. Just got depressed and checked out. From all that information. And the bad guys were winning. In America anyway. That mean Republican machine, those greedy pricks. She put the mink and then the fox into storage. A defiantly empty political gesture. Hell, they had no resale value. Who the fuck wanted used fur? And more to the point: who the fuck wanted to be offed by a rabid animal-rights activist?

Wouldn't it be something if the Chinese young reinformed the rest of the world what was really worth fighting and dying for? What it was really like to be brave? Might inspire kids Kate's age. To do what? Buy guns. Christ almighty . . .

Sometimes she wanted to ask her daughter: What do you really think about your future? She didn't have the heart.

'You think Mike Ovitz worries about China?' she asked Stuart, who claimed to be moved by the shot of the guy in front of the tanks.

'Only if there's a two-picture deal for one of his clients . . .' and he hung up . . .

Richard Gere. He flies out to meet Mike, Ileen, and me, to talk us into involving him in the development of *The Vampire Lestat*. We all know he's a bad idea, but he's so passionate, so charming, so committed . . .

'All actors are liars,' he tells me at dinner one night. I

should listen more carefully. Richard *acts* smart. He is lying. We start ambitiously enough. The first thing Richard does is score us a meeting with Oliver Stone. Oliver seems interested but reluctant. He asks if it would be too much trouble to import Anne Rice for a little talk.

The meetings are casual, conducted mostly in and around my house. We are unable to hold on to Stone for more than a week. Undaunted, Richard and I continue to hang out. I even take him to a Eurythmics concert, which he seems to enjoy.

I try my Dreyfuss dialogue, the dialogue that says I've been slogging through the mire for five years while you've been making two, three million dollars on one bad picture after another; you ain't making more on this than me if it's a hit. He says something lamely about you work for years and years to establish a price, which in this case is 2.3. In the end, he blows himself off the deal over less than a hundred grand, and blames me. He snubs me in restaurants . . . *Plus ça change*, etc.

Rob Cohen leaves Taft Barish to become the director he's always wanted to be. Ileen departs within weeks. Unencumbered with moderately honorable staff, Keith reneges on the deal for *Interview*. We force him to pay us off on *Lestat* and give it back in turnaround.

Ileen goes to Lorimar with supermanager Bernie Brillstein. Anne Rice and I go to see them. Me in black leather and studs, her in her Catholic schoolgirl traveling outfit: beige skirt, blue serge jacket, white blouse with ruffles. We wow them once again and go into negotiations. She is at the brink of sitting down to write *The Queen of the Damned* and writes a fifty-page synopsis to help sell them. The negotiation gets assigned to Charles Melnicker, a Jewish Prince more concerned with making himself the star of the process than closing. He gets a cold; we provide the tissues.

Pissed about the time, Mike Levy and I go to see Jeff Berg, now ICM's chairman. I wear hightoppers and a Joseph Tricot miniskirt and top. Right in front of us, he calls Paramount and Warners, tells them they're blowing *Star Wars* for the nineties.

I notice that he has very few pieces of art on the walls. One of them is the one sheet for *Taxi Driver*. Every time he makes a call I get up and do a cheer. Boomalacka boomalacka . . .

He walks us to the elevators, turns to me: 'See, I'm not so bad,' he says, all little-boy.

'I never said you were bad, Jeff. I said you were good; I just didn't know why you weren't being good for me . . .' kissing ass. Whatever's good for the project, I tell myself, but I feel rancid. I don't wanna I don't wanna . . .

The deal goes down at Lorimar and we actually get them to pop for Anne Rice writing a 'bible' for a series of movies. Just as she starts, another writer's strike . . .

I swig back the Optifast I have in a thermos and offer it to Mones, who makes the sign of the cross and the Pee-wee Herman u-u-u-gh sound simultaneously. He laughs good-humoredly, more at his joke than at mine. This is what I get high on now. I walk real fast on the treadmill in my bedroom at the Ritz Carlton and I go on Optifast for a week.

Everyone is now straight to one degree or another. Sobriety has replaced drugs as a bonding mechanism. I do not find it as much fun. But it is neither as painful nor expensive as the other, and we are all getting older; fun is not so much fun anymore.

Mones's looks, brain, and humor (as purveyor and appreciator) almost make up for the fact that he behaves as if he is the center of the universe. A year before, when Kate, on the brink of being a teenager, was prefacing every word with ba-a-a-ba-ay, she referred to him as Baby Mones, and it stuck. For awhile everyone was calling him Baby Mones. It was a matter of if the shoe fits.

It has been a rough year. For me, it is a watershed. I am making myself spend far too much money and soul on this little picture with this semiprofessional financier named Vestron Pictures. I have put up at the Ritz Carlton for far too long, but I couldn't hack the Mayflower. I'd have slashed my wrists. I wonder if this other trip is the long, slow version that Ozzie Janiger used to mention.

I feel like I still have that little part of me that is a demon and when it isn't committing psychological homicide it makes me want to kill myself. It lives there all the time. In past times, I have harnessed it in the service of making great movies or great personal melodrama. Neither turns me on anymore, and I am trying to find a useful outlet, so that I can turn it into a resource. A retread in movies isn't the answer.

I love Mones because we agree on everything. He and I worry about the world and exchange horror stories and outrage and facts. I love Mones but *The Beat* isn't *Taxi Driver* and Mones isn't Marty. Not even Schrader. But this is only his first movie, and it probably would be better if I had fought for him to keep the original title, *Voorhas*. More I think about it, in fact, keeping the title would have at least assured heavy-metal kind of traffic. Heavy metal keeps getting bigger and bigger. Heavy metal, as Victor once said about acid when Brooke announced, wide-eyed, that it was making a come-back, never went away.

Fact is, though, I have gotten enmeshed in *Voorhas* as an afterthought. It was Mones's book, *A Song for Modern Man*, I really wanted to get off the ground. Its themes dovetail with my worldview: the end is here and only magic will save us. Mones and I spend three weeks making it a professional manuscript and enjoy each other's work style so much we end up making this movie. Nobody wants to publish the book, although they all comment on the strength of the writing.

New York is wearing on me and I am glad this picture is coming to a close. Mones is an actor as well as a director, so every time I suggest a change, he rolls the film back and forth in the Steenbeck, over and over, past the point of reacting to the idea; I feel he is *acting* what the director would do. I have to keep my impatience in check constantly, so it is just as well I'm fasting. Less physical impact from the process.

'Take your moments,' I have heard Mones say to his young actors when they get too worked up and wave their hands instead of modulating their voices. I love a man who heeds his own advice . . .

*

Holly Knight calls from L.A. She's on her way through New York to Italy and then back through New York. I say, great, I could use the company. We spend half an evening on her way to Italy, and a day and a half on her way back. She brings me beautiful black leather gloves with a gold paisley cuff, and the *pièce de résistance*: a T-shirt with Jonathan Frid, from *Dark Shadows* days, blood dripping from his fangs, emblazoned in front.

Holly Knight is a Jewish girl from New Jersey with fat thighs, a lousy nose job, and a real gift for writing hit songs. Like a score of rock 'n' rollers who keep asking for meetings, she's obsessed by the Vampire books, and when she heard I controlled them, she came at me. I had already been through a meeting with Sting and Bryan Ferry, but I admire her music, so I figure what the fuck, and have dinner with her at Mortons.

When I met Holly Knight, even though she wrote broad-appeal, strong-women songs, I had every hope that I would be creating a combination, with Sting, or Brian Ferry, or Barry Gibb, that no one but me would think of, and which would turn out to be brilliant. That would be a Julia Phillips-like gesture. And Holly, a bit on the voluble side (Better living through chemistry? Nah, I probably just made her nervous.) seemed so forthcoming, that I thought, well, this could really be something – a working association with a woman that doesn't foul itself with female poison. Hah!

It starts with Holly furious that I have met Daryl Hall in New York when she's been trying to get to him for a year. Holly's thirty, so she's still at that point in her career where she uses her cachet to meet people who might provide romantic diversion as well. She'd deny that to herself, of course, but I think she's never really interested in collaborating with anyone who doesn't turn her on. There is a kind of creative energy that can flow that is like sex but is not sex, and that can lead to collaborations of doom. She had that for many years with her writing partner, Michael Chapman, before she wanted to try it all on her own. I had that with Steven, with Marty, even Erica for a nanosecond.

I had to pick Daryl up at Columbus. All we West Coasters feel so comfortable at Columbus. A little more out-front than our watering holes: button men, pols, and stars really do rub shoulders. In L.A., we each have our different hangouts. Actually, he and his manager, whom I know, pick me up. A cute scumbag named Jeb Brian, who works for Tommy Mottola, and cuts his hair like their client, John Cougar, né Mellencamp. It's another case of Please meet my client, he loves the Vampire books. The old me would have said, That's because they're the only books he's ever read, the new me says, Sure, why not?

Daryl Hall, outside of his music and completely noncharismatic performances on stage, turns out to be a pretty good guy. Plus he has a long, lanky body with long, lanky strawberry blond hair and green slanty eyes. I have a little trouble with the double chin, and I notice he does, too; he's always holding his head down.

I ask him if he's self-conscious about his chin, and he says yes, and I blurt one of those awful Jewish Princess lines: 'With all the money you've made I don't see why you don't have that taken care of. You know, a plastic surgeon could take care of that . . .' I think that just makes him more self-conscious. I like him a lot at Columbus, and less in my suite. Probably mutual . . .

No matter what I say, Holly thinks I've slept with Daryl Hall. I come close but in the end, when he finally asks at four in the morning if he should send his driver away, I reply, Only if you want to walk home.

As I pull up to valet park, grabbing a five out of my pocket: 'T'ang you, missy fi' dolla, hab a ni' deener . . .' I see Steven and Amy chatting with Peter Morton. When they see me, Peter and Steven smile, Amy gets tight-lipped. Hey, babe, better a has-been than a never-was . . .

'Hey, Jul-ee-a, you look cool . . .' Steven smiles. I am in black-and-gold Alaïa and Porsche sunglasses. High heels. Goddamn right. Cooler than you. I keep my sunglasses on. 'Let's go in together . . .' he says affably.

Amy wishes she could disattach herself, but she walks in with us. She goes right to their table. He.stands at the front with me. Both of us are so Hollywood we know everyone is watching. Take your moment . . . He says, 'I'm having dinner with Menno Mayess . . . come join us later . . .' Not on a bet.

I am meeting Holly. She is already there. Next to us, at Peter's table, a guy waits patiently for his date to arrive. Nibbles at bread. Sips at a Perrier. He waits a long time. His date finally arrives, a rock 'n' roll princess who was big in the seventies and now is just big. Gigantic.

She alights at the table for a millisecond, then heads for the ladies' room. Both Holly and I need to pee, but this woman is a famous junkie and neither one of us wants to take a chance on finding her dead in the bathroom. We keep shooting odds and evens until she returns to the table. I win. There are works, with blood, discarded carelessly in the sink . . .

Steven and I have our separate dinners, and as we get up to leave, we bump into each other again. 'Why don't you give me a call, come see the compound . . .' he suggests.

The next day I give him a call at Universal, hating myself all the time, and make a lunch date. I wear a lot of Commes des Garçons violet and lavender for the lunch.

'You've never looked better.' He beams. That's 'cause you didn't know me when I was fifteen, I think but don't say. He shows me around Amblin'. He is especially proud of his child-care center. Steven, that great lover of children . . . user of children, I amend. As I ooh and aah over this and that, I think about how insincere I am. This half-in, half-out of the business is wearing me down . . .

I think I should take a vacation immediately after this lunch.

We go to his private dining room and are served large salads by a private chef. Shades of Dan Melnick. Neither of us eats much. The chef brings homemade cookies and coffee for me. The subject of the end of *Close Encounters* raises its ugly head . . .

'You let me down,' I hear him saying. What!#@?

'I let myself down . . .' I hear myself responding.

'You let yourself down,' he parrots, stuttering my words at me. I grab a cookie. He does, too. I let me down, you let me down. I never let you down. Little Putz. But I say:

'Water under the bridge . . .' and eat a few more cookies.
   I guess the lunch works, though; I get a Christmas card that year, after being off the list a long time. Picture of the baby, Max. Blond and smiling . . .

Inevitably, Holly and I go to war over Brooke, which must frighten and astonish him. It all starts at my forty-third birthday party. Holly, Brooke, and Billy Wirth arrive early for support. What a laugh . . .
   I've made myself unnecessarily tense over this party, and I've made it unnecessarily large and expensive. I know it's a hot ticket when Billy Gerber, a mini-mogul at Warners, calls to ask if Bruce Willis can come as his date. I flash on Bruce's behavior at Melanie's.
   'Only if he behaves . . .' Billy promises he will.
   I'm not at my thinnest, but I manage to squeeze into a very flattering red sequined Vicky Thiel dress for the occasion. I get a lot of unnecessarily large and expensive gifts, but the best present is from Rutger Hauer. It is a compass on a pin, which he puts on my dress, over my heart, saying, solemnly, 'So you will always know where you are going . . .'
   At some point in the evening, Brooke, Holly, and Billy disappear. There are three hundred people drinking laughing dancing, but I search the sea of faces singing Happy Birthday Dear Julia and can't find them. Gee thanks, guys, for the support . . . At two thirty in the morning, I retreat into my office. Ace alternative-rock manager Gary Kurfirst finds me.
   'Is anyone left?' I ask.
   'Yeah . . .'
   'Well, you're the manager . . . make them go home . . .' I have passed the point of drunk and disorderly into hangover, and it isn't the morning after the night before yet.

Holly tries to make a production deal with Brooke, papers drawn, etc., but it never comes off. I do, after all, have fifteen years on her . . .

'You're not rock 'n' roll enough,' Holly says in our last conversation.

I laugh at her. Are you kidding? I was there when it began.

Todd Smith is so short and with such perfect little features and little miniature suits and shoes, he is almost like a toy. He is not a toy. He is a CAA agent, and a good one, too. I had met him right at the beginning of the eighties, when I was at MGM; he intrigues me. I am a spotter of trends; he is a trend. I have lunch with this adorable CAA agent-toy. One of the things he says at lunch is, 'You're never dead in this business until you're really dead,' which I find encouraging. The other is, 'I love being an agent.' I have never heard anyone say that. He loves being an agent. What the fuck does that mean, I wonder. Welcome to the eighties, Jools.

He likes *The Fling*, one of the first scripts I develop under my overall deal at MGM, and he tries mightily to help me with it. It never happens. It is very nearly a go before the strikes; when they are over, it is never brought up again.

Peter Locke, David Debin's partner at the time, has done a hell of a lot of work bringing the budget down, and I have actually entertained the notion of firm offers to Candice Bergen and Jackie Bisset. How the mighty have become like everybody else. We have cut out a truly funny nuclear-holocaust/dream-sequence finale that is the heart of the movie, but we save three million dollars. At one point I have to remind Peter Locke that there can be no fat, not even for stealing.

'You've taken the fun out of film making.' He smiles, and I think, holier-than-thou, That's the difference between you and me. (Five years later, I am going broke and he is sitting on top of a fortune built principally on afternoon television offerings like *Divorce Court*, to which Kate is briefly addicted during a period of illness.)

The failure of *The Fling* notwithstanding, Todd and I stay in touch, and when his client Sean Penn marries Madonna, he calls me. 'They want to do a black comedy together . . . I couldn't think of anyone funnier or blacker than you . . .' I mention Bill Cosby and Eddie Murphy and Richard Pryor before he gave up drugs. Lose Richard Pryor, because he is not funny anymore. He laughs in an obligatory fashion and tells me this is deadly serious. I know that. I'll think of something, I tell him. I wonder to myself if now that he is representing Madonna it is okay to think of him as my little CAA agent boy toy.

Later in the day, when I am talking to Mike Levy about a new approach to get *Interview with the Vampire* onto the Broadway stage, I mention the Sean/Madonna call. I figure Todd has called dozens of people. Levy is one of those guys from the old school. You tell him about a deal in search of a story and he finds writers for you. Two days later, we are meeting with a hot new couple who have a comedy deal at Touchstone: Alex Gorby and Andy Rose.

Alex is the extrovert and does all the talking. Andy says nothing. I figure he does all the real work. The old inside/outside-man boogie. It is easier to love Alex, especially after a brief discussion of *Less than Zero*; it was recommended to me by Joan Didion, which I don't understand, because it reads like a poor Joan Didion rip-off. I have been sufficiently upset by the book, on behalf of Kate's adolescence, to want to pack my bags and leave this terrible place called Beverly Hills, and I say so. Alex pooh-poohs the book's accuracy.

'Bret Easton Ellis never knew anyone or did anything cool,' he says morosely, probably because the book is selling like hotcakes and Alex is jealous. Precocity is very competitive. At least that hasn't changed.

'I want to do a takeoff.' I laugh. 'You know, a true novel of the seventies . . .'

'You could call it *More than Two*,' Alex says. Okay, so you were born too late, I think, you're still fun. I'll play with you. Jesus, I hope Andy can write.

We pitch out a pretty funny story with a lot of dead bodies and big parts for Sean and Madonna. We call it *I Am Furious (Yellow)* because her character hates that color. When I think we have enough to talk about, I call Todd and ask if he wants to hear it. Apparently no one else has taken his call seriously, because he makes time for us right away.

I work out pretty intensely before I go up there. CAA's offices have a negative effect on me, like positive ions or the Santa Ana winds. They give me the vapors and make me murderous at the same time. They are all in a line, these star agents, like at an insurance company. I think this environment is a sure manifestation of the kinds of movies they put together – how can your vision soar in these square little cubicles? But I'm a crazy claustrophobe. I've been in churches that felt too cramped.

I suppress my prejudice and show up on time. We aren't kept in the reception area more than five minutes, which gives me time to check out the picture of the old guy from William Morris who is supposed to be the inspiration for this wild corporate success. Todd comes out and ushers us into a small conference room, there are so many of us.

We pass the pitch around the four of us with only a few stumbles, and Todd graces us with a chortle or two. At the end, we look at him expectantly. 'I love this,' he says with a straight face. Well, just what do you mean by that? I mean, this is a guy who loves being an agent.

'You love this?' I'm not certain about anything anymore. Define your terms, Todd.

He smiles in a proprietary fashion, the old guy in the room. 'I love this,' he reiterates simply. We roll this news around silently.

'So, now what?'

'Now I set up a date for you to tell it to her manager . . .' Ah, the next step in the everlasting dance, ooo-eee, doin' the Hollywood shuffle.

'Okay,' I say.

'I'll set it up for right away . . .'

'I've gotta go to New York . . .' Mike interjects, then changes his mind. 'You can do this meeting without me . . .' Gee, thanks, I thought that's what I was doing now. I have thought this before about Mike Levy, once especially in a meeting with Mark Canton and David Debin about *Edgar*, a fabulous rock 'n' roll horror story, but that was because he had a drink at lunch. My fault. He wanted to be cool, like me and Debin. Have a drink at lunch. He fell asleep on the couch, but it was the third pitch on a poisonous Valley day. It didn't matter; Canton put it into development.

He assigned us Billy Gerber and Allyn Stewart to shepherd us through the WB maze. We went through two drafts with Debin, who did his best work. But it wasn't familiar enough for the two junior executives, so on the third go-around, they hooked us up with a guy named Dan O'Bannon whose name is on *Alien*. He in turn did some of the worst work in his life. The yuppies had kneaded it and kneaded it until it became, as Grady Rabinowitz used to say, a piece of shit. It went flatline at Warners. If I had to put a tag on my friendship with Debin, I would say it was on *Edgar*'s demise. And greed. Always greed with these guys.

The point is, contrary to his afternoon nap, Mike Levy surprises me by turning out to be intuitive, supportive, and honorable. Not greedy. Not stupid. Ego, but not much, considering he is a man, which I see as his only negative quality. A great partner. If that is not a contradiction in terms. Family. I am supposed to be creative in meetings. That is the deal; that's why it is okay for me to do the meeting with the writers and the manager while he is in New York. Todd sets the meeting with the manager from the conference room, right in front of us, 'I'm sitting here with blank and blank and blank, and blah blah blah . . . Ten-thirty Tuesday?' Everyone nods. 'Your place?' Everybody nods.

I meet Alex and Andy at ten at Hamburger Hamlet. This is not my time of day. It has fucked with my biorhythms, my alpha waves, and my shitting cycle, but I am here because a deal's a deal's a deal. Besides, I like this black comedy. It has really been invented with these two people in mind, and it has a nice psycho/social spin that I think is weirdly commercial. I am wearing a neon-red sleeveless wool minidress and long sweater that is from among the last of early Steven Sprouse. I am even wearing the neon yellow and red tights, also by Steven Sprouse, which Kate bought me for a birthday long past. I have felt a great need to wear red, perhaps to wake myself up for an outside meeting at this hideous hour, perhaps as some sort of protection.

The boys point out Sean at another table. I have met him before, once at Le Dome with Joyce Hiser and Jamie Foley; Jamie once told me he ran *Taxi Driver* a half dozen times before he started *Reckless*. Apparently to little effect. While I'm having dinner with Ronee Blakley, I spot them at the bar and beckon them to come over for a drink. I am real friendly because Ronee is boring and depressing – this is a woman who has stayed married to Wim Wenders for years past being with him – and I do not plan to spend too many more evenings out with her.

I'm fond of Joyce and Jamie and I think Sean Penn is a big talent. The closest of all of them to being a De Niro-like presence. They tell me about a project they are trying to put together called *At Close Range*, which De Niro has just turned down because it is 'too dark.' I say it must be black as darkest Africa for De Niro to say that, and we all laugh.

I do not know that drinking is a problem for Sean Penn. I only know that he's a knockout on screen. I do not say hello in Hamburger Hamlet. If we get past the manager the next step will be Himself and Herself anyway, but it is kind of vibey that he should be here where we are meeting to go to a meeting with her manager. I have lived far too long in California. I am actually beginning to think in vibes.

We walk across the street to the Luchman Building, which is replete with manager-tenants, and soar to the penthouse to meet one Freddy DeMann – is Freddy, d'man? I wonder. I am prepared to like this guy. How could you not like a guy whose name is a pun?

The office is in high-tech blackgraychrome with a lot of plants. I feel like I'm in a restaurant on Melrose. Veronica, his assistant – very English (how typical) shows us to his office, which overlooks Sunset through huge tinted windows. The shading makes the neon red I'm wearing the kind of spectacular hue I only see on mushrooms. Somehow the color helps me focus on making small talk about show business, what a star Madonna is, how we all got together on this idea.

Freddy is a dapper little guy with brilliantined hair and a

mustache. He dresses the way I would if I were a guy. Right outta Maxfield's. He has large, sad eyes. We like each other immediately, although at a certain point in the meeting I stop sitting on the couch and pace in front of the windows so that I don't have to figure out a new way to cross my legs so that he will stop looking up my very short skirt. Hey, I wore it. Something made me pull it out of the back of the closet. We toss the Frisbee of this story around quite effectively and when we finish Freddy says, without hesitation, 'I love it!'

'Y-a-a-ay!' We dance around the room, me and the boys. 'Now what?'

'I think you should pitch it to them,' Freddy says.

That afternoon I get calls from Mark Canton, now president of Warners, and Jeff Katzenberg, president at Disney, about this pitch. These guys do not call me on a regular basis. Freddy DeMann has been a busy little boy. I know these are bullshit calls, but I also know Freddy has been giving me nice press, so I call him to say thanks and we make a date for dinner at Mortons.

At dinner, he grabs my attention by telling me that I knock him out as a person and a talent, and that he knows that I've had a rough time from this town. If a guy in movies were talking this way to me, I'd ignore it, but when a guy from music talks this way, I believe him. I assume he is tougher than movies or television or publishing. Balls are inverse to pecking order. I assume. Isn't this sad-eyed fashion plate the man who resuscitated Michael Jackson's career after his voice changed (until he was fired by the father) and who is managing Madonna, the hottest tamale to come along since Barbra Streisand?

I can tell two things: one, he has a big crush on me and if he weren't already married, this is the sort of guy whom I should consider good boyfriend material; and two, he has a serious problem with depression. I am infinitely more comfortable with conversation about the depression than the crush, so I ask him about it. He tells me that in his family it is known as the Glickman Curse. His mother's maiden name.

The fact that I understand his depression only makes him love me more. I am seriously worried about being this loved, because in my experience, the more they love me the more they hate me. By the end of dinner, I am sorry I let him pick me up at my house in his hot Porsche, and I start looking for a table I can join. Thank God, Ileen Maisel is there, and I can grab a ride home with her. Freddy is courtly about it, and we take an option on being friends.

He arranges an early get-together with the Prince and Princess and declines an invitation to attend. Between lunch and dinner at Le Dome far enough hence for Mike Levy to return from New York and recover from his jet lag. Alex and Andy are excited to meet Madonna. They are, after all, her age. It seems like a lot of people to put at my table, which works best for four, but who am I to deny the writers? I should take my cue from Freddy, but I miss it.

Mike is so insecure about my being on time that he picks me up from my house to make this six o'clock meeting. I wear my gold Harriet Selwyn blazer with matching vest and an old pair of poison-green Krizia pants. In preparation, I do a double session with Rebecca at an aerobic rate, but it does nothing for my toxins. In the light, I have underbumps all over my face, but I cover them with makeup and pray for an early sunset.

We are the first ones there. I go through a moment of crisis about giving up my back-to-the-wall seat, but I know the rules: the star gets the most protection at the table, even if it is your table. I decide to keep it warm for her and sip on a Perrier.

I always like to play the game with new people about how late they will be. How fucking insecure are you, I say to them in my mind: ten, twenty, thirty minutes? The all-time record being Redford, who once kept me waiting an hour. Unless you count Don Simpson, or Craig Baumgarten, who never showed up at all. So far, everyone is doing fine, because Mike has gotten us here so early.

Then, there is Andy, in his jeans and his blue shirt, to set off his eyes, because the rest of his face is pointy and birdlike, under the beard . . . and Alex. I gasp. Alex, who has a large lumbering quality to begin with, is wearing bear-claw slippers on his feet, bracelets up to his elbow, and a goofy expression on his face. He looks, not cool, not hip, not trendy – just bizarre. Maybe this is the way he thinks it is appropriate to dress for a meeting with Madonna.

I decide a martini will be helpful in overcoming this Alex-hurdle. It arrives just as Madonna and Sean do and I am torn for a moment between saying hello, changing seats, and taking a nice long sip. I do all three without embarrassing myself. She is dyed platinum and dressed from head to toe in black leather. She looks adorable. I like that she is into her image and is dressed in Madonna gear. He is in jeans and leather jacket, what a surprise. He is a dim bulb in her supernova aura.

She has the same amazing pale perfect skin that Barbra Streisand has. I have always imagined that Marilyn Monroe's skin was like that, too. It is impossible not to think of Marilyn Monroe when you see Madonna, even if you know that that's because she has designed herself so that you will think that way.

Everyone is introduced and she sits down in my seat. He sits squoonched in tight to her left, with Andy an unthreatening presence on his left. I sit to her right, and Mike sits to my right. This puts Alex directly opposite her at the table. Smack dab in her eyeline. He ogles her, and she shifts in her chair. The waiter hovers, and I ask if they want anything to drink. They hold hands tightly, sometimes resting on her knee, sometimes on his. Todd and Freddy have both said this is a real love affair. It would seem so.

She orders Perrier in a thin, clear voice. He eyes my martini, starts to order a beer, but she squeezes his knee and he changes his mind. He smiles, shy, abashed. They seem sweet together. We chat for a moment or two about how hard it is to be a star and have people pointing cameras at you all the time. They seem particularly disturbed by a guy who keeps getting them in the bathroom. I can relate, but only intellectually. I am one of those faces that the paparazzi think they should know and then decide that they don't.

When that subject is exhausted, she and I discuss the

relative merits of aerobics. I have just sold my Lifecycle to an ex-runner who is now an actor and needs to reduce his thighs. I know about the thighs because when he showed up for work one day in shorts, I looked at him coldly and told him never again to show up for work in short pants. She swears by it. I tell her I am trying a treadmill instead.

I am not real good at small talk and I am so hyped from working out, that I launch into the pitch almost immediately after these trifling pleasantries. Of course, since this will be her next movie after *Desperately Seeking Susan*, we have designed a part for her that does call for her to sing on screen, à la Streisand in her first two *Funny* movies.

'I don't wanna sing,' she whines softly. Oh dear. I wonder if Todd and Freddy know this. I am tempted to ask if she wants to do Ibsen instead, but I press on. They smile politely and uncomfortably. Alex continues to ogle. She leans over to me and says under her breath, 'This guy is making me real uncomfortable . . .'

I whisper back, 'Me, too,' and we touch eyes. 'I thought I should bring the writers . . . my mistake,' I add. I want Alex to evaporate, but the more I want him gone, the larger he looms. The Abominable Writer. The old me would not take the I don't wanna sing to heart. The old me would argue with her and tell her it is the best way for her to make the transition from rock concert to screen. The new me backs off from the issue and finishes the pitch. I am dripping head sweat by the end, but no one but me knows. I take a big swig on my perfectly watered-down drink, and let the others' aimless chatter carry me off my anxiety wave. I look around. See, Jools, all normal here, there is Carlo the waiter hovering discreetly.

On the drive home, Levy says, 'I don't think that marriage is gonna last.'

'Why?' They seem like a real . . . couple.

'He's very jealous of her . . . jealous about her, jealous of her . . .' Levy always bolts me out of whatever torpor I'm in with incisive remarks like this.

562

'I feel bad about the writers . . .'

'Fuck the writers! So the deal doesn't work out . . . the important thing is that you were a star!' I was? Old Julia City? 'A fucking star! You were always the star . . .' He lowers his voice to agent-telling-a-secret-level. 'Don't ever repeat this, but remember when George Roy Hill insisted Michael be the one on the line?'

I grind my teeth, yes I remember . . . 'Well, Zanuck told me the reason he chose him is that you were too much for him to handle. He was afraid you would be up his ass all the time!' Now he tells me. I could've saved a coupla thou in therapy over that one issue alone. And then I think: Am I supposed to be flattered here?

After *I Am Furious* dies, Freddy and I stay in touch. I keep telling him there is a great movie to be made in a female version of *Carnal Knowledge*. I finally get him to rent it. He calls, claiming that it doesn't work on his VCR. I'll run it on my big screen, I say. Wanna see it here? Me and Freddy'll watch the movie, then have a bite at Morts. He arrives as my assistant, Karen, is about to leave. Some instinct in me asks her to stay. I start to thread up the movie, pile a bunch of pillows on my bed for his head.

My cat jumps on the bed in front of Freddy's face, and he jerks back, surprised.

'I always wanted to see your pussy but I didn't know it would be so soon . . .' What? What?#@! I get uptight instead, beg Karen to stay. We watch the movie. It is only ninety-six minutes, but it feels like two hours. I don't care. It's brilliant. It would be just as great with two women. Particularly with Madonna as Jack Nicholson. I think the sky's the limit with her, even though I keep saying to Freddy, I have two words for you . . . acting lessons . . . drama coach . . .

Freddy's pretty depleted from the movie, so he's happy to leave when it's over. He insists on driving me down in his Porsche. Black. Porsche. Once we're in public I like him again and I feel safe getting excited about the movie I have in my mind. I look around the restaurant and spot Ileen.

It will be the second time she drives me home from a date with Freddy . . .

Madonna gives Freddy permission to pitch 'Female Carnal Knowledge' to Warners. He sends me alone. Mark Canton has populated his office with three or four veepees. I pitch the female carnal knowledge concept; he calls it The Two Chicks Story. Smiling, I amend that to Chicks and Pricks, get a laugh from various and sundry. Amend it again to Chicks and Dicks – we'll name all the male characters Richard.

Rand Halston, who is Freddy's agent at CAA, negotiates a development deal which is only a tad less generous than the one I already have with Warners on *Edgar*. I start a writer search, lunch with Sandra Bernhard, Carrie Fisher . . .

Couple of weeks after the deal finally closes, Freddy calls, concerned. Amy Heckerling, another CAA client, has gotten wind of our project and is threatening to sue, on the grounds that an old project of hers, called *Making Out*, covers the same turf. I read it, and harumph, Not likely, but Freddy is adamant that we should back off. He doesn't want us to be sued, but given our current comparative financial status, he has more to lose than I. Warners reverts the rights to me. So much for balls in inverse pecking order to the system . . .

.   .   .

The only time I was ever involved with a picture that was in the competition at Cannes was in 1976 with *Taxi Driver*, which won.

I was shooting *Close Encounters*, so I didn't go, and by the time *Close Encounters* was invited, I wasn't. Going to Cannes for the festival was one of those things I never got around to doing. I just had this Palme d'Or as a souvenir. And a litho in blue and lavender. Of a place I'd never been to.

Crashing off freebase one night, Rottweiler got mad at me and decided to take it out on all my awards. The Oscar and all those film-editing awards were indestructible, and the Di Donatello award with the gay guy perched on a chunk of malachite was on too high a shelf. The Italians had lobbied pretty heavily for somebody associated with *Close Encounters* to show up, but it was a summer filled with kidnapping and assassination, and there was no way I was going. They sent it by United Parcel. By that time, awards meant nothing to me.

Frustrated, Rottweiler palmed the Palme, as it were, and hurled it against a filing cabinet. He broke off its thumb, which later, remorseful, he volunteered to glue together, but we couldn't remember where the severed member had been stashed. Besides, I liked it better that way. Broken, damaged, but still shiny, like me.

So I go to Cannes on *The Beat*. Forget about first prize. It can't even make it into any sort of competition – not the main, not the Director's Fortnight, nothing. It was a struggle to get Vestron to send us. I humiliated all my former selves begging the underqualified, overfed Bill Quigley, now president of Vestron Pictures, for two first-class and two business-class round-trip tickets to Cannes. For me and Nick and Kilik and Mones. He really put me through the ringer on it, made me crawl, and then never came across with the dough.

(My first great crawl was across a room because I fell off my platform shoes and had to do something. You have a choice at moments like that. Do you suffer loud pain, or do you make it a pratfall and go for the joke? I went for the joke. *Steelyard Blues*' release schedule had just been reversed due to our efforts and bravery, and we were going into Frank Wells's office to thank him, even though he'd done little but say yes. Now that I think of it, that's big. Yes. No. Tony and Michael and I made our cute entrance and I started to move across that vast expanse of carpet toward that Tall Handsome Gentile Man, whom I've always thought of as Supergoy. And I fell off my shoe and tripped down a stair. It was very painful. Humiliating, too. I turned onto my stomach and crawled and kissed his ankle, muttering thankyou thankyou thankyou. It got big, uncomfortable laughs.)

I put the four round-trip-to-Nice plane tickets, two first, two business, on my account with Hoffman Travel. It never occurs to me, after my accomplished crawling, that I might not be reimbursed. Every time I get off a phone call with Quigley I find myself muttering gorgeous phrases, like 'that fat fuck,' to myself. Bill Quigley is one of those angry, insecure guys who seem infuriated by my existence. (What do they want? Ileen cried. They want you dead, I said back. . . . Me, too, I think, therefore I know.)

Nick and I fly to New York, lay over for a day, and the four of us go to the airport together in a limo on my Dav-El house account. (Something else for which I will never be repaid.) The flight over is populated by numerous indie prods, semi-names, and on-the-fringers. Shep Gordon of Island/Alive sits kitty-corner from me and Mones with a vaguely familiar traveling companion who stares at me every chance he gets. His name is Dennis Marini, a legend-in-his-own-mind type who owns acres on Maui and keeps Shep grounded. Who knows with what chemical aids? Mones and I have popped some Restoril, compliments of Stuart, and doze without much commitment.

We arrive in Nice the next day. In a holdover from my traveling-with-Mr.-Wald days, I have ordered a car with a bilingual driver. He is waiting for us at the airport. Olivier. The Big O, we christen him, even though he is slight of build and Dutch. We make our way to Cannes to find M. J. Pekos, Vestron's head of marketing, who has rented a villa for the four of us. This is the only part of the plan that worries me. I have been in business with Vestron for two years and they've never done anything right on their own, or right the first time. We pick M.J. up at the hotel, and she directs Olivier through the back part of town, around circuitous rotaries and up over the harbor along picturesque streets, which smell of sewage.

I keep my gold-and-silver Porsche sunglasses on, even though they feel heavy and the declivity they make on the bridge of my nose will take an hour to disappear. Maybe for protection. We finally locate the street on which we are to live for the next week or so, and with trembling hands, M.J. opens the front gate.

When we enter, the smell of shit gives me a solid whack in the nose. The visuals are on a par. We are in a polyester paean to S & M. Whips and chains and velvet paintings. Purple velvet and fake leopardskin throws with a fine silt of dust-covered couches and ottomans and a chair out of *Star '80*. Not

566

a single bathroom that is complete, not a shower in sight. Beds covered by moth-worn canopies. And a beautiful view of the harbor, which hardly balances out the rest.

I encamp myself there and look soulfully at the sea. What have I done to deserve this? I begin to think that I have only paid off karma on a past life and haven't even started on this one. That might account for having to cope with this 'villa.' Mones goes from room to room exploding Pee-wee Herman noises. Nick and Kilik look frightened.

'M.J., you don't seriously expect four grown people of different sexes who are used to their space to live here, do you?' I say, dripping irony.

'Listen,' she says, her voice stern and her eyes frantic, 'I had to lay a couple grand more on this guy just so he wouldn't rent it out from under me . . .'

'Well, that would appear to be throwing good money after bad,' I shoot back. This is starting to make me furious. Where are we going to find rooms in this crowded paradise? 'I don't know about the boys, but I ain't stayin' here . . .'

'Well, I've already spent ten grand on this place . . .'

I gape in astonishment.

'After you saw it?' I am beginning to think these people are not really evil and incompetent, just stoopid. Mones is still going from room to room doing Pee-wee Herman impressions. Yeah, right, you expostulate and I cope. 'M.J., we can't stay here . . . in fact, I can't stay here another minute . . .'

Olivier has opened the trunk and is getting ready to start unloading but I shoot him a look, and he closes the trunk. Smart, Olivier. Maybe *you* can find us rooms.

We all get back in the car and head back toward the Majestic. When we get there, M.J. points us in the direction of the patio and says to have some lunch on her. She wanders off, I hope in search of rooms for us. I duke the guy who runs the patio a hundred dollars and tell him I am M.J. Pekos and will be dining here daily. I have made a decision that this incompetent bitch will pay for my lunch every day. I never used to think this way.

I've been traveling in an Issey Miyake catsuit, and I am beginning to feel too warm and extra funky. I take my glasses

567

off and rub my nose. I order a martini, which will not make this wonderful headache I'm getting any better. Fuck it, I think, vodka will be good for my soul. If I still have one. I'd rather have a room.

We all go to the buffet and load up on French food; when we come back to the table my glasses are gone. *Quel* drag. They are prescription and I hope whomever took them goes blind. Larry Kasinoff is suddenly standing over us.

'What did you do to M.J.?' he squeaks accusingly at me.

'What did I do to M.J.?' I explode and bark harsh laughter.

'She's up in her room crying . . .'

'At least she has a room to cry in.' Mones chuckles, saying my words for me. I crack a thin smile.

'Wanna join us, Lar, have a little food? Or would you rather make a few calls on our behalf, find us some rooms. Maybe use some of your influence at this terrific place.' The Majestic looks grand downstairs, but I bet there are roaches in the rooms and that they're a little yellow-shag-carpet.

Larry sits down. 'Welcome to Cannes . . .' Does this mean you'll be picking up the check? Larry is one of those skinny guys who is a hell of an eater. These days of course that could mean he throws up after every meal. Beautiful people doing beautiful things.

I check out the passing parade around the pool. There's Jerry Tokofsky over there with Dick Richards. Some bimbo with implants and bad teeth is posing in a bikini that has no straps but is held up with bones. She looks very uncomfortable. A seminame French actress sits with her legs apart, the fringe of her stained skirt just covering her privates. Photographers flash away. As always, they hesitate around me – should I know her? – then move on.

Larry Mortoff stops by to say hello. He has pretty blue eyes, but he is never working at a company that seems really credible. He is dining with Mike Greenfield, an obnoxious fatso who represents TV stars. I try to avoid him, but when he sees me, he comes bustling right over. He is the kind of guy who never speaks, he yells, and when he does he sprays spit on you. It's the closest I've been to a shower in a day. This is just too much. I put my head down on my arms and close my eyes. There's a tap on my shoulder.

'There are some people who'd like to meet you,' Dick Richards says, and indicates Bo and John Derek hidden discreetly under a tree. Why not? Why the fuck not?

M.J. finds us rooms at the Holiday Inn in Nice. We drive fifty miles, check in on my platinum. I take a shower, short circuit my dryer. The boys want to go back into Cannes. I say, fine, but not with me. I lie down on my bed and watch boring French television. I fall asleep early . . .

Kenny Friedman tells us there are plenty of empty rooms at Loew's La Napole. Not to mention a casino in the basement. I suss out the situation, grab three singles and a pretty baby-pink suite, which I take for myself. I produce platinum and fifty-dollar bills, and the staff ensconces us *toute de suite*.

We go to a party that night, and a very handsome dude glombs onto me with his steel-gray eyes. I turn away, think better of it, turn back. I have to follow him through the crowd, but he is easy to spot. Tall. Drunk. I think certain people cross your path at certain times for a reason. He crosses mine to remind me that it is very easy to become a drunk. That first night he misbehaves so badly that I throw him out of my car. The next day he bothers me some more. I tell him, Get sober and I'll hang with you. I'm too busy for this.

Vestron has shipped all sorts of materials, but they are ineffectual in the extreme when it comes to extracting them from Customs. It falls to Olivier to rescue their pathetic one-sheets and synopses and bios. They still don't have a theater to run the picture. In a hyperkinetic frenzy, Mones runs all over town with Kilik, putting up posters. We have a big meeting with all the parties, Vestron's international crew, Marion Billings, M.J., us. It is going nowhere. The Drunk walks in. He looks good.

'I'm sober,' he says, and everybody stands up and applauds. We go to lunch at the Majestic. The maître d' smiles at 'Miz Peckos' and seats us at a poolside table. I know he wants a drink, but he refrains . . .

I do some interviews set up by Marion Billings. I feel she is doing a marginally better job than Vestron, but not a really good job. I have caved to Mones on this matter; I wanted Lois Smith, but she didn't mother him enough. The Old Julia wouldn't have let him make this mistake, the New Julia doesn't care enough . . .

The trip to Cannes costs me fifty grand out of pocket, for which I'm never reimbursed. Vestron has now cost me nearly one hundred fifty thousand dollars to make a picture I'm not even sure I like. I see the Drunk once or twice stateside, but his handsome loser qualities, which would have fascinated me before, seem boring and sad. God knows, I don't need to be around somebody who makes me sadder . . .

The Beat is released with little fanfare in off-the-beaten-path cities near the end of '87. It is Mones's *Steelyard Blues*. He gets a lot of writing assignments out of it.

Kilik becomes the line producer on *Do the Right Thing*.

Billy McNamara, one of our stars, gets hot for three minutes, and I steer him first to Andrea at ICM, later to Todd Smith at CAA when the first choice doesn't work out. He takes a part in *Island Son* playing Richard Chamberlain's younger brother. I see a few minutes one night and know it won't last. That's okay. He's young, he'll survive.

In one of life's little ironies, Nick's next picture, *sex, lies and videotape* wins the Palme d'Or two years later. I go to a screening. I can't make it past twenty-five minutes and I wander through the Academy waiting for it to end. *Thirty-something* for the big screen . . . Christ, I think, now these guys are making movies about their own lives. I get back to my seat just in time to see the dedication to Anne Dollard.

'I didn't like it, but I think it'll be a huge hit,' I tell Nick, relieved when it opens to big numbers that I still know how to spot 'em . . .

So does Nick. One day, after lunch at Le Dome, he plays me a rough mix of an album by Michael Penn. A couple of years ago Mones and I went to see Michael Penn at Madame Wong's and begged Nick to drop him. He has stuck with

Michael Penn for seven years. He is in a high state of giggle when he pushes the cassette into the tape player. Smog rests heavily over our view. We pass a joint. 'What if I were Romeo in black jeans, What if I were Heathcliff it's no myth . . .' I get the chills and a small tear in the corner of my eye. *Où sont les* John Lennons of yesteryear . . .

That summer the album comes out and is a smash, along with another film of Nick's, *Drugstore Cowboy*, one of the few movies I deign to see in the theater. It seems that Nick's integrity in his work is in inverse proportion to that of his lifestyle.

The theater is filled with junkies and people who go to AA. When there is a closeup of a bottle of dilaudid, the audience sighs wistfully. As one. As it were. My friend Lee has given up smoking and drinking. Outside of meetings and chewing Nicorette gum, he doesn't do much anymore. Except go to this movie with me. Which is probably not making him feel better.

'It's the stars,' he declares as we walk out of the theater into a funky part of town and race to the car. 'Probably the moon's in Anus . . .' I laugh, try to be supportive.

'I think you're doing just great. You're my hero, my role model . . .' I almost mean it.

'I'm giving up pissing and breathing next week,' he says morosely.

'It's the eighties,' people started to tell each other as if that sentence alone imparted greater meaning. She changed real-estate agents. She changed business managers, she changed lawyers, she changed hairdressers. People still took her on for her past glories and her potential. The past loomed farther and farther back and she didn't have a clue what the potential was going to do.

So she worked out more. She ran long dictances on her treadmill with the doors open and MTV blaring. She could look at the people's park she had created on her property or what Anne Rice called soft core violo-porn. The music helped her keep pushing and the images on television went with the addictive aspects of the entire endeavor. Christ, she thought, more and more absorbed by the MTV fare, I have to be the oldest person who watches this station. How do I feel about that? Good and bad, like with everything.

She was not a morning person, but she got up earlier and earlier to be able to accommodate her run. She chatted to Mones about it, who had so much rage that he, who wrote all day, had escalated himself to an eighteen-mile run. Per day. Rage seemed too small a word for what drove her. Every other day she worked out with weights as well. She liked how high she got and she liked how strong it made her. Once in awhile, when she ran too hard or too long her ankle would get a little swollen or a little painful.

She got herself up to four and a half miles an hour. She started to run six miles and smoke three packs a day, so clearly the running was a sheer act of will. After she ran she would cough up shit that was as appalling as anything that ever came out of her lungs when she was smoking freebase, and that included burnt-through pieces of screen. Maybe she was staying even with the smoking by running. Fat chance.

She accepted all the information about the damaging effects of smoking, but it didn't make much sense to give up one of her last pleasures when she lived in L.A. and breathed air that ranged in color from violet to shit brown and was so thick you could bite it. Why didn't people get as worked up about the poison, the nuclear, and the viral infection of it all as they did about smoking? She expected that she was more likely to die of gunshot wounds inflicted by a rabid antismoker than of lung cancer. Particularly here in L.A., land of the young and the beautiful and the non-no-antismoking?

Because they are stupid and they are greedy, she thought as she ran, little icicles of pain running from her ankle bone to her shin. Good, I'm in pain, I must still be alive. Had she figured out a new and exciting addiction? Given that they were all addictions to pain in one way or another, she had to admire the directness of this particular route. She liked its clarity. Nothing complex here.

'Run through it,' Mones, an ex-druggie himself, advised. 'You'll get very high.' She started to notice that after the pain, the ankle would bliss out. Then she could pour it on for a while, get the rhythm. Nothing but her and the music and the rhythm and her thoughts. Then the pain would come back. Then it would go numb again. Painumb, painumb – a physiological mantra, as it were.

'Little jolts all along the way,' she reported to Mones, who would laugh with deep understanding. 'Like a solution of Librium and meth in a time-release drip. Librium, meth, Libriummeth, Libriumeth.' Painumb, painumb, painumb. The truth was that some days she loved it almost as much as drugs and others it made it possible for her to do some unfamiliar tasks that she now performed on a daily basis. House and land chores, a shopping list that included: Changing light bulbs in impossible places both in- and outdoors. Bringing the garbage cans up from the road. Tilting the Sparkletts into its closet without a drop of spillage. Sudsing porcelain clean because she could afford Marie only twice, then once, a week. Negotiating with creditors. Watching her spending.

'These are a few of my fa-vor-ite things,' she sang while she ran, and had to stop, she cracked up so hard. Actually, though, she was pretty good at all this stuff, and she liked the feeling that she was finally beginning to be able to take care of herself in a complete sort of way. She'd always been smart and verbal, so people took it for granted that she was competent and self-assured. If she could move mountains, it was assumed she could move molehills, like this petty shit. Frankly, she thought she had made herself good at the grand so she would never have to do the small. Not until now. This was stuff she should have learned years ago, like making the bed, sewing a hem, and taking out the garbage, but she was too busy thinking her great thoughts or doing her great business.

Wow . . . real life. I'm getting to pay my dues backwards, she thought, and smiled to herself philosophically.

'Put ice on it before and after,' Mones advised, but sometimes after she ran her ankle was blown up and painful. She continued to run. That and smoking were keeping her together while she walked along the precipice of what she had come to regard as the docudramedy that was her life. One day she woke up and couldn't put any weight on her right leg. Her ankle was exploding and discolored.

She went to the orthopedist who had straightened Kate's pigeon-toed walk and who had set her own broken wrist in a cast that went from thumb to armpit and looked like a swan. He was now a hot doctor, but in view of her past relationship with his office, he took her that day. She heard the orthopedist dictate to the mini-recorder into which he intoned endless diagnoses that she had a hairline fracture of the tibia, something he called an addicted runner's injury. What kind of shoes was she wearing? Get Tiger Gels. Was she running outdoors? She should wear a brace and stay off the foot for awhile. He held up his hands as if to fend off her panic.

'Do something else. I understand, I'm an addicted runner, too.'

'What? What?'

'Swimming, stationary bike . . .' She made a Valleygirl vomitface. 'I know, I know,' he commiserated, 'but if you do it, I'll have you running again in six weeks to two months. It's better than never running again and being in constant pain.'

'Call it a toss-up.' She looked at the brace he was shoving on her ankle ruefully and wondered which outfits in her closet would work with it. What possible fashion statement could be developed from this material? Thank goodness it was still winter – she could wear tights and tight little Gaultier dresses with low boots. An elegant elf, Brooke called her. With another broken wing.

She rented a Tunturi stationary bike from Abbey Rents. She was so poor she had to think twice about buying it for two hundred fifty dollars. Fuck it, I'll never be that poor. And I'll never get rich again if I turn into a fat tub of goo. She wrote a check on the little OD account City National had set up so obligingly years ago when the money was just pouring in, and wondered how obliging they felt now. She set the tension to ten and moved the seat around a dozen times so that her knees wouldn't lock. It made her pour sweat within seconds and the seat bit into her cunt in a most unwanted way. This was not going to be an easy adjustment.

'Put a towel on it,' a friend who was a bike freak advised re: the seat, 'and keep the tension real low and the reps real high,' re: the sweat factor. She pointed it exactly at the television, in front of the treadmill, and turned up MTV.

One day, she managed to ride for an hour. She got off, sweating like from a run, and then felt the endorphins kick in. Her twat was numb for ten minutes after she got off the bike, but this was okay, this could work for the time being. Besides, she didn't have to turn the television up so loud.

Another thing. She could close her eyes on the bike, and play voice twin. Did Axl Rose know that he sounded just like Janis Joplin? Did Bobby Brown know that he was really Sly Stone? Had Culture Club ever heard 'Subterranean Homesick Blues'? Did Mike Ovitz know that Bryant Gumbel was his long lost bro?

One day Dick deBlois, her new business manager, called and said, 'Wouldn't we rather owe City National than the IRS?' He had been the one getting the notices and the phone calls, so presumably he knew that this was the right thing to do, kind of like having oat bran for breakfast instead of Sugar Pops.

Steven Reuther fucks himself into a job at Vestron. He almost marries the woman, but they split up badly instead. She, who was there first, and helped Austin build the company, loses an executive war with Bill Quigley and is fired.

Austin has Quigley do the dirty deed. Steven, meanwhile, goes up the executive ladder. His credit is on a dozen turkeys and one hit, *Dirty Dancing*. Within weeks after he and Ms. Vestron have split, he hooks up with Natalie Zimmerman, who is a more beautiful version of her predecessor. Tall dark and handsome I want to say.

When I return from Cannes, I try to enlist his aid in my reimbursement campaign. The figure is now one-five-oh grand. His lips say yes yes yes but his eyes say no no no. Re: My Money. It is business by nonresponse, an eighties phee-nom, perfected by rinky dink outfits like Vestron. So Steve Reuther is not just a sleaze. He is a pussy sleaze. Bit by bit we fall completely out of each other's lives.

Later, when I am running out of money, I call in the shopping-spree-at-Giorgio's debt. Rather, I have Dick deBlois call in his debt. He sends the check to me with a formal handwritten note thanking me for my generosity. Hey, it would've been nice if you could've convinced Austin or Bill to cut me a check for the money they owed me instead of this lousy pittance, I say to his letter.

Steve and Natalie live together for quite a while, and after an appropriate interlude she gets pregnant, which has become the New Order these days. They throw themselves a big Hollywood wedding. I am not invited . . .

Kate writhes on the floor of the emergency room. Her pediatrician, Dr. Levin, looks annoyed. We both speak to her in sharp voices, as if this will snap her out of her pain. He pokes and she writhes.

'Kate, you're behaving like a four-year-old,' I hear myself say angrily.

'Well, it's not appendicitis . . . my suggestion is you take her home, and let's see what happens in a couple of hours . . .'

'Shouldn't we be keeping her here?' My voice is tremulous.

'Ordinarily, if a kid showed up with these symptoms' – he means the pain and the all-night puking – 'I'd put her on an IV and keep her here for twenty-four hours of observation, but,' he gestures toward Kate, who is still not acting the perfect progeny, 'the hospital seems to be having a negative effect.'

Kate and Jackie and I get in the car and go home for a couple of hours. The pain gets worse, so we all decide Kate needs to be put into the hospital. By the time she is all checked in it is eight o'clock at night. Over the next three days, through the miracle of magnetic imaging (thank you, George Lucas) we learn that one of Kate's fallopian tubes is filled with fluid and flopping over on itself and perform a laparoscopy. Nothing is removed but the excruciating pain. Dr. Levin brings Kate a volume of Emily Dickinson poems by way of apology. *This is my letter to the World / That never wrote to Me . . .*

Three months later, on a Saturday morning, just after I have taken two hits off my all-time favorite roach, the phone rings. I let the machine pick up: 'Mom, Mommy – if you're there, pick up the phone . . .' It is Kate, and I don't like the way her voice sounds. I pick up and she immediately starts to cry. 'Mommy, I have that pain again, and Daddy was shooting at night' (his first feature since *The Flamingo Kid*). 'They won't let me wake him. They gave me a Tylenol and codeine . . .'

How Kate and I ever survived the holistic ministrations of Michael's second wife, Liv, an insane ex-model who took marriage as permission to become obese, I will never know. I do know that from the time the joint custody started, Kate has always called me during medical emergencies, because I seem to be the only adult in her life who still believes in the occasional visit to the doctor. I decide this is an emergency.

'Get dressed. I'm coming over . . .'

'What're you going to do?'

'I'm going to take you to Dr. Levin . . .' After the fallopian emergency had passed, we had been told the condition could become chronic and needed to be watched carefully. Kate had just had a sonogram last week. I pull on some exercise clothes and hop in the car. My heart is racing. We fly to the doctor's, who takes one look and says, 'We need to put her in the hospital.' I call Michael, who has wakened from his beauty sleep. Why am I calling you? I wonder.

I drive Kate back to Michael's to pack a bag. It is agreed that she should go in on his insurance this time. I am still struggling with my insurance company to pay off the bills incurred by the last emergency. In the car down, Kate says, 'Mommy, I'm so scared . . .'

'Me, too,' I say. 'Let's list the fears in order.'

'Well, I'm scared I'll have to have surgery, I'm afraid I'll get left back in school . . .' It is right in the middle of finals.

'I'm scared of the same things, but if you do need surgery, better out than in, and I'm sure all the teachers will be cooperative about this sort of an emergency . . .' I'm scared of cancer, I think, and shoo the word into the corner of my conscious mind. I pull into the emergency lot and the attendant waves to us in recognition. Celebrity parking at Cedars.

Kate is put on the gynecological floor this time, instead of the pediatric floor. Not as happy a place, given that one side is devoted to maternity (festive) and the other to oncology (not festive). Women with turbans on their heads and pale, drawn faces walk painfully up and down the hall. Too late, I think. Poor poor Mommy. Please forgive me . . .

Kate is in a lot of pain, and they do nothing for it. God forbid they should mask the symptoms until her doctor arrives. He has taken his son to a Lakers game, so we get to wait most of the day. He finds me in the cafeteria forcing down a morsel of trafe and tells me that they have all looked at the sonogram and the tube has to come out.

'Where did this come from?' I want to know, and of course he tells me that it is probably congenital. The eye, the shoulder, the tube. It's all my fault.

Congenital.

Michael and I accompany her to pre-op. It is the worst twenty minutes to spend with your child. She is old enough now to be aware that things get fucked up during surgery sometimes. She has already discussed this with the resident. 'I'm afraid something might go wrong . . .' she has said. She has a laugh over us in our shower caps and rubber booties. Then she is wheeled away. We wait in the visitors' lobby with Jackie.

Twenty minutes later the doctor comes out with a silver dish and something that looks like a half a chicken. It is the offending tube, and I wonder why he has brought us this piece of our child to survey. He explains that he has left pieces of tube at each end. 'They'll be able to connect it with plastic by the time she wants children,' he says. Phew! I have sutured the future and it is plastic. Thanks, Dad . . .

They give her a morphine drip that she can operate by herself and for the next two days I watch her dose herself and scratch.

Congenital.

Scott calls to see how Kate is, how I am, and, without really thinking, I ask if he is busy for dinner. After all, Mortons is just down the block from Cedars. 'I feel the need for male company,' I tell him. What does that mean, exactly? I am certainly not looking to get laid. Maybe it is just a reaction to the femaleness of the medical emergency. I smoke a joint and order a martini. I feel better.

'It's all my fault . . .'

'What, Julia, the state of the world as we know it?'

'There's that, too . . .' Scott smiles. That's why I have come to dinner with him. He's such a gentle man. A gentleman, too. He's gotta be the last guy on earth who stands up every time you go to the ladies' room.

'It's my fault that she's had this medical crisis . . .'

'Why is that?'

'Because the first two months I was pregnant I did drugs, I was on the road with *Steelyard Blues* and I did uppers downers inbetweeners . . . I didn't know I was pregnant until I got home . . .'

'I knew you were going to say that . . .'

'Well, where does that stuff have an effect: respiratory, nervous – '

'Reproductive . . .'

'Exactly.' We sip at our drinks.

'Feel better now?'

'The only thing that makes me feel better is something I've gotten quite into from reading *Scientific American* . . .'

'I know what it is . . .' No way, I think. I've been dining out on this for a month. 'Oh really . . .'

'Yup. It's the Great Attractor . . .'

My mouth drops open. Nobody in Hollywood but me is supposed to know about this. 'How'd you know that?'

'It's been all over the papers, Julia. I knew you'd like it because of the name . . .' I think of my dinner with Michelle Phillips and Carl Parsons a month ago. I'd just read an article in *Scientific American*, which was replete with lots of pretty pictures. The concept of the Great Attractor had come up with the mapping of the stars that the Smithsonian and Harvard were doing. Because of new technology it was now possible to map up to four maybe five hundred galaxies in the universe, instead of the four galaxies closest by. What had developed in this mapping, even when one accounted for the Doppler effect, red and blue shifts, gravitational and magnetic pulls, was that everything seemed to be going from one place to another.

'I'm so glad to know we're going somewhere,' Michelle had said after I regaled her with this dissertation.

I had a long conversation with Anne Rice about the Great Attractor and she asked what I thought it was.

'Well, I know what you'll say,' I retorted. 'You'll say it's God . . .' this to little Annie Rice, from the Irish Channel, as she called herself.

'Julia, I don't believe in God . . .' This was big news to me and took me a second to absorb.

'I can't tell you how much better this makes me feel,' I said after a long silence. 'I feel so much less alone . . .'

'So, since you know all about the Great Attractor, I can't dazzle you with my explanation of same,' I say now to Scott, who is smiling with pride at being one-up on me.

'Well, you probably know more about it from *Scientific American* than I do from the *Times*. New York or L.A . . .'

'Please, it's a miracle I understand anything about it at all. I have to call my father and ask him what it means . . .' At least it gives me something to talk about to my father. Well, that isn't strictly true; actually, me and my father are finding a great deal to talk about now that I am middle-aged and he is old. And my mother is dead. Dead people, dead people. Have they all gone toward the white light of the Great Attractor? 'There was an interesting little postscript on this article though. One of the guys instrumental in the mapping was killed in a freak motorcycle accident . . . young, too . . .'

'Maybe we're getting too close to the truth.' Scott smiles.

'Yeah, that would be the movie way of thinking . . .'

'So, what do you think the Great Attractor is?' Scott smiles again.

'I think it's probably the Great Attractress.' I smile back.

Michael hadn't invited me to his second wedding, although, God knows, I heard enough about it from those who did attend. Bookie dished over lunch that the new wife, Liv Faret, whom we called ferret in my house, was a part of a crowd of international girls: actress/model/whatever (AMW's Barry Beckerman called them) who made a pact in 1969 to marry rich, whatever else they did with their lives. She was married to some sort of Scandinavian baron for awhile, but had pretensions to woman-producerness, so she left him and got adopted by Verna Fields. I guess that's how she met Michael.

I never met Liv when she was a great beauty. She was already turning to fat when she swept past me one day, contempt all over her high-cheekboned face, to visit little Kate in the hospital when she had her tonsils removed. It's true, I was doing a great deal of blow at the time, and had left Hollywood in disgrace, but as far as I was concerned, she was just a hooker with an accent who was enjoying the fruits of my labors, and I wanted her to get that look off her face before I had to take it off in some physical fashion. I split instead, exhausted as I was by having been the pre-op sleep-over parent. Kate hadn't slept a wink and neither had I.

Liv left in disgrace in the middle of the night with jewelry and china, a classy gesture, and I didn't have to interact with her again until Kate had her teenage hospital emergencies. She had by then blown up to about two hundred fifty pounds, which shocked and horrified me, although I couldn't ever really forgive her for her treatment of me or Kate.

I got to give her that same look back, only she didn't have the presence of mind to split. Well, nobody ever said she was smart. Shrewd, maybe. Perfect match for Michael.

Now, Michael is going to get married again. On New Year's Eve, no less. To another person with a foreign accent. Juliana Maio. A lawyer. Between the English-as-a-second-language, and the career, no sense of humor. What is it with Michael and these dang furr'ners? I wonder. The old *plus ça change* boogie, I guess.

At least Juliana is small, and she has the class to request a dinner alone before we see each other again at their wedding. I presume they are getting married on New Year's Eve so they'll never forget their anniversary. As far as I am concerned, that is okay, it gives me something to do. I ask Stuart to be my escort on the grounds he will be supportive, as opposed to Brooke, who would be a chore. As it turns out, Dreyfuss is a no-show and Michael says it is okay to bring them both. Which is a good thing, because Stuart has been celebrating with his downstairs neighbor for a considerable period before coming to get me. His mouth is working overtime traveling all over his face and he keeps getting lost on his way to the bathroom.

Michael Douglas is also a no-show. Months later, he slips out of his partnership with Michael. I knew that would happen. Otherwise, he'd have found a way to get out of Aspen and come to the Bel Air Hotel. I think it's a lousy gesture. More and more, I am taking Michael's side in any perceived battles he is having with the world. Interesting . . .

I wear a Fabrice strapless black minidress with sparkles down the front and a matching bolero jacket, and I sip Perrier all night. I've also been invited to a New Year's Party Freddy DeMann is throwing; I call him in the afternoon to tell him I don't think I could make it and he sounds sad.

'I was really looking forward to seeing you . . .'

'Okay, I'll leave the second the ceremony is over . . .'

This doesn't occur till nearly one o'clock, but by now I've had enough of interacting with all of Michael's family and bunches of other people I haven't seen in years: Blumenthal, Freddy Gordon, Deborah Raffin, and Michael Viner . . . At one point Stuart and Brooke and I dance with Kate and her best friend, Amanda, and that is the most family bonding I can bear on a New Year's without bawling my eyes out and embarrassing myself and my daughter in front of all these many Phillipses . . .

When we get ready to say our goodbyes, Stuart wanders off. Of course, I don't realize this until I am already in my car. Brooke has to go back to find him. Now your brother . . . etc., etc . . . By the time we get to Freddy's, it is nearly one thirty.

There is a party of adults, downstairs, and a party of teenagers, upstairs. Freddy shows me around the house that Madonna built. Every time we go into a room with teenagers, he yells a warning. They are always spraying room deodorant. I hope they are smoking nothing more hazardous to their health than pot. I don't know any of the grownups at the party; I recognize Lionel Richie, though, and charm him by telling him I've just come from my ex-husband's wedding.

'I've always admired your work,' I lie. It is hard to tell, but I believe I see him blushing. Behind him, situated on the staircase where no one can see them, Brooke and Stuart pantomime fingers down throats and I almost smirk. Lionel rewards me with a person-to-person 'Outrageous' and I nearly guffaw.

It is late enough to make excuses, and we start to leave. Bruce Willis is coming into the party with Joel Silver, who sweeps past me, and his pregnant wife, Demi Moore, who also sweeps, but Bruce and I get stuck face to face in the door. Clean and Sober. We give each other big hugs, and he goes into the party and I leave. Brooke and Stuart and me head home to my house and I make us breakfast. At four we all crash, me alone in my bed, them in Kate's and Jackie's rooms.

The next day we have the last of some magic mushrooms and Stuart gets so loose he takes off all his clothes.

'E-e-eu-u-uw, Stuart, gross,' I say, trying to find someplace to give him a dirty look that won't offend me.

We never have the fight that's brewing, but he splits. Brooke, who's only been a witness, leaves shortly thereafter. I feel guilty and bereft.

Happy fucking New Year.

Later on, Stuart calls and we make up by phone, on the grounds we don't want to start the year out with a fight, but I make a mental note: no more Michael weddings, no more Freddy DeMann parties, no more psychedelics with Stuart.

I guess these count as resolutions . . .

Time's Man of the Year is Gorbachev. Gorbachev and Reagan. Michael and me. Détente . . .

I go to Brooke's gym with him just to see the difference between machines and the free weights to which I have become addicted. Like all gyms, there's entirely too much cruising; after the tenth person gives Brooke the eye, he says, 'People fuck you with just a glance, don't they?' 'Welcome to the nineties,' I reply. 'No, in the nineties they'll fuck themselves, in the mirror,' he says. Well, he should know, the little disco brat. I weigh 107 pounds, but of course when I look in the mirror all I see is a small deposit of fat on my hips in a spot nobody else I have ever met has a deposit of anything.

I am in hot pink shorts and a T-shirt and Brooke is in basic street combat gear and T-shirt when we decide the thing to do is to have red meat at Mortons, our outfits notwithstanding. My table stands at the ready at 6:30.

I am in a nondrinking, noneating sort of mode, but I get off watching Brooke having a little bit of everything. We are done as the restaurant starts to crank up its dinner crowd.

The big round table in front has filled up with Sherry Lansing, Martha Latrell, Jimmy Wiatt, and Anne Archer, Adrian Lyne and his wife, Samantha, and Michael Douglas. Sherry and Michael have touched my shoulder on the way in.

Since it is clearly a *Fatal Attraction* pre-Oscar celebration, I have sent over a good bottle of champagne.

On my way out I go over to say hello. Michael Douglas is surprisingly affectionate. In fact they all are, and Sherry says come and join us for a drink. They are about halfway through their dinner and clearly in their cups. I feel ridiculous and perfect in my hot pink shorts and T.

Brooke wants to go and walks me to my car where I have stashed a hot pink Harriet Selwyn summer cotton sweater. I tie it around my waist. 'You should go have a drink with them,' he says. I kiss Brooke goodbye and go back in.

There is champagne on the table and in the bucket and everyone is having a hard-liquor drink. I order a Smirnoff martini on the rocks with a twist and look around the table. For the first time, I notice Sherry is wearing a cream-colored version of the sweater I have tied around my waist. With pearls.

I don't know why Sherry has never annoyed me the way she annoys all the other women. Sherry is very pretty, but she has never had any style. She never really looks pulled together to me. At least she's gotten rid of the haircut, the Marilyn Quayle flip that she wore for years. Now it is in a long, curly bob. I'm at her power dinner in workout clothes and I'm having the nerve to think about her lack of style. Sometimes I appall even myself.

'You're getting too thin,' Jimmy Wiatt says, eying my arms. He looks a bit porky to me, and I want to say, Define your terms, fatso! but I say:

'There is no such thing, you know . . .' I make a muscle forward and back and squint my eyes at him. Look at the cut, look at the tone, look past me to another table . . .

There's Jack Nicholson having a quiet tête-à-tête with Keith Barish. An *Ironweed* dinner.

They signal and wave and Michael Douglas excuses himself. Then Wiatt. Then Adrian. Oh please.

Everyone is getting very drunk. One toast after another. Anne Archer cries saluting Adrian. Martha cries saluting Sherry. Carried away, I disgust myself by toasting Sherry: 'If it has to go from "only" to "first" I'm glad it's you.' Tears all around. Liar liar pants on fire! Boomalackaboomalacka.

Am I the only one in Hollywood who gets to go broke and cold turkey? Lackaboomboomboom . . .

Re: the quintessential rock 'n' roll manager. He is either short or tall, and probably balding. In either case, he is not really sure of himself. He beats you up to whatever degree he is unsure of himself. Whether his assault is physical or verbal it is always an intense emotional experience. It seems to get him off. He is aggressively vulgar, but he is also intelligent; there is often something elegant about his mind, even if he prostitutes it for more money for his client. Chances are he's from the Bronx and probably attended DeWitt Clinton High School. He likes to 'dese' and 'dose' you, if only for effect.

He aspires to be bigger than life. He is either very funny himself or a great appreciator of the funny. He is considered, therefore, to have a good sense of humor. He is not in touch with his feelings, if he still has them. If he could have them surgically removed, he would. He is often married, and has been married to the same woman for a long time. He fucks bimbos a lot. Badly.

He loves to party, but as he gets older he tends to binge rather than have a good time. He is anywhere from pretty powerful to very powerful. He is not happy. He fights the same fights every day and doesn't appear to get bored. Usually for money. As it were.

He acquires art. He has good taste, he picks well. He tells himself it is a good investment. He does not want to admit to himself he likes to look at the pictures. He will never sell them. He vaguely remembers when he loved music. He stopped loving music years ago.

He is a social climber: he wants to be on top, so he flirts with going into the film business. Hollywood pecking order: Music TV Movies. He loves movies, but he's never really serious about making them. His clients take up too much of his time, and that's where the real money is. In the for-love-or-money horse race money always wins by a nose.

Poor little self-made rich boy. His wife/lover doesn't understand him. Probably from time to time he beats her up. Then the wife/lover shops on Rodeo Drive with fierce intensity and they make peace. Women are stars or hookers on the good-looking hand, or dykey dogs on the other hand. He is not used to women like me. Whatever the fuck that is . . . At first he goes for me, then lets me down. And I thought I was being so charming, so charismatic, so major league. Probably hated me behind my back.

That's the quintessential. Then there's Gary Kurfirst. Gary has made a career of being a diamond in the rough who handles tasty bands. He has also produced a movie I really admire called *Siesta*, so he and I get friendly. Gary likes blondes. I know that before it is borne out by evidence: Tina Weymouth, Mary Lambert, Debbie Harry, even his wife, Phyllis, a childhood sweetheart whom he married a long time ago and kept salted away somewhere in area code 914. Nevertheless, I get to him. Sheer brain power, I figure.

Gary puts me together with Mary Lambert, the director of *Siesta*. She has paid her dues making topnotch music videos with big-timers: Sting, Madonna, the Ramones. She is small and thin, with a broad, high forehead and deep-set blue eyes. Thin determined lips and a strong chin. A sister under the skin. She paints large vistas in beautiful strong colors, alternating with steamy intimate portraits, a propitious start for a director. In some parallax way, she reminds me of Marty Scorsese.

I've been sent a wonderfully disturbing surreal novel by a woman named Emily Praeger called *Clea and Zeus Divorce*, and it just feels like something that Mary would like to do and that she would do well. I give the book to Gary right away and he gives it to Mary. On faith, he says. She flips. She and I meet several times while he is out of town. I talk to the agent for the book, an old friend from New York, an impossible screamer named Ron Bernstein, who has a great eye for material and a big heart, and he says he thinks I should talk to the author.

I don't like the bitch at all on the phone; I sense a cold paranoia that makes for good stories and bad negotiations. We arrange for her to see *Siesta*, which she likes, and *The Beat*, which she doesn't. She can hardly keep the contempt out of her voice: 'I took a young male friend, who liked it,' she says dully. Oh yeah, well I'm starting to like this book less and less, too, but I press on, being gracious and keeping Mary and her talking, albeit by long distance. I don't wanna do this anymore, I don't wanna do whatever's good for the project. But . . .

Mary says she has friends on *Saturday Night Live* who say the woman is weird with a big head and a little body (a physical description of the character Clea in the book). I'm not surprised. For some reason this piece of information seems like the signal not to attenuate the process anymore, so I tell both Mary and Gary that I think we should option the book, or get out of the *Clea and Zeus* business right away. Mary and I want to go go go, and Gary says he will come out to meet with us.

'You girls get your act together and I'll come out,' is what he says. Girls? *Pardonnez-moi*, but are you talking to me?

So Mary and I reconnoiter at my table at Le Dome.

'I always see you in the same table at Le Dome at lunch,' Jack Gilardi once said, a tinge of envy in his voice. Jack Gilardi, an agent from way back, one of the old school, ex-husband to Annette Funicello, the Mouseketeer with tits. Jack Gilardi, who grossed more than me in a good year, and still didn't have a house account at Mortons. Jack Gilardi, who liked me for two seconds when the *Trax* deal was going, and then smiled distantly from across the room when it fell out. Which was a blessing, because he wore far too much cologne, and when he cheek-kissed it always gave me the sneezes. *Où sont les* Jack Gilardis of yesteryear?

'Oh, my car is on a little computer.' I smiled. 'I get in and I say "lunch" and it drives to Le Dome. When it's dark outside, I say "dinner" and it drives to Mortons . . .'

Mary and I sit at the table and play with our silverware. It is the holiday season and the place is jumping with semifamous writers, directors, and actors. Lots of forced gaiety. Lots of clothes, jewels, and makeup. Lots of champagne.

Paula Abdul, who has choreographed several of Mary's videos, comes over to say hello, and we invite her to sit down. Within a minute, she is pouring her heart out to Mary about the lousy treatment she's received from Janet Jackson, who has not acknowledged Paula's contribution to her videos or her stardom. She must have been truly hurt to be so open in front of a complete stranger. The old Hollywood boogie.

We commiserate and she brightens somewhat. The rest of her career is going just fine, she says. She is actually starting to sing a little herself. But she gets sad again, the thought of Janet undoubtedly running through her mind. It is, after all, the Christmas season, a time to focus on all the failed relationships of the past year. Me, I'm into the failed relationships of past lives. *Plus ça change*, etc. (A year later Paula Abdul's album would have four hit singles and soar to number one. Had she become a star because another star rejected her? A case of fuck me? no fuck you . . . No doubt.)

Just as Paula and her tale of woe depart, Gary arrives. All smiles. Mary smiles back. Are they lovers? I wonder. If they are, that makes my situation anywhere from difficult to untenable. Am I getting addicted to all this weirdness, or do other people find themselves in strange equations too? I mean, other people in Peoria. Civilians. Gary sits down and kisses us both. We babble – like girls? – about how excited we are getting about this project, and he dumps cold water all over our nicely coiffed heads right away.

'I don't want to be involved in this,' he says, kinda flatly.

'What?!@' Mary and I explode simultaneously.

'I just don't think this is commercial and I don't wanna be involved . . . you can go ahead on your own . . .' Mary's thin lips tremble a little on this last piece of dialogue. I am getting afraid she might cry right at the table. Definitely some hidden agendas here. Oh poor me poor me.

'Gary,' Mary says in her thin southern voice, 'part of the whole excitement about this was that the three of us would do it together . . .' Now, she is getting tears in her eyes. This is

589

really too much. I'm not hungry anymore. I propel myself out of the chair before I think about what to do next.

'This is personal between you two,' I say, more anger in my voice than I really feel. I have reached the point where basically this sort of nonsense just makes me tired. 'Let me know what you guys decide . . . I can go either way, but right now, I think I'll go home . . .' If I had long hair, I'd have tossed my curls. Then, I'm gone. And within days, so is the project.

Lynn Nesbit calls one day to say that an erstwhile English manager, Barry Krost, has been sneaking around, trying to put together a package on *Interview with the Vampire* behind our backs. After Taft Barish reneged, I had spoken to David Geffen about the possibility of his mounting such an enterprise. He has been exceptionally successful in his Broadway ventures, and I know through Howard Rosenman that he loves *Interview*. He expresses interest, says if he gets involved he wants to put up his own money.

'Why?' I ask. 'I thought the point of being a producer was to put up other people's money . . .'

'Not on Broadway. If you don't put up your own money, you don't make anything . . .' I have noticed that outside of Michael, David Geffen is the most money-obsessed person I know. 'And Julia,' he adds, 'you should put up some of your own money, too . . .'

What money????

I'd rather be in business with Geffen on Broadway than Barry Krost, so I head him off at the pass, and he prevails on me to arrange a dinner, instead, for me, Anne, himself and Bernie Taupin, one half of the Bernie-Elton John equation. This duo interests me. I check it out with Geffen and he acts interested, too. Back to the Broadway show, this time with Bernie and Elton John.

The day of the big dinner my *Vanity Fair* arrives. There is a big story in it about Lori Rodkin, a groupie in manager's clothing. One of those people that stars love because they are the mirror that tells the star: You are a star. I had lunch with

Lori once, during which time she gave me a résumé around the men she'd lived with. I must have made a face, because she said: 'Don't you think I can earn my own Mercedes?'

'Well, you've just given me your star-fucking lineage . . .' I respond, and Harlan, who has arranged this little tête-à-tête, sinks lower into his chair.

The article in *Vanity Fair* is an exact duplication of her riff at lunch. One of the legion of ex-boyfriends mentioned is Bernie Taupin. Dinner is going very well, but I just must say to him, 'So Bernie, have you read the article about Lori in *Vanity Fair* . . .'

He freaks out, recites a litany of responses to every one of her allegations about him. All the way back to her hotel in the car, Anne keeps going: 'I don't believe you did that, I don't believe you did that . . .'

The next month there is a long letter in *Vanity Fair* reiterating everything he said at the table. It gives me a tiny chuckle.

We have a meeting in Elton's suite the Four Seasons: Anne, Elton, Bernie, Mike, Barry, and me. When we mention David Geffen, assuming he is an asset, Elton's face clouds over, and he allows they don't get along that well. This nasty tidbit notwithstanding, we toast the Broadway opening of *Interview* . . .

Lorimar is merged into Warners. David Geffen, who has been staying in touch with me about these books, has a relationship with Warners. I ask him to read Anne's bible. He says he likes it. He asks if we have a problem with the rights being assigned to his company. I confer with Mike and we agree that being in business with this guy is the closest we will ever be to getting the fucker made.

After *Queen of the Damned* goes to number one on *The New York Times* bestseller list, Geffen calls to say he doesn't think it's smart to proceed with the musical. I concur with him on creative grounds, but I have a bad feeling that he is putting the kibosh on it because of Ancient History with Elton. *Queen of the Damned*, my ass . . .

It is left to me to blow them off, which I do on the phone with Barry Krost. 'You know why he's doing this!' he sputters. Did I ask a question here? 'When *Cats* was opening in New York, David wanted Elton there. Elton was on a world tour and didn't want to come. David begged, pleaded, cajoled, told Elton to take the Concorde. Elton was tired, didn't show . . . his next three albums were on Geffen. David torpedoed them, then didn't renew his contract . . .'

I call David to tell him the dirty deed is done. We arrange a meeting . . .

Time's Man of the Year is Planet of the Year: Endangered Earth. David Geffen's logo is the globe and he is the Endangered Man.

'He's selfish, self-centered, egomaniacal, and worst of all – greedy.' Geffen, who seems always to dress in polo shirts and jeans, presumably to impress you with what a casual guy he is, is telling me his impressions of Steven Spielberg; I think it is a pretty good description of him.

To my credit, I only smile and say, 'You're telling me?' Fuck, I taught the little prick he deserved limos before he even knew what it was like to travel in a first-class seat on a plane. My stomach is very knotted in spite of the fact that Mike Levy and I have met at the Hamburger Hamlet an hour before this meeting to go over our directors' list and have a little something to take the edge off.

For Levy, the edge is taken off by some antibiotic and a Perrier. For me, a salad and vodka and tomato juice. We have come up with a directors list of doom – everyone from Zemeckis to David Lynch, and we have a couple of good laughs. We are dreading this meeting. We have pushed and manipulated to end up with this guy, and deep down we know that it is going to be a nightmare.

We walk to his building. Unusual in L.A. Emblazoned over

the door it says THE DAVID GEFFEN COMPANY. Think this guy's got an ego problem? I ask and tug at my leather skirt. We enter laughing, which disarms the receptionist, a pleasant boy with a pierced ear. We are asked to wait a moment, what a surprise, and Levy, ever the agent, makes a call. I pace and make friends with the receptionist.

Levy is still on the phone when we are summoned, so I pace some more. Finally, I tell him that God wants to see us, and at that moment, Lisa Henson, daughter of Jim, a yuppie exec from Warners, arrives. I have been shining her on for weeks with this drink date and that lunch, and I am surprised she has been invited, but I don't care, except to trip on my aggravation on the way up the stairs.

We keep going up and up stairs and then we arrive at another office that says DAVID GEFFEN on the door. It reminds me of Grady describing working with Burt Reynolds years ago: 'Think about it, Julia, he gets up every morning and puts a toupee on his head, lifts in his shoes, and a girdle around his waist, and sits at a desk that has a nameplate that says BURT REYNOLDS on it,'

The meeting is very long, almost three hours, which means that David Geffen is having what is called *fun* in Hollywood. This generally means running someone around the room, preferably someone more talented and less powerful than you. That gets to be me in this particular instance, and it surprises me how unattached I am to the experience. I change position many times. The skirt is a little tight. I keep thinking, I'm never eating again, a chronic mantra for me, and it removes the desire for drugs.

I have gotten up out of a sickbed for this (another Oriental flu – I am convinced the heathen Chinese are testing a new germ, but I don't drink the water. Only Evian – I am the wave of the future; soon we will all be drinking water you have to pay for) and I can feel my fever rising along with my desire for drugs. This guy is really pissing me off.

I can tell which way the wind is blowing by the directors he exes out – Kubrick, Steven, even Zemeckis he is fighting me on. Anyone more powerful than him gets taken off the list. We get a couple of vetoes, too, so Adrian Lyne and Sidney

Lumet bite the dust. In fact, this whole process is very like jury selection. Prosecution exes someone, so the defense does, too.

At one point, we ask Lisa Henson, who has been participatory in a yes/no kind of way, if there is anyone missing whom she wants to see considered and she says Jim Cameron, who directed *Terminator, Aliens*. Hey, I like his work, too, but this shows such a deep misunderstanding of the material and movies in general that I have an epiphanal moment in which I understand completely why I haven't gone to the movies much in the last five years.

The pattern of Geffen's vetoes tend to go along with how much he thinks he will be 'allowed to be involved,' i.e., whom he can control. I've always been a pretty hands-on producer myself, but have no hesitation to hand this over to Kubrick, even if his selection was the only input I would ever have. Does David Geffen really think that he is a better film maker than Kubrick?

And fuck it, if I'm willing to hand it over to Steven Spielberg, whom I detest, if he wants to do it, or even Bob Zemeckis, whom I had known in his pre-protégé days as an incredible pest on the set of *Close Encounters*, who the fuck is he to veto Stanley fucking Kubrick?

Then I answer myself: He is David Geffen, a powerful force in Hollywood January 1989, the Donald Trump of Show Business. Jesus, these guys are taking the fun out of everything. I noticed the week before, knee deep in the flu, that Donald Trump had written a letter of protest to *People* magazine because the week before they had, in an article about Merv Griffin, said that Trump had been bested by Griffin in the Resorts International deal. Jesus, was Donald Trump so insecure as to personally write a letter about that shit? Aren't you supposed to be above that sort of thing if you're Donald Trump?

Geffen, and his collagened face, remind me of Trump. It's kind of puffed out. Makes them both look like middle-aged babies, I think, as Geffen uses the 'I' word again, referring to Meryl Streep as a 'very good friend of mine.' She is wrong, he says, for some picture he claims David Lynch is dying to do.

That's where we are ending up, after this director's list of doom. David Lynch.

Here I am, sitting in overcommercialized, insubstantial, trend-following Hollywood, and this genius, David Geffen, is touting a director who is probably brilliant, at the very least, talented, but the word *anti-commercial* springs to mind right as I hear his name repeated. I wonder if David Lynch is telling David Geffen Meryl Streep so they can disagree on something besides each other, and he can pass without insulting Geffen. If I were David Lynch I'd jump all over the Vampire project, and then I would get down on my knees to me and thank me for such great material.

'This could be a career maker for him,' I say, trying to look on the bright side, speaking in a jargon that David Geffen will hear. Wash your mouth out with soap, girl. He yells out to Linda, a long-suffering middle-aged woman who has kept his act together for twenty years, to call Rick Nicita, David Lynch's agent at CAA. All these guys have a woman like that. I wonder if she has a piece of the pie. Not likely . . .

Nicita is in a meeting with a client and will call back. Maybe David Geffen isn't as hot as I thought, never mind as he thought. If that's the case then why am I staying here? Why don't I just jump up, tell him he doesn't know dick, and storm out? I got to go far the first time around with behavior like that. Until they had a chance to make me go away and eat worms forever. I pull at my skirt and crack my neck. I might have to pace pretty soon.

We get to Stephen Frears, whose movies I personally admire very much. I had stayed up two nights ago with a 102-degree fever to watch *Prick Up Your Ears* on Z, so I would know everything about Steven Frears for this meeting. Geffen had mentioned him on the phone.

Liaisons just released, is doing very very well. His name seems a very this-week kind of idea, as Michael Des Barres commented, when I asked him what he thought. *My Beautiful Laundrette* had been swell, too. The problem is that this guy likes the closeup, and all his movies are essentially about the gay lifestyle. The material is faggy enough; my instinct is to cast away from that. Make the vampires' desire and longing more universal, more androgynous. Which is more or less what I say to Geffen.

'Don't you want to see any broad vista, David?' I wonder if he has any idea what I mean.

'See, you like all that ancient history. I don't. I love *Interview* . . . I want to do that book as a movie.' Then why did you say you liked the bible Anne Rice wrote for Lorimar? The one that combined *Interview* and *Lestat*? I guess you lied. So we would go to the meeting at Warners and say: Geffen Geffen he's our man, if he can't do it no one can!

'That book came out in 1976. Don't you think it's been superseded by events?' Toxic waste, cancer, AIDS . . .'I just always had in mind something more epic – something that covered time, that answered the questions posed in *Interview*. That was more elevated.'

'I want to make a personal relationship movie about people who happen to be vampires . . .' he says tersely, annoyed. Oh, don't give me that bullshit relationship jive . . . do you know how many years I've been hearing that phrase and how much territory it covers?

'I like the vista – I always wanted to make the *2001* of vampire movies . . .' with Stanley Kubrick directing it . . .

'You always say that . . . what do you mean by that?' he smirks.

'Here's what I mean.' I lean forward and look at him from under my lashes, so he can see how much I want to please and convince him. 'If *2001* was really three separate movies, a little past, a little present, a little future, with the monoliths there as the linkage the glue – then the vampire epic would be three separate movies, only instead of going forward go back, the monoliths are the blood-sucking vampires themselves – the link. And by the way, all movies are about relationships – these just cover centuries, and I want to provide backdrop for that concept . . .' I take a breath and continue. This may be the last time he lets me talk this long. 'I think you'd be making a real mistake to ever forget our characters are vampires. They don't just *happen* to be vampires – it is the central fact about them . . .' How's that for a little *explication du texte*?

You didn't go to Mount Holyoke College, did you? Stoopid doodyhead.

'Yeah, but I don't want to make one of those big-budget movies . . . I want to keep this pared down.' Great, you want to remake *The Hunger*. Which I always think of as *From Hunger*.

'Even if you just use *Interview*, which, in all fairness, I should tell you is an idea that Anne Rice herself favors, you're still covering broad vista. Plus, there are some effects from the other books that are just great for movies and fit in with the alternativeness of her vampire mythology, which we would be crazy to blow off. . .'

'Like what, for instance?' Is he really asking or just pissed?

'Oh, like the flying, the cacophony of human voices because of their telepathy, the way their features freeze, the interlacing of the heartbeats with the kill . . .'

'Fine, fine . . .' Oh, I get it. We're not discussing a movie here. We're negotiating. A moment of silence. He grabs for his phone and dials. 'Yes, it's David Geffen calling him again . . . he made another call first? Ask him to call me the second he's off the phone . . .' He swivels back to us. 'Rick Nicita's calling us right back . . .'

'What was going on there?' I needle.

'Oh, just a secretary with a little attitude.' He's unperturbed. Well, that's nice. Usually guys this insecure are rough on the help. Fiedler, Baumgarten, Dawn Steele . . . but they aren't David Geffen, are they?

The phone rings, and Linda hollers from the other room that Nicita is on the phone. David wheels and swivels to the phone. I permit myself the image of him alone, wheeling and swiveling around the room, a big bad boy in his expensive nursery. 'Listen, I just want to tell you again how passionate I am about the material and how passionate I am about working with David . . .' he says fervently into Rick's ear. He listens. 'Yeah, but this could be a career maker . . .'

Well, fuck you. The guy is so blatant he's ripping off my line, without attribution, right in front of me. He hasn't gone out of his way to mention that we're in the room, either. Usually conversations in circumstances like this tend to start:

'I'm sitting in the room with blah blah blah and we were just talking about blah blah blah and we think etc. etc. etc.' I'm surprised I'm even noticing this, much less taking offense. I thought I was beyond the reach of such petty jealousies. This is how niggers must feel all the time. Fuck me? Fuck you! He gets off the phone to report on the other side of the conversation.

Norman Garey once said that one of the things he was starting to notice about Hollywood was that a lot of phone calls were third-party items: i.e., reporting the result of one conversation on another phone call. Then you would have to call the first person back to report on the reaction of the person in the second phone call, etc.

'Well, of course, you're a lawyer, isn't that what you do?' I said, and Norman looked wounded. Well, in his way, Norman the Lawyer was more of a film maker than this Big Macher rolling around his office in his toy chair, but you play the hand you're dealt.

Or stop gambling.

Throw in the deck.

Cash in your chips.

Like Norman.

Levy and I commiserate on the walk back to our cars, parked over at Hamburger Hamlet.

'Is it time to get paid off and go away?' I ask, hating the thought.

'Not yet,' Levy says. 'I'll know when it's the right time . . .' It bothers me that he hasn't said: *if* it's the right time . . . 'Besides, he likes you . . .'

'Yeah, Close Encounters of the Codependent Kind . . .' and while Levy laughs, I think, not for the first time: Balls, said the Queen, if I had them I'd be . . . King David! Played by Richard Gere.

I call Anne Rice when I get home to report on the meeting. I tell her everything. We're friends. She gets very upset. 'If he ends up, after all this time, making a movie about two hairdressers pissing on each other, I won't just sue, I'll kill him!'

A week later, Geffen calls to tell me that he has sent the book to Stanley Kubrick. I am shocked but pleased. Oh, I get the picture, I think, when I get off the phone. You run me around in front of other people, then in the privacy of the back of your car, being driven to your house at the beach, you have a conversation with yourself and change your mind. Some part of me finds this endearing behavior. As in: he's an asshole, but he's my asshole . . .

Just when I'm getting over hating Michael for doing evil things to me, he starts to do all those things to Kate. And then I have to start hating him again. It is good. It keeps me earthbound, like antiabortionists. The greedy Jews have that effect on me, too: people like Ivan Boesky and Dennis Levine, and Mike Milken. They have played to the prejudice lurking beneath the surface of the American soul and hordes of farmers in the Middle West are going to form groups and kill the Jews for taking their farms away.

Lately, though, I am getting cosmic.

I am thinking Big Thoughts about the Big Picture.

I have been moving in that direction a long time, but present events are hastening the process. I have burned out on the process of making pictures. I hate the new guys. The new guys are just like the guys in the news who keep being indicted. Men have really screwed it up, I keep thinking. I read the news and I hate them globally as much as I hate them personally. Marching backward. Making silly pathetic wars with more and more lethal weapons. Who'da thunk there would be something more terrifying than nuclear. Germ and poison gases in the hands of Islamic fundamentalists. Religion! These are all male games and male myths. Jesus.

The people, they need a leader.

I know the shrink will say thinking cosmic, let alone global, is just a bullshit way of not coping with your own earthly existence, so I am kind of glad when Michael keeps fucking up in the emergency-care arena. Well, he wanted the joint custody and we have stuck to the deal, which made me cry every other Monday in the beginning when she would go to him.

Instead of rushing to the doctor or the emergency room, he yells at her for being sick. Which is what takes place over one particularly odious weekend when she is at his house. I am on call, coaching him through the process as her fever rises and the doctor shines him on. Finally, midnight Sunday, she spikes a fever of one-oh-five and even the doctor agrees they should meet at Cedars Emergency. The next day she returns to me for a prolonged visit. She has been diagnosed with mononucleosis and hepatitis. She is fifteen. Same age, same diseases. The karmic/genetic tie is almost too much to bear, but I bear it. For the first two weeks she is so weak she has to be reminded by me constantly that she really wants to live.

Well, at least Michael has been brought up to speed on illness, I think comfortingly to myself one night while I strain to hear if she is breathing . . .

I take a break from Kate's illness, have a fast lunch with Lee. Friday at Le Dome. Kitty-corner from Jackie Collins and her Hollywood Wives. I'm expostulating on the End of the World:

'I'm telling you, man, if there is a God, he's going "Strike the set, strike the set. Tornado here, earthquake there, bigger hurricanes . . ."' Lee pushes back the dip in his extraordinary Veronica Lake hairdo and smiles.

'Maybe He's just giving us warnings. You know, Like that article he wrote for *Time* magazine at the beginning of the year . . .'

She didn't go out much anymore. Everything felt stale repetitive alienating. Once in awhile though, she just had to dress up and run around with good-looking people. The last two times she had gone out she had freaked out so badly that it took weeks to recover each time. The first time was in the middle of Kate's mono-hep recovery. Nick Wechsler wanted her to meet John Lydon, aka Johnny Rotten, so they had a drunken dinner at Le Dome. Lydon and his wife, Nora, a good-natured Kraut, which seemed like a contradiction in terms and who was easily fifteen years older than he was, went on with her and Scott to BC, the hot new happening club that had been opened by Brett and Chris a couple of weeks ago. Well, actually, only Brett, because Chris had died of an O.D. the weekend before the opening. Aspirated on his vomitus, a phrase she had picked up during the CNN broadcasts of Claus von Bulow's second trial.

The club was beautiful but empty, and they had moved on with Matt Dillon in tow to a reggae club in Santa Monica. But not before she had put her life on the line from carelessness. Milling around outside, a black dude in a bright blue jacket pulled up in a black car that she thought to be Scott's. She got in and he took off. She checked out his eyes. They were glazed. He kept saying, 'You such a pretty lady. Lemme take you to breffass . . .'

It took two blocks and John and Nora screaming at her, Get out of the car this instant! for her to realize that she had absentmindedly stepped into not Scott's car, but the car of a man who was probably a crack dealer. He stopped at a red light and she took off for Lydon's car across four lanes of traffic. Later, when she told the story to Kate during one of

601

their you-have-to-want-to-recover-let's-talk-about-it-at-Hamburger-Hamlet excursions, Kate said, 'That was a very meish thing to do,' and she didn't sleep for days worrying about her daughter.

The second time she had gone out she was again at BC, this time with Brooke and Michelle. They had shared a couple of mushrooms, and smuggled vodka in in an Evian bottle. Marty Bauer and Brian De Palma thought Michelle was her daughter, which had her bummed for awhile, but the vibe was pretty nice and civilized, and the guys had done a great job on the décor and ambience of the interior. The food was not bad, either. She ran into Beverly d'Angelo and Pamela Des Barres, both of whom looked pale and weathered compared to her, so she cheered up.

They left to go to a party and came back in an hour. The place had completely changed. Music blared and trash was everywhere. They danced very hard because the mushrooms were now in full swing, and she stopped suddenly and thought, I will give myself a heart attack, and she took up a position at a front booth. Timmy and Barbara Leary leaned over to say hello. They looked drawn and grim and she thought, They look like they are waiting for their dealer. They sat down and Timmy said, his mouth tight and cranky, 'We're waiting for our dealer . . .' *Plus ça change plus c'est la même* dead people.

The next time I go out, it will be to catch a plane to the South of France, she thought, smiling benignly at Timmy.

'You're a horrible example for your daughter,' Geffen says emphatically, eying my vodka on the rocks. Right, like you know so much about child rearing, I think but don't say. We're having lunch at 11 Giardino, because the restaurant is on a square city block that he's just acquired. I am not wrong to think of him and Donald Trump together. The last time I was here, I ended up with raw egg dripping down the front of my favorite little black cocktail dress. I feel the same now.

He has his hands on my arm and my knee. Is that to show how close he feels to me, to provide comfort, to restrain me? I keep wanting to say: You're like a bad Jewish mother, but it doesn't work on me my bad mother was another kind of bad Jewish mother, but it's not worth the effort. This guy thinks he has me pegged: all that AA, codependent, West Coast bullshit.

We are having this fabulous little get-together because Michael Levy has been pressuring me to arrange a meeting. Geffen refuses to meet with Levy without Sean Daniels. Geffen says, 'I had to reach pretty far and pay a lot of money to bring this guy over from Universal, and I won't have this sort of meeting without him . . . On the other hand, if you want to have a little lunch, alone, I'm available.'

Hollywood Games. I tell Levy the truth, and he tells me to go alone. So now I'm here on a hot day relating to a man who has no sense of humor as far as I can tell. I think Levy and he are the infinitely better pairing.

Everyone seems to like Geffen but me. Gary, Freddy, everyone says he's a good guy. I don't see it, but I feel like I'm at a party and everyone is telling me I'm too drunk to drive. I see this lunch as taking a cab home. I'm deferring to common wisdom. Mostly, I'm worried that David wants to make a movie about two hairdressers pissing on each other.

'Why don't you like *Lestat* . . .'

'You mean the rock 'n' roll? It's never worked,' he says.

'There's always a first time,' I say, thinking, All the movies that I made that were great were also first. 'You know why you don't like the rock 'n' roll? Cause you're in the music business . . .' Dummy. Man, if I were a three-hundred-year-old creature coming back into the end of the twentieth century, I'd be Mick Jagger . . . for sure . . . especially now that Mick wasn't really Mick anymore . . .

'If you can't be first, be best; if you can't be best, be first . . . why not both?' Geffen smiles fondly, like, Silly thing . . .

'Look, I'm not creative and intellectual and educated, like you,' he says, waving these attributes away with his hand, so

603

much annoying dust, 'but I'll tell you what I bring to the table . . .'

'Hey, you're the mogul,' I interrupt, meaning it.

'I know what's wrong!' he exclaims.

I. KNOW. WHAT'S. WRONG???

Well, it is the *fin de siècle*, and things have degenerated to such a point, I suppose that's a talent. An ability, at least.

'I know exactly what you mean . . .' I lie. But does that mean you know what's right? Right and wrong. He wouldn't be interested in these fine points unless there was a lot of money in them.

'Have you thought about writers?' he asks fake-politely. For a thousand years . . .

'Well, all the guys who are really perfect for it have turned it down: Peter Schaffer, David Hare . . .'

'You know who would be perfect?'

'Who?' I really want to know . . .

'David Mamet!' David. Mamet! Who writes your dialogue?

'That's a terrible idea,' I blurt and know immediately from the shadow that passes across his face I've made a big mistake, but I go on anyway, 'David Mamet writes small, earthy plays in argot; he would be the exact opposite of the perfect writer . . .' I wonder if he knows what I mean, 'but hey, I've got an open mind . . .'

People keep coming over to the table. They want to say hello to him, but he doesn't know their names; I tell him their names. When the fourth obeisant slave retreats he says, 'Why can't I remember anybody's name?'

'Contempt,' I say before I think.

'O-o-o-o-hhh,' he says, blushing and smiling, and I like him for the first time. Christ, a year from now, I'll probably be so grateful for his existence I'll be singing his praises. By the end of lunch we agree that the next step is for me and Mike Levy to set up a meeting, by the book, with Sean Daniels and Cari-Esta Albert, Sean's assistant, to come up with a writers' list. Is my foot half-in this door of show business or half-out?

A little of both.

*

but the mogul thinks with some fabulous coordinated merchandising effort combined with some tie-ins with eateries and a tour in ten cities of the various acts on the soundtrack that he can make a lot of money. He gives himself a go go go.

He is sure of everything.

Freddy calls a couple of days before the invitation to his party arrives. Possibly to see if the Julia Phillips referred to in Army Archerd's column that morning is me. She is marrying someone named John Putch, which makes me think it is a nasty plant: i.e., Putz, but I laugh instead:

'You don't think I would even dream of getting married without asking your permission, do you?'

'I'm having a big bash birthday party – you'll be getting the invitation in a couple of days . . .'

'Forty already?' He laughs weakly.

'Nope. The big Five-Oh . . .'

'So you're having two hundred of your nearest and dearest . . .' I flash on the party I gave myself for my forty-third birthday, when I finally acknowledged I was in my forties . . .' You're going to be suicidal by two o'clock,' I say, projecting.

'So you'll come . . .' Ohmigod no, do I have to?

'A-a-a-r-r-r-g-g-g-h.'

'Is that yes?'

'I hate those things . . .' Beg me.

'You'll come?' Good enough.

'I'm there . . .'

Two days later the invitation arrives: black envelope, silver handwriting to Julia Philips and Guest. If I'm so fucking important, can't you spell my name right? I open it. It is a foldout of some sort, made to look like film, I can see the sprockets drawn on either side. I open it this way and that, but it takes a good thirty seconds to register that it is a Madonna and Candy DeMann Production of Freddy's 18,250th day. I multiply 365 by 50 and notice that Madonna's name is slightly larger and thicker than Freddy's wife's. Jesus.

I pan down. There is a picture of Freddy, probably from his bar mitzvah. Black Tie. Dinner and Dancing. Oy. A little card falls out to inform me that in lieu of gifts a contribution to Greenpeace would be in order. Herself's charity of the moment. Oy oy oy.

I RSVP yes, and hate myself for the rest of the day.

I wonder for a moment if I should invite Stuart, but he let me down New Year's Eve. I call Nick.

'No no no,' he says, adding, 'I don't do that stuff anymore . . . no more shmoozing . . .' Liar liar pants on fire, but I don't push it. I call Pat Lucas, head of movie soundtracks at SBK. Big, tall, exotic mulatto Pat Lucas. That oughtta set Freddy's mind rolling. She laughs and says, Sure, but I have to wear the tux.

It is overcast the day of the party and I decide definitely the tux. Also, I can wear low heels. When Gary Kurfirst calls midafternoon I can tell he's looking for an invitation; I tell him I booked Pat Lucas as my date a month ago, but I'll call Freddy and see if it's okay for him to tag along. Freddy tells me in an uptight voice that it is a sitdown dinner for three hundred people with a tent and food and bars and a dance floor . . . in other words, no last-minute guests. I apologize for even asking.

'All I want to see is you,' he says in his Glickman Curse voice. I bet you say that to all the girls.

'I'm there . . .' When I get off the phone, I realize that my stomach is curling over on itself. Sitdown dinner for three hundred people?@*! With a tent, and dance floor? Must be on his tennis court. I'll have to go down all those steps . . . Definitely the tux with the low heels. Definitely a two-drink two-joint enterprise. Definitely sorry I said yes.

When we arrive, not by limo, but by trusty old gray Mercedes four five oh – SLC – there is a line of paparazzi interspersed with the line of Chuck's Valet parkers. Yuck, that kind of a party. People in black tie are lining up at the front of the house. There is a table with guest cards and table numbers, silver pen on black, and a dish full of buttons that

says: I KNOW FREDDY DEMANN PERSONALLY . . . I look around.
Better than you . . .

We are pressed into a line that files past Freddy. He has
that freaked-out stuntman acidflash look in his eyes. I say hi
and I'm not sure he even recognizes me so I give him a hug.
He responds with tiny pressure. I know his eyes are already
over my shoulder in search of the next hello.

The guests form an endless meandering line out of the house
and then down several landings. Briefly, standing above, it
looks to me like a long black-tie human snake. The party is
skewed heavily toward business. Lawyers, agents, CEOs. This
party is so heavy it is going to topple of its own weight.
Wishful thinking. Pat Lucas keeps a smile fixed on her face.
She knows more people here than I do . . .

I find a bartender and order a greyhound. I run into Mr.
Wald, clean and sober. short and grim. Gary Stiffelman. See
but don't know John Branca. Little Irving and his little wife
Shelley. Joel Schumacher. Mary Lambert, also *sans* Gary
Kurfirst. Good Girl.

I keep moving with the line. The Hostess is standing near a
bar on the next landing. She is hard to miss. She looks just
like she's supposed to. Her skin is so porcelain it glows. I
wonder for a moment if she is on a first-name basis with the
Vampire Lestat. If anyone is, it is she.

There is a short, bespectacled man with good hair standing
next to her. It takes me a moment to recognize Warren.
Warren is usually tall and dominates a room, but in this
situation he is a dim bulb in the aura of her supernova. He
looks like Ron Meyer, star of CAA, not Warren, Star. I touch
his arm and he smiles. He is glad to see me. I lean across her
to exchange kisses in the air. She ignores me.

'I don't believe you're here,' I say. Because I don't, even
though as I think about it I realize there is a ridiculous
inevitability to Warren and Madonna. He looks down at his
shoes.

'I'm here,' he says to the ground. I straighten up to half-
look in her direction. She ignores me. She is in a skin-tight
halter dress that stops above the knee and is somewhere
between flesh-tone and gold lamé. She is wearing very high

609

heels, with sparkles up the heel. Her hair is white. She looks great, and it is better to look good than to feel good. She puff-puffs at a Virginia Slim.

'Warren Beety,' she says in an exaggerated New York whine, 'let's move down to the next level . . .' This is the way the world ends, not with a bang but a simper . . .

Outside of these two I don't see any star types. I wonder who the paparazzi intend to shoot. As I scan the crowd, it seems more and more like a convention of dentists. Then I hear my name being called and look in that direction, and it is Howard Rosenman, with Barry Diller, Sandy Gallin, and David Geffen. Welcome to the nineties. I wave. Barry smiles thinly, Sandy looks beyond me. Howard and David are friendly. I walk over, so with them at the level above me, I am at their feet. Howard and David lean over the rail to exchange more air kisses. David whispers in my ear, 'So, we closed with Michael Cristofer . . .' Information I already know. Then I return to Pat's side; she is easy to find, because in her heels she's six feet, easy, and she's the only black person I can see, except for Clarence Avant, although I did notice place cards for Quincy Jones and Lionel Richie . . .

This party is making me defiant. I find a bathroom and, for no reason, smoke two hits on a joint I don't want. I pour the greyhound down the toilet. When I emerge, I can see people are making their way down endless candlelit steps to a huge tent below. I signal Pat, and we move with the crowd.

Just as I start to think, this is like a bar mitzvah at Leonard's in Great Neck, there is a picture of Freddy, blown up, at the entrance to the tent. It looks like his bar mitzvah photo. There is also another picture of Freddy with his dad, whom I notice is a very handsome man. I say something and the couple behind me, who have obviously known Freddy all his life, mutter 'too bad he died so young.' For a moment, I think they are talking about Freddy, then realize they are speaking of his dad. Everybody knows a lot of dead people.

We find our table. It is ringside to a dance floor that no one but Sandra Bernhard and a woman dressed like a belly dancer use. I am at a table with Bookie and his girlfriend, Amy Grossman, daughter of Ernie; Jim Brooks and his wife; Joe

Smith, who is the president of Capitol Records. I make small talk with Bookie and Amy. The last time I saw him was at lunch, and he was going through separation from the French wife. Now he tells me that they are getting a divorce and there is some problem about whether she will leave and take the baby back to France. I don't wanna do this anymore . . .

I go to the bar and get another greyhound. I bump into Mary Macucci, caterer extraordinaire. We've done quite a few parties together. One of them was a fancy do celebrating the engagement of Bookie and his now ex-French-wife.

'So, ya keepin' off the sauce?' Mary wants to know in extreme Brooklynese. If I close my eyes she sounds like Madonna. I look deep into my drink . . . there goes my eyeball into your highball . . . then, I look her dead in the eye.

'I do whatever I want,' I say.

'Well, ya look great . . .' Better than you.

I walk outside the party and find the portable bathrooms. The light doesn't go on in the stall I select. I take it as an omen. When I get back to the table, Bookie and Amy are getting up to leave. I check my watch.

'Pat, we've been here two hours . . . let's go . . .' She laughs. She's ready. 'I gotta find Freddy and say goodbye . . .'

'If we're sneaking out, we should just sneak . . .'

'Nah, I wanna get credit for my two hours . . .' We follow Bookie, threading our way through people. A CAA group chats with each other. Photographers are taking their pictures. I thought they wanted to be low profile. Sooner or later, everyone in Hollywood wants to be a star, see his picture in the papers . . .

I spot Irving Azoff, and back in the crowd away from the noise, Sid Sheinberg. He looks as happy as he did at Norman's funeral. I fantasize Irving on Sid's shoulder, Universal's Master Blaster, and know I have gone way past the time I should have left. I search the crowd . . .

'You've ignored me twice,' Ron Meyer – the real Ron Meyer – says. I smile weakly and kiss air.

'Hello,' I say. 'I don't know why I didn't recognize you . . . you're getting so famous.' There has been a spate of articles

611

in the New York and L.A. *Times* about Ron Meyer's nasty divorce and CAA. He doesn't look at all happy to be famous . . . Ron Meyer is the only CAA agent I have a personal fondness for, probably the result of a hot lunch in the early eighties on the patio at Jimmy's, where he regaled me with colorful tall tales of compulsive gambling. He is such a good agent, though, that I have always wondered if they were just stories, told to relate to me on my level.

Finally, I see Freddy chatting with another interchangeable yuppie.

'I gotta go . . .' I say and Freddy looks perturbed.

'But it hasn't even started yet . . .' I look back toward the party. It ain't ever gonna start. Everybody looks like he has a migraine. I kiss him goodbye . . .

Pat and I hit Mortons. I think I want a drink, but order a hot fudge sundae instead.

'Why are you so angry?' she asks.

'I dunno . . .'

'Because you went, right?' I nod assent and scarf down the sundae. The chocolate is a foreign substance in my gut, and I have to hit the nouvelle ladies' immediately. I pray for no works in the sink; too on the nose.

'Well, thanks for taking me,' Pat sums up. 'I got to meet people tonight I only read about in the papers . . .'

It takes me two days to feel guilty about Freddy and his party. I call him at the office to apologize. I offer to take him to lunch. We go the next day. My table. Le Dome. I wear Gaultier spandex and a short-sleeved leather jacket. I haven't been there in a while. but nothing's changed. We do a little postpartum on the party. I needle him by asking why certain people weren't there: Dawn Steele, Jerry Moss. He says they declined. We talk about his d.j., Matt Robinson, and he tells me they're starting a record label together. Nothing but rap . . . Perfect, the Jew makes money off the niggers, I think, but don't say.

'Gonna sign NWA?' Fuck tha police, fuck tha police . . .

'I'm impressed you know who NWA is . . .' Probably before

you did, thanks to Stuart. I smile at the thought of Stuart making me stop at the record store to buy the tape, *Straight Outta Compton*.

'You gotta hear this, Jools, a million and a half units sold and no airplay . . .' Stuart said. Now I work out to them. Their anger drives me.

'So, Freddy, how come you gave yourself this big bash . . .'

'It was an announcement . . .' I used to give big parties about once every two years, usually for somebody else's occasion: David and Jean's wedding reception, Bookie's engagement, Tarnoff's birthday. I always thought they were announcements, too. I'm here, let's do some business.

'Well, if you're really doing a rap label, will you please look at Brooke's tape? Kind of a whiteboy novelty rap? Pretty please?'

'Sure, okay, drop it off. . .'

I actually drop the tape off at his house on my way to dinner. I call to see if he's watched it and he makes an excuse. I call again after a couple of weeks have gone by. He still hasn't watched it.

'Freddy, we're talking less than five minutes, here . . .'

'I know,' he says in a really downtrodden Glickman Curse voice.

'Maybe you're just resistant to this idea . . .' Whatsa matta? too young? too hip? too handsome?

'Yeah, maybe . . .' *This is my letter to the World* . . .

Dear Freddy: I know a lot of dead people and one of them is . . . thee . . .

'Whoo whoo,' went the owl, and the dog down the street woofwoofed wildly. But then, that dog was always woofing wildly. The owner, a neighbor, was away at work all day, so

613

the dog bemoaned his loneliness and howled mournfully all day. Then the owner would come home and the dog would bark loud, excited greetings. For some reason, this annoyed the neighbor, so he would yell at the dog. If the dog kept it up he would hit the dog.

Once his girlfriend screamed loudly, 'What do you want? I don't know what you want,' and he hit her, too. The woman cried and the dog howled, a pretty noisy Sunday all in all. She thought about community responsibility, and should she call the cops, and then she Kitty Genovesed the situation.

Debin came to pick her up so they could go off and do something social that involved drinking, and he said as they got in the car, referring to the violence and the noise, 'Is that what love is?' in that thin, sarcastic tone of his, which made everything droll, and she answered yes without hesitation or amplification, but she thought, woman against man, 'It is in my experience, mothafucka . . .'

Some days, when she was really morose, and thinking of buying a gun but glad she didn't have one, given the number of times she would wake up to another what's-the-point day, she would think, but if I ever *do* own a gun I will kill that dog first, and the neighbor second . . .

She walked outside and checked out a rare bright, starlit sky. Who, indeed, she thought, peering at the trees on her property and looking for the owl that she could hear but never see. The best thing about this canyon was living in unthreatening nature. The worst thing was that she didn't have a view. No ocean for the day, no city for the night. She had done the best with what she had, which was a sort of rustic-at-one-with-nature bullshit show-biz mini-manse.

She had bought a house in Hawaii that was a newer upscale version, but that had both the city and the ocean. She loved that house. She had nearly gone mad in that house. That house had had a little too much nature, though – giant spiders and bullfrogs and roaches. Actually, if you left them alone they would go away.

And if you really wanted to be rid of them, you had to do it yourself, because most guys in Hollywood were pretty squeamish about woodland animals and spiders and vermin.

She was always carrying out the odd dead bird or rat or killing the giant spider. One of the benefits of being a solitary dame. It was either that or move to a condo with a doorman. Eeeeoooouuu. Why not buy a station wagon while you're at it and throw in the towel?

'Whoo,' went the owl, and she squinted for better focus; at least catch a glimpse of those beautiful eyes.

Once, after she cleaned up, there had been a terrible ruckus in the oak tree over the deck, and she had gone out to see what the commotion was about. Nine hundred catbirds were cawing and screeching and something large and taupe was rustling in the tree. It was five o'clock on a summer afternoon. A sloth, maybe.

Kate came out to see what was going on, and they started up the steps together, to the deck, to get a better view. All of a sudden, the large taupe thing moved, and then it took off, and it was a big beautiful owl, with a ten-foot wing-span. It flew out of the tree and swooped down over them, so low that they actually ducked.

'I had to wait thirty-eight years to see such a sight,' she said excitedly. 'You are very lucky to be eight and see it.'

'Eight and a half,' Kate said precisely but her eyes were dancing.

She wondered now if this was the same owl.

She took off down the driveway in her sweats. I don't care if it's the middle of the night. I'll do my Deep Canyon run. If the skateboarders can be there at three ay-em then I can, too. It'll be just me and the animals . . .

She had always gotten along with animals, from the time she was very small. She had been one of those little girls to share ice-cream cones with strange dogs, or to lick the one part on a cat's chest it couldn't reach with its own tongue. She had always preferred cats, but she could get along just fine with dogs.

When she was a teenager and her family drove to Florida for Christmas she made her father stop along the side of the road around several farms where there were baby pigs. To this day, she just loved the way baby pigs looked. She had not especially been a *Call of the Wild* kind of youngster (although it was one of her favorite books – she had liked Jack London almost as much as she liked animals).

When she was a kid in Brooklyn and had a pet hamster, she used to take it to school in the pocket of her peajacket. She liked to take it out in the elevator going up to her apartment, just to see if the ladies in the elevator would scream. And she didn't mind white mice or spiders or any of the creatures that most people disliked.

She had a science teacher in seventh grade named Mr. Kelly whose mission in life seemed to be teaching children that snakes were dry and warm not cold and slimy and damp. So the best thing about her current venue, and why she thought she had continued to stay, year after year, was that Benedict Canyon was still wild enough for her to stay in touch and in tune with the forces of nature at work.

She had always understood environment and ecosystem. From her father. The scientist. And her mother. The immigrant. The thinker. Thinking had been bad for her mother's health. Not thinking had been bad for Mankind. But worse for the animals.

She realized that she had always known it was over. Because of her father working on the bomb and her mother's inability to censor any thought, no matter how terrifying it might be for a child. Her father had been screaming about holes in the Van Allen Belt when she was a little girl. He had been certain then that we were going to die under a mountain of shit.

She was so pissed off at her parents' informed cynicism that she had found Michael to marry, someone who had been brought up by people who believed that you should sacrifice truth for pleasantness if you had to. Michael was steeped in upwardly striving middle-class values, and they seemed refreshing to her when she met him. Denial denial denial.

Her parents had been right all along of course; the eighties had made everything worse. Sometimes she thought that if everyone had a change of heart and woke up tomorrow prepared to separate garbage and heat with solar power and build homes for the homeless and stop murdering each other

– even then – it was still over. The only thing that kept her from clinical depression was her daughter, and this relationship she had with nature.

So when she ran down her driveway too early in the morning, for her uphill Deep Canyon torturejog, and saw the Mexican-in-distress standing next to his shabby red Camaro, she automatically followed his gaze. It was the black cat from across the street, the one who bedeviled her cats, the one she was always chasing away from their food. It was at the side of the road, hunched up, wheezing.

'I t'ing da ca's be' heet . . .' he screamed, and involuntarily she raced across the street to the cat, thinking, Bullshit, you hit this cat. It was making a horrible noise and blood was coming from its mouth. It locked her eyes and its eyes said: I am alive and suffering. Save me. This is your fault, Freddy. She ran up the driveway and banged on her neighbor's door. A frightened male voice asked, 'Who is it?'

'Wayne*, it's Julia, your cat's been hit. Open the door!' She banged on it, rather more emphatically than necessary. He did, this ancient old queen in a dirty red velvet bathrobe who was her neighbor. He was having trouble focusing, and when he did, he had fear in his bloodshot, hungover eyes. She had to pull at his arm to get him moving. The cat had dragged itself halfway up the driveway. There was a trail of blood behind it. Wayne froze in his spot. 'Omigod . . . Damian*,' he whispered hoarsely.

'Where's Sam*?' she screamed through his panic. Where's Sam. Asleep of course. She raced through the house and banged on closed doors. Sam came out, brushing last night's sins from his eyes. She explained the situation briefly and he raced out to the front of the house, where Wayne stood rooted to his spot. The Mexican was bent over the cat.

Sam scooped the cat up and headed for his car. He got in with the cat on his lap and flew out the driveway. The Mexican headed for his car and Wayne went into the house with the paper. She ran up Deep Canyon, vibing the cat. Don't die, Damian.

She returned later in the day, because she didn't have their

617

number. The cat was on IVs and the vet was afraid of internal damage . . .

Memo for today: What I did. I ran up Deep Canyon. I saved the cat. I may have saved a life, she thought, as she walked back across the street. Not a bad day.

'So you'll be there?' Stuart had his nervous-roadie-reconfirming-the-backup-singers voice.

'Me and the Posse . . . it'll probably cost me two hundred dollars. We have a whole plan to make sure I show . . . me, Taylor, Brooke 'n' Corey . . . Mortons eight thirty, then on to Stu-Babes . . .' M. Hollywood's gonna be thirty-five. Someone a decade younger than she was getting old.

She sagged on her bed, wishing for tomorrow. Young Hollywood Party. Oh, sigh. Well, at least Nelson Mandela was getting out of jail. Never mind that they took his entire life as a man away from him. God knows, she could relate.

She had already worked out hard, triple sets, all afternoon. No more trainers. 'Full Circle Fitness,' Rebecca had said. 'You go full circle, you graduate.' Self-discipline. Well, better than being punished by an outsider. Besides, she might want to wear something sleeveless; always looked better if you pumped iron before. Brooke, not Rebecca, had taught her that.

Brooke and Corey pick her up. Brooke and she smoke a joint on the patio. Corey loves it, but turns it down. Corey freaked by other Corey's bust. Clean and sober. Lean and mean . . . But tell me, Cor, does the music sound the same? Hey, just kidding . . .

Moral conflict, puffing in his face. Kate hangs out with them. More conflict.

Brooke is full-time babysitting/managing Corey. That's cool. Keeps him straight. Doing good job. Yeah, Jools. Boomalacka boomalacka.

Mixed feelings about Corey. Love him. Detest him too, or at least that manipulative part that knew how to make people twice his age snap to. He was only eighteen and a teen heart throb. Christ, he'd already been in more movies than she'd ever made. Baby stars . . . teevee . . . too weird . . .

'Ladygod, okay for me to take Kate out sometime?' Ladygod . . . ooh, that was good. Corey knows: the people, they need a leader . . .

'Why don't you ask her . . .' Smile, then, too quickly: 'But she doesn't like people who like pot . . .'

KATE: 'That's not true, Mom, I like you . . .' Teenagers: two; Mom: zip . . .

Kate splits. Them, too. Down to the driveway. Only the gray Mercedes in the garage now. When it was the gray and the black, people would ask: Why two of the same car? So I can go eeny meeny miney mo . . .

When she sold the black, Brooke said: 'So now, it's just eeny, eeny, eeny . . .'

She backs eeny out the driveway and they follow her to the restaurant . . .

Re: the quintessential child/teen star: He/she is defined by his parents' wishes for themselves. The parents are variously: foreign, southern, ex-hippies, in, or wanna be in, the Business. The kids'll always tell you that ever since they were two, they wanted to perform. Right. A lot of times, they are ripped off by their parents, who often decide to manage their kid's careers. Some see their kid's gigs as a dating service: get to location, check out the crew, and fuck a grip for eight weeks.

Drew Barrymore used to show up in heavy makeup at Helena's back in the mid-eighties when Helena's was happening, with her other teenage friends, and we, parents ourselves, would go, Isn't that too bad, isn't that terrible? like we hadn't participated in the creation of such a pheenom . . .

What is it with America and her preoccupation with child stars? Just a tiny step to the right and it's kiddie porn. I grow old, I grow old, I will bare my midriff . . . rolled.

They had a blast at Mortons. Always did when Doug was at the door. And Darryl serving. Doug's apprentice. Blond, tan,

California boys. It would be a big give-up, not seeing that look, when and if she moved. Next week, for sure. Darryl was a bit preoccupied with Mike Tyson's defeat and not attentive enough. She had to smack him around a little. Practice. For what? Breaking in waiters at Mortons.

And then, Taylor's friend had arrived with the last of the magic mushrooms. They changed tables and stuck the dust on a butter plate, passed it around, licking their fingers, dipping them in the dust, sucking their fingers. Just a bunch of kids getting the last of the cookie batter. It tastes like puffed wheat. Little espresso, little alcohol, kick the mother in . . .

Blast over to the house on Sunset Plaza Drive. Traffic thick. Lotsa lights. Sunset beginning to look like a video game. Talk on the car phone with Corey and Brooke, who follow her insecurely. As in: right up her ass.

Big Party. Real black people there. Stuart, who started out on the road with Chic and Patti LaBelle, made it a point to stay in touch with the brothers . . .

Young people everywhere. Up-and-comers. Good party. For a party. She was comfortable walking up the stairs, threading her way through strangers toward Stuart and the bar, which were in reasonable proximity to each other. With the boys. Three sixty for the first time: not too many dead people here. Is it live or is it . . . memomushroom? Who cares?

Black bartender with white hair, Morgan Freeman in *Driving Miss Daisy*. Good stiff drink. To Mandela! she salutes in her mind. She swears his eyes well up with tears in response. Swing through the party once. Barely know anyone there; recognize from restaurants.

See yuppie agent with great hair and eyes across room. They wend toward each other. Brooke shoots her a look: He's a lox, and she shoots back: But he's so-o-o-o handsome. He shrugs his shoulders philosophically, makes a toking gesture with his fingers to his mouth: Do we have any pot left? Without a cue they head to the part of the house that looks like it leads to the pool.

620

By the time they are outside there are eight or nine of them: the group from dinner, the host, the agent, and a client of the agent's, an upandcoming comic with star potential. He has a frail, beautiful blonde in tow. They pass the joint around and pretend they're still in high school.

Too old. Too cold. Back inside. Thread through again. Taylor mincing and mingling. His friend hovering. Lean against the wall. Deep yoga breaths. Brooke is talking to Lori Rodkin. In the overhead light Lori's skin looks mottled.

She talks to the agent, who shifts uncomfortably from foot to foot. To be honest, the pot is making me paranoid, he says. He starts every sentence: To be honest. Makes her think he's not. You're safe with me, she tells him, trying to be nice, but he features her with a look that reminds her that men don't feel safe around her. As a rule. Unless they're very smart, very stoopid, or very stoned. Brooke is right, this guy's a lox. Brooke is behind her, she nudges him and he turns. From his smile, she can tell he doesn't mind being drawn away from Lori's net.

'Ready to go?'

'Ready to walk outside anyway . . .' Start to move. Hand on her arm. Lori. Oh no. Are you and Brooke still together? Lori queries sotto voce. We never were . . . Brooke grabs her hand and Lori's look says: Yeah, right. Should I bother to explain? Nah . . .

Pick up members of the posse on their way out. More and more people coming in. Little log jam at front door. Claus-tro-pho-bia.

Blast out into chill night air. Doesn't matter. Little heat lamps within her skin to keep her warm. Down the steps. Fumble for a roach. Pass it around. The gesture is what counts. They sit down, spread out decoratively along the steps, with their cool clothes and their cool shoes and their cool dos. She turns around.

Is this my movie?

OVO: Harumph! Not likely.

SHE: And did I have fun?

ME: I can't remember.

'Ah,' she smiles broadly, feeling every muscle of her lower

621

face pull – how interesting, maybe just do this for a while –
nahh – and says, 'The B-o-y-e-e-z-z.' Laughs all around. I
don't know, Marty, there's a good Mickey Spillane movie
downtown. Oh no, I'm a dude. Why didn't somebody tell me?

Corey smiles his easy heart-throb smile. 'Poor Jools . . .
how many parties, how many times . . . how many boyeez?'
Excuse me, but are you *really* eighteen? Who does your
dialogue? Who does your hair? Time for a sudden move.

'I have to go now,' she says. Disap*poin*ted! Hey, always
leave before you're ready to do whatever's good for the
project. Tentative title: *Ladygod and the Boyeez* . . . they'll
learn . . . what is truth what is truth . . .

Drive v-e-e-r-r-ry carefully down Sunset . . . back to
Benedict, back to nature, back to CNN, see Mandela when he
walks out of prison . . .

Maybe take a shower . . .

'You could build a city if you wanted to,' her mother said and
threw the pieces from the Erector Set on the floor. Her
brother built real structures: beginnings, middles, ends. She
created fantasies. Sometimes she didn't finish them.

'You could build a city if you wanted to,' guys were always
telling her as they watched her make *Close Encounters* and
didn't help much.

And then they hated you behind your back, she thought.
Cities, she thought. I could've built cities. Nah. Bridges. And
then burned them behind me . . .

At least I would've built something, she added in her
defense, ruminating on the daily announcements in the trades,
each deal bigger, each dick larger. All the dialogue during
inappropriate talkshow interviews centering on how much
money the participants would make, not on how great their
movies would be.

Did anybody else play with the names so that it became
Peter's goober, Guber's peter? They're making movies and
I'm doing puns and anagrams . . . words seemed more trust-
worthy than movies did, now, anyway. I don't like movies

anymore . . . certainly not this gilded turd *Batman*, which everyone told her she'd like because it was so dark. Not dark, she wanted to tell them. More . . . *corrupt* than dark. More . . . *shiny*, more . . . *big* than . . . visionary. Call it the Trump Tower of movies.

'I loved Jack Nicholson,' Kate told her after she saw it.

'Oh, Kate,' she'd said despondently, 'he's been over the top for fifteen years . . .'

'He's over the top, but he has such a good time doing it, I had a good time with him!'

'Oh, I don't think it was really *with* him. More like at your expense . . . you don't know any better . . .'

'Don't blame me for my taste. It's not my fault. I was born into Sequel Hell . . .'

Later, Kate read her a paper on *The Great Gatsby*. My heart soars like an eagle . . . she was so moved at the end, she almost sobbed out loud. Instead: 'So whaddya think of the "lost generation"?'

Kate thought for a moment, looked at her toes, then straight on: 'I think it's made a comeback . . .'

Her lips moved but she did not say the words. She had internalized this endless conversation with herself for so many years, this eternal negotiation, this struggle for – what? The next step. She let the water beat down on every aching part of her body, muscle group by muscle group, making little moves back and forth in the shower. She let it bang away across her shoulders and neck for an especially long time.

'That's where the people pressure lives,' trainer after trainer told her, kneading away at her knotted neck. Tell me about it. I burned out on people years ago, she thought, pressing on a spot somewhere between the back of her neck and the top of her head that Mr. Fearless had located for her the first week they were shooting *Close Encounters* in Wyoming.

I think I'm beginning to make sense out of this.

She twisted her neck around and around, slowly, like chiro after chiro had shown her. If she did it just right she would

623

hear cracks and see stars. Ah, there they were, crack after crack, star after fucking star. Do I feel better? Definitely. And then she said it out loud:

'F-u-u-ck me-e-e-e?' she said. 'Fu-u-u-ck you!' It would be like shooting a movie, building a city. She would construct it. Word after word. Sentence upon sentence. Paragraph ensuing paragraph.

You'll never get to make movies again, she thought. That's okay, I'm not making any now.

You won't have any friends left, she continued. That's okay, I don't have any now. I'll make new friends. That's what I'm good at . . .

She had known the title for years; she would call it *You'll Never Eat Lunch in This Town Again*. As in: You'll never eat shit in this town again. 'You'll never eat lunch in this town again,' she said thoughtfully, dispassionately, already on the outside looking over the work. Prophetic, no doubt.

That's okay, I'm always on a diet.

Besides, I'm not so hungry anymore.

And, fuck it, the people, they need a leader, or they will all go to hell . . .

She dried herself off hastily and grabbed a yellow pad and a pen. Yo! MTV Raps needled incessantly in the background. I'd be pissed off if I was a nigger, too, she thought. Well, you are a nigger; you're a woman, aren't you? And then she wrote, with more assurance than she expected: He swung himself up onto the kitchen counter and said, 'I think I was an abused child . . .'

> *Ther saugh I first the derke ymaginyng*
> *Of Felonye, and al the compassyng:*
> *The crueel Ire, reed as any gleede;*
> *The pykepurs, and eek the pale Drede;*
> *The smylere with the knyf under the cloke . . .*

It was from the Knight's Tale, in *The Canterbury Tales*. She looked it up one night, after coming home from Mortons. Ah,

Mortons on a Friday night. An enchanting mixture of Hollywood and Valley power and money with a generous assortment of trash interspersed. The women were anorectic and the men seemed gay.

Not too many people here who even knew who Geoffrey Chaucer was. 'Oh, Geoff Chaucer,' she imagined them saying, 'isn't he the guy who made a housekeeping deal at Paramount?' Just kidding . . .

Mortons: Peter Morton's living room for the rich and powerful. The famous came there, too, but it was really a haven for those who pulled the strings that operated the rich and famous, from Mike Ovitz, the Valley viper who spearheaded CAA into prominence in the eighties, to bald-headed men with peeled-onion eyes like Peter Lorre's who looked like they trafficked in guns and drugs. Probably most of them just arranged leveraged buyouts and hostile takeovers. She always thought of Ovitz as Mike Ozymandias Ovitz, particularly now that he had caused this I.M. Pei structure to be erected: the old 'Look upon my works Ye Mighty and Despair' syndrome.

Craig, a previous maître d', told her once that Mortons was Peter's vanity, yielding less than a two percent return. It was the Hard Rock Cafés that made him the kind of money that supported the art on the walls.

There was a very famous Bacon, which was definitely two men embracing, reportedly worth one and a half mil, that hung discreetly in the back, the section of the restaurant that she called Heaven, where the rich nobodies sat. She'd heard that Peter and his ex-wife had fought over it.

A lot of divorced or divorcing couples fought more over the art nowadays than the house, the cars, the kids. Back in the seventies, when she and Michael were splitting up, their arguments seemed to center more around credit, but maybe they were a special case, and besides the big money and the attention hadn't started to roll in; they just knew it would.

They never got the chance to buy the art to have a fight over later.

Her personal favorite for art fights was the one that was

probably still going on between Elliot Roberts and his ex-wife, Gwen. Elliot was a major rock 'n' roll manager, handling such luminaries as Tom Petty, Joni Mitchell, Jackson Browne, when he started to collect paintings by Escher.

While Elliot was becoming the owner of the largest collection of Eschers, which were getting more and more valuable, his wife, Gwen, was in solitary confinement at Terminal Island. Elliot kept organizing benefits for the prisoners so he could visit her. Then she got out and they got married, had some kids. Then they split up. The night he left, he took three hangers with some shirts and pants. He left the Eschers on the walls. He never got them back. She guessed even tough rock 'n' roll managers were no match for a woman who made it through solitary.

She checked out the dark imagining:

Marvin Davis and his family gathered around the first big table on the right. She wondered if he had his own special chair here, like he did at Fox in the old days.

Alan Ladd and his wife of the moment were dining quietly with the Zanucks over on the four against the window. She squinted at Lili Zanuck, Academy Award winner extraordinaire. No more 'only,' just 'first.' If you can't be first be best, and vice versa . . . Had to happen sometime . . .

Ed Limato imbibed a martini straight up while Richard Gere drank gallons of expensive red wine. He snubbed her now, never talked to her since he had blown himself off *The Vampire Lestat*.

And now, here was the Beges, wrinkles a-crinkle, departing an early get-together with Walter Matthau and Billy Wilder. The laughing dinosaurs. She stood up to hug him. Why are we always so happy to see each other? she wondered. Because we're alive and kicking . . .

And Brian Grazer, one half of Imagine Entertainment, with Tom Pollack of Universal, laughing too loudly – what could they possibly have to say to each other that was funny?

Back at the table Peter used for his little dmner parties was a gathering of vampires: Richard Perry, Stan Dragoti, Mike Gruskoff, Victor Drai, Nick . . . Partaking of the meal before the meal. As it were. Maybe Richard should go drink wine – or the blood of young girls – with them.

Not to mention David Geffen confabbing with Marlo Thomas on another two meant for four. Yo, as long as there are scalpels and collagen, may you stay forever young! He'd sold the record and publishing company for $545 million. Probably just about what a billion used to be . . . Enough? she'd asked him and he'd thought for a moment, crossed his arms over his chest. Enough, he'd said uncertainly.

On the opposite side, near the bar, were Sean Penn with De Niro, Art Linson, and Brian De Palma. She sent them a bottle of wine so she wouldn't have to walk over and say hello. At least Brooke and Stuart got to meet De Niro out of it . . .

Later, after Ed and Richard left, Peter came in with Lorne Michaels.

'Anyone ever call you Forlorn?' she'd asked Lorne during their one and only long lunch. It was a particularly hot day and they were out on the terrace outside the Polo Lounge, throwing back vodka and tomato juice like the world was going to end the second they left their table.

'All the time,' he said crossly. They were needling each other, him with dialogue about the perfect woman for him, which was someone in her mid-twenties whom he could mold, her with dialogue about how they all must end up leaving him. Once they were molded . . .

'How are you?' Peter asked, not really wanting to know.

'Great,' she smiled. 'I sold my book . . .' In seven hours and fifteen minutes. Way to go, Joni! Thank you, Lynn. Bless you, Phyllis. Joni said: We're gonna go to the moon together, and she had said: I've been there, let's go farther . . .

'That's nice . . .' Peter smiled. Well, at least I can pay your bill, she thought. Not to mention, save the house, the car, the kid . . . 'What's it about?' She three-sixtied the room with squinted eyes.

Everything.

Well, most of it.

Actually, only some.

Sixty/forty, my best offer, take it or leave it . . .

Cogito, ergo sum. I am, I am . . . just a speck of sand. Under . . . Incogito, ergo SUMbuddy . . . hey, babe, be your own best friend . . . boomalacka boomalacka . . .

'Mortons,' she said.

She glances past his right ear and out the WINDOW, toward the night sky, thinking this movie is too static, THE THIRD MAN THROUGH THE DOOR will die from boredom not bullets . . .

FOLLOW her eyes . . .

The CAMERA, traveling outside on her gaze, WHIP PANS one-eighty, then JETTISONS in the opposite direction. Faster and faster. Away from Mortons, the neon sign is a dot, and then BEV HILLS, L.A., the WORLD, EARTH. THE SOLAR SYSTEM.

Wait a second, just whose movie is this?

THE CAMERA accelerates with the blue shift, warp-speeding through the GALAXY, faster than anything even imagined by Steven or George or Marty . . .

And then it settles somewhere in DEEP SPACE for just a moment.

A SHADOW enters screen left. It moves slowly, inexorably, devouring everything in its path.

Is it A MOTHER SHIP? This script needs a polish.

A BIG BANG? Get me another writer!

THE GREAT ATTRACTOR? Maybe replace the cameraman?

THE END OF THE UNIVERSE? Fire the director!#@*?!

GOD? Mommy, did you lie to me? That's okay, I forgive you . . .

It looks like – it is – A GIANT RED . . .

FINGERNAIL!

And it cover the SCREEN and BURNS BRIGHT RED for an instant. Then it FADES TO BLACK and as Mick Jagger HOWLS – oh no – SATISFACTION . . .

Credits Begin . . .

For my mother. Enough? Already. R.I.P.

House Lights Up

ACKNOWLEDGMENTS

For those who saw me through the painful and arduous task of rendering an entertaining autobiography, some special thanks:

To Kate, my daughter, and Jackie Smith, her nanny, for going through hell-and-back with me. To my dad, Adolph Miller, and my stepmother, June, for their confidence, support, and financial assistance.

To Michael Phillips, who didn't love the concept, and never stood in my way.

To my cats, Raps and Ramona, for hanging tough and hanging tight.

To Karen Baumer, my friend, my sister, my assistant. Poor baby . . .

To Joni Evans, inspirer, publisher, friend, liege. Phyllis Levy, our mutual mentor. Lynn Nesbit, my agent and protector – my idol – and Lew Grimes, friend and collector-of-money-without-portfolio.

To Julie Grau, my muse, confidante, ally, editor, and partner-in-crime. Couldn't have done it without her.

To Leslie Oelsner, who reminded me of the principles of fiction, 'nuff said.

To my few loyal friends and supporters:

Roz Heller, who always believed in me and never gave up – or in. Stuart Griffen and Lance Tendler, eighties guys with heart. Brooke McCarter, Corey Haim, and Billy McNamara, the sons I never had. Mones, Kilik, Wechsler and Kramer, Mother's Younger Brothers every one. My real younger brother, Matthew, for just existing in all his smartness. Ditto, Gary Kurfirst. To David Debin and Gary Devore, my role models, and Lee Ramstead and Marcia Selwyn, my heroes. Michelle Meier, my little sister.

To Norman and Judy Leaf for checking up on me, and John Ptak, a knight in shining armor.

To the two Annes: Rice and Thompson, writers themselves who kept saying, You can do it, try this, try that . . .

To Mike Sherman for negotiating the deal, and Chris Cuddy for closing it.

To Dick deBlois for maintaining my financial life, such as it is, and Marie Martignon, Forthill Construction, and Angel Plumbing for keeping my house clean and sober.

To Drs. Sellars, Siegel, Dornfeld, Kanengiser, and Feuer for keeping body and soul reasonably functional, along with Rebecca Eastman and Cathy Donavan for teaching me the kind of physical discipline that works so well with writing.

To the Writer's Computer Store especially Jesse Douma – for bringing me into the latter half of the twentieth century with minimal trauma.

To Harlan Goodman and Bob Goldstein for pitching out the title with me.

To the guys and gals at Mortons, Le Dome, the Polo Lounge, Adriano's, Sushi Ko, and Hamburger Hamlet for holding my tables even when I couldn't afford them, and to Janet at Maxfield's and Rena at Madeleine Gallay for keeping me in designer armor. Manny at H. Lorenzo, when I was really hurting . . .

To Terre Bridgham for upkeep on fingers and toes, and Victor Sortino, Daley Henderson, and Peter Nagai for my haircuts – short, chic, and to the point.

To the IRS and World Savings and Loan and City National Bank for providing constant financial imperative, and last, and maybe most of all, to the eighties moguls who made me so mad, I just had to tell the tale . . .

Index

Fictitious names are indicated by asterisks.

Abdul, Paula, 589
Abraham, Marc, 481
Academy Awards, iii–xx, 20–1,
    167, 272, 341, 369, 371, 459
Adams, Douglas, 186
Addis, Keith, 530, 547
Adjani, Isabel, 540
Aherne, Kay, 393–4, 471–2
AIDS, 503–4
Alati, Vincent, 316–17
Albert, Cari-Esta, 604–5
Albert, Prince*, 416–18, 460
Alcoholics Anonymous (AA),
    436, 521, 523
Allen, Herbie, 227–9, 293, 351,
    380, 397, 487
Alonzo, John, 352
Alves, Joe, 253–4, 292, 295
American Graffiti, vii, 211
Amy (cook), 435–6, 484
Anish, Larry, 310
Antonioni, Michelangelo, 194
Apocalypse Now, 257, 541
Arbogast, Roy, 296, 304
Archer, Anne, 584–5
Ariel*, 346–7, 382, 390
Arkin, Alan, 55, 106
Army-McCarthy hearings, 31,
    42
Ashby, Hal, 196, 205–6, 208,
    267

Ashley, Ted, 118, 122
Ashley Famous, 92, 93
Aubrey, Jim, 139
Avildsen, John, 149
Azoff, Irving, 370–1, 374, 525,
    611

Baba Sheek, 351, 355–61
Bach, Alice, 82–3
Bailey, Pearl, 211
Balaban, Bob, 302, 352, 356
Balistreri, Chicky, 438
Barrett, Rona, 342–3, 389
Barrymore, Drew, 619
Bart, Peter, xiii, 93
Baskin, Richard, 14, 498, 502,
    506, 509
Bauer, Marty, 602
Baumgarten, Craig, 456–7, 527,
    560
Baxley, Craig, 536–7
Beat, The, 85, 530–40, 548–9,
    565, 570
Beatles, 180, 370
Beatty, Warren, 179, 181,
    194–5, 196, 540–2, 609–10
Beaupre, Lee, 99–100, 124
Beckerman, Barry, 91, 581
Bedtime Story (Robinson),
    192–3

Begelman, David, 65, 95–101, 104–5, 136, 151, 155–7, 179, 201–2, 205–8, 209–13, 218, 225–6, 230–1, 235, 241–4, 246–9, 254, 258, 261, 265, 283, 306–9, 314–16, 366, 367, 371, 375, 379–90, 439, 463–4, 473–6, 517, 626
Begelman, Gladyce, 371
Begelman, Lee, 99
Bellucci, Eunice, 94
Belushi, John, 260
Berenson, Berry, 187
Berg, Jeff, 8, 474, 496,
Bergman, Marilyn, 498–502, 523–4, 528, 547–8
Berman, Shelley, 55
Bernstein, Larry, 284
Bernstein, Penny, 284–5
Bernstein, Ron, xv, 186, 587
Big Bus, The, 190–1, 452, 514
Bill, Antoinette, vi–vii, ix, xiii, xvii, 104
Bill, Tony, iv, vii, ix, xiii, xiv, xv, xvii, 87, 105–13, 115, 117, 119–22, 139–47, 194, 202, 239, 241, 402, 565
Billings, Marion, 570
Bill/Phillips Productions, 109–47
  congratulatory telegrams of, vii–viii
  splitting up of, vii, xvii, 147
Birdt, Marvin, 91–5, 104, 171
Birnbaum, Roger, 383
Blakley, Ronee, 509, 558
Blau, Louis C., 272, 307–8
Blauner, Steve, 111
Bloom, Jim (J. B.), 302, 352, 355, 357, 358, 362, 363, 364
Blumenthal, George, 443
Bochner, Hart, 460
Bologna, Joe, 192

bookies, 31–2, 35, 44, 89
Bookman, Bob, 151–3, 456
Boone, Richard, 146
Boonshaft, Hope, 500
Bornstein, Judy, 252
Boulting, Ingrid, 525
Bound for Glory, 205, 267
Boyd, Steven, 146
Boyle, Peter, xv, xix, 110, 111, 113, 124, 129, 132, 134, 146, 174, 260
Brackman, Jake, 116, 119
Brackman, Leon, 488
Brando, Marlon, 241–2
Brandon, Michael, 506, 507–8
Brazzi, Lucca, 528
Bregman, Marty, 248
Bremmer, Arthur, 300
Breslauer, Gerry, 86
Bressler, Sandy, 247
Brian, Jeb, 551
Brillstein, Bernie, 547
Briscoe, Jim, 86, 421
Brodkey, Harold, 150
Brokaw, Norman, 527
Brooke, 6–14, 19–22, 38, 352, 504–5, 549, 553, 582–5, 602, 618–19
Brooklyn Paramount, 44, 51
Brooks, Albert, 219
Brown, David, 111, 121, 139–42, 130–45, 147, 149
Brown, Jerry, 470
Brown, Michael, 180–1
Bruce, Lenny, 55, 65, 80, 150, 262–3, 405
Buchman, Caitlin, 39
Burbank Studios, 231, 235
Burstyn, Ellen, 119, 241, 242
Bury My Heart at Wounded Knee, 241–2
Butch Cassidy and the Sundance Kid, 144, 149

634

Caan, James, 248–9
Calley, John, iii, 240–1, 415
Cameron, Jim, 594
Cameron, Julia, 256, 257
Candidate, The, 122
Cannes, 564–9
Cannon, Dyan, 199, 207
Cantamesa, Gene, 280
Canton, Mark, 135, 496, 556, 559
Cantwell, Colin, 277
Carnal Knowledge, 238–9
   female version of, 563–4
Carr, Alan, 172–3, 174
Carradine, Keith, 113
Carroll, Gordon, 349
Carsell, Richie, 123
Carter, John Mack, 89
CBS Pictures, 527–8
Cecilia (Harlan's assistant), 481, 482
Chamberlain, Dorothy, 76
Chapman, Michael, 550
Charles Rivers Mice and Rats, 94
Chase, Chevy, 260–1, 475
Cheese, the (bookie), 89
Chetwyn, Lionel, 69
Childhood's End (Clarke), 458–9
Chinatown, 233
Christie, Julie, 180–1, 196
Clark, Betty Anne, 153–4
Clarke, Arthur C., 458, 462–6, 467–70, 488
Clayburgh, Jill, 131, 172
Clea and Zeus Divorce (Praeger), 587
Clinton, George, 384
Clockwork Orange, A, 122
Close Encounters of the Third Kind, 65, 156, 161, 182, 192, 201, 205, 206–7,

210–13, 219, 225–9, 236–7, 252–6, 261, 265–8, 272–309, 311–17, 319, 327–8, 350–68, 375–90, 396, 475–6, 536–8, 552–3, 564–5
CMA, 96, 105, 109, 113, 118
cocaine, 167, 183, 190, 345–6, 367, 416
   on carpet, 334–6, 387
   facial appearance and, xvi, 18
   gums and, 393
   JP's use of, v, viii, x, xi, xv–xvi, xviii, xx, 14, 15, 52, 84, 181, 186, 188, 197, 199, 221, 257–8, 261, 286, 323–4, 333–43, 386–9, 393
   at parties, xv–xvi, 186, 196–9
   quality of, v, xvi, 221, 333–4, 344
   Rolling stones and, 221
   see also freebase
Coelho, Tony, 502
Coen, Chuck, 71–2
Cohen, Larry, 191
Cohen, Rob, 458, 529, 547
Cohen, Sid, 441
Cohn, Sam, 109–11
Colbert, Bob, 87, 176–7, 309, 310, 318
Columbia Pictures, 144, 155, 193, 202, 205–6, 213, 230, 243–6, 252, 254–6, 347, 383, 390, 474–6, 487
Come Blow Your Horn, 105
Connelly, John, 313–14
Coppola, Francis Ford, xiii, 252, 257–9, 369, 513
Corday, Barbara, 499
Cotelo, Celia, 493–4
Crapsey, Adelaide, 490
Creative Artists Agency (CAA), 452, 518, 554–7, 564, 570, 595, 611–12

Crichton, Michael, 137
Cristofer, Michael, 605, 610
Cro-Mags, 533–5
Cronkite, Walter, 327–8
Cuddy, Chris, 265, 482
Curtis, Jamie Less, 509
Curtis, Tony, 208

d'Angelo, Beverly, 602
Daniels, Sean, 603, 604–5
Danielson, Connie, 96, 99, 206,
    207, 243, 248, 306, 388
Danner, Blythe, 118
Darrach, Brad, 135
Dattila, Bob, 284
David, 75, 83, 133
Davidson, Marty, 92
Davis, Clive, 383–4
Davis, Frank, 140
Davis, Marvin, 480–1, 485–6,
    489, 492, 626
Davis, Sammy, Jr., 173
Davoe, Arthur, 320
Day for Night, 273
Deadhead Miles, 106
Debbie*, 427, 432–3
Debin, David, 330, 396, 481,
    485, 487, 515, 519, 556–7,
    614
deBlois, Dick, 576
De Laurentiis, Dino, 91, 517–19
DeMann, Candy, 607
DeMann, Freddy, 332, 558–64,
    582–3, 607–8, 617
De Niro, Robert, 157, 237, 239,
    240–1, 245–6, 252, 255,
    298, 558, 627
Dennison, Sally, 273, 275
De Palma, Brian, 79, 115, 118,
    170, 180, 237, 241, 253,
    364–5, 602, 627
Dern, Bruce, 119
Des Barres, Michael, 329–32,
    595

Des Barres, Pamela, 602
Devore, Gary, 513–20
Diamond, Marsha, 459, 498
Diamond, Neil, 459, 498
Dickinson, Angie, 473
Dickinson, Emily, 60, 577
Didion, Joan, xvi, 116, 142, 346,
    347–8, 398, 496–7, 555
Diller, Barry, 187, 191, 457, 610
Dillon, Melinda, 267–8, 279–80,
    282, 296, 304
Doctors in Hollywood, 450,
    474–6
Dodds, Pat, 184, 189, 198, 243,
    256
Dollard, Anne, 69–70, 570
Donen, Josh, 136
Donovan, Arlene, 137–8
Don Smollen, 313
Dornfeld, Leslie, 9–10, 453,
    457, 458, 513
Douglas, Michael, 66, 582,
    584–5
Drai, Victor, 517, 626
Dreyfuss, Richard, 137, 196,
    198, 246–50, 254, 261–2,
    286, 290, 291, 296, 300,
    302–5, 321, 337, 455, 582
  drinking of, 293, 304
  drug use of, 304–5
Drugstore Cowboy, 571
Duffy, Martha, 250–1
Dullea, Keir, 118
Dunaway, Faye, 93, 233, 365
Dunn, Michael, 174
Dunne, John Gregory, v, xvi,
    115, 150, 164–5, 168, 342,
    347, 348, 371, 398–9, 497
Dylan, Bob, 73, 75, 99, 116, 264

Eagles, 370–1, 373, 388
Eastman, Andrea, xv, 92, 93–4,
    139, 142–4, 183–4, 194,

636

213–14, 339–42, 412, 460, 570
Eastman, Carole, 93, 232
Eastman, John, 382
Eastman, Rebecca, 17–18, 560, 618
Easy Rider, 99–100, 110, 119, 124, 224, 255
Ebert, Jose, 512
Edgar, 556–7
Eisenhower, Dwight D., 7, 49, 53
Elliot, Cass, 170–4
Ellis, Bret Easton, 555
Engelberg, Mort, 392
English, Priscilla, 530
Erlichman, Marty, 102
Ertegun, Ahmet, 222, 224
Esterhaus, Joe, 605
Evans, Bob, xiii, 94, 179, 230, 231, 257, 473
Evans, Joni, 102, 488, 544
exercise, 17–18, 447, 511, 560, 562, 572–3
Exorcist, The, iii, x, xii, 102
Eyes of Laura Mars, The, 365

Faret, Liv, 577, 581–2
Farha, Sandra, 499
Fawcett, Farrah, 239, 512
Fearless, Mr*, 281, 283, 306, 310–11, 536, 623
Fear of Flying (Jong), 65, 151–6, 163, 182, 193, 196, 201–2, 205, 206, 210, 211, 218, 230, 232–5, 248–9, 265, 267–8, 270, 283–4, 348–9, 457, 487
Ferry, Brian, 550
Field, David, 483
Fields, Freddie, 97, 179, 398, 478, 488
Fields, Randy, 389
Fields, Verna, 211, 375, 581

Finkel, Terry, 77
Finslander*, 10, 86, 415–16, 418–21, 432, 454–5
First Artists, 97–108, 112, 127, 137
Fischer, Carrie, 527
Fisher, Joe, 313, 366–8, 378
Fiskin, Jeffrey, 147, 157
Flately, Guy, 309
Fling, The, 450, 477, 554
Foley, Jamie, 558
Fonda, Jane, 110, 111, 113, 121, 131, 208–9, 230, 500, 532
Ford, Betty, 525, 526
Ford, Gerald, 235
Foreman, John, 108
Foster, Jodie, 246, 252, 369–70
400 Blows, The, 273
Fox, 68, 176–7, 481–5, 487–9, 492, 495, 496–7
Frawley, Jim, 191–2
Frears, Stephen, 595
freebase, 7, 15, 17, 21, 65, 86, 400–10, 412, 417, 418–19, 421–8, 436–7, 440–8, 454, 505–6
    dreams about, 14, 447–8
    recipes for, 401–4
Freed, Alan, 44, 51
Freedman, Mitch, 85, 160–1, 539, 543
Freeman, Fred, 191
French, Jesse, 142
French, Robin, 139–43, 190–1, 192
French Connection, The, 124–5
Frey, Glen, 374, 388
Friedkin, Billy, xii
Friedman, Kenny, 481, 491, 541, 569
Frost, Robert, 391
Fuchs, Ellen, 543–4
Furie, Sidney, 207

Gaines, John, 146
Gandhi, Indira, 351, 356
Garey, Barbara, 481–2, 487
Garey, Jerry, 517
Garey, Norman, x, 65–6, 85–6,
    119, 142–3, 157, 168, 247,
    258, 269–72, 283, 312,
    342–3, 348, 354, 373–4,
    408, 410–11, 426, 446, 473,
    481–5, 489, 598
Garner, James, 208
Garr, Teri, 266, 302
Gaye, Marvin, 466–7
Geffen, David, 590–9, 602–4,
    610, 627
Gerard, Manny, 118
Gerber, Billy, 136, 553, 557
Gere, Richard, 453–4, 458,
    546–7, 626
Getaway, The, (Thompson), 108
Ghost Town, 450–3, 458–9,
    463–70
Gibb, Barry, 542, 550
Gilardi, Jack, 520, 588
Giler, David, 156, 173, 233–5,
    348–50, 517
Gimble, Roger, 241
Gimme Shelter, 534
Gittes, Harry, 232
Glazner, Dick, 284
Godfather, The, xiii, 148, 257
Goldberg, Leonard, 525–6, 527
Goldberg, Wendy, 525–6, 527
Goldberg, Whoopi, 500
Gold Brothers, 124, 150
Golden Globes, 368–9, 372
Goldman, Bo, 486
Goodrow, Gary, 113
Gorbachev, Mikhail, 584
Gorby, Alex, 555, 557, 560–2
Gordon, Freddy, 89
Gordon, Larry, xv, 64–7, 68,
    212

Gould, Jason, 101
Graduate, The 92
Grant, Cary, 15
Grant, Lee, 196
Grazer, Brian, 626
Great Attractor, 580–1
'green' (drug), 263–4, 265
Greenfield, Leo, iii, 121, 122,
    148–9
Greenfield, Mike, 568
Greenlaw, Charlie, 241
Gregory, Maia, 95
Griffen, Stuart, 330
Grode, Susan, 256, 502
Grossman, Arny, 610–11
Grossman, Ernie, 125–6, 133
Guber, Peter, 209–12, 255,
    453–4, 622
Guc, David, 513–15
Guest, Christopher, 509
Guffey, Cary, 298–9
Guys, The, 67–8

Hackman, Gene, 124, 247, 497
Hahn, Helene, 496
hair, hairdressers, 56, 79, 131,
    192, 232, 511–12
Haldeman, Barry, 176, 482
Haley, Jack, 368
Hall, Daryl, 550–1
Halston, Rand, 564
Hamlisch, Marvin, x
Harlan (assistant), 160, 324,
    481–5, 489, 494, 528, 591
Harmon, Johnny, 47
Harmon, Sandy, 192, 219, 220
'arriet and 'enry*, 466–7
Harris, Barbara, 55
Harris, Johnny, 11–12, 71
Harris, Susan, 459–60
hash, 186, 240, 358, 362–4
Hauer, Rutger, 553
Hawaii, 393–9, 458–9, 460,
    471–2, 492–5, 614

638

Hawn, Goldie, 188, 194–6, 199–200, 212, 217, 219–25, 230, 456, 472
Hayden, Tom, 208
Hayes, Helen, 34, 52
Hayman, Gale, 451, 452
Hayward, Billy, 461
Heckerling, Amy, 564
Hefner, Hugh, 316
Heller, Roz, 39, 155, 157, 203, 209–10, 232
Henderson, Jocko, 52
Henley, Don, 374, 388
Henson, Lisa, 593, 594
heroin, 196, 201, 214
Herrmann, Bernard, 236–7, 384
Hesseman, Howard, 113
Heston, Charlton, 532
Higgins, Colin, 498
Hill, George Roy, vii, xii, xiv, 106, 143–50, 157, 274, 475, 563
Hill, Luisa, 150
Hinckley, John, 262
Hipwell, Connie, 477–8
Hirsch, Barry, 489
Hirsch, Richard, 43
Hirschfield, Alan, 118, 226–9, 288–9, 291, 293, 308, 313–17, 319–20, 351, 364–5, 383, 385, 389, 396, 397, 479–80, 483–8, 537
Hitchhiker's Guide to the Galaxy (Adams), 186
Hoffman, Abbie, 546
Hoffman, Dustin, 92
Hollywood Women's Coalition, 500–2
Hollywood Women's Political Committee, 502
homosexuality, 61, 73, 331, 468
Hooper, Tobe, 455
Hopkins, Anthony, 187

Hopper, Dennis, 99
Horowitz, Eli, 246
Houdini deal, 246
Howard, Ken, 117
How to Save Your Own Life (Jong), 347–9
Hunt, Baker, 62, 545
Hurt, Mary Beth, 251
Huston, John, xii
Hyams, Joe, 122
Hyams, Nessa, 154–5, 157, 174, 194, 201–2
Hyams, Peter, 163, 488
Hyneck, Alan, 267, 311–12, 390

I Am Furious (Yellow), 555–63
International Creative Management (ICM), 92, 142, 151, 153, 156, 451, 519, 547, 570
International Famous Agency (IFA), 139, 144, 191
Interview with the Vampire (Rice), 493–6, 527, 529,–30, 542, 547, 555, 590, 591–9
Ipcress File, The, 207
Irving, Amy, 296, 297, 371–3, 551
Island, Mary Jane, 433
Island, Ray, 430–1, 433
Ives, Burl, 28–9

Jackson, Jesse, 39
Jaffe, Marc, 95
Jaffe, Stanley, 243–5, 251–6, 258, 278, 282–3, 293–4, 537
Jagger, Bianca, 221
Jagger, Mick, 220–3, 225, 477, 603, 629
Jane, 72–3, 83, 133
Janiger, Ozzie, 15–16, 548
Jaws, 148, 206, 211, 219, 327, 328, 357

Jeremiah Johnson, 244
Jeremy*, 13, 103, 181–6,
    187–93, 195–201, 208,
    212–18, 234, 257, 282, 323,
    325, 344, 457
Jews, 23–4, 51, 68, 187, 599
    drinking and, xvi, 293, 516
    suicidal behavior of, 16–17
    white-bread, 154
John, Elton, 590, 591–2
Johnson, Lamont, 240
Jones, Reice, 405, 439–40, 444
Jong, Erica, 127, 152–5, 186,
    193–4, 196, 205, 218,
    248–9, 265, 268, 270,
    283–4, 347–9, 414

Kael, Pauline, 250, 251, 252
Kahn, Mike, 367, 376, 377, 379
Kamen, Stan, 195, 212–13, 475
Kane, Josh, 43–4
Kane, Michael (Killer), 451–3,
    463
Kartiganer, Larry, 398
Kasdan, Larry, 15
Kasinoff, Larry, 540, 567
Kass, Artha, 516
Katzenberg, Jeff, 135, 192, 495,
    559
Keane, Andy, 385
Kelley, Patrick, 97, 112
Kendall, 262, 274, 282, 289–93,
    300, 309, 310, 336–9, 366,
    380, 390
Kennedy, John F., 71, 73, 151
Kennedy, Ted, 473
Kershner, Irv, 239–40
Kidder, Margot, 115, 117–18,
    170, 172, 176, 233–4
Kilik, 536, 537, 539, 565–70
King of Marvin Gardens, The,
    86, 119–20, 262
Kingsley, Pat, 298, 301, 308,
    309, 396

Kirkpatrick, David, 136
Klute, 110 131
Knight, Holly, 550–4
Koch, Howard, Sr., 190, 192,
    427–8
Konigsberg, Frank, xv
Kovacs, Laszlo, 352
Kramer, Deena, 348
Kroll, Jack, 250
Krost, Barry, 590–2
Kubrick, Stanley, 122, 277, 470,
    473–4, 514, 593–6, 599
Kup's Show, 532–3
Kurfirst, Gary, 553, 587–90, 609

Ladd, Alan, Jr., 156, 626
Ladies' Home Journal, 62–3, 88,
    91, 93, 350
Lady and the Hunk, The, 450,
    477
Lambert, Mary, 587–90, 609
Landis, John, 536, 538
Lansing, Sherry, 479, 483, 498,
    500, 584–6
Latrell, Martha, 584–5
Laurents, Arthur, 103
Lauter, Dick, 85–6
Lawford, Peter, 394
Lazarus, Paul, 137, 183–4,
    213–14, 234
Lazarus, Robert, 213–14, 519
Leary, Barbara, 491, 496, 602
Leary, Timothy, 15, 173, 490–1,
    496, 602
Lederer, Dick, 121–2, 124,
    148–9, 218
Lemmele, George, 238
Lemmon, Jack, xi, xii, xiv
Lenny, 262–3
Less Than Zero, (Ellis), 555
Levin, Alan, 527–8
Levine, David, 35–6
Levine, Emily, 39, 481, 4956,
    499

Levine, Hank, 85, 397
Levy, Mike, 495–6, 527, 547,
    555–7, 560–3, 592–3, 598,
    603, 604–5
Levy, Norman, 255, 258, 381–5,
    388–9, 398, 479–81, 483
Levy, Phyllis, 91, 412
Lewis, Fiona, 461, 530
Librium, 431, 433
Liddy, Gordon, 490–2
Limato, Ed, 453–4, 626
Linda (weekend nanny), 419–21
Lindsay, John V., 138–9, 145
lithium, 440, 445
Lloyd Weber, Andrew, 542
Locke, Peter, 554
Loren, Sophia, 368–9
Lorimar, 547–8, 591, 596
Lozoff, Penny, 58, 59
Lucas, George, viii, 480–1, 577
Lucas, Marcia, 211, 236–9
Lucas, Pat, 608–12
Lumet, Sidney, 207, 593–4
Lydon, John (Johnny Rotten),
    601
Lydon, Nora, 601
Lynch, David, 592, 594–5
Lyne, Adrian, 584–5, 593
Lyne, Samantha, 584

McCall's Magazine, 76, 82
McCarey, Leo, 202
McCarthy, Joseph, 41–2
McCarthy, Tom, 374
McCartney, Linda, ix
McCartney, Paul, ix, 382
McElwaine, Guy, 156–7, 199,
    448
McGrath, Earl, 222, 224
McGraw, Ali, 62, 92
McLean, Nick, 280, 285, 288,
    290, 291, 297, 306, 310, 347,
    360, 383, 455

McLean, Sydney, 60–1, 70, 88
McNamara, Billy, 570
MacPherson, Izzy*, 212, 264–5,
    268–71, 282, 287, 296–7,
    306, 309
McQueen, Steve, 62
Macucci, Mary, 611
Maday, Mike, 413–14, 420, 425,
    435, 449
Madonna, 554–5, 559–64, 607,
    609
magic mushrooms, 583–4, 602,
    620
Maio, Juliana, 582
Maisel, Ileen, 526–9, 546, 547,
    560, 563–4, 566
Malick, Terry, 106
Mamet, David, 604, 605
Manchester, Melissa, 500
Mann, Corinne, 69
Manny's, 31–2, 35, 44
Manson, Charles, 324
Mara*, 17, 204, 605
March, Don, 458
Marco and His Brothers, 458
Margolin, Janet, 117
marijuana, v, x, xviii, 12, 13, 51,
    87, 95, 127, 185, 188–9,
    224, 339, 341–2, 391–2,
    394–6, 415–16, 455–6, 491,
    507, 524–5
Marini, Dennis, 566
Marks, David, 349–50, 386
Marlowe, Miss, 33–4
Marquette University, 61
Marshall, Noel, 218
Martin, Hy, 149
Matthau, Walter, xiv, 626
Mayo Clinic, Alcohol and Drug
    Dependence Unit of
    (ADDU), 424, 426–35
Mazursky, Paul, 207
Mean Streets, 240, 244

Meatballs, 474

Medavoy, Mike, 109, 110, 111, 139–44

Mehta, Zubin, 119

Melnick, Dan, 137–40, 142–5, 256, 366, 375, 378–9, 381–2, 388, 390, 483, 484, 486–7, 496

Melnicker, Charles, 547

Mengers, Sue, 230–1, 475, 497–8

Meredith, Scott, 488

Merrick, David, 92

Meyer, Ron, 611–12

Meyerson, Mark, 76–7, 224

MGM, 137, 139–42, 144, 450–3, 463–76, 554

MGM/UA, 439, 445

Michaels, Lorne, 627

Mighty Mo*, 329, 435, 436–7

Milius, Jon, 66, 122–3, 137, 140, 157, 180, 244, 257, 395–6

Miller, Adolph (father), vi, xix, 16, 24–6, 28–30, 32–3, 34, 40–54, 59, 60–1, 63, 79, 105, 198–9, 257, 308, 319–23, 360, 397, 414–15, 437–8, 545, 580–1, 616
   JP's avoiding of, 436–7
   JP's borrowing from, 161

Miller, Chris, 76–7, 459

Miller, Elias (grandfather), 23, 79

Miller, Harvey, 262

Miller, Henry, 268, 348, 414

Miller, Mae (sister-in-law), 438

Miller, Matthew (brother), 28, 29, 36–7, 40–3, 45–7, 50, 57, 74, 311, 322–3, 415, 436, 437–8, 459

Miller, Tanya (mother), xix, 16, 22–33, 34–7, 40–54, 56–9, 76, 78, 87, 88, 117, 198–9,
   231, 257, 259, 284–5, 308, 317–20, 616, 629
   anti-Semitism of, 24, 29, 35, 48
   cancer of, 73, 352–3, 360, 362, 381, 396–7, 489
   crying of, 22, 25, 30, 57, 59, 319
   death of, 414–15, 437, 479
   as eccentric, 70
   familial estrangement of, 23, 24–5
   husband's surgery and, 321–3
   JP as possession of, 70
   medicine cabinet of, xv, xvi, 15
   Naked Maja position of, 50, 214, 410
   pill use of, 23, 30, 58, 314
   racism of, 35, 224
   smoking of, 32–3, 47, 58, 214
   unhappiness of, 26, 27, 29, 30, 58–9

Minelli, Liza, x, xiv, 115, 298, 368–9

Mirisch, 94–5, 97

Mishkin, Meyer, 246–9

Mitchell, John, 355

Mitchell, Steven Paul, 52, 53

Mobile, Ala., location shooting, 278, 286, 306

Mogul, Artie, 386, 389

Monash, Buddy, 487

Mones, Paul, 330, 478, 534–6, 539–41, 548–9, 565–70, 573–4

money, 68, 83–8, 350–1, 507
   business managers and, 85–8, 159–61, 424
   drug, 345–6
   father's advice about, 63, 82
   fear of, 87–8, 189
   JP's problems with, 83–8, 159–62, 507, 576

Moore, Demi, 583
Moore, Paul, 209
Moore, Sara Jane, 235
Moore, Susannah, 208, 530
Morris, Kiki, 501
Morse, Robert, 427–8, 431
Mortoff, Larry, 568
Morton, Peter, 551–2, 625–8
Moss, Jerry, 386, 398, 525, 527, 612
Motion Picture Association of America (MPAA), 243–6, 251, 252
Mottola, Tommy, 551
Mount Holyoke College, 59–61, 70-5, 138, 154
Munshin, Jules, 34
Murphy, Judge Thomas J., 249, 265, 390
Murray, Bill, 475
Myers, Chuck, 289
Myerson, Alan, 110–13, 120–1

Nasitir, Marcia, 62–3, 170, 239
Nelson, Willie, 460, 462
Nesbit, Lynn, 153, 494–5, 590
Newcombe, Pat, 396
Newman, Paul, 97, 107–8, 145–6, 274
New Yorker, 150–1
New York New York, 297–8
New York Times, iii, 55, 71, 75, 306–9, 453, 487, 591
Nice, 565–9
Nichols, Mike, 342
Nicholson, Jack, 119, 173, 247–8, 563, 585, 623
Nicita, Rick, 595, 597
Niven, David, xiii
Nixon, Richard, 175
Norpramin, 16, 17
nuclear power, 26, 49–50, 450
Nyro, Laura, 101

O'Bannon, Dan, 557
Obst, Linda, 332
O'Hare, Joe, 265–6, 300
Oliver, Jane, 92, 93, 96, 102, 105, 111, 183
Olivier (driver), 566, 567, 569
O'Neal, Ryan, 199
Operation Intercept, 391
Ordinary People, 456–7
O'Reilly, Reilly*, 19, 165–7, 170, 174–9, 195, 338, 416, 419
Ovitz, Mike, 135, 136, 157, 474–5, 546, 625
Owl and the Pussycat, The, 102, 104

Pacino, Al, 172, 241, 247–8, 257
Paltrow, Bruce, 117–18
Paramount Pictures, 63, 91, 94, 106, 190–2, 454, 495, 527, 547
Pardon Mon Affaire, 451, 453
Parent, Gail, 452–3, 475–6, 481
Parks, David, 405, 408–9, 411, 412, 425–7, 435, 439, 441–4, 445, 447, 463–4
Passer, Ivan, 102
Pattiz, Norm, 525
Paylow, Clark, 265, 278, 281, 286, 290, 294–5, 302, 376, 378
Peckerman, Joe, 482
Peckinpah, Sam, 164
Peellaert, Guy, 255
Pekos, M. J., 566–9
Penn, Michael, 570–1
Penn, Sean, 554–5, 558–62, 627
Performance, 100, 409
Perkins, Tony, 187
Perry, Richard, 101, 626
Peters, Ellie, 540
Peters, Jon, 232, 365–6, 384, 500

Petersdorf, Rudy, 141–4
Peyton, Harley, 543
Phil*, 177
Phillips, Julia:
  Academy Awards and, iii–xv,
    179, 272
  adolescence of, 48–59, 625–16
  ambition of, 136, 218
  anxiety and nervousness of,
    iv, vi, xi, 8, 21, 64, 73, 78,
    89, 142, 148, 160, 196, 222,
    353, 453
  bad driving of, xx, 15, 178,
    179–80, 310, 339
  bad press of, 306–9
  birth of, 7
  boredom of, 6, 27, 45, 58, 83,
    181, 194, 460
  childhood of, 24–7, 40–8
  claustrophobia of, 54, 113,
    114
  concussions of, 59, 251–2
  cultural education of, 34, 52
  decision making of, 63, 286,
    318
  depressions of, 8, 14–18, 22,
    74, 112, 168, 181, 204, 221,
    355, 414, 440, 453, 490,
    492–3
  dieting of, 9–10, 11, 453, 548,
    624
  directing of, 65-6, 195–6,
    206–7, 210, 218, 231, 235,
    458
  disappointments of, 22, 389
  dreams of, 14, 17, 82, 344,
    447–8
  drinking of, x, xv, xvi, 14, 46,
    179, 281, 301, 493, 508, 511,
    516–17, 553, 568, 602, 603
  drug bust of, 339–43, 354
  drug rehabilitation efforts of,
    7, 8, 14, 423–36, 439–48

  drug use of, iv–v, vi, viii, x,
    xi, xv–xviii, xx, 7, 12–18,
    20, 52, 65, 68, 84–6, 95,
    127, 134, 175–6, 179, 181,
    186, 188–90, 195–7, 199,
    221, 236, 240, 257, 261,
    263–6, 270, 271, 281, 286,
    316, 323–4, 325, 333–41,
    362–4, 386–90, 393–6,
    400–10, 414, 418, 421–9,
    435–48, 454–6, 490,
    491,505, 507–8, 523–5, 545,
    578–9
  drug wanderings of, 393–4
  education of, 30–1, 33–4, 40,
    41–3, 48, 57–61, 70–5, 376
  family background of, 22–6
  fear of flying of, 269–70,
    283–5, 296, 353, 531
  firings of, 86–7, 95, 112
  gambling of, 31–2, 35, 40, 44,
    300–1
  grief and mourning of, 14,
    162–3, 390–1, 448
  guilt of, 545, 578–9, 612
  headaches of, 89–90, 95, 108,
    116–17,
  hepatitis of, 54–9
  income of, 63, 76–7, 82, 91,
    98
  insomnia of, 14, 17, 26–7,
    143, 162, 353
  introspection of, 22, 24, 31,
    35, 38–9, 62–4
  as Jewish, xiv, xvi, 16, 30,
    40–1, 48, 100, 154
  lateness of, 188, 316, 339, 372,
    386, 390, 399, 414
  loneliness of, 57, 199, 324, 325
  lying of, 44, 98, 155, 218, 387,
    456, 583, 604
  marriage of, see Phillips,
    Michael

middle age of, 8, 14, 62, 204,
433, 545, 580
mobility of, 26–7, 155, 459
near-strangulation experiences
of, xiii, xiv, 12–13
pregnancies of, 134, 147,
150–2, 240, 421–2, 579
rage and anger of, 8, 14, 22,
37–9, 59, 68, 74, 75–6, 98,
242, 430–1, 479, 482, 572
rashes of, xx, 29, 44, 47–8
restlessness of, 59, 100, 137
as Rich Bitch, 297–8
sexism encountered by,
109–13, 125–6, 151
sexual behavior of, 19–20, 68,
72, 78, 131–2, 175, 179–80,
256, 260, 280–1, 287, 326,
346, 400, 435, 459–61,
476–7, 480, 504–8
shyness of, 208, 212, 224–5
speeches of, 268–71, 501
success of, 20–1, 33–4, 163–4
suicidal behavior of, 15–17
surgery of, 12, 152
therapy of, 112, 285, 441, 450,
476, 479, 488, 510
toothache of, 289, 291, 321
vision of, 149
weight gain of, 9, 17, 70, 134,
171, 181, 220, 448, 451, 453
weight loss of, 70, 90, 171,
424, 428, 432, 453, 454
writings awards of, 60–1, 70
writing of, 57, 60–1, 70, 82–3
Phillips, Kate (daughter), v,
xviii, xix, 67, 86, 163, 182,
188, 195, 214–15, 219–20,
230, 251, 325, 327, 344, 393,
396, 399, 418–25, 428–9,
435, 442, 443–50, 474,
504–5, 506-10, 542, 546,
548, 554, 557, 576-9, 581,

583, 599–61, 615, 618–19,
623
birth of, 150–2, 240
as deterrent to suicide, 17
horoscope of, 346–7
Phillips, Larry (father-in-law),
vii, xix, 71, 79, 465
Phillips, Michael, iii–viii, x,
xiii–xx, 13, 87, 89, 99,
107–15, 118–24, 132–4,
139–47, 156–9, 161, 167,
173–4, 190, 194, 246–7,
254, 262–4, 319–20, 348,
375–6, 447, 448–9, 459,
537, 538, 565
custody battle with JP, 443–4,
445–6, 447
JP's borrowing from, 161
JP's breakups with, xx, 72–5,
77, 78, 108, 158–9, 162–4,
170–1, 263–4, 625
JP's business problems with,
201–2, 210–11, 236, 334,
375–6, 434–5
JP's career picked up by, 67
JP's dating of, 72–3, 137
JP's marriage to, 72–3, 78–82,
616
JP's missing of, 188, 189
JP's stock sold by, 397–8
marital problems and fights
of, v, xviii, xix, 79, 89–90,
95, 115, 158, 162–3, 167,
170, 284, 285, 419
second marriage of, 582–3
Taxi Driver and, 192, 201,
236, 241, 250–1, 255,
257–8, 260, 283
therapy of, 195
third marriage of, 582–3
as 'wrong Phillips,' 66, 79
Phillips, Michelle, xv, 173, 174,
234, 461, 580

645

Phillips, Sherry (mother-in-law), vii, xviii, 74, 86–7, 114, 465
Platoon, 541
Poitier, Sidney, 97
Pollack, Sydney, 94, 98, 105, 117, 127–8, 207
Pollack, Tom, 626
Poltergeist, 455
Poster, Steve, 352
Powell, Charlie, 255
Praeger, Emily, 587–8
Presley, Elvis, 81, 297
Price, Frank, 474, 475–6
Price, Wesley, 88–9
Prince, Steven, 256
Principal, Victoria, 286
Professional Films, 124–8
Profile Records, 533
Pryor, Richard, 212, 555
Ptak, John, xv, 153, 176, 435, 475
Purdy, James, 203
Puzzle of a Downfall Child (Eastman), 93

Quaaludes, 14, 68, 87, 160, 236, 257, 265, 436, 490
Queen of the Damned, The (Rice), 547, 591–2
Quigley, Bill, 565–6, 575–6
Quine, Richard, 173

Rabinowitz, Grady*, 65, 165–70, 173, 174, 252–7, 259–62, 264–5, 269, 270, 287, 296, 334–41, 344, 376, 389, 509, 557, 593
Rabinowitz, Mrs Grady*, 260–1, 262, 269, 287, 344, 509
Rafael, David, 108–9
Rafael, Mickey, 460–3
Rafelson, Bob, 111, 119

Raisner, Bernie, 89–90
Ramer, Bruce, 376
Randall, Florence, 45
Randall, Tony, 45–6
Randy* (Jeremy's friend), 183
Reagan, Ronald, 262, 324, 391, 532, 584
Reddy, Helen, 459–60, 462, 463, 465, 469, 471
Redford, Robert, x, 101–9, 111, 115, 127–31, 308, 560
  broken thumb of, 125
  JP slighted by, 457, 560
  The Sting and, xii, 140, 143–7
  Streisand and, 103–5
Reiss, Bonnie, 502
Reitman, Ivan, 474, 475
Reuther, Steve, 330–1, 506, 508, 509, 510. 523
Rhodes, Shari, 267
Rice, Anne, 7, 527–31, 547–8, 572, 580, 591, 596–9
Rice, Susan, 19
Rice, Tim, 542
Richards, Dick, 568, 569
Richards, Keith, 221, 222–3
Richie, Lionel, 583
Ricky* (friend), 333, 334
Rimbaldi, Carlos, 375
Ringwald, Molly, 540
Rissner, Dan, 483
Roberts, Eliot, 524, 626
Roberts, Gwen, 626
Robinson, Bill, 121
Rodkin, Lori, 590–1, 621
Rolling Stones, x, 219–25, 429
Rose, Andy, 555, 557, 560–1
Rosenfeld, Frank, 488
Rosenfeld, Mike, 452–3
Rosenhouse, Matty, 313, 315
Rosenman, Howard, xv, 186–7, 215, 590, 610
Rosenthal, Abner, 43

Rosenthal, John, 90, 92, 94–5
Ross, Artie, 181, 338
Rothman, Arlyne, 231
Rottweiler*, 86, 400–1, 402, 405, 409, 412–15, 418–21, 437, 564–5
Ruddy, Al, xiii
Rudin, Scott, 64–5, 66
Rutman, Mickey, 85–8, 451
Rydell, Mark, 95, 98

Sackheim, Bill, 211
Safronsky, Bernie, 527–8
Salt, Jennifer, 115, 118, 131, 170, 172, 233–4
Salt, Waldo, 118
Sardi's, 91–2, 187
Sargent, Herb, 261
Sarrazin, Michael, 170–1
Saunders, George, 478
Savage, John, 113
Savio, Mario, 71
Schatzberg, Jerry, 93
Schiff, David, 526
Schillig, Chris, 71–2
Schneider, Bert, 111, 119–20, 261–2, 301
Schneider, Harold, 120, 121, 142, 606
Schrader, Geneen, 157, 256
Schrader, Paul, xv, 137, 157, 179–80, 206, 237–8, 239, 241, 256, 300, 376, 453
Schuck, Victoria, 138
Schumacher, Joel, iv, xi, 8, 39
Schwartz, Marion*, 33, 34
Scorsese, Martin, 115, 137, 157, 235–46, 252, 256, 257, 260, 298, 368, 587
Scott, 69, 579–81, 601
Scott, Ridley, 542
Scott-Fox, Judy, 605
Scotti Brothers, 384–5

Sellers, Al, 193, 216
sex, lies and videotape, 570
Sexton, Anne, 348
Shagan, Betty, 119
Shagan, Steve, ix, 119
Shampoo, 194–5, 233
Shapiro Ken, 191, 514
Shapiro, Mike, 301, 385
Shaw, Robert, 146
Shaw, Tommy, 211
Sheinberg, Sid, vii, viii, 148, 486, 611
Shepherd Cybill, 237, 239
Shepherd, Dick, iii
Sherman, Bobby, 176
Sherry, Val, 102, 111
Short Strokes, 450, 477
Sidewater, Fred, 518, 519
Siegel Ron, 15–16, 404, 442–7, 506, 509
Silberman, Peter, 308
Silver, Joel, 64–5, 66, 583
Simon, Carly, 230–1
Simpson, Don, xv–xvi, xvii, 66–7, 123–33, 192, 454, 560
Singer, Isaac Bashevis, 102
Slocombe, Doug, 352, 355, 359, 362
Smith, Howard K., 328
Smith, Jackie, 219, 251, 278–81, 340, 341, 344, 393, 396, 418–19, 424, 435, 447, 506–7, 509, 510, 578
Smith, Lois, 251, 298, 309, 321, 542, 570
Smith, Michael, 57, 58, 70
Smith, Todd, 554–6, 561–2, 570
Smithline, Mort, 176
Sobieski, Carole, 233
Sonya, v, xix, 188, 214–15
Spector, Phil, 99
Spielberg, Steven, 86, 115, 137, 148, 155–7, 169, 172, 199,

206, 210–11, 219, 227–9,
  240, 241, 246–9, 250–1,
  252–3, 254, 256–7, 272–7,
  280–4, 285–309, 313–15,
  319–20, 321, 327–8, 342–3,
  351–5, 357–64, 365–83,
  386–90, 455–7, 475–6,
  537–8, 551–3, 592–4
Spratlin, Jack*, 64, 189–90,
  323–7, 333–4, 338, 343–6,
  371–2, 385, 387–8, 393–400
Sprouse, Steven, 557
Squiers, Conrad, 82, 83, 89
Stark, Ray, 104, 129, 131, 151,
  246, 405–12, 480
Starr, Ringo, 416
Steele, Dawn, 514, 612
Steelyard Blues, 108–15, 120–4,
  133, 139, 141–2, 451–2, 532,
  565
Stein, Jules, 320
Steiner, Jerry, 113
Stevenson, Adlai, 49–50
Stewart, Allyn, 557
Stewart, Rod, 472
Stieffel, Arnold, 189
Sting, 530, 542, 550
Sting, The, iii–xx, 21, 87, 107,
  109, 120, 124, 125, 127, 131,
  132, 139–51, 157, 189, 255,
  265, 328, 341, 346, 459–60
Stout, Tom, 270, 425–6
Streep, Meryl, 251, 595
Streisand, Barbara, 86, 97,
  101–5, 111, 113, 127–9, 131,
  175, 194, 232, 497–8, 500,
  502, 506, 509
Stripes, 474
Stuart, 8–9, 11, 14, 61–2, 135,
  136, 566, 583–4, 608, 618
Sugarland Express, The, 194
Sun Valley, 506–10
Surtees, Robert, 157

Susskind, David, 137–8
Sutherland, Donald, 109–11,
  113, 120, 121, 274, 538
Sweeney, Mary Anne, 269, 271
Sylbert, Anthea, 499, 502
Sylbert, Dick, 192, 208–9, 342,
  372
Sylk, Kenny, 506

Taft Barish, 529–30, 542, 547,
  590
Talent Associates, 137–8
Tanen, Ned, 148, 398
Tarnoff, John, 330
Taupin, Bernie, 590–1
Taxi Driver, 85, 155, 170, 182,
  201, 205, 209, 236–46,
  250–1, 252, 255, 257–62,
  283, 310, 346, 369, 535, 548,
  564
Taylor, Elizabeth, xiii–xv
Taylor-Young, Leigh, 448
television, 42, 165, 260–1,
  527–8, 532–4, 545–6, 554
Tennant, Bill, 390
Terrail, Patrick, 462
Terrell, Tammy, 467
Thalians, 215–16
Thiele, David, 216–17
Third Man Through the Door,
  The (TMTTD), 334, 371,
  373, 388
Thomas, Marlo, 147, 627
Thompson, Jim, 108
Tim*, 433, 435
Time, 51, 311
  Man of the Year of, 7, 53, 60,
    83, 107, 158, 329, 439, 510,
    584, 592
  Women of the Year of, 252
Tokofsky, Jerry, 568
Tomlin, Lily, 17–18, 198
Towne, Robert, 173, 215–16,
  232–3, 261

Tramont, Jean-Claude, 497
Trax, 517–20, 531, 588
Truffaut, François, 272–7, 283, 290, 301–2, 305–9, 321, 352, 356–8, 362, 366, 410
Trumball, Doug, 213, 254, 277, 281, 292–3, 294–7, 347, 366–8, 378, 390
Turner, Kathleen, 512–15
Turner, Pete, 288, 313
Twentieth Century-Fox, 68, 176–7, 481–5, 487–9, 492, 495, 496–7
2010, 470, 472, 473
Tyler, Grace, 70–1

Ueberroth, Peter, 501
Ufland, Harry, 240, 241–2, 456, 485, 486, 496
UFOs, 311–12, 327, 329
United Artists (UA), 95, 97
Universal, iii, vii, viii, 142, 144, 147, 148, 552
Updike, John, 151
Uricich, Dick, 289, 352

Vaccaro, Brenda, 195
Vadim, Roger, 113
Vadim, Vanessa, 113
Valium, v, viii, x, xi, 264
Vampire Lestat, The (Rice), 527, 603–4, 626
Vegas (Dunne), 163–8
Veitch, John, 237, 293–4, 303, 306, 308, 361, 374, 378, 396
Verdict, The, 487
Vestron Pictures, 530–1, 538, 539–40, 548, 565, 566, 569–70, 576
Victor, 79, 131, 192, 222, 317, 318, 347, 432, 466, 487–8, 503, 512, 549
Vidgin, Robin, 358, 360, 364

Vietnam War, 77, 82, 90, 135, 204, 238, 449, 514
Volker, Dr, 427–31, 434

Wagner, Robert, 212
Wald, Mr Jeff, 459–73, 481, 495, 499, 500, 506, 523–7, 609
Wald, Traci, 524, 525
Walden, Bobby, 501
Walker, Katherine, 251
Wallace, George, 300
Wallerstein, Bob, 517, 519–20, 538, 539
Walsh, Joey, 156, 349
Walter*, 402–5
Ward, Chris, vi, vii, viii, xvii, 157
Ward, David, vi, vii, ix, x–xi, xiv, xvii, 87, 107, 109, 110, 111, 120, 139, 142, 144–5, 146, 157
Warden, Jack, 196
Warner, Frank, 385, 389
Warner, Jack, 532–3
Warner Bros, iii, 66, 111, 118, 120, 121, 122, 123–4, 142, 144, 149, 154, 241, 373, 547, 557, 564, 591
Wasserman, Lew, vii, viii, 141, 499
Watergate, 155, 158
Waterston, Chick, 359–60, 362
Watts, Charlie, 223
Way We Were, The, 103–4, 127–30
Webb, Charles, 92
Wechsler, Nick, 533, 536–42, 565-71, 601, 608
Weinseir, Carol, 48–9
Weinstein, Paula, 271, 388, 499–502, 528
Weis, Gary, 478, 515, 526
Welch, Joseph, 42

Wells, Frank, 111, 114, 374, 388, 565
Wenders, Wim, 558
Wexler, Jerry, 224
White, Sue, 72
Whitney, John, 277
Wiatt, Jimmy, 451, 453, 463, 517, 519–20, 584–5
Wickstrom, Linda, 342
Wilder, Billy, 94, 626
Williams, John, 290–1
Williams, Paul, 116–17, 181
Willie, 36–7
Willis, Bruce, 543–4, 553, 583
Winkler, Irwin, 136
Wirth, Billy, 553
Wish You Were Here, 514, 517
Wizan, Joe, 489, 496
Wolf, Wally, 118–19
women's liberation, 238, 499
Wood, Ronnie, 221–2, 385

Wowie, Sir Mauie*, 395–6
Wynn, Tracey Keenan, 538

Yablans, Frank, 148, 487–8, 500
Yates, Peter, 94, 97, 98
'Yentl the Yeshiva Girl' (Singer), 102
Young, Buddy, 255
You're a Big Boy Now, 105
Yuppie 1, 460–1
Yuppie 2, 460–1

Zacharia, Don, 488
Zanuck, Dick, vii, 111, 121, 139–45, 149, 524
Zanuck, Lili, 626
Zemeckis, Bob, 592–4
Zimmerman, Natalie, 530, 576
Zimmerman, Vernon, 106, 120
Zsigmond, Vilmos, 265, 287, 290, 295, 302, 303, 305, 351–2, 362

A Selected List of Non-Fiction Available from Mandarin

While every effort is made to keep prices low, it is sometimes necessary to increase prices at short notice. Mandarin Paperbacks reserves the right to show new retail prices on covers which may differ from those previously advertised in the text or elsewhere.

The prices shown below were correct at the time of going to press.

☐	7493 0109 0	**The Warrior Queens**	Antonia Fraser	£4.99
☐	7493 0108 2	**Mary Queen of Scots**	Antonia Fraser	£5.99
☐	7493 0010 8	**Cromwell**	Antonia Fraser	£7.50
☐	7493 0106 6	**The Weaker Vessel**	Antonia Fraser	£5.99
☐	7493 0014 0	**The Demon Drink**	Jancis Robinson	£4.99
☐	7493 0016 7	**Vietnam – The 10,000 Day War**	Michael Maclear	£3.99
☐	7493 0061 2	**Voyager**	Yeager/Rutan	£3.99
☐	7493 0113 9	**Peggy Ashcroft**	Michael Billington	£3.99
☐	7493 0177 5	**The Troubles**	Mick O'Connor	£4.99
☐	7493 0004 3	**South Africa**	Graham Leach	£3.99
☐	7493 0254 2	**Families and How to Survive Them**	Creese/Skynner	£5.99
☐	7493 0060 4	**The Fashion Conspiracy**	Nicolas Coleridge	£3.99
☐	7493 0179 1	**The Tao of Pooh**	Benjamin Hoff	£2.99
☐	7493 0000 0	**Moonwalk**	Michael Jackson	£2.99

All these books are available at your bookshop or newsagent, or can be ordered direct from the publisher. Just tick the titles you want and fill in the form below.

Mandarin Paperbacks, Cash Sales Department, PO Box 11, Falmouth, Cornwall TR10 9EN.

Please send cheque or postal order, no currency, for purchase price quoted and allow the following for postage and packing:

UK — 80p for the first book, 20p for each additional book ordered to a maximum charge of £2.00.

BFPO — 80p for the first book, 20p for each additional book.

Overseas including Eire — £1.50 for the first book, £1.00 for the second and 30p for each additional book thereafter.

NAME (Block letters) ....

ADDRESS ....

....

....